GIL KANE

THE ART OF THE COMICS

BY DANIEL HERMAN

HERMES PRESS

NESHANNOCK, PENNSYLVANIA

GIL KANE

HERMES PRESS

THE ART OF THE COMICS

BY DANIEL HERMAN

NESHANNOCK, PENNSYLVANIA

Published by Hermes Press
2100 Wilmington Road
Neshannock, Pennsylvania 16105

Cover design by Daniel Herman
Book design by Daniel Herman

Library of Congress Control Number: 2001088750
Limited edition hardcover ISBN 0-9710311-1-8
Trade softcover ISBN 0-9710311-2-6

Front cover: original artwork for: the cover for *Green Lantern* #26, the splash page for *The Atom* #6, unused cover for *His Name is...Savage* #1, the splash page for *The Amazing Spider-Man* #100, an interior page from *Blackmark*, and the cover for *The Mighty Marvel Western* #44. All artwork, Gil Kane, pencils. ©2001, DC Comics, The Estate of Gil Kane, and Marvel Characters, Inc. Back cover: original artwork for: the cover for *Green Lantern* #60, an interior page from *Blackmark*, and the cover for *Edge* #2. Also pictured, the logo art from the Sunday *Star Hawks* strip. All artwork, Gil Kane, pencils. ©2001 DC Comics, The Estate of Gil Kane, The Estate of Gil Kane and Steven Grant, and United Features Syndicate, Inc.

Printed in Canada

ACKNOWLEDGMENTS

Many people gave valuable assistance in the preparation of this book. First and foremost, this book would not be possible without the help of Gil and Elaine Kane. In 1998, when I first approached Gil and told him I was working on a monograph about his work, he agreed to speak with me on a regular basis. Arrangements were made, and I called him every Saturday morning thereafter. These lengthy discussions/interviews were conducted for a period of four months. Gil was extremely ill during that time, but he graciously made time to answer my questions and give his views and opinions, without hesitation. After Gil passed away, Elaine helped clarify remaining questions and made herself available whenever information or guidance was needed in finalizing this book.

I would also like to thank John Romita, Roy Thomas, and Julius Schwartz, who consented to be interviewed in the preparation of this book.

A number of comic art collectors graciously allowed reproduction of artwork from their collections. I would like to thank: Scott Dunbier, Mike Burkey, Ethan Roberts, Jeremy Radisich, Enrico Salvini, Al Bigley, and Tom Horvitz. I would also like to thank Alex Chun for making available the photograph he took of Gil, seen on page 145.

Special thanks to Mitch and Mary Itkowitz, of Graphic Collectibles, for providing artwork for reproduction in this book and for helping in other ways too numerous to mention.

The layout and composition of this book was greatly aided by the never ending assistance of Diana Petrella. Assistance in editing and proof reading the text was provided by Barbara McGeoch and Lillian Geer. My office staff, Lori Geramita (who typed and retyped the manuscript), Fran Occhibone, and Elaine DeVivo, helped above and beyond the call.

Finally, without the help of my wife, Louise, and my daughter, Sabrina, this project never would have come to fruition.

For Louise and Sabrina

GIL KANE THE ART OF THE COMICS

TABLE OF CONTENTS

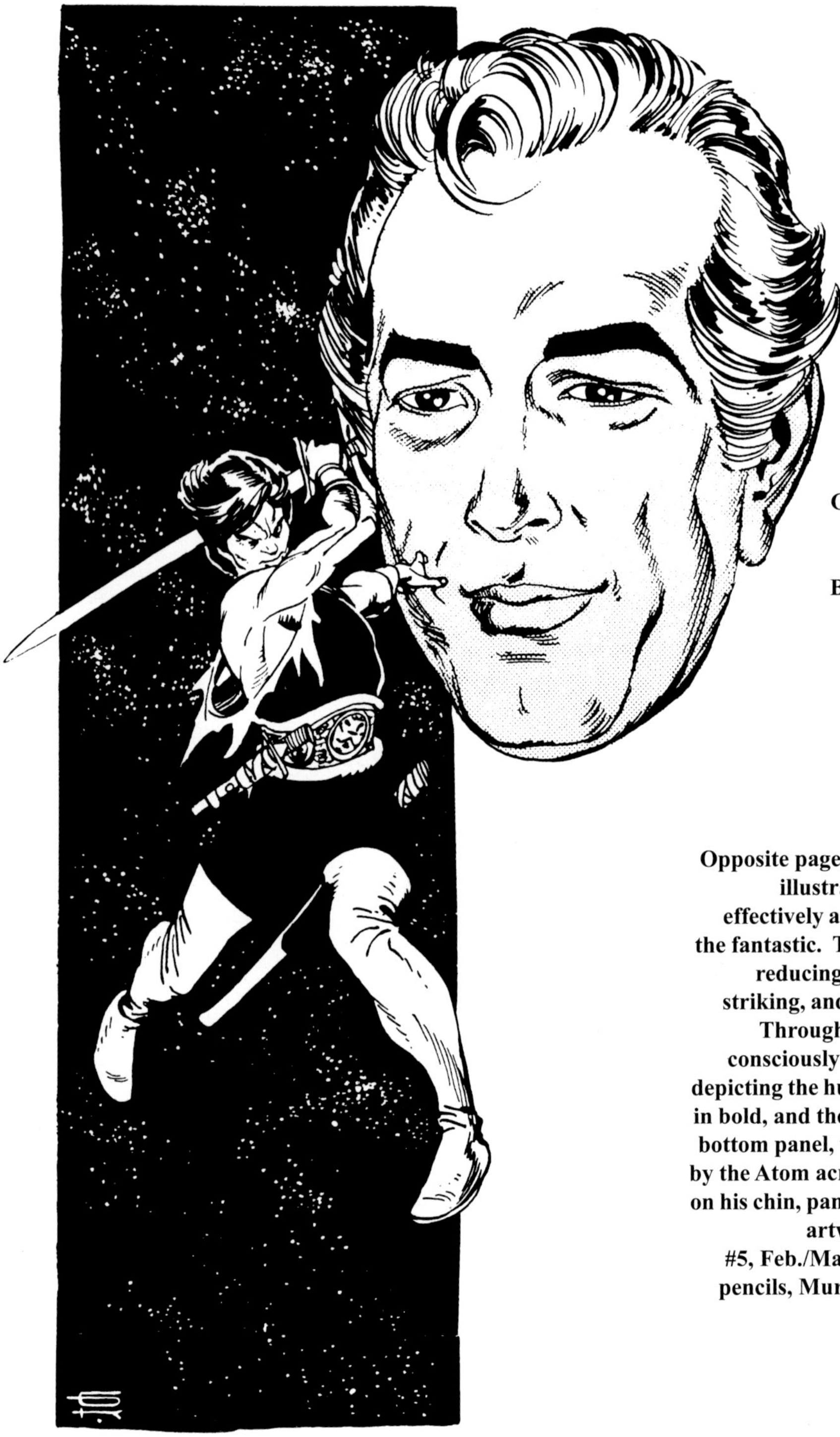

Gil Kane, circa 1971, in a self-portrait, seen with his hero Blackmark, from the last page of *Blackmark*, 1971, ©2001 The Estate of Gil Kane.

Opposite page, center and bottom: illustrates how Kane could effectively and simply dramatize the fantastic. The hero transforms, reducing in size- - in just one, striking, and eye-catching panel. Throughout his career, Kane consciously developed the art of depicting the human form in action, in bold, and theatrical ways. In the bottom panel, the villain is stopped by the Atom acrobatically bouncing on his chin, panels from the original artwork from *The Atom* #5, Feb./March, 1963, Gil Kane, pencils, Murphy Anderson, inks, ©2001 DC Comics.

INTRODUCTION

Comic books are just for kids, right? Wrong. Not only are they for kids of **all** ages, but through the work of artists like Gil Kane, comic books now address **mature** audiences. At their best, comic books transcend being creations for commerce and present images and stories that reach across all ages and backgrounds. This premise, however, requires that comic books be looked at and read, something it appears the critics of the medium have not done.

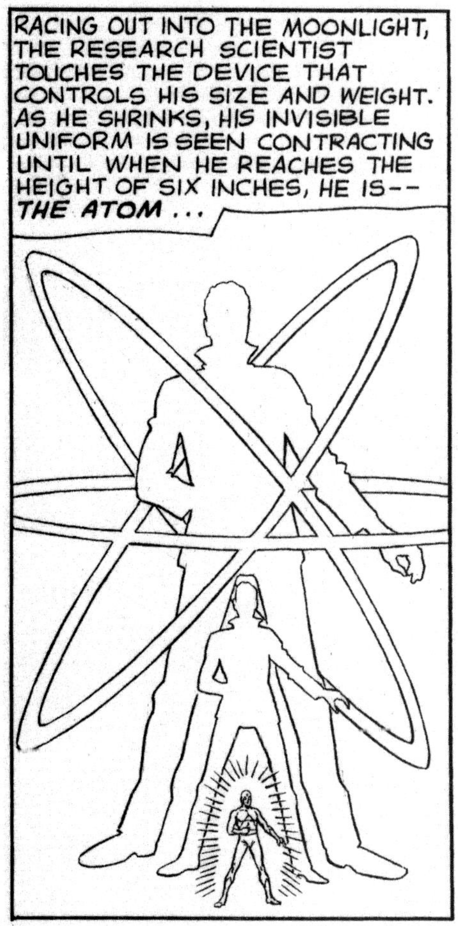
RACING OUT INTO THE MOONLIGHT, THE RESEARCH SCIENTIST TOUCHES THE DEVICE THAT CONTROLS HIS SIZE AND WEIGHT. AS HE SHRINKS, HIS INVISIBLE UNIFORM IS SEEN CONTRACTING UNTIL WHEN HE REACHES THE HEIGHT OF SIX INCHES, HE IS-- THE ATOM ...

The comic book in America has had a complicated genesis. Comic books are the product of a contrast between the commercial and the artistic. They reflect the artists who drew and wrote them, and the time and place when most of the great comic book artists were reaching towards their maturity, beginning at the end of the depression, and coalescing in New York City.

This book is about one of the foremost artists of comic book stories, Gil Kane. Kane's development

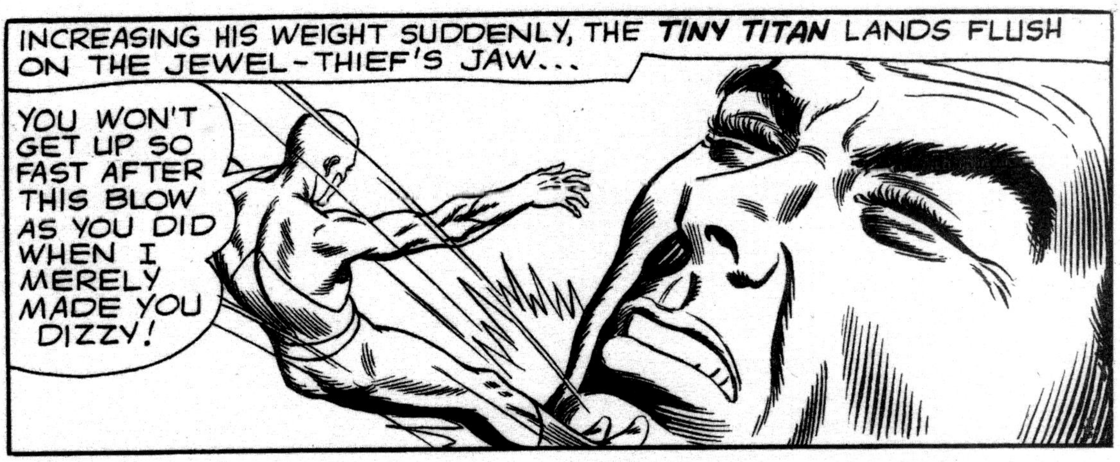
INCREASING HIS WEIGHT SUDDENLY, THE TINY TITAN LANDS FLUSH ON THE JEWEL-THIEF'S JAW...
YOU WON'T GET UP SO FAST AFTER THIS BLOW AS YOU DID WHEN I MERELY MADE YOU DIZZY!

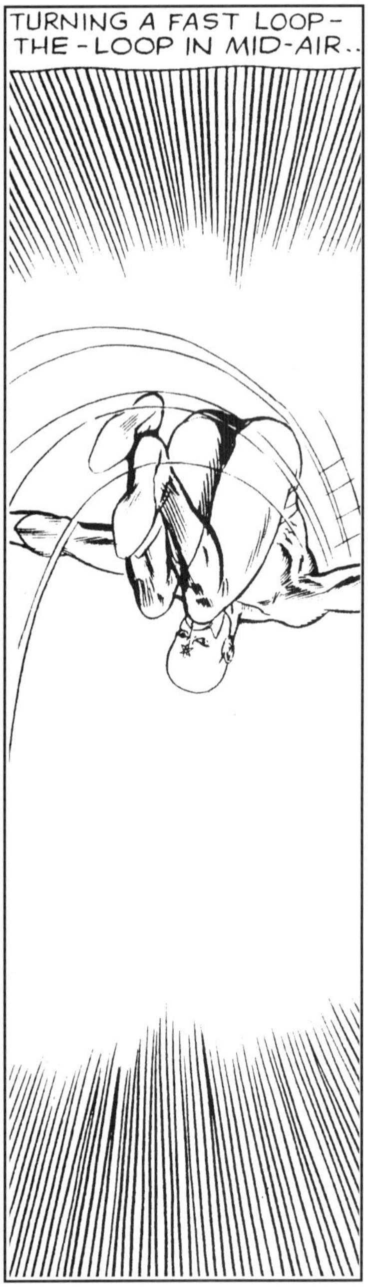
TURNING A FAST LOOP-
THE-LOOP IN MID-AIR..

as an artist and as a graphic storyteller grew and matured contemporaneously with the comic book medium. Kane, who died during the preparation of this book, was an articulate advocate of the art of comic books. Through his efforts, the medium was forced to grow and mature. Kane's work in comic books, graphic novels, and comic strips was and **still is** influential to artists in the medium, and continues to be good reading and good looking work.[1] Kane was also influential as a mentor, critic, and commentator about the history of comic books.

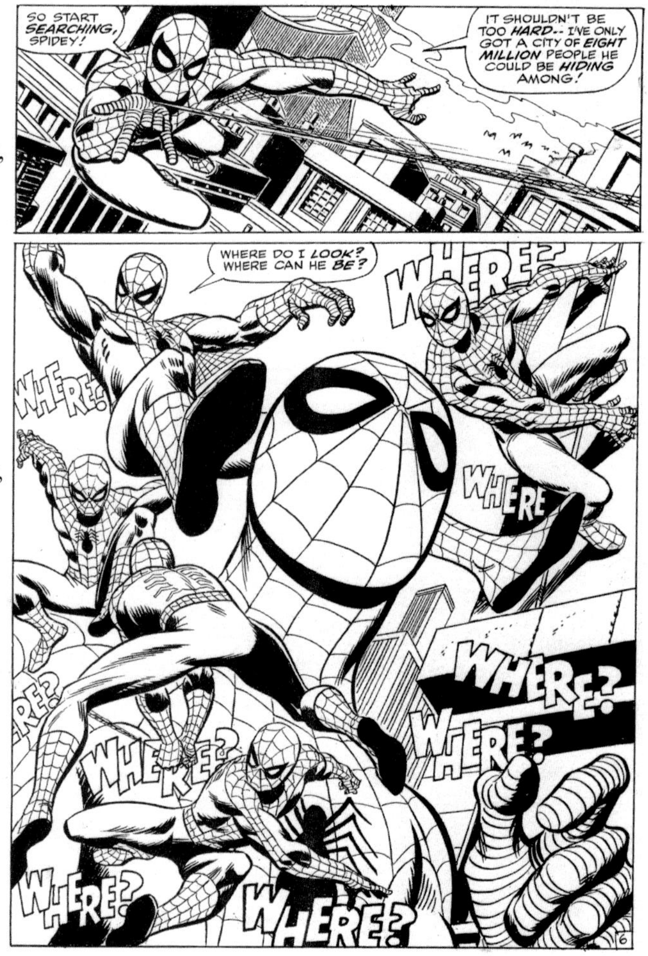
SO START SEARCHING, SPIDEY!
IT SHOULDN'T BE TOO HARD-- I'VE ONLY GOT A CITY OF EIGHT MILLION PEOPLE HE COULD BE HIDING AMONG!
WHERE DO I LOOK? WHERE CAN HE BE?
WHERE?
WHERE?
WHERE
WHERE?
WHERE?
WHERE?
WHERE?
WHERE?
WHERE?

In approaching Kane's work and the subject of American comic book art, one difficulty in assessing these subjects becomes readily apparent: the lack of significant serious analysis and criticism of this unique area of American art. The vacuum of serious analysis of the art of the comics is due, in part, to the academic art world's use of comic art and comic books as examples of

Above left: Kane's Atom dramatically somersaults, panel from the original artwork, Gil Kane, pencils, Murphy Anderson, inks, *The Atom* #5, Feb./March, 1963, ©2001 DC Comics. Right: Kane uses unusual camera angles and montage, a Kane trademark, to pace a Spider-Man story, Gil Kane, pencils, John Romita, inks, from the original artwork, from page 6, from *The Amazing Spider-Man* # 89, Oct., 1970, ©2001 Marvel Characters, Inc.

Below: Kane designed covers which showcased the dramatic use of composition. The cover art for *Green Lantern* #60, the "Lamplighter Cover," could easily be a movie poster or a book cover, as it is not only an attractive cover image, but also, an effective piece of graphic design. The cover design for *Green Lantern* #41, is equally as effective, and could have been used in advertising or in other commercial venues.

low art and kitsch. No medium, whether serious or commercial, is free of good and bad practitioners, and comic art is no exception. Many comic artists over the last 75 years have, beyond any doubt, and by any standard, created an imagery that demands serious attention and admiration. Gil Kane stands among the ranks of the best of the comic book artists.

To fully understand Kane's growth and contribution as a comic artist, it is first necessary to put comic art within the context of twentieth century culture and art.

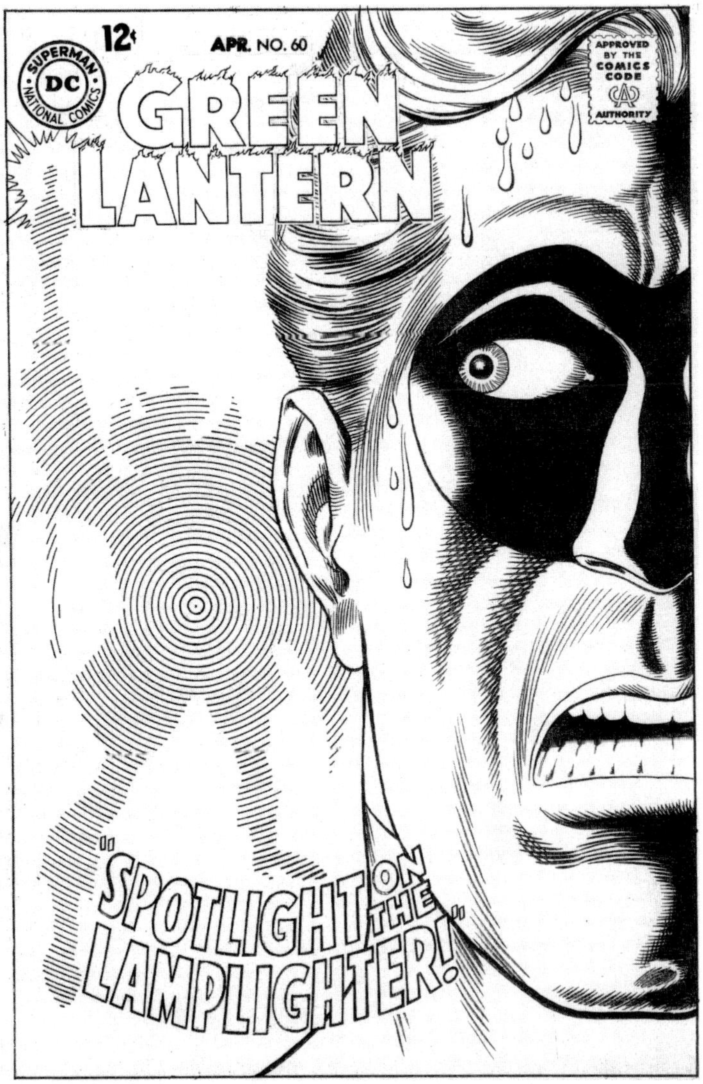
12¢
APR. NO. 60
APPROVED BY THE COMICS CODE AUTHORITY
GREEN LANTERN
"SPOTLIGHT ON THE LAMPLIGHTER!"

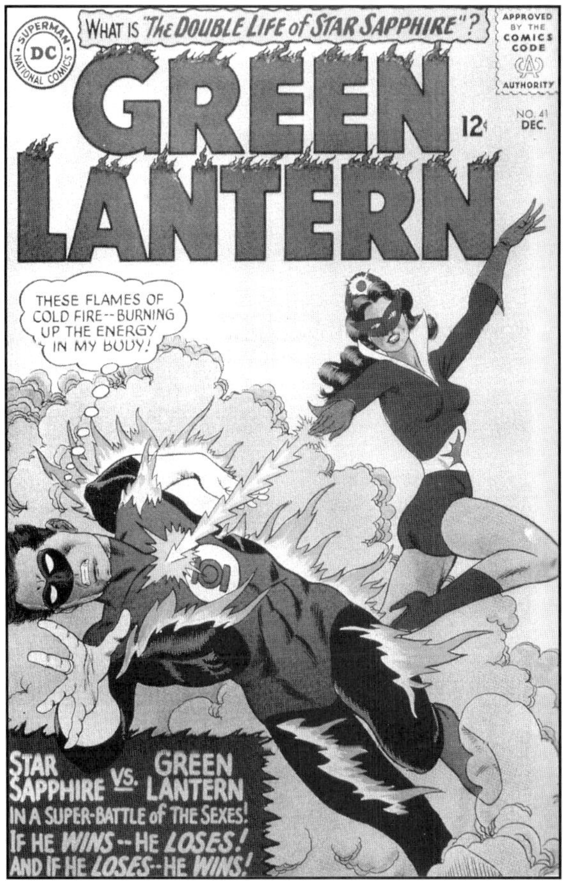
WHAT IS "The DOUBLE LIFE of STAR SAPPHIRE"?
APPROVED BY THE COMICS CODE AUTHORITY
GREEN LANTERN
12¢
NO. 41 DEC.
THESE FLAMES OF COLD FIRE--BURNING UP THE ENERGY IN MY BODY!
STAR SAPPHIRE VS. GREEN LANTERN
IN A SUPER-BATTLE of THE SEXES!
IF HE WINS--HE LOSES!
AND IF HE LOSES--HE WINS!

Left: original artwork for the cover for *Green Lantern*, #60, April, 1968, Gil Kane, pencils, Murphy Anderson, inks. Above: cover for *Green Lantern* #41, Dec., 1965, Gil Kane, pencils, Sid Greene, inks, both covers, ©2001 DC Comics.

1 COMIC ART AS ART

Although art was once primarily defined by the disciplines of painting and sculpture, the twentieth century witnessed a dynamic expansion of the definition of just what, art is. The term "art" has been expanded to include such commercial endeavors as graphic and industrial design, advertising, illustration, cinema, and newspaper

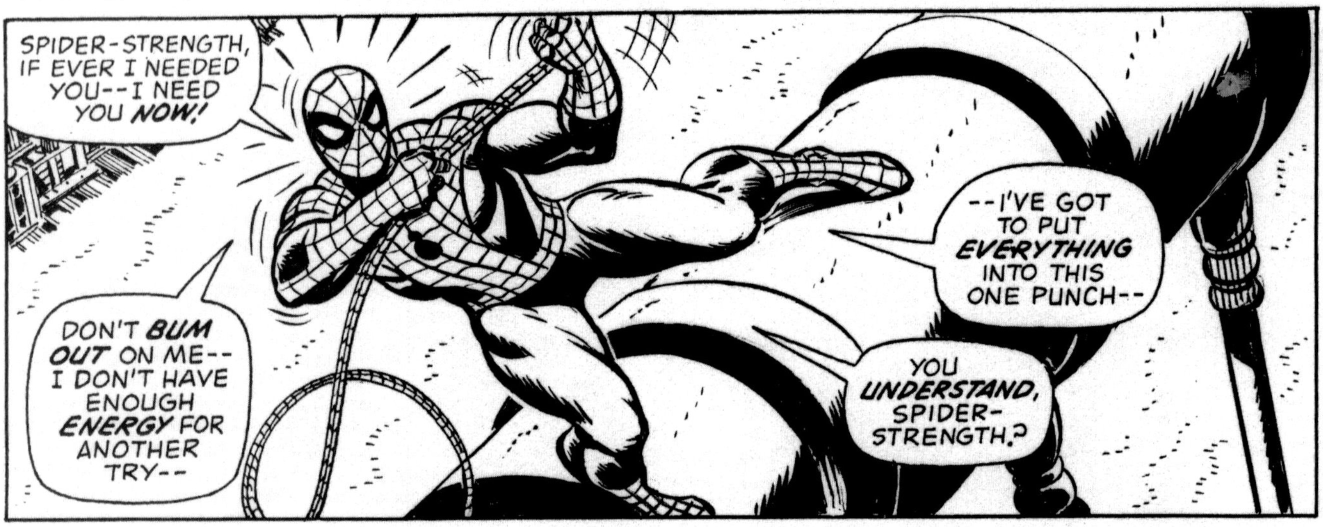
SPIDER-STRENGTH, IF EVER I NEEDED YOU--I NEED YOU NOW!
DON'T BUM OUT ON ME-- I DON'T HAVE ENOUGH ENERGY FOR ANOTHER TRY--
--I'VE GOT TO PUT EVERYTHING INTO THIS ONE PUNCH--
YOU UNDERSTAND, SPIDER-STRENGTH?

comic strips.

Newspaper comic strips have received attention and praise, but this medium is severely limited in conveying cohesive narrative imagery.[1] Comic books have provided, for a few talented artists who can exploit the art form, a forum to tell stories with pictures which is unparalleled in the print medium.

Twentieth century art has had as one of its driving forces the

Kane employs skewed camera angles, above, and forced perspective, opposite page, to create archetypal images which transcend comic books. The panel above is the top panel, and the opposite page panel is the bottom panel, both which form the complete page for page 22, from *The Amazing Spider-Man* #121, June, 1973, Gil Kane, pencils, John Romita, inks, ©2001 Marvel Characters, Inc.

urge to reduce the pictorial image. Cubism flattened images and forms by compressing the spatial picture plane while simplifying the overall image. The Fauves simplified composition by emphasizing the primacy of color and reduction of form. The twentieth century also witnessed the genesis of artists and artisans who believed that society could be influenced through art and industrial design. Among these movements were Constructivism in Russia, De Stijl in the Netherlands, and the Bauhaus in Germany. All of these movements shared a common concept, which integrated art and design for everyday use. Ultimately, the lessons espoused by these movements found their way into American art and design and were clearly influential in dictating the graphic nature of American comic books and comic art.

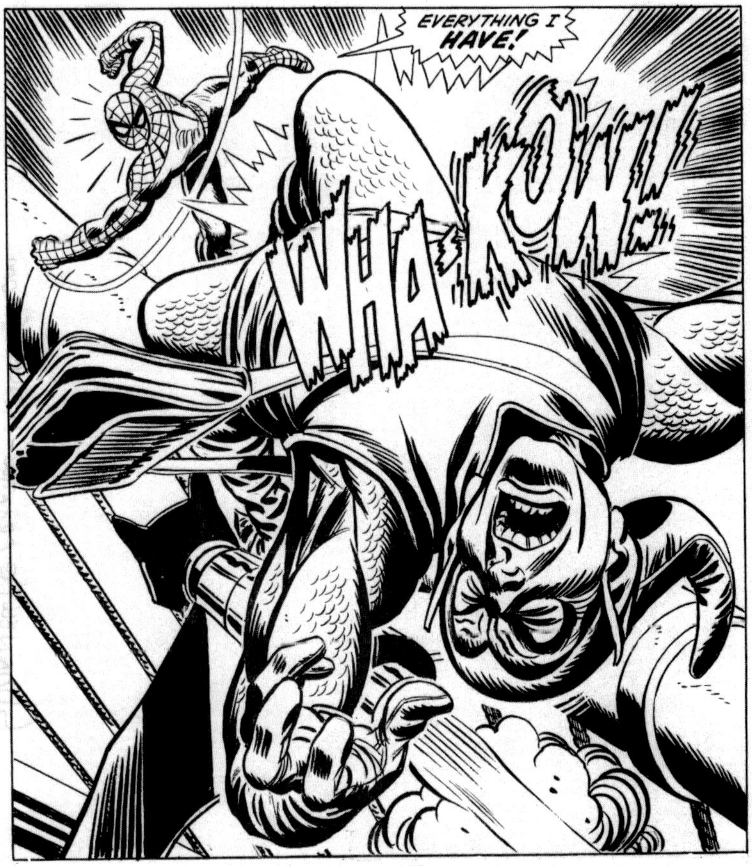
EVERYTHING I HAVE!
WHAKOWW!

Thrown into this mix of influences were developments in popular culture, such as pulp novels and movies. Comic books and their art represent a unique amalgam of many elements: lighting and camera angles from the movies, plots from the pulp novels, and simplified design elements and bold colors from high art. As the abstract painters of the first half of the century struggled to develop personal, pictorial languages through their art, the first generation of comic book artists strove to create a personal pictorial language which took comic art away from the realm of illustration and in a different and more modern direction.

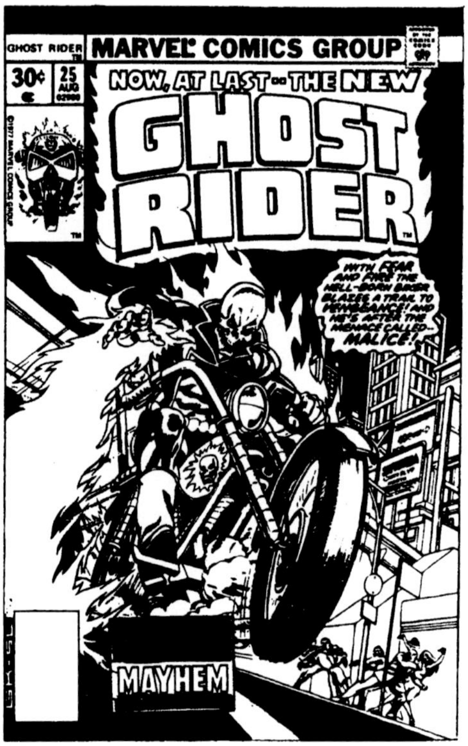
GHOST RIDER
MARVEL COMICS GROUP
30¢
25 AUG
NOW, AT LAST--THE NEW
GHOST RIDER
WITH FEAR AND FIRE THE HELL-BORN BIKER BLAZES A TRAIL TO VENGEANCE! AND HE'S AFTER THE MENACE CALLED-- MALICE!
MAYHEM

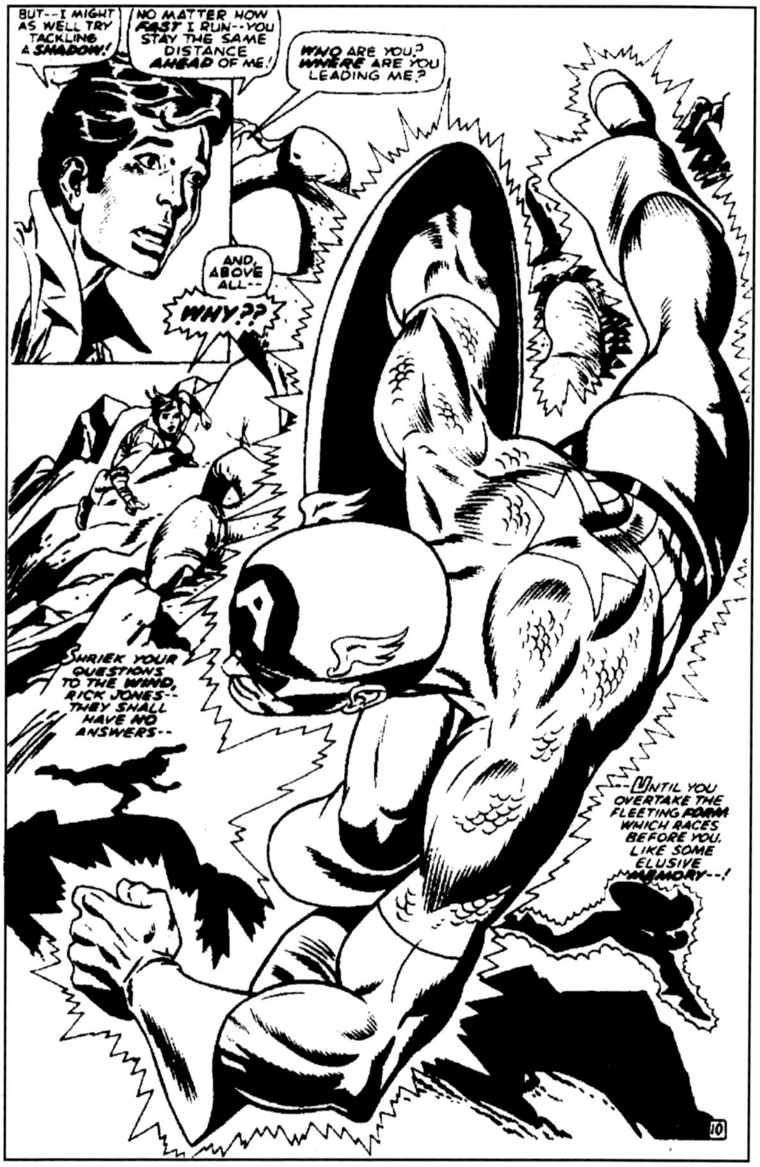
BUT--I MIGHT AS WELL TRY TACKLING A SHADOW!
NO MATTER HOW FAST I RUN--YOU STAY THE SAME DISTANCE AHEAD OF ME!
WHO ARE YOU? WHERE ARE YOU LEADING ME?
AND, ABOVE ALL--
WHY??
SHRIEK YOUR QUESTIONS TO THE WIND, RICK JONES--THEY SHALL HAVE NO ANSWERS--
--UNTIL YOU OVERTAKE THE FLEETING FORM WHICH RACES BEFORE YOU, LIKE SOME ELUSIVE MEMORY--!
10

Above: original cover art for *Ghost Rider* #25, Aug., 1977, Gil Kane, pencils, Steve Leialoha, inks. Right: Kane creates a dramatic interior splash page, original artwork from *Captain Marvel* #17, page 10, Oct., 1969, Gil Kane, pencils, Dan Adkins, inks, both ©2001 Marvel Characters, Inc.

2 COMIC ART AND THE FIRST GENERATION

The first generation of artists who drew comic book stories were primarily young men, many still in their teens, who wanted to depict ideas, graphically, that were a combination of pulp science fiction, newspaper strips, and movies. These influences coupled with the uncertainties of the depression and the escalating heat of international affairs during the 1930s, gave inspiration to these artists. The first comic book artists were in the vanguard of an art form that was just being created and for which there were no rules. The conditions they worked under were like an assembly line: one artist would pencil, one would ink, another would clean up the page while others did the writing and editorial. There was nothing

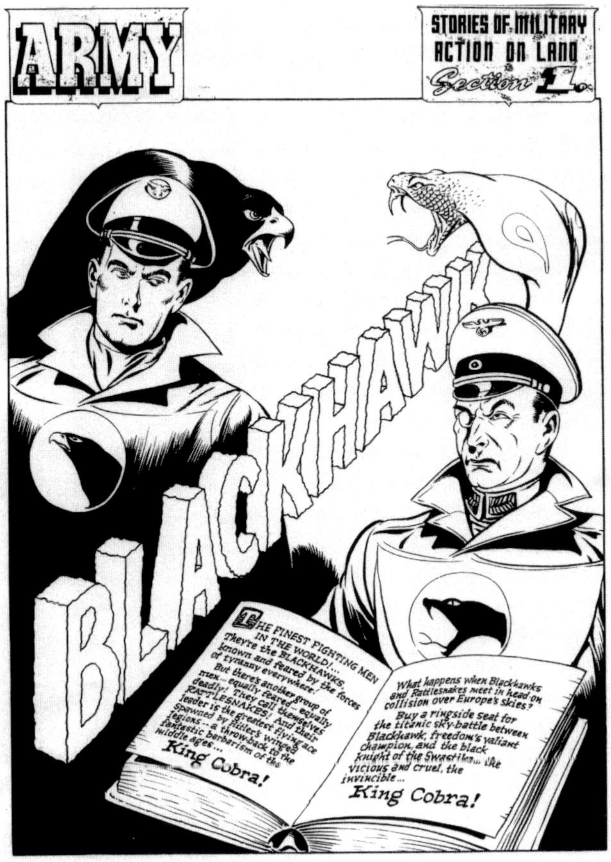
ARMY
STORIES OF MILITARY ACTION ON LAND
Section 1
BLACKHAWK
THE FINEST FIGHTING MEN IN THE WORLD!... They're the BLACKHAWKS, known and feared by the forces of tyranny everywhere! But there's another group of men... equally feared... equally deadly! They call themselves RATTLESNAKES! And their leader is the greatest flying ace spawned by Hitler's winged legions... a throw-back to the fantastic barbarism of the middle ages...
King Cobra!
What happens when Blackhawks and Rattlesnakes meet in head-on collision over Europe's skies? Buy a ringside seat for the titanic sky-battle between Blackhawk, freedom's valiant champion, and the black knight of the Swastika... the vicious and cruel, the invincible...
King Cobra!

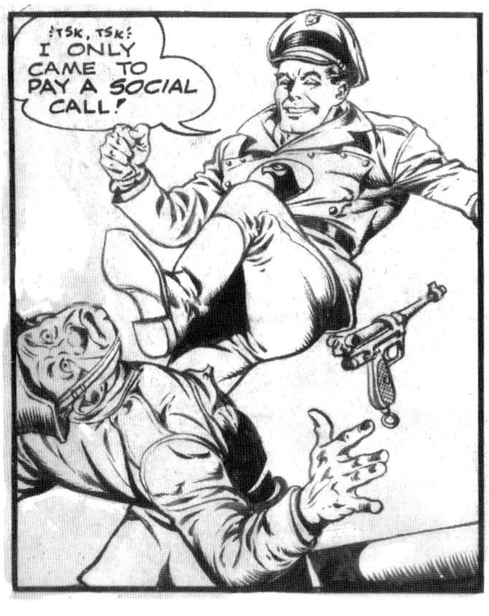
TSK, TSK! I ONLY CAME TO PAY A SOCIAL CALL!

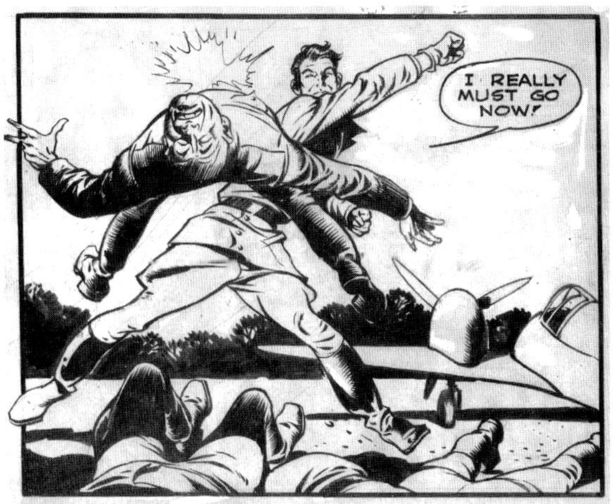
I REALLY MUST GO NOW!

Reed Crandall was admired by many comic book artists for his early work for *Blackhawk*, in *Military Comics*. Left: the original artwork for the striking splash page for *Military Comics* #19, May, 1943, Reed Crandall, pencils and inks. This splash page makes dramatic use of both text and pictures. Below: two panels from the original artwork for page 3 from *Military Comics* #14, Dec., 1942, in which Crandall shows his dramatic flair and orchestration of action, Reed Crandall, pencils and inks, all artwork ©2001 DC Comics.

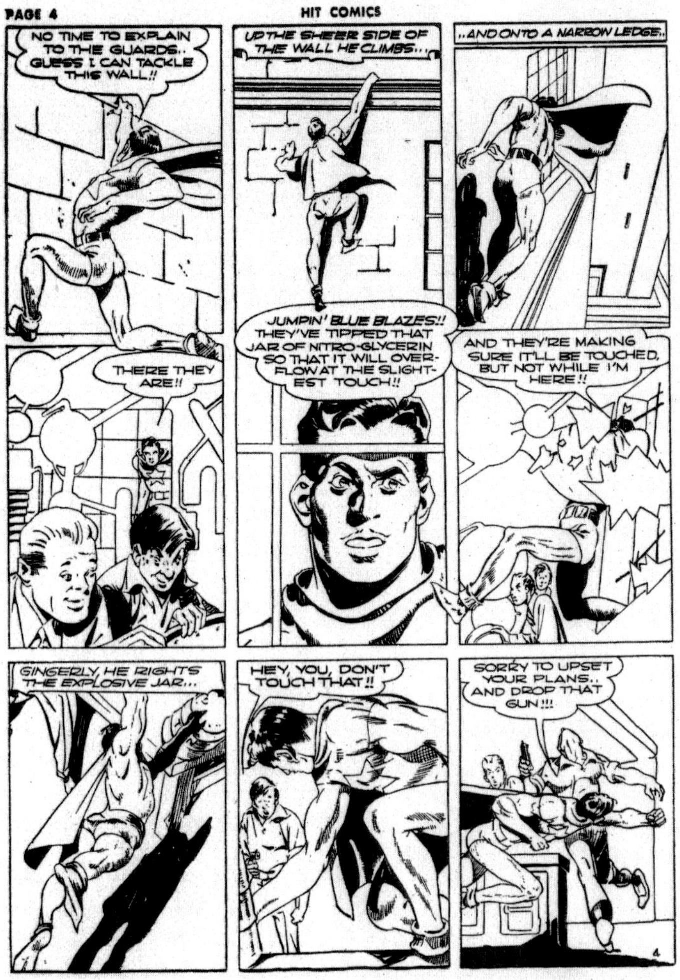
PAGE 4
HIT COMICS
NO TIME TO EXPLAIN TO THE GUARDS.. GUESS I CAN TACKLE THIS WALL!!
UP THE SHEER SIDE OF THE WALL HE CLIMBS...
..AND ONTO A NARROW LEDGE.
THERE THEY ARE!!
JUMPIN' BLUE BLAZES!! THEY'VE TIPPED THAT JAR OF NITRO-GLYCERIN SO THAT IT WILL OVER-FLOW AT THE SLIGHT-EST TOUCH!!
AND THEY'RE MAKING SURE IT'LL BE TOUCHED, BUT NOT WHILE I'M HERE!!
GINGERLY, HE RIGHTS THE EXPLOSIVE JAR...
HEY, YOU, DON'T TOUCH THAT!!
SORRY TO UPSET YOUR PLANS.. AND DROP THAT GUN!!!

Classic Lou Fine artwork for *Stormy Foster*, from *Hit Comics* #22, June, 1942, for Quality. Fine's elegant figure work, where violence was choreographed as if it were ballet, influenced Kane and every other comic artist who saw his work. ©1942 the respective copyright holder.

romantic about being an artist for the comics but of these pioneers, a talented handful of artists had an optimism and vitality which came through in their work. During these early years there was excitement and adventure in being an artist of comic book stories that attracted many to this infant industry.[1] Foremost among the first generation of comic book artists were Joe Shuster, Jerry Robinson, Bernard Bailey, Will Eisner, Lou Fine, Mac Raboy, Reed Crandall, Mort Meskin, Jack Cole, Joe Simon and Jack Kirby.

The progenitors of the first generation of comic book artists were the newspaper "strip" artists. Historically the American newspaper comic strip was initially developed in 1892, but the medium did not seriously begin to develop as an "art" until later. Although Winsor McCay and George Herriman made important contributions to the art of the comic strip, their influences were of minor import upon the first generation of comic book artists.

The first significant developments in newspaper comics that were influential upon the first generation of comic book artists came with the adaptation from the pulp magazine *Amazing Stories* of *Buck Rogers* and with the creation and development of Roy Crane's *Wash*

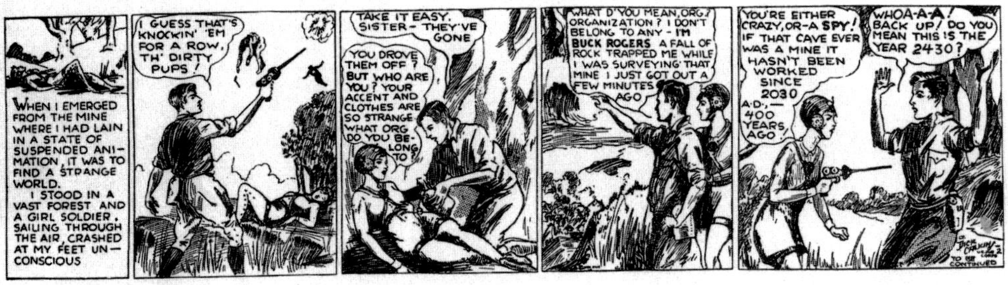
WHEN I EMERGED FROM THE MINE WHERE I HAD LAIN IN A STATE OF SUSPENDED ANI- MATION, IT WAS TO FIND A STRANGE WORLD.
I STOOD IN A VAST FOREST AND A GIRL SOLDIER, SAILING THROUGH THE AIR, CRASHED AT MY FEET UN- CONSCIOUS
I GUESS THAT'S KNOCKIN' 'EM FOR A ROW, TH' DIRTY PUPS!
TAKE IT EASY, SISTER - THEY'VE GONE
YOU DROVE THEM OFF? BUT WHO ARE YOU? YOUR ACCENT AND CLOTHES ARE SO STRANGE. WHAT ORG DO YOU BE- LONG TO?
WHAT D'YOU MEAN, ORG? ORGANIZATION? I DON'T BELONG TO ANY - I'M BUCK ROGERS A FALL OF ROCK TRAPPED ME WHILE I WAS SURVEYING THAT MINE I JUST GOT OUT A FEW MINUTES AGO
YOU'RE EITHER CRAZY, OR - A SPY! IF THAT CAVE EVER WAS A MINE IT HASN'T BEEN WORKED SINCE 2030 A.D., — 400 YEARS AGO!
WHOA-A-A! BACK UP! DO YOU MEAN THIS IS THE YEAR 2430?
TO BE CONTINUED

Tubbs II. *Buck Rogers* was enormously influential, not because of the quality of its art, but because its story mesmerized the American public. *Buck Rogers* was a tale of a man who while investigating a mysterious

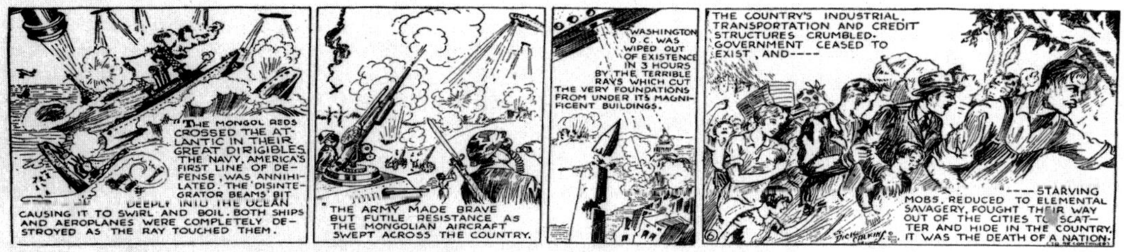
"THE MONGOL REDS CROSSED THE AT- LANTIC IN THEIR GREAT DIRIGIBLES. THE NAVY, AMERICA'S FIRST LINE OF DE- FENSE, WAS ANNIHI- LATED. THE 'DISINTE- GRATOR BEAMS' BIT DEEPLY INTO THE OCEAN CAUSING IT TO SWIRL AND BOIL. BOTH SHIPS AND AEROPLANES WERE COMPLETELY DE- STROYED AS THE RAY TOUCHED THEM.
"THE ARMY MADE BRAVE BUT FUTILE RESISTANCE AS THE MONGOLIAN AIRCRAFT SWEPT ACROSS THE COUNTRY.
WASHINGTON D.C. WAS WIPED OUT OF EXISTENCE IN 3 HOURS BY THE TERRIBLE RAYS WHICH CUT THE VERY FOUNDATIONS FROM UNDER ITS MAGNI- FICENT BUILDINGS.
THE COUNTRY'S INDUSTRIAL, TRANSPORTATION AND CREDIT STRUCTURES CRUMBLED. GOVERNMENT CEASED TO EXIST, AND----
"----STARVING MOBS, REDUCED TO ELEMENTAL SAVAGERY, FOUGHT THEIR WAY OUT OF THE CITIES TO SCAT- TER AND HIDE IN THE COUNTRY. IT WAS THE DEATH OF A NATION.

gas in a deep mine is put in suspended animation and awakens in a future earth torn by war. The man, Buck Rogers, joins a resistance movement of freedom fighters who fight not only the bad guys on earth (the Mongols) but also invaders from Mars (the Tiger Men). *Buck Rogers* made its appearance as a daily comic strip on January 7, 1929, and was written by Phil Nowlan with rather crude art by Dick Calkins.

Two early examples of the *Buck Rogers* strip. The first, top, is the second strip in the continuity from January 8, 1929. The second, below, was clearly influential in its depiction of the destruction of Washington D.C. by alien invaders, from January, 13, 1929. Artwork, Dick Calkins, ©1929 National Newspaper Syndicate, Inc.

The strip was an adaptation of Nowlan's pulp magazine story *Armageddon 2419 A.D.* The importance of *Buck Rogers* cannot be underestimated. The strip introduced the American public to the ideas of pulp science fiction. *Buck Rogers* captivated not only children but **adults**. It helped make science fiction popular with the American public. *Buck Rogers* also helped interest many first generation comic book artists in science fiction and introduced many of the most important comic book artists of the second generation to science fiction/fantasy. *Buck Rogers* became a national craze and its characters, their space ships, and ray guns became part of the American lexicon.

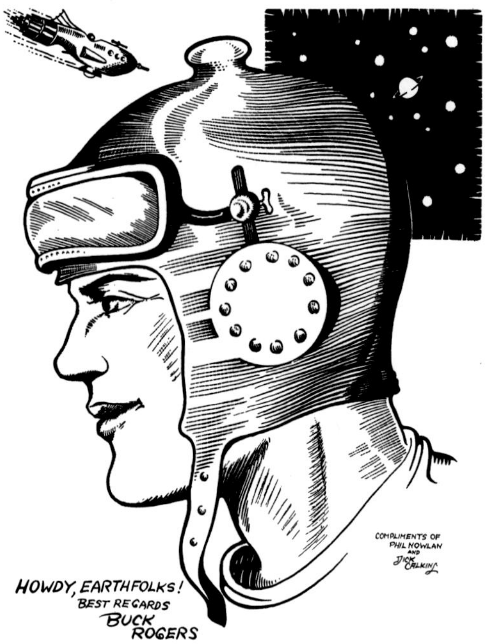
HOWDY, EARTHFOLKS!
BEST REGARDS
BUCK ROGERS
COMPLIMENTS OF PHIL NOWLAN AND DICK CALKINS

Left: a publicity portrait of Buck Rogers. Below: the corresponding portrait of Buck's girlfriend, and fellow freedom fighter, Wilma Deering, artwork, Dick Calkins, © 1929 National Newspaper Syndicate, Inc.

While Buck Rogers was saving the earth every day in the newspaper strip, Roy Crane was developing a milestone in newspaper adventure strips with *Wash Tubbs II*. *Wash Tubbs* had an exciting story, exotic locations, heroic

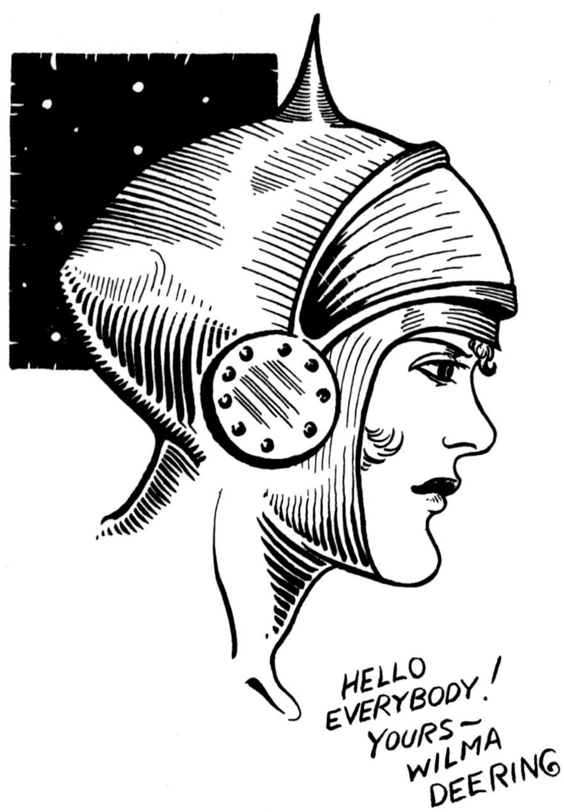
HELLO EVERYBODY!
YOURS—
WILMA DEERING

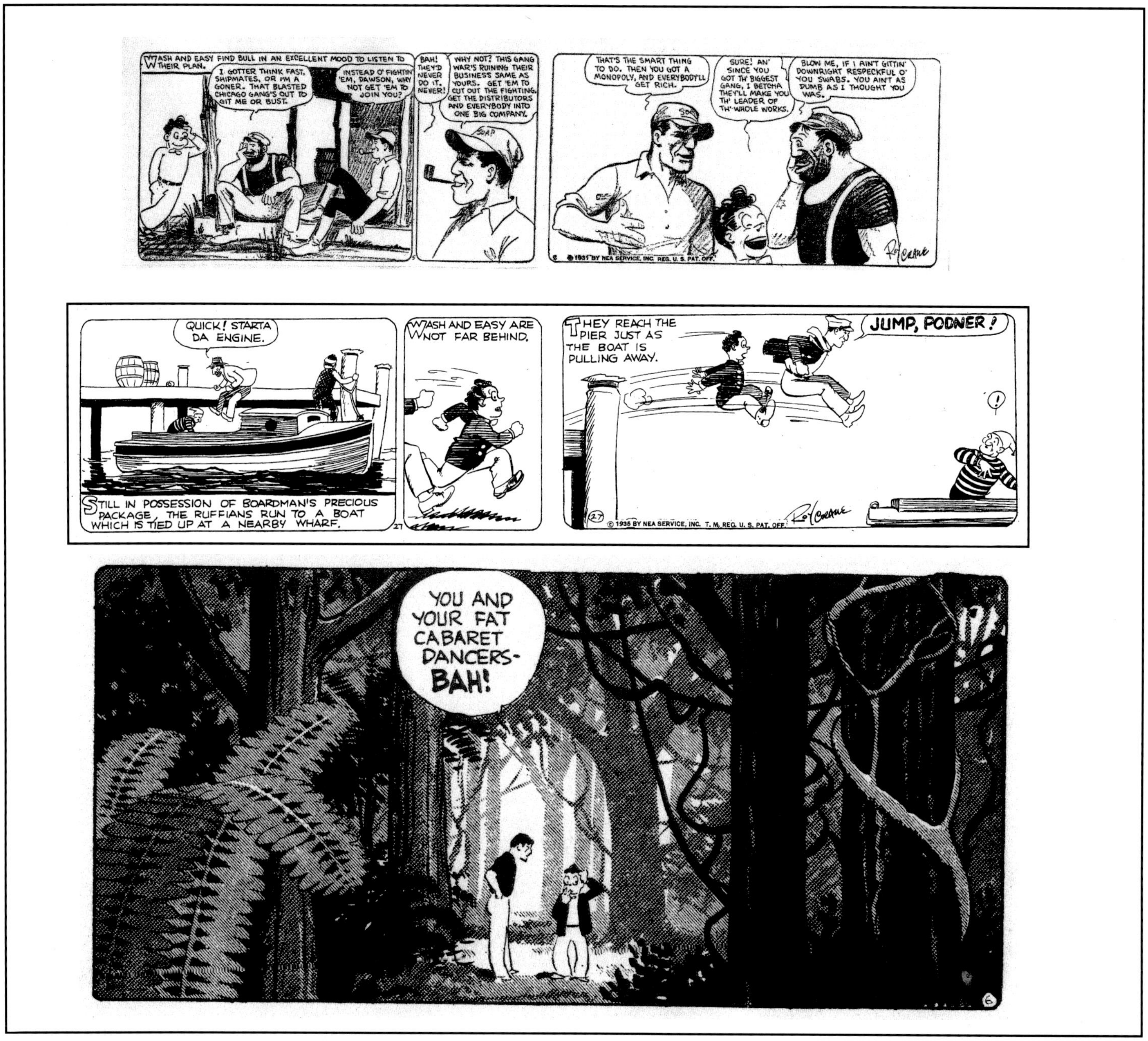
WASH AND EASY FIND BULL IN AN EXCELLENT MOOD TO LISTEN TO THEIR PLAN.
I GOTTER THINK FAST, SHIPMATES, OR I'M A GONER. THAT BLASTED CHICAGO GANG'S OUT TO GIT ME OR BUST.
INSTEAD O' FIGHTIN' 'EM, DAWSON, WHY NOT GET 'EM TO JOIN YOU?
BAH! THEY'D NEVER DO IT. NEVER!
WHY NOT? THIS GANG WAR'S RUINING THEIR BUSINESS SAME AS YOURS. GET 'EM TO CUT OUT THE FIGHTING. GET THE DISTRIBUTORS AND EVERYBODY INTO ONE BIG COMPANY.
THAT'S THE SMART THING TO DO. THEN YOU GOT A MONOPOLY, AND EVERYBODY'LL GET RICH.
SURE! AN' SINCE YOU GOT TH' BIGGEST GANG, I BETCHA THEY'LL MAKE YOU TH' LEADER OF TH' WHOLE WORKS.
BLOW ME, IF I AIN'T GITTIN' DOWNRIGHT RESPECKFUL O' YOU SWABS. YOU AIN'T AS DUMB AS I THOUGHT YOU WAS.
© 1931 BY NEA SERVICE, INC. REG. U. S. PAT. OFF.
QUICK! STARTA DA ENGINE.
STILL IN POSSESSION OF BOARDMAN'S PRECIOUS PACKAGE, THE RUFFIANS RUN TO A BOAT WHICH IS TIED UP AT A NEARBY WHARF.
WASH AND EASY ARE NOT FAR BEHIND.
THEY REACH THE PIER JUST AS THE BOAT IS PULLING AWAY.
JUMP, PODNER!
© 1935 BY NEA SERVICE, INC. T. M. REG. U. S. PAT. OFF.
YOU AND YOUR FAT CABARET DANCERS- BAH!

characters and was beautifully drawn and composed. Crane's strip made its debut on April 21, 1924 under the title, *Washington Tubbs II. Wash Tubbs* was not immediately a breakthrough, however. It was not until 1929, with the strip's introduction of the character Captain Easy, that *Wash Tubbs* began to distinguish itself. In 1932, the strip was

Three examples showcasing the range of Roy Crane's early work on *Wash Tubbs*. The first, top, is drawn in grease pencil and dates from May 5, 1931. The second, middle, is from the original artwork, from 1935. The third, bottom, is a gorgeous example of how Crane utilized craftint paper to achieve atmospheric effects. Crane's work on *Wash Tubbs,* influenced most artists working in comic strips and comic books at the time. His work is an encyclopedia of effective ways to handle action and adventure material. Artwork, Roy Crane, ©2001 Newspaper Enterprise Association (NEA).

renamed *Captain Easy.* From 1928 onward, Crane began to distinguish the strip artistically. He experimented with different shading effects and in 1936 started using craftint doubletone paper (paper which when exposed to a liquid developer reveals different shades of gray dots, giving the art a shaded, nuanced character). Crane also experimented with the use of uniform gray dots, called ben day dots, which give the

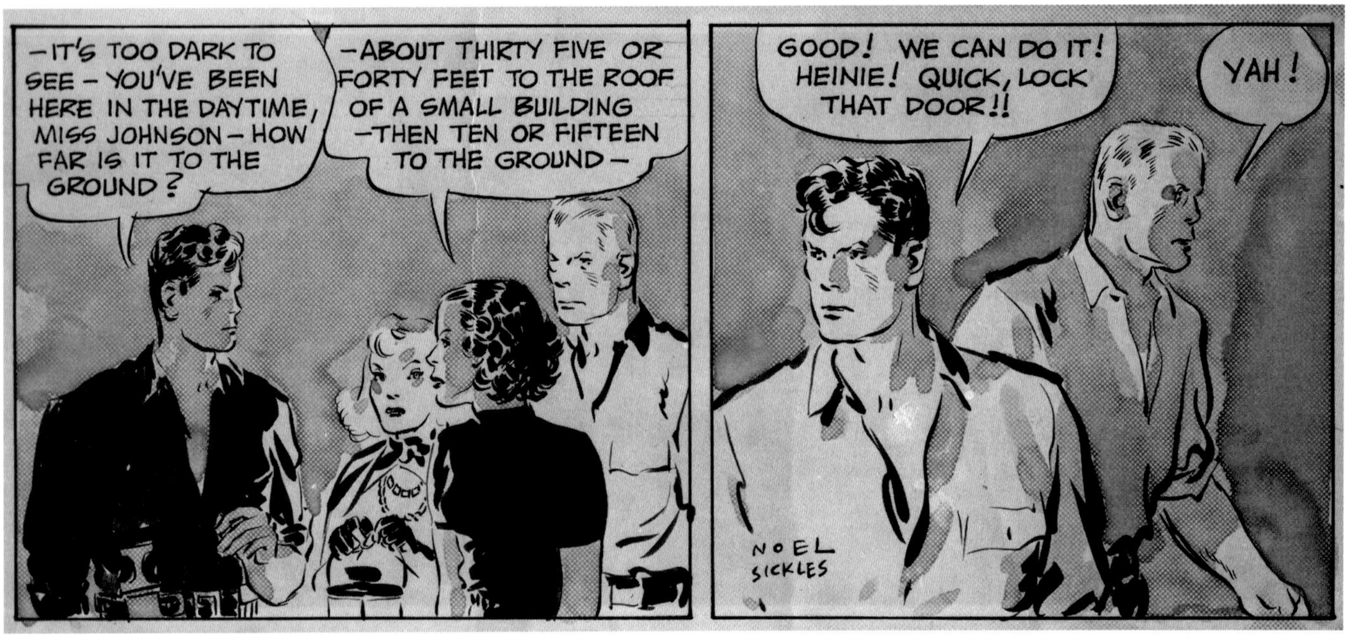
-IT'S TOO DARK TO SEE - YOU'VE BEEN HERE IN THE DAYTIME, MISS JOHNSON - HOW FAR IS IT TO THE GROUND?
-ABOUT THIRTY FIVE OR FORTY FEET TO THE ROOF OF A SMALL BUILDING -THEN TEN OR FIFTEEN TO THE GROUND -
GOOD! WE CAN DO IT! HEINIE! QUICK, LOCK THAT DOOR!!
YAH!
NOEL SICKLES

appearance of a monochromatic texture.

Crane's work influenced budding cartoon strip artists such as Milton Caniff, who commented that he read the strip while he was in college at Ohio State University, and also influenced a generation of comic strip and comic book artists including Gil Kane.

Noel Sickles' ground breaking work with *Scorchy Smith* influenced Milton Caniff's work for *Terry and the Pirates.* Above: two panels, from a four panel daily, highlighting Sickles' use of lighting and his simplicity of line. Work of this caliber has rarely been equalled. From the original artwork, Noel Sickles, *Scorchy Smith*, May 28, 1936, ©1936 The Associated Press.

It is also obvious that *Captain Easy* impressed Joe Shuster and Jerry Siegel, the creators of Superman, because another of their characters, Slam Bradley, closely resembled Captain Easy (as did Clark Kent and Superman).

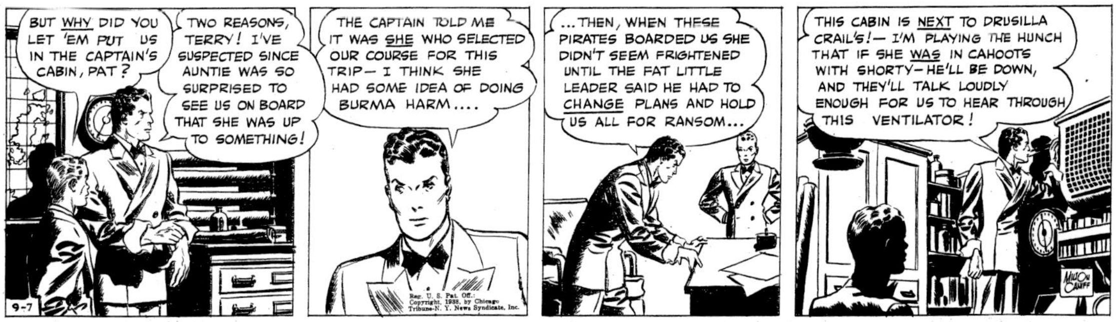
BUT WHY DID YOU LET 'EM PUT US IN THE CAPTAIN'S CABIN, PAT?
TWO REASONS, TERRY! I'VE SUSPECTED SINCE AUNTIE WAS SO SURPRISED TO SEE US ON BOARD THAT SHE WAS UP TO SOMETHING!
THE CAPTAIN TOLD ME IT WAS SHE WHO SELECTED OUR COURSE FOR THIS TRIP— I THINK SHE HAD SOME IDEA OF DOING BURMA HARM....
...THEN, WHEN THESE PIRATES BOARDED US SHE DIDN'T SEEM FRIGHTENED UNTIL THE FAT LITTLE LEADER SAID HE HAD TO CHANGE PLANS AND HOLD US ALL FOR RANSOM...
THIS CABIN IS NEXT TO DRUSILLA CRAIL'S!— I'M PLAYING THE HUNCH THAT IF SHE WAS IN CAHOOTS WITH SHORTY—HE'LL BE DOWN, AND THEY'LL TALK LOUDLY ENOUGH FOR US TO HEAR THROUGH THIS VENTILATOR!
9-7
MILTON CANIFF

Above: original artwork, Milton Caniff, *Terry and the Pirates*, September 7, 1938, ©1938 Chicago Tribune-N.Y. News Syndicate, Inc.

Another significant development in comic strips, from the perspective of comic book artists, was the creation of a language of form for depicting the characters and stories that was simple and nuanced. The two men primarily responsible for this development were Noel Sickles and Milton Caniff. Sickles and Caniff were both employees of the Associated Press and close collaborators and friends. Together, they developed an abbreviated shorthand for depicting characters and stories that gave the appearance of simplicity but which presented a nuanced and visually effective method of graphic

Below: one of Caniff's most famous characters, the "Dragon Lady," in a daily dating from May 19, 1939. The Dragon Lady was an archetypal character who served as the basis for many comic strip and comic book villians, who were more complex and multifaceted than antagonists in previous comic strip fiction, ©1939 Chicago Tribune-N.Y. News Syndicate, Inc.

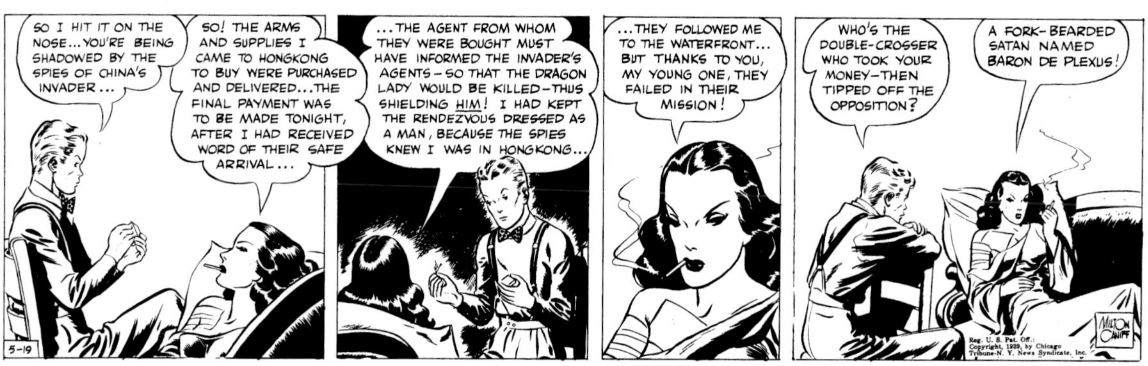
SO I HIT IT ON THE NOSE...YOU'RE BEING SHADOWED BY THE SPIES OF CHINA'S INVADER...
SO! THE ARMS AND SUPPLIES I CAME TO HONGKONG TO BUY WERE PURCHASED AND DELIVERED...THE FINAL PAYMENT WAS TO BE MADE TONIGHT, AFTER I HAD RECEIVED WORD OF THEIR SAFE ARRIVAL...
...THE AGENT FROM WHOM THEY WERE BOUGHT MUST HAVE INFORMED THE INVADER'S AGENTS—SO THAT THE DRAGON LADY WOULD BE KILLED—THUS SHIELDING HIM! I HAD KEPT THE RENDEZVOUS DRESSED AS A MAN, BECAUSE THE SPIES KNEW I WAS IN HONGKONG...
...THEY FOLLOWED ME TO THE WATERFRONT... BUT THANKS TO YOU, MY YOUNG ONE, THEY FAILED IN THEIR MISSION!
WHO'S THE DOUBLE-CROSSER WHO TOOK YOUR MONEY—THEN TIPPED OFF THE OPPOSITION?
A FORK-BEARDED SATAN NAMED BARON DE PLEXUS!
5-19
MILTON CANIFF

storytelling. So attractive was their style that it was quickly copied and assimilated by the majority of artists working on comic strips dealing with mystery, intrigue, and action.

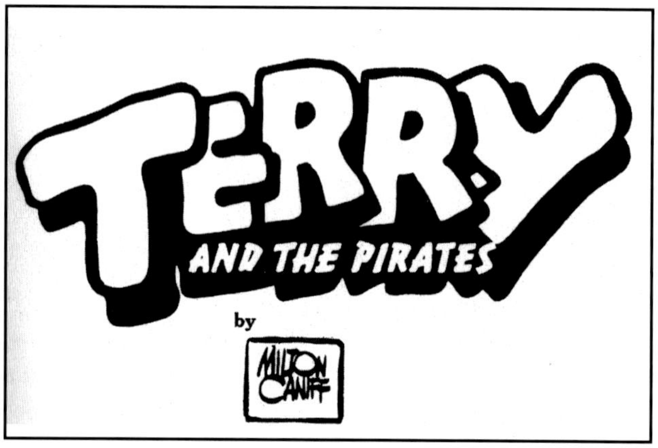

The logo designed by Noel Sickles for the Sunday continuity of Milton Caniff's *Terry and the Pirates*, ©2001 Chicago Tribune-N.Y. News Syndicate, Inc.

Sickles and Caniff met during the 1930s at the offices of the *Columbus* (Ohio) *Dispatch*. Both became fast friends and eventually went to New York to work in the art department of the Associated Press. Caniff first found work at the AP and through his help, Sickles was also hired. In 1933, Sickles took over an action strip called *Scorchy Smith*. By this time both men were sharing a studio in New York and had already worked on various projects together. In October 1934, Caniff began work on *Terry and the Pirates*. It is clear that the distinctive look of both *Scorchy* and *Terry* can be credited to Sickles, whose style and technique dramatically influenced Caniff. Caniff, however, continued to grow and mature in his art while Sickles quit the *Scorchy* strip and went into a successful career in illustration. Sickles, however, briefly returned to comic strips in an uncredited continuity of

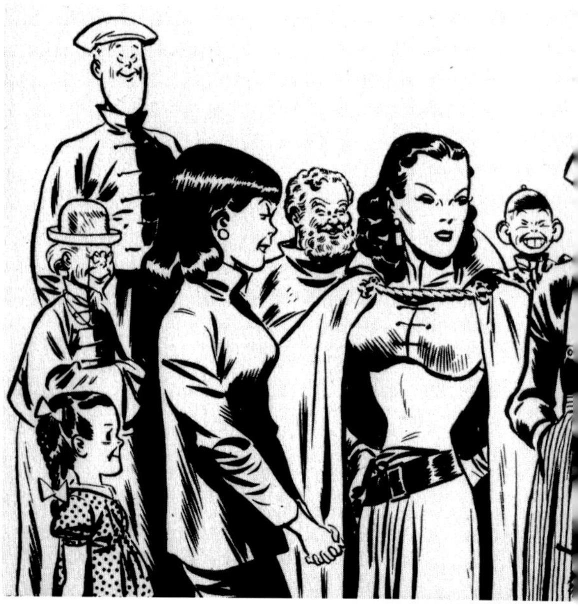

The cast of characters who populated the world of *Terry and the Pirates*, Milton Caniff, ©2001 Chicago Tribune-N.Y. News Syndicate, Inc.

Terry and the Pirates for Caniff. The influence of both Sickles' work on *Scorchy* and Caniff's work on the early years of *Terry and the Pirates* was extremely important to all cartoon pencillers and inkers for the next 25 years.

Alex Raymond's hero, Flash Gordon, swings into action in this panel which conveys the energy of the strip, © 2001 King Features Syndicate, Inc.

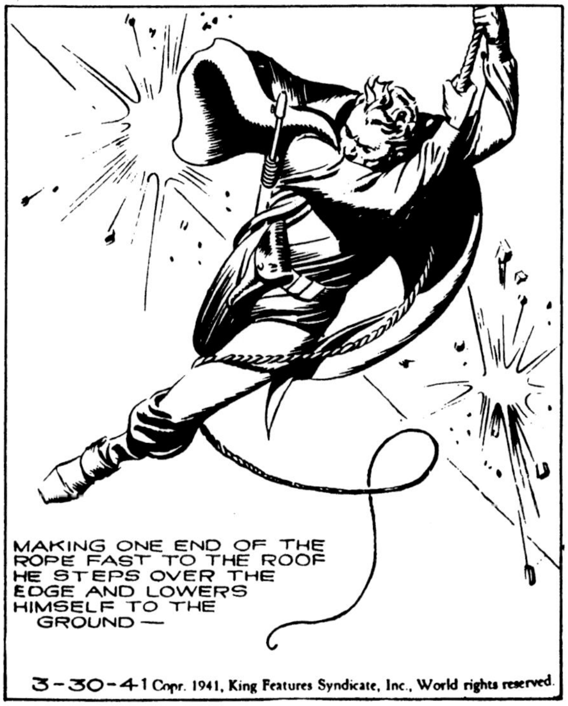
MAKING ONE END OF THE ROPE FAST TO THE ROOF HE STEPS OVER THE EDGE AND LOWERS HIMSELF TO THE GROUND —
3-30-41 Copr. 1941, King Features Syndicate, Inc., World rights reserved.

Sickles and Caniff created a style for the simplification of drawing and inking. This was accomplished by reducing the drawing of the figures to only the essential line, and inking, delineated by the depth of the brush stroke. Background detail was depicted utilizing shadow effects, which made use of the dramatic placing of black against white. Sickles and Caniff also focused attention on the graphic design of the logos for their newspaper strips and the style and appearance of their signatures in the strips. Sickles designed the logo for Caniff's *Terry and the Pirates* Sunday strip and later designed the title for Caniff's *Steve Canyon.*

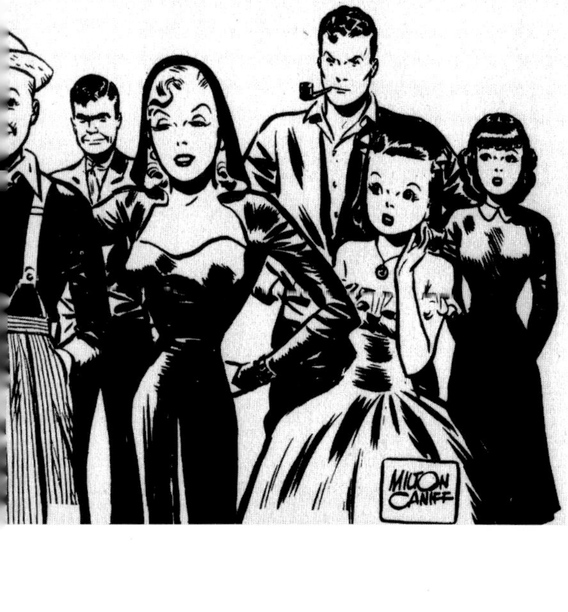
MILTON CANIFF

At almost the same time a young artist working for the King Features Syndicate, Alex Raymond, who had been drawing a strip called

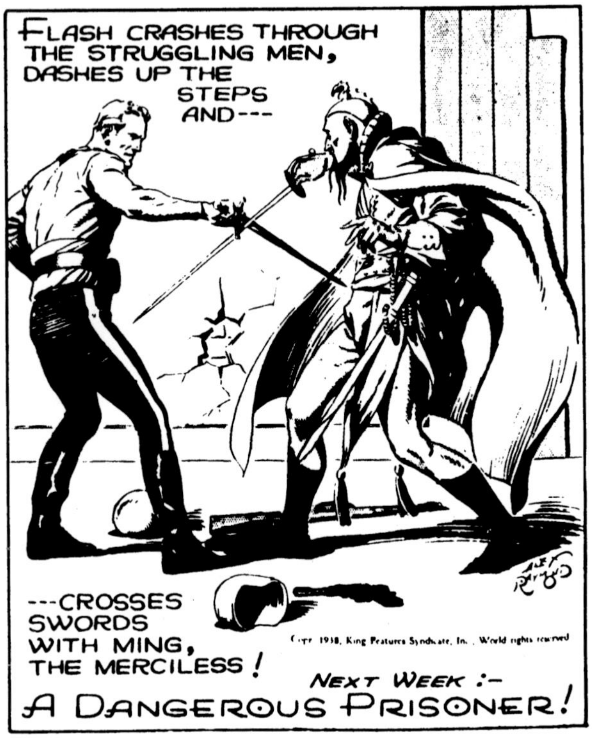
FLASH CRASHES THROUGH THE STRUGGLING MEN, DASHES UP THE STEPS AND---
---CROSSES SWORDS WITH MING, THE MERCILESS!
Copr. 1938, King Features Syndicate, Inc., World rights reserved
NEXT WEEK :-
A DANGEROUS PRISONER!

Two panels depicting classic confrontations, from Alex Raymond's *Flash Gordon*, ©2001 King Features Syndicate, Inc.

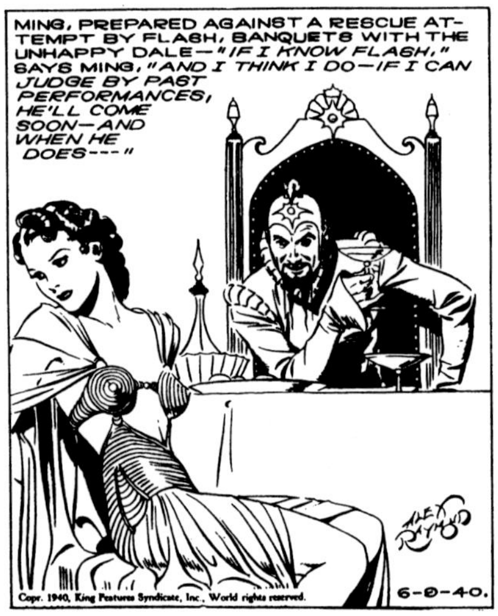
MING, PREPARED AGAINST A RESCUE ATTEMPT BY FLASH, BANQUETS WITH THE UNHAPPY DALE—"IF I KNOW FLASH," SAYS MING, "AND I THINK I DO—IF I CAN JUDGE BY PAST PERFORMANCES, HE'LL COME SOON—AND WHEN HE DOES---"
Copr. 1940, King Features Syndicate, Inc., World rights reserved.
6-8-40.

Secret Agent X–9, got the job of illustrating a strip called *Flash Gordon*. *Flash Gordon* was the Syndicate's reaction to the enormous popularity of Buck Rogers. *Flash Gordon* proved to be enormously influential to the first generation of comic book artists, and was the vehicle for Raymond to hone his craft and to mature into a truly significant comic strip artist.

Sickles, Caniff and Raymond were not the only comic strip artists whose work made an impact on the first and second generation of comic book artists. Chester Gould, the creator of *Dick Tracy*, which premiered in the *Chicago Tribune* in 1931, created a tough and highly stylized world and developed characterizations and concepts which influenced many comic book artists. Gould flattened the look of his characters, inked with a bold line and embraced the surreal possibilities of urban violence by creating characters and story lines that were memorable and bizarre. Gould created his hero, Dick Tracy, with an unmistakable profile and gave the strip villains that were hard to forget and who were archetypes for many comic book villains. Gould's *Dick Tracy* embraced the fantastic and the eccentric and made it popular to a wide audience. Sixty years after the creation of such villains as Flattop, Pruneface and Mumbles, these characters are still influential archetypes. Gould also depicted Dick Tracy's Chicago as a dark gotham city besieged by criminals, a concept that was not lost on comic book artists.

Also of import was the work done by Hal Foster, who introduced Tarzan to the comic pages and later created the still running strip *Prince Valiant*. Foster, who was an illustrator, had been formally trained at the Art Institute of Chicago, National Academy of Design and the Chicago Academy of Fine Arts. Initially, Foster drew illustrations with a lengthy text for an adaptation of *Tarzan* which ran in newspapers from January to March of 1929. This was not, however, the end of the strip. After a second false start under another artist, Foster returned to

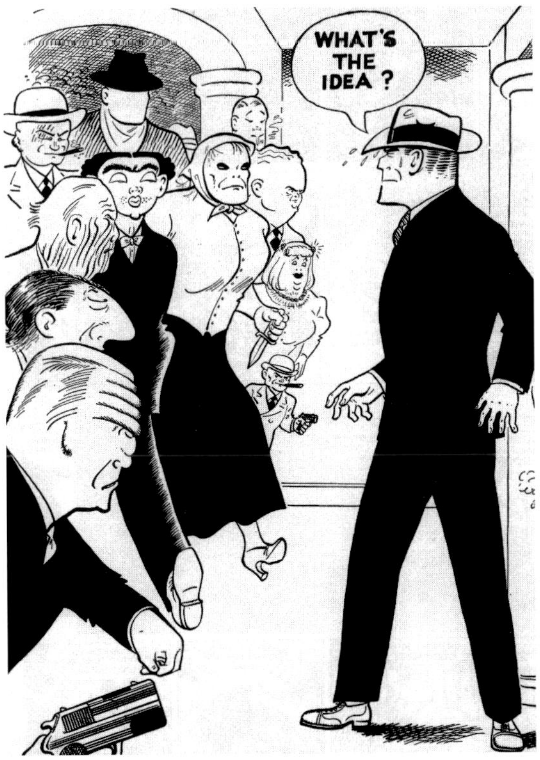
WHAT'S THE IDEA ?

Tarzan on September 27, 1931. With Foster's work on the subsequent *Tarzan* Sundays, he created a continuity with the strip which is still memorable and impressive. Using the size allowed the Sunday strip, coupled with his skill as an illustrator, Foster utilized many different methods to tell his story integrating

Specially drawn for *Life* magazine in 1944, this illustration, by *Dick Tracy* creator Chestor Gould, shows Tracy confronted by a gallery of his criminal foes, ©2001 Tribune Media Services, Inc.

cinematic techniques into the strip. He used unusual angle shots. He cut back and forth in the same scene to show different perspectives. Foster orchestrated the development of his stories by creating panels where he would pull back and frame the shot, to show the entire scene, and then cut back to isolated action. Foster's skill as an **artist/ storyteller** distinguished *Tarzan* as a significant development in graphic storytelling which would have an important effect on other artists, including those among the first generation of comic book artists.

Foster was, however, not content to continue with *Tarzan* and developed his own strip, *Prince Valiant*. Due to Foster's popularity with William Randolph Hearst, the owner of the King Features Syndicate, *Prince Valiant* made its debut as a Sunday strip (it ran only as a Sunday strip) on February 13, 1937. With *Prince Valiant*, Foster developed his storytelling techniques and abilities even further.

The influence of the *Tarzan* strip was not over, however.

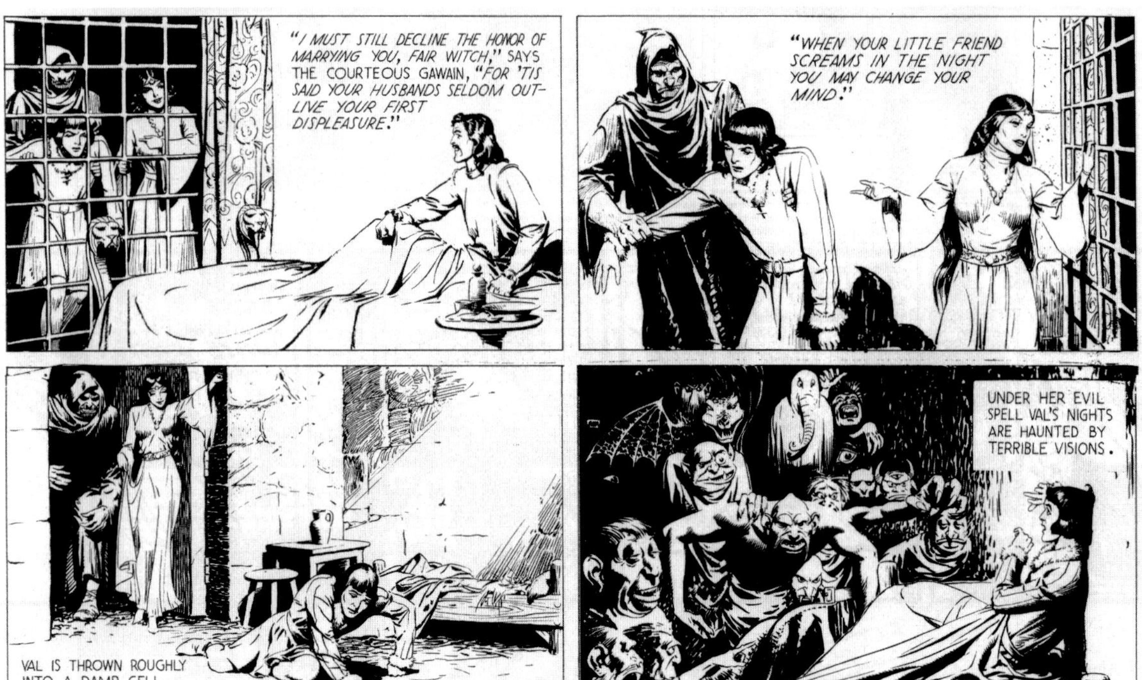
"I MUST STILL DECLINE THE HONOR OF MARRYING YOU, FAIR WITCH," SAYS THE COURTEOUS GAWAIN, "FOR 'TIS SAID YOUR HUSBANDS SELDOM OUTLIVE YOUR FIRST DISPLEASURE."
"WHEN YOUR LITTLE FRIEND SCREAMS IN THE NIGHT YOU MAY CHANGE YOUR MIND."
VAL IS THROWN ROUGHLY INTO A DAMP CELL.
58 3-19-38
UNDER HER EVIL SPELL VAL'S NIGHTS ARE HAUNTED BY TERRIBLE VISIONS.

A handsome *Prince Valiant* Sunday from early in the series, artwork, Hal Foster, February 13, 1937, ©2001 King Features Syndicate, Inc.

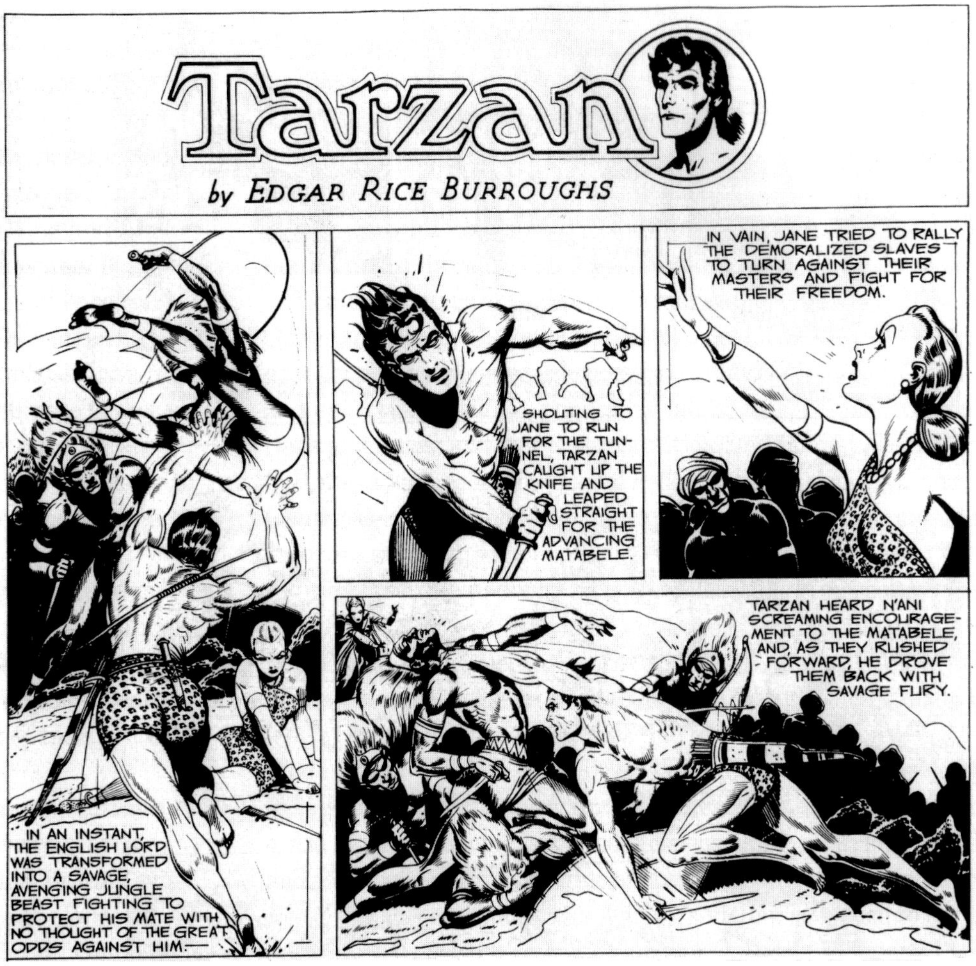
TARZAN
by EDGAR RICE BURROUGHS
IN AN INSTANT, THE ENGLISH LORD WAS TRANSFORMED INTO A SAVAGE, AVENGING JUNGLE BEAST FIGHTING TO PROTECT HIS MATE WITH NO THOUGHT OF THE GREAT ODDS AGAINST HIM.—
SHOUTING TO JANE TO RUN FOR THE TUNNEL, TARZAN CAUGHT UP THE KNIFE AND LEAPED STRAIGHT FOR THE ADVANCING MATABELE.
IN VAIN, JANE TRIED TO RALLY THE DEMORALIZED SLAVES TO TURN AGAINST THEIR MASTERS AND FIGHT FOR THEIR FREEDOM.
TARZAN HEARD N'ANI SCREAMING ENCOURAGEMENT TO THE MATABELE, AND, AS THEY RUSHED FORWARD, HE DROVE THEM BACK WITH SAVAGE FURY.

A *Tarzan* Sunday, showing the energy Burne Hogarth harnessed in the strip, which was so attractive to artists in comic books and comic strips, April 4, 1948, ©2001 Edgar Rice Burroughs, Inc.

Burne Hogarth, who took over from Foster, inevitably found his own voice with the strip. With Hogarth's work on the *Tarzan* Sundays from 1947 to 1950, he surpassed Foster's original work on the continuity and became an important influence on the second generation of comic book artists.

The precedents set by these artists served to guide and influence those who began work on the first comic books.

Although many of the first comic books offering original material, rather than strip reprints from newspapers, were clumsy looking and inarticulate, this was quickly remedied by the up-and-coming artists of the first generation. These artists included Jerry Robinson, who pencilled and inked some of the most memorable Batman covers ever created, and Jack Kirby, who put so much energy

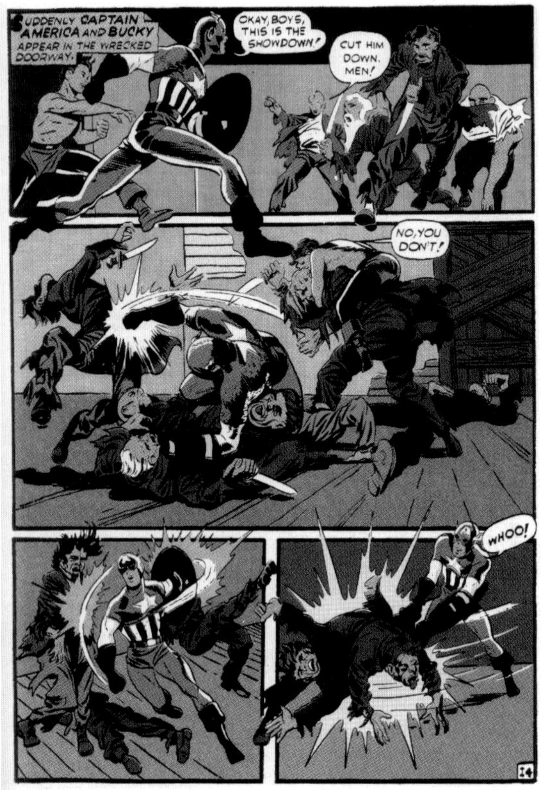

SUDDENLY CAPTAIN AMERICA AND BUCKY APPEAR IN THE WRECKED DOORWAY.
OKAY, BOYS, THIS IS THE SHOWDOWN!
CUT HIM DOWN, MEN!
NO, YOU DON'T!
WHOO!

Jack Kirby's *Captain America* was innovative and lively. Kirby's powerful art attracted readers and drew the admiration of artists for its energy and spirit. Kirby introduced a double spread splash page in *Captain America*, and set a very high standard for those who followed him on the feature. Interior page from *Captain America* #4, June, 1941, Jack Kirby, pencils, Joe Simon, inks, ©2001 Marvel Characters, Inc.

into his artwork that his characters literally came out of the pages at the viewer. What comic books were and could be, were defined by these artists. As Robinson focused his skills on design, Lou Fine and Mac Raboy focused their attention on imparting grace and elegance to their characters with compositions that could not be copied or equaled. Will Eisner developed the plots to his stories featuring the Spirit with great intelligence. He defined the uses of the first page in a comic book story, called a splash page, by integrating the logos and text of the story into the page design itself. With Eisner, the text became an element of the story. Words were used not only to further the story but as compositional elements. All of these young artists helped define the fledgling art of the comics. It was now up to the second generation, the generation to which Gil Kane belonged, to build on this foundation and to further refine, with those who remained from the first generation, the advances that would come in graphic storytelling.

Below: a Will Eisner splash page from the *Spirit*, June 26, 1949. The *Spirit* ran as a comic book/newspaper section in Sunday newspapers, and was innovative in its use of the splash page. This example integrates the feature's title into the artwork, with Eisner's characteristic sense of humor, ©2001 Will Eisner.

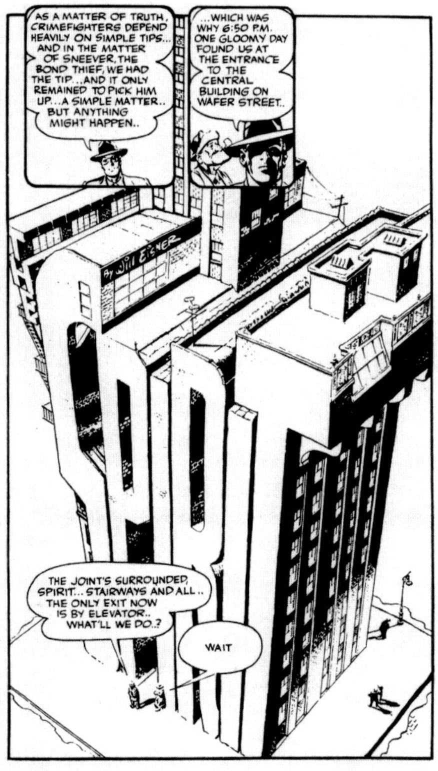

AS A MATTER OF TRUTH, CRIMEFIGHTERS DEPEND HEAVILY ON SIMPLE TIPS... AND IN THE MATTER OF SNEEVER, THE BOND THIEF, WE HAD THE TIP... AND IT ONLY REMAINED TO PICK HIM UP... A SIMPLE MATTER.. BUT ANYTHING MIGHT HAPPEN..
...WHICH WAS WHY 6:50 P.M. ONE GLOOMY DAY FOUND US AT THE ENTRANCE TO THE CENTRAL BUILDING ON WAFER STREET..
THE JOINT'S SURROUNDED, SPIRIT... STAIRWAYS AND ALL.. THE ONLY EXIT NOW IS BY ELEVATOR.. WHAT'LL WE DO..?
WAIT

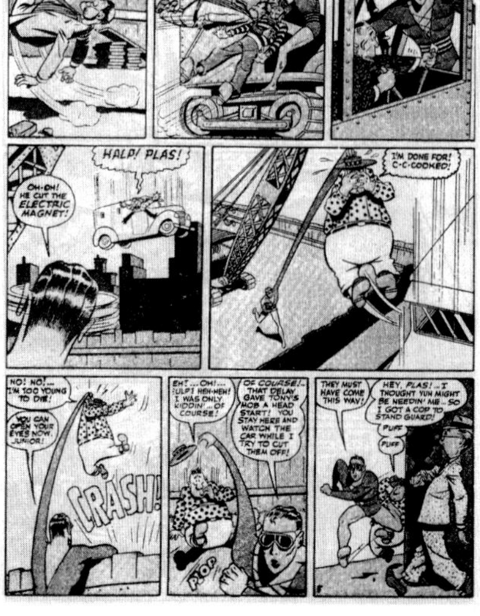

PAGE 20
PLASTIC MAN
JUST TO MAKE SURE THAT.....
...NONE OF YOUR PALS CAN GET AWAY!
YOU'VE GOT ME, PLASTIC MAN... BUT I'LL FIX THAT FAT FRIEND O' YOURS!
WHAT TH---??
HALP! PLAS!
OH-OH! HE CUT THE ELECTRIC MAGNET!
I'M DONE FOR! C-C-COOKED!
NO! NO!... I'M TOO YOUNG TO DIE!
YOU CAN OPEN YOUR EYES NOW, JUNIOR!
CRASH!
EH? ...OH!... GULP! HEH-HEH! I WAS ONLY KIDDIN' ...OF COURSE!
OF COURSE!.. THAT DELAY GAVE TONY'S MOB A HEAD START! YOU STAY HERE AND WATCH THE CAR WHILE I TRY TO CUT THEM OFF!
PLOP
THEY MUST HAVE COME THIS WAY!
HEY, PLAS! ...I THOUGHT YUH MIGHT BE NEEDIN' ME... SO I GOT A COP TO STAND GUARD!
PUFF
PUFF

Right: Jack Cole's Plastic Man. Cole's character was drawn with panache and humor, and this page, from *Plastic Man* #2, Feb., 1944, shows Cole's genius for shifting the action and shooting from different camera angles, all while pacing the strip effortlessly, and drawing the feature aplomb. Kane would later pay homage to Cole with an attempt to bring the character back in 1966, ©2001 DC Comics.

3 ELI KATZ

Gil Kane started out life as Eli Katz. He was born on April 6, 1926, in Riga, Latvia. In 1930, at the height of the depression, he and his family moved to New York City where his father worked as a poultry merchant. Kane grew up in the Brownsville section of Brooklyn, going to movies and reading pulp magazines, newspaper strips and comic books. Indeed, Kane was in the perfect place to be exposed to one of the most stimulating environments of the twentieth century: Pre-World War II, New York City. As a boy Kane read *Buck Rogers, Tarzan, Dick Tracy, Terry and the Pirates, Flash Gordon,* and every comic book he could get his hands on. He also saw as many movies as he could afford (he especially loved Errol Flynn swashbuckler films). He was living in the highly charged, competitive, and optimistic world of immigrants who had come to New York because of the freedom and potential it offered them and their families. New York was also the center of the comics world. The "shops" that supplied art to comic book publishers were all located in New York and the

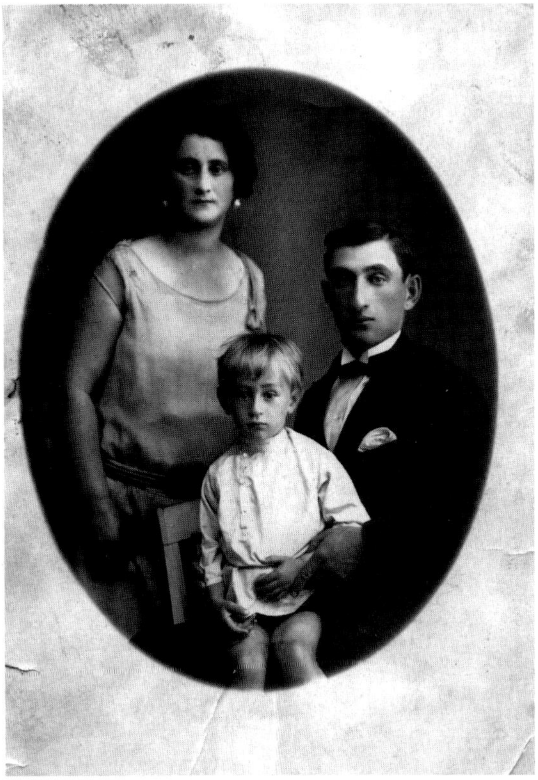

Eli Katz, with his mother and father, before the family emigrated to the United States.

surrounding area (with the exception of the shop set up by Superman creators Siegel and Shuster which started in Cleveland and was inevitably absorbed by DC Comics and moved to New York)[1]. These shops were similar to many other assembly line businesses in New York, which cranked out a product, using a system where work was distributed to many different workers. The pay in the shops was meager and the goal of many of the artists was to find work in advertising or in mainstream newspaper comic strips. In 1941, at the age of fifteen, with his portfolio of samples in hand, Kane tried to break into the comic book business making the rounds to numerous shops. While, initially, he did not find work, the persistence and desire to improve, which characterized his work and marked his career, eventually landed him a job less than a year later, at the age of 16. Kane would later observe that working in the

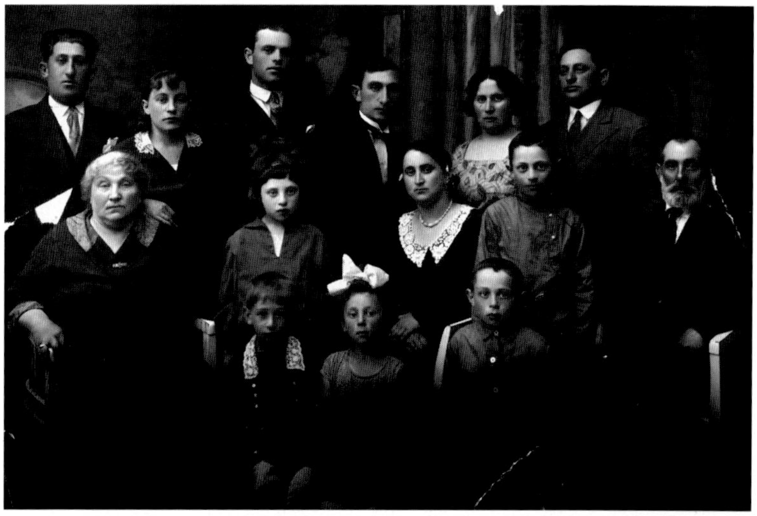

Kane, front, left, with his parents and relatives, before coming to the United States. Everyone in this picture, except Kane and his parents, was killed in the holocaust.

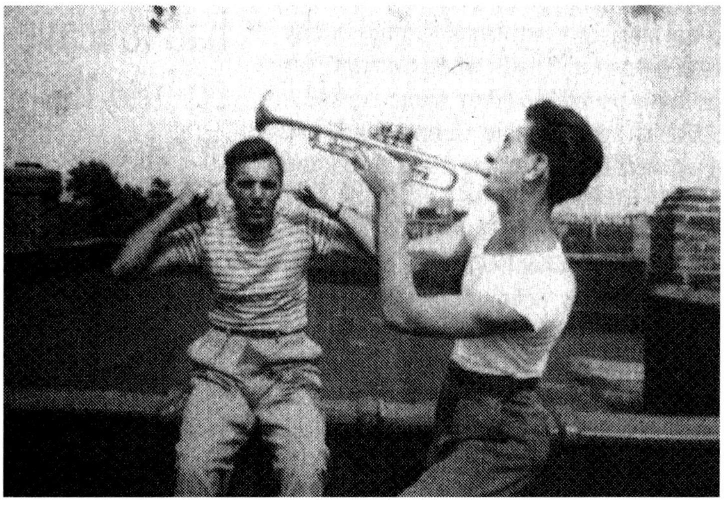

Kane, as a boy, showing off his musical talent.

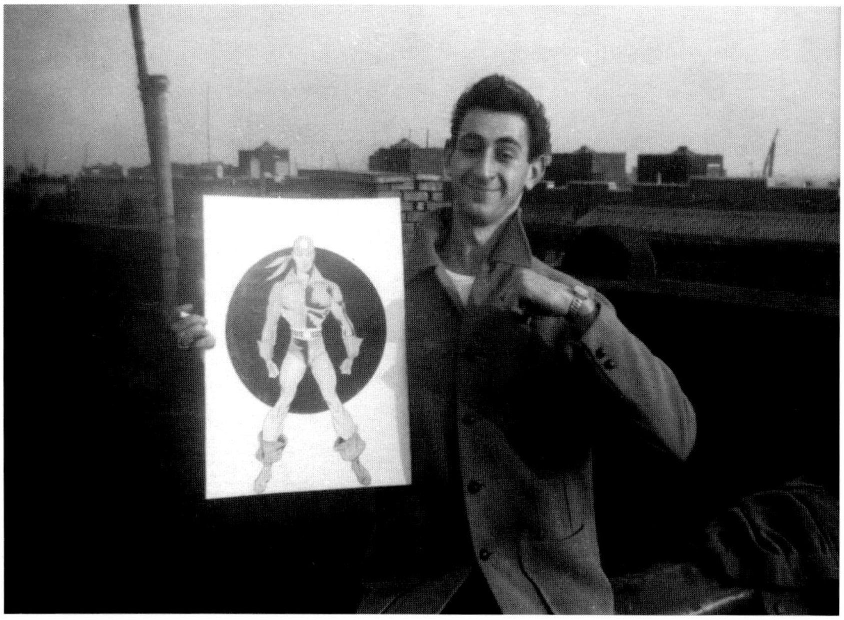

shops was his college education. This was a common opinion held by many of the second generation of comic artists who came to prominence in the late 1950s. Many of these artists viewed their work in the shops as invaluable in understanding not only the craft of the comics but the **art of the comics**.

The second generation of comic book artists included: Dan Barry, Jack Davis, Steve Ditko, Will Elder, Lee Elias, Russ Heath, Carmine Infantino, Bernie Krigstein, Joe Kubert, Harvey Kurtzman, Joe Orlando, John Severin, Alex Toth, Al Williamson, and Wally Wood.

In 1942, Kane got his first job doing clean-ups on comic book pages for MLJ. M, L, and J,

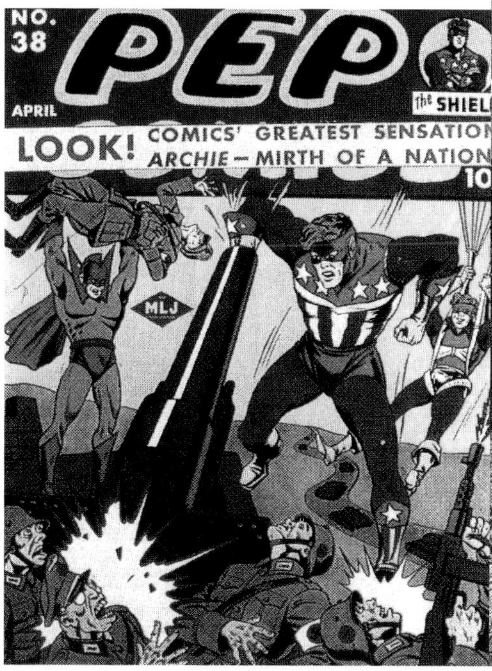

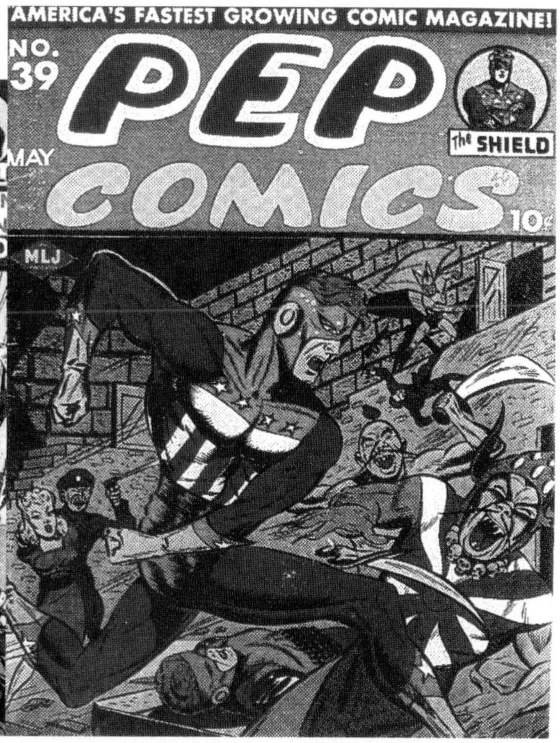

Covers to *Pep Comics* #38, April, 1943, and *Pep Comics* #39, May, 1943, ©2001 Archie Comics, Inc. Kane did not draw these covers, but contributed to the interior artwork.

were the initials of the three men who were the principals of the shop, Morris Coyne, Louis Silberkleit and John Goldwater. The MLJ comic line was later renamed Archie Comics. Kane's job was actually a free-lance assignment. His job required him to take pencilled pages of comic book stories home, put borders on the pages, draw word balloons, and erase marks and corrections from the pages. He was paid a fixed rate for each page on which he worked. Kane's first assignment was for a strip called *Inspector Bentley of Scotland Yard* in the comic book *Pep Comics*. After just three weeks he was fired. Almost immediately, Kane landed another job, with more responsibility, in the Jack Binder shop, pencilling pages. For the next two years, Kane worked at a number of shops and came under the tutelage of some of the most talented artists from the first generation of comic book artists. During this period, Kane got a job working for Joe Simon and Jack Kirby, pencilling pages for such strips as the *Boy Commandos,* the *Newsboy Legion* and the *Sandman*. These were popular and important titles in comics at that time, and Jack Kirby

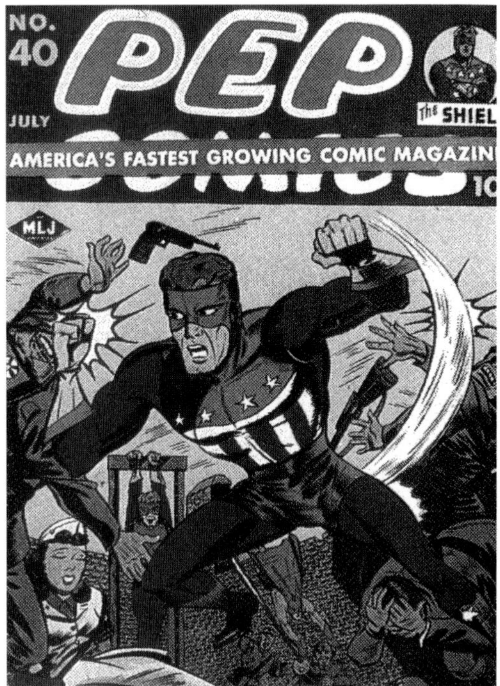

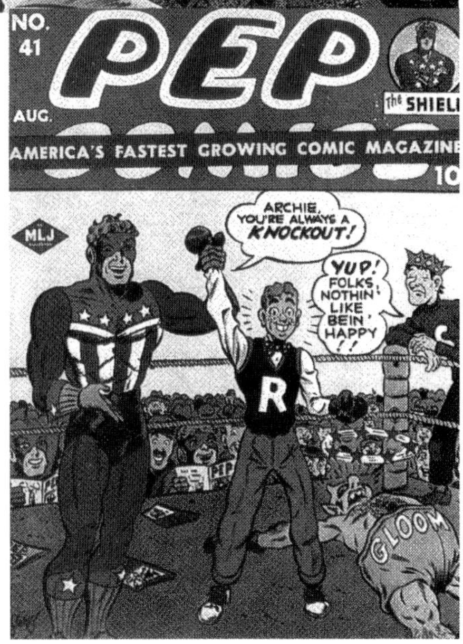

Covers to *Pep Comics* #40, July, 1943, and *Pep Comics* #41, August, 1943, ©2001 Archie Comics, Inc. Kane did not draw these covers, but contributed to the interior artwork.

was developing into one of the finest comic artists in the field. Kane worked with Kirby for approximately six months, at which time Kirby was drafted. It was while Kane was working for Simon and Kirby at DC Comics that he became familiar with Mort Meskin. Meskin became a highly respected first generation artist, who was well known for his desire to depict his characters in unique and unusual ways. Meskin was not content to reuse figures in the manner of an assembly line, or to fall back upon time tested formulas. He challenged his imagination and his work was admired by other comic book artists.

Kane also found work for Bernard Bailey. Bailey, who was a partner with artist Mac Raboy, produced work for Fawcett, which included art for the character Captain Marvel Jr. Raboy was renowned for his elegant figure work, solid cover designs, and layout.

When he was not trying to solicit more free-lance work pencilling comic pages, Kane worked all night finishing his assignments. By day, he attended the School of Industrial Art, which later became

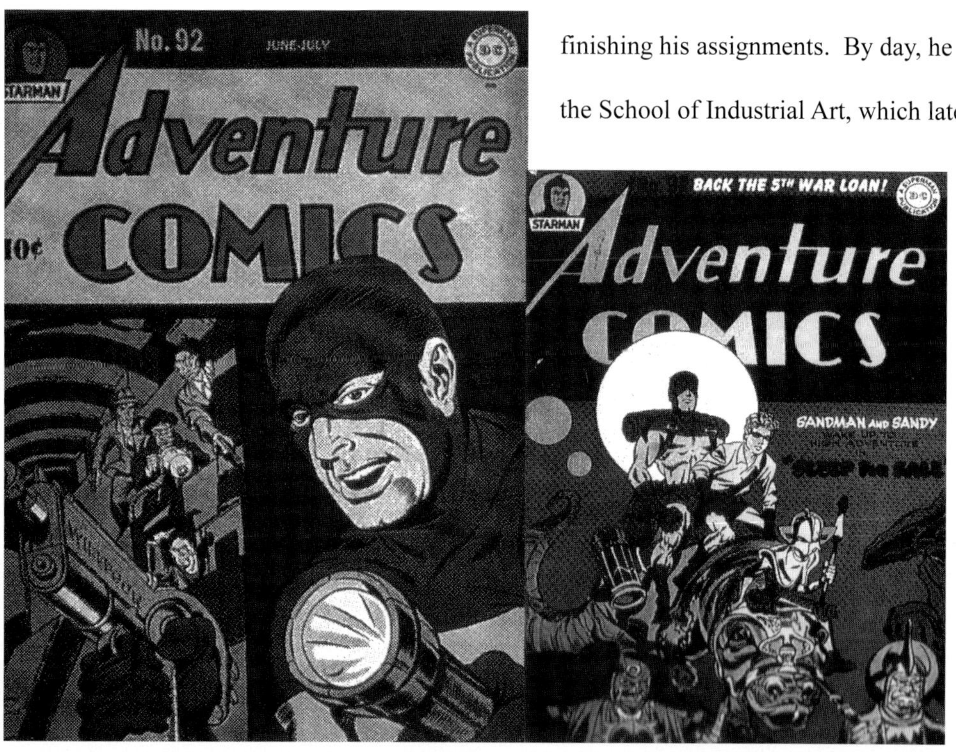

Covers to *Adventure Comics* #92, June/July, 1944, and *Adventure Comics* #93, Aug./Sept., 1944, ©2001 DC Comics. Kane did not draw the art for these covers, but worked as an assistant to Jack Kirby, pencilling the interior artwork.

the School for Art and Design. Kane was not the only aspiring comic artist at his school. Carmine Infantino and Harvey Kurtzman were classmates of Kane's, and they would subsequently work with Kane and distinguish themselves in the comics and publishing industries. While working in Bailey's shop, Kane and Infantino teamed up. Kane pencilled stories and Infantino inked them. They produced stories for several different shops and for DC Comics. The partnership did not continue due to Kane and Infantino's competitiveness with each other.

Kane, ever industrious, even set up his own studio for a short time on Vanderbilt Avenue in New York City, but it soon closed and Kane returned to working at his parent's home. Kane was spending the majority of his time soliciting work with different shops and working to complete his assignments. He felt that he was establishing himself as an artist. In an effort to devote full time to his craft, he quit school in early 1943. Kane's education did not stop, however. He sought out other artists and writers to expand his understanding of comic art, art, science, philosophy, and literature.

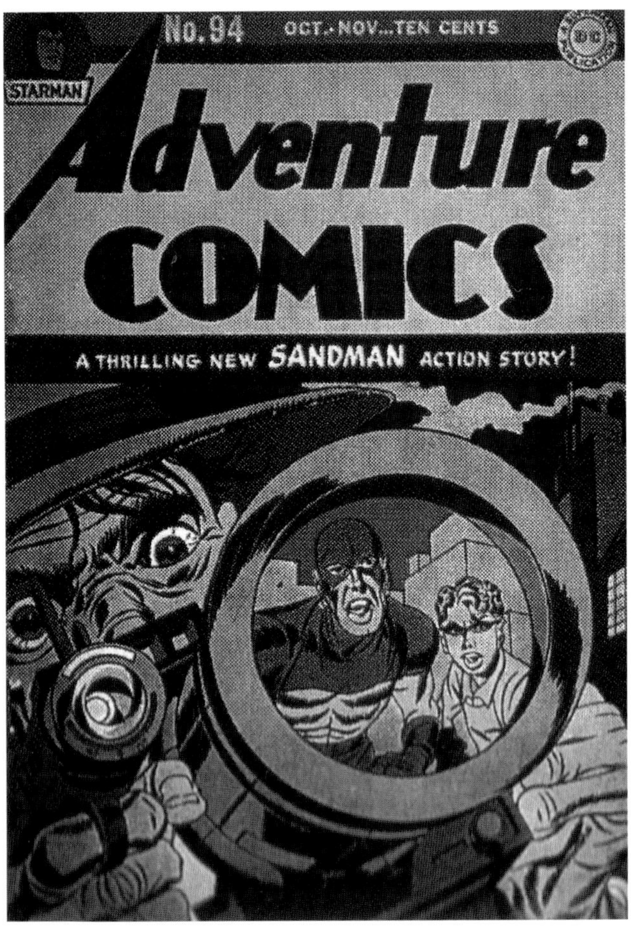

Cover art for *Adventure Comics* #94, Oct./Nov., 1944, ©2001 DC Comics. Kane did not draw the cover art, but worked as an assistant to Jack Kirby on the interior artwork.

He read voraciously, worked to hone his craft, and continued to do so until the end of his life. He also regularly attended the movies, which added even more fuel to his already active imagination.

Kane, with friends, in the Army, circa 1944.

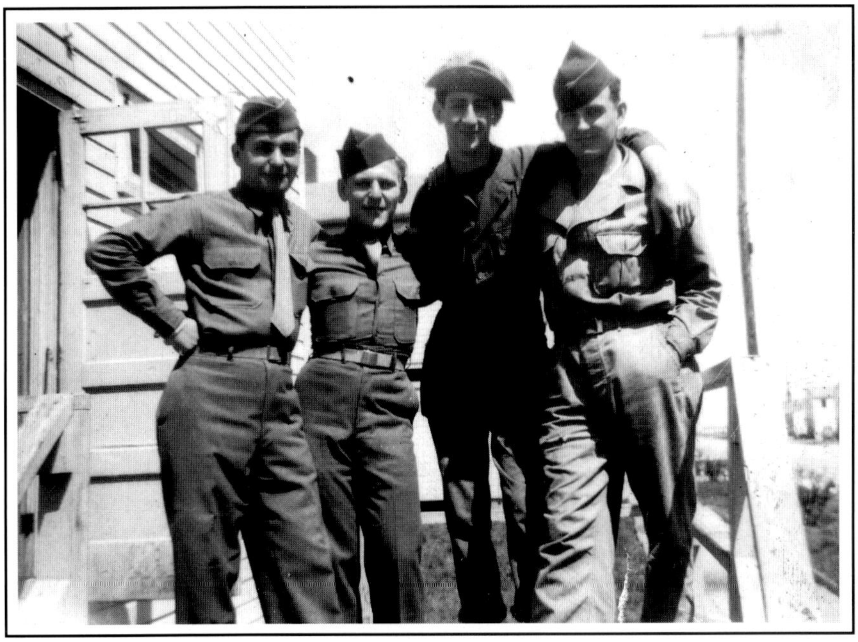

International tensions were heating up and this would effect everything. The comics industry would rise to support the war effort and many of the finest comic book artists of the first generation would go off to war. When Jack Kirby was drafted, he gave Kane the script to a *Newsboy Legion* story to be pencilled. When Kane returned the finished story, he was fired by DC Comics.

Early in 1944, Kane registered in the United States Army. He went home, told his parents and went out to find more work. Two months later, he was called into active service and was sent to Fort Dix.

Ten days later, he was assigned to Camp Abilene in Texas where he tried to get work as a cartoonist on the camp newspaper. The best he could do was to contribute cartoons, as he was unable to secure a full-time job. D-day, the invasion of Europe, was on the horizon, and Kane thought he would be sent to Europe, but instead he was sent to California, and then to the Philippines. Upon arriving in the Philippines, Kane came down with dengue fever, which made him sick for weeks. The war was ending, and so was Kane's nineteen months of service. He returned to New York in December, 1945, ready to start back as a comic book artist.

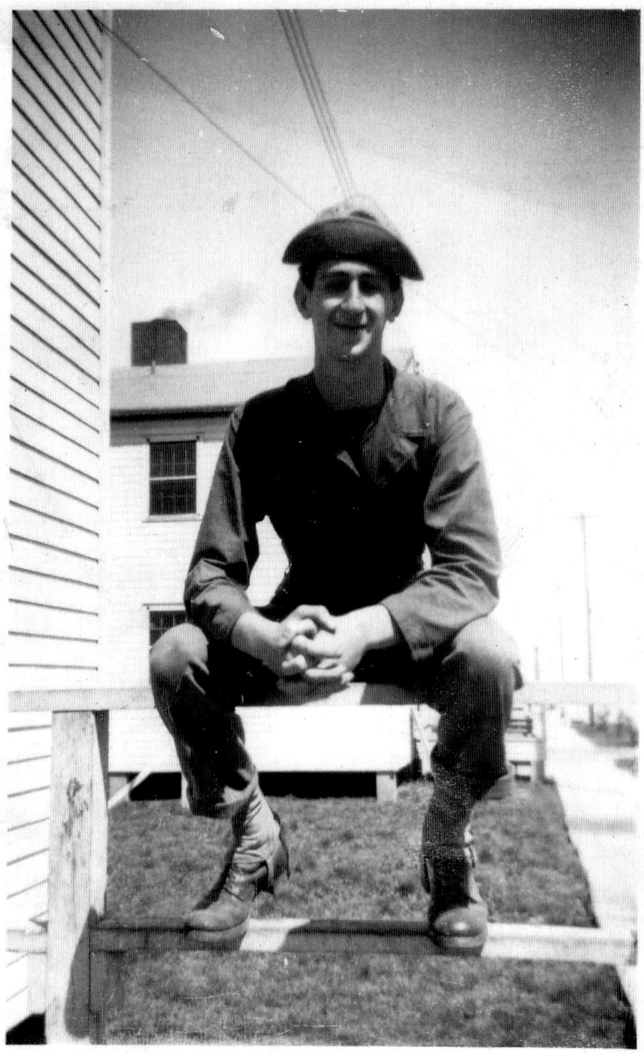

Kane, in the Army, circa 1944.

4 HONING HIS CRAFT

The comic industry experienced constant expansion during the war, despite wartime restrictions and paper shortages. One of the reasons for this increase was the popularity of comic books with American soldiers in the European and Pacific theaters of operation. To better serve this audience, the shops and publishers adapted their product and made it funnier, more sexual, and violently explicit. In 1945, superheroes were still popular but other subjects were beginning to prove potentially profitable as well. Jungle tales with scantily attired women, romance stories, westerns, and comedy would shortly become popular properties. It was into this atmosphere that Gil Kane was thrust when he re-entered the comic book business.

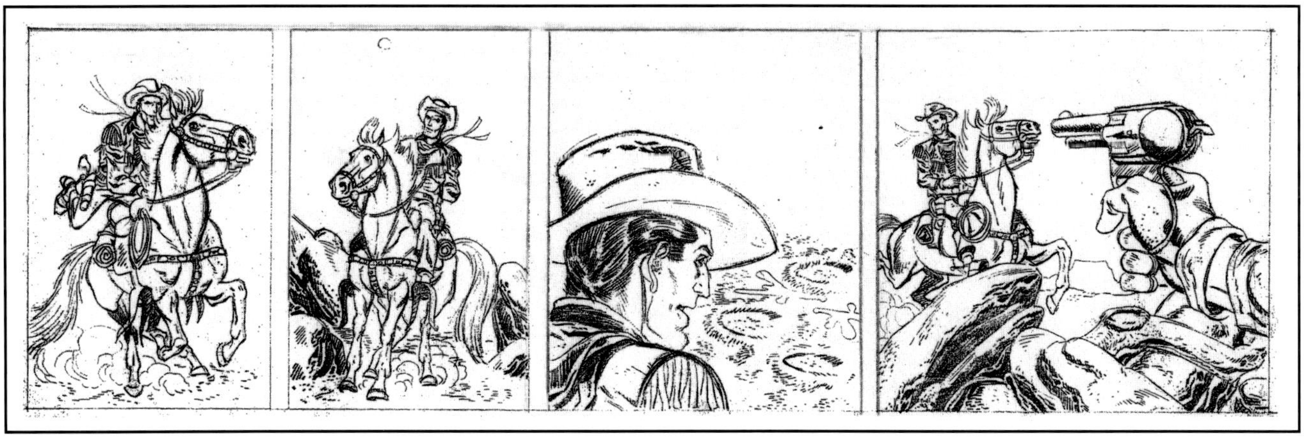

Kane, who had gone under a number of pseudonyms, including Pen Star, Scott Edward, and Gil Stack, ultimately adopted the name Gil Kane, borrowing his first name from a performer and actor,

Above: a sample for a proposed daily strip entitled, *Whip Horne*, drawn by Kane in the mid 1940s, ©2001 The Estate of Gil Kane. One of the earliest surviving pieces of Kane's original artwork, this daily, pencils only, is clearly the work of an apprentice. The pencilling is stiff and clumsy. The composition is confused and unsure. Kane persisted in mastering his craft, and in less than five years had developed into a seasoned professional.

Gil Lamb. Indeed, Kane's taking a new name was indicative of his desire to reinvent himself, a compulsion which was a driving force for the rest of his life. For work, Kane went back to the Bailey shop pencilling pages. He also went back to free-lancing for other shops, and continued to make the rounds looking for work. Kane was now working in as many genres as he could. He worked on westerns, adventure, science fiction, comics about movie stars and musicians, and, of course, superheroes. No one, including Kane, was prepared for the radical changes that would alter the industry. The first generation of artists, who had formed comic books and their content, were growing, maturing, and leaving the business. Lou Fine, who had worked in the Eisner shop and had imparted élan and verve to comic book characters, was lured into advertising and would never again produce the brilliant and inspired work he had created in the comics. Mac Raboy took over the *Flash Gordon* Sunday strip in 1948, which he

An interior page from the original artwork from *All-Star Western* #59, June/July, 1951, Gil Kane, pencils, Bernard Sachs (?), inks, ©2001 DC Comics. By 1951, Kane was a consummate professional, as this page amply demonstrates. He was developing an individual style which he would further hone over the next fifteen years. Clearly, this excellent example of Kane's early work is both polished and confident.

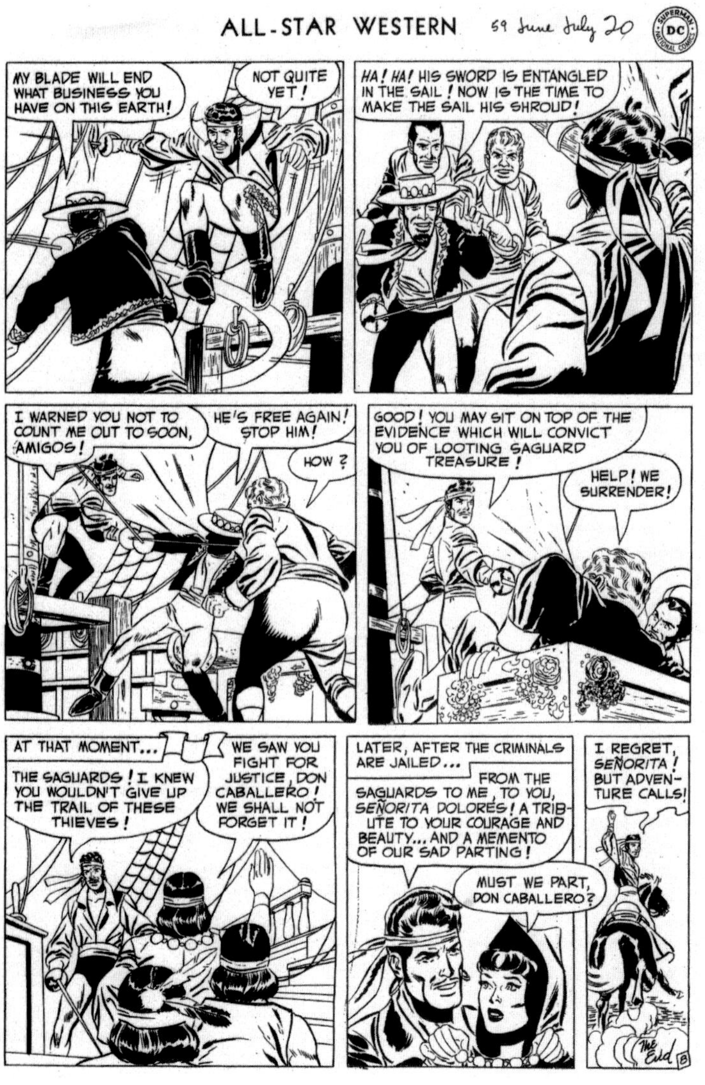
ALL-STAR WESTERN
MY BLADE WILL END WHAT BUSINESS YOU HAVE ON THIS EARTH!
NOT QUITE YET!
HA! HA! HIS SWORD IS ENTANGLED IN THE SAIL! NOW IS THE TIME TO MAKE THE SAIL HIS SHROUD!
I WARNED YOU NOT TO COUNT ME OUT TO SOON, AMIGOS!
HE'S FREE AGAIN! STOP HIM!
HOW?
GOOD! YOU MAY SIT ON TOP OF THE EVIDENCE WHICH WILL CONVICT YOU OF LOOTING SAGUARD TREASURE!
HELP! WE SURRENDER!
AT THAT MOMENT...
THE SAGUARDS! I KNEW YOU WOULDN'T GIVE UP THE TRAIL OF THESE THIEVES!
WE SAW YOU FIGHT FOR JUSTICE, DON CABALLERO! WE SHALL NOT FORGET IT!
LATER, AFTER THE CRIMINALS ARE JAILED...
FROM THE SAGUARDS TO ME, TO YOU, SEÑORITA DOLORES! A TRIBUTE TO YOUR COURAGE AND BEAUTY... AND A MEMENTO OF OUR SAD PARTING!
MUST WE PART, DON CABALLERO?
I REGRET, SEÑORITA! BUT ADVENTURE CALLS!

worked on until his death in 1967, and rarely equalled his inspired work in comics. Within several years, many more of the greatest and most influential first generation artists would be unable to find work, or leave comics for other opportunities. Fawcett, which had the *Captain Marvel* line of comic books, had been in protracted litigation over copyright infringement with the owner of Superman, DC Comics, due to alleged similarities between the characters, and would withdraw from the publication of comic books as much as a result of this litigation as from market conditions. Jack Cole, perhaps one of the most creative comic artists ever, would leave comics and would eventually find a home drawing cartoons for Hugh Hefner at *Playboy*.

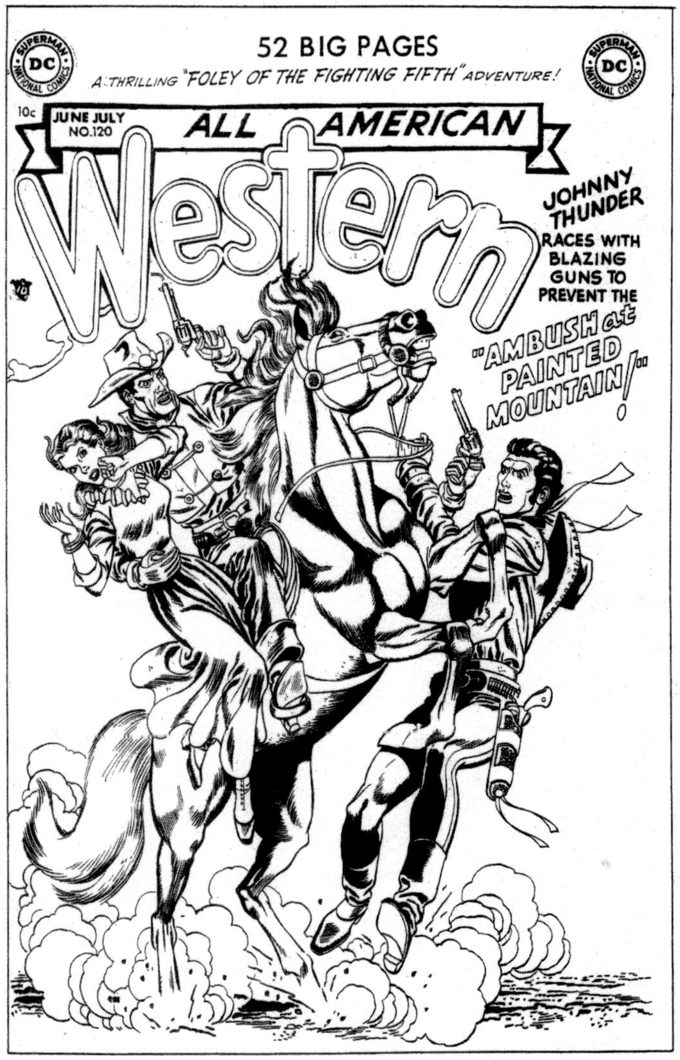
52 BIG PAGES
A THRILLING "FOLEY OF THE FIGHTING FIFTH" ADVENTURE!
10c
JUNE JULY NO.120
ALL AMERICAN
Western
JOHNNY THUNDER RACES WITH BLAZING GUNS TO PREVENT THE
"AMBUSH at PAINTED MOUNTAIN!"

Original artwork for the cover for *All-American Western* #120, June/July, 1951, Gil Kane, pencils, ©2001 DC Comics. Kane spent a significant amount of time drawing western stories for comic books and had a long standing affection for the genre, which continued throughout his career.

By 1949 superheroes were dead. The shop system had ended.

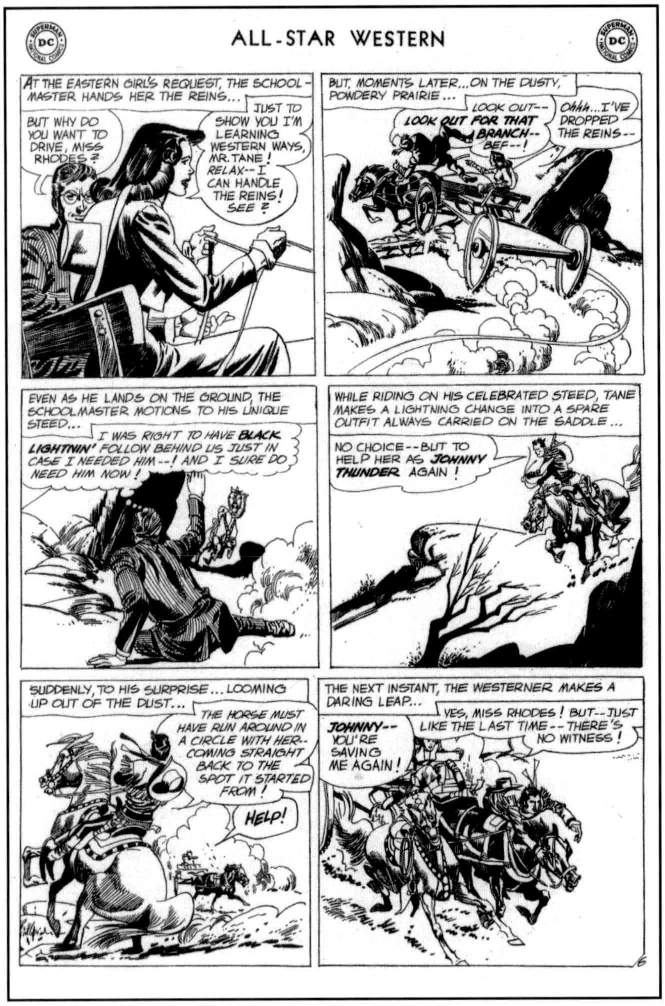
ALL-STAR WESTERN
AT THE EASTERN GIRL'S REQUEST, THE SCHOOL-MASTER HANDS HER THE REINS...
BUT WHY DO YOU WANT TO DRIVE, MISS RHODES?
JUST TO SHOW YOU I'M LEARNING WESTERN WAYS, MR. TANE! RELAX--I CAN HANDLE THE REINS! SEE?
BUT, MOMENTS LATER...ON THE DUSTY, POWDERY PRAIRIE...
LOOK OUT-- LOOK OUT FOR THAT BRANCH-- BEF--!
Ohhh...I'VE DROPPED THE REINS--
EVEN AS HE LANDS ON THE GROUND, THE SCHOOLMASTER MOTIONS TO HIS UNIQUE STEED...
I WAS RIGHT TO HAVE BLACK LIGHTNIN' FOLLOW BEHIND US JUST IN CASE I NEEDED HIM--! AND I SURE DO NEED HIM NOW!
WHILE RIDING ON HIS CELEBRATED STEED, TANE MAKES A LIGHTNING CHANGE INTO A SPARE OUTFIT ALWAYS CARRIED ON THE SADDLE...
NO CHOICE--BUT TO HELP HER AS JOHNNY THUNDER AGAIN!
SUDDENLY, TO HIS SURPRISE...LOOMING UP OUT OF THE DUST...
THE HORSE MUST HAVE RUN AROUND IN A CIRCLE WITH HER--COMING STRAIGHT BACK TO THE SPOT IT STARTED FROM!
HELP!
THE NEXT INSTANT, THE WESTERNER MAKES A DARING LEAP...
JOHNNY--YOU'RE SAVING ME AGAIN!
YES, MISS RHODES! BUT--JUST LIKE THE LAST TIME--THERE'S NO WITNESS!
6

Original artwork for an interior page featuring Johnny Thunder, from *All-Star Western*, Gil Kane, pencils, ©2001 DC Comics.

Major superhero titles had been transformed into western titles, but Kane still managed to find work. In fact, despite the hard times visited upon the industry, Kane continued to work and develop his craft. He also made contacts and connections with writers, artists, and editors that would serve him for the rest of his life. In 1947, he again landed work with DC Comics. It was at this time that he met Robert Kanigher and Julius Schwartz, who both later became editors at DC Comics and would be responsible for assigning artists to stories. After working for about six months for DC Comics Kane was, yet again, fired. He immediately found work for the comic book *Famous Funnies*. Subsequently, Schwartz brought Kane back to DC Comics in 1949, giving and getting him work on a long-term basis. Kane's association with DC Comics would last, on and off, until Kane's death.

Indeed, it was Kane's relationship with Schwartz that resulted in Kane's most famous collaborations in commercial comics a decade later. Schwartz was aware

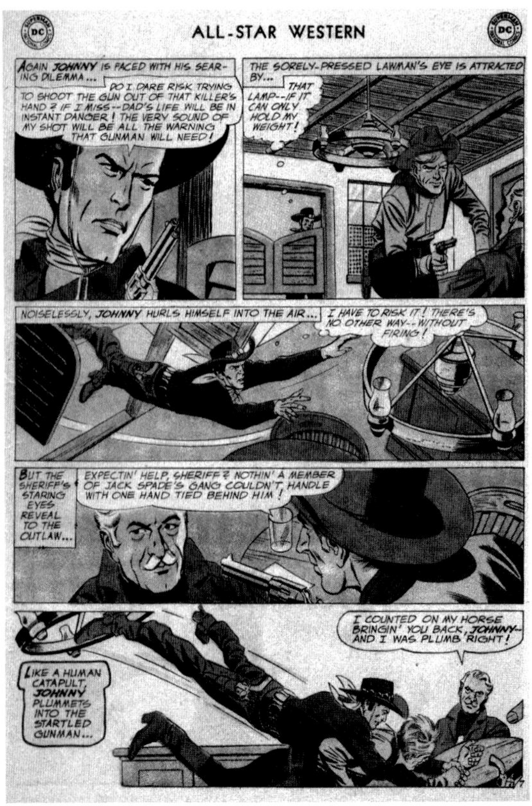
ALL-STAR WESTERN
AGAIN JOHNNY IS FACED WITH HIS SEARING DILEMMA...
DO I DARE RISK TRYING TO SHOOT THE GUN OUT OF THAT KILLER'S HAND? IF I MISS--DAD'S LIFE WILL BE IN INSTANT DANGER! THE VERY SOUND OF MY SHOT WILL BE ALL THE WARNING THAT GUNMAN WILL NEED!
THE SORELY-PRESSED LAWMAN'S EYE IS ATTRACTED BY...
THAT LAMP--IF IT CAN ONLY HOLD MY WEIGHT!
NOISELESSLY, JOHNNY HURLS HIMSELF INTO THE AIR...
I HAVE TO RISK IT! THERE'S NO OTHER WAY--WITHOUT FIRING!
BUT THE SHERIFF'S STARING EYES REVEAL TO THE OUTLAW...
EXPECTIN' HELP, SHERIFF? NOTHIN' A MEMBER OF JACK SPADE'S GANG COULDN'T HANDLE WITH ONE HAND TIED BEHIND HIM!
LIKE A HUMAN CATAPULT, JOHNNY PLUMMETS INTO THE STARTLED GUNMAN...
I COUNTED ON MY HORSE BRINGIN' YOU BACK, JOHNNY--AND I WAS PLUMB RIGHT!

A typical Kane western story, interior page, from *All-Star Western* #109, Oct./Nov., 1959, Gil Kane, pencils, Joe Giella, inks, ©2001 DC Comics.

of Kane's talents and abilities, and had a rapport with Kane which worked to the advantage of both men. Over the many years they worked together, Kane knew he could rely on Schwartz and the two men developed a strong friendship.

It was during this period, that Kane seriously began to practice his craft, and to dedicate himself to drawing. Previously, Kane had closely followed the lead of other influential comic artists. He had learned his craft rather than developing a language of form and composition of his own. During the late 1940s and early 1950s the second generation of comic book artists were searching for an identity. Many of these artists, including Kane, had worked in the shops during the first generation and had been no

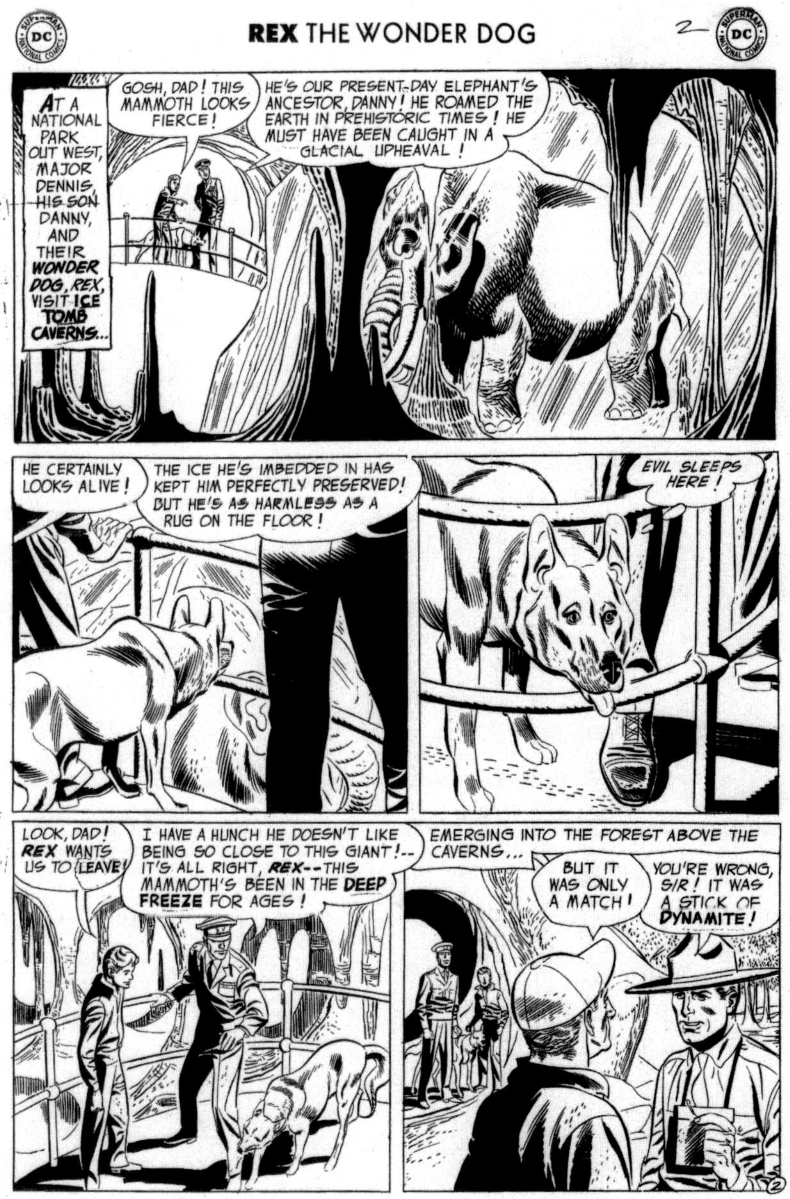
REX THE WONDER DOG
AT A NATIONAL PARK OUT WEST, MAJOR DENNIS, HIS SON DANNY, AND THEIR WONDER DOG, REX, VISIT ICE TOMB CAVERNS...
GOSH, DAD! THIS MAMMOTH LOOKS FIERCE!
HE'S OUR PRESENT-DAY ELEPHANT'S ANCESTOR, DANNY! HE ROAMED THE EARTH IN PREHISTORIC TIMES! HE MUST HAVE BEEN CAUGHT IN A GLACIAL UPHEAVAL!
HE CERTAINLY LOOKS ALIVE!
THE ICE HE'S IMBEDDED IN HAS KEPT HIM PERFECTLY PRESERVED! BUT HE'S AS HARMLESS AS A RUG ON THE FLOOR!
EVIL SLEEPS HERE!
LOOK, DAD! REX WANTS US TO LEAVE!
I HAVE A HUNCH HE DOESN'T LIKE BEING SO CLOSE TO THIS GIANT!-- IT'S ALL RIGHT, REX--THIS MAMMOTH'S BEEN IN THE DEEP FREEZE FOR AGES!
EMERGING INTO THE FOREST ABOVE THE CAVERNS...
BUT IT WAS ONLY A MATCH!
YOU'RE WRONG, SIR! IT WAS A STICK OF DYNAMITE!

Original artwork for an interior page from *The Adventures of Rex the Wonder Dog* #21, May/June, 1955, Gil Kane, pencils, Bernard Sachs (?) inks, ©2001 DC Comics. Kane worked on a number of strips during the 1950s and had a long association with the *Rex the Wonder Dog* strip. Kane took over duties on this strip from Alex Toth, just as he had taken over from Toth on the *Johnny Thunder* strip.

more than cogs in the assembly line. Kane readily acknowledged that while he started in the shop system, his artistic identity did not begin to mature until the1950s. Indeed, the second generation of comic book artists gleaned many lessons from the first generation as well as from the great strip artists.[1]

Original artwork for an interior page from *Strange Adventures* #55, April, 1955, Gil Kane, pencils, Bernard Sachs, inks, ©2001 DC Comics.

Kane, along with other second generation artists, consciously or not, inherited the desire to advance the art of the comics. Only a handful of first generation artists remained active and influential

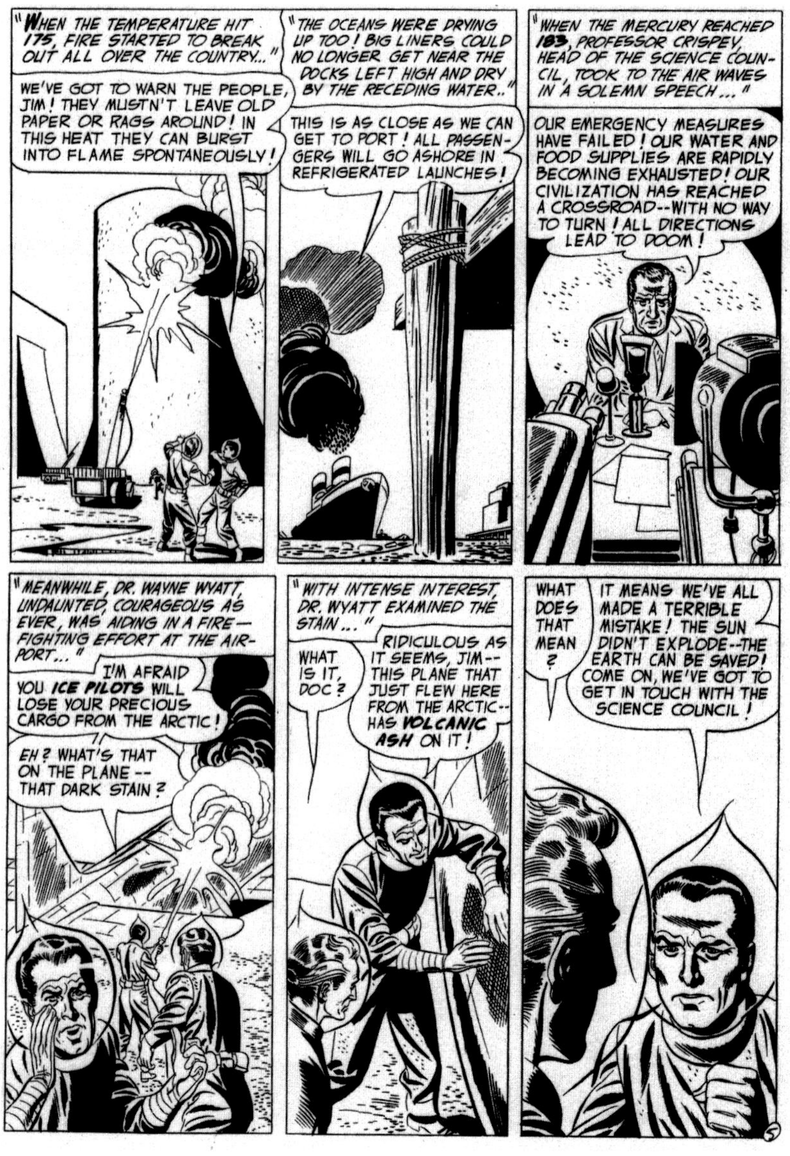
"WHEN THE TEMPERATURE HIT 175, FIRE STARTED TO BREAK OUT ALL OVER THE COUNTRY..."
WE'VE GOT TO WARN THE PEOPLE, JIM! THEY MUSTN'T LEAVE OLD PAPER OR RAGS AROUND! IN THIS HEAT THEY CAN BURST INTO FLAME SPONTANEOUSLY!
"THE OCEANS WERE DRYING UP TOO! BIG LINERS COULD NO LONGER GET NEAR THE DOCKS LEFT HIGH AND DRY BY THE RECEDING WATER.."
THIS IS AS CLOSE AS WE CAN GET TO PORT! ALL PASSENGERS WILL GO ASHORE IN REFRIGERATED LAUNCHES!
"WHEN THE MERCURY REACHED 183, PROFESSOR CRISPEY, HEAD OF THE SCIENCE COUNCIL, TOOK TO THE AIR WAVES IN A SOLEMN SPEECH..."
OUR EMERGENCY MEASURES HAVE FAILED! OUR WATER AND FOOD SUPPLIES ARE RAPIDLY BECOMING EXHAUSTED! OUR CIVILIZATION HAS REACHED A CROSSROAD--WITH NO WAY TO TURN! ALL DIRECTIONS LEAD TO DOOM!
"MEANWHILE, DR. WAYNE WYATT, UNDAUNTED, COURAGEOUS AS EVER, WAS AIDING IN A FIRE-FIGHTING EFFORT AT THE AIRPORT..."
I'M AFRAID YOU ICE PILOTS WILL LOSE YOUR PRECIOUS CARGO FROM THE ARCTIC!
EH? WHAT'S THAT ON THE PLANE -- THAT DARK STAIN?
"WITH INTENSE INTEREST, DR. WYATT EXAMINED THE STAIN..."
WHAT IS IT, DOC?
RIDICULOUS AS IT SEEMS, JIM-- THIS PLANE THAT JUST FLEW HERE FROM THE ARCTIC-- HAS VOLCANIC ASH ON IT!
WHAT DOES THAT MEAN?
IT MEANS WE'VE ALL MADE A TERRIBLE MISTAKE! THE SUN DIDN'T EXPLODE--THE EARTH CAN BE SAVED! COME ON, WE'VE GOT TO GET IN TOUCH WITH THE SCIENCE COUNCIL!

including Will Eisner, Jack Kirby and Joe Simon and to a smaller extent Reed Crandall.

In an effort to further develop his art, Kane set about rereading the pulp novels that had fascinated him when he was young. By his own account, he reread all of the *Shadow* and *Doc Savage* novels available to him. Kane also began reading F. Scott Fitzgerald and Ernest Hemingway. Kane did not stop

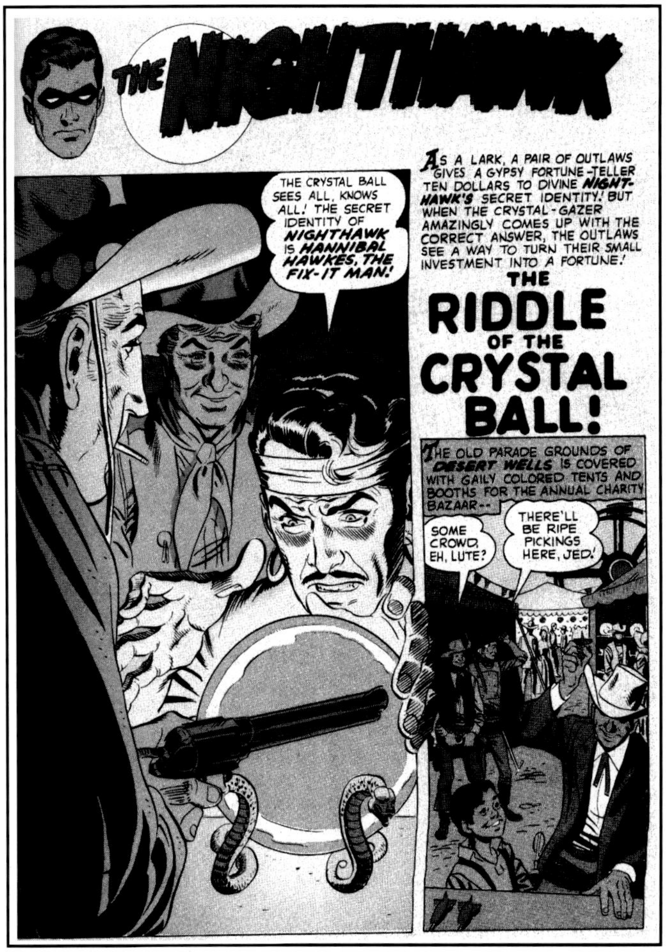
THE NIGHTHAWK
AS A LARK, A PAIR OF OUTLAWS GIVES A GYPSY FORTUNE-TELLER TEN DOLLARS TO DIVINE NIGHT-HAWK'S SECRET IDENTITY! BUT WHEN THE CRYSTAL-GAZER AMAZINGLY COMES UP WITH THE CORRECT ANSWER, THE OUTLAWS SEE A WAY TO TURN THEIR SMALL INVESTMENT INTO A FORTUNE!
THE CRYSTAL BALL SEES ALL, KNOWS ALL! THE SECRET IDENTITY OF NIGHTHAWK IS HANNIBAL HAWKES, THE FIX-IT MAN!
THE RIDDLE OF THE CRYSTAL BALL!
THE OLD PARADE GROUNDS OF DESERT WELLS IS COVERED WITH GAILY COLORED TENTS AND BOOTHS FOR THE ANNUAL CHARITY BAZAAR--
SOME CROWD, EH, LUTE?
THERE'LL BE RIPE PICKINGS HERE, JED!

Above: splash page from *Western Comics* #72, December, 1958, Gil Kane, pencils, Bernard Sachs, inks, ©2001 DC Comics.

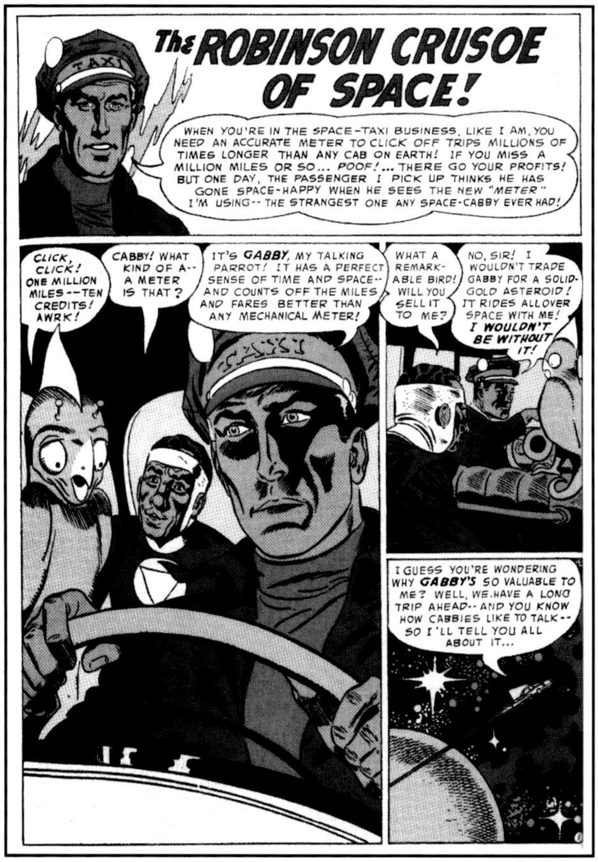
THE ROBINSON CRUSOE OF SPACE!
WHEN YOU'RE IN THE SPACE-TAXI BUSINESS, LIKE I AM, YOU NEED AN ACCURATE METER TO CLICK OFF TRIPS MILLIONS OF TIMES LONGER THAN ANY CAB ON EARTH! IF YOU MISS A MILLION MILES OR SO... POOF!... THERE GO YOUR PROFITS! BUT ONE DAY, THE PASSENGER I PICK UP THINKS HE HAS GONE SPACE-HAPPY WHEN HE SEES THE NEW "METER" I'M USING-- THE STRANGEST ONE ANY SPACE-CABBY EVER HAD!
CLICK, CLICK! ONE MILLION MILES--TEN CREDITS! AWRK!
CABBY! WHAT KIND OF A-- A METER IS THAT?
IT'S GABBY, MY TALKING PARROT! IT HAS A PERFECT SENSE OF TIME AND SPACE-- AND COUNTS OFF THE MILES AND FARES BETTER THAN ANY MECHANICAL METER!
WHAT A REMARK-ABLE BIRD! WILL YOU SELL IT TO ME?
NO, SIR! I WOULDN'T TRADE GABBY FOR A SOLID-GOLD ASTEROID! IT RIDES ALLOVER SPACE WITH ME! I WOULDN'T BE WITHOUT IT!
I GUESS YOU'RE WONDERING WHY GABBY'S SO VALUABLE TO ME? WELL, WE HAVE A LONG TRIP AHEAD-- AND YOU KNOW HOW CABBIES LIKE TO TALK-- SO I'LL TELL YOU ALL ABOUT IT...

Above: splash page from *Mystery in Space* #30, Feb./March, 1955, Gil Kane, pencils, Bernard Sachs, inks, ©2001 DC Comics.

there, however, he also read Edgar Rice Burroughs. While he had always been impressed with the work of Hal Foster and later Burne Hogarth on the Tarzan strips, he was equally impressed with the original stories.

Kane was coming of age as an artist during a seminal point in world art history, and the atmosphere around New York was not lost on him.

In the 1950s, New York was the undisputed center of the world of modern art. New York was also the center of art criticism. Kane, being aware of this, was regularly reading the *Partisan Review* and the *Saturday Review*. He was keenly aware that comics were a

Interior page from *Sensation Comics* #107, Jan./Feb., 1952, Alex Toth, pencils, Sy Barry, inks, ©2001 DC Comics. Note the layout and panel design of this page, which cuts from character to character with close-ups and then, dramatically pulls the camera back.

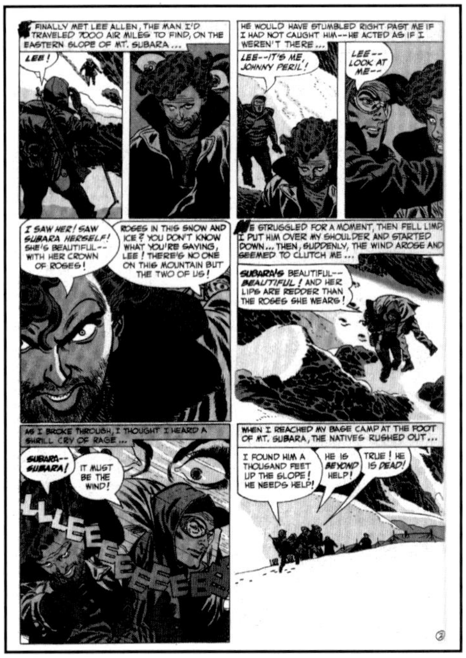
FINALLY MET LEE ALLEN, THE MAN I'D TRAVELED 7000 AIR MILES TO FIND, ON THE EASTERN SLOPE OF MT. SUBARA...
LEE!
HE WOULD HAVE STUMBLED RIGHT PAST ME IF I HAD NOT CAUGHT HIM--HE ACTED AS IF I WEREN'T THERE...
LEE--IT'S ME, JOHNNY PERIL!
LEE--LOOK AT ME--
I SAW HER! SAW SUBARA HERSELF! SHE'S BEAUTIFUL--WITH HER CROWN OF ROSES!
ROSES IN THIS SNOW AND ICE? YOU DON'T KNOW WHAT YOU'RE SAYING, LEE! THERE'S NO ONE ON THIS MOUNTAIN BUT THE TWO OF US!
E STRUGGLED FOR A MOMENT, THEN FELL LIMP. I PUT HIM OVER MY SHOULDER AND STARTED DOWN... THEN, SUDDENLY, THE WIND AROSE AND SEEMED TO CLUTCH ME...
SUBARA'S BEAUTIFUL--BEAUTIFUL! AND HER LIPS ARE REDDER THAN THE ROSES SHE WEARS!
AS I BROKE THROUGH, I THOUGHT I HEARD A SHRILL CRY OF RAGE...
SUBARA--SUBARA!
IT MUST BE THE WIND!
LLLEEEEEEEEE
WHEN I REACHED MY BASE CAMP AT THE FOOT OF MT. SUBARA, THE NATIVES RUSHED OUT...
I FOUND HIM A THOUSAND FEET UP THE SLOPE! HE NEEDS HELP!
HE IS BEYOND HELP!
TRUE! HE IS DEAD!

storytelling medium which needed not only good writing, but good storytelling which integrated the art and the story seamlessly. In the late 1940s there was very little which was intelligent about the comics. There were isolated examples of brilliance, with Jack Cole's *Plastic Man,* but by and large, comic books and art were aimed at the lowest common denominator. This, however, was changing.

Wally Wood and Alex Toth were developing highly different and influential styles, which integrated a number of influences. Toth had admired, studied, and synthesized elements from Crane, Sickles, and Caniff. Wood drew inspiration from the work of Eisner, Raymond and Foster. Comic books and comic book pages were now being designed by more ambitious artists. Kane was conscious of these developments and his art from this period shows that he was tightening his craft. In the early 1950s Kane began to develop a personal language of design and layout which would serve as the basis for his art for the rest of his career. Kane's comic book stories, while severely limited by the

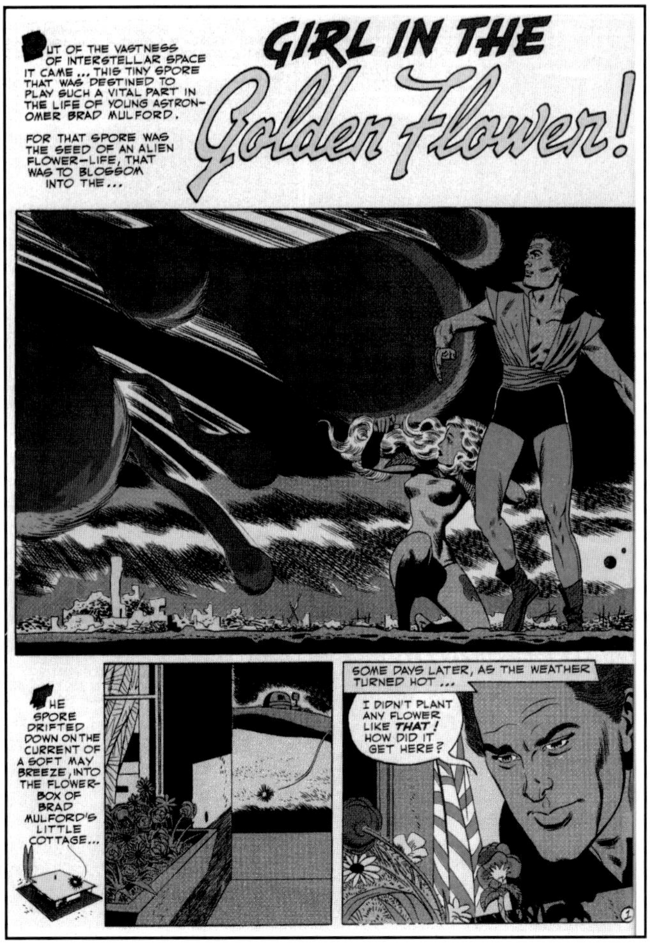
UT OF THE VASTNESS OF INTERSTELLAR SPACE IT CAME... THIS TINY SPORE THAT WAS DESTINED TO PLAY SUCH A VITAL PART IN THE LIFE OF YOUNG ASTRONOMER BRAD MULFORD.
FOR THAT SPORE WAS THE SEED OF AN ALIEN FLOWER-LIFE, THAT WAS TO BLOSSOM INTO THE...
GIRL IN THE Golden Flower!
HE SPORE DRIFTED DOWN ON THE CURRENT OF A SOFT MAY BREEZE, INTO THE FLOWER-BOX OF BRAD MULFORD'S LITTLE COTTAGE...
SOME DAYS LATER, AS THE WEATHER TURNED HOT...
I DIDN'T PLANT ANY FLOWER LIKE THAT! HOW DID IT GET HERE?

Left: *Strange Adventures* #18, March, 1952, Alex Toth, pencils, Sy Barry, inks, ©2001 DC Comics. Toth was a great influence on other comic artists in the second generation, including Kane. Kane carefully studied his work, as Kane took over for Toth on several strips. Kane, who was always improving his craft, discussed the art of the comics with Toth and watched the progress of his work, absorbing many of Toth's examples.

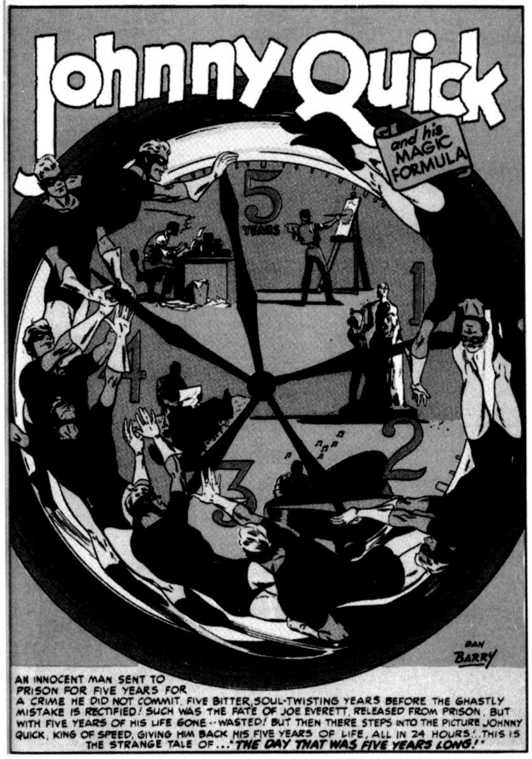
Johnny Quick
and his MAGIC FORMULA
DAN BARRY
AN INNOCENT MAN SENT TO PRISON FOR FIVE YEARS FOR A CRIME HE DID NOT COMMIT. FIVE BITTER, SOUL-TWISTING YEARS BEFORE THE GHASTLY MISTAKE IS RECTIFIED! SUCH WAS THE FATE OF JOE EVERETT, RELEASED FROM PRISON, BUT WITH FIVE YEARS OF HIS LIFE GONE--WASTED! BUT THEN THERE STEPS INTO THE PICTURE JOHNNY QUICK, KING OF SPEED, GIVING HIM BACK HIS FIVE YEARS OF LIFE, ALL IN 24 HOURS!..THIS IS THE STRANGE TALE OF..."THE DAY THAT WAS FIVE YEARS LONG!"

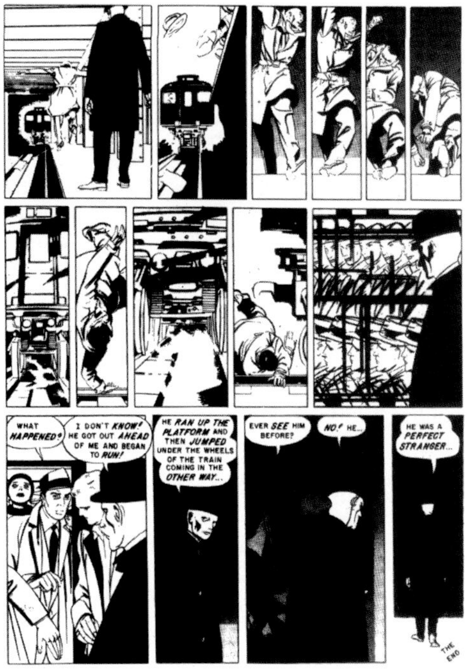
WHAT HAPPENED?
I DON'T KNOW! HE GOT OUT AHEAD OF ME AND BEGAN TO RUN!
HE RAN UP THE PLATFORM AND THEN JUMPED UNDER THE WHEELS OF THE TRAIN COMING IN THE OTHER WAY...
EVER SEE HIM BEFORE?
NO! HE...
HE WAS A PERFECT STRANGER...
THE END

Left: interior page from one of the most famous stories in a comic book, "The Master Race," from *Impact* #1, EC Comics, March, 1955, Bernie Krigstein, pencils and inks, ©2001 William M. Gaines. This story's panel design and layout was of enormous influence on Kane and other artists. Krigstein used this type of layout in many stories, which explored how to break down time, panel by panel.

grids imposed by his editors, showed his experimentation with different angles and perspective.

Above: splash page for Adventure Comics #144, September, 1949, Dan Barry, pencils and inks, ©2001 DC Comics. Barry's clean, simple, style was highly attractive and influential with the artists at DC Comics. Barry went from working on comic book stories to newspaper strips, first working on *Tarzan* and then on to *Flash Gordon*.

Kane, as was his practice, was not content to work for only one publisher. During the late 1940s and 1950s, Kane worked for numerous publishers including Atlas, Ziff Davis, Fawcett, and Avon. Kane also ghosted at least three newspaper strips for other artists and shopped his own strip ideas to various syndicates (without success). During this time Kane worked in every comic book genre and further practiced his composition and drawing. He was now regularly drawing stories and covers for the major comic book publishers and yet he was not satisfied with his work.

Kane had steady work during the

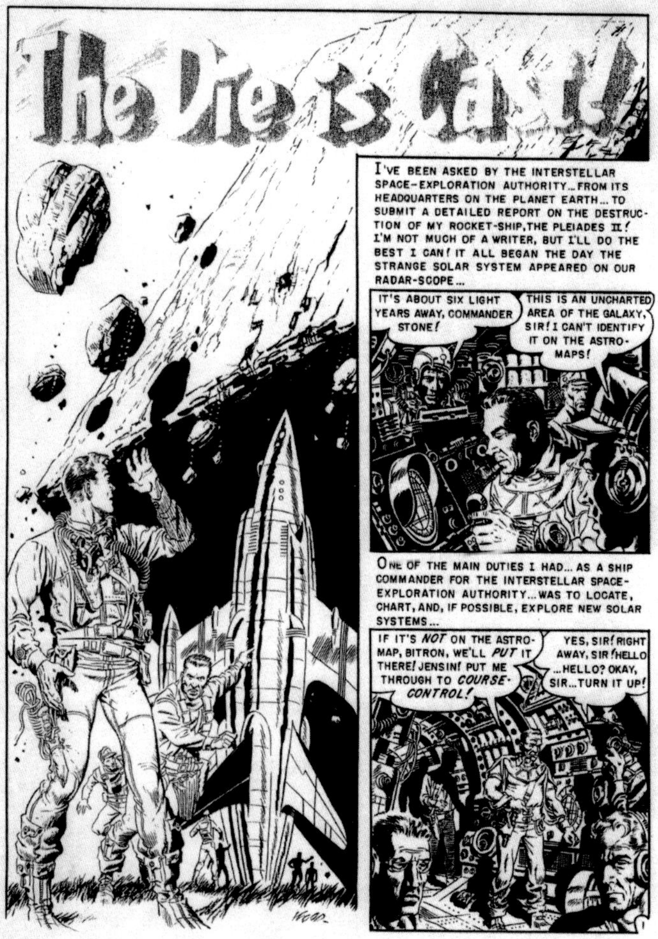
The Die is Cast!
I'VE BEEN ASKED BY THE INTERSTELLAR SPACE-EXPLORATION AUTHORITY...FROM ITS HEADQUARTERS ON THE PLANET EARTH...TO SUBMIT A DETAILED REPORT ON THE DESTRUCTION OF MY ROCKET-SHIP, THE PLEIADES II! I'M NOT MUCH OF A WRITER, BUT I'LL DO THE BEST I CAN! IT ALL BEGAN THE DAY THE STRANGE SOLAR SYSTEM APPEARED ON OUR RADAR-SCOPE...
IT'S ABOUT SIX LIGHT YEARS AWAY, COMMANDER STONE!
THIS IS AN UNCHARTED AREA OF THE GALAXY, SIR! I CAN'T IDENTIFY IT ON THE ASTRO-MAPS!
ONE OF THE MAIN DUTIES I HAD...AS A SHIP COMMANDER FOR THE INTERSTELLAR SPACE-EXPLORATION AUTHORITY...WAS TO LOCATE, CHART, AND, IF POSSIBLE, EXPLORE NEW SOLAR SYSTEMS...
IF IT'S NOT ON THE ASTRO-MAP, BITRON, WE'LL PUT IT THERE! JENSIN! PUT ME THROUGH TO COURSE-CONTROL!
YES, SIR! RIGHT AWAY, SIR! HELLO ...HELLO? OKAY, SIR...TURN IT UP!

Right: splash page from the original artwork from *Weird Fantasy* #12, March/April, 1952, Wally Wood, pencils and inks, EC Comics, ©2001 William M. Gaines. Wood was greatly admired by artists and readers for his style, which blended Hal Foster and Will Eisner. Wood went on, in the late 1960s, to work with Kane, as an inker, with very successful results.

Below left: splash page from *All-Star Western* #109, Oct./Nov., 1959, Gil Kane, pencils, Joe Giella, inks, ©2001 DC Comics. Right: cover from *Showcase* #17, December, 1958, Gil Kane, pencils and inks, ©2001 DC Comics.

early 1950s. He was pencilling and inking western stories for DC Comics during this period. He worked on *Hopalong Cassidy, Western Comics (*the *Nighthawk* and *Matt Savage* strips*), All-Star Western (*the *Don Caballero, Trigger Twins, Johnny Thunder* and *Foley of the Fighting 5th* strips*), All-American Western,* and *Jimmy Wakley.* He also contributed continuing work on the *Adventures of Rex the Wonder Dog, Strange Adventures,* and *Mystery in Space.* Many of the elements that would define his work were becoming evident. Moreover, also working at DC Comics were Dan Barry, Mort Meskin, Alex Toth and Lee Elias, who all had an enormous impact upon him. Toth's assimilation of the techniques of Noel Sickles and Milton Caniff,

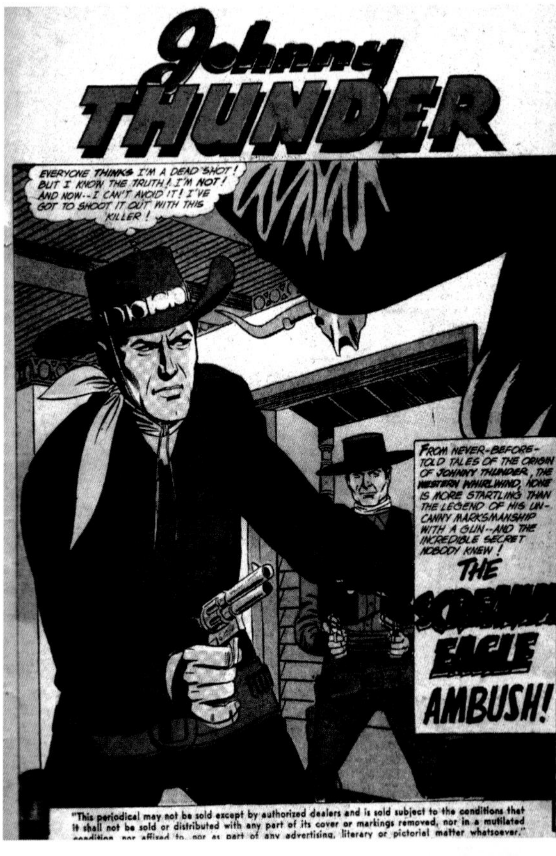
Johnny THUNDER
EVERYONE THINKS I'M A DEAD SHOT! BUT I KNOW THE TRUTH! I'M NOT! AND NOW--I CAN'T AVOID IT! I'VE GOT TO SHOOT IT OUT WITH THIS KILLER!
FROM NEVER-BEFORE-TOLD TALES OF THE ORIGIN OF JOHNNY THUNDER, THE WESTERN WHIRLWIND, NONE IS MORE STARTLING THAN THE LEGEND OF HIS UNCANNY MARKSMANSHIP WITH A GUN--AND THE INCREDIBLE SECRET NOBODY KNEW!
THE
EAGLE
AMBUSH!
"This periodical may not be sold except by authorized dealers and is sold subject to the conditions that it shall not be sold or distributed with any part of its cover or markings removed, nor in a mutilated

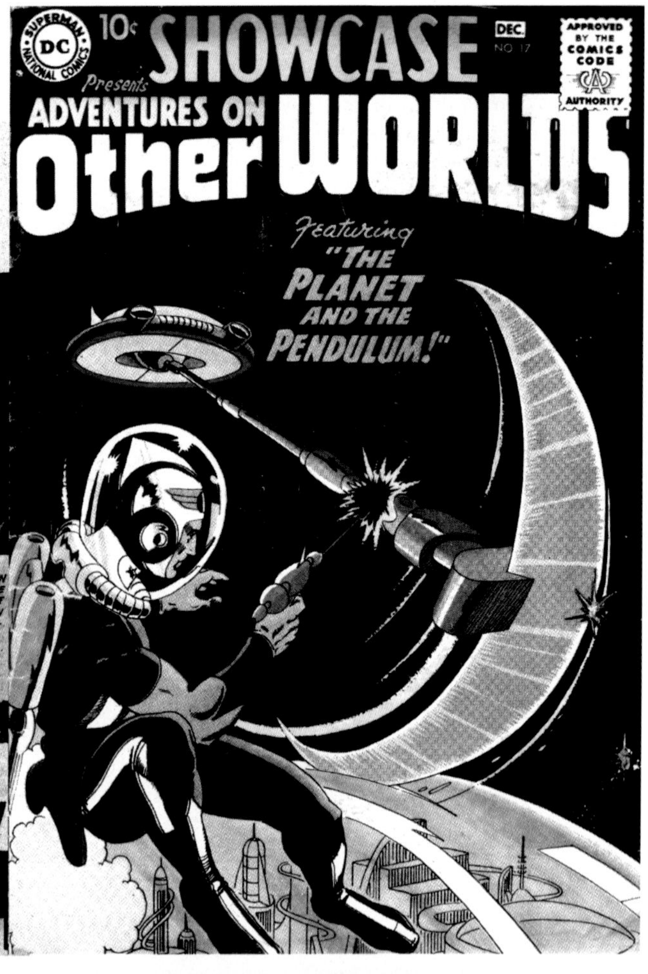
10¢
SHOWCASE
DEC. NO. 17
APPROVED BY THE COMICS CODE AUTHORITY
Presents
ADVENTURES ON Other WORLDS
Featuring "THE PLANET AND THE PENDULUM!"

Below: cover from *Showcase* #18, February, 1959, Gil Kane, pencils, Bernard Sachs, inks, and cover from *Showcase* #19, April, 1959, Gil Kane, pencils, Bernard Sachs, inks, both ©2001 DC Comics. Kane worked in a number of genres during the 1950s, as these covers attest, from science fiction to westerns.

presenting characters and locales using a shorthand of form emphasizing the depth of line, and the use and contrast of black and white, can be seen clearly as registering in Kane's work at this time. Indeed, the art of comic books was maturing. This was best demonstrated by the groundbreaking work of William Gaines at Entertaining Comics (EC). In just three short years, Gaines helped transform comic books. Using second generation artists Wally Wood, Al Feldstein, Al Williamson, Bernie Krigstein, Harvey Kurtzman, John Severin, Jack Davis, and Reed Crandall, Gaines integrated art with interesting story-lines which had intelligence and wit, something the majority of comic books at DC Comics lacked. Although DC Comics' product was directed primarily at 6 to 10 year olds, EC was much more broad ranged and

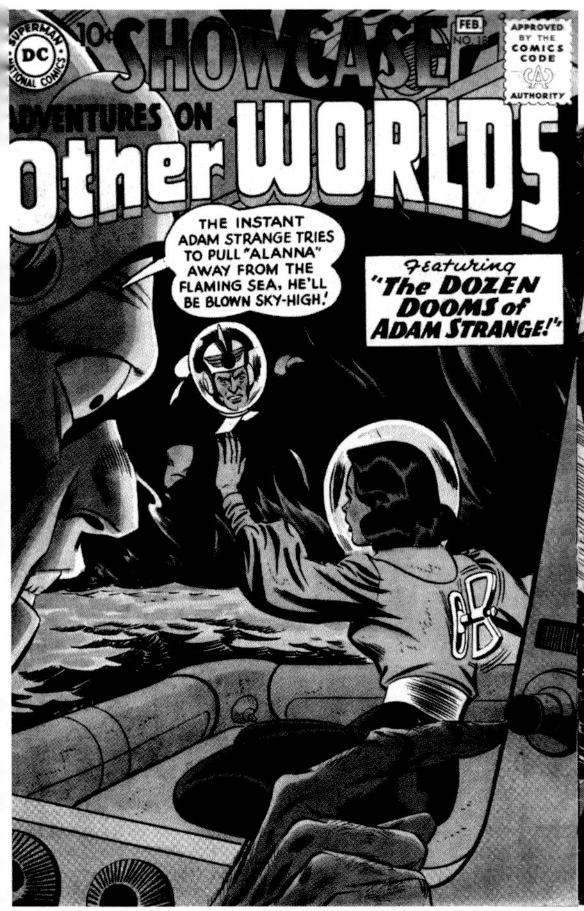
10¢ SHOWCASE
FEB. NO. 18
APPROVED BY THE COMICS CODE AUTHORITY
ADVENTURES ON Other WORLDS
THE INSTANT ADAM STRANGE TRIES TO PULL "ALANNA" AWAY FROM THE FLAMING SEA, HE'LL BE BLOWN SKY-HIGH!
Featuring "The DOZEN DOOMS of ADAM STRANGE!"

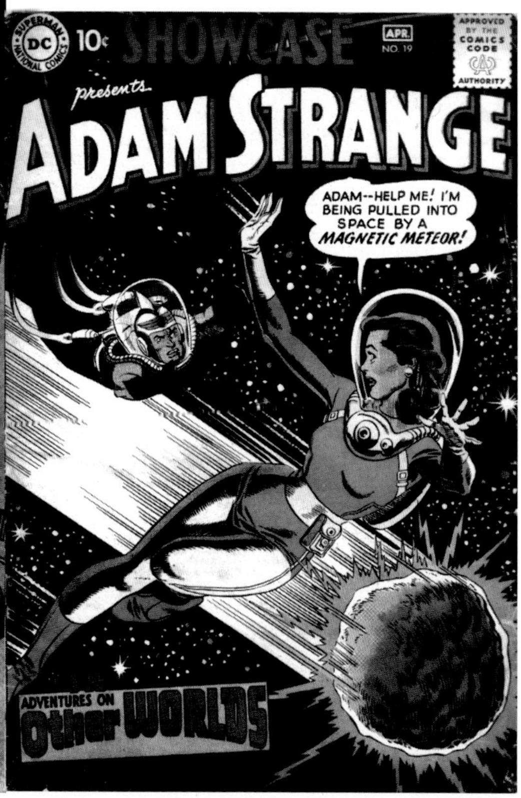
10¢ SHOWCASE
APR. NO. 19
APPROVED BY THE COMICS CODE AUTHORITY
presents ADAM STRANGE
ADAM--HELP ME! I'M BEING PULLED INTO SPACE BY A MAGNETIC METEOR!
ADVENTURES ON Other WORLDS

Kane's version of Johnny Thunder rides again, ©2001 DC Comics.

could actually be appreciated by adults. EC pushed the acceptable limits of the 1950s by dealing with sex, violence, and horror (EC was by no means the worst offender in graphically depicting violence - - one of the most famous illustrations in comic books comes from Jack Cole in *True Crime* #2, where a hypodermic needle is plunged into the eye of the addicted main character).

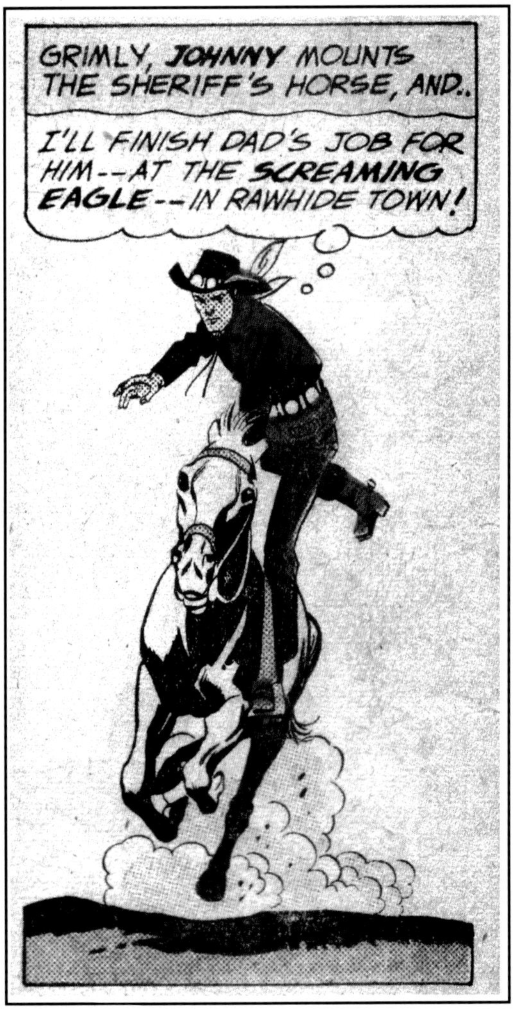
GRIMLY, JOHNNY MOUNTS THE SHERIFF'S HORSE, AND..
I'LL FINISH DAD'S JOB FOR HIM--AT THE SCREAMING EAGLE--IN RAWHIDE TOWN!

EC also dealt with politically unpopular subjects such as racial prejudice and intolerance. EC produced adaptations of the work of Ray Bradbury, and with the help of Harvey Kurztman created haunting and disturbing war comic books. Kurtzman and EC Publisher William Gaines also created a comic book that would live on long after the EC line of comic books had vanished: *MAD*.

Kane and everyone in the industry were placed in peril by the unfavorable light that would be focused on comic books. In 1954, United States Senators Thomas Hennings and Estes Kefauver held hearings at the Federal Courthouse in New York to examine the contents and effect of comic books on young readers. Some of the criticism leveled at the comics industry was justified, but the general

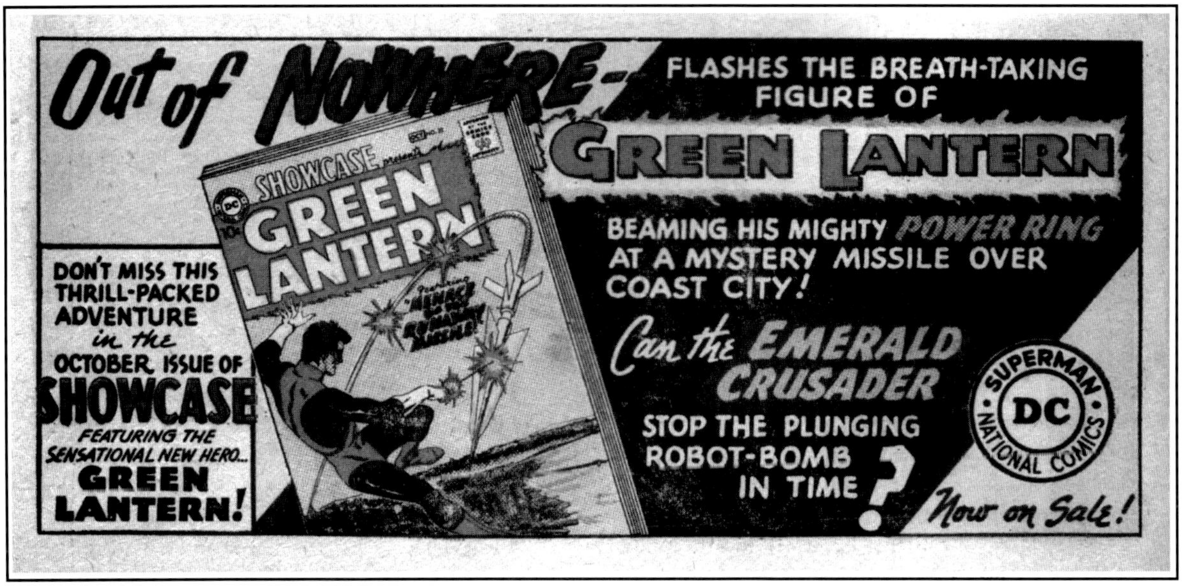
Out of NOWHERE--
FLASHES THE BREATH-TAKING FIGURE OF
GREEN LANTERN
SHOWCASE
GREEN LANTERN
DON'T MISS THIS THRILL-PACKED ADVENTURE in the OCTOBER ISSUE OF SHOWCASE
FEATURING THE SENSATIONAL NEW HERO... GREEN LANTERN!
BEAMING HIS MIGHTY POWER RING AT A MYSTERY MISSILE OVER COAST CITY!
Can the EMERALD CRUSADER STOP THE PLUNGING ROBOT-BOMB IN TIME?
SUPERMAN DC NATIONAL COMICS
Now on Sale!

attack leveled at the entire industry was overzealous and unfair. The parents' groups, religious groups and politicians assailing the comics industry were misguided and uninformed about comic books and were whipped into a frenzy by material taken out of context. The results of these hearings and the public furor generated crippled the comics

Above: the advertisement which ran in DC comic books heralding the introduction of a new character, the Green Lantern. In the comics world, this feature would bring Kane fame for the rest of his life. This advertisement, a "house ad," ran in DC comic books distributed in June and July, 1959, ©2001 DC Comics.

industry, and set the art form back a decade.[2] Mainstream comics, which had been bland and intellectually uncontroversial, became even more inoffensive. Kane found that many of the titles where he had found steady work were gone, or changing frequently, to deal with the changes mandated as a result of the Senate hearings. Censorship, in the form of the Comics Code Authority, was accepted by publishers to avoid public regulation. The great advances in the art of the comics would now come from outside the mainstream, including the pioneering work to be done by Kane. This, however, was far off in the future.

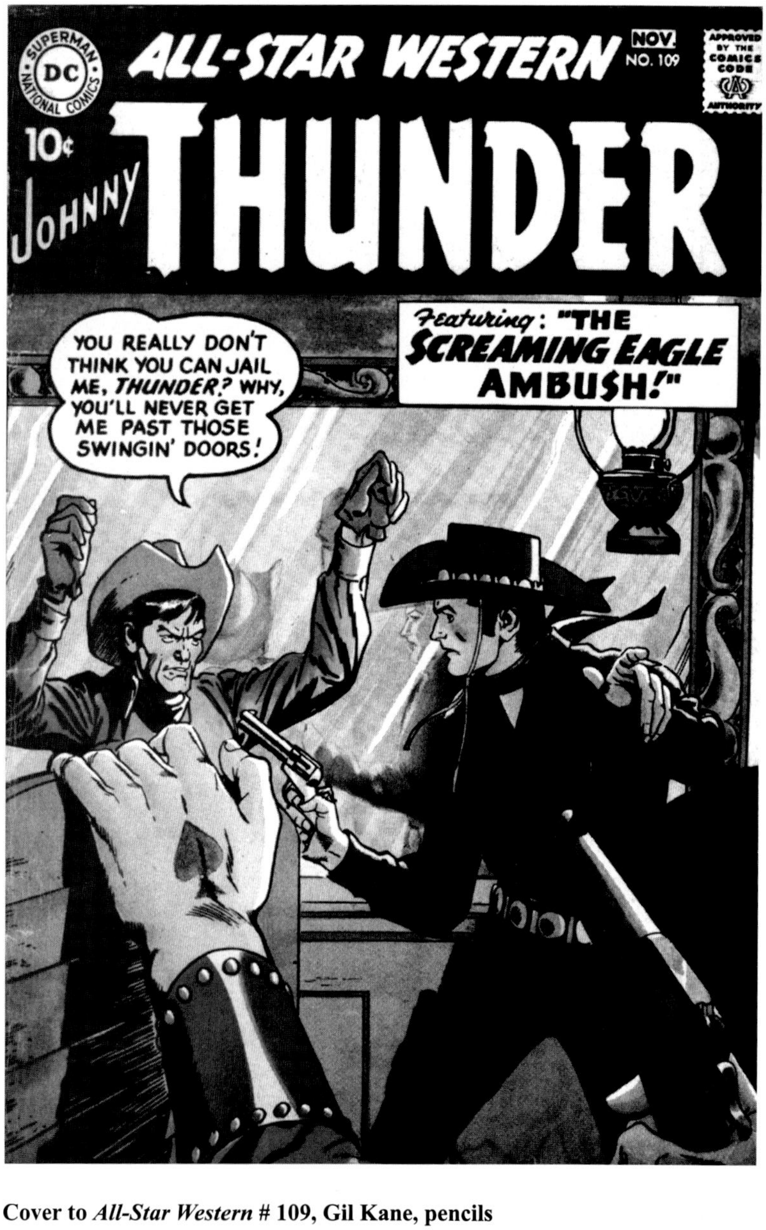
ALL-STAR WESTERN
NOV. NO. 109
10¢
JOHNNY THUNDER
Featuring: "THE SCREAMING EAGLE AMBU$H!"
YOU REALLY DON'T THINK YOU CAN JAIL ME, THUNDER? WHY, YOU'LL NEVER GET ME PAST THOSE SWINGIN' DOORS!

Cover to *All-Star Western* # 109, Gil Kane, pencils and inks, Oct./Nov., 1959, featuring Johnny Thunder, ©2001 DC Comics.

5 SUPERHEROES

After the creation of the Comics Code Authority in 1954, the comics industry was hit hard. Many publishers closed down for good. DC Comics continued, but was forced to reduce its titles. Marvel Comics, which at the time was known as Atlas, was forced to cancel a majority of its titles. Kane, however, continued to work, although he observed that this was an "anxious" time for him. By the end of the 1950s DC Comics was attempting, through two titles of comic books, *Showcase* and *The Brave and the Bold,* to test the marketplace with new ideas. Under editor Julius Schwartz, DC Comics had updated one of its 1940s superheroes, the Flash, with increasing success. Next, Schwartz decided to repackage another 1940s superhero, the Green Lantern.[1] Schwartz picked Kane to redesign the hero's costume and to draw the character. For

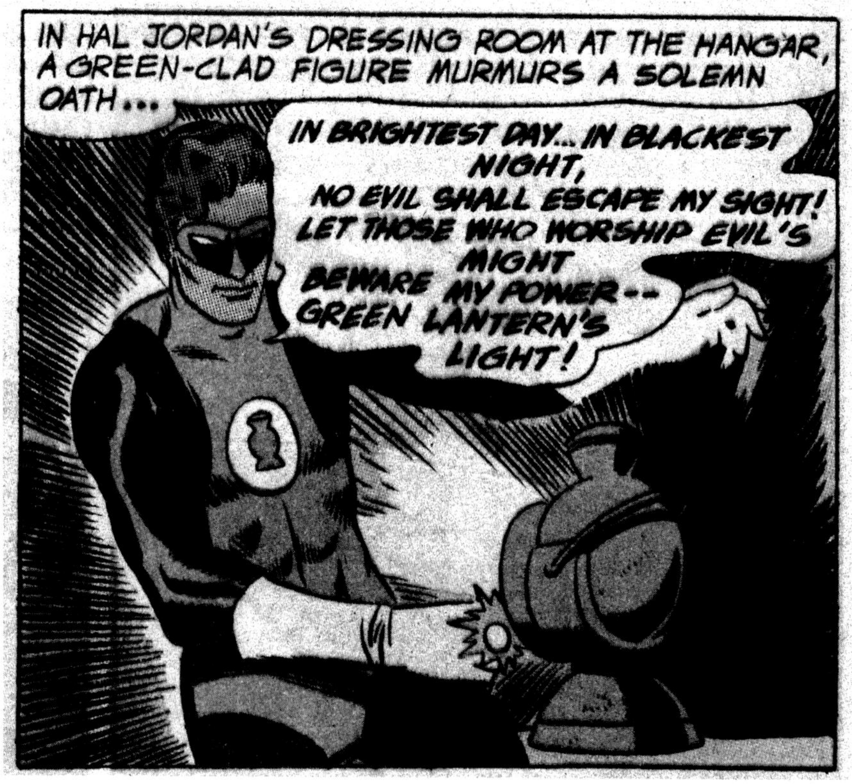
IN HAL JORDAN'S DRESSING ROOM AT THE HANGAR, A GREEN-CLAD FIGURE MURMURS A SOLEMN OATH...
IN BRIGHTEST DAY... IN BLACKEST NIGHT, NO EVIL SHALL ESCAPE MY SIGHT! LET THOSE WHO WORSHIP EVIL'S MIGHT BEWARE MY POWER-- GREEN LANTERN'S LIGHT!

Above: the Green Lantern takes his oath for the first time, interior page panel from *Showcase* #22, Sept./Oct., 1959, Gil Kane, pencils, Joe Giella, inks, ©2001 DC Comics.

better or worse, Kane's involvement with the Green Lantern would bring him a kind of fame in the comic book business, and among the fans of comic books, reserved for very few artists. For the rest of Kane's life, he would be identified with the Green Lantern. Despite his many significant accomplishments to come, when Kane died, many of his obituaries ran his cover art for the 1959 issue of *Showcase,* featuring the Green Lantern.[2] Kane complained that his best work was not done in the superhero genre, but inevitably it was the fame that followed him from his work on the Green Lantern, due to his design and artwork on the character, that allowed him to

Below: cover for *Showcase* #22, Sept./Oct., 1959, Gil Kane, pencils and inks, ©2001 DC Comics. Among fans of comic books, this cover is synonymous with the artwork of Gil Kane.

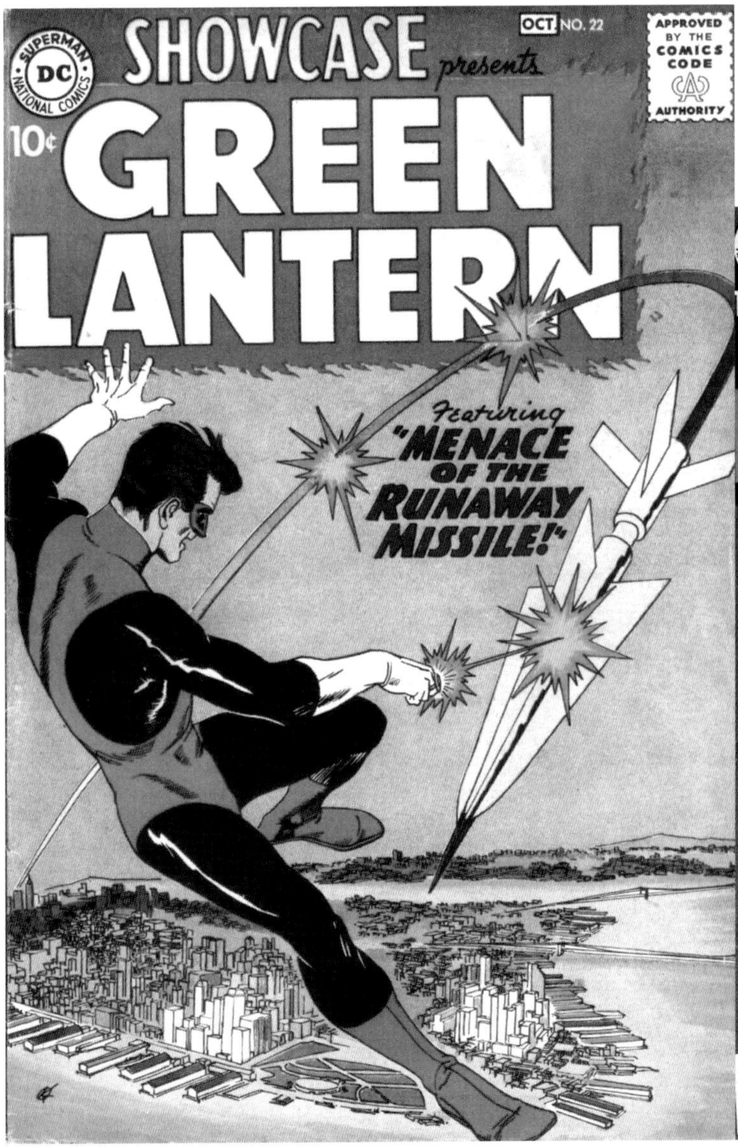

Below: cover for *Showcase* #23, Nov./ Dec., 1959, Gil Kane, pencils, Joe Giella, inks, ©2001 DC Comics.

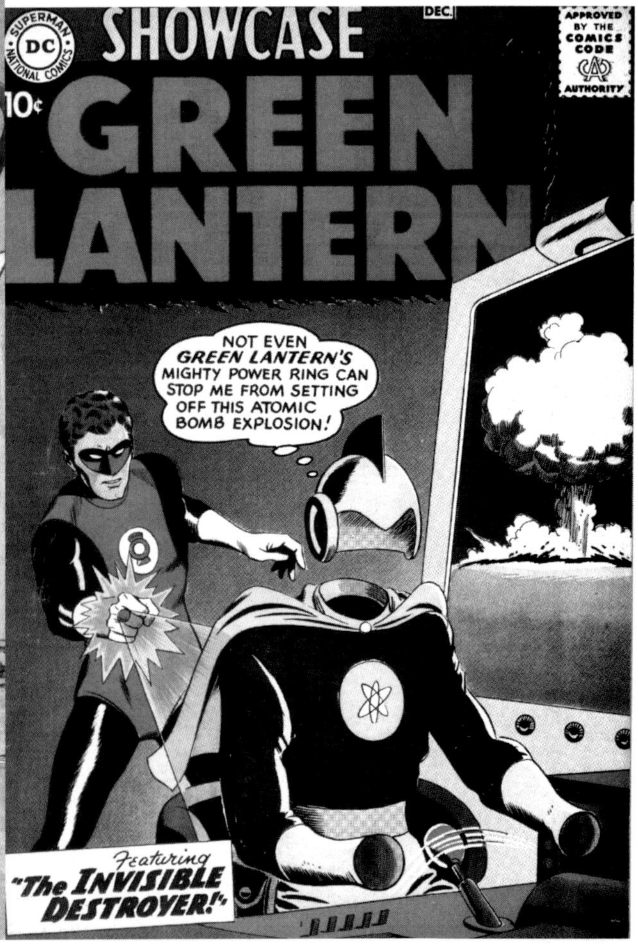

venture into other less popular comic venues. Drawing the Green Lantern forced Kane to focus more on drawing the human figure. In the process he was able to create many different techniques for depicting the human form in ways that were elegant and graceful. Kane, and the best of the second generation of comic book artists, were not trying to be illustrators, but were seeking to define a method of telling their stories using a style of drawing that compressed figure composition down only to its essential elements. To comic book fans, the introduction of the Flash and Green Lantern started a "Silver Age." The same fans had christened the period starting with the premier of Superman in 1938, to the end of the Second World War, as the "Golden Age." No matter how this period of the late 1950s/early 1960s is described, this was the opportunity Kane had been looking for. It was at this juncture that Kane began to formulate a personal aesthetic which would drive his art for the rest of his career.

Below far left: cover for *Green Lantern* #2, Sept./Oct., 1960, Gil Kane, pencils, Joe Giella, inks. Below middle: cover for *Green Lantern* #4, Jan./Feb., 1961, Gil Kane, pencils, Joe Giella, inks. Below right: cover for *Green Lantern* #22, July, 1963, Gil Kane, pencils, Murphy Anderson, inks. All cover ©2001 DC Comics.

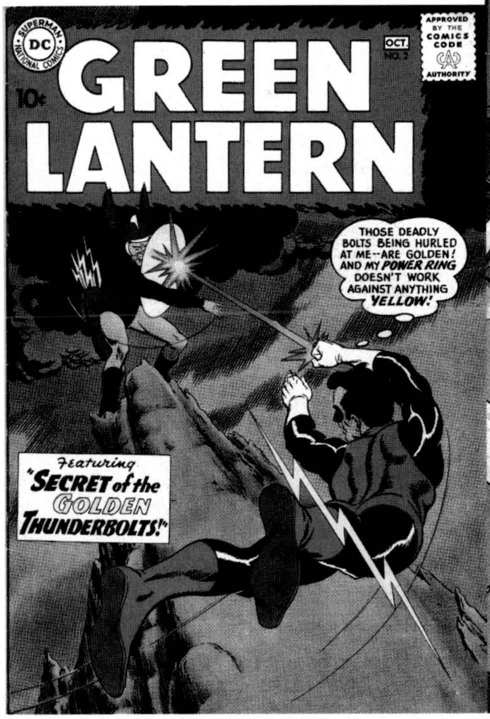
10¢
GREEN LANTERN
OCT. NO. 2
APPROVED BY THE COMICS CODE AUTHORITY
THOSE DEADLY BOLTS BEING HURLED AT ME--ARE GOLDEN! AND MY POWER RING DOESN'T WORK AGAINST ANYTHING YELLOW!
Featuring "SECRET of the GOLDEN THUNDERBOLTS!"

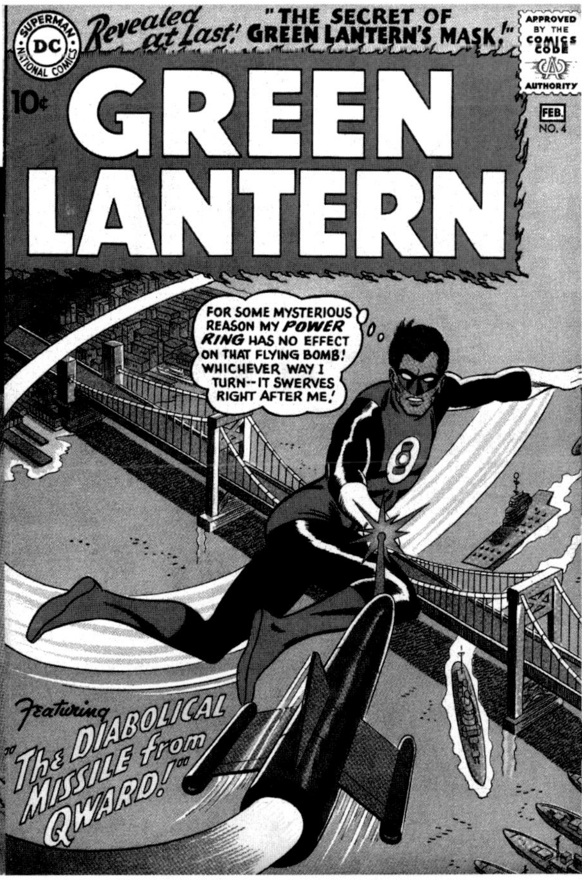
Revealed at Last! "THE SECRET OF GREEN LANTERN'S MASK!"
APPROVED BY THE COMICS CODE AUTHORITY
10¢
GREEN LANTERN
FEB. NO. 4
FOR SOME MYSTERIOUS REASON MY POWER RING HAS NO EFFECT ON THAT FLYING BOMB! WHICHEVER WAY I TURN--IT SWERVES RIGHT AFTER ME!
Featuring "The DIABOLICAL MISSILE from QWARD!"

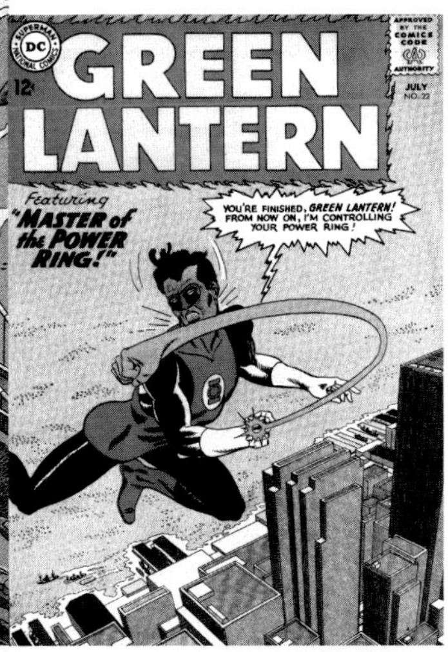
12¢
GREEN LANTERN
Featuring "MASTER of the POWER RING!"
YOU'RE FINISHED, GREEN LANTERN! FROM NOW ON, I'M CONTROLLING YOUR POWER RING!

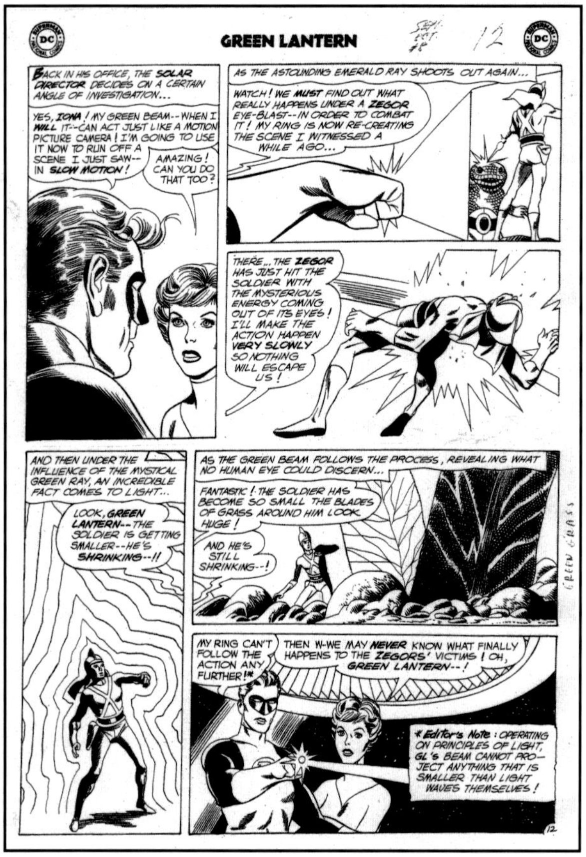
GREEN LANTERN
BACK IN HIS OFFICE, THE SOLAR DIRECTOR DECIDES ON A CERTAIN ANGLE OF INVESTIGATION...
YES, IONA! MY GREEN BEAM--WHEN I WILL IT--CAN ACT JUST LIKE A MOTION PICTURE CAMERA! I'M GOING TO USE IT NOW TO RUN OFF A SCENE I JUST SAW-- IN SLOW MOTION!
AMAZING! CAN YOU DO THAT TOO?
AS THE ASTOUNDING EMERALD RAY SHOOTS OUT AGAIN...
WATCH! WE MUST FIND OUT WHAT REALLY HAPPENS UNDER A ZEGOR EYE-BLAST--IN ORDER TO COMBAT IT! MY RING IS NOW RE-CREATING THE SCENE I WITNESSED A WHILE AGO...
THERE... THE ZEGOR HAS JUST HIT THE SOLDIER WITH THE MYSTERIOUS ENERGY COMING OUT OF ITS EYES! I'LL MAKE THE ACTION HAPPEN VERY SLOWLY SO NOTHING WILL ESCAPE US!
AND THEN UNDER THE INFLUENCE OF THE MYSTICAL GREEN RAY, AN INCREDIBLE FACT COMES TO LIGHT...
LOOK, GREEN LANTERN--THE SOLDIER IS GETTING SMALLER--HE'S SHRINKING--!!
AS THE GREEN BEAM FOLLOWS THE PROCESS, REVEALING WHAT NO HUMAN EYE COULD DISCERN...
FANTASTIC! THE SOLDIER HAS BECOME SO SMALL THE BLADES OF GRASS AROUND HIM LOOK HUGE!
AND HE'S STILL SHRINKING--!
GREEN GRASS
MY RING CAN'T FOLLOW THE ACTION ANY FURTHER!*
THEN W-WE MAY NEVER KNOW WHAT FINALLY HAPPENS TO THE ZEGORS' VICTIMS! OH, GREEN LANTERN--!
*Editor's Note: OPERATING ON PRINCIPLES OF LIGHT, GL'S BEAM CANNOT PROJECT ANYTHING THAT IS SMALLER THAN LIGHT WAVES THEMSELVES!
12

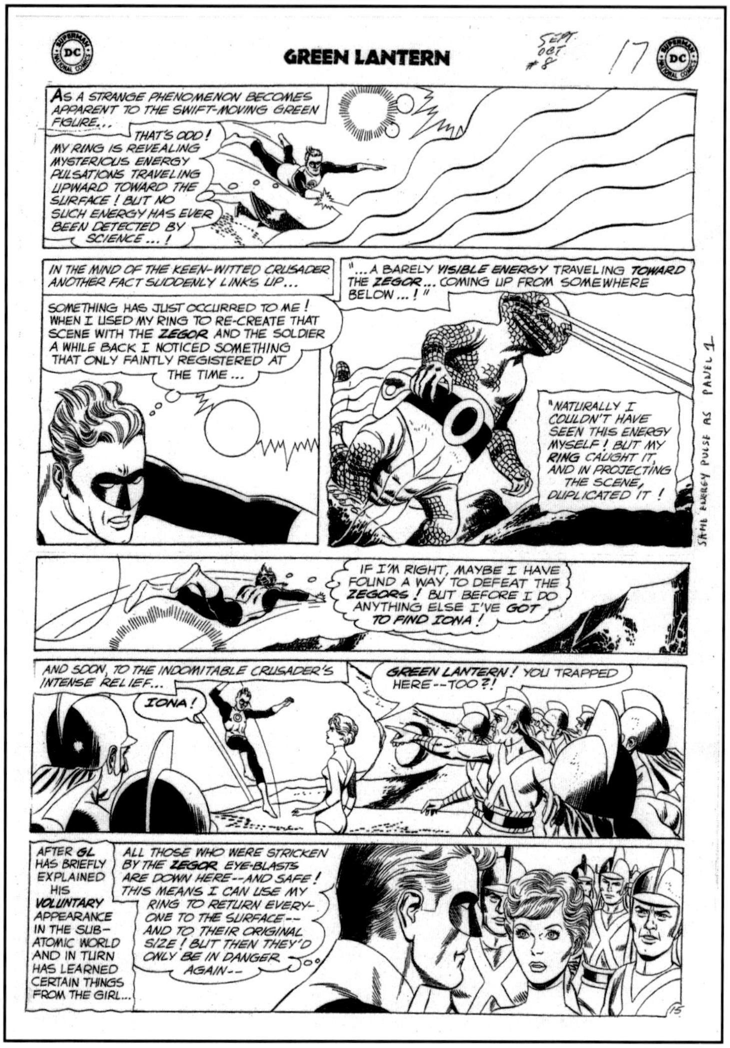
GREEN LANTERN
SEPT OCT #8
17
AS A STRANGE PHENOMENON BECOMES APPARENT TO THE SWIFT-MOVING GREEN FIGURE...
THAT'S ODD! MY RING IS REVEALING MYSTERIOUS ENERGY PULSATIONS TRAVELING UPWARD TOWARD THE SURFACE! BUT NO SUCH ENERGY HAS EVER BEEN DETECTED BY SCIENCE...!
IN THE MIND OF THE KEEN-WITTED CRUSADER ANOTHER FACT SUDDENLY LINKS UP...
SOMETHING HAS JUST OCCURRED TO ME! WHEN I USED MY RING TO RE-CREATE THAT SCENE WITH THE ZEGOR AND THE SOLDIER A WHILE BACK I NOTICED SOMETHING THAT ONLY FAINTLY REGISTERED AT THE TIME...
"...A BARELY VISIBLE ENERGY TRAVELING TOWARD THE ZEGOR... COMING UP FROM SOMEWHERE BELOW...!"
"NATURALLY I COULDN'T HAVE SEEN THIS ENERGY MYSELF! BUT MY RING CAUGHT IT, AND IN PROJECTING THE SCENE, DUPLICATED IT!
SAME ENERGY PULSE AS PANEL 1
IF I'M RIGHT, MAYBE I HAVE FOUND A WAY TO DEFEAT THE ZEGORS! BUT BEFORE I DO ANYTHING ELSE I'VE GOT TO FIND IONA!
AND SOON, TO THE INDOMITABLE CRUSADER'S INTENSE RELIEF...
IONA!
GREEN LANTERN! YOU TRAPPED HERE--TOO?!
AFTER GL HAS BRIEFLY EXPLAINED HIS VOLUNTARY APPEARANCE IN THE SUB-ATOMIC WORLD AND IN TURN HAS LEARNED CERTAIN THINGS FROM THE GIRL...
ALL THOSE WHO WERE STRICKEN BY THE ZEGOR EYE-BLASTS ARE DOWN HERE--AND SAFE! THIS MEANS I CAN USE MY RING TO RETURN EVERY-ONE TO THE SURFACE--AND TO THEIR ORIGINAL SIZE! BUT THEN THEY'D ONLY BE IN DANGER AGAIN--
15

Above: two non-sequential interior pages, for the original artwork from *Green Lantern* #8, Sept./Oct., 1961, Gil Kane, pencils, Joe Giella, inks, ©2001 DC Comics. These two pages demonstrate how Giella's inks were in tune with Kane's pencils, following Kane's line, without overpowering it. Unfortunately, many times Giella's inks for *Green Lantern* appear rushed and cursory. On balance, however, Giella closely followed Kane's pencils. Murphy Anderson, on the other hand, who inked the cover for *Green Lantern* #26, which is illustrated in this section, added too much of his own personality in inking Kane's work, and often lost the flow of Kane's line.

In commenting on his early work on the *Green Lantern* series, Kane observed that he was clearly not capable of fully exploring the graphic possibilities of the character and the stories. Kane felt that he needed to further refine his drawing and choreography. Kane's early efforts on *Green Lantern* were further hampered by collaborators who did not fully understand what he was trying to accomplish. It was established practice at DC Comics to have one

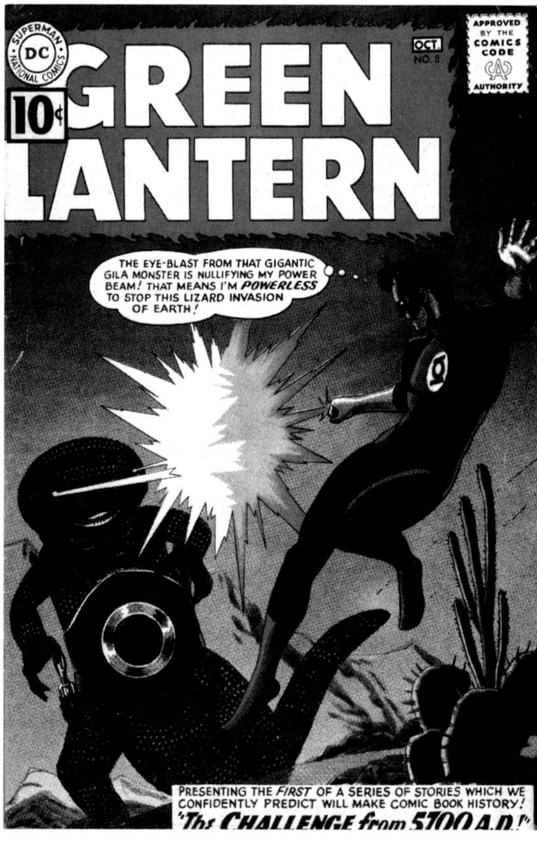
GREEN LANTERN
10¢
OCT. NO. 8
APPROVED BY THE COMICS CODE AUTHORITY
THE EYE-BLAST FROM THAT GIGANTIC GILA MONSTER IS NULLIFYING MY POWER BEAM! THAT MEANS I'M POWERLESS TO STOP THIS LIZARD INVASION OF EARTH!
PRESENTING THE FIRST OF A SERIES OF STORIES WHICH WE CONFIDENTLY PREDICT WILL MAKE COMIC BOOK HISTORY!
"The CHALLENGE from 5700 A.D.!"

Cover for *Green Lantern* #8, Sept./Oct., 1961, Gil Kane, pencils, Jack Adler, finishes,©2001 DC Comics.

Right: covers for *Green Lantern* #30, July, 1964, Gil Kane, pencils, Murphy Anderson, inks; *Green Lantern* #32, Oct., 1964, Gil Kane, pencils, Murphy Anderson, inks; and *Green Lantern* #49, Dec., 1966, Gil Kane, pencils and inks. All covers ©2001 DC Comics.

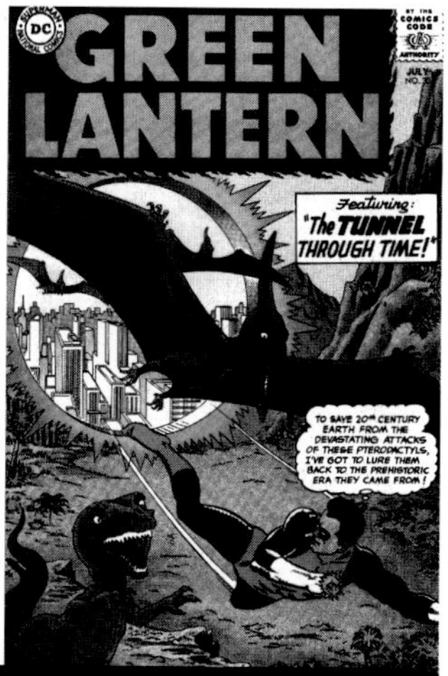
GREEN LANTERN
Featuring: "The TUNNEL THROUGH TIME!"

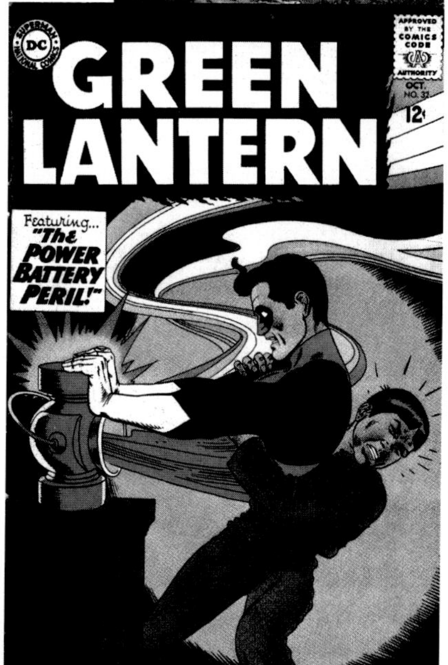
GREEN LANTERN
12¢
Featuring... "The POWER BATTERY PERIL!"

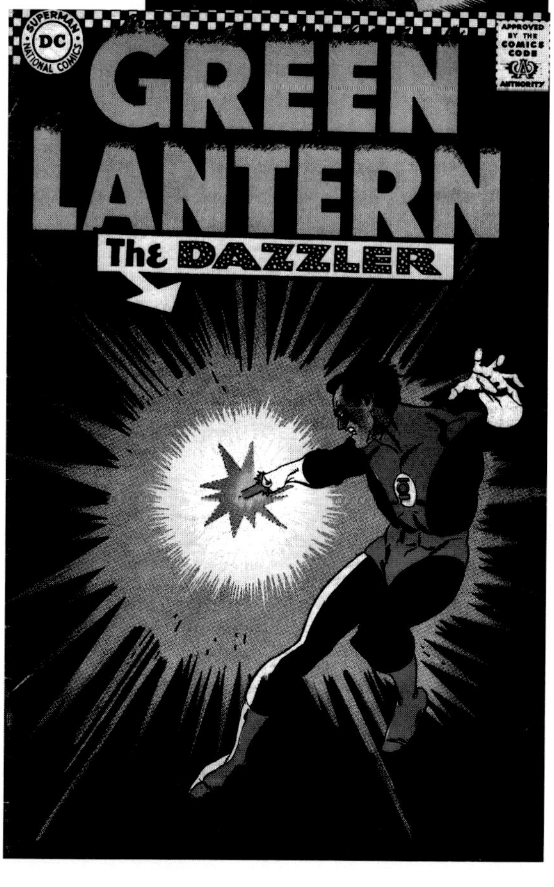
GREEN LANTERN
The DAZZLER

artist pencil artwork, and to have another artist ink the work. This separation of labor led to many difficulties, when the inker was not sensitive to the artist's intentions. The division of effort in the production of artwork was developed in the shops to facilitate turning out the most product on a tight schedule.[3] During the early run of *Green Lantern*, Kane was primarily paired with two inkers, Joe Giella and Murphy Anderson. Giella underwhelmed Kane's work, by failing to capture the flow of the figures Kane intended. Anderson, on the other hand, overwhelmed the work. Anderson, who inked primarily with a pen, was a strong inker, whose personality became primary when he worked. His inking, while competent, lacked

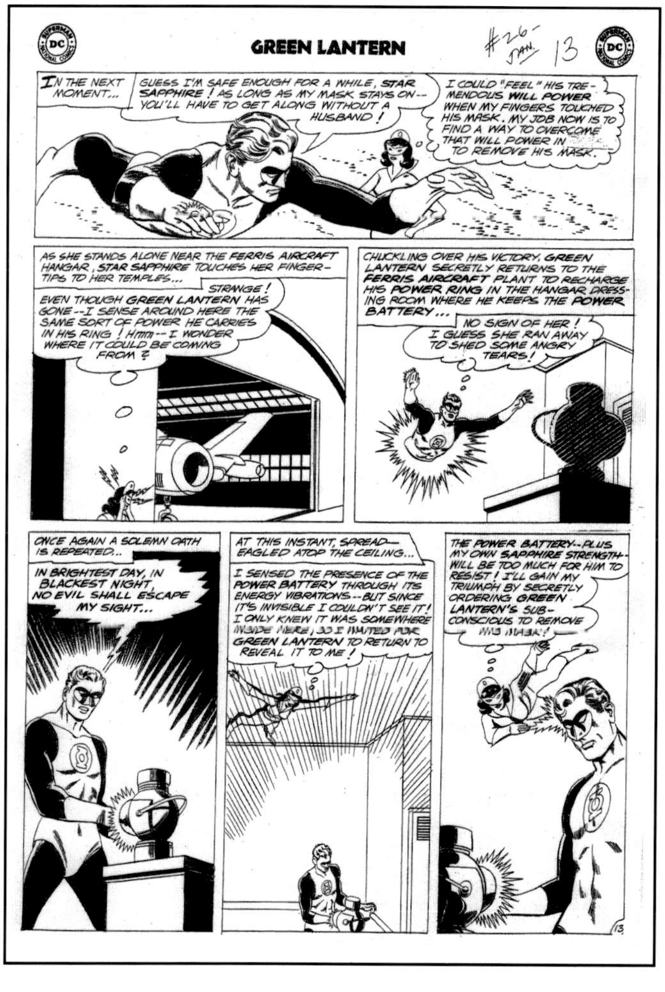
GREEN LANTERN
#26-JAN. 13
IN THE NEXT MOMENT...
GUESS I'M SAFE ENOUGH FOR A WHILE, STAR SAPPHIRE! AS LONG AS MY MASK STAYS ON-- YOU'LL HAVE TO GET ALONG WITHOUT A HUSBAND!
I COULD "FEEL" HIS TREMENDOUS WILL POWER WHEN MY FINGERS TOUCHED HIS MASK. MY JOB NOW IS TO FIND A WAY TO OVERCOME THAT WILL POWER IN TO REMOVE HIS MASK.
AS SHE STANDS ALONE NEAR THE FERRIS AIRCRAFT HANGAR, STAR SAPPHIRE TOUCHES HER FINGERTIPS TO HER TEMPLES...
STRANGE! EVEN THOUGH GREEN LANTERN HAS GONE--I SENSE AROUND HERE THE SAME SORT OF POWER HE CARRIES IN HIS RING! Hmm--I WONDER WHERE IT COULD BE COMING FROM?
CHUCKLING OVER HIS VICTORY, GREEN LANTERN SECRETLY RETURNS TO THE FERRIS AIRCRAFT PLANT TO RECHARGE HIS POWER RING IN THE HANGAR DRESSING ROOM WHERE HE KEEPS THE POWER BATTERY...
NO SIGN OF HER! I GUESS SHE RAN AWAY TO SHED SOME ANGRY TEARS!
ONCE AGAIN A SOLEMN OATH IS REPEATED...
IN BRIGHTEST DAY, IN BLACKEST NIGHT, NO EVIL SHALL ESCAPE MY SIGHT...
AT THIS INSTANT, SPREAD-EAGLED ATOP THE CEILING...
I SENSED THE PRESENCE OF THE POWER BATTERY THROUGH ITS ENERGY VIBRATIONS--BUT SINCE IT'S INVISIBLE I COULDN'T SEE IT! I ONLY KNEW IT WAS SOMEWHERE
GREEN LANTERN TO RETURN TO REVEAL IT TO ME!
THE POWER BATTERY--PLUS MY OWN SAPPHIRE STRENGTH--WILL BE TOO MUCH FOR HIM TO RESIST! I'LL GAIN MY TRIUMPH BY SECRETLY ORDERING GREEN LANTERN'S SUBCONSCIOUS TO REMOVE

Original artwork for an interior page from *Green Lantern* #26, Jan., 1964, Gil Kane, pencils, Joe Giella, inks, ©2001 DC Comics. Another example of Giella inking Kane's pencils.

Right: original artwork for the cover for *Green Lantern* #26, Gil Kane, pencils, Murphy Anderson, inks, January, 1964, ©2001 DC Comics. A striking, simple, and classic example of a 1960s DC Comics cover. This cover is reproduced showing the artboard that was given to artists for cover compositions. In the process of photographing and printing the cover, usually some of the artwork was cropped off. See the final color version of this cover in the color section in this book: *Art in Color*.

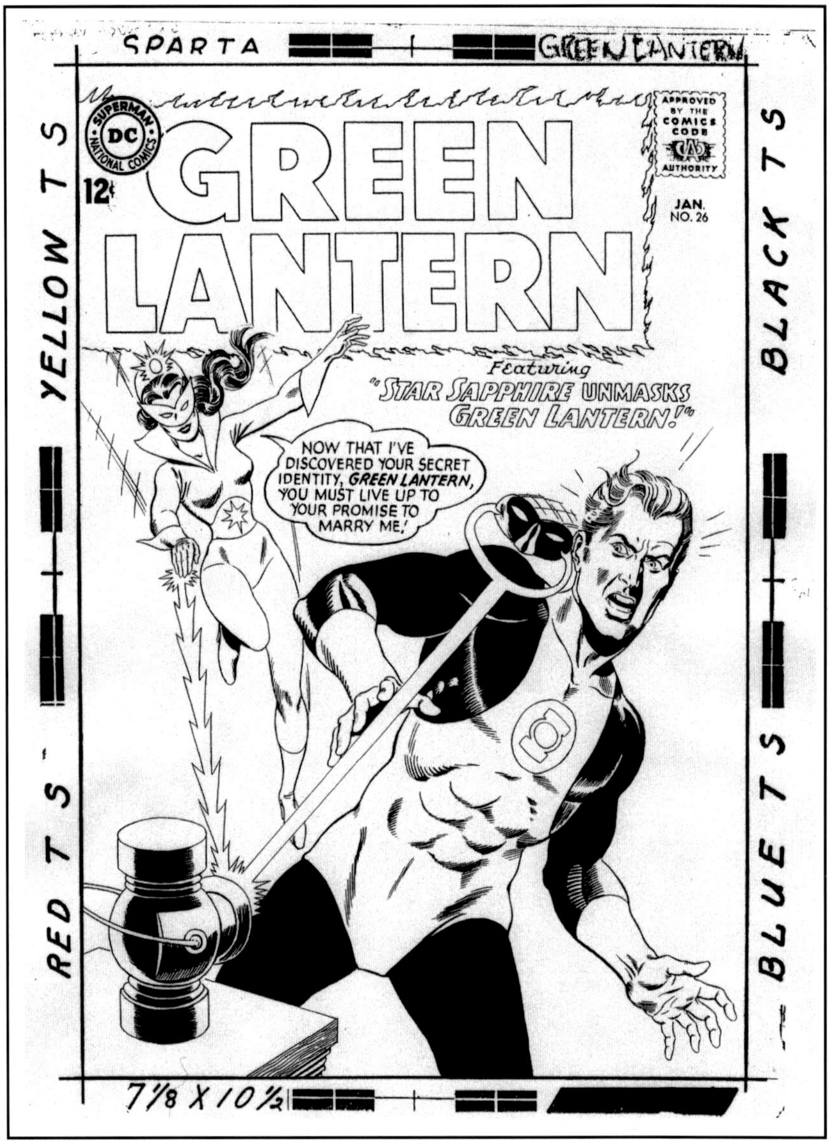
SPARTA
GREEN LANTERN
DC
SUPERMAN NATIONAL COMICS
12¢
GREEN LANTERN
APPROVED BY THE COMICS CODE AUTHORITY
JAN. NO. 26
Featuring
"STAR SAPPHIRE UNMASKS GREEN LANTERN!"
NOW THAT I'VE DISCOVERED YOUR SECRET IDENTITY, GREEN LANTERN, YOU MUST LIVE UP TO YOUR PROMISE TO MARRY ME.'
YELLOW TS
RED TS
BLACK TS
BLUE TS
7 1/8 X 10 1/2

grace, but ultimately made Kane's work more appealing. Of the two inkers, Giella, at his best, better served Kane. Finally, in the mid 1960s Kane was paired with Sid Greene who, more than any other inker before, seemed to understand him. Kane also received an inking assist from Wally Wood, in 1968. Wood, who was no longer in top form, nevertheless served Kane, and the Green Lantern well. By the mid 1960s Kane had also tightened his work and significantly modified his composition and drawing. The combination of Kane's maturation,

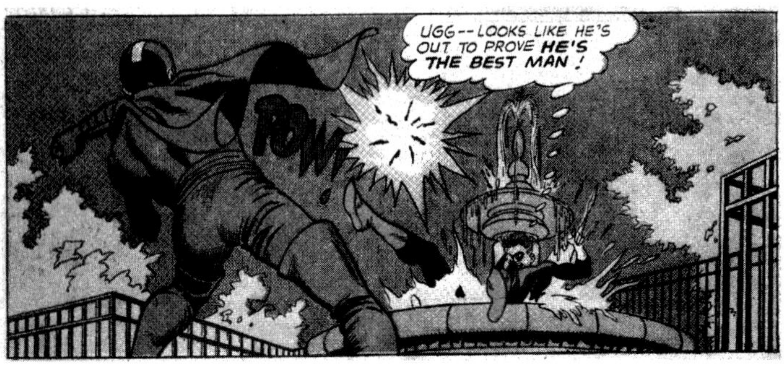
UGG--LOOKS LIKE HE'S OUT TO PROVE HE'S THE BEST MAN!
POW!

A panel which displays Sid Greene's inking of Kane's pencils from *Green Lantern* #39, Oct., 1965, ©2001 DC Comics.

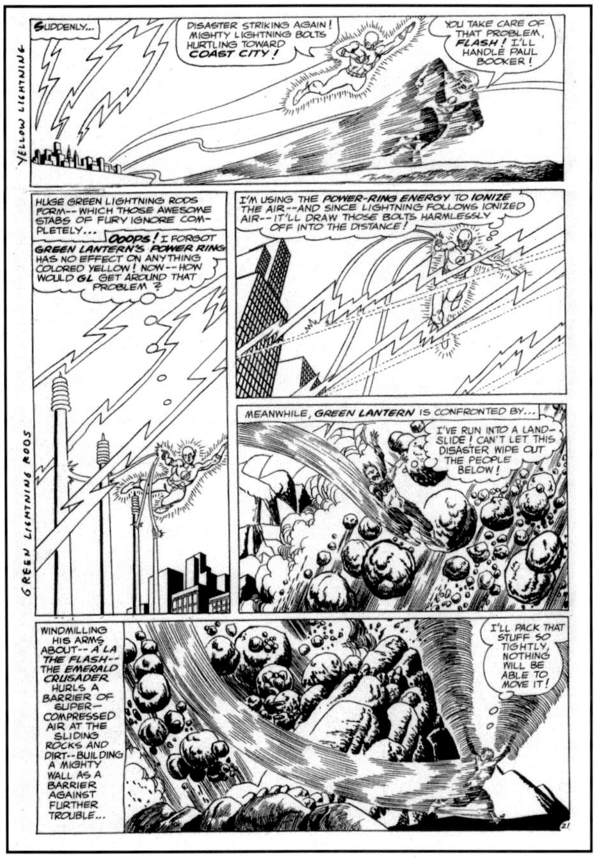
YELLOW LIGHTNING
SUDDENLY...
DISASTER STRIKING AGAIN! MIGHTY LIGHTNING BOLTS HURTLING TOWARD COAST CITY!
YOU TAKE CARE OF THAT PROBLEM, FLASH! I'LL HANDLE PAUL BOOKER!
GREEN LIGHTNING RODS
HUGE GREEN LIGHTNING RODS FORM-- WHICH THOSE AWESOME STABS OF FURY IGNORE COMPLETELY...
OOOPS! I FORGOT GREEN LANTERN'S POWER RING HAS NO EFFECT ON ANYTHING COLORED YELLOW! NOW--HOW WOULD GL GET AROUND THAT PROBLEM ?
I'M USING THE POWER-RING ENERGY TO IONIZE THE AIR--AND SINCE LIGHTNING FOLLOWS IONIZED AIR-- IT'LL DRAW THOSE BOLTS HARMLESSLY OFF INTO THE DISTANCE!
MEANWHILE, GREEN LANTERN IS CONFRONTED BY...
I'VE RUN INTO A LANDSLIDE! CAN'T LET THIS DISASTER WIPE OUT THE PEOPLE BELOW!
WINDMILLING HIS ARMS ABOUT-- A LA THE FLASH-- THE EMERALD CRUSADER HURLS A BARRIER OF SUPER-COMPRESSED AIR AT THE SLIDING ROCKS AND DIRT--BUILDING A MIGHTY WALL AS A BARRIER AGAINST FURTHER TROUBLE...
I'LL PACK THAT STUFF SO TIGHTLY, NOTHING WILL BE ABLE TO MOVE IT!
21

Left: original artwork from an interior page for *Green Lantern* #43, Gil Kane, pencils, Sid Greene, inks, March, 1966, ©2001 DC Comics. This page demonstrates how Greene, more than Kane's prior inkers on the feature, sensitively finished his pencils, rather than overpowering them.

coupled with Greene's more sensitive inking, created some very memorable work.

Kane, never one to sit still, was further expanding artistically. In 1961 he pitched the concept of resuscitating another superhero owned by DC Comics, the Atom. Kane designed the concept, and it was approved and put into production.[4] The Atom, as the name of the character implied, was a scientist who through the use of "white dwarf star matter" could reduce his size to minimal proportions, thus facilitating the action

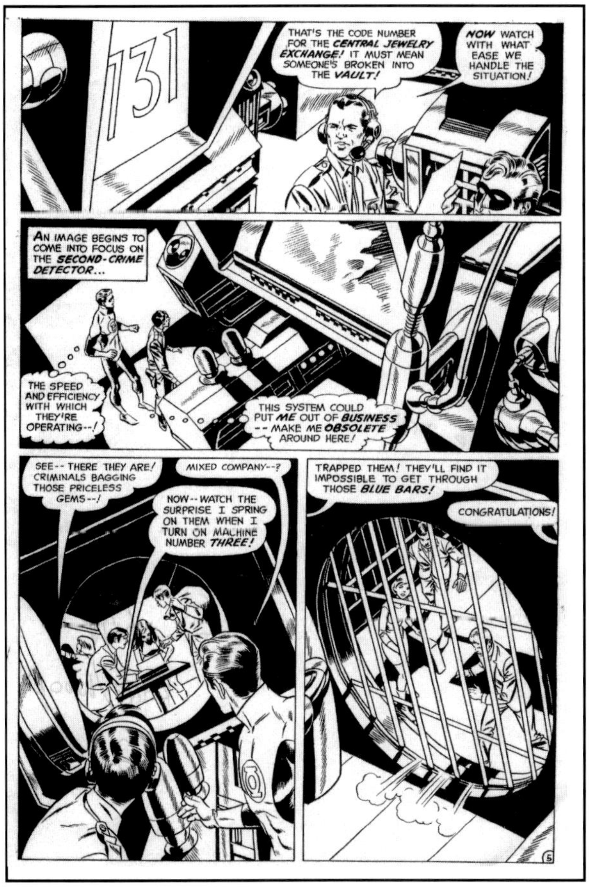
731
THAT'S THE CODE NUMBER FOR THE CENTRAL JEWELRY EXCHANGE! IT MUST MEAN SOMEONE'S BROKEN INTO THE VAULT!
NOW WATCH WITH WHAT EASE WE HANDLE THE SITUATION!
AN IMAGE BEGINS TO COME INTO FOCUS ON THE SECOND-CRIME DETECTOR...
THE SPEED AND EFFICIENCY WITH WHICH THEY'RE OPERATING--!
THIS SYSTEM COULD PUT ME OUT OF BUSINESS --MAKE ME OBSOLETE AROUND HERE!
SEE--THERE THEY ARE! CRIMINALS BAGGING THOSE PRICELESS GEMS--!
MIXED COMPANY--?
NOW--WATCH THE SURPRISE I SPRING ON THEM WHEN I TURN ON MACHINE NUMBER THREE!
TRAPPED THEM! THEY'LL FIND IT IMPOSSIBLE TO GET THROUGH THOSE BLUE BARS!
CONGRATULATIONS!
5

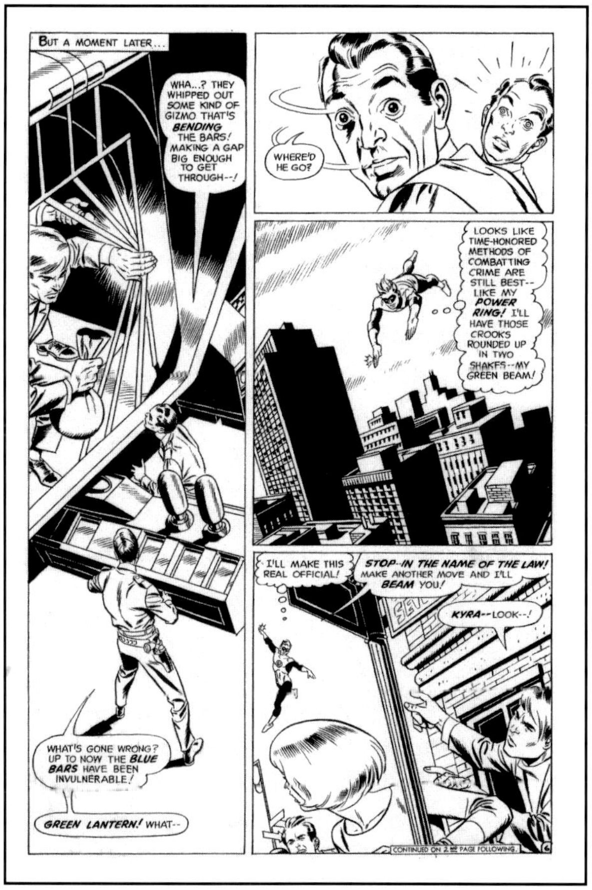
BUT A MOMENT LATER...
WHA...? THEY WHIPPED OUT SOME KIND OF GIZMO THAT'S BENDING THE BARS! MAKING A GAP BIG ENOUGH TO GET THROUGH--!
WHERE'D HE GO?
LOOKS LIKE TIME-HONORED METHODS OF COMBATTING CRIME ARE STILL BEST-- LIKE MY POWER RING! I'LL HAVE THOSE CROOKS ROUNDED UP IN TWO SHAKES--MY GREEN BEAM!
WHAT'S GONE WRONG? UP TO NOW THE BLUE BARS HAVE BEEN INVULNERABLE!
GREEN LANTERN! WHAT--
I'LL MAKE THIS REAL OFFICIAL!
STOP--IN THE NAME OF THE LAW! MAKE ANOTHER MOVE AND I'LL BEAM YOU!
KYRA--LOOK--!
CONTINUED ON 2ND PAGE FOLLOWING.
6

Left and right: two sequential pages from the original artwork for *Green Lantern* #69, Gil Kane, pencils, Wally Wood inks, June, 1969, ©2001 DC Comics. These pages demonstrate how Wally Wood added lighting effects, which were usually absent, to Kane's pencils. Wood's inks gave the artwork a bold quality which prior inkers were unable to capture.

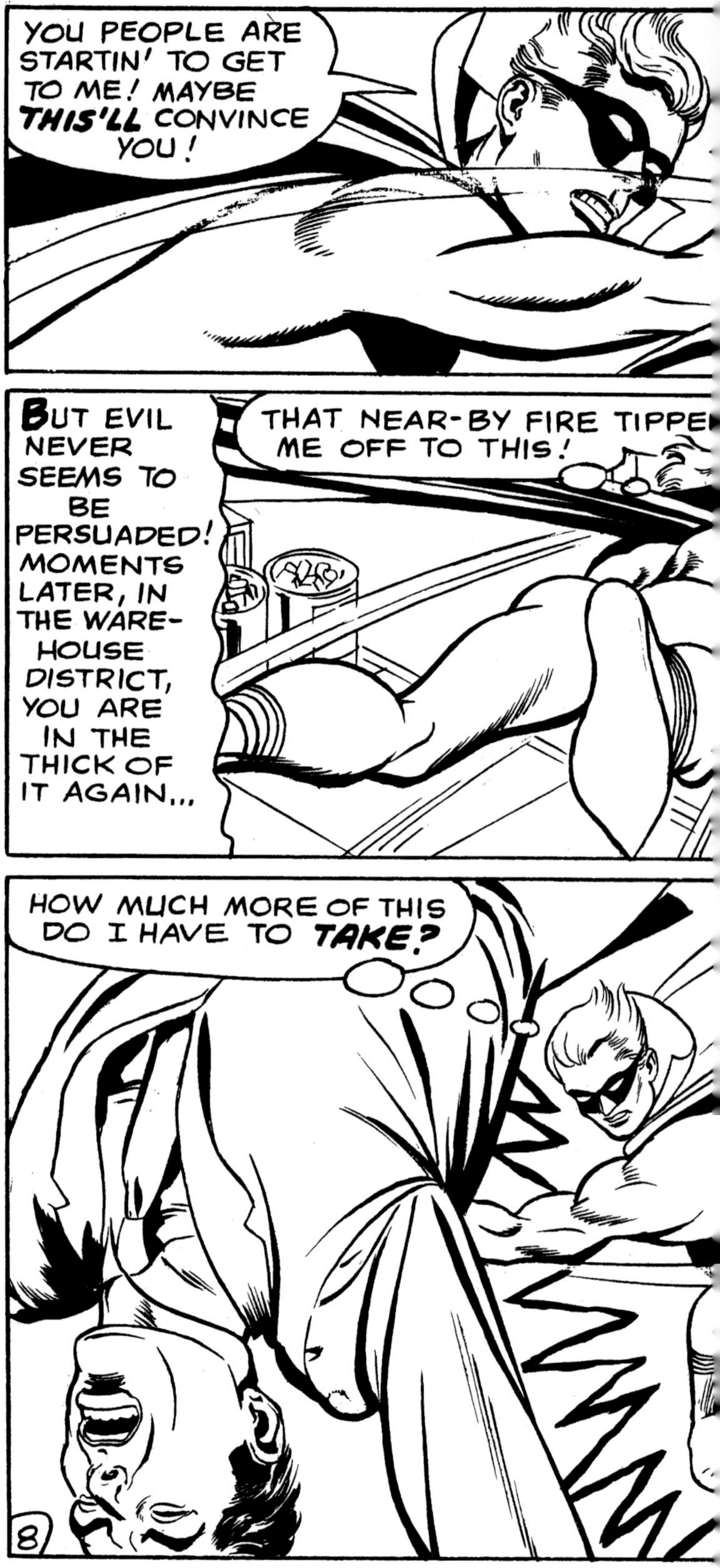
YOU PEOPLE ARE STARTIN' TO GET TO ME! MAYBE THIS'LL CONVINCE YOU!
BUT EVIL NEVER SEEMS TO BE PERSUADED! MOMENTS LATER, IN THE WARE-HOUSE DISTRICT, YOU ARE IN THE THICK OF IT AGAIN...
THAT NEAR-BY FIRE TIPPE ME OFF TO THIS!
HOW MUCH MORE OF THIS DO I HAVE TO TAKE?
8

of the story. Kane, unfortunately, was not permitted to write for either the *Green Lantern* or *The Atom.* Although the art in these comic books shows Kane maturing, the scripts for these stories, conceptualized by Julius Schwartz and written primarily by John Broome (*Green Lantern*) and Gardner Fox (*The Atom*) was frequently not inspired. At their best, the stories were fanciful, and sometimes clever. Kane consistently provided memorable art, for both titles, for almost seven years. In his work on *Green Lantern* and *The Atom*, Kane made memorable use of his

Center: an interior page from the original artwork for *Green Lantern* #61, June, 1968, Gil Kane, pencils, Sid Greene, inks, ©2001 DC Comics. At almost the actual size of the original drawing (comic artwork was drawn two times larger than the actual comic book until the middle 1960s, when, due to cost saving measures, it was reduced to one-and-a-half times the size of the comic book), this is an excellent example of Kane and Greene working together. Kane's figures achieve a fluidity which spills the energy of the drawing off the page, right at the reader.

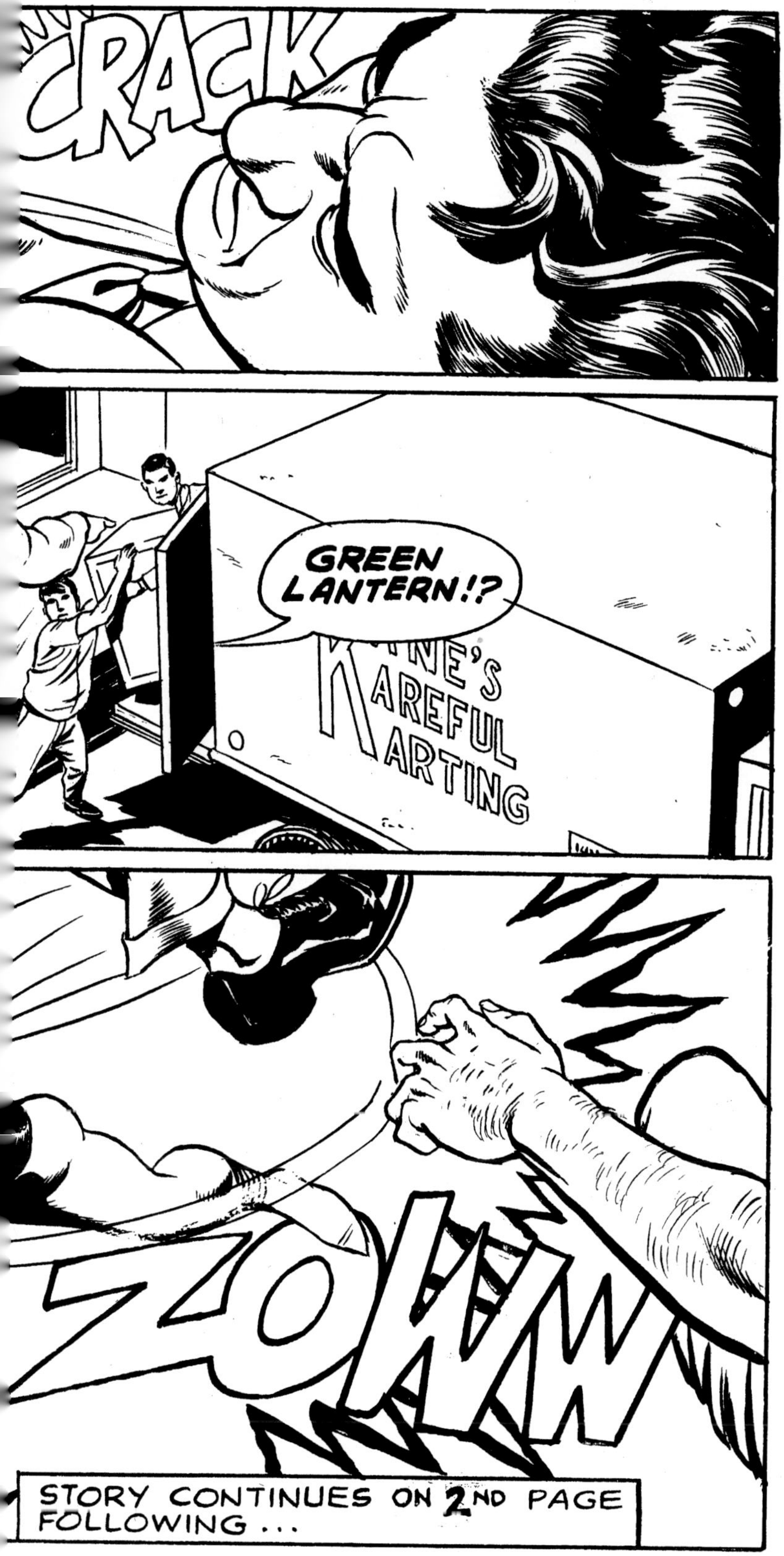
CRACK
GREEN LANTERN!?
KANE'S KAREFUL KARTING
ZOWN
STORY CONTINUES ON 2ND PAGE FOLLOWING ...

figure drawing and composition. Comic books, which have always been associated with slam/bang action, fights, fantastic villains, robots, and maidens in distress, were never served any better than by Kane's work on these titles. *Green Lantern* and *The Atom* are, in many respects, archetypal comics. Putting aside all pretension, they revel in being nothing more than **comic book stories**. These titles did little to advance the art of the comics, and

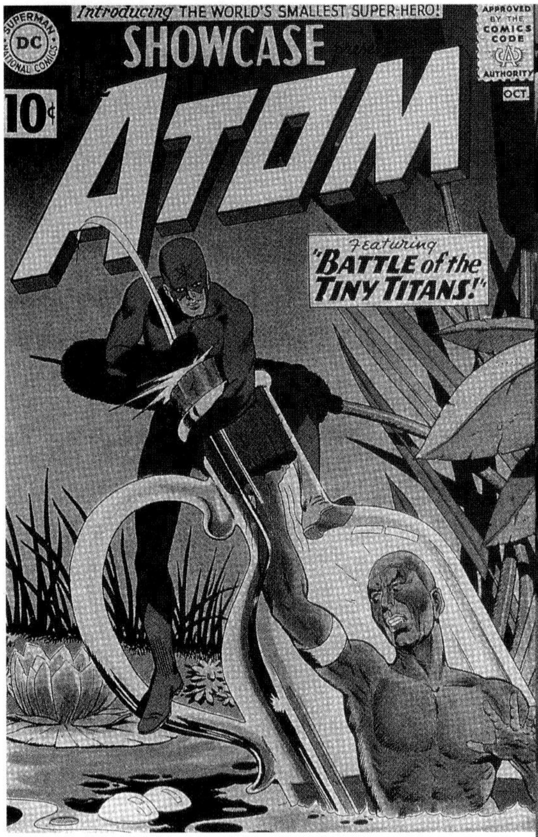
Introducing THE WORLD'S SMALLEST SUPER-HERO!
SUPERMAN DC NATIONAL COMICS
SHOWCASE
APPROVED BY THE COMICS CODE AUTHORITY
OCT.
10¢
ATOM
Featuring "BATTLE of the TINY TITANS!"

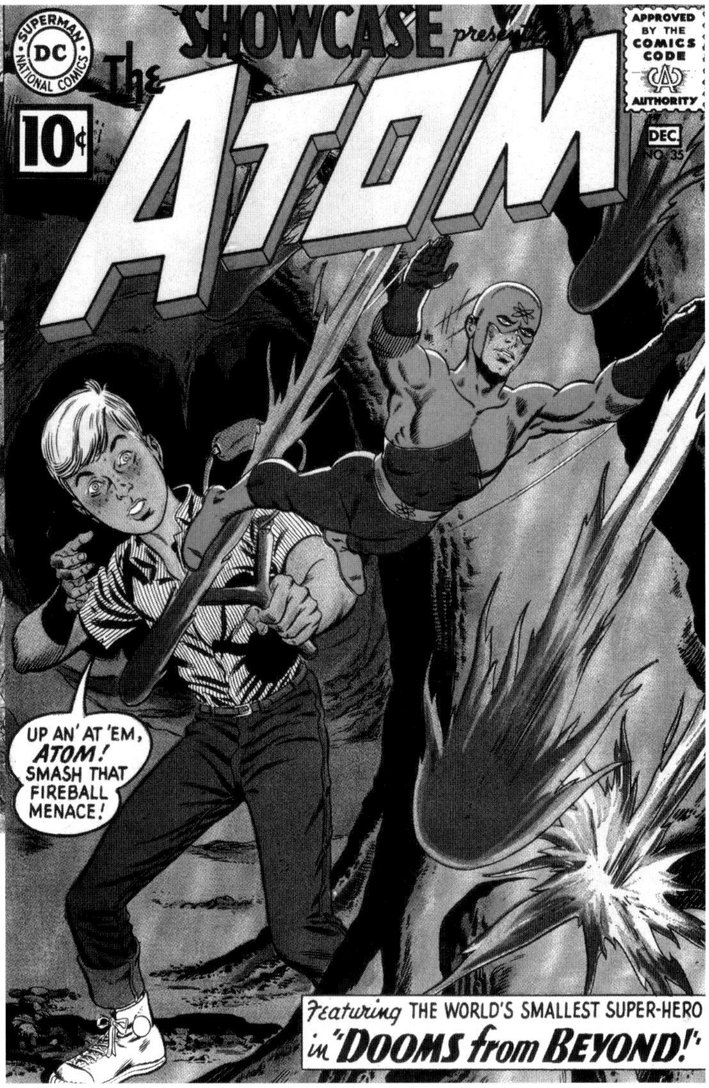
SUPERMAN DC NATIONAL COMICS
SHOWCASE presents
The ATOM
APPROVED BY THE COMICS CODE AUTHORITY
10¢
DEC NO. 35
UP AN' AT 'EM, ATOM! SMASH THAT FIREBALL MENACE!
Featuring THE WORLD'S SMALLEST SUPER-HERO
in "DOOMS from BEYOND!"

Above left and right: covers for *Showcase* #34, Sept./Oct., 1961 and #35, Nov./Dec., 1961, both, Gil Kane, pencils and Murphy Anderson, inks, both ©2001 DC Comics. The first and second appearance of Kane's new, and improved Atom. Kane borrowed the name of the character from a 1940s DC Comics superhero, who had an "atomic punch," and gave his new Atom a different ability, the power to shrink to diminutive size, taking this element of the character from Doll Man, a character created by Will Eisner in 1939, and initially drawn by Lou Fine, and later by Reed Crandall. The new Atom was updated by Kane and Editor Julius Schwartz to be in step with the 1960s.

most assuredly did not advance Kane's agenda: to create something of his own which made use of all of his ambition and talent.

The 1960s witnessed a change in the mores of certain segments of American society. Kane, who was still living in New York, was again in the center of these developments. *Playboy, Esquire,* Pop Art, the Civil Rights movement, and a relaxation in certain formal aspects of American culture were all spinning forward.

James Warren, who at the time was beginning to publish three black and white magazines influenced by EC, *Creepy, Eeire,* and

Right: original artwork for the splash page from *The Atom* #2, Aug./Sept., 1962, Gil Kane, pencils, Murphy Anderson, inks, ©2001 DC Comics.

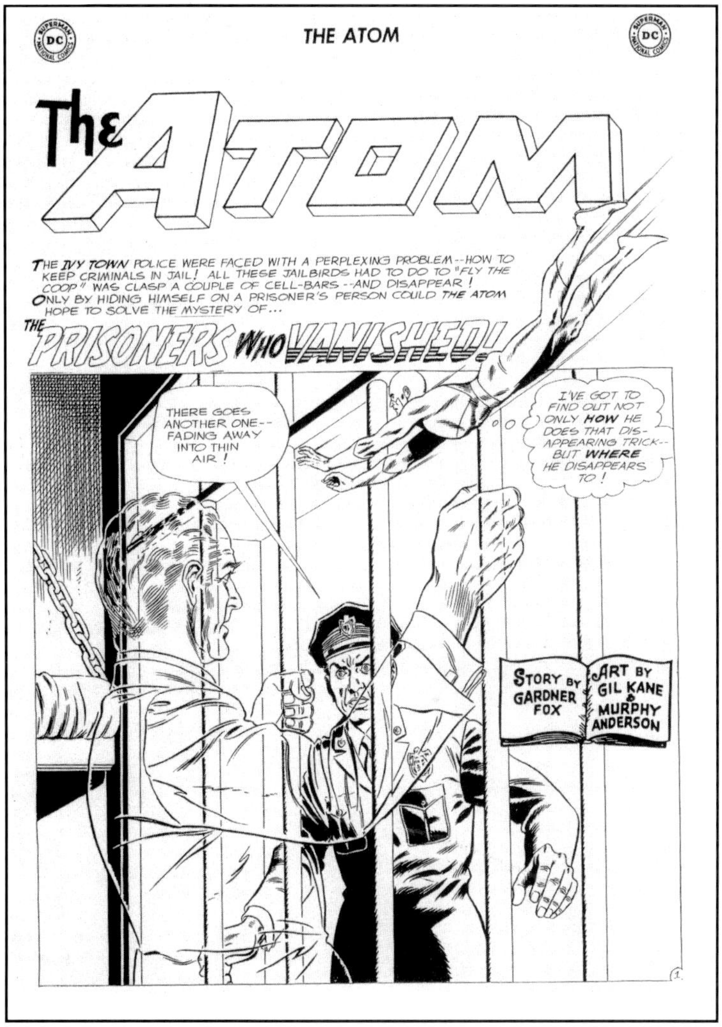
THE ATOM
The ATOM
THE IVY TOWN POLICE WERE FACED WITH A PERPLEXING PROBLEM--HOW TO KEEP CRIMINALS IN JAIL! ALL THESE JAILBIRDS HAD TO DO TO "FLY THE COOP" WAS CLASP A COUPLE OF CELL-BARS--AND DISAPPEAR! ONLY BY HIDING HIMSELF ON A PRISONER'S PERSON COULD THE ATOM HOPE TO SOLVE THE MYSTERY OF...
THE PRISONERS WHO VANISHED!
THERE GOES ANOTHER ONE-- FADING AWAY INTO THIN AIR!
I'VE GOT TO FIND OUT NOT ONLY HOW HE DOES THAT DISAPPEARING TRICK-- BUT WHERE HE DISAPPEARS TO!
STORY BY GARDNER FOX
ART BY GIL KANE & MURPHY ANDERSON

Blazing Combat, was trying to establish himself in comic books. In 1965, Kane was approached by Warren, to work on a comic book which dealt with teenagers, and was to be similar to the comics published by Archie Comics. Warren, whose offices were in New York, provided Kane with a studio in his building on 47th Street and 2nd Avenue, called Embassy House. Like Hugh Hefner, Warren lived in his offices and entertained with a nod towards Hefner's philosophy of open sexuality. It was through Kane's association with

Below: covers to *The Atom* #2, Aug./Sept., 1962, *The Atom* #18, April/May, 1965, and *The Atom* #25, June/July, 1966, all Gil Kane, pencils and all Murphy Anderson, inks, all ©2001 DC Comics.

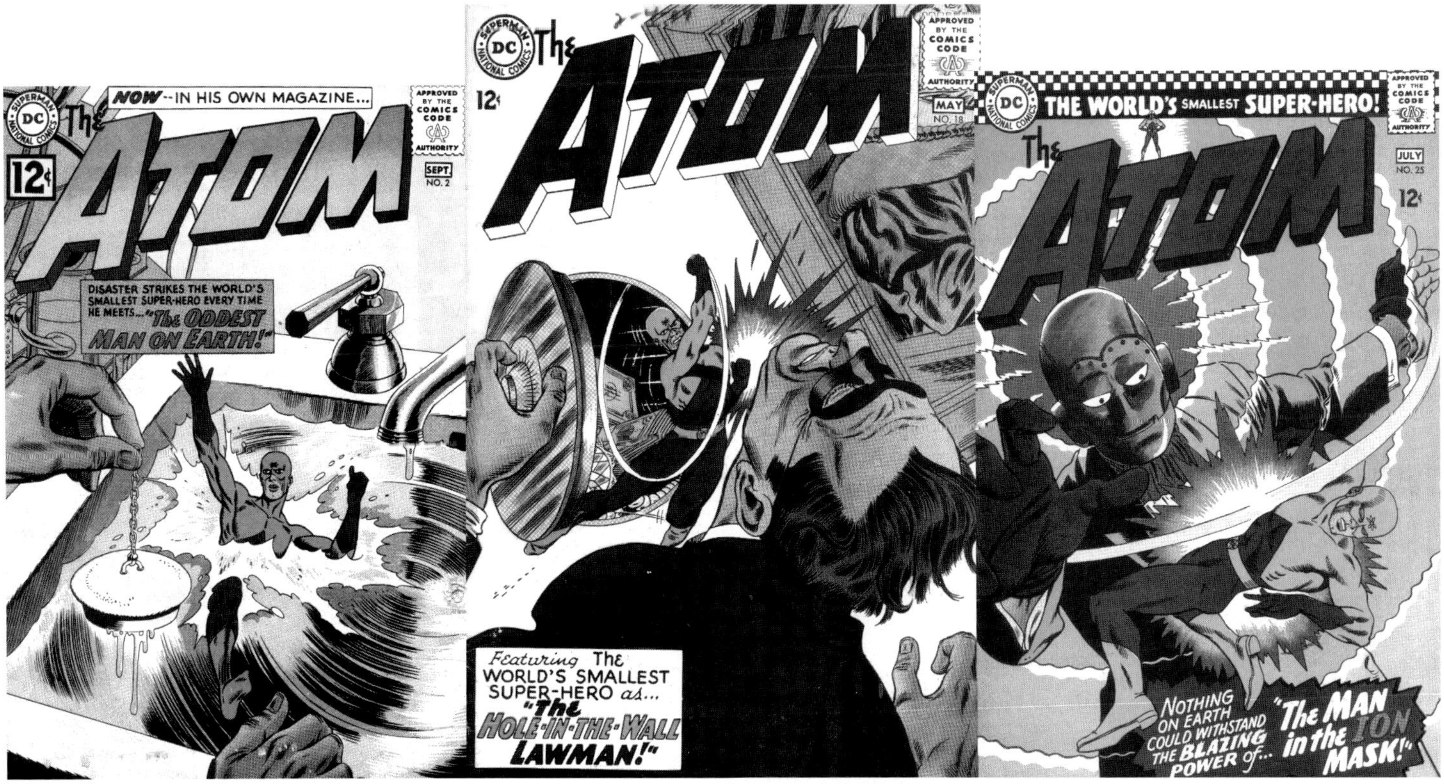
NOW--IN HIS OWN MAGAZINE...
The ATOM
12¢
SEPT. NO. 2
DISASTER STRIKES THE WORLD'S SMALLEST SUPER-HERO EVERY TIME HE MEETS... "The ODDEST MAN ON EARTH!"
The ATOM
12¢
MAY NO. 18
Featuring The WORLD'S SMALLEST SUPER-HERO as... "The HOLE-IN-THE-WALL LAWMAN!"
THE WORLD'S SMALLEST SUPER-HERO!
The ATOM
JULY NO. 25
12¢
NOTHING ON EARTH COULD WITHSTAND THE BLAZING POWER of... "The MAN in the ION MASK!"

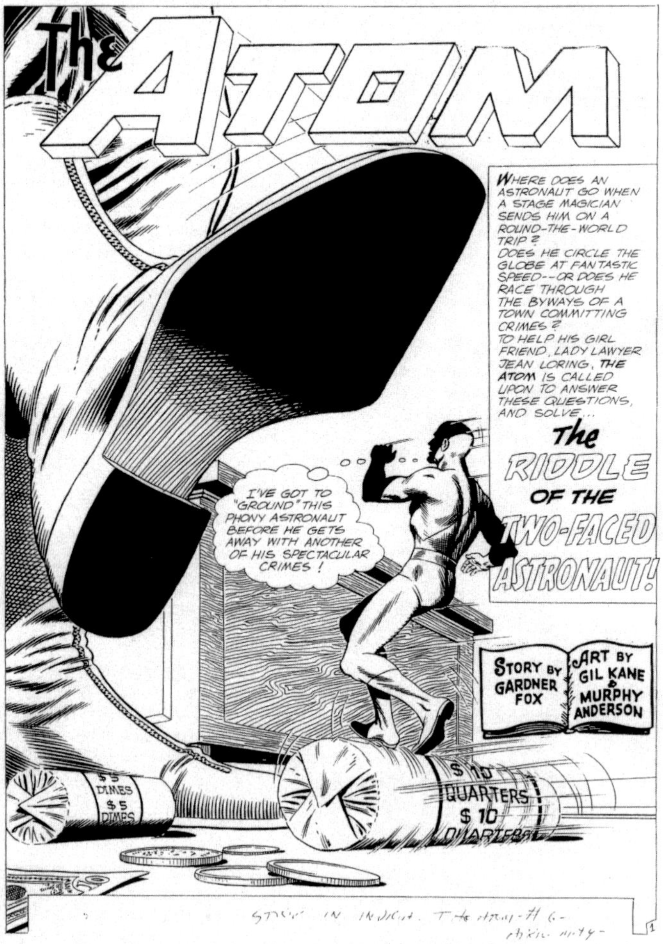
The ATOM
WHERE DOES AN ASTRONAUT GO WHEN A STAGE MAGICIAN SENDS HIM ON A ROUND-THE-WORLD TRIP? DOES HE CIRCLE THE GLOBE AT FANTASTIC SPEED--OR DOES HE RACE THROUGH THE BYWAYS OF A TOWN COMMITTING CRIMES? TO HELP HIS GIRL FRIEND, LADY LAWYER JEAN LORING, THE ATOM IS CALLED UPON TO ANSWER THESE QUESTIONS, AND SOLVE...
The RIDDLE OF THE TWO-FACED ASTRONAUT!
I'VE GOT TO "GROUND" THIS PHONY ASTRONAUT BEFORE HE GETS AWAY WITH ANOTHER OF HIS SPECTACULAR CRIMES!
STORY BY GARDNER FOX
ART BY GIL KANE & MURPHY ANDERSON
$5 DIMES $5 DIMES
$10 QUARTERS $10 QUARTERS

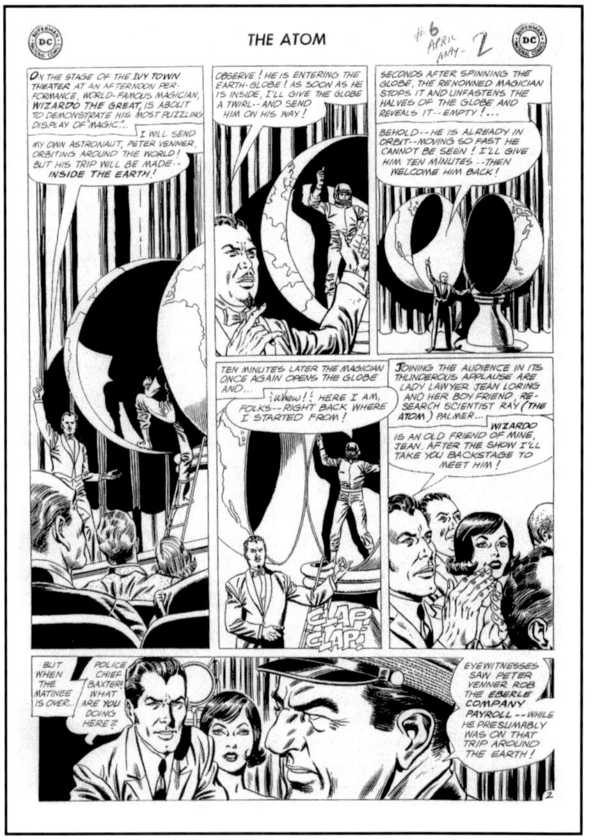
THE ATOM
#6 APRIL MAY- 2
ON THE STAGE OF THE IVY TOWN THEATER AT AN AFTERNOON PERFORMANCE, WORLD-FAMOUS MAGICIAN, WIZARDO THE GREAT, IS ABOUT TO DEMONSTRATE HIS MOST PUZZLING DISPLAY OF "MAGIC"...
I WILL SEND MY OWN ASTRONAUT, PETER VENNER, ORBITING AROUND THE WORLD! BUT HIS TRIP WILL BE MADE--INSIDE THE EARTH!
OBSERVE! HE IS ENTERING THE EARTH-GLOBE! AS SOON AS HE IS INSIDE, I'LL GIVE THE GLOBE A TWIRL--AND SEND HIM ON HIS WAY!
SECONDS AFTER SPINNING THE GLOBE, THE RENOWNED MAGICIAN STOPS IT AND UNFASTENS THE HALVES OF THE GLOBE AND REVEALS IT--EMPTY!...
BEHOLD--HE IS ALREADY IN ORBIT--MOVING SO FAST HE CANNOT BE SEEN! I'LL GIVE HIM TEN MINUTES--THEN WELCOME HIM BACK!
TEN MINUTES LATER THE MAGICIAN ONCE AGAIN OPENS THE GLOBE AND...
¡WHEW!¡ HERE I AM, FOLKS--RIGHT BACK WHERE I STARTED FROM!
CLAP! CLAP!
JOINING THE AUDIENCE IN ITS THUNDEROUS APPLAUSE ARE LADY LAWYER JEAN LORING AND HER BOY FRIEND, RESEARCH SCIENTIST RAY (THE ATOM) PALMER...
WIZARDO IS AN OLD FRIEND OF MINE, JEAN. AFTER THE SHOW I'LL TAKE YOU BACKSTAGE TO MEET HIM!
BUT WHEN THE MATINEE IS OVER...
POLICE CHIEF BAXTER! WHAT ARE YOU DOING HERE?
EYEWITNESSES SAW PETER VENNER ROB THE EBERLE COMPANY PAYROLL--WHILE HE PRESUMABLY WAS ON THAT TRIP AROUND THE EARTH!

GIL KANE

THE ART OF A STORY

Next four pages: complete original artwork for a thirteen page story from *The Atom* #6, April/May, 1963, Gil Kane, pencils, Murphy Anderson, inks, ©2001 DC Comics. This story is typical of Kane's work in the 1960s. It is presented here, in its entirety, to demonstrate the dynamics of comic book storytelling. This story presents an encyclopedia of devices which effectively move the story towards its conclusion.

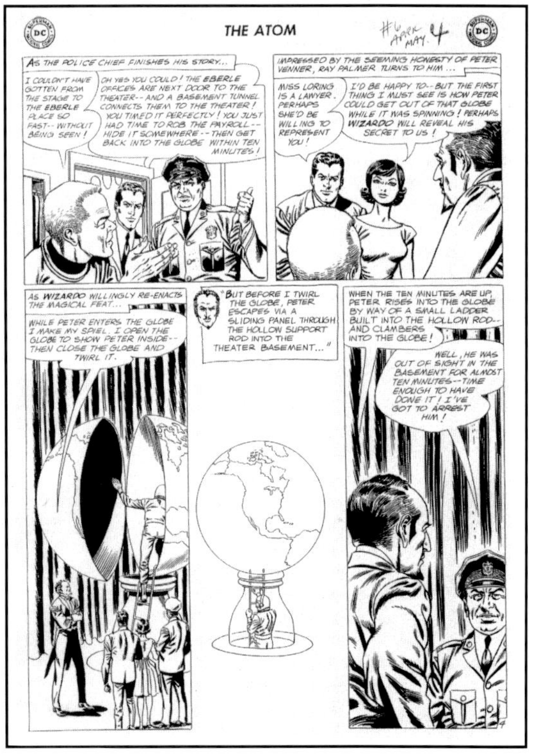
THE ATOM
#6 APRIL MAY. 4
AS THE POLICE CHIEF FINISHES HIS STORY...
I COULDN'T HAVE GOTTEN FROM THE STAGE TO THE EBERLE PLACE SO FAST--WITHOUT BEING SEEN!
OH YES YOU COULD! THE EBERLE OFFICES ARE NEXT DOOR TO THE THEATER--AND A BASEMENT TUNNEL CONNECTS THEM TO THE THEATER! YOU TIMED IT PERFECTLY! YOU JUST HAD TIME TO ROB THE PAYROLL--HIDE IT SOMEWHERE--THEN GET BACK INTO THE GLOBE WITHIN TEN MINUTES!
IMPRESSED BY THE SEEMING HONESTY OF PETER VENNER, RAY PALMER TURNS TO HIM...
MISS LORING IS A LAWYER. PERHAPS SHE'D BE WILLING TO REPRESENT YOU!
I'D BE HAPPY TO--BUT THE FIRST THING I MUST SEE IS HOW PETER COULD GET OUT OF THAT GLOBE WHILE IT WAS SPINNING! PERHAPS WIZARDO WILL REVEAL HIS SECRET TO US!
AS WIZARDO WILLINGLY RE-ENACTS THE MAGICAL FEAT...
WHILE PETER ENTERS THE GLOBE I MAKE MY SPIEL. I OPEN THE GLOBE TO SHOW PETER INSIDE--THEN CLOSE THE GLOBE AND TWIRL IT.
"BUT BEFORE I TWIRL THE GLOBE, PETER ESCAPES VIA A SLIDING PANEL THROUGH THE HOLLOW SUPPORT ROD INTO THE THEATER BASEMENT..."
WHEN THE TEN MINUTES ARE UP, PETER RISES INTO THE GLOBE BY WAY OF A SMALL LADDER BUILT INTO THE HOLLOW ROD--AND CLAMBERS INTO THE GLOBE!
WELL, HE WAS OUT OF SIGHT IN THE BASEMENT FOR ALMOST TEN MINUTES--TIME ENOUGH TO HAVE DONE IT! I'VE GOT TO ARREST HIM!

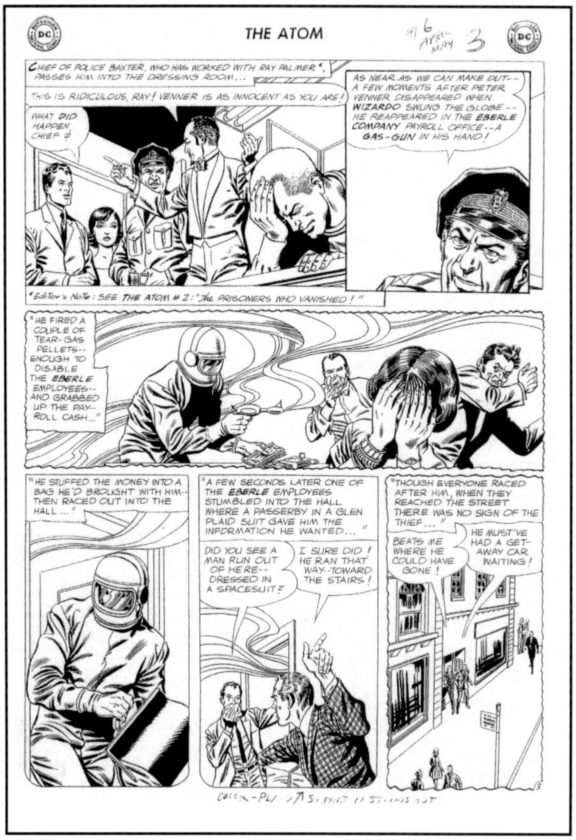
THE ATOM
#6 APRIL MAY 3
CHIEF OF POLICE BAXTER, WHO HAS WORKED WITH RAY PALMER*, PASSES HIM INTO THE DRESSING ROOM...
THIS IS RIDICULOUS, RAY! VENNER IS AS INNOCENT AS YOU ARE!
WHAT DID HAPPEN, CHIEF?
AS NEAR AS WE CAN MAKE OUT-- A FEW MOMENTS AFTER PETER VENNER DISAPPEARED WHEN WIZARDO SWUNG THE GLOBE -- HE REAPPEARED IN THE EBERLE COMPANY PAYROLL OFFICE--A GAS-GUN IN HIS HAND!
*Editor's Note: SEE THE ATOM #2: "The PRISONERS WHO VANISHED!"
"HE FIRED A COUPLE OF TEAR-GAS PELLETS-- ENOUGH TO DISABLE THE EBERLE EMPLOYEES-- AND GRABBED UP THE PAY-ROLL CASH..."
"HE STUFFED THE MONEY INTO A BAG HE'D BROUGHT WITH HIM-- THEN RACED OUT INTO THE HALL ..."
"A FEW SECONDS LATER ONE OF THE EBERLE EMPLOYEES STUMBLED INTO THE HALL WHERE A PASSERBY IN A GLEN PLAID SUIT GAVE HIM THE INFORMATION HE WANTED..."
DID YOU SEE A MAN RUN OUT OF HERE-- DRESSED IN A SPACESUIT?
I SURE DID! HE RAN THAT WAY--TOWARD THE STAIRS!
"THOUGH EVERYONE RACED AFTER HIM, WHEN THEY REACHED THE STREET THERE WAS NO SIGN OF THE THIEF..."
BEATS ME WHERE HE COULD HAVE GONE!
HE MUST'VE HAD A GET-AWAY CAR WAITING!

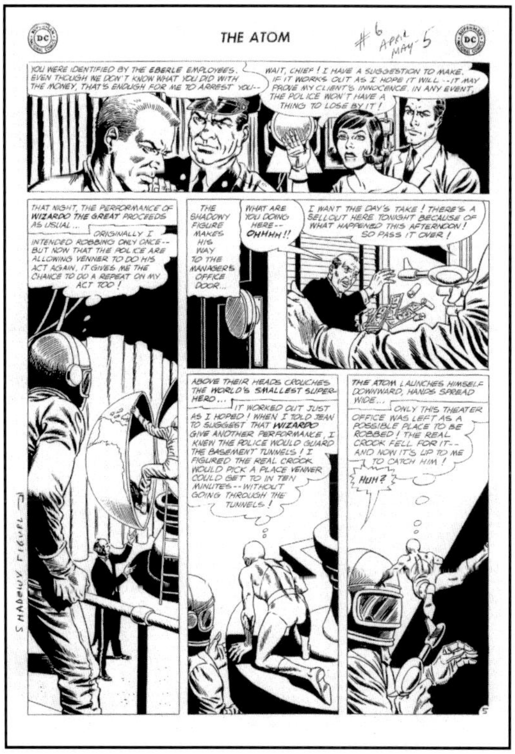
THE ATOM
#6 APRIL MAY 5
YOU WERE IDENTIFIED BY THE EBERLE EMPLOYEES. EVEN THOUGH WE DON'T KNOW WHAT YOU DID WITH THE MONEY, THAT'S ENOUGH FOR ME TO ARREST YOU--
WAIT, CHIEF! I HAVE A SUGGESTION TO MAKE. IF IT WORKS OUT AS I HOPE IT WILL --IT MAY PROVE MY CLIENT'S INNOCENCE. IN ANY EVENT, THE POLICE WON'T HAVE A THING TO LOSE BY IT!
THAT NIGHT, THE PERFORMANCE OF WIZARDO THE GREAT PROCEEDS AS USUAL...
ORIGINALLY I INTENDED ROBBING ONLY ONCE-- BUT NOW THAT THE POLICE ARE ALLOWING VENNER TO DO HIS ACT AGAIN, IT GIVES ME THE CHANCE TO DO A REPEAT ON MY ACT TOO!
THE SHADOWY FIGURE MAKES HIS WAY TO THE MANAGER'S OFFICE DOOR...
WHAT ARE YOU DOING HERE-- OHHHH!!
I WANT THE DAY'S TAKE! THERE'S A SELLOUT HERE TONIGHT BECAUSE OF WHAT HAPPENED THIS AFTERNOON! SO PASS IT OVER!
ABOVE THEIR HEADS CROUCHES THE WORLD'S SMALLEST SUPER-HERO...
IT WORKED OUT JUST AS I HOPED! WHEN I TOLD JEAN TO SUGGEST THAT WIZARDO GIVE ANOTHER PERFORMANCE, I KNEW THE POLICE WOULD GUARD THE BASEMENT TUNNELS! I FIGURED THE REAL CROOK WOULD PICK A PLACE VENNER COULD GET TO IN TEN MINUTES--WITHOUT GOING THROUGH THE TUNNELS!
THE ATOM LAUNCHES HIMSELF DOWNWARD, HANDS SPREAD WIDE...
ONLY THIS THEATER OFFICE WAS LEFT AS A POSSIBLE PLACE TO BE ROBBED! THE REAL CROOK FELL FOR IT-- AND NOW IT'S UP TO ME TO CATCH HIM!
HUH?

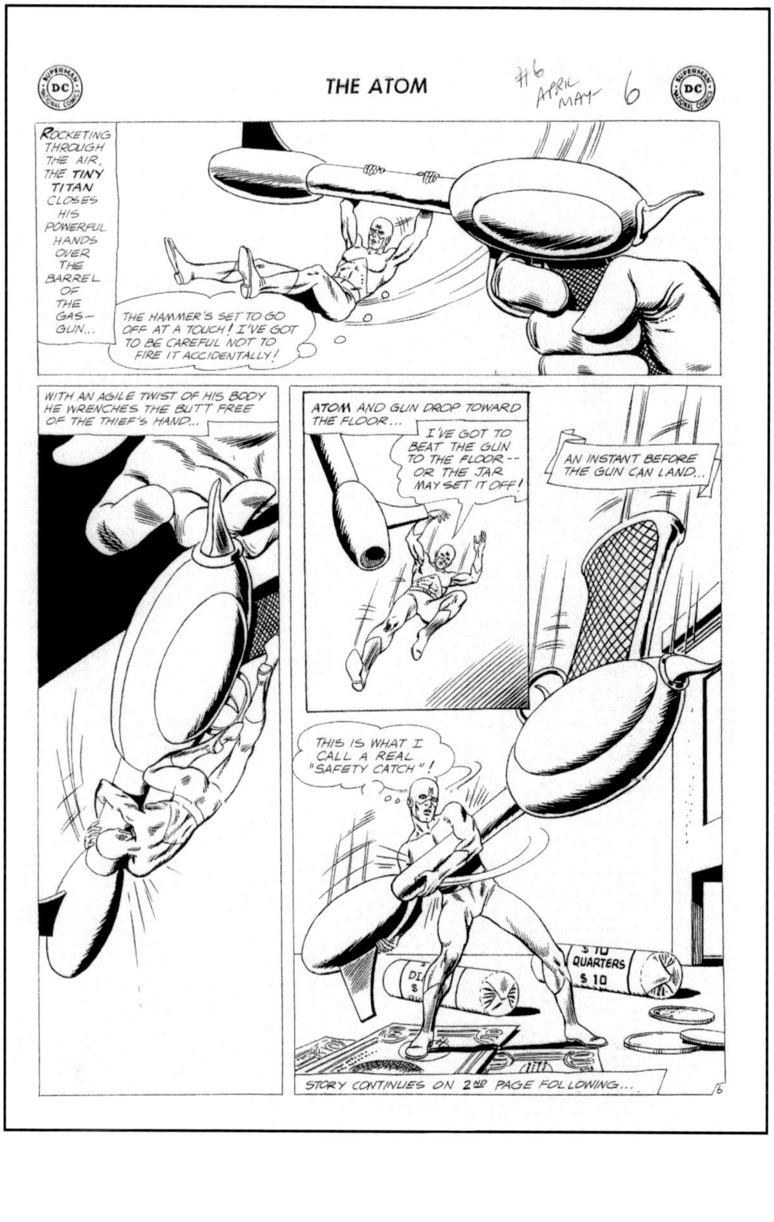
THE ATOM
#6 APRIL MAY 6
ROCKETING THROUGH THE AIR, THE TINY TITAN CLOSES HIS POWERFUL HANDS OVER THE BARREL OF THE GAS-GUN...
THE HAMMER'S SET TO GO OFF AT A TOUCH! I'VE GOT TO BE CAREFUL NOT TO FIRE IT ACCIDENTALLY!
WITH AN AGILE TWIST OF HIS BODY HE WRENCHES THE BUTT FREE OF THE THIEF'S HAND...
ATOM AND GUN DROP TOWARD THE FLOOR...
I'VE GOT TO BEAT THE GUN TO THE FLOOR-- OR THE JAR MAY SET IT OFF!
AN INSTANT BEFORE THE GUN CAN LAND...
THIS IS WHAT I CALL A REAL "SAFETY CATCH"!
QUARTERS $10
STORY CONTINUES ON 2ND PAGE FOLLOWING...

At the time this story was created, Kane was still restrained by his editors in his page/panel layout. Kane's layout, in this story, was not unique, but made good use of each page. Kane distinguished this story by effective pacing and creative staging. Page 6, above, is an especially fine example of Kane's work at the time, and hints at how he was developing his art.

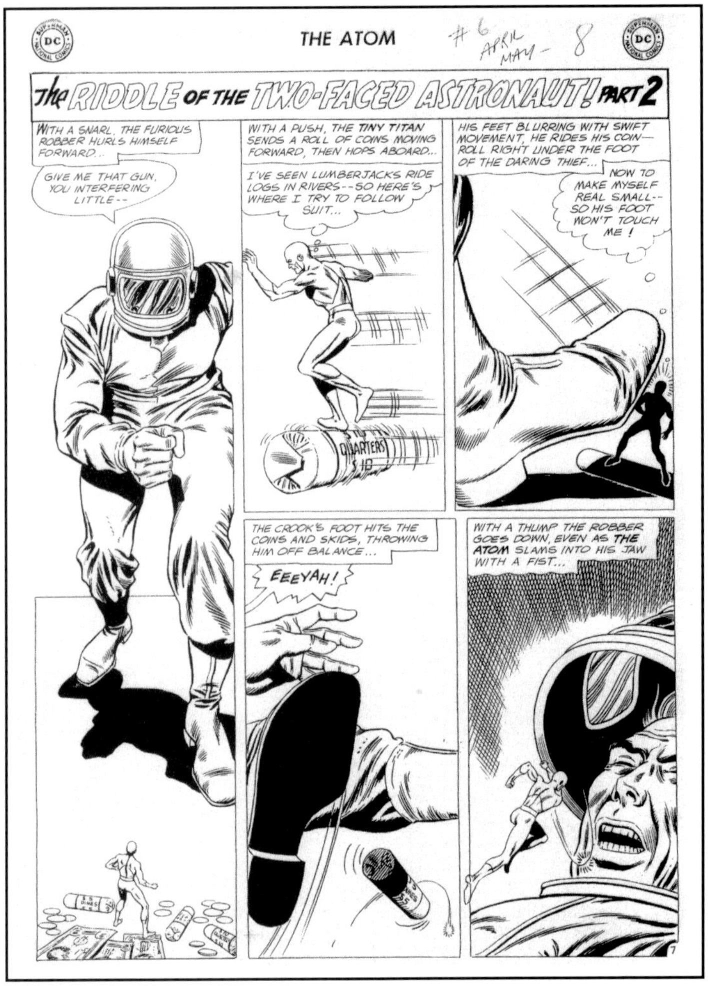
THE ATOM
#6 APRIL MAY- 8
The RIDDLE OF THE TWO-FACED ASTRONAUT! PART 2
WITH A SNARL, THE FURIOUS ROBBER HURLS HIMSELF FORWARD...
GIVE ME THAT GUN, YOU INTERFERING LITTLE--
WITH A PUSH, THE TINY TITAN SENDS A ROLL OF COINS MOVING FORWARD, THEN HOPS ABOARD...
I'VE SEEN LUMBERJACKS RIDE LOGS IN RIVERS--SO HERE'S WHERE I TRY TO FOLLOW SUIT...
QUARTERS $10
HIS FEET BLURRING WITH SWIFT MOVEMENT, HE RIDES HIS COIN-ROLL RIGHT UNDER THE FOOT OF THE DARING THIEF...
NOW TO MAKE MYSELF REAL SMALL--SO HIS FOOT WON'T TOUCH ME!
THE CROOK'S FOOT HITS THE COINS AND SKIDS, THROWING HIM OFF BALANCE...
EEEYAH!
WITH A THUMP THE ROBBER GOES DOWN, EVEN AS THE ATOM SLAMS INTO HIS JAW WITH A FIST...

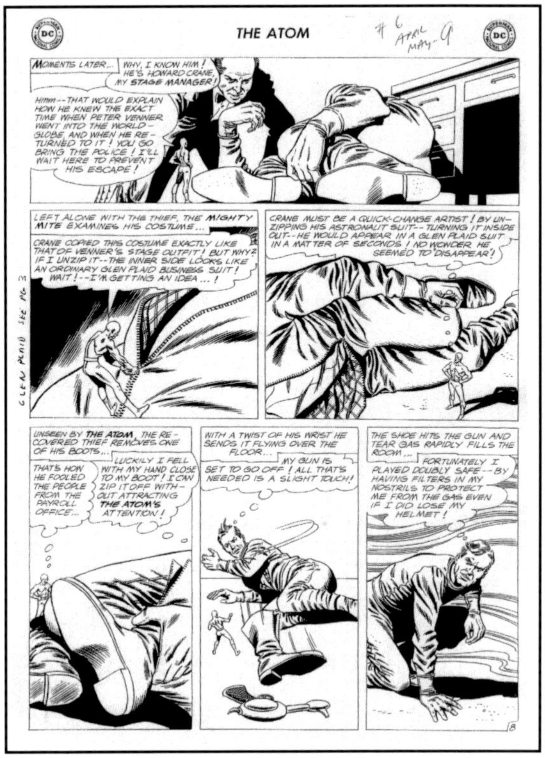
THE ATOM
#6 APRIL MAY- 9
MOMENTS LATER...
WHY, I KNOW HIM! HE'S HOWARD CRANE, MY STAGE MANAGER!
HMM--THAT WOULD EXPLAIN HOW HE KNEW THE EXACT TIME WHEN PETER VENNER WENT INTO THE WORLD-GLOBE, AND WHEN HE RETURNED TO IT! YOU GO BRING THE POLICE! I'LL WAIT HERE TO PREVENT HIS ESCAPE!
LEFT ALONE WITH THE THIEF, THE MIGHTY MITE EXAMINES HIS COSTUME...
CRANE COPIED THIS COSTUME EXACTLY LIKE THAT OF VENNER'S STAGE OUTFIT! BUT WHY? IF I UNZIP IT--THE INNER SIDE LOOKS LIKE AN ORDINARY GLEN PLAID BUSINESS SUIT! WAIT!--I'M GETTING AN IDEA...!
GLEN PLAID SEE PG 3
CRANE MUST BE A QUICK-CHANGE ARTIST! BY UNZIPPING HIS ASTRONAUT SUIT--TURNING IT INSIDE OUT--HE WOULD APPEAR IN A GLEN PLAID SUIT IN A MATTER OF SECONDS! NO WONDER HE SEEMED TO "DISAPPEAR"!
UNSEEN BY THE ATOM, THE RECOVERED THIEF REMOVES ONE OF HIS BOOTS...
THAT'S HOW HE FOOLED THE PEOPLE FROM THE PAYROLL OFFICE...
LUCKILY I FELL WITH MY HAND CLOSE TO MY BOOT! I CAN ZIP IT OFF WITHOUT ATTRACTING THE ATOM'S ATTENTION!
WITH A TWIST OF HIS WRIST HE SENDS IT FLYING OVER THE FLOOR...
MY GUN IS SET TO GO OFF! ALL THAT'S NEEDED IS A SLIGHT TOUCH!
THE SHOE HITS THE GUN AND TEAR GAS RAPIDLY FILLS THE ROOM...
FORTUNATELY I PLAYED DOUBLY SAFE--BY HAVING FILTERS IN MY NOSTRILS TO PROTECT ME FROM THE GAS EVEN IF I DID LOSE MY HELMET!

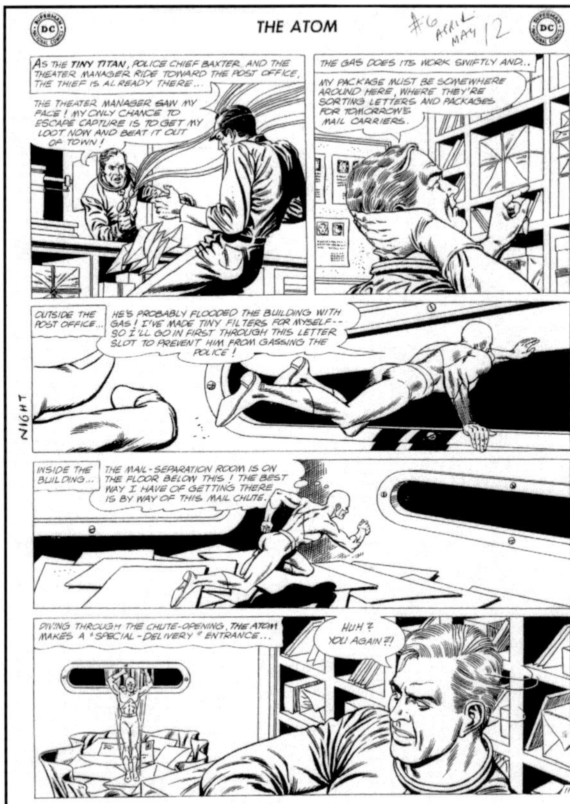
THE ATOM
#6 APRIL MAY 12
AS THE TINY TITAN, POLICE CHIEF BAXTER AND THE THEATER MANAGER RIDE TOWARD THE POST OFFICE, THE THIEF IS ALREADY THERE...
THE THEATER MANAGER SAW MY FACE! MY ONLY CHANCE TO ESCAPE CAPTURE IS TO GET MY LOOT NOW AND BEAT IT OUT OF TOWN!
THE GAS DOES ITS WORK SWIFTLY AND...
MY PACKAGE MUST BE SOMEWHERE AROUND HERE, WHERE THEY'RE SORTING LETTERS AND PACKAGES FOR TOMORROW'S MAIL CARRIERS.
OUTSIDE THE POST OFFICE...
HE'S PROBABLY FLOODED THE BUILDING WITH GAS! I'VE MADE TINY FILTERS FOR MYSELF--SO I'LL GO IN FIRST THROUGH THIS LETTER SLOT TO PREVENT HIM FROM GASSING THE POLICE!
NIGHT
INSIDE THE BUILDING...
THE MAIL-SEPARATION ROOM IS ON THE FLOOR BELOW THIS! THE BEST WAY I HAVE OF GETTING THERE IS BY WAY OF THIS MAIL CHUTE.
DIVING THROUGH THE CHUTE-OPENING, THE ATOM MAKES A "SPECIAL-DELIVERY" ENTRANCE...
HUH? YOU AGAIN?!

GIL KANE

THE ART OF A STORY

The remainder of the story from the previous pages. Take note of page 12 (which has a "13" at the top, which denotes the page count of the comic book, not the story), far right, which breaks split seconds in time down into separate panels to heighten the action, and takes the story to its conclusion.

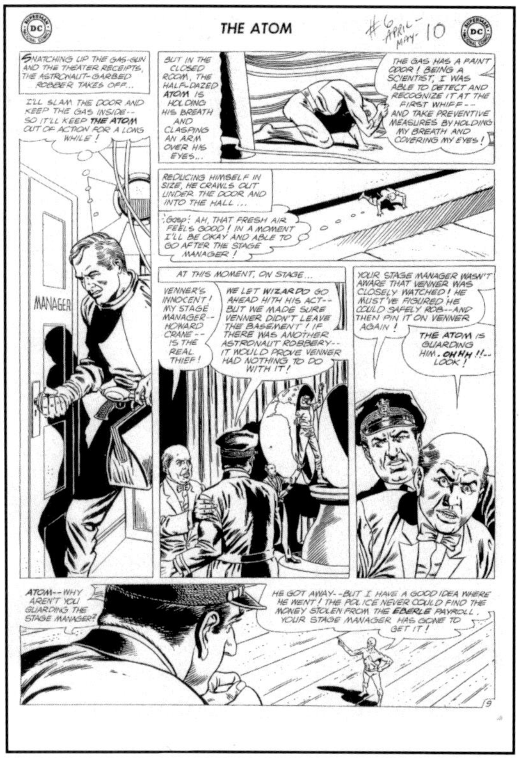
THE ATOM
SNATCHING UP THE GAS-GUN AND THE THEATER RECEIPTS, THE ASTRONAUT-GARBED ROBBER TAKES OFF...
I'LL SLAM THE DOOR AND KEEP THE GAS INSIDE-- SO IT'LL KEEP THE ATOM OUT OF ACTION FOR A LONG WHILE!
BUT IN THE CLOSED ROOM, THE HALF-DAZED ATOM IS HOLDING HIS BREATH AND CLASPING AN ARM OVER HIS EYES...
THE GAS HAS A FAINT ODOR! BEING A SCIENTIST, I WAS ABLE TO DETECT AND RECOGNIZE IT AT THE FIRST WHIFF-- AND TAKE PREVENTIVE MEASURES BY HOLDING MY BREATH AND COVERING MY EYES!
MANAGER
REDUCING HIMSELF IN SIZE, HE CRAWLS OUT UNDER THE DOOR AND INTO THE HALL...
GASP! AH, THAT FRESH AIR FEELS GOOD! IN A MOMENT I'LL BE OKAY AND ABLE TO GO AFTER THE STAGE MANAGER!
AT THIS MOMENT, ON STAGE...
VENNER'S INNOCENT! MY STAGE MANAGER-- HOWARD CRANE-- IS THE REAL THIEF!
WE LET WIZARDO GO AHEAD WITH HIS ACT-- BUT WE MADE SURE VENNER DIDN'T LEAVE THE BASEMENT! IF THERE WAS ANOTHER ASTRONAUT ROBBERY-- IT WOULD PROVE VENNER HAD NOTHING TO DO WITH IT!
YOUR STAGE MANAGER WASN'T AWARE THAT VENNER WAS CLOSELY WATCHED! HE MUST'VE FIGURED HE COULD SAFELY ROB--AND THEN PIN IT ON VENNER AGAIN!
THE ATOM IS GUARDING HIM. OHHH!!-- LOOK!
ATOM-- WHY AREN'T YOU GUARDING THE STAGE MANAGER?
HE GOT AWAY--BUT I HAVE A GOOD IDEA WHERE HE WENT! THE POLICE NEVER COULD FIND THE MONEY STOLEN FROM THE EBERLE PAYROLL. YOUR STAGE MANAGER HAS GONE TO GET IT!
9

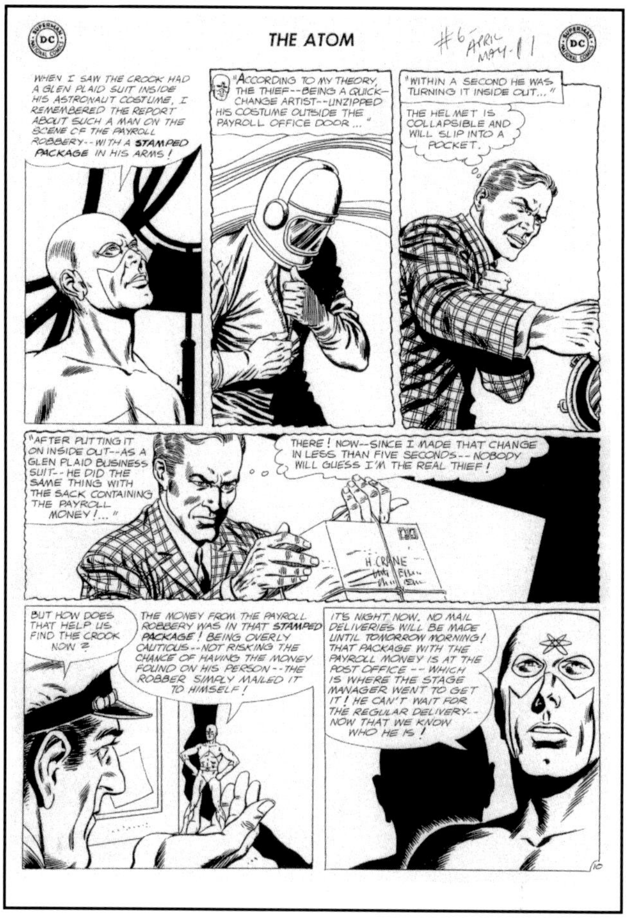
THE ATOM
WHEN I SAW THE CROOK HAD A GLEN PLAID SUIT INSIDE HIS ASTRONAUT COSTUME, I REMEMBERED THE REPORT ABOUT SUCH A MAN ON THE SCENE OF THE PAYROLL ROBBERY--WITH A STAMPED PACKAGE IN HIS ARMS!
"ACCORDING TO MY THEORY, THE THIEF--BEING A QUICK-CHANGE ARTIST--UNZIPPED HIS COSTUME OUTSIDE THE PAYROLL OFFICE DOOR..."
"WITHIN A SECOND HE WAS TURNING IT INSIDE OUT..."
THE HELMET IS COLLAPSIBLE AND WILL SLIP INTO A POCKET.
"AFTER PUTTING IT ON INSIDE OUT--AS A GLEN PLAID BUSINESS SUIT--HE DID THE SAME THING WITH THE SACK CONTAINING THE PAYROLL MONEY!..."
THERE! NOW--SINCE I MADE THAT CHANGE IN LESS THAN FIVE SECONDS--NOBODY WILL GUESS I'M THE REAL THIEF!
H. CRANE
BUT HOW DOES THAT HELP US FIND THE CROOK NOW?
THE MONEY FROM THE PAYROLL ROBBERY WAS IN THAT STAMPED PACKAGE! BEING OVERLY CAUTIOUS--NOT RISKING THE CHANCE OF HAVING THE MONEY FOUND ON HIS PERSON--THE ROBBER SIMPLY MAILED IT TO HIMSELF!
IT'S NIGHT NOW. NO MAIL DELIVERIES WILL BE MADE UNTIL TOMORROW MORNING! THAT PACKAGE WITH THE PAYROLL MONEY IS AT THE POST OFFICE--WHICH IS WHERE THE STAGE MANAGER WENT TO GET IT! HE CAN'T WAIT FOR THE REGULAR DELIVERY--NOW THAT WE KNOW WHO HE IS!
10

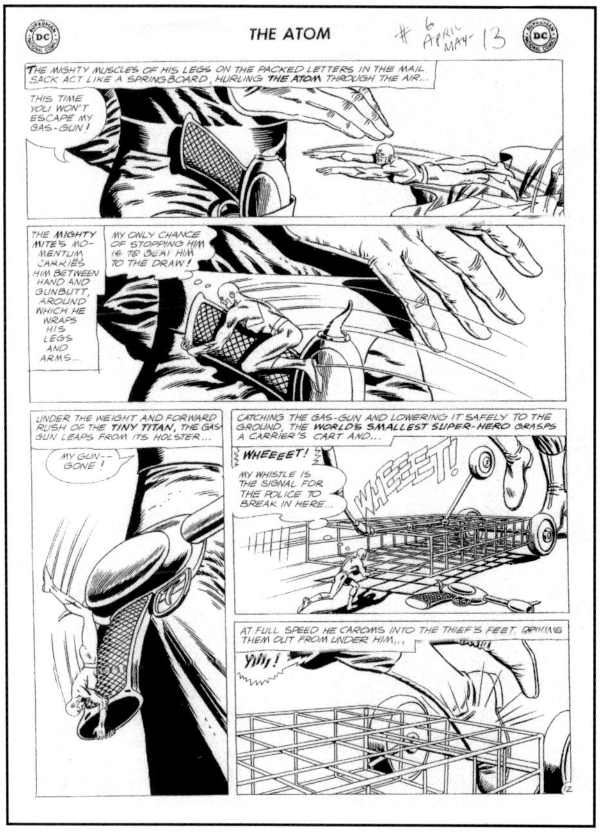
THE ATOM
THE MIGHTY MUSCLES OF HIS LEGS ON THE PACKED LETTERS IN THE MAIL SACK ACT LIKE A SPRINGBOARD, HURLING THE ATOM THROUGH THE AIR...
THIS TIME YOU WON'T ESCAPE MY GAS-GUN!
THE MIGHTY MITE'S MOMENTUM CARRIES HIM BETWEEN HAND AND GUNBUTT, AROUND WHICH HE WRAPS HIS LEGS AND ARMS...
MY ONLY CHANCE OF STOPPING HIM IS TO BEAT HIM TO THE DRAW!
UNDER THE WEIGHT AND FORWARD RUSH OF THE TINY TITAN, THE GAS-GUN LEAPS FROM ITS HOLSTER...
MY GUN-- GONE!
CATCHING THE GAS-GUN AND LOWERING IT SAFELY TO THE GROUND, THE WORLD'S SMALLEST SUPER-HERO GRASPS A CARRIER'S CART AND...
WHEEEET!
MY WHISTLE IS THE SIGNAL FOR THE POLICE TO BREAK IN HERE...
WHEEET!
AT FULL SPEED HE CAROMS INTO THE THIEF'S FEET, THEM OUT FROM UNDER HIM...
YIII!
12

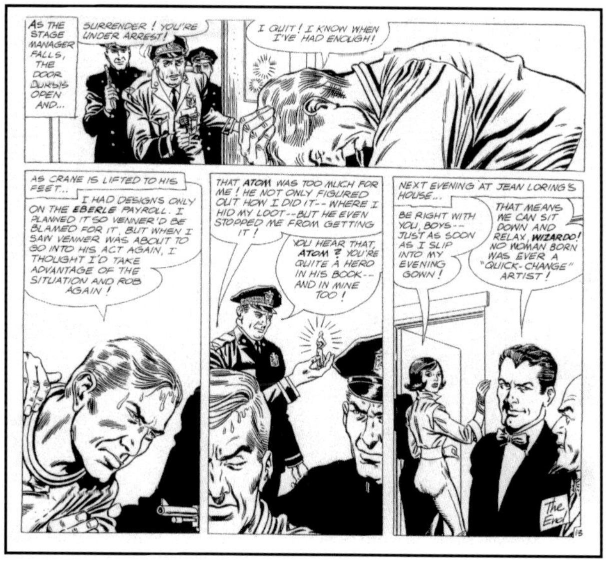
AS THE STAGE MANAGER FALLS, THE DOOR BURSTS OPEN AND...
SURRENDER! YOU'RE UNDER ARREST!
I QUIT! I KNOW WHEN I'VE HAD ENOUGH!
AS CRANE IS LIFTED TO HIS FEET...
I HAD DESIGNS ONLY ON THE EBERLE PAYROLL. I PLANNED IT SO VENNER'D BE BLAMED FOR IT, BUT WHEN I SAW VENNER WAS ABOUT TO GO INTO HIS ACT AGAIN, I THOUGHT I'D TAKE ADVANTAGE OF THE SITUATION AND ROB AGAIN!
THAT ATOM WAS TOO MUCH FOR ME! HE NOT ONLY FIGURED OUT HOW I DID IT--WHERE I HID MY LOOT--BUT HE EVEN STOPPED ME FROM GETTING IT!
YOU HEAR THAT, ATOM? YOU'RE QUITE A HERO IN HIS BOOK--AND IN MINE TOO!
NEXT EVENING AT JEAN LORING'S HOUSE...
BE RIGHT WITH YOU, BOYS--JUST AS SOON AS I SLIP INTO MY EVENING GOWN!
THAT MEANS WE CAN SIT DOWN AND RELAX, WIZARDO! NO WOMAN BORN WAS EVER A "QUICK-CHANGE" ARTIST!
13

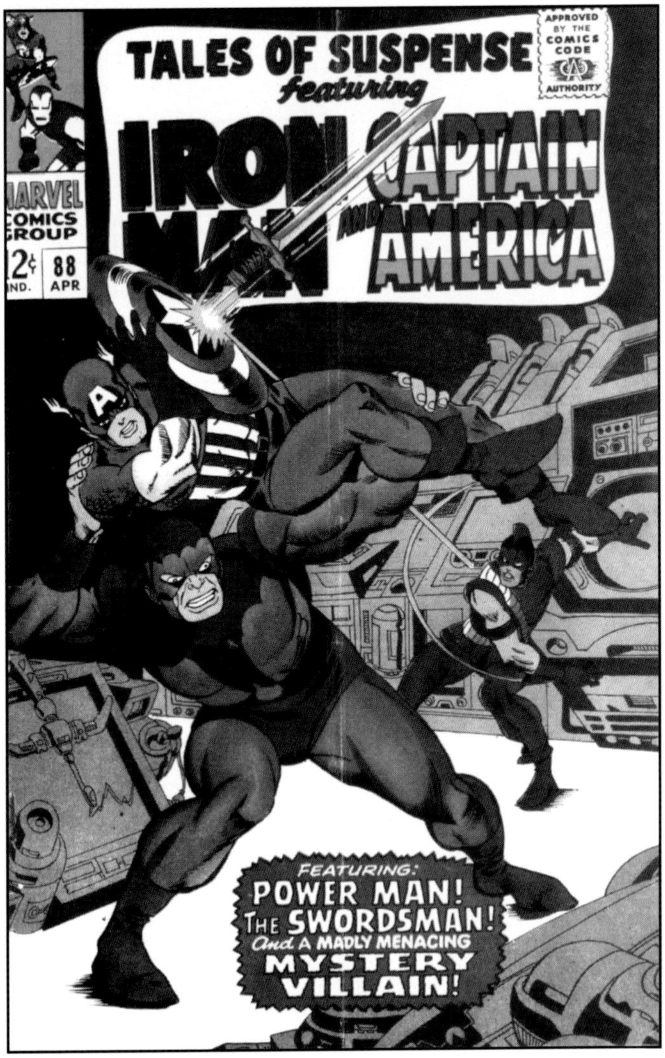
APPROVED BY THE COMICS CODE AUTHORITY
TALES OF SUSPENSE
featuring
IRON MAN
and
CAPTAIN AMERICA
MARVEL COMICS GROUP
12¢ 88 APR
FEATURING:
POWER MAN!
THE SWORDSMAN!
And A MADLY MENACING
MYSTERY VILLAIN!

Left: cover for *Tales of Suspense* #88, April, 1967, Gil Kane, pencils and inks, ©2001 Marvel Characters, Inc.

Warren that he met Archie Goodwin. Goodwin was shortly to become an important collaborator with Kane. While Kane's association with Warren did not bear fruit, he was imbued with the desire to produce and create something of his own. During the mid and late 1960s Kane continued to work for a number of publishers. He worked for Marvel, and helped Wally Wood in his effort to create a line of superhero/action/adventure comic books for Tower Comics. Wood, who was

Below: two sequential pages from *The Atom* #36, April/ May, 1968, Gil Kane, pencils, Sid Greene, inks, ©2001 DC Comics. Compare these two pages to the previous thirteen page story. These two pages demonstrate the development of Kane's art in just five years. Kane used a more dynamic panel layout, and his drawing was more dynamic. Kane's art was further assisted by Greene's sympathetic inking.

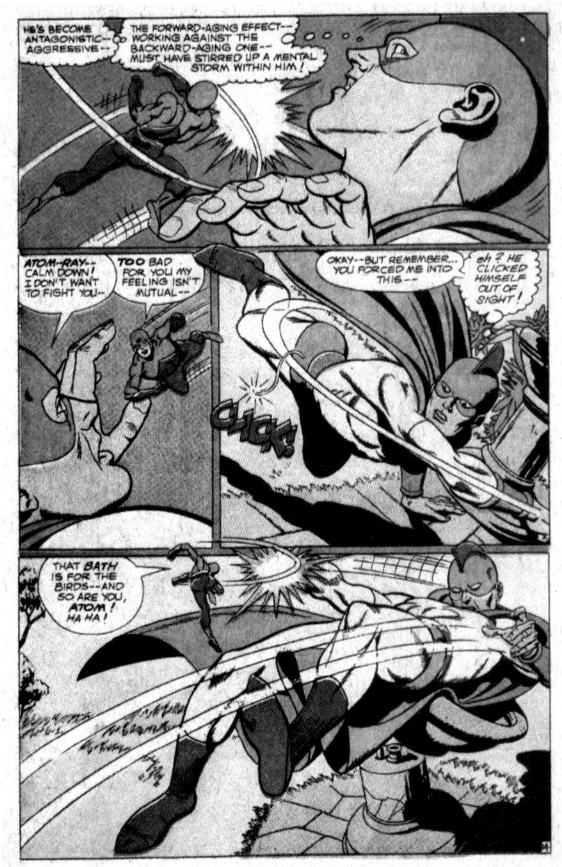
HE'S BECOME ANTAGONISTIC--AGGRESSIVE--
THE FORWARD-AGING EFFECT--WORKING AGAINST THE BACKWARD-AGING ONE--MUST HAVE STIRRED UP A MENTAL STORM WITHIN HIM!
ATOM-RAY--CALM DOWN! I DON'T WANT TO FIGHT YOU--
TOO BAD FOR YOU MY FEELING ISN'T MUTUAL--
OKAY--BUT REMEMBER... YOU FORCED ME INTO THIS--
eh? HE CLICKED HIMSELF OUT OF SIGHT!
CLICK!
THAT BATH IS FOR THE BIRDS--AND SO ARE YOU, ATOM! HA HA!

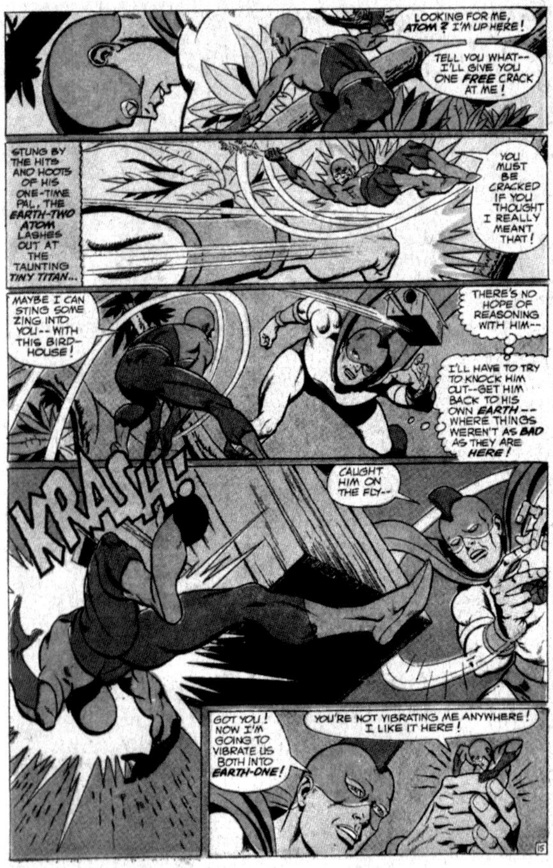
LOOKING FOR ME, ATOM? I'M UP HERE!
TELL YOU WHAT--I'LL GIVE YOU ONE FREE CRACK AT ME!
STUNG BY THE HITS AND HOOTS OF HIS ONE-TIME PAL, THE EARTH-TWO ATOM LASHES OUT AT THE TAUNTING TINY TITAN...
YOU MUST BE CRACKED IF YOU THOUGHT I REALLY MEANT THAT!
MAYBE I CAN STING SOME ZING INTO YOU--WITH THIS BIRD-HOUSE!
THERE'S NO HOPE OF REASONING WITH HIM--
I'LL HAVE TO TRY TO KNOCK HIM OUT--GET HIM BACK TO HIS OWN EARTH--WHERE THINGS WEREN'T AS BAD AS THEY ARE HERE!
KRASH!
CAUGHT HIM ON THE FLY--
GOT YOU! NOW I'M GOING TO VIBRATE US BOTH INTO EARTH-ONE!
YOU'RE NOT VIBRATING ME ANYWHERE! I LIKE IT HERE!

outspoken about artists in comics being given more opportunities to create their own material without editorial interference, was conceptualizing his own self-published effort. Both Wood and Kane were in accord that for the art of the comics to progress, artists had to be free of the artistic and editorial control imposed by publishers. Kane had become bored with what he saw as the "banality of mainstream comics." He not only wanted, but artistically needed, another outlet for the stories he wanted to tell. It was during this time that Kane began planning what would be one of the most significant works of his career, and an important development in the art of the comics, the creation of an adult comic story,

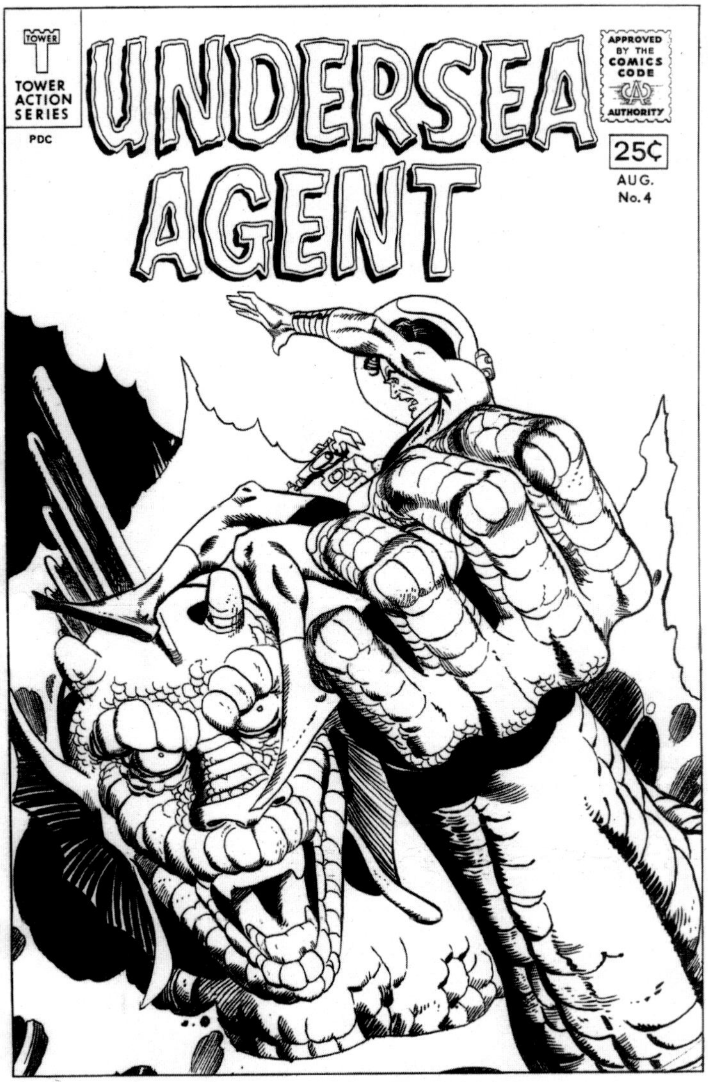
TOWER
TOWER ACTION SERIES
PDC
UNDERSEA AGENT
APPROVED BY THE COMICS CODE AUTHORITY
25¢
AUG. No. 4

Left: original cover artwork for *Undersea Agent* #4, August, 1966. Below: splash page from *Thunder Agents* #14, July, 1967. Both, Gil Kane, pencils and inks, both ©2001 Tower Comics, Inc.

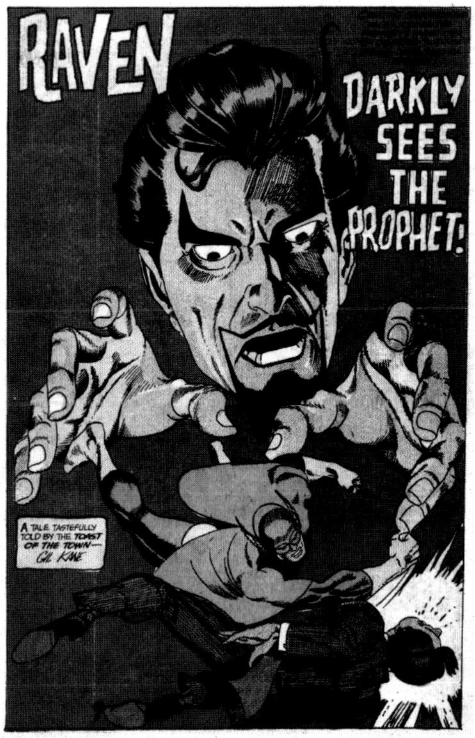
RAVEN
DARKLY SEES THE PROPHET!
A TALE TASTEFULLY TOLD BY THE TOAST OF THE TOWN— GIL KANE

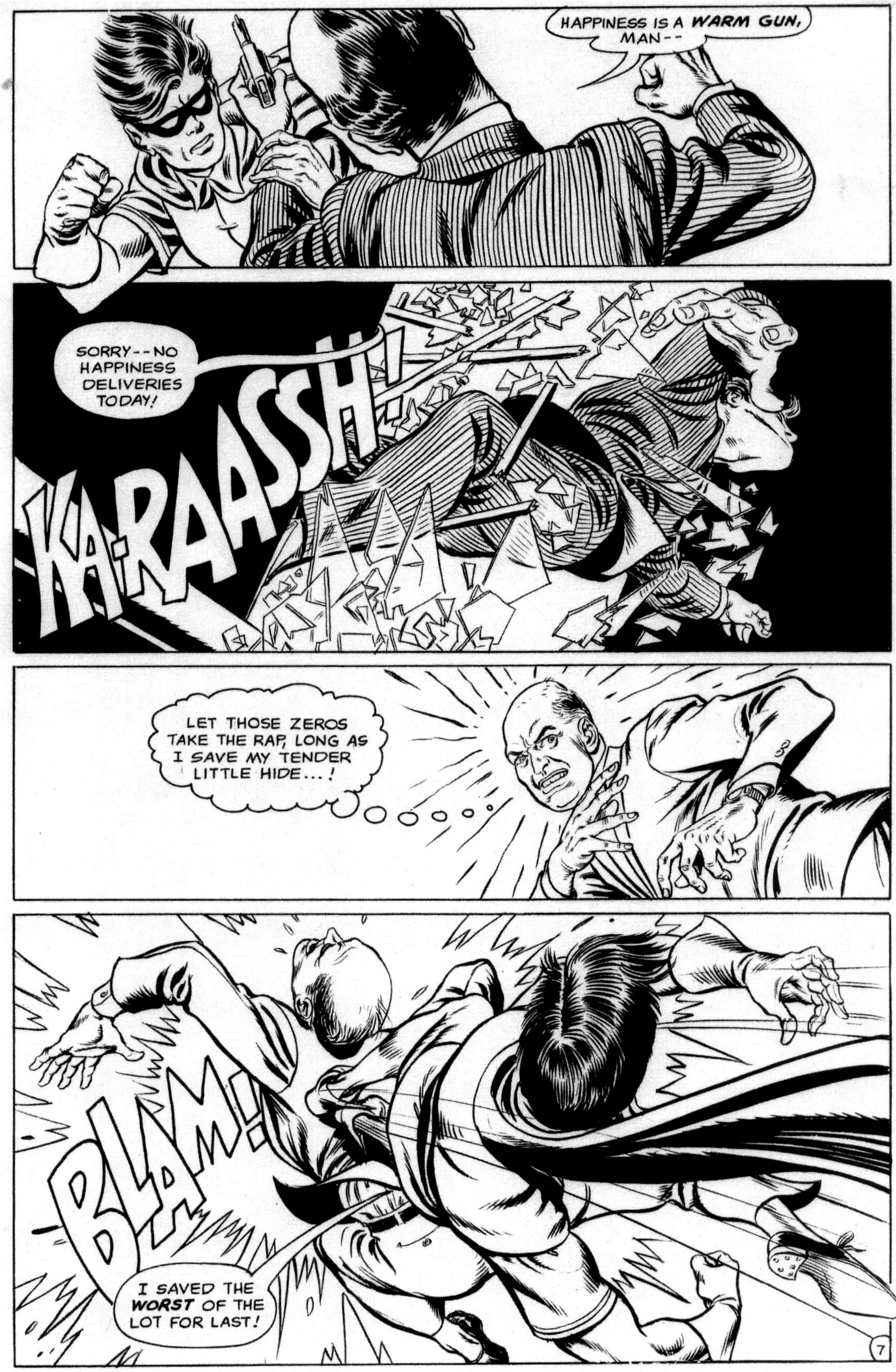
HAPPINESS IS A WARM GUN, MAN--
SORRY--NO HAPPINESS DELIVERIES TODAY!
KA-RAASSH!
LET THOSE ZEROS TAKE THE RAP, LONG AS I SAVE MY TENDER LITTLE HIDE...!
BLAM!
I SAVED THE WORST OF THE LOT FOR LAST!
7

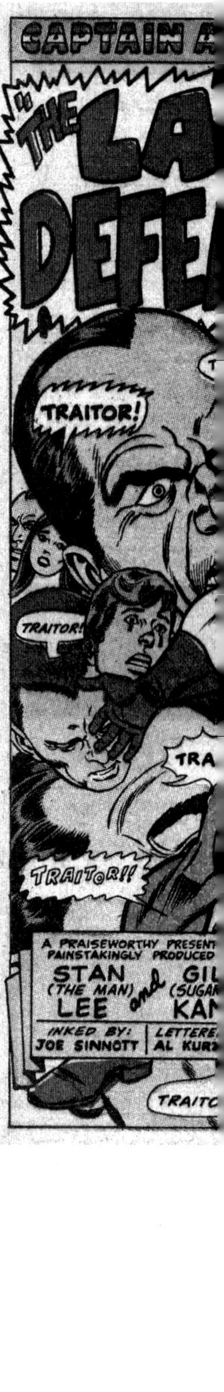
TRAITOR!
TRAITOR!
TRAITOR!!
STAN (THE MAN) LEE
INKED BY: JOE SINNOTT

Above: original artwork for an interior page from *Detective* #391, December, 1969, Gil Kane, pencils, Murphy Anderson, inks, ©2001 DC Comics. Right center: splash page from *Tales of Suspense* #91, July, 1966, Gil Kane, pencils, Joe Sinnott, inks, ©2001 Marvel Characters, Inc.

Right: dynamic cover for *Detective* #180, Gil Kane, pencils, Murphy Anderson, inks, May, 1966, ©2001 DC Comics.

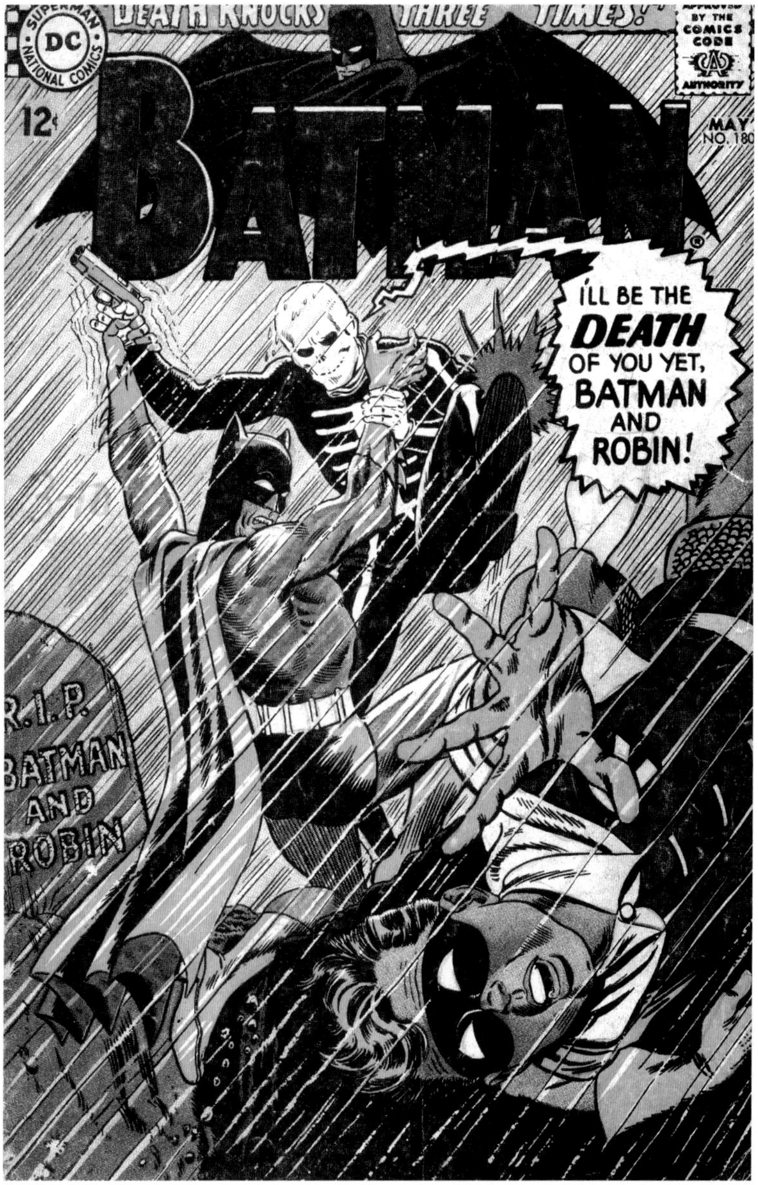
DEATH KNOCKS THREE TIMES!
SUPERMAN DC NATIONAL COMICS
APPROVED BY THE COMICS CODE AUTHORITY
12¢
BATMAN
MAY NO. 180
I'LL BE THE DEATH OF YOU YET, BATMAN AND ROBIN!
R.I.P. BATMAN AND ROBIN

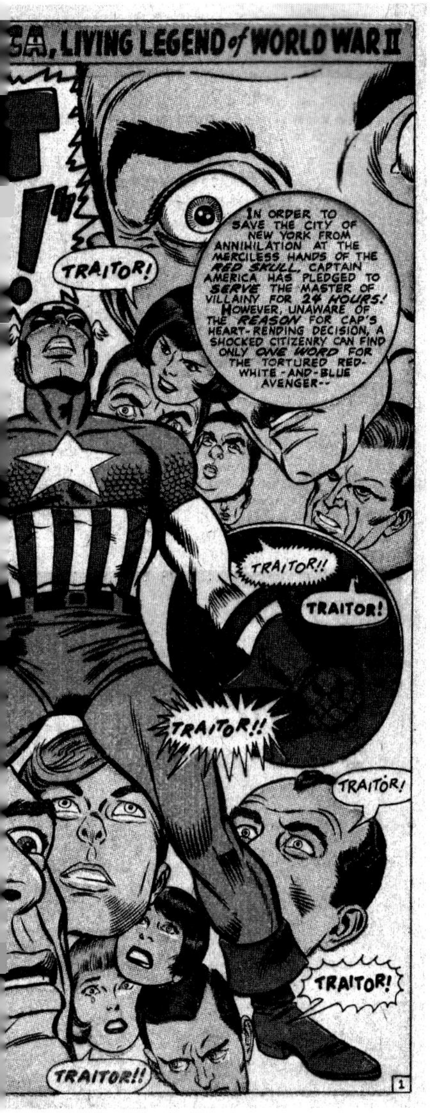
LIVING LEGEND of WORLD WAR II
IN ORDER TO SAVE THE CITY OF NEW YORK FROM ANNIHILATION AT THE MERCILESS HANDS OF THE RED SKULL, CAPTAIN AMERICA HAS PLEDGED TO SERVE THE MASTER OF VILLAINY FOR 24 HOURS! HOWEVER, UNAWARE OF THE REASON FOR CAP'S HEART-RENDING DECISION, A SHOCKED CITIZENRY CAN FIND ONLY ONE WORD FOR THE TORTURED RED-WHITE-AND-BLUE AVENGER--
TRAITOR!
TRAITOR!!
TRAITOR!
TRAITOR!!
TRAITOR!
TRAITOR!
TRAITOR!!

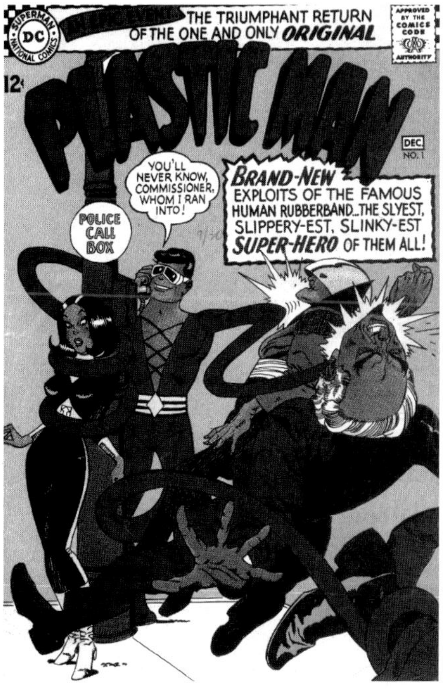
THE TRIUMPHANT RETURN OF THE ONE AND ONLY ORIGINAL
APPROVED BY THE COMICS CODE AUTHORITY
12¢
PLASTIC MAN
DEC. NO. 1
YOU'LL NEVER KNOW, COMMISSIONER, WHOM I RAN INTO!
BRAND-NEW EXPLOITS OF THE FAMOUS HUMAN RUBBERBAND...THE SLYEST, SLIPPERY-EST, SLINKY-EST SUPER-HERO OF THEM ALL!
POLICE CALL BOX

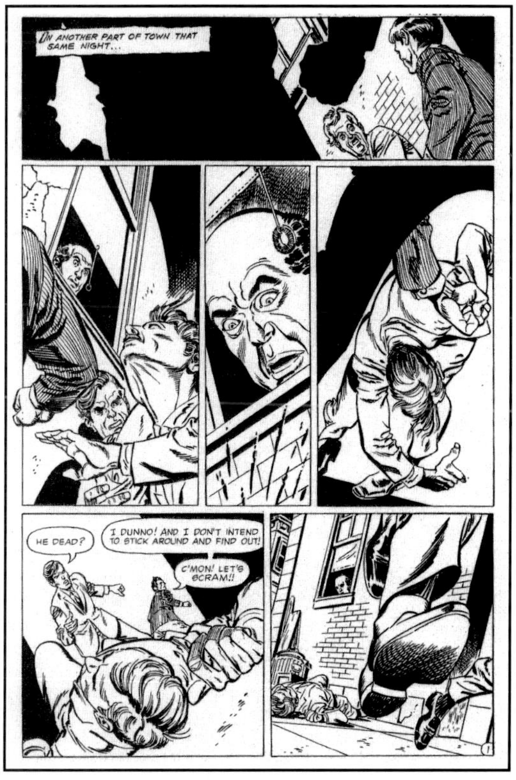
IN ANOTHER PART OF TOWN THAT SAME NIGHT...
HE DEAD?
I DUNNO! AND I DON'T INTEND TO STICK AROUND AND FIND OUT!
C'MON! LET'S SCRAM!!

Right: Kane's homage to Jack Cole's Plastic Man, cover to *Plastic Man* #1, Nov./Dec., 1966, Gil Kane, pencils and inks. Far right: interior page from *Hawk and Dove* #3, Dec./Jan., 1969, Gil Kane, pencils, Sal Trapani, inks, all ©2001 DC Comics.

in an extended narrative form. Kane planned to create a "B-movie" in extended comic book form, intended for teenagers and adults, now commonly referred to as a "graphic novel." At almost the same time, Kane was planning to create a myth of the distant future using the same extended narrative form. In both of these projects, Kane would use Goodwin to translate his story and plot outlines into dialogue and text. Their collaboration

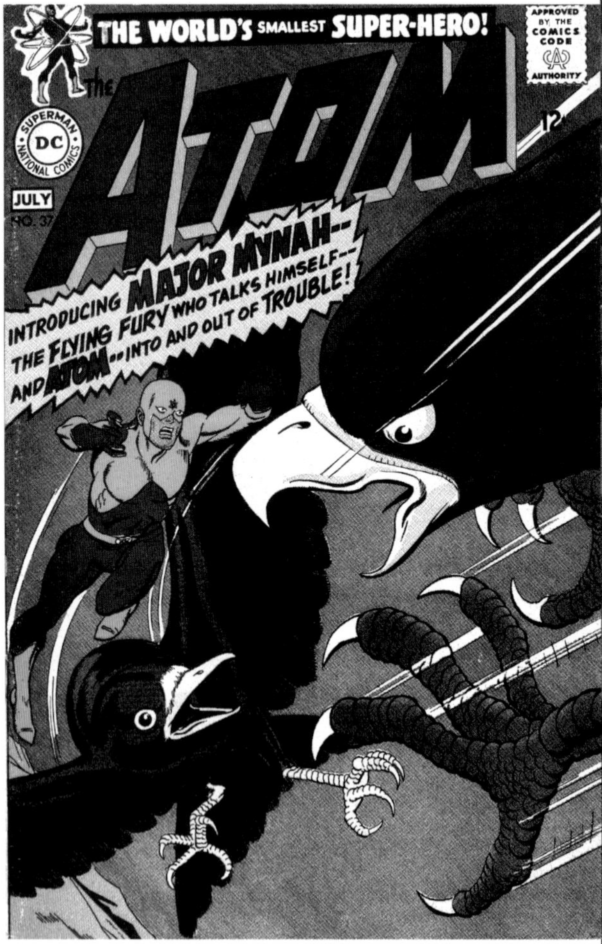
THE WORLD'S SMALLEST SUPER-HERO!
APPROVED BY THE COMICS CODE AUTHORITY
ATOM
JULY
INTRODUCING MAJOR MYNAH--
THE FLYING FURY WHO TALKS HIMSELF--
AND ATOM--INTO AND OUT OF TROUBLE!

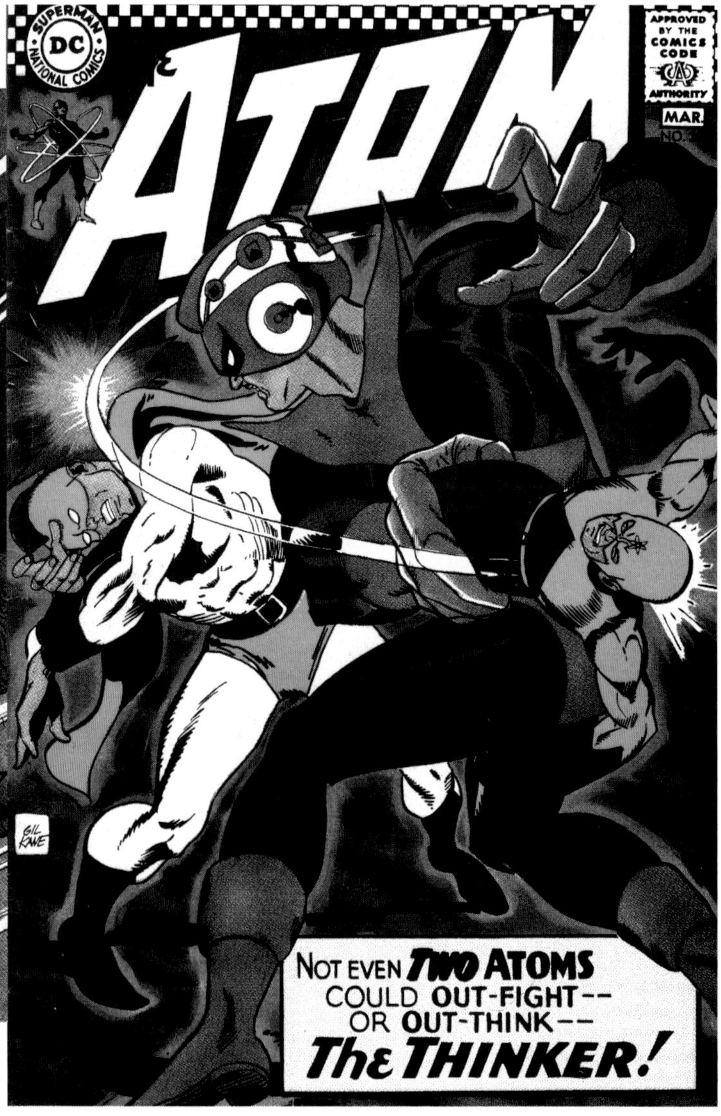
APPROVED BY THE COMICS CODE AUTHORITY
ATOM
MAR.
GIL KANE
NOT EVEN TWO ATOMS
COULD OUT-FIGHT--
OR OUT-THINK--
The THINKER!

Above: cover for *The Atom* #37, Gil Kane, pencils, Sid Greene, inks, June/July, 1968. Right: cover for *The Atom* #29, Gil Kane, pencils and inks, Feb./March, 1967, all ©2001 DC Comics.

resulted in the graphic novels *His Name is…Savage* and *Blackmark*, which both would break new ground, advancing the art of graphic storytelling.

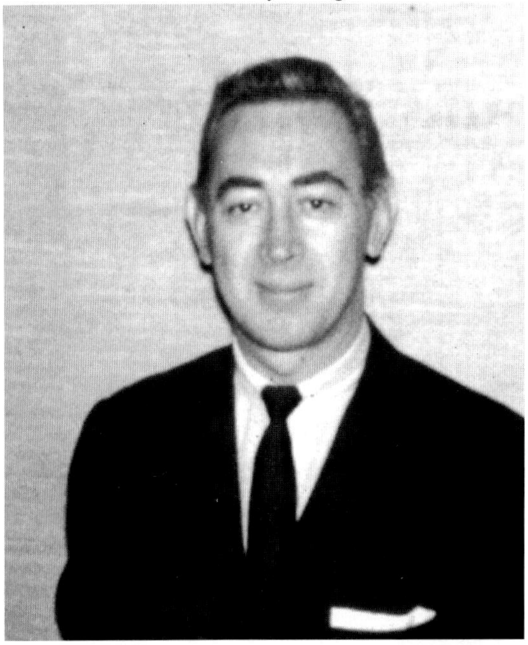

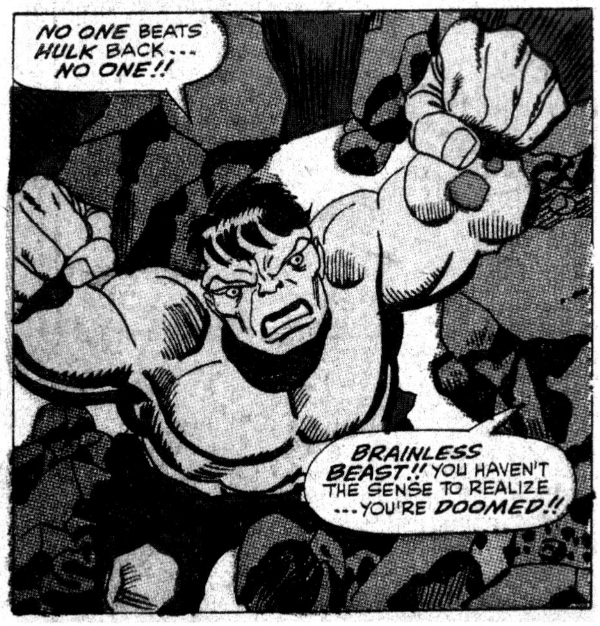
NO ONE BEATS HULK BACK... NO ONE!!
BRAINLESS BEAST!! YOU HAVEN'T THE SENSE TO REALIZE ...YOU'RE DOOMED!!

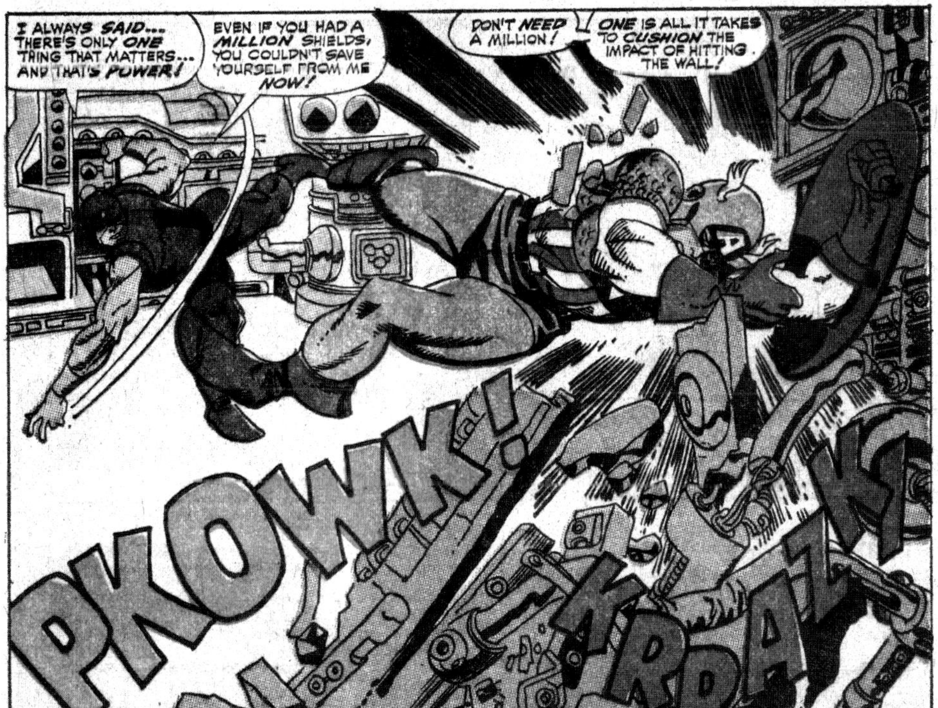
I ALWAYS SAID... THERE'S ONLY ONE THING THAT MATTERS... AND THAT'S POWER!
EVEN IF YOU HAD A MILLION SHIELDS, YOU COULDN'T SAVE YOURSELF FROM ME NOW!
DON'T NEED A MILLION!
ONE IS ALL IT TAKES TO CUSHION THE IMPACT OF HITTING THE WALL!
PKOWK!
KRRAZK

Above: Gil Kane, circa 1966. Right: dynamic panel from *Tales to Astonish* #90, April, 1967, Gil Kane, pencils and inks. Bottom: more action from Kane from *Tales of Suspense* #88, April, 1967, Gil Kane, pencils and inks, both ©2001 Marvel Characters, Inc.

6 HIS NAME IS...SAVAGE

Kane had now developed his craft for almost 25 years. In the late 1950s he had begun to think about **writing** and drawing his own material. His work for DC Comics, drawing and inking western genre comics, had given him the desire to control his own work. While working on the *Green Lantern* and *Atom* titles, he had been denied the opportunity to write his own material, despite his desire to do so. Indeed, Kane had been searching for material that he could use as the basis for his own comic books. He had always been attracted to the pulps and had made a conscious attempt to analyze

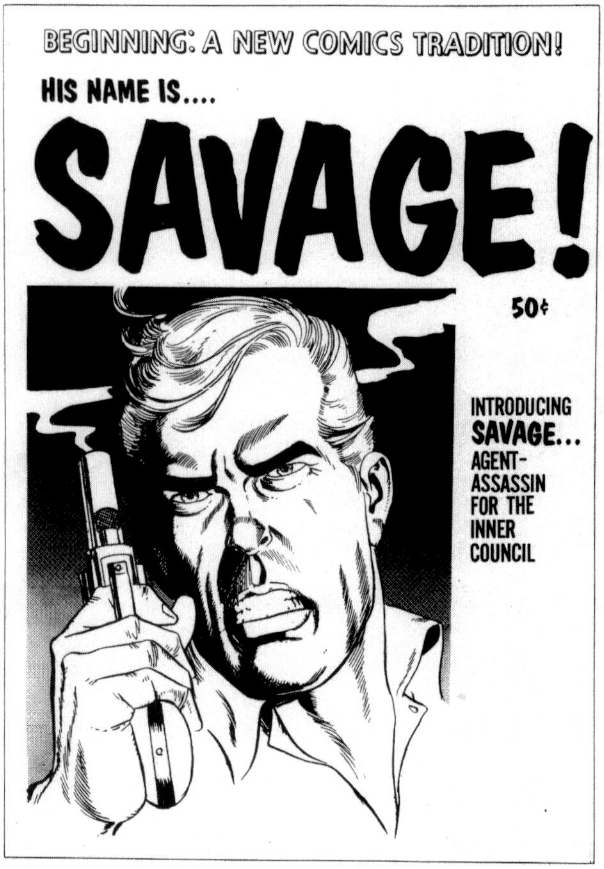
BEGINNING: A NEW COMICS TRADITION!
HIS NAME IS....
SAVAGE!
50¢
INTRODUCING SAVAGE... AGENT-ASSASSIN FOR THE INNER COUNCIL

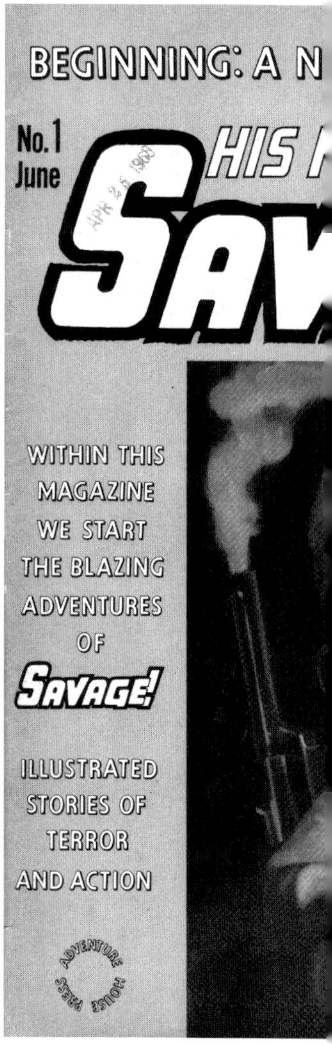
No. 1
June
WITHIN THIS MAGAZINE WE START THE BLAZING ADVENTURES OF
SAVAGE!
ILLUSTRATED STORIES OF TERROR AND ACTION
ADVENTURE HOUSE PRESS

Above: original artwork for the unused cover for *His Name is...Savage*, ©2001 The Estate of Gil Kane. Center: published cover for *His Name is...Savage*, June, 1968, painting by Robert Foster, ©2001 The Estate of Gil Kane.

the writing of pulp stories by rereading the *Doc Savage* and *Shadow* novels. He had also become interested in the *Conan* books of Robert E. Howard. So interested, in fact, that he sought out Howard's agent and was given possession, for a time, of many Howard manuscripts, together with correspondence and other records. Kane poured over this material, with the idea of using the

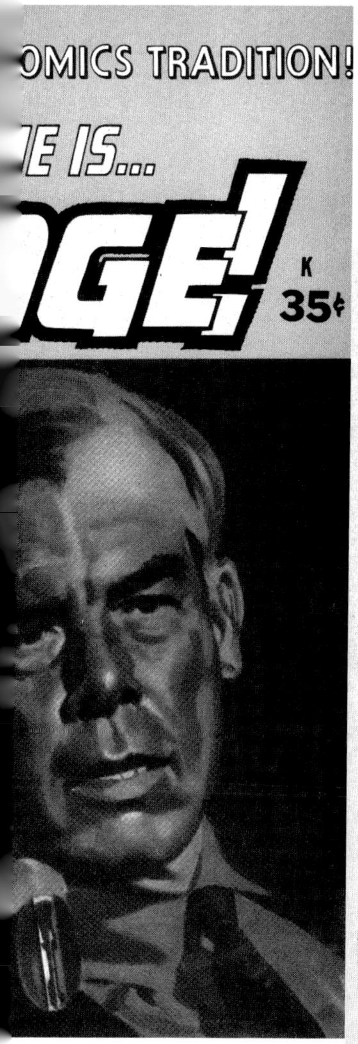

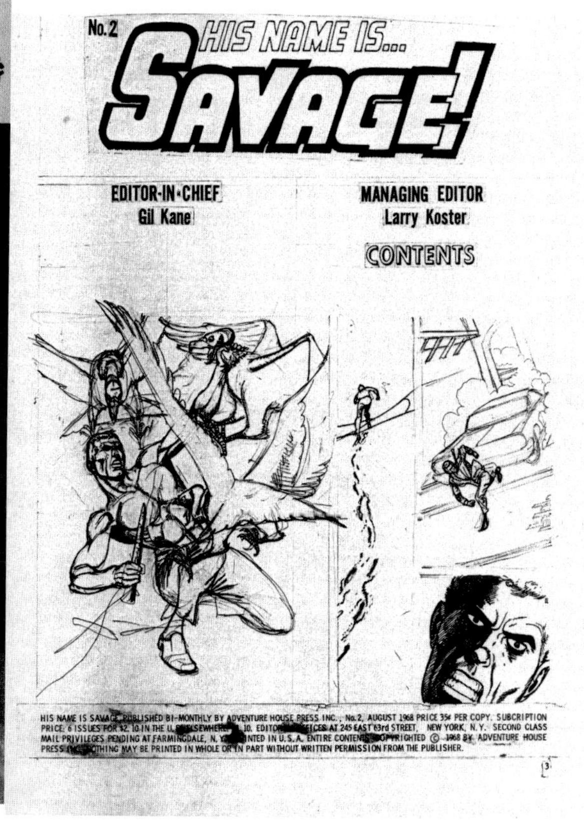

Conan character in an extended narrative comic book story. Kane wanted to tell a complete story, rather than relate an episode or parable, as had been the practice at the time with all comic book stories. He wanted to develop characters with personalities and motivations, within

Above: original artwork for the unused cover for *His Name is...Savage* #2, Gil Kane, pencils and partial inks, ©2001 The Estate of Gil Kane.

the structure of one story, told primarily with pictures. He also began to conceptualize a character of his own for use in an extended comic book format. Ultimately, this character would be named Savage. Although Kane had begun to expand his attention to the writing of serious authors, he nevertheless continued his love for romantic, adventure material. Kane was drawn to the mythical, whether it was with the Arthurian legend, adventure material, such as Conan, or to mystery and detective novels. Despite criticism that he would not explore "serious" material, Kane maintained the position that if the material was done correctly it would stand on its own.

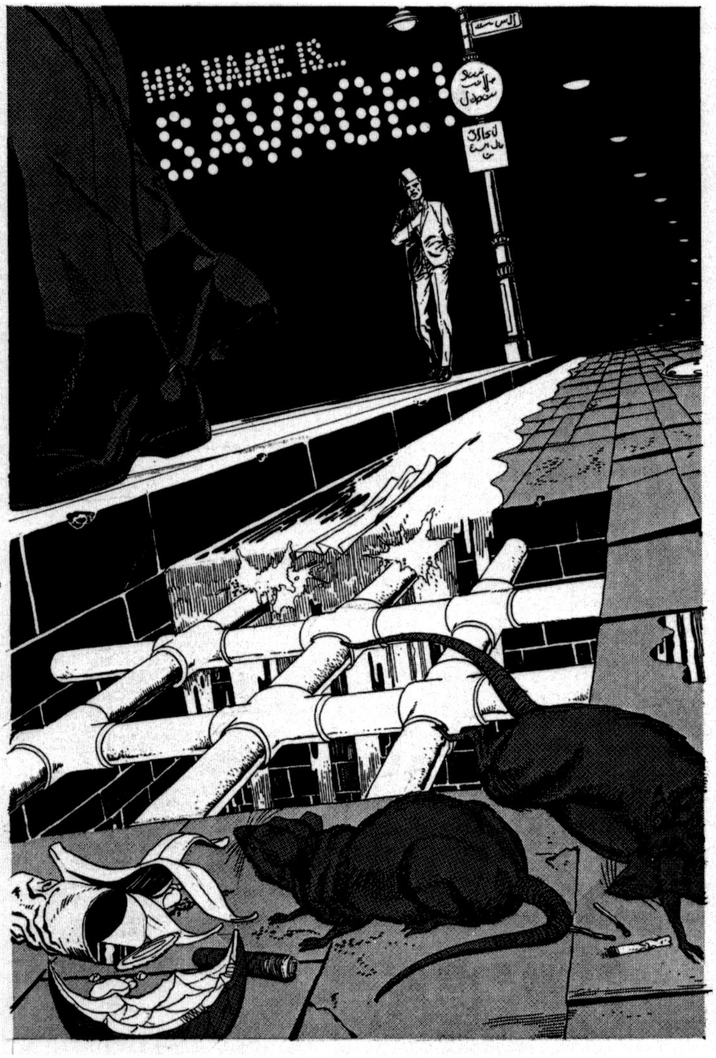
HIS NAME IS...
SAVAGE!

In planning his comic book novels, Kane crystallized his thoughts on the composition of the comic book page, and the orchestration of the plot, by reviewing the layouts used in

Original artwork for the unused cover for *His Name is...Savage* #3, Gil Kane, pencils, ©2001 The Estate of Gil Kane. This unused cover offers an arresting image, with a classic Kane camera angle, looking up from ground level, while at the same time presenting an obvious homage to Will Eisner.

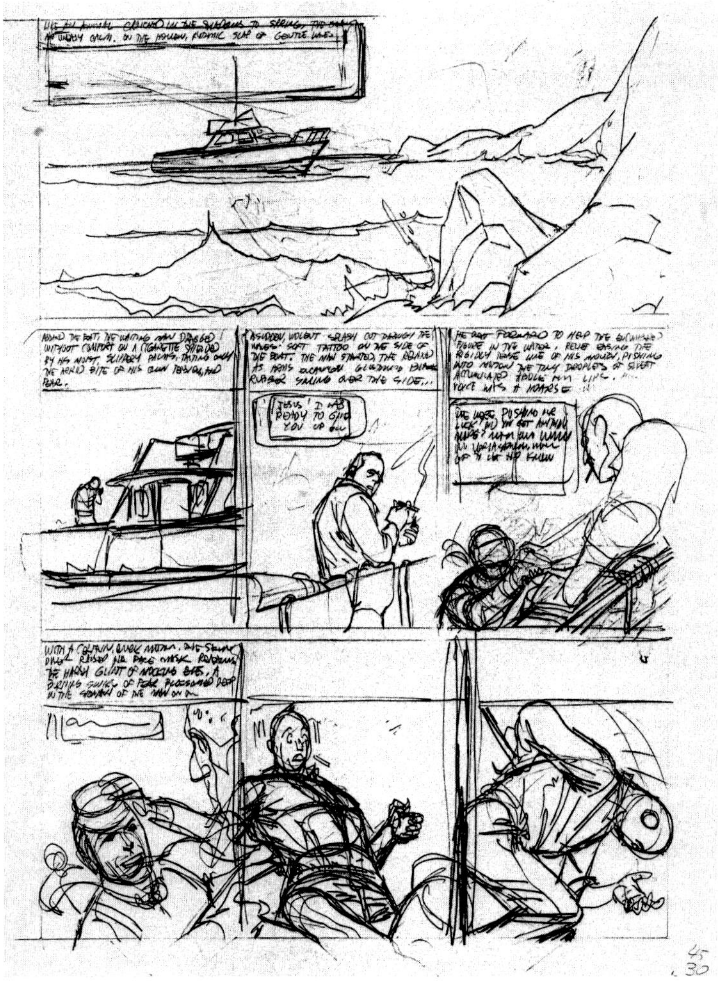

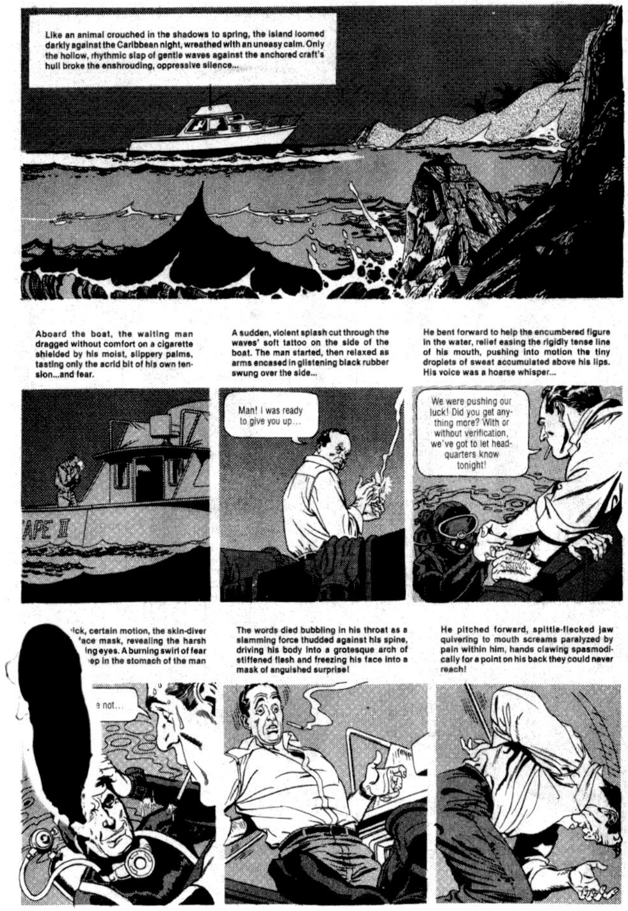
Like an animal crouched in the shadows to spring, the island loomed darkly against the Caribbean night, wreathed with an uneasy calm. Only the hollow, rhythmic slap of gentle waves against the anchored craft's hull broke the enshrouding, oppressive silence...
Aboard the boat, the waiting man dragged without comfort on a cigarette shielded by his moist, slippery palms, tasting only the acrid bit of his own tension...and fear.
A sudden, violent splash cut through the waves' soft tattoo on the side of the boat. The man started, then relaxed as arms encased in glistening black rubber swung over the side...
Man! I was ready to give you up…
He bent forward to help the encumbered figure in the water, relief easing the rigidly tense line of his mouth, pushing into motion the tiny droplets of sweat accumulated above his lips. His voice was a hoarse whisper...
We were pushing our luck! Did you get anything more? With or without verification, we've got to let headquarters know tonight!
certain motion, the skin-diver
face mask, revealing the harsh
eyes. A burning swirl of fear
in the stomach of the man
not…
The words died bubbling in his throat as a slamming force thudded against his spine, driving his body into a grotesque arch of stiffened flesh and freezing his face into a mask of anguished surprise!
He pitched forward, spittle-flecked jaw quivering to mouth screams paralyzed by pain within him, hands clawing spasmodically for a point on his back they could never reach!

Above: the first page from *Savage*, in its original layout form, and as a finished page. All artwork in this chapter, Gil Kane, pencils and pencils and inks. All artwork in this chapter, ©2001 The Estate of Gil Kane. Throughout his career, Kane always started work on a story by making detailed layout drawings or "breakdowns." These layout drawings, from *Savage*, layout camera angles, frame scenes, and place the figures. These drawings allowed Kane to fine-tune his pages and to crystallize his thoughts before actually pencilling the final page. Kane took these layout drawings and put them on a lightbox, a piece of opaque glass with a light behind it. He placed a clean sheet of paper over the layout drawing, and used it as a guide. In this way, he could make adjustments while drawing, by consulting the drawing in the layout underneath the page he was finishing. Using this method, Kane was able to produce a clean finished page, while still completely developing the overall story composition and drawing. The next ten pages of this chapter document nine sequential pages from *Savage*. These images show how dynamic Kane's uninked pencils were.

a number of publications, including commercial magazines and design publications. Kane used this analysis in the layout of the first modern extended narrative comic book story: *His Name is… Savage.*

Kane first had the idea of doing a novel in comic book form while he was working for James Warren. After Kane parted company from Warren, he set up a studio near Embassy House at 63rd Street between 2nd and 3rd Avenues in New York. For the next five years, Kane worked, on and off, on two groups of comic book novels that revolutionized comic books by demonstrating the potential of narrative

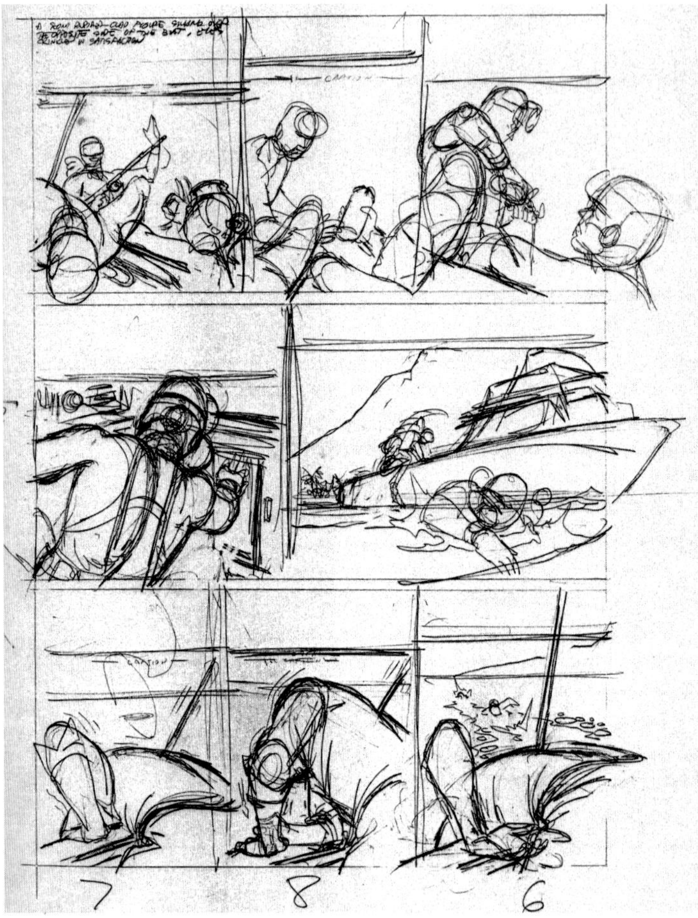

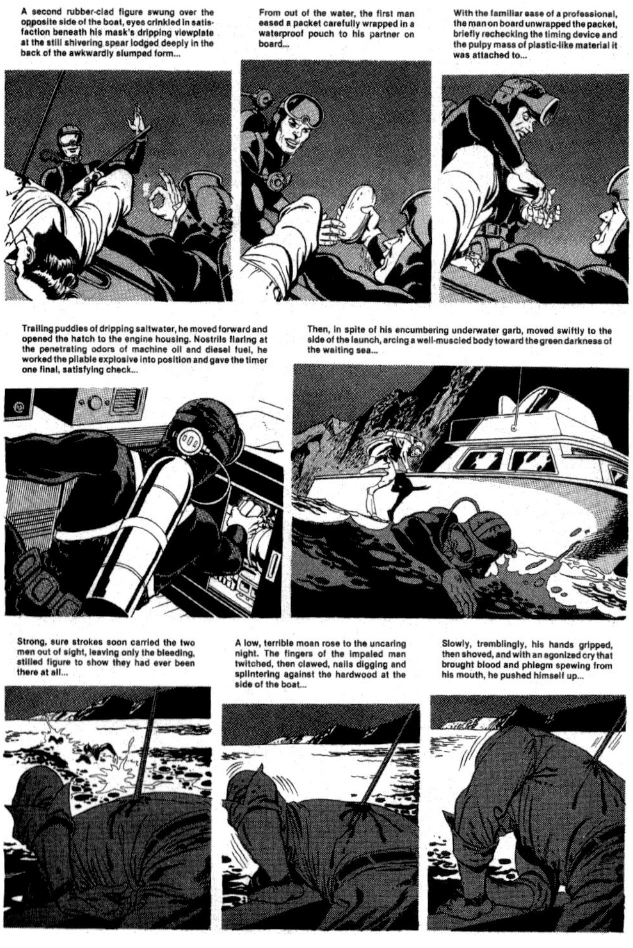
A second rubber-clad figure swung over the opposite side of the boat, eyes crinkled in satisfaction beneath his mask's dripping viewplate at the still shivering spear lodged deeply in the back of the awkwardly slumped form...
From out of the water, the first man eased a packet carefully wrapped in a waterproof pouch to his partner on board...
With the familiar ease of a professional, the man on board unwrapped the packet, briefly rechecking the timing device and the pulpy mass of plastic-like material it was attached to...
Trailing puddles of dripping saltwater, he moved forward and opened the hatch to the engine housing. Nostrils flaring at the penetrating odors of machine oil and diesel fuel, he worked the pliable explosive into position and gave the timer one final, satisfying check...
Then, in spite of his encumbering underwater garb, moved swiftly to the side of the launch, arcing a well-muscled body toward the green darkness of the waiting sea...
Strong, sure strokes soon carried the two men out of sight, leaving only the bleeding, stilled figure to show they had ever been there at all...
A low, terrible moan rose to the uncaring night. The fingers of the impaled man twitched, then clawed, nails digging and splintering against the hardwood at the side of the boat...
Slowly, tremblingly, his hands gripped, then shoved, and with an agonized cry that brought blood and phlegm spewing from his mouth, he pushed himself up...

Left: page 2 in its rough form and in its finished form. Note the use of text and artwork to tell the story. *Savage* cinematically tells its story, unlike traditional comic books.

storytelling in an extended format.

For years, Kane had felt limited by his editors at DC Comics. He was not allowed to explore the choreographic potentials of violence. As with many of the film directors of the 1960s, Kane saw the cinematic possibilities of telling stories about adventure and intrigue without censorship. These types of stories, by their very nature, involve violence, and Kane was intrigued by the thought of depicting such a story as a novel in comic book form. As his inspiration, Kane looked to the movies of his day. He took note of the popular spy movies of the time, and of the movie, *"Point Blank,"* which starred Lee Marvin. Marvin served as the starting point for Kane's hero, Savage, just as a decade earlier, Paul Newman had served as the starting point for the civilian identity of the Green Lantern (at the time Newman and Kane were neighbors). Kane conceptualized Savage as a modern day Conan. After Kane had outlined the plot of the first Savage book, he brought Archie Goodwin on board to write the dialogue.

Kane had several objectives to accomplish with *Savage*. He wanted to utilize prose and word balloons to augment the visual development of the story. Kane hoped to be able to integrate these elements, together with a method of laying out the visuals, to develop the story more completely. Ultimately, Kane used many more panels per page than comic books to pace the story more like a movie. There were more angles per scene, more quick cuts, more

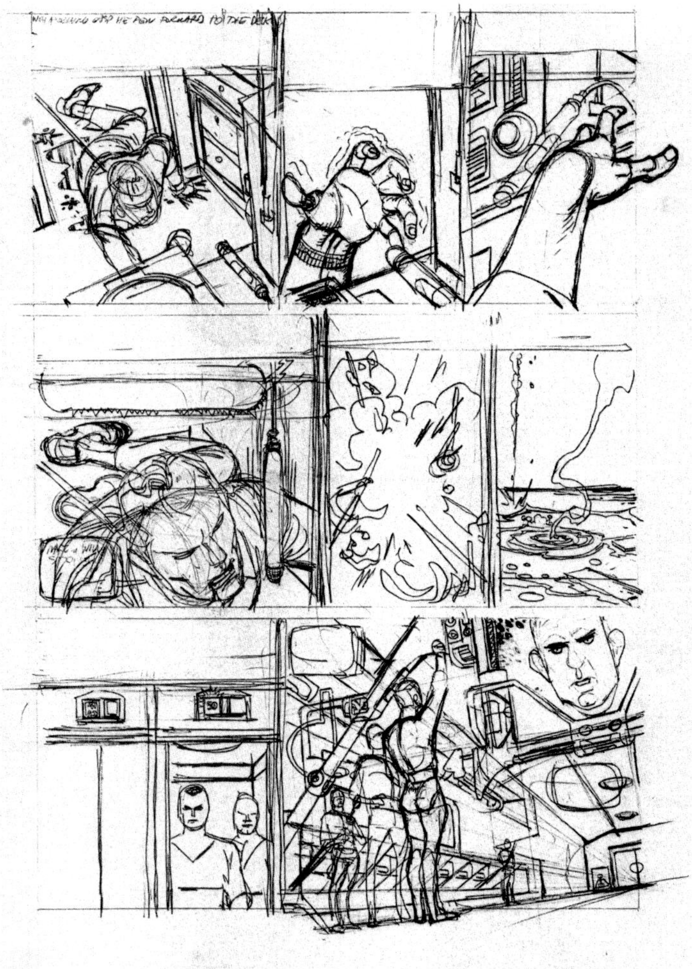

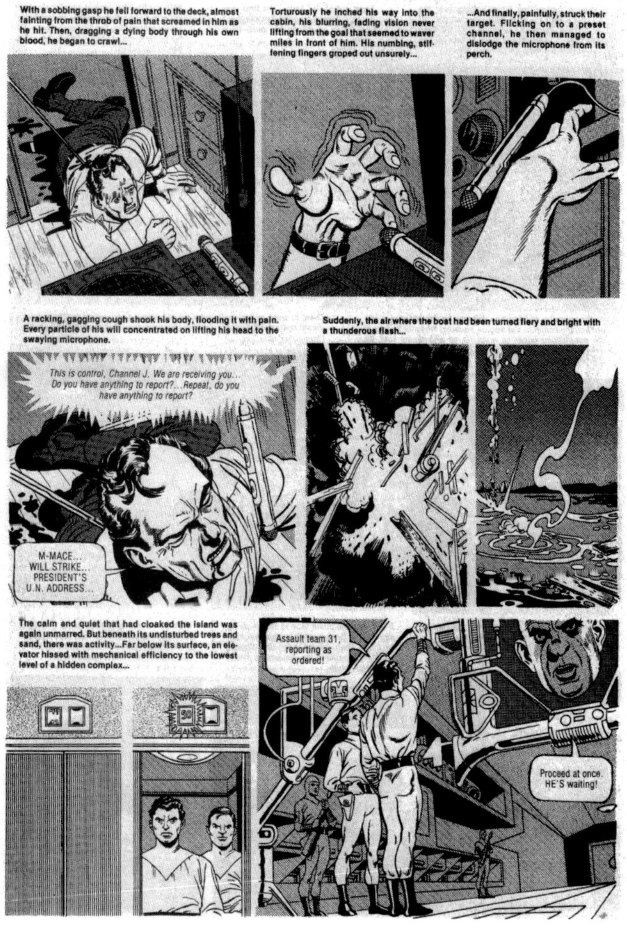
With a sobbing gasp he fell forward to the deck, almost fainting from the throb of pain that screamed in him as he hit. Then, dragging a dying body through his own blood, he began to crawl...
Torturously he inched his way into the cabin, his blurring, fading vision never lifting from the goal that seemed to waver miles in front of him. His numbing, stiffening fingers groped out unsurely...
...And finally, painfully, struck their target. Flicking on to a preset channel, he then managed to dislodge the microphone from its perch.
A racking, gagging cough shook his body, flooding it with pain. Every particle of his will concentrated on lifting his head to the swaying microphone.
This is control, Channel J. We are receiving you... Do you have anything to report?...Repeat, do you have anything to report?
M-MACE... WILL STRIKE... PRESIDENT'S U.N. ADDRESS...
Suddenly, the air where the boat had been turned fiery and bright with a thunderous flash...
The calm and quiet that had cloaked the island was again unmarred. But beneath its undisturbed trees and sand, there was activity...Far below its surface, an elevator hissed with mechanical efficiency to the lowest level of a hidden complex...
Assault team 31, reporting as ordered!
Proceed at once. HE'S waiting!

Right: page 3, in its rough, breakdown and in finished form. This page clearly demonstrates Kane's complete control of the images and the story.

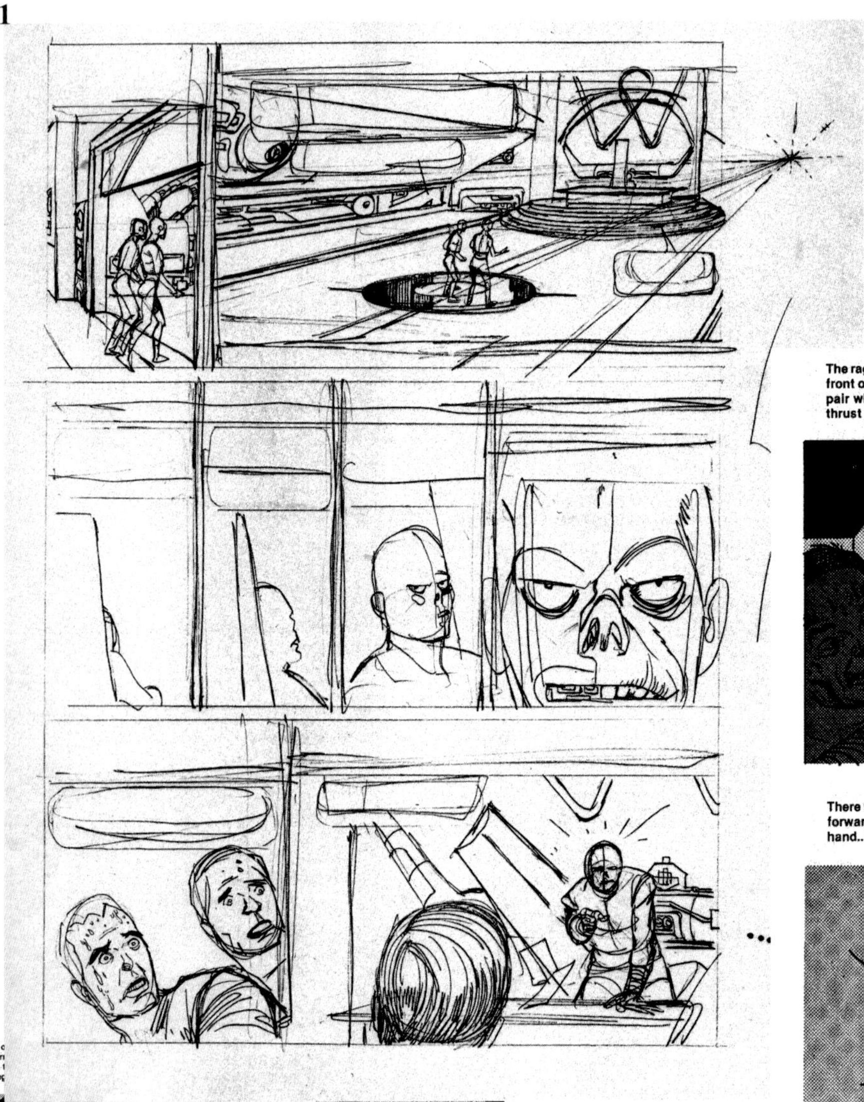

The artwork on these pages clearly demonstrates the amount of rigorous planning and design necessary to develop the narrative required to support such a fully developed comic book story. Until *Savage*, American comic books had never attempted to completely develop a story which expanded the potential of the plot and characters.

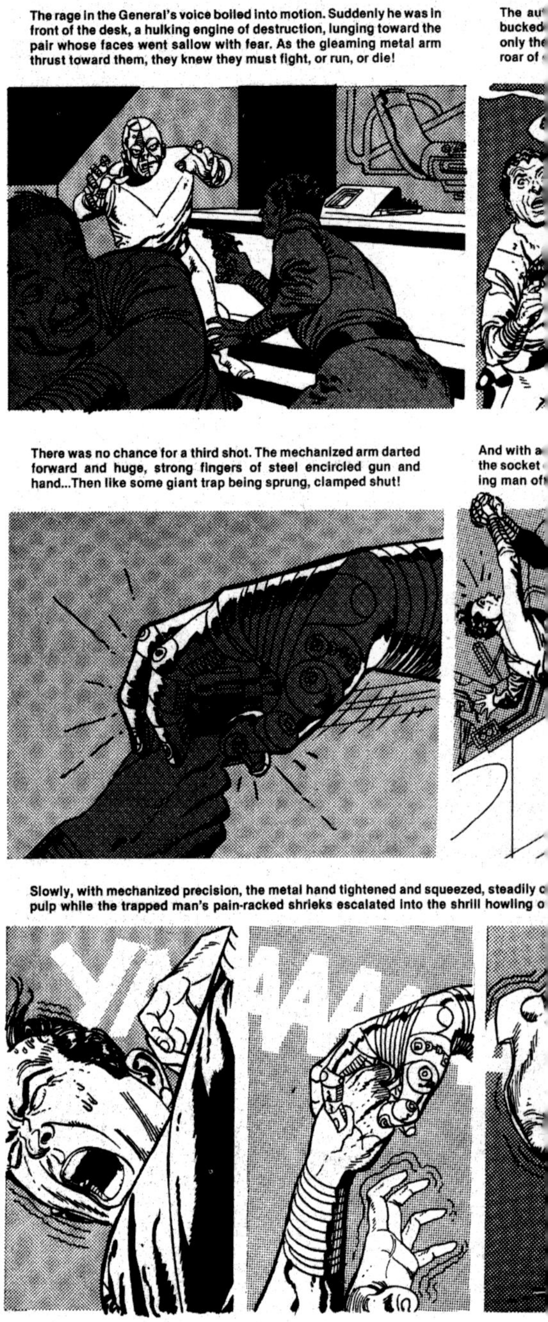
The rage in the General's voice boiled into motion. Suddenly he was in front of the desk, a hulking engine of destruction, lunging toward the pair whose faces went sallow with fear. As the gleaming metal arm thrust toward them, they knew they must fight, or run, or die!
There was no chance for a third shot. The mechanized arm darted forward and huge, strong fingers of steel encircled gun and hand...Then like some giant trap being sprung, clamped shut!

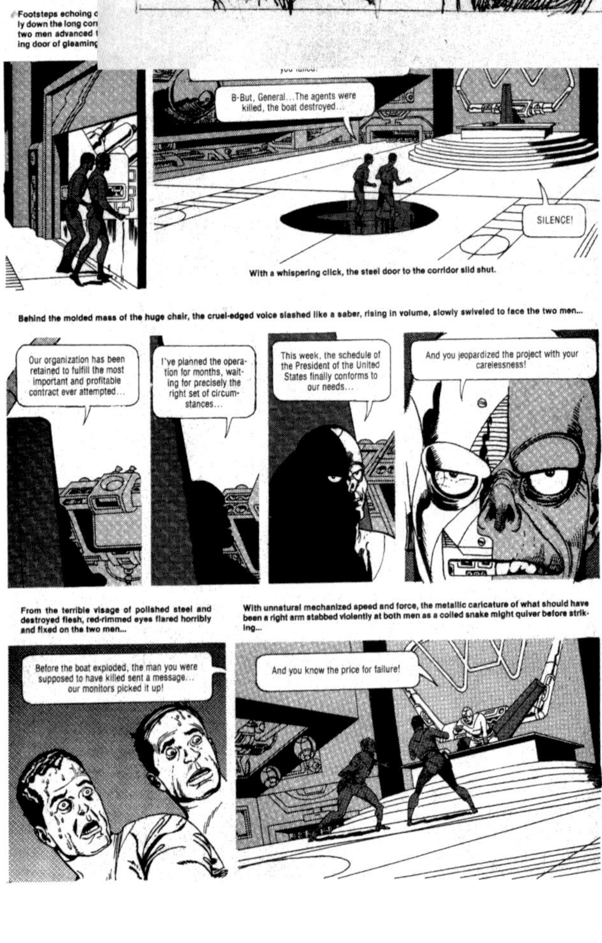
B-But, General...The agents were killed, the boat destroyed...
SILENCE!
With a whispering click, the steel door to the corridor slid shut.
Behind the molded mass of the huge chair, the cruel-edged voice slashed like a saber, rising in volume, slowly swiveled to face the two men...
Our organization has been retained to fulfill the most important and profitable contract ever attempted...
I've planned the operation for months, waiting for precisely the right set of circumstances...
This week, the schedule of the President of the United States finally conforms to our needs...
And you jeopardized the project with your carelessness!
From the terrible visage of polished steel and destroyed flesh, red-rimmed eyes flared horribly and fixed on the two men...
Before the boat exploded, the man you were supposed to have killed sent a message... our monitors picked it up!
With unnatural mechanized speed and force, the metallic caricature of what should have been a right arm stabbed violently at both men as a coiled snake might quiver before striking...
And you know the price for failure!

Left: Page 4, layout drawing and finished page.

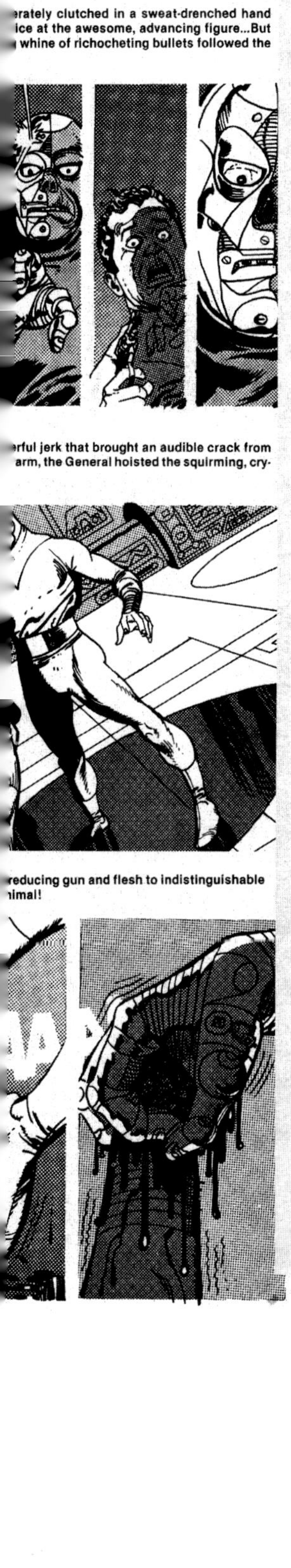

erately clutched in a sweat-drenched hand
ice at the awesome, advancing figure...But
whine of richocheting bullets followed the
erful jerk that brought an audible crack from
arm, the General hoisted the squirming, cry-
reducing gun and flesh to indistinguishable
nimal!

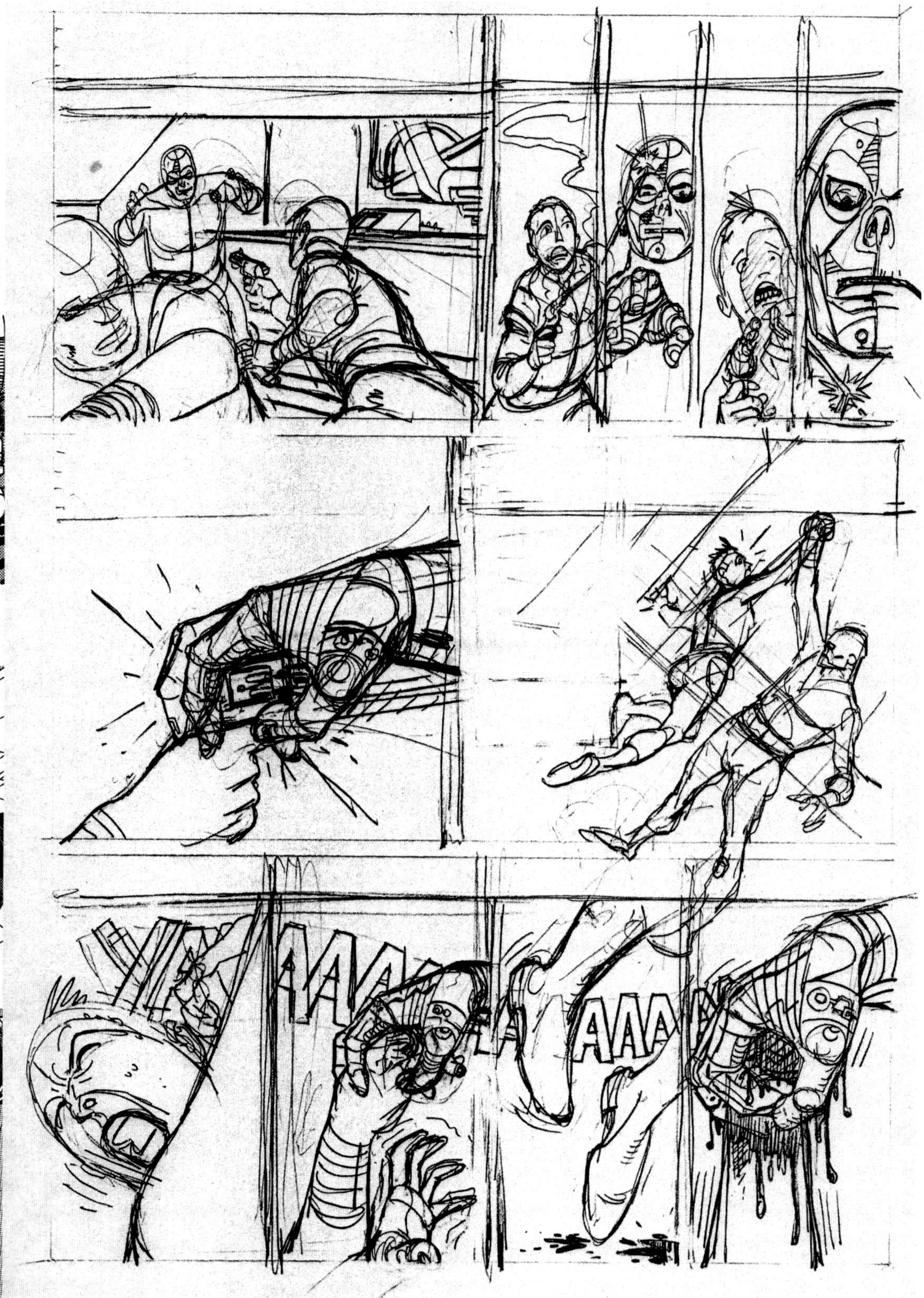

Above: page 5, finished page and layout drawing. This page is a tour-de-force in action storytelling, integrating everything Kane had been learning, in the development of the story.

pull backs, and more pans in the layout of the story. The composition of *Savage* is visually jam-packed with different storytelling elements.[1] The plot to *Savage* was hardly ground breaking: a megalomaniac kidnaps the President and impersonates him at the United Nations, in an attempt to start a third world war. The success of *Savage,* however, is not in the plot, but in the storytelling. Indeed, as with Alfred Hitchcock, the method of developing the story and moving the characters and action toward the climax distinguishes the work, rather than the plot elements themselves. Although *Savage* was criticized in 1968, and later in 1982, when it was re-released by

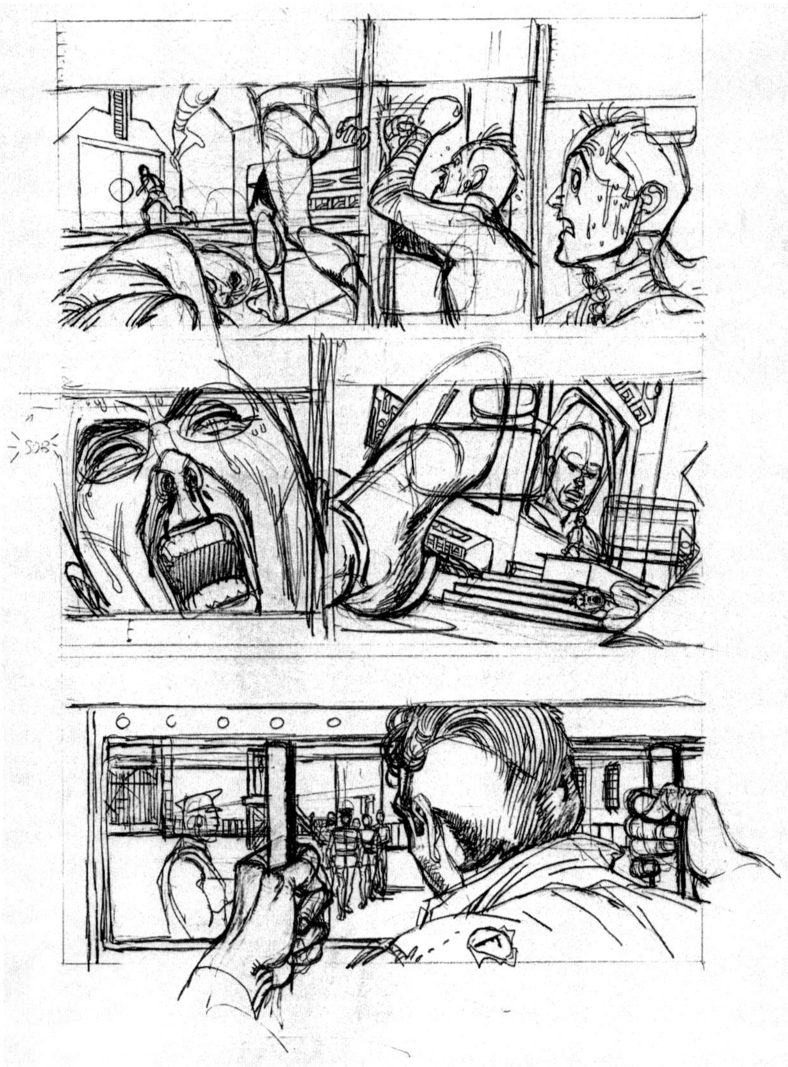

Above: page 6, layout drawing and finished page.

Fantagraphics, as *Gil Kane's Savage,* those dissatisfied missed the point. *Savage* was an archetypal comic book. It embodied all that comic books were and showed what they could be. Just as many B-

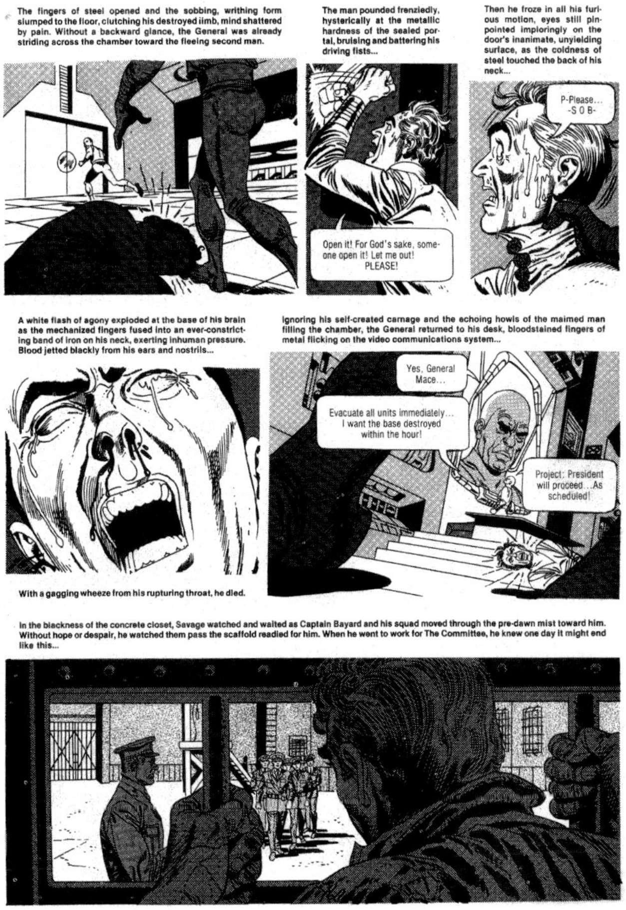
The fingers of steel opened and the sobbing, writhing form slumped to the floor, clutching his destroyed iimb, mind shattered by pain. Without a backward glance, the General was already striding across the chamber toward the fleeing second man.
The man pounded frenziedly, hysterically at the metallic hardness of the sealed portal, bruising and battering his driving fists...
Open it! For God's sake, someone open it! Let me out! PLEASE!
Then he froze in all his furious motion, eyes still pinpointed imploringly on the door's inanimate, unyielding surface, as the coldness of steel touched the back of his neck...
P-Please... -S O B-
A white flash of agony exploded at the base of his brain as the mechanized fingers fused into an ever-constricting band of iron on his neck, exerting inhuman pressure. Blood jetted blackly from his ears and nostrils...
With a gagging wheeze from his rupturing throat, he died.
Ignoring his self-created carnage and the echoing howls of the maimed man filling the chamber, the General returned to his desk, bloodstained fingers of metal flicking on the video communications system...
Yes, General Mace...
Evacuate all units immediately... I want the base destroyed within the hour!
Project: President will proceed...As scheduled!
In the blackness of the concrete closet, Savage watched and waited as Captain Bayard and his squad moved through the pre-dawn mist toward him. Without hope or despair, he watched them pass the scaffold readied for him. When he went to work for The Committee, he knew one day it might end like this...

movies transcended their meager budgets to create something new and memorable, *Savage* showed those who were willing to look the potential that comics had. *Savage* is more than an interesting experiment because, as a hardboiled adventure yarn, it works.

Ultimately, Kane used *Savage* as an opportunity to do everything he was not allowed to do in mainstream comics. With *Savage*, Kane amplified the action and violence of the story and frenetically paced the plot, pulling out all of the stops. Kane described the experience of creating and composing *Savage* as "liberating."

Savage, however, almost never made it to the newsstands.

The layout drawings and finished artwork on these pages demonstrate how Kane carefully and thoughtfully choreographed the action in *Savage*. Like contemporary cinema and literature of the time, *Savage* made violence one of its primary elements. Violence was not new to comic books, but the violence in *Savage* is cinematic and not gratuitous. Violence is a plot element which defines the main characters and perpetuates the action of the story.

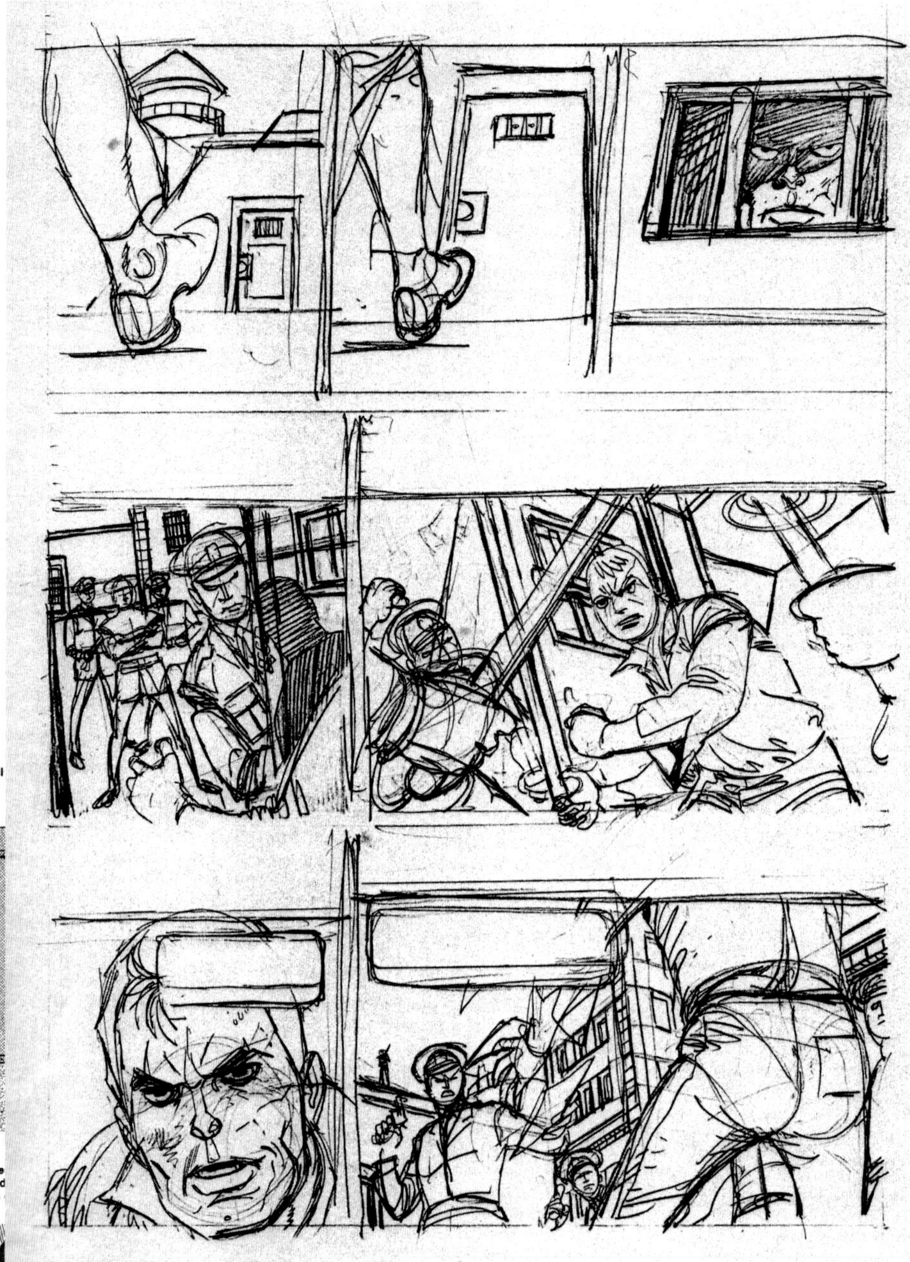

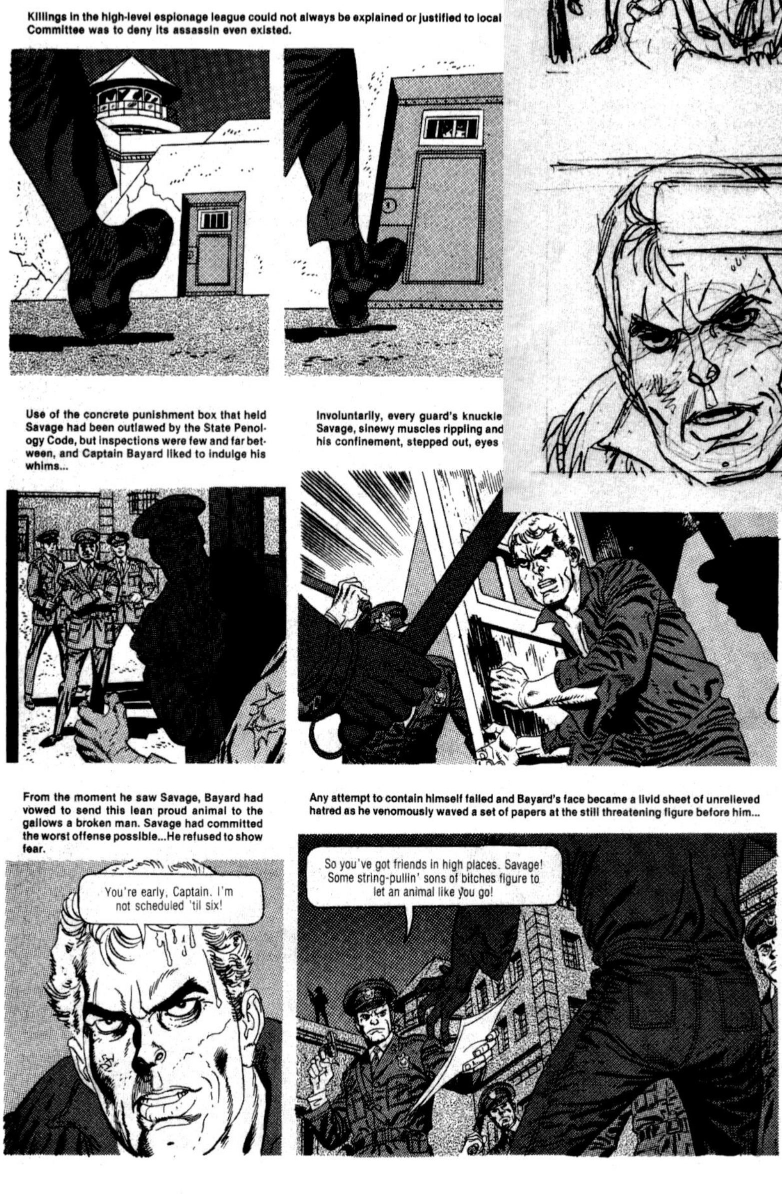
Killings in the high-level espionage league could not always be explained or justified to local
Committee was to deny its assassin even existed.
Use of the concrete punishment box that held Savage had been outlawed by the State Penology Code, but inspections were few and far between, and Captain Bayard liked to indulge his whims...
Involuntarily, every guard's knuckle
Savage, sinewy muscles rippling and
his confinement, stepped out, eyes
From the moment he saw Savage, Bayard had vowed to send this lean proud animal to the gallows a broken man. Savage had committed the worst offense possible...He refused to show fear.
You're early, Captain. I'm not scheduled 'til six!
Any attempt to contain himself failed and Bayard's face became a livid sheet of unrelieved hatred as he venomously waved a set of papers at the still threatening figure before him...
So you've got friends in high places. Savage! Some string-pullin' sons of bitches figure to let an animal like you go!

Left and above: page 7, layout drawing and finished page. This page, coupled with the page on the right, form a sequence which address a broad range of storytelling techniques, which are amplified by the plasticity of Kane's drawing.

The layout drawings on these pages and in the chapter, show Kane's high degree of sophistication in his page breakdown of panels, his confident staging of each page, and his supple drawing.

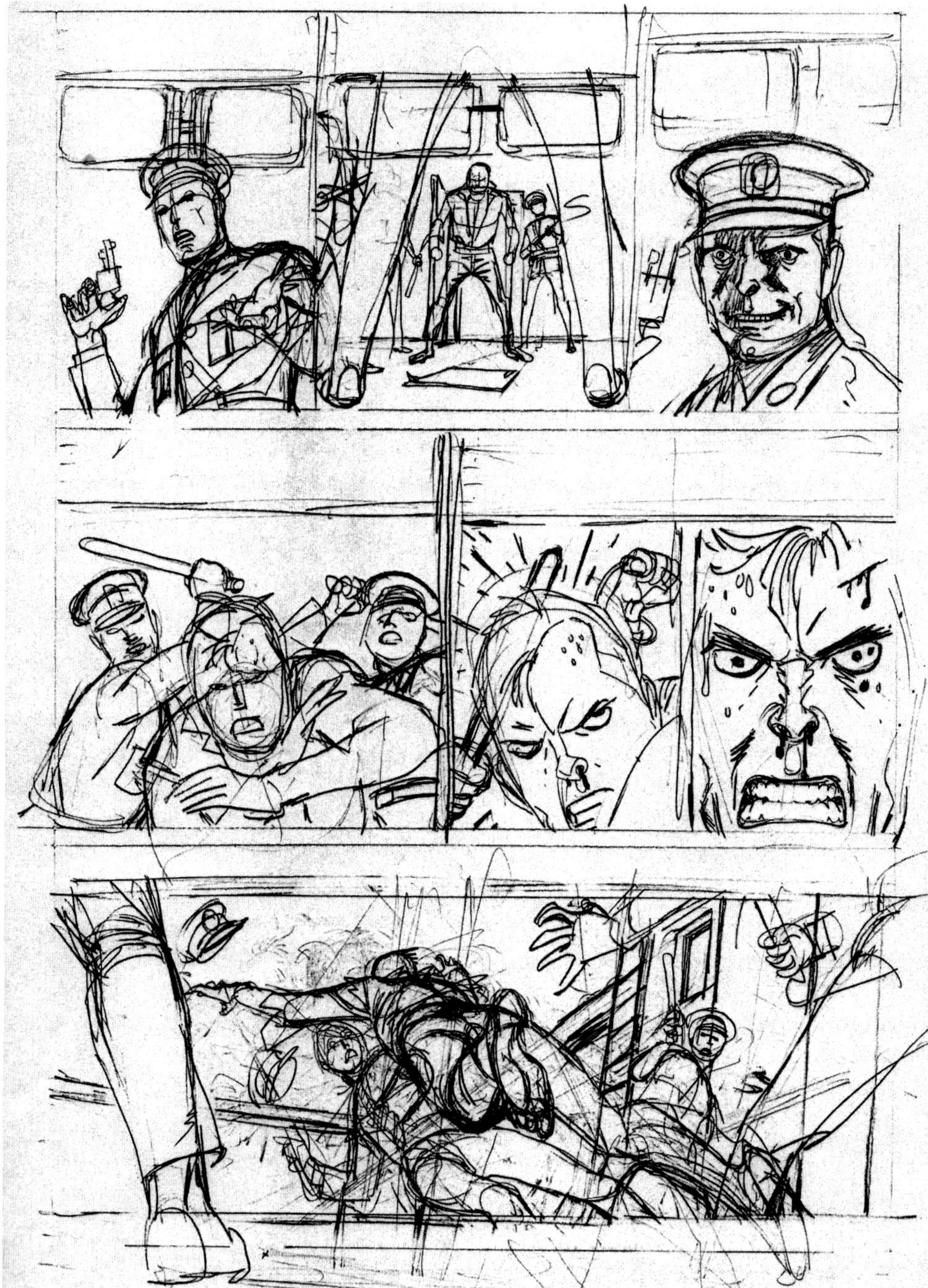

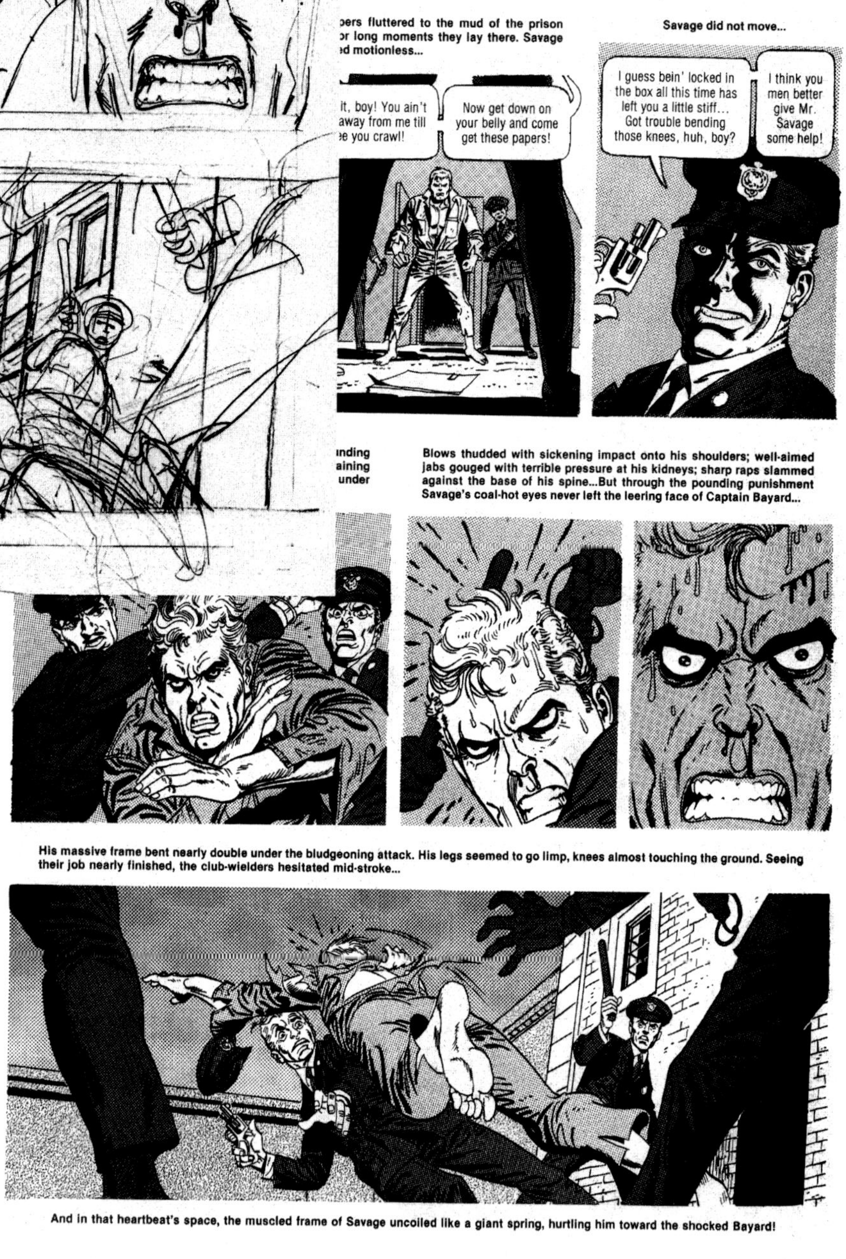
Now get down on your belly and come get these papers!
Savage did not move...
I guess bein' locked in the box all this time has left you a little stiff... Got trouble bending those knees, huh, boy?
I think you men better give Mr. Savage some help!
Blows thudded with sickening impact onto his shoulders; well-aimed jabs gouged with terrible pressure at his kidneys; sharp raps slammed against the base of his spine...But through the pounding punishment Savage's coal-hot eyes never left the leering face of Captain Bayard...
His massive frame bent nearly double under the bludgeoning attack. His legs seemed to go limp, knees almost touching the ground. Seeing their job nearly finished, the club-wielders hesitated mid-stroke...
And in that heartbeat's space, the muscled frame of Savage uncoiled like a giant spring, hurtling him toward the shocked Bayard!

Above and right: page 8, layout drawing and finished page. More non-stop action from Kane.

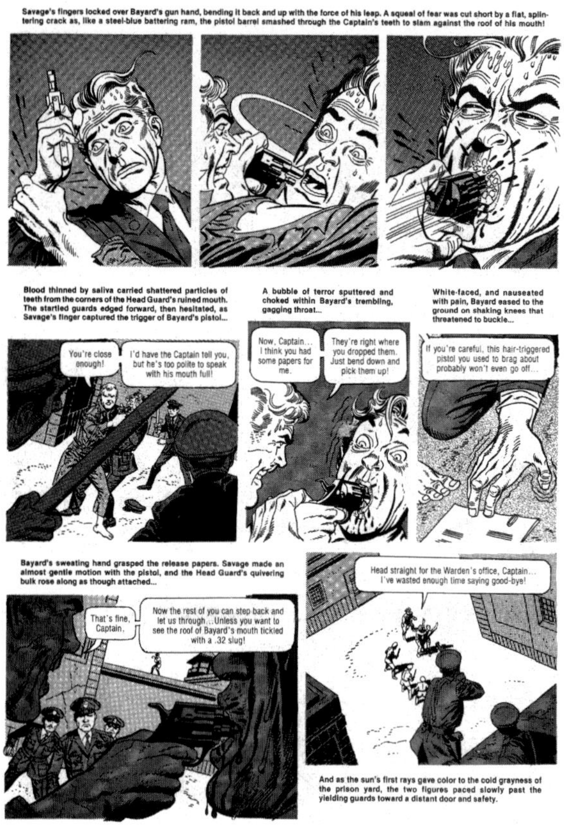
Savage's fingers locked over Bayard's gun hand, bending it back and up with the force of his leap. A squeal of fear was cut short by a flat, splintering crack as, like a steel-blue battering ram, the pistol barrel smashed through the Captain's teeth to slam against the roof of his mouth!
Blood thinned by saliva carried shattered particles of teeth from the corners of the Head Guard's ruined mouth. The startled guards edged forward, then hesitated, as Savage's finger captured the trigger of Bayard's pistol...
You're close enough!
I'd have the Captain tell you, but he's too polite to speak with his mouth full!
A bubble of terror sputtered and choked within Bayard's trembling, gagging throat...
Now, Captain... I think you had some papers for me.
They're right where you dropped them. Just bend down and pick them up!
White-faced, and nauseated with pain, Bayard eased to the ground on shaking knees that threatened to buckle...
If you're careful, this hair-triggered pistol you used to brag about probably won't even go off...
Bayard's sweating hand grasped the release papers. Savage made an almost gentle motion with the pistol, and the Head Guard's quivering bulk rose along as though attached...
That's fine, Captain.
Now the rest of you can step back and let us through...Unless you want to see the roof of Bayard's mouth tickled with a .32 slug!
Head straight for the Warden's office, Captain... I've wasted enough time saying good-bye!
And as the sun's first rays gave color to the cold grayness of the prison yard, the two figures paced slowly past the yielding guards toward a distant door and safety.

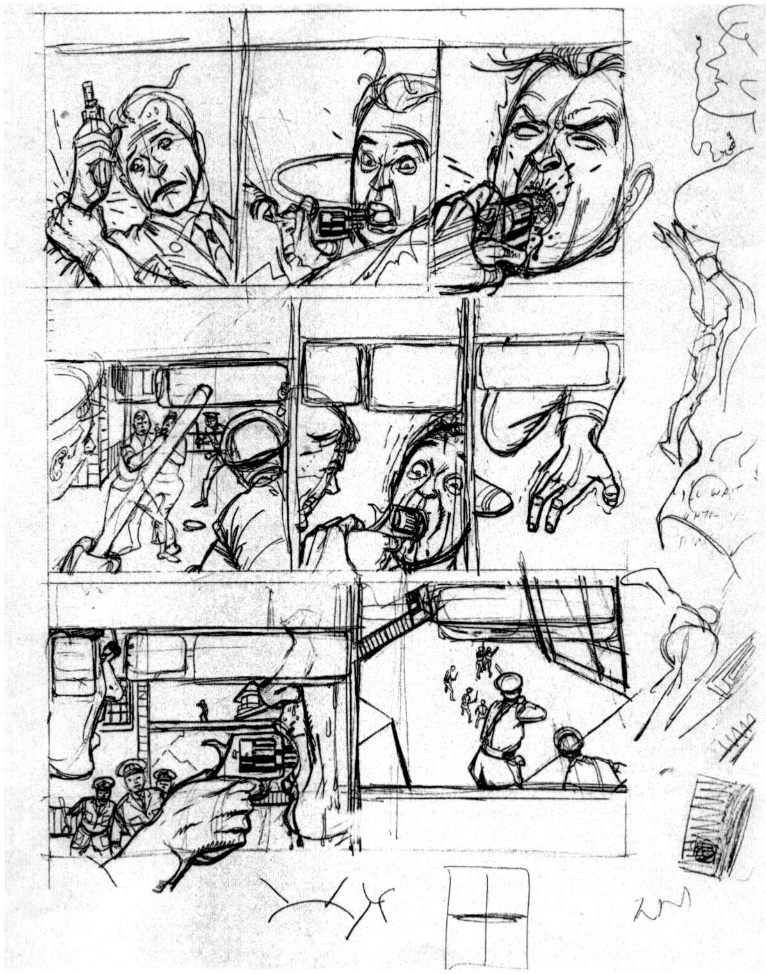

Kane pitched the idea of *Savage* to Cable Distributing (the distributor for Warren's magazines). Cable agreed to pay the costs of printing, and nothing more. In exchange, it would receive 60 percent of any revenue generated. Kane received no fees or advances and would only profit if the magazine generated money. *Savage* was to be printed under Kane's imprint, Adventure House Press, Inc. The printing of *Savage* ran into problems created by its not being approved by the Comics Code Authority. The first company slated to print *Savage* called Kane and demurred on the grounds that it had been advised that *Savage* was pornographic. Nothing could have been further from the truth, but in quickstep Kane

Above: page 9, layout drawing and finished page. The last page in the sequence, where Kane brings the action to its climax. There is no question by this point in the story that Savage is a very tough anti-hero. In *Savage*, Kane used violence to develop the story and the character of Savage. *Savage* never would have been possible in mainstream comic books at the time.

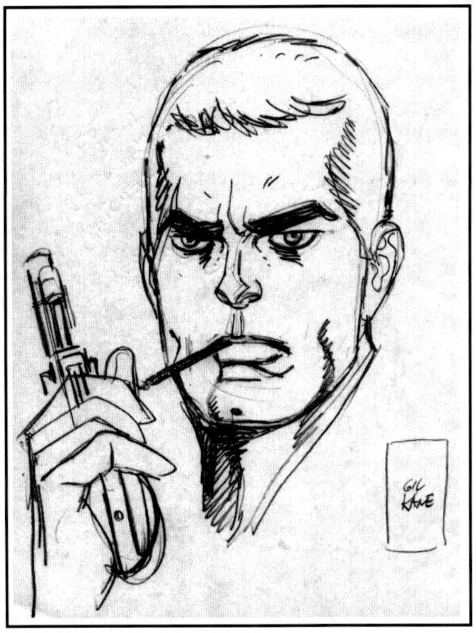

found that the second company which had agreed to print *Savage* was also withdrawing, citing similar concerns. By Kane's account, these printers were scared away by supporters of the Comics Code who saw a magazine outside their control as posing a threat. *Savage,* moreover, was not for 6 to 10 year olds, but for teenagers and adults. Kane was not trying to talk down to his audience, he was just trying to effectively tell a story. As with the comics published by EC, over a decade earlier, anything which was more than pabulum was seen by the established publishers as a threat to order and control in the comic book industry. Finally, Kane found a printer who did not care what *Savage* was about, and even beat the price for printing quoted by the other printers. Just when Kane thought he could get *Savage* to the newsstands, he learned that the many local distributors that had to pick up the magazine for sale were being told that there were problems with *Savage*. Everyone stayed away except Cable. Of the print run of 200,000, Kane estimated only 20,000 copies

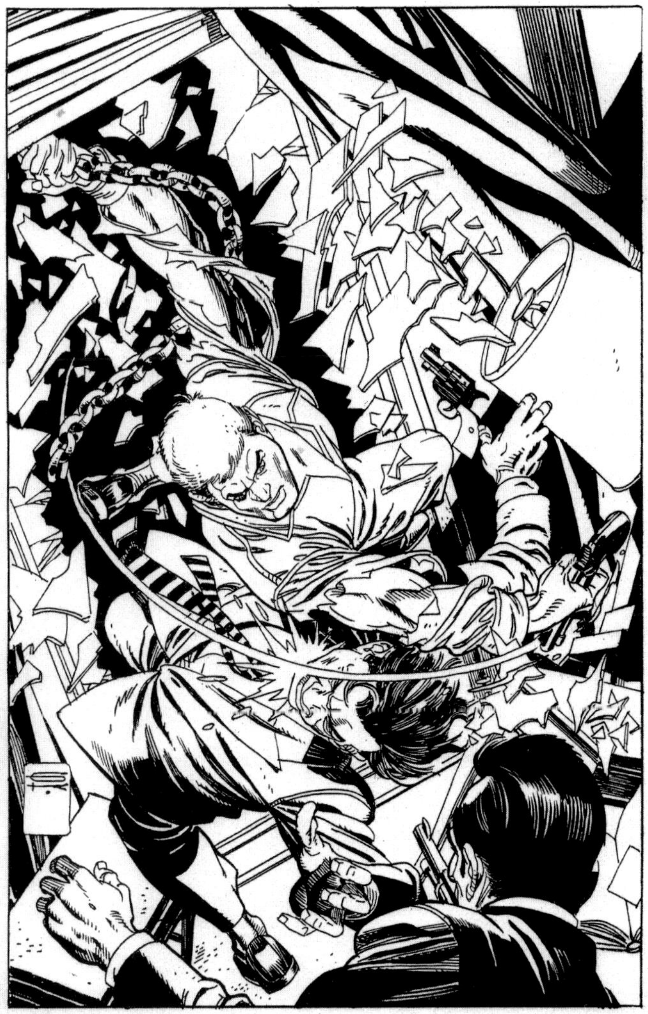

Above and right: Two pieces of original *Savage* artwork created when Kane later revisited the character.

made it to the newsstands. *Savage* and the two follow-up stories died. Kane had even prepared two more covers and plot lines, but they never saw the light of day. The original cover planned by Kane was not used due to concerns that its depiction of Savage was too close to Lee Marvin, a painted cover was used in its place. This cover, nevertheless, also bore a strong resemblance to Marvin. More importantly, Kane had planned an extended graphic story using Howard's Conan, which also died along with *Savage.*

Savage was more than just a noble experiment that bucked the comic book establishment. It was the assimilation of Kane's years of experience and self-education. *Savage* transformed Kane's art from merely being the archetype of DC Comics' house style, to an art which exceeded the sum of its parts. Kane had been trying to develop a singular identity as an artist and with *Savage* he came of age. Kane used these lessons on his next personal adventure into the extended story form with his novel, *Blackmark.*

The advertisement which ran in *Savage*, for planned comic books that, sadly, were never realized.

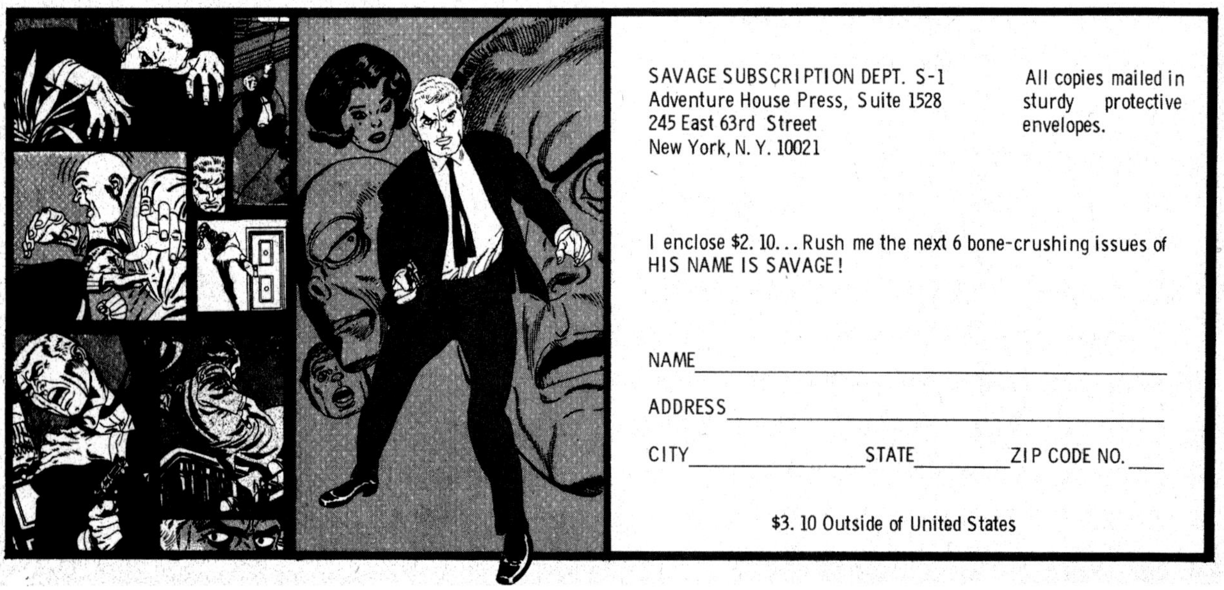
SAVAGE SUBSCRIPTION DEPT. S-1
Adventure House Press, Suite 1528
245 East 63rd Street
New York, N. Y. 10021
All copies mailed in sturdy protective envelopes.
I enclose $2. 10... Rush me the next 6 bone-crushing issues of HIS NAME IS SAVAGE!
NAME
ADDRESS
CITY
STATE
ZIP CODE NO.
$3. 10 Outside of United States

7 BLACKMARK, ART, AND MAKING A LIVING

Kane had always struggled to make a living, and the time while he was creating *Savage* was no exception.[1]

Since he was not being paid to create *Savage* he continued to work for both DC Comics and Marvel, and to pitch new projects. The work he was producing gave a hint of what he was planning, but was still standard comic book fare. When Kane moved into his new studio he needed an assistant to help him work on his different projects. For this, Roger Brand was hired.[2] Brand's services proved invaluable because six weeks after Kane had the go ahead from Cable Distributing to begin work on *Savage*, he also received a commitment from Bantam Books to begin work on another extended narrative story to be titled *Blackmark*, although production on

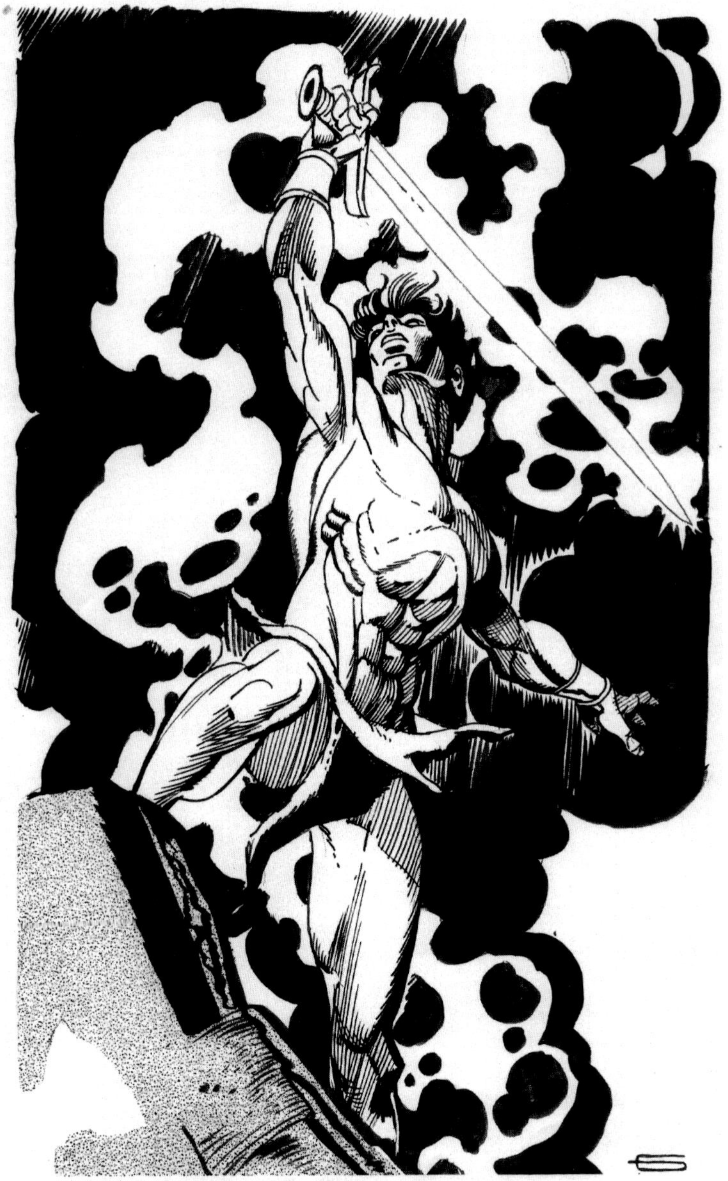

Interior page from the original artwork for Chapter IV, of *Blackmark*, 1971, ©2001 The Estate of Gil Kane.

This page and the next: a four page continuity from *Blackmark*, 1971, Gil Kane, pencils and inks. All artwork in this chapter is © 2001 The Estate of Gil Kane. These pages demonstrate how graphic novels use text, dialogue, and pictures to develop a story, giving the reader a more developed plot and characters, unlike conventional comic books.

this project would not begin until later.

Kane had convinced the Chairman of Bantam Books to back *Blackmark* as a series of extended comic book novels. Kane had arranged to pitch various proposals, and had been given fifteen minutes to make his presentation. After more than one-and-a-half hours of talking, he had a commitment to do four books. Later, Bantam's commitment on the books was extended to eight installments. Bantam's arrangement was extremely beneficial for them, because they were only paying Kane $3,500.00 in advance for his book, which had to be inked, lettered, and camera ready. Even though these terms were highly advantageous for Bantam, Kane jumped at the opportunity to completely craft his own story. Due to the effort involved in producing such a large amount of finished art,

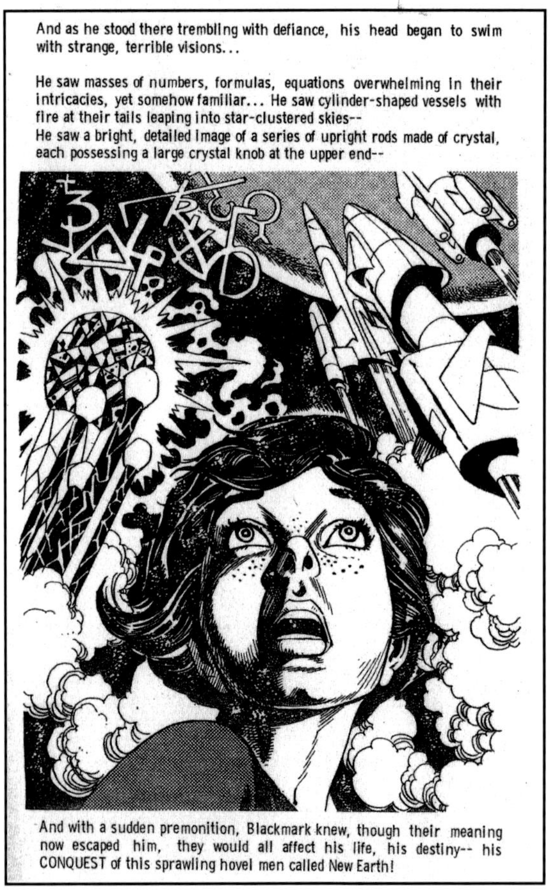
And as he stood there trembling with defiance, his head began to swim with strange, terrible visions...
He saw masses of numbers, formulas, equations overwhelming in their intricacies, yet somehow familiar... He saw cylinder-shaped vessels with fire at their tails leaping into star-clustered skies--
He saw a bright, detailed image of a series of upright rods made of crystal, each possessing a large crystal knob at the upper end--
And with a sudden premonition, Blackmark knew, though their meaning now escaped him, they would all affect his life, his destiny-- his CONQUEST of this sprawling hovel men called New Earth!

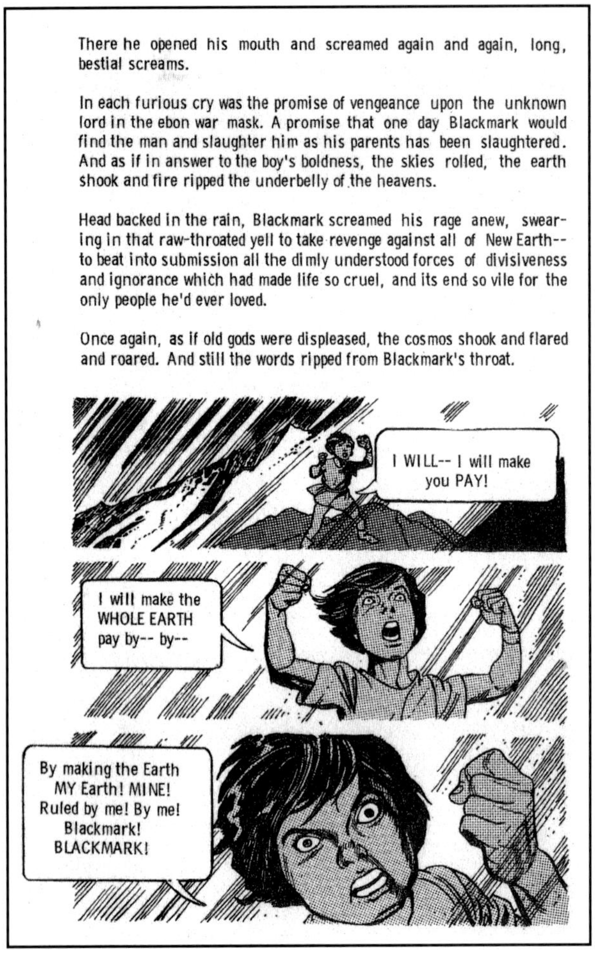
There he opened his mouth and screamed again and again, long, bestial screams.
In each furious cry was the promise of vengeance upon the unknown lord in the ebon war mask. A promise that one day Blackmark would find the man and slaughter him as his parents has been slaughtered. And as if in answer to the boy's boldness, the skies rolled, the earth shook and fire ripped the underbelly of the heavens.
Head backed in the rain, Blackmark screamed his rage anew, swearing in that raw-throated yell to take revenge against all of New Earth-- to beat into submission all the dimly understood forces of divisiveness and ignorance which had made life so cruel, and its end so vile for the only people he'd ever loved.
Once again, as if old gods were displeased, the cosmos shook and flared and roared. And still the words ripped from Blackmark's throat.
I WILL-- I will make you PAY!
I will make the WHOLE EARTH pay by-- by--
By making the Earth MY Earth! MINE! Ruled by me! By me! Blackmark! BLACKMARK!

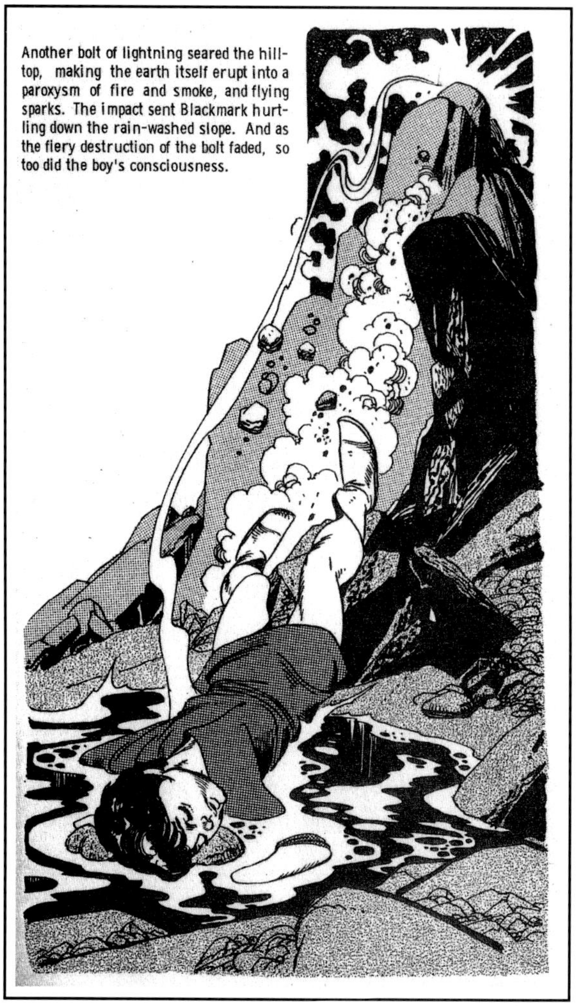
Another bolt of lightning seared the hill-top, making the earth itself erupt into a paroxysm of fire and smoke, and flying sparks. The impact sent Blackmark hurtling down the rain-washed slope. And as the fiery destruction of the bolt faded, so too did the boy's consciousness.

Kane relied on Brand for assistance in adding the zip-a-tone shading to all of the pages (which is extremely time consuming).[3] Kane's use of black and white, rather than color, perfectly suited the art. Finally, Kane was beginning to feel that his many years of work were paying off. He would be able to craft his own characters and stories. He could now focus his attention on designing stories, characters, and art that were one complete concept.

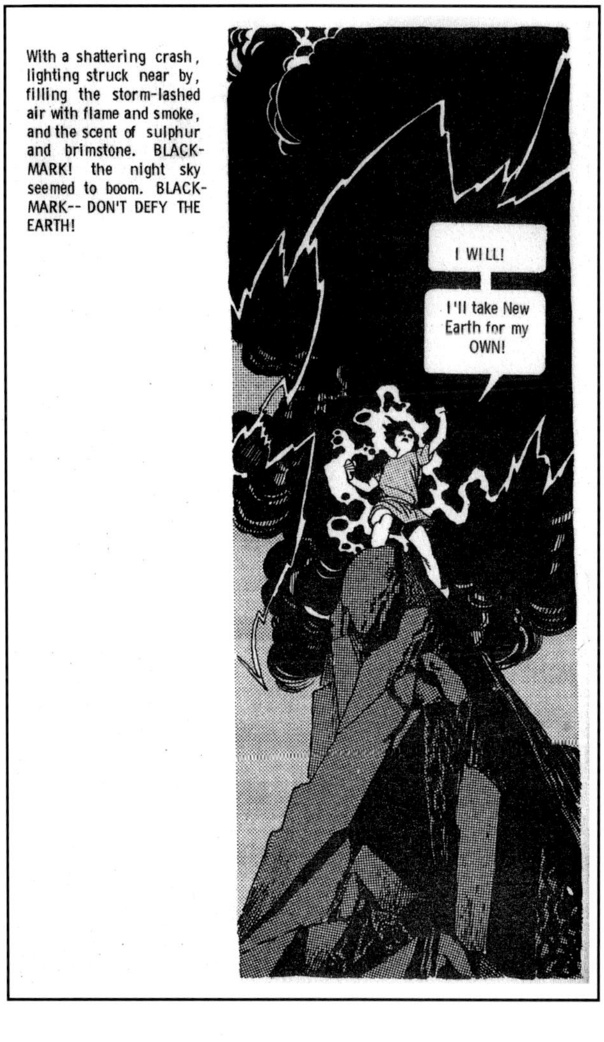
With a shattering crash, lighting struck near by, filling the storm-lashed air with flame and smoke, and the scent of sulphur and brimstone. BLACK-MARK! the night sky seemed to boom. BLACK-MARK-- DON'T DEFY THE EARTH!
I WILL!
I'll take New Earth for my OWN!

Blackmark was a story set in the post apocalyptic future, when society had disintegrated into chaos. Man occupied an earth beset by mutants where science was feared and outlawed. The hero of the story, Blackmark, is conceived with the help of science and given his destiny while still unborn. *Blackmark* is an amalgam of all Kane's favorite mythical themes.

As with *Savage*, Kane wrote the

plot outline and then called upon Archie Goodwin to write the actual text and dialogue.

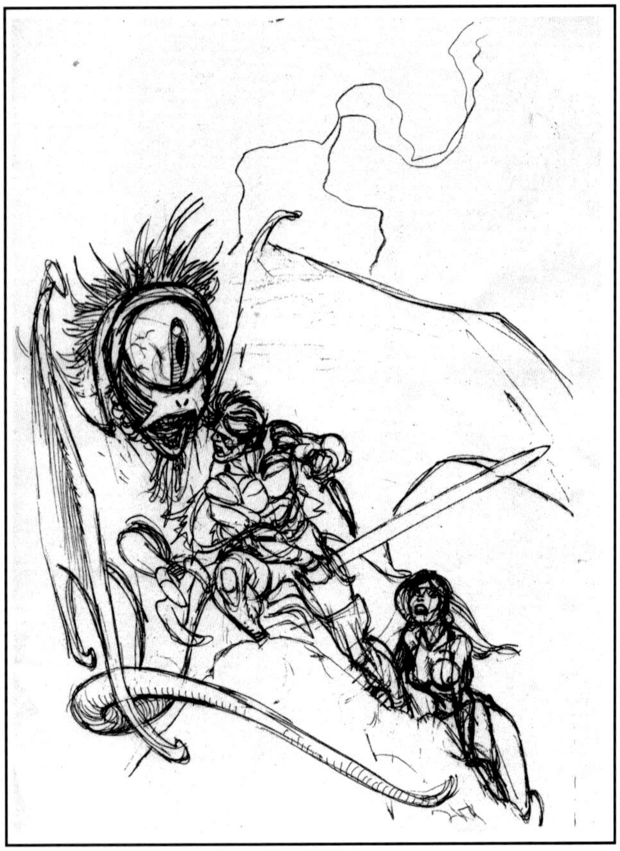

Cover "rough" for the unpublished cover for the second Blackmark graphic novel, *The Mind Demons*, Gil Kane, pencils.

Kane used *Blackmark* to further his experiments with page composition and the integration of narrative text, pictures, and dialogue. Kane spent a significant amount of time composing his panel layout for *Savage,* and it showed. In *Savage,* Kane did the initial page layout on 18 inch by 24 inch sheets of paper, which allowed him to design pages which contrasted many different panel sizes on one page, and to break down time and action to develop the story in a number of ways. With *Blackmark,* however, Kane was limited by the standard size of a pocket book, 4 $^1/_4$ inches by 7 inches, with artwork produced on pages which were 9 inches by 12 inches. Despite these limitations, Kane composed each page with a panel layout that played off the

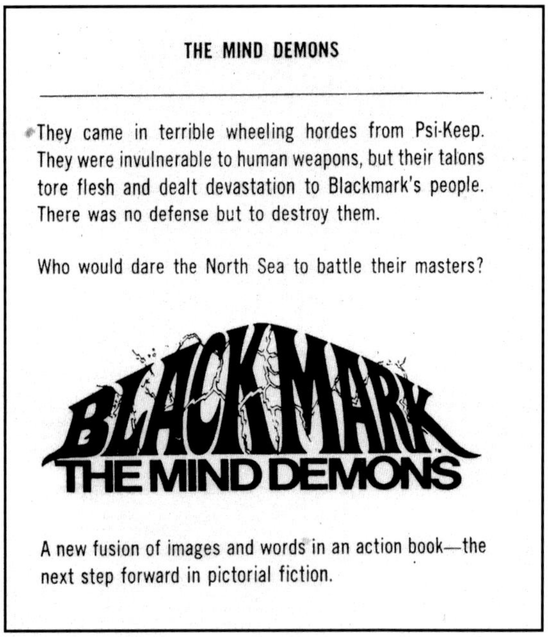

THE MIND DEMONS

They came in terrible wheeling hordes from Psi-Keep. They were invulnerable to human weapons, but their talons tore flesh and dealt devastation to Blackmark's people. There was no defense but to destroy them.

Who would dare the North Sea to battle their masters?

BLACKMARK
THE MIND DEMONS

A new fusion of images and words in an action book—the next step forward in pictorial fiction.

Title page for the original version of the second Blackmark graphic novel.

next page, thereby keeping the look of the book interesting. Despite Kane's efforts, the final product was too small, and the dramatic effect of the artwork and story was severely limited by the format. Kane also felt that the installments of *Blackmark* should be released in quick succession, in serial format. Indeed, Kane had two books completed, with one additional book almost completely pencilled. Kane had planned to release the first two installments at one time. Bantam only released the first book, however. Although *Blackmark* is clearly influenced by Conan, something Bantam wanted, Bantam did not know how to classify the book, as it was something very unusual: a story for mature readers, told entirely in **pictures, words, and text.**

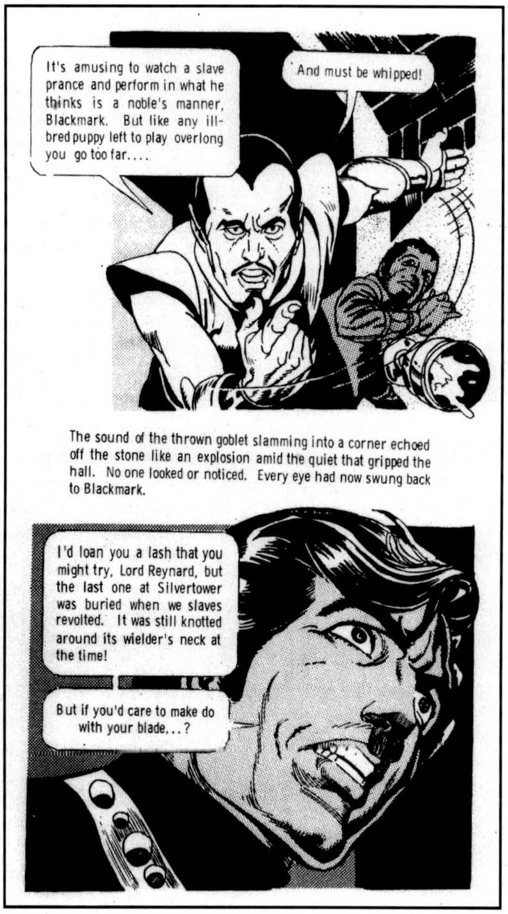
It's amusing to watch a slave prance and perform in what he thinks is a noble's manner, Blackmark. But like any ill-bred puppy left to play overlong you go too far....
And must be whipped!
The sound of the thrown goblet slamming into a corner echoed off the stone like an explosion amid the quiet that gripped the hall. No one looked or noticed. Every eye had now swung back to Blackmark.
I'd loan you a lash that you might try, Lord Reynard, but the last one at Silvertower was buried when we slaves revolted. It was still knotted around its wielder's neck at the time!
But if you'd care to make do with your blade...?

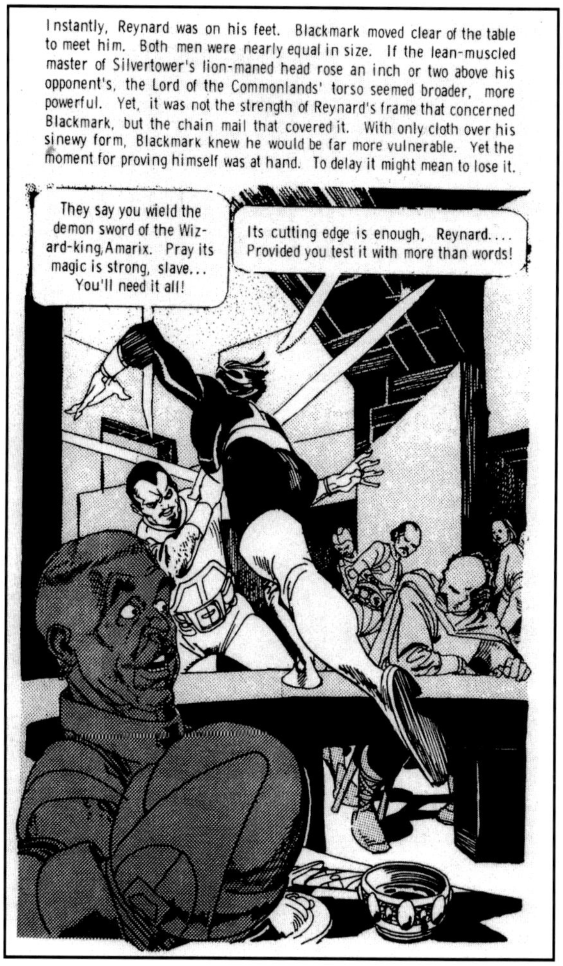
Instantly, Reynard was on his feet. Blackmark moved clear of the table to meet him. Both men were nearly equal in size. If the lean-muscled master of Silvertower's lion-maned head rose an inch or two above his opponent's, the Lord of the Commonlands' torso seemed broader, more powerful. Yet, it was not the strength of Reynard's frame that concerned Blackmark, but the chain mail that covered it. With only cloth over his sinewy form, Blackmark knew he would be far more vulnerable. Yet the moment for proving himself was at hand. To delay it might mean to lose it.
They say you wield the demon sword of the Wizard-king, Amarix. Pray its magic is strong, slave... You'll need it all!
Its cutting edge is enough, Reynard.... Provided you test it with more than words!

Above: the first two pages from an eight page continuity, previously unpublished in its original form, from *The Mind Demons*. This continuity shows Kane's graphic storytelling at its most effective. By the time this story was completed, Kane's art was fully mature, as these pages attest.

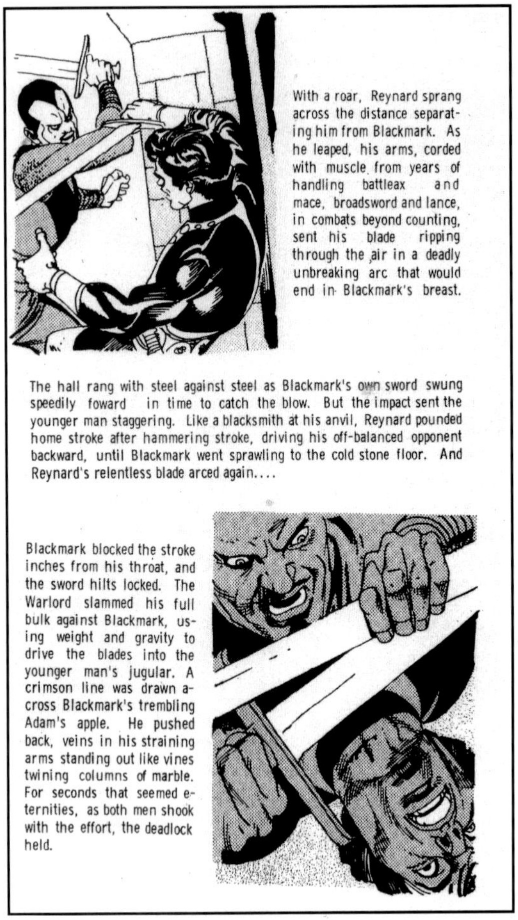
With a roar, Reynard sprang across the distance separating him from Blackmark. As he leaped, his arms, corded with muscle from years of handling battleax and mace, broadsword and lance, in combats beyond counting, sent his blade ripping through the air in a deadly unbreaking arc that would end in Blackmark's breast.
The hall rang with steel against steel as Blackmark's own sword swung speedily foward in time to catch the blow. But the impact sent the younger man staggering. Like a blacksmith at his anvil, Reynard pounded home stroke after hammering stroke, driving his off-balanced opponent backward, until Blackmark went sprawling to the cold stone floor. And Reynard's relentless blade arced again....
Blackmark blocked the stroke inches from his throat, and the sword hilts locked. The Warlord slammed his full bulk against Blackmark, using weight and gravity to drive the blades into the younger man's jugular. A crimson line was drawn across Blackmark's trembling Adam's apple. He pushed back, veins in his straining arms standing out like vines twining columns of marble. For seconds that seemed eternities, as both men shook with the effort, the deadlock held.

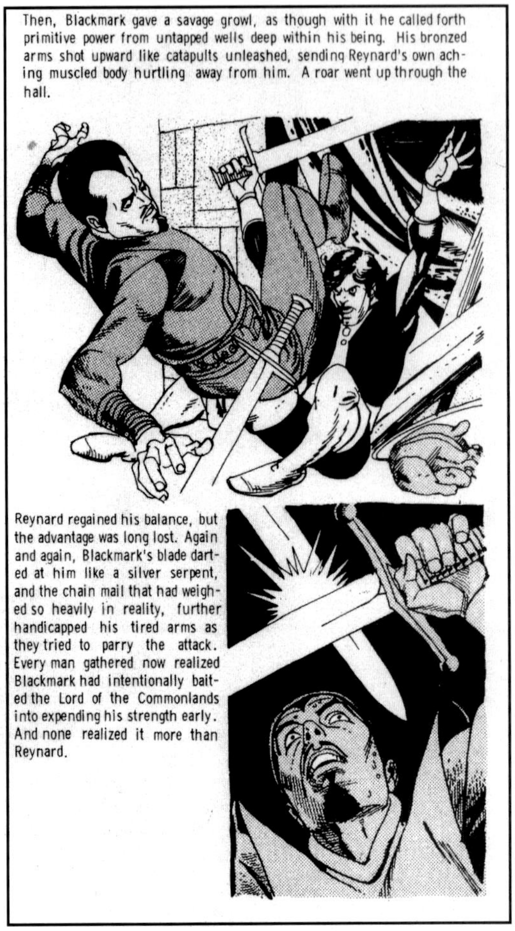
Then, Blackmark gave a savage growl, as though with it he called forth primitive power from untapped wells deep within his being. His bronzed arms shot upward like catapults unleashed, sending Reynard's own aching muscled body hurtling away from him. A roar went up through the hall.
Reynard regained his balance, but the advantage was long lost. Again and again, Blackmark's blade darted at him like a silver serpent, and the chain mail that had weighed so heavily in reality, further handicapped his tired arms as they tried to parry the attack. Every man gathered now realized Blackmark had intentionally baited the Lord of the Commonlands into expending his strength early. And none realized it more than Reynard.

Bantam also was unsure as to how to market *Blackmark*. Due to these uncertainties, Bantam did not market *Blackmark* effectively. While the sales figures indicated close to a sixty percent sale of the book, Bantam shelved the project after only one installment was published.

Blackmark was published in 1971 and it took more than eight years for the second installment to be

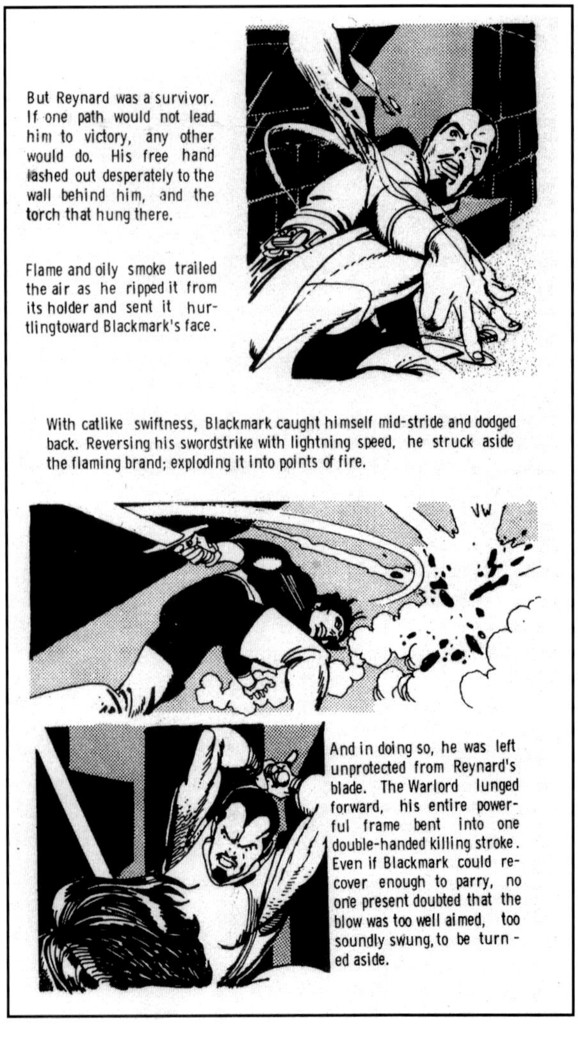
But Reynard was a survivor. If one path would not lead him to victory, any other would do. His free hand lashed out desperately to the wall behind him, and the torch that hung there.
Flame and oily smoke trailed the air as he ripped it from its holder and sent it hurtlingtoward Blackmark's face.
With catlike swiftness, Blackmark caught himself mid-stride and dodged back. Reversing his swordstrike with lightning speed, he struck aside the flaming brand; exploding it into points of fire.
And in doing so, he was left unprotected from Reynard's blade. The Warlord lunged forward, his entire powerful frame bent into one double-handed killing stroke. Even if Blackmark could recover enough to parry, no one present doubted that the blow was too well aimed, too soundly swung, to be turned aside.

The continuing three pages of the continuity, highlighting how Kane focused on the design of each page, completely integrating the story with pictures and text.

published, this time by Marvel Comics in *Marvel Preview* #17. Because *Marvel Preview* was a magazine format, Kane was forced to alter the original layout, which does a disservice to the story, and to his carefully crafted layout composition. A comparison of the original art for the story, versus the final presentation of the story, makes it clear that the original format was much more effective. If the books had been released *together,* as Kane had planned and in their full size, *Blackmark* would have artistically been more successful. The financial failure of *Savage,* due to internal

The next two pages in the continuity from *The Mind Demons.*

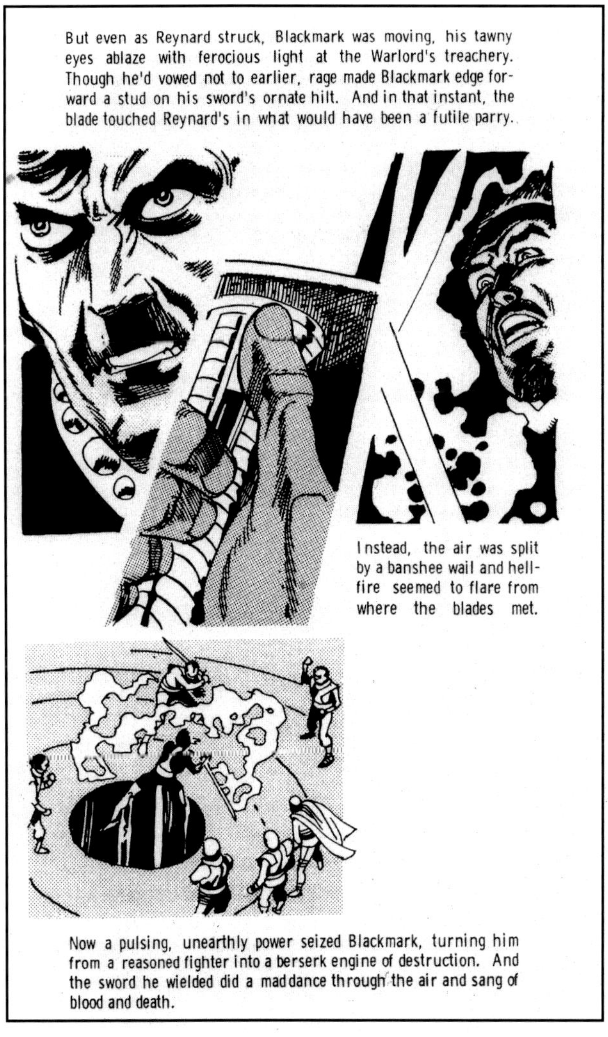
But even as Reynard struck, Blackmark was moving, his tawny eyes ablaze with ferocious light at the Warlord's treachery. Though he'd vowed not to earlier, rage made Blackmark edge forward a stud on his sword's ornate hilt. And in that instant, the blade touched Reynard's in what would have been a futile parry.
Instead, the air was split by a banshee wail and hell-fire seemed to flare from where the blades met.
Now a pulsing, unearthly power seized Blackmark, turning him from a reasoned fighter into a berserk engine of destruction. And the sword he wielded did a maddance through the air and sang of blood and death.

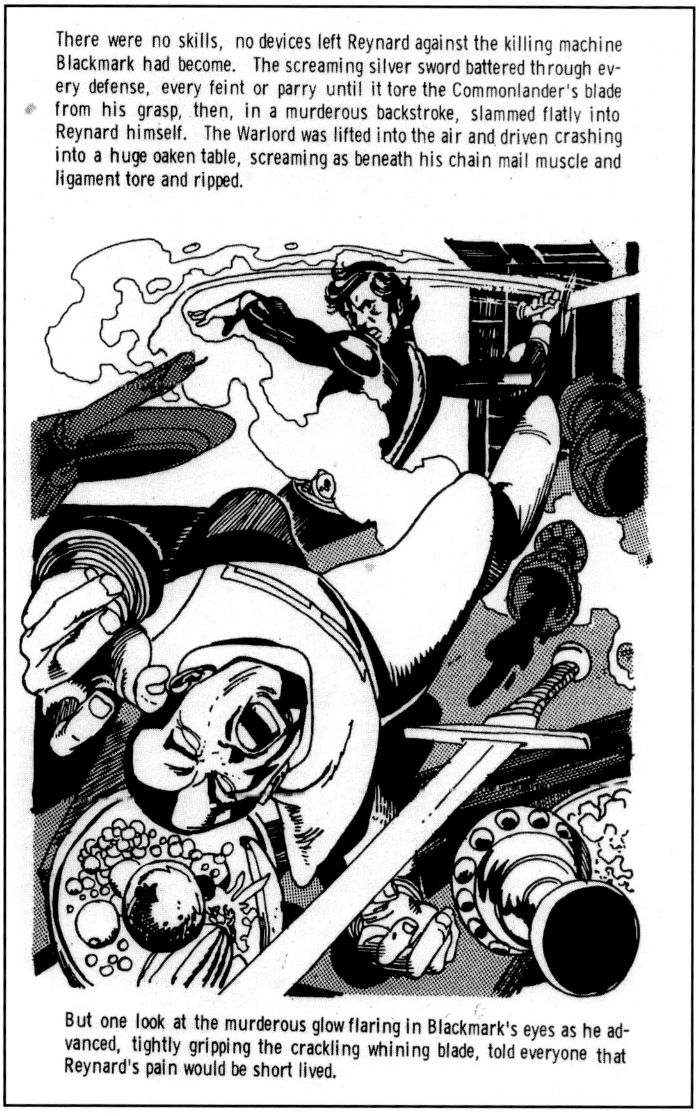
There were no skills, no devices left Reynard against the killing machine Blackmark had become. The screaming silver sword battered through every defense, every feint or parry until it tore the Commonlander's blade from his grasp, then, in a murderous backstroke, slammed flatly into Reynard himself. The Warlord was lifted into the air and driven crashing into a huge oaken table, screaming as beneath his chain mail muscle and ligament tore and ripped.
But one look at the murderous glow flaring in Blackmark's eyes as he advanced, tightly gripping the crackling whining blade, told everyone that Reynard's pain would be short lived.

politics in the comics industry, and the lack of support *Blackmark* received from Bantam, forced Kane to return to mainstream comics. The five year period which had experienced the genesis and completion of *Savage* and *Blackmark* had been an exciting and exhausting time for Kane. He had been very close to achieving the artistic success he had strived for, but ultimately he had been too early with developments which were not yet appreciated by the industry, or the fans of comics.

Artistically, Kane's art had matured and grown significantly. *Savage* had pushed his limits, and even thirty years later, mainstream and independent comics have very rarely exceeded Kane's great B-movie comic book novel, *His Name is…Savage*. *Blackmark*, due to the limitation of the format and Bantam's refusal to release it as Kane had envisioned, has not fared

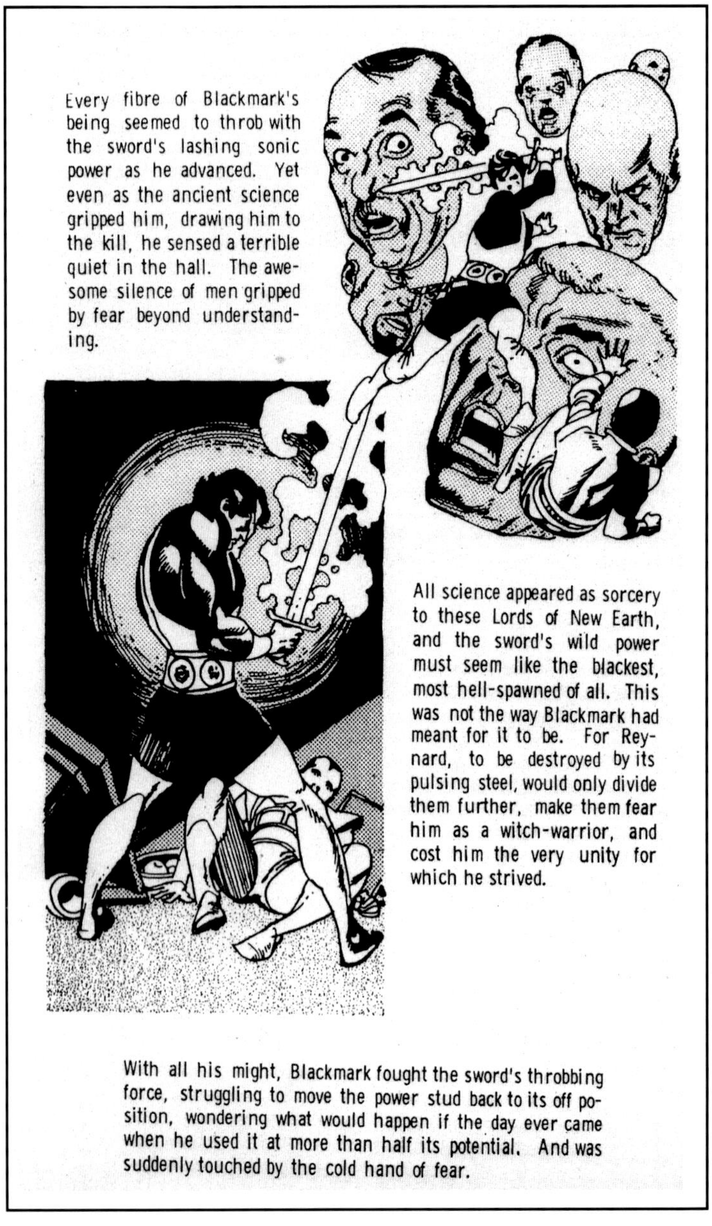
Every fibre of Blackmark's being seemed to throb with the sword's lashing sonic power as he advanced. Yet even as the ancient science gripped him, drawing him to the kill, he sensed a terrible quiet in the hall. The awe-some silence of men gripped by fear beyond understand-ing.
All science appeared as sorcery to these Lords of New Earth, and the sword's wild power must seem like the blackest, most hell-spawned of all. This was not the way Blackmark had meant for it to be. For Rey-nard, to be destroyed by its pulsing steel, would only divide them further, make them fear him as a witch-warrior, and cost him the very unity for which he strived.
With all his might, Blackmark fought the sword's throbbing force, struggling to move the power stud back to its off po-sition, wondering what would happen if the day ever came when he used it at more than half its potential. And was suddenly touched by the cold hand of fear.

The last page in the eight page continuity, where Kane uses his signature montage.

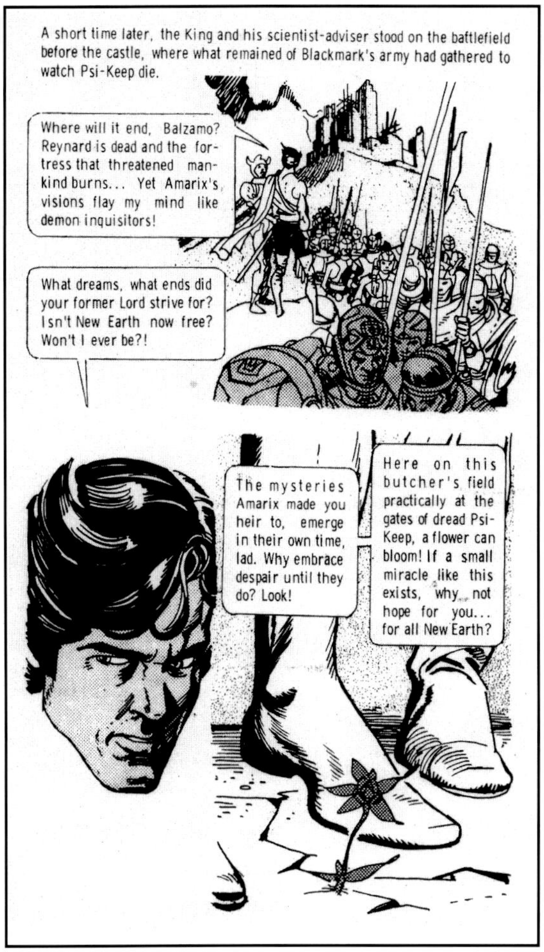
A short time later, the King and his scientist-adviser stood on the battlefield before the castle, where what remained of Blackmark's army had gathered to watch Psi-Keep die.
Where will it end, Balzamo? Reynard is dead and the fortress that threatened mankind burns... Yet Amarix's visions flay my mind like demon inquisitors!
What dreams, what ends did your former Lord strive for? Isn't New Earth now free? Won't I ever be?!
The mysteries Amarix made you heir to, emerge in their own time, lad. Why embrace despair until they do? Look!
Here on this butcher's field practically at the gates of dread Psi-Keep, a flower can bloom! If a small miracle like this exists, why not hope for you... for all New Earth?

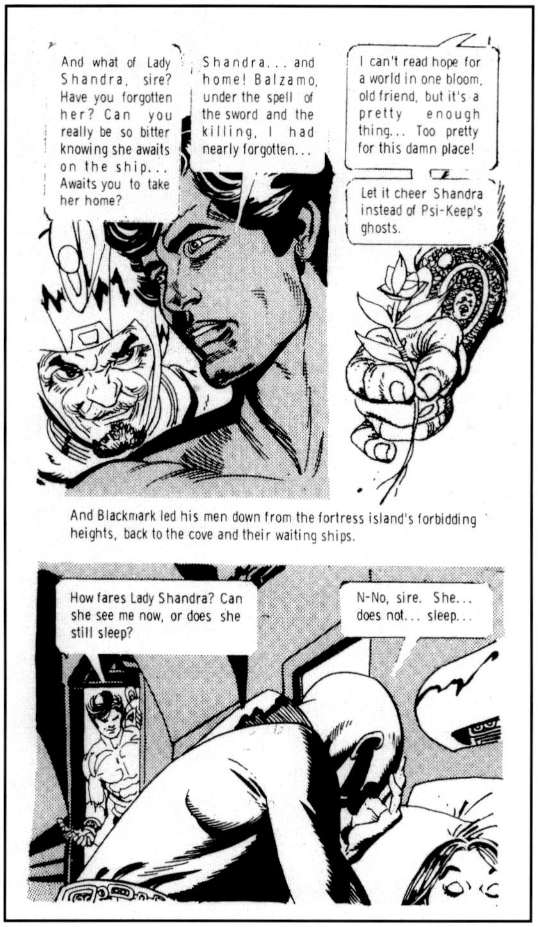
And what of Lady Shandra, sire? Have you forgotten her? Can you really be so bitter knowing she awaits on the ship... Awaits you to take her home?
Shandra... and home! Balzamo, under the spell of the sword and the killing, I had nearly forgotten...
I can't read hope for a world in one bloom, old friend, but it's a pretty enough thing... Too pretty for this damn place!
Let it cheer Shandra instead of Psi-Keep's ghosts.
And Blackmark led his men down from the fortress island's forbidding heights, back to the cove and their waiting ships.
How fares Lady Shandra? Can she see me now, or does she still sleep?
N-No, sire. She... does not... sleep...

as well. Only in its original version, with the two extant stories united and in their full size, does the story begin to have any real impact.

Toward the end of the 1960s the entire comic book industry began experiencing changes reflecting the momentous events being experienced by the country. The struggle against racial discrimination and the Vietnam war brought into question many of the social tenants which had been taken for granted. Vocal dissent against the government, and all things established, was commonplace. In an attempt to inject relevance into comics, DC Comics and Marvel both attempted to tackle "serious" subjects such as drug abuse, prejudice, racism, and the anti-government sentiment which was echoed by the newspapers, magazines, and television, daily. Kane had left his tenure with the *Green Lantern* to work on *Savage* and was finally replaced by artist, Neal Adams, with the stories written by Denny O'Neil. These stories represented an attempt to inject relevance

Above: the first two, in a continuity of four pages, previously unpublished in their original form, from Kane's *The Mind Demons*.

into the Green Lantern character by confronting him with the inadequacies of being a superhero and with the bigger perspective of social problems. Although these comic books were embraced by fans, they ultimately failed artistically because they were self-conscious and preachy. The stories printed by EC, almost twenty years earlier, had been more honest, and dealt with these issues in a less obvious, but more effective manner. Marvel also had attempted to be relevant. One of these attempts involved the issue of drug addiction which was featured in the comic book *The Amazing Spider-Man.* These Spider-Man stories were not

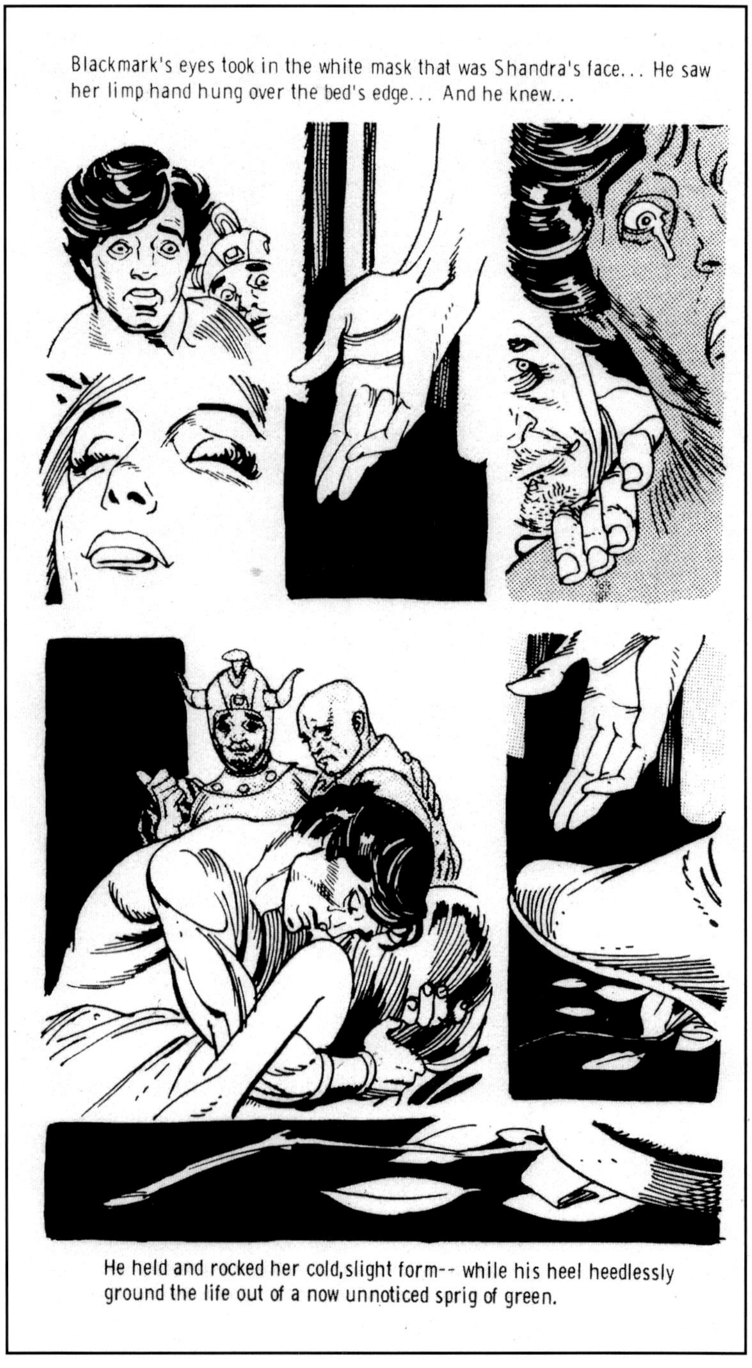
Blackmark's eyes took in the white mask that was Shandra's face... He saw her limp hand hung over the bed's edge... And he knew...
He held and rocked her cold, slight form-- while his heel heedlessly ground the life out of a now unnoticed sprig of green.

Right: Kane deftly and dramatically handles a key moment in *The Mind Demons*. While there is a minimum of text, the pictures tell the reader everything.

approved by the Comics Code. Kane pencilled these issues and had input into the story, but Stan Lee is generally credited with coming up with the idea to tackle the issue of drug use in these stories. Fans of comics generally see these issues of *The Amazing Spider-Man* as a watershed of sorts, but these stories are, at best unremarkable and not particularly memorable. Comics were also being used as a vehicle by the counterculture, in what came to be known as "underground comix." These comics dealt with graphic sex, violence, and drugs and were bitterly sarcastic and contemptuous of the "establishment." Underground Comix avoided the controls of the Comics Code by being sold in stores stocked and run by the counterculture itself. Interestingly, a few of these comics took the art of comic books forward and helped continue the maturation of the comics. Kane, however, was a traditional romantic and while he appreciated some of the art and the artists of underground comix, he continued to work in the mainstream.

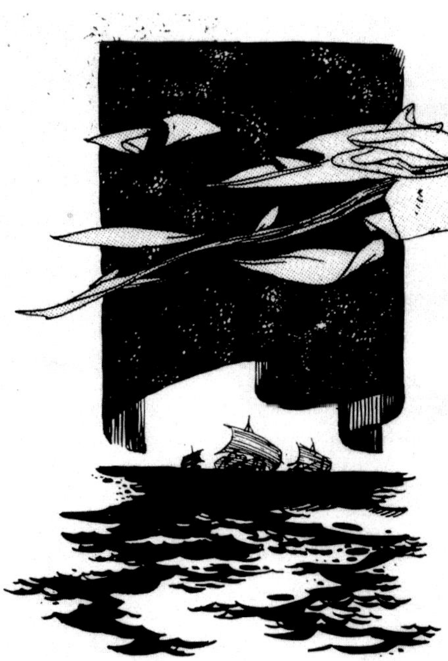

8 WORKING IN THE MAINSTREAM

During his work on *Savage* and *Blackmark*, Kane did have opportunities, at DC Comics and Marvel, to put his personal stamp on comics in the mainstream. Kane had worked consistently for DC Comics since 1949. Shortly, however, this association came almost to a standstill. The reasons for this were two-fold. First, Kane had developed an extremely close relationship with an up-and-coming power at Marvel Comics, Roy Thomas. Thomas, who published a comic fan magazine, *Alter Ego* (called a "fanzine"), in 1969 published one of the first print interviews with Kane. This interview, conducted by John Benson, explored Kane's **opinions** on the art and developments of comic books and strips. After being involved as an active fan of comic books, Thomas went on to write stories for DC Comics, and then to work for Marvel, as a writer and as an unofficial associate editor. It is clear that Thomas held Kane

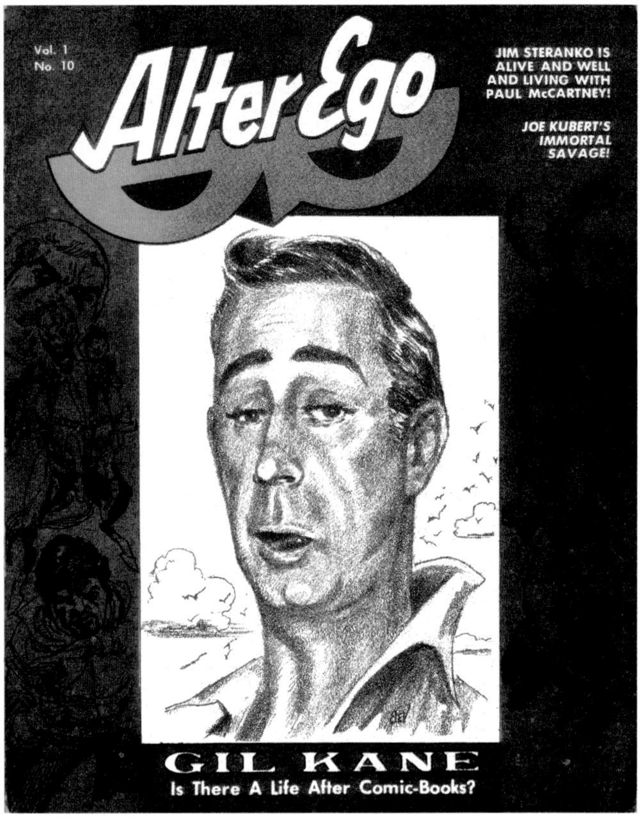
Vol. 1
No. 10
Alter Ego
JIM STERANKO IS ALIVE AND WELL AND LIVING WITH PAUL McCARTNEY!
JOE KUBERT'S IMMORTAL SAVAGE!
GIL KANE
Is There A Life After Comic-Books?

Cover for *Alter Ego* #10, 1969, ©2001 Roy Thomas. In addition to the portrait of Kane, by comic artist and colorist Marie Severin, the cover contains a border of characters Kane drew which were associated with him.

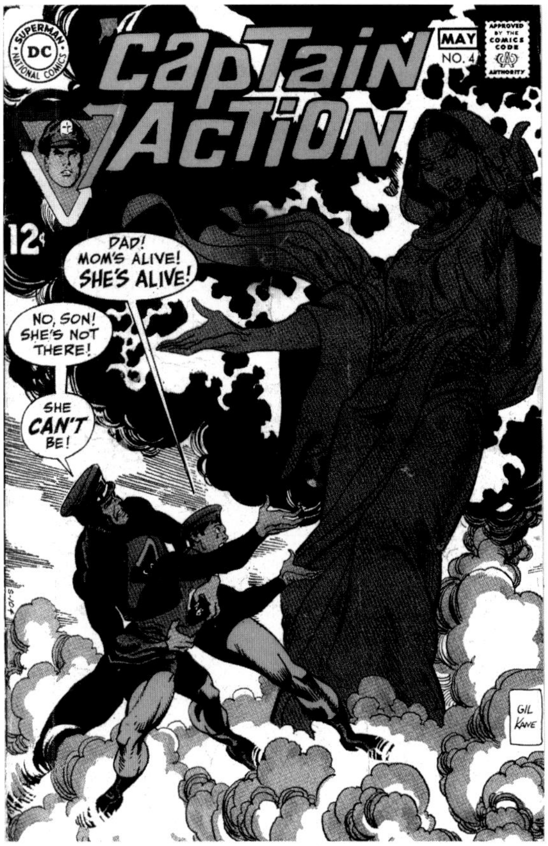
SUPERMAN
DC
NATIONAL COMICS
CapTain
ACTiON
MAY
NO. 4
APPROVED BY THE COMICS CODE AUTHORITY
12¢
DAD! MOM'S ALIVE! SHE'S ALIVE!
NO, SON! SHE'S NOT THERE!
SHE CAN'T BE!
GIL KANE

in high regard artistically and also, intellectually. Kane was also held in high regard by one of Marvel's primary artists, John Romita, who had recommended that Kane be assigned the duty of pencilling *The Amazing Spider-Man* strip. The second reason was Carmine Infantino. Infantino, who had always been competitive with Kane since they were boys in high school, was ascending through the ranks of management at DC Comics. Infantino was less than kind to his old classmate, and Kane felt that Infantino's attitudes toward him did not make for a comfortable working relationship.[1] Kane continued to work for DC Comics during

Above: cover for *Captain Action* #4, April/May, 1969, Gil Kane, pencils and inks, ©2001 DC Comics. At the time he began work on *Captain Action*, Kane had been reading George Bernard Shaw's, *Man and Superman*. The third act of the play, which is entitled *Don Juan in Hell*, inspired Kane to interpolate elements of the play into the script for *Captain Action* #4. Rarely had comic books had such source material as their inspiration. Left: two sequential pages from *Captain Action* #4.

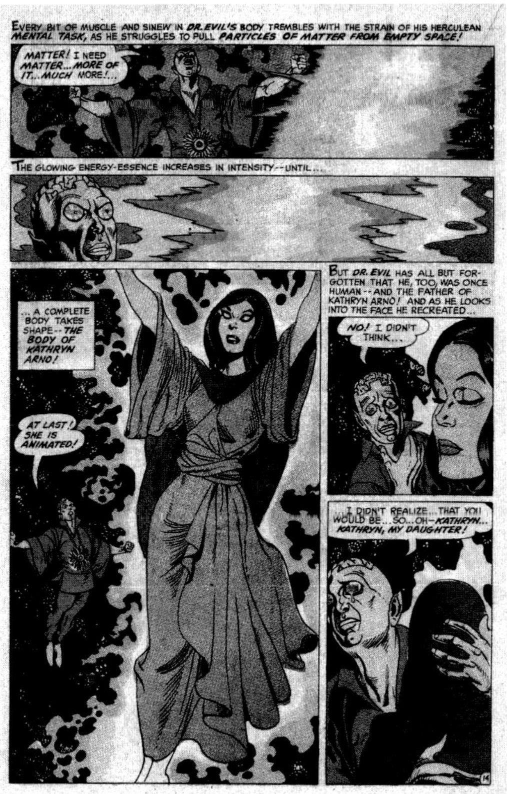
EVERY BIT OF MUSCLE AND SINEW IN DR. EVIL'S BODY TREMBLES WITH THE STRAIN OF HIS HERCULEAN MENTAL TASK, AS HE STRUGGLES TO PULL PARTICLES OF MATTER FROM EMPTY SPACE!
MATTER! I NEED MATTER...MORE OF IT...MUCH MORE!...
THE GLOWING ENERGY-ESSENCE INCREASES IN INTENSITY--UNTIL...
... A COMPLETE BODY TAKES SHAPE--THE BODY OF KATHRYN ARNO!
AT LAST! SHE IS ANIMATED!
BUT DR. EVIL HAS ALL BUT FORGOTTEN THAT HE, TOO, WAS ONCE HUMAN--AND THE FATHER OF KATHRYN ARNO! AND AS HE LOOKS INTO THE FACE HE RECREATED...
NO! I DIDN'T THINK...
I DIDN'T REALIZE...THAT YOU WOULD BE...SO...OH--KATHRYN... KATHRYN, MY DAUGHTER!
14

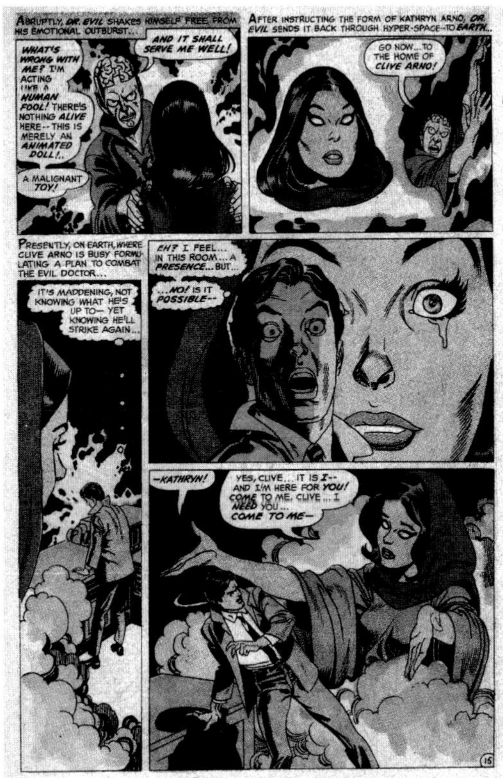
ABRUPTLY, DR. EVIL SHAKES HIMSELF FREE FROM HIS EMOTIONAL OUTBURST...
WHAT'S WRONG WITH ME? I'M ACTING LIKE A HUMAN FOOL! THERE'S NOTHING ALIVE HERE--THIS IS MERELY AN ANIMATED DOLL!..
A MALIGNANT TOY!
AND IT SHALL SERVE ME WELL!
AFTER INSTRUCTING THE FORM OF KATHRYN ARNO, DR. EVIL SENDS IT BACK THROUGH HYPER-SPACE--TO EARTH...
GO NOW...TO THE HOME OF CLIVE ARNO!
PRESENTLY, ON EARTH, WHERE CLIVE ARNO IS BUSY FORMULATING A PLAN TO COMBAT THE EVIL DOCTOR...
IT'S MADDENING, NOT KNOWING WHAT HE'S UP TO-- YET KNOWING HE'LL STRIKE AGAIN...
EH? I FEEL... IN THIS ROOM....A PRESENCE...BUT...
...NO! IS IT POSSIBLE--
-KATHRYN!
YES, CLIVE... IT IS I-- AND I'M HERE FOR YOU! COME TO ME, CLIVE... I NEED YOU... COME TO ME--
15

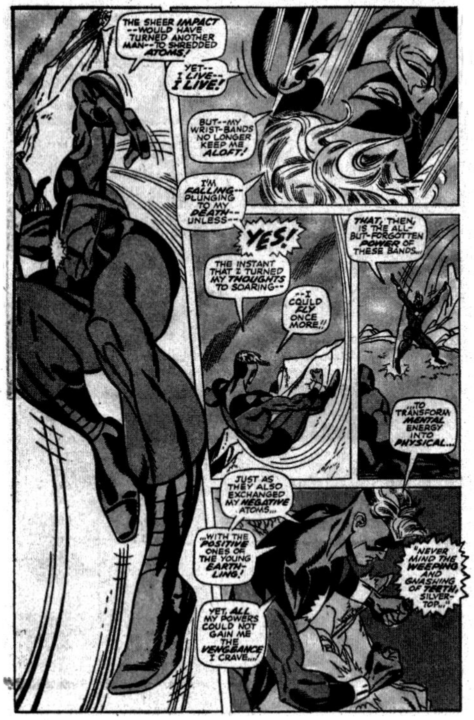
THE SHEER IMPACT --WOULD HAVE TURNED ANOTHER MAN--TO SHREDDED ATOMS!
YET-- I LIVE-- I LIVE!
BUT--MY WRIST-BANDS NO LONGER KEEP ME ALOFT!
I'M FALLING-- PLUNGING TO MY DEATH-- UNLESS--
YES!
THE INSTANT THAT I TURNED MY THOUGHTS TO SOARING--
--I COULD FLY ONCE MORE!!
THAT, THEN, IS THE ALL-BUT-FORGOTTEN POWER OF THESE BANDS...
...TO TRANSFORM MENTAL ENERGY INTO PHYSICAL...
JUST AS THEY ALSO EXCHANGED MY NEGATIVE ATOMS...
...WITH THE POSITIVE ONES OF THE YOUNG EARTH-LING!
"NEVER MIND THE WEEPING AND GNASHING OF TEETH, SILVER-TOP..."
YET, ALL MY POWERS COULD NOT GAIN ME THE VENGEANCE I CRAVE...!

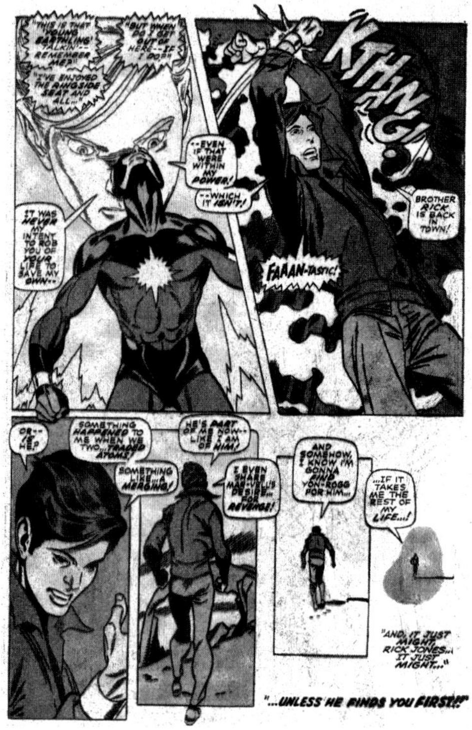
"I'VE ENJOYED THE RINGSIDE SEAT AND ALL..."
--EVEN IF THAT WERE WITHIN MY POWER!
--WHICH IT ISN'T?!
IT WAS NEVER MY INTENT TO ROB YOU OF YOUR LIFE TO SAVE MY OWN--
KTHANG!
BROTHER RICK IS BACK IN TOWN!
FAAAN-TASTIC!
OR-- IS HE?
SOMETHING HAPPENED TO ME WHEN WE TWO... TRADED ATOMS!
SOMETHING LIKE... A MERGING!
HE'S PART OF ME NOW-- LIKE I AM OF HIM!
AND SOMEHOW, I KNOW I'M GONNA FIND YON-ROGG FOR HIM...
...IF IT TAKES ME THE REST OF MY LIFE...!
"AND, IT JUST MIGHT, RICK JONES... IT JUST MIGHT..."
"...UNLESS HE FINDS YOU FIRST!!"

Two sequential pages from *Captain Marvel* #17, October, 1969, Gil Kane, pencils and Dan Adkins, inks, ©2001 Marvel Characters, Inc. Adkins succeeded in perfectly matching Kane's pencils in his inking for Captain Marvel.

Infantino's tenure as Editorial Director, and later as Publisher, but only sporadically. Before leaving DC Comics for his extended commitment with Marvel, Kane did make some noteworthy contributions. He contributed handsome artwork to the *Teen Titans* title and, more importantly, wrote and drew several issues of a comic book called *Captain Action. Captain Action* was a toy doll for boys, and DC Comics was doing a comic book tie-in for the doll. Kane's work on the book had very little to do with the toy. One of the story lines dealt with Captain Action's wife returning from the dead (in form only), through the efforts of her inhuman (once mortal, now transformed)

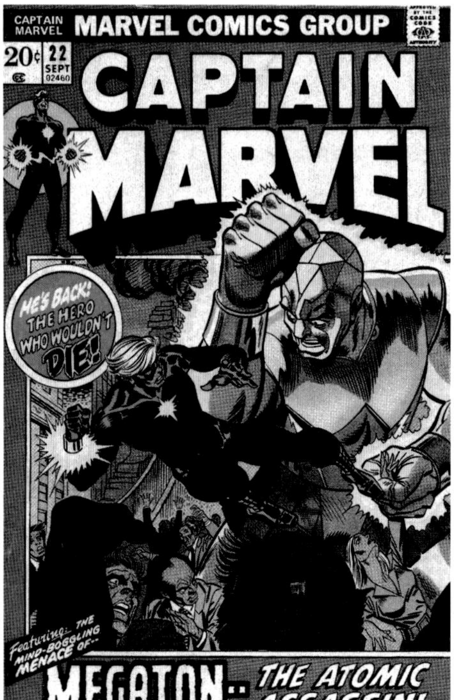
CAPTAIN MARVEL
MARVEL COMICS GROUP
20¢ 22 SEPT
CAPTAIN MARVEL
HE'S BACK! THE HERO WHO WOULDN'T DIE!
Featuring... THE MIND-BOGGLING MENACE OF--
MEGATON.. THE ATOMIC ASSASSIN!

Cover for *Captain Marvel* #22, September, 1972, Gil Kane, pencils, Dan Adkins, inks, ©2001 Marvel Characters, Inc.

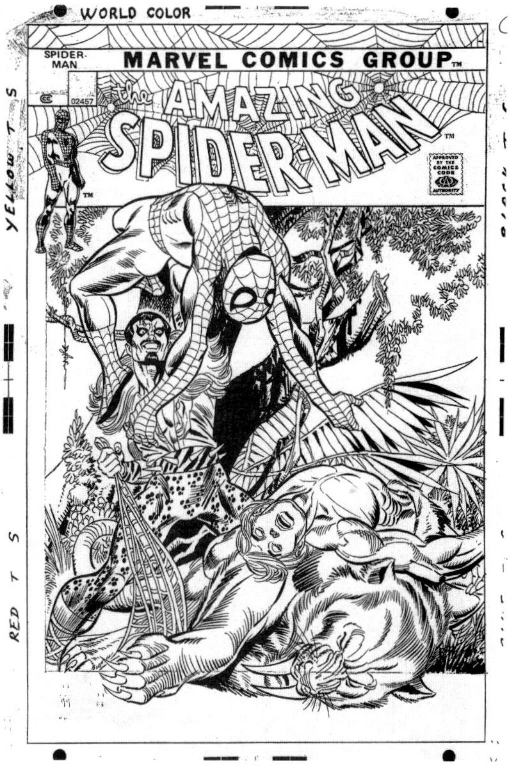
WORLD COLOR
SPIDER-MAN
MARVEL COMICS GROUP
THE AMAZING SPIDER-MAN

Original art for the cover for *The Amazing Spider-Man* #104, January, 1972, Gil Kane, pencils, Frank Giacoia, inks, ©2001 Marvel Characters, Inc.

father, to manipulate the Captain in his struggle to save the human race. The story, while short on development, is unusual for a comic book, as it has many elements which are uncharacteristic for mainstream comics efforts at the time. The art is effectively staged and rendered, and is quite cinematic. The story juxtaposes text, dialogue, and art and utilizes panel breakdowns Kane developed in *Savage* and *Blackmark*. The comic book ran only for five issues (Kane worked on four of them). Kane's work on the last three is extremely handsome and interesting. Kane received his assignment on *Captain Action* in mid 1968. He received sporadic work from DC Comics through 1970, at which time for all intents and purposes, his relationship with DC Comics was severed.

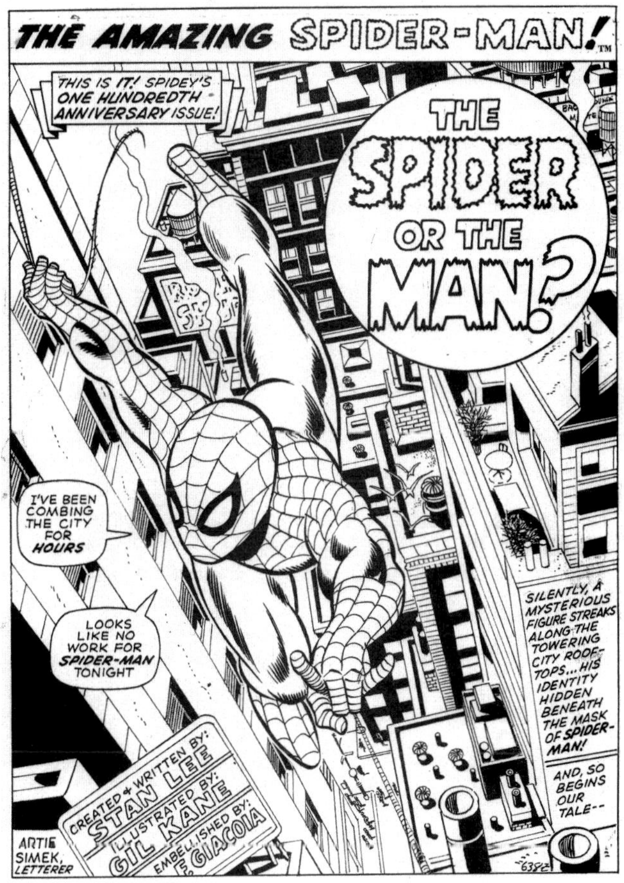
THE AMAZING SPIDER-MAN!
THIS IS IT! SPIDEY'S ONE HUNDREDTH ANNIVERSARY ISSUE!
THE SPIDER OR THE MAN?
I'VE BEEN COMBING THE CITY FOR HOURS
LOOKS LIKE NO WORK FOR SPIDER-MAN TONIGHT
SILENTLY, A MYSTERIOUS FIGURE STREAKS ALONG THE TOWERING CITY ROOF-TOPS... HIS IDENTITY HIDDEN BENEATH THE MASK OF SPIDER-MAN!
AND, SO BEGINS OUR TALE--
CREATED & WRITTEN BY: STAN LEE
ILLUSTRATED BY: GIL KANE
EMBELLISHED BY: F. GIACOIA
ARTIE SIMEK, LETTERER

Original artwork for the splash page for *The Amazing Spider-Man* #100, September, 1971, Gil Kane, pencils, Frank Giacoia, inks, ©2001 Marvel Characters, Inc.

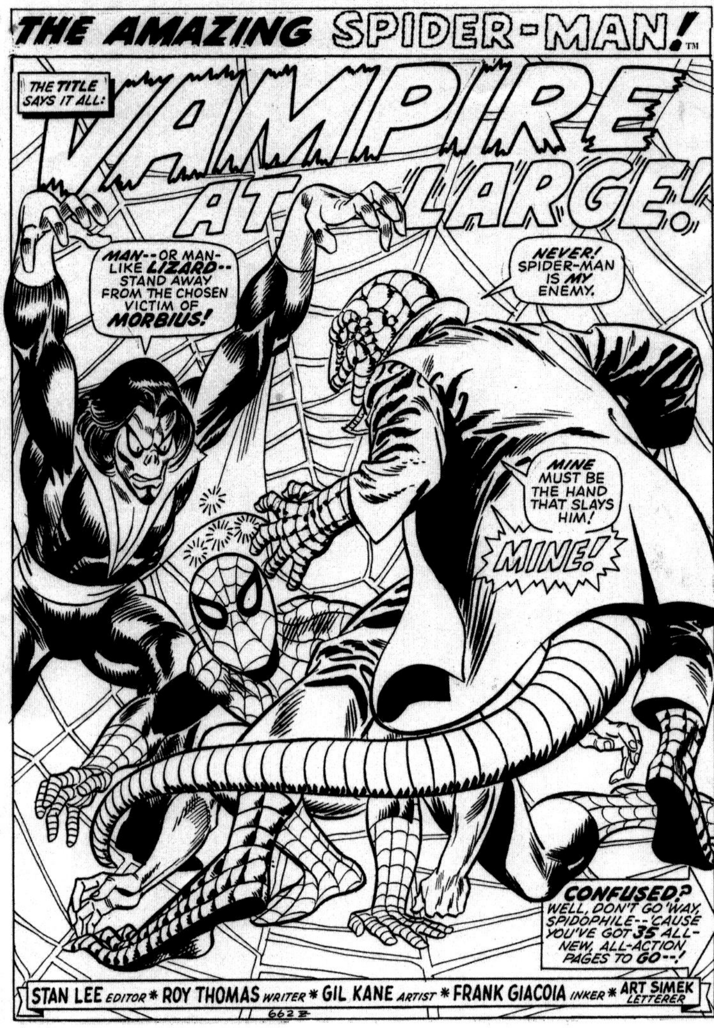
THE AMAZING SPIDER-MAN!
THE TITLE SAYS IT ALL:
VAMPIRE AT LARGE!
MAN--OR MAN-LIKE LIZARD--STAND AWAY FROM THE CHOSEN VICTIM OF MORBIUS!
NEVER! SPIDER-MAN IS MY ENEMY.
MINE MUST BE THE HAND THAT SLAYS HIM!
MINE!
CONFUSED? WELL, DON'T GO 'WAY, SPIDOPHILE--'CAUSE YOU'VE GOT 35 ALL-NEW, ALL-ACTION PAGES TO GO--!
STAN LEE EDITOR * ROY THOMAS WRITER * GIL KANE ARTIST * FRANK GIACOIA INKER * ART SIMEK LETTERER

Left: original artwork for the splash page from *The Amazing Spider-Man* #102, Gil Kane, pencils, Frank Giacoia, inks, November, 1971. Below: original artwork for the cover for *Sub-Mariner* #46, February, 1972, Gil Kane, pencils, Mike Esposito, inks. All artwork on these pages, ©2001 Marvel Characters, Inc.

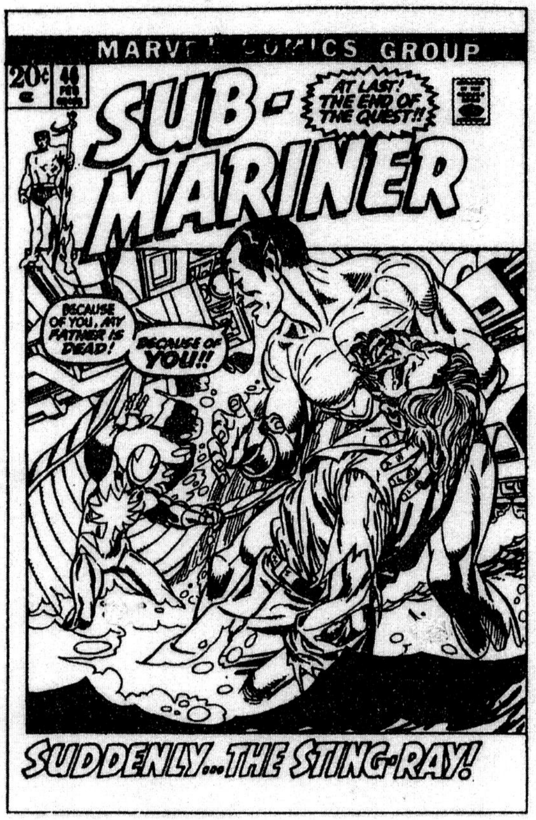
20¢
46 FEB
SUB-MARINER
AT LAST! THE END OF THE QUEST!!
BECAUSE OF YOU, MY FATHER IS DEAD!
BECAUSE OF YOU!!
SUDDENLY...THE STING-RAY!

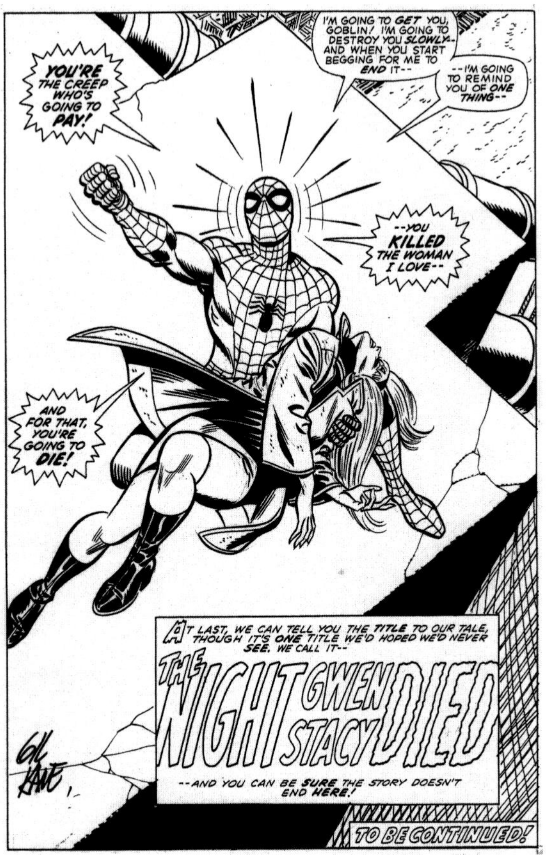
YOU'RE THE CREEP WHO'S GOING TO PAY!
I'M GOING TO GET YOU, GOBLIN! I'M GOING TO DESTROY YOU SLOWLY--AND WHEN YOU START BEGGING FOR ME TO END IT--
--I'M GOING TO REMIND YOU OF ONE THING--
--YOU KILLED THE WOMAN I LOVE--
AND FOR THAT, YOU'RE GOING TO DIE!
AT LAST, WE CAN TELL YOU THE TITLE TO OUR TALE, THOUGH IT'S ONE TITLE WE'D HOPED WE'D NEVER SEE. WE CALL IT--
THE NIGHT GWEN STACY DIED
--AND YOU CAN BE SURE THE STORY DOESN'T END HERE!
TO BE CONTINUED!

Left: original artwork for the last page for *The Amazing Spider-Man* #121, June, 1973, Gil Kane, pencils, John Romita, inks. Right: original artwork for the splash page for *The Amazing Spider-Man* #122, July, 1973, Gil Kane, pencils, John Romita, inks.

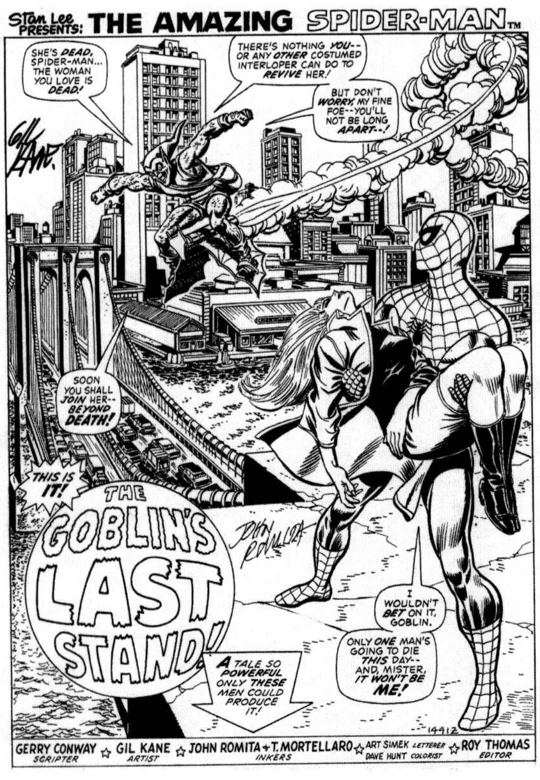
STAN LEE PRESENTS: THE AMAZING SPIDER-MAN
SHE'S DEAD, SPIDER-MAN... THE WOMAN YOU LOVE IS DEAD!
THERE'S NOTHING YOU--OR ANY OTHER COSTUMED INTERLOPER CAN DO TO REVIVE HER!
BUT DON'T WORRY, MY FINE FOE--YOU'LL NOT BE LONG APART--!
SOON YOU SHALL JOIN HER--BEYOND DEATH!
THIS IS IT!
THE GOBLIN'S LAST STAND!
I WOULDN'T BET ON IT, GOBLIN.
ONLY ONE MAN'S GOING TO DIE THIS DAY--AND, MISTER, IT WON'T BE ME!
A TALE SO POWERFUL ONLY THESE MEN COULD PRODUCE IT!
GERRY CONWAY SCRIPTER ☆ GIL KANE ARTIST ☆ JOHN ROMITA + T. MORTELLARO INKERS ☆ ART SIMEK LETTERER DAVE HUNT COLORIST ☆ ROY THOMAS EDITOR

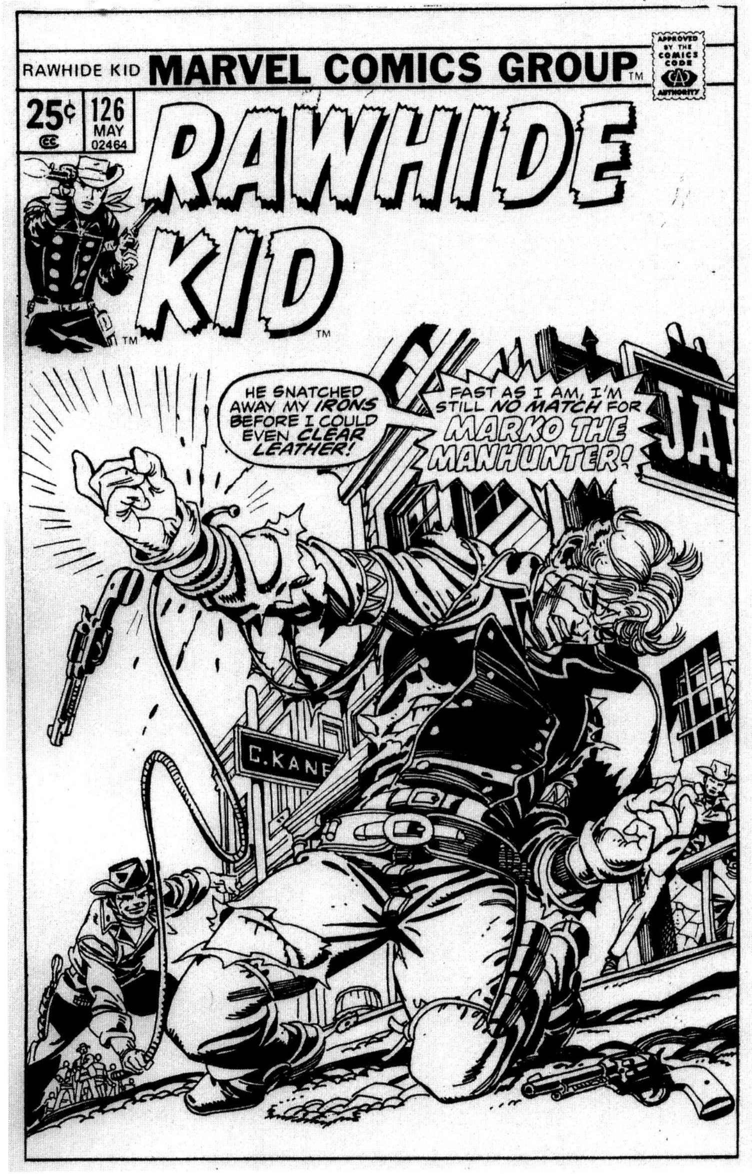
RAWHIDE KID
MARVEL COMICS GROUP
APPROVED BY THE COMICS CODE AUTHORITY
25¢ 126 MAY 02464
RAWHIDE KID
HE SNATCHED AWAY MY IRONS BEFORE I COULD EVEN CLEAR LEATHER!
FAST AS I AM, I'M STILL NO MATCH FOR MARKO THE MANHUNTER!
C. KANE

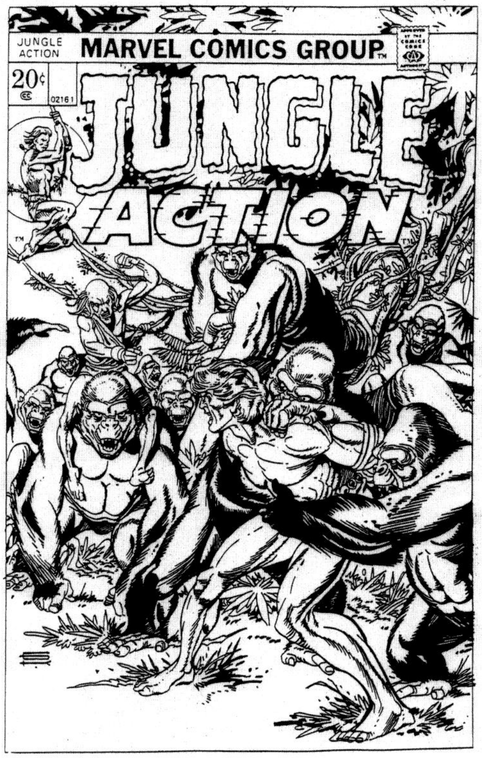
JUNGLE ACTION
MARVEL COMICS GROUP
20¢
02161
JUNGLE ACTION

Original artwork for an unpublished cover for *Jungle Action*. Kane pencilled many covers that were not used, or that were significantly modified by his editors from their original form.

Original artwork for *Rawhide Kid* #126, May, 1975, Gil Kane, pencils and inks. Below: original artwork for *Iron Man* #74, May, 1975, Gil Kane, pencils, Mike Esposito, inks. Right: original artwork for *Omega* #9, July, 1977, Gil Kane, pencils, Mike Esposito, inks.

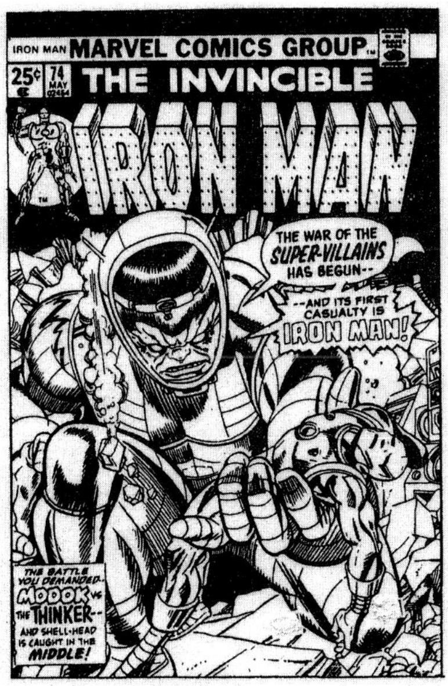
IRON MAN
MARVEL COMICS GROUP
25¢ 74 MAY
THE INVINCIBLE
IRON MAN
THE WAR OF THE SUPER-VILLAINS HAS BEGUN--
--AND ITS FIRST CASUALTY IS IRON MAN!
THE BATTLE YOU DEMANDED-- MODOK vs THE THINKER-- AND SHELL-HEAD IS CAUGHT IN THE MIDDLE!

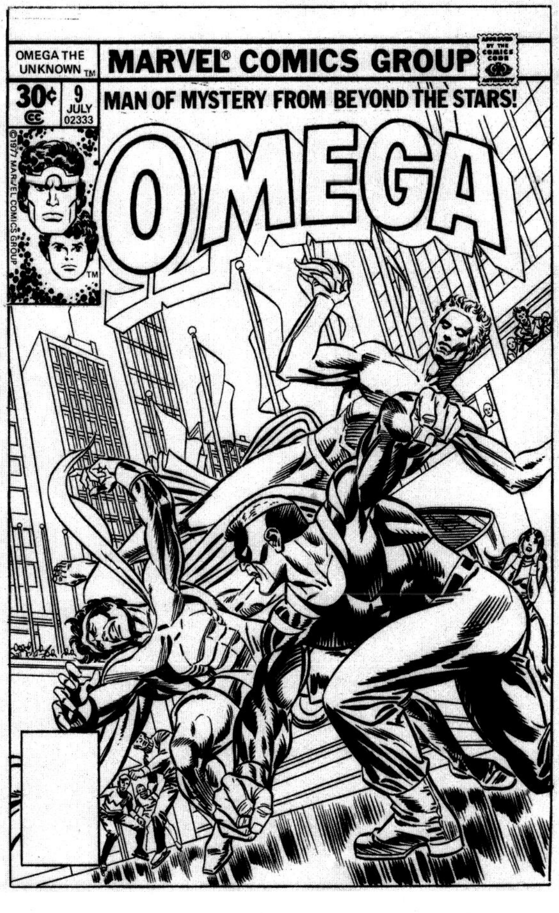
OMEGA THE UNKNOWN
MARVEL® COMICS GROUP
30¢ 9 JULY 02333
MAN OF MYSTERY FROM BEYOND THE STARS!
OMEGA

Kane was much happier working for Marvel. Indeed, he quickly began receiving assignments to do covers. Ultimately Kane became Marvel's chief cover artist turning out over 800 covers during his tenure. As the artist of so many covers, Kane had an obvious hand in helping mold the Marvel house style. Just as he had helped create the archetypal look of the art for DC Comics in the 1960s, Kane was again proving equally influential with a new generation of readers and artists with his work at Marvel. Just as Jack Kirby had dominated the style of Marvel comics throughout the 1960s, Kane had a significant impact upon Marvel in the 1970s. Indeed, Kane was one of the few

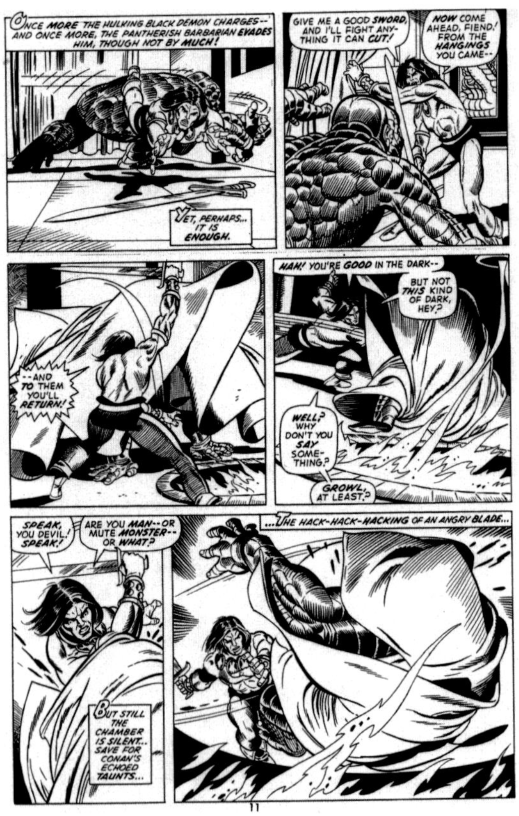
ONCE MORE THE HULKING BLACK DEMON CHARGES-- AND ONCE MORE, THE PANTHERISH BARBARIAN EVADES HIM, THOUGH NOT BY MUCH!
YET, PERHAPS... IT IS ENOUGH.
GIVE ME A GOOD SWORD, AND I'LL FIGHT ANY-THING IT CAN CUT!
NOW COME AHEAD, FIEND! FROM THE HANGINGS YOU CAME--
--AND TO THEM YOU'LL RETURN!
HAH! YOU'RE GOOD IN THE DARK--
BUT NOT THIS KIND OF DARK, HEY?
WELL? WHY DON'T YOU SAY SOME-THING?
GROWL, AT LEAST?
SPEAK, YOU DEVIL! SPEAK!
ARE YOU MAN--OR MUTE MONSTER-- OR WHAT?
BUT STILL THE CHAMBER IS SILENT... SAVE FOR CONAN'S ECHOED TAUNTS...
...THE HACK-HACK-HACKING OF AN ANGRY BLADE...
11

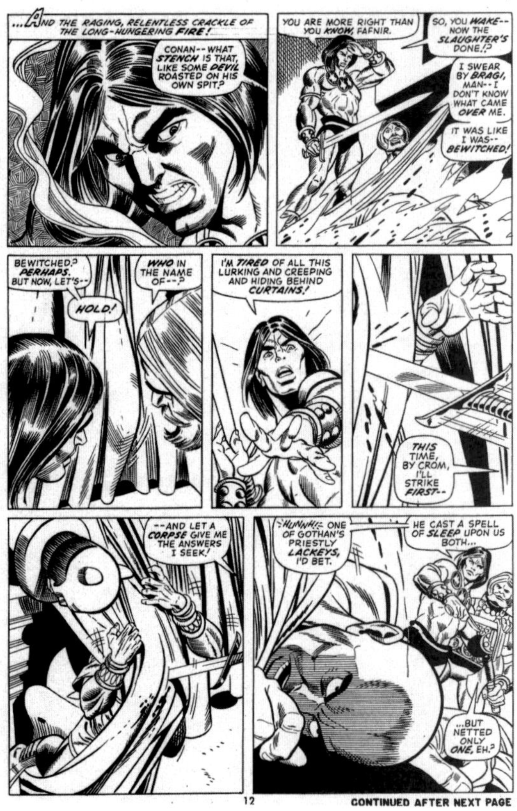
...AND THE RAGING, RELENTLESS CRACKLE OF THE LONG-HUNGERING FIRE!
CONAN--WHAT STENCH IS THAT, LIKE SOME DEVIL ROASTED ON HIS OWN SPIT?
YOU ARE MORE RIGHT THAN YOU KNOW, FAFNIR.
SO, YOU WAKE-- NOW THE SLAUGHTER'S DONE!?
I SWEAR BY BRAGI, MAN--I DON'T KNOW WHAT CAME OVER ME.
IT WAS LIKE I WAS-- BEWITCHED!
BEWITCHED? PERHAPS. BUT NOW, LET'S--
HOLD!
WHO IN THE NAME OF--?
I'M TIRED OF ALL THIS LURKING AND CREEPING AND HIDING BEHIND CURTAINS!
THIS TIME, BY CROM, I'LL STRIKE FIRST--
--AND LET A CORPSE GIVE ME THE ANSWERS I SEEK!
HUNNH! ONE OF GOTHAN'S PRIESTLY LACKEYS, I'D BET.
HE CAST A SPELL OF SLEEP UPON US BOTH...
...BUT NETTED ONLY ONE, EH?
12
CONTINUED AFTER NEXT PAGE

Original artwork for two sequential pages from *Conan the Barbarian* #78, Sept., 1977, Gil Kane, pencils, Ernie Chan, inks, ©2001 Marvel Characters, Inc.

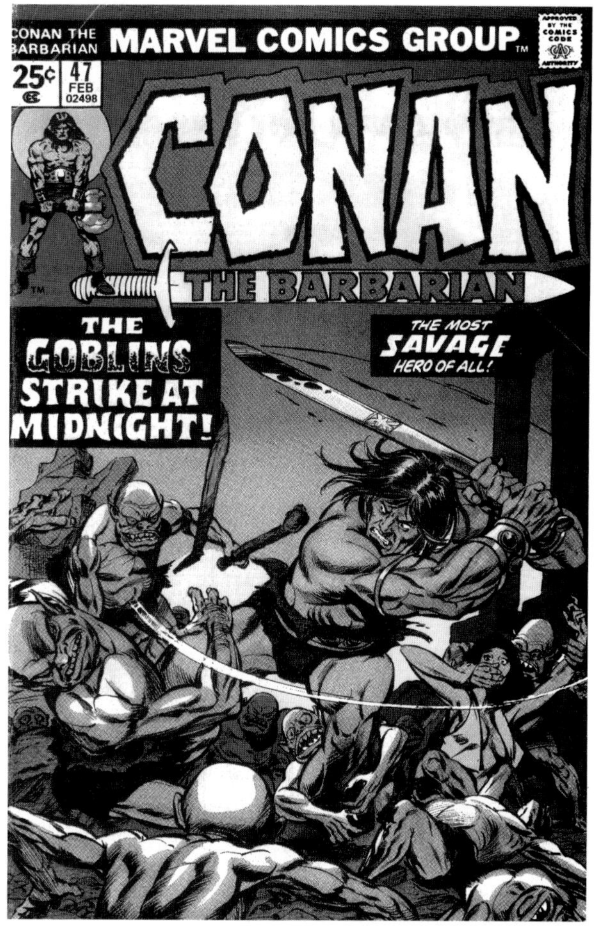

artists during the 1970s to publicly compliment Jack Kirby and acknowledge his importance as a major force in comics. During Kane's tenure at Marvel, he built on Kirby's dynamic approach, made Marvel's covers more fluid and refined, and established a singular style which was purely his own. Kane's cover work with Marvel had a level of quality which rivaled, and even surpassed Kirby's.

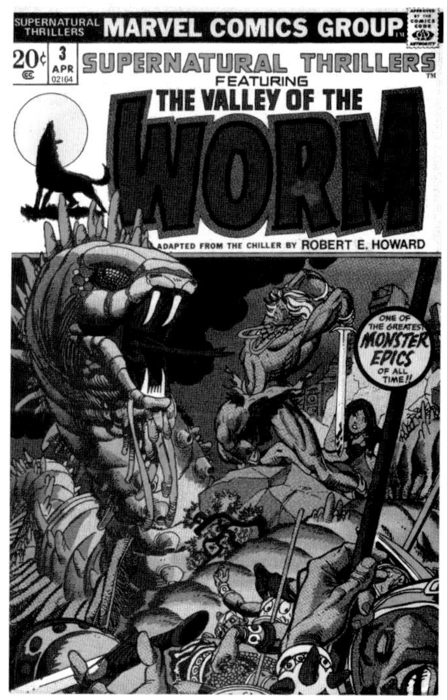

Kane was influential while at Marvel in other ways. He began to advocate Marvel's use of the *Conan* character, and, according to Kane, used his influence with the estate of Robert E. Howard to secure the rights to use the character for Marvel. Kane's passionate recommendations to use the character were not lost upon Thomas and Marvel's management.[2] In 1970 Marvel published a comic book utilizing the Conan character with art by Barry Windsor Smith and scripts by Thomas. Marvel's release of a Conan title sparked new and intense interest in the

Covers for *Conan the Barbarian* #47, Feb., 1975, Gil Kane, pencils, and *Supernatural Thrillers* #3, April, 1973, Gil Kane, pencils, Ernie Chan, inks, both ©2001 Marvel Characters, Inc.

Cover for *Marvel Premiere* #16, July, 1974, Gil Kane, pencils, Klaus Janson, inks. All covers in this section ©2001 Marvel Characters, Inc.

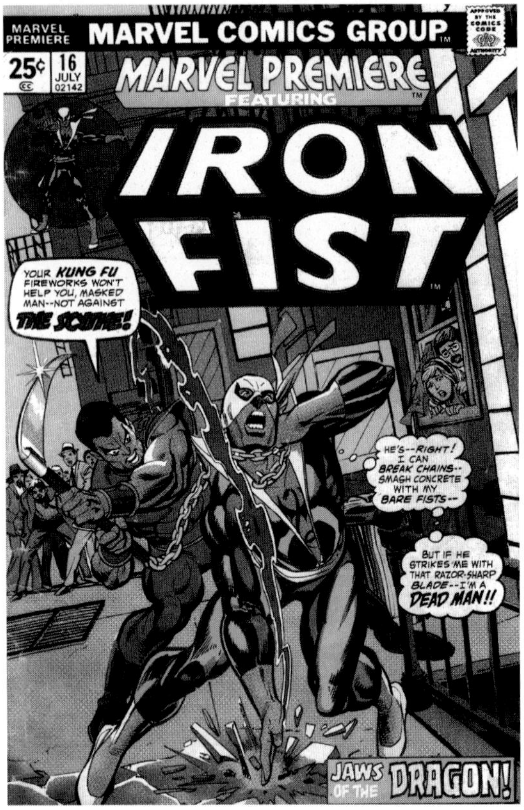

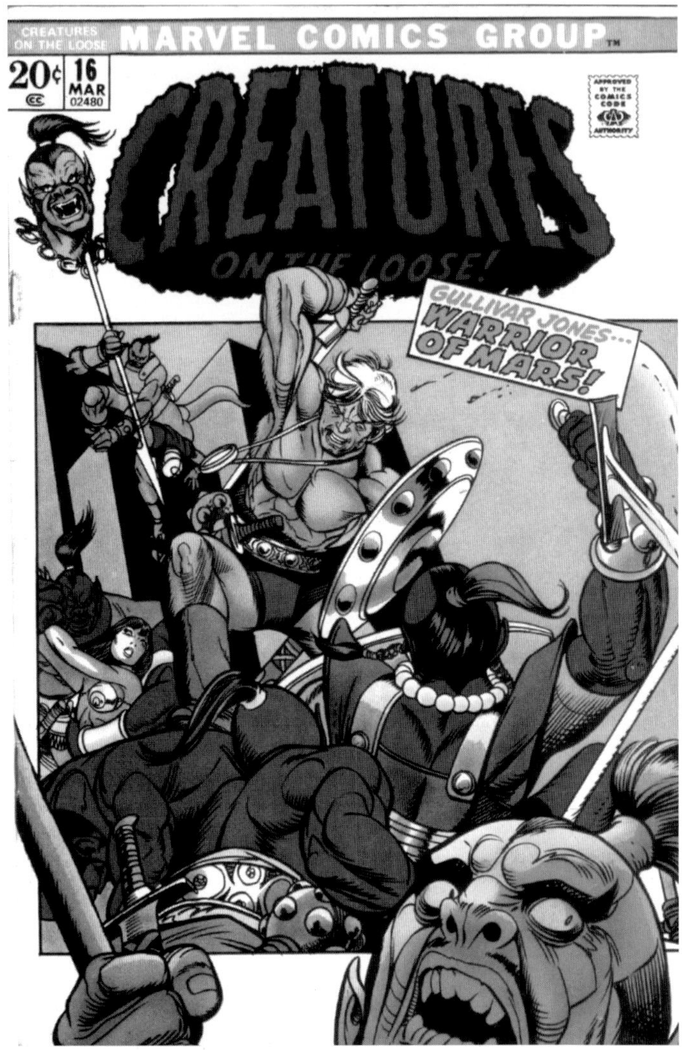

Cover for *Creatures on the Loose* #16, March, 1972, Gil Kane, pencils and inks.

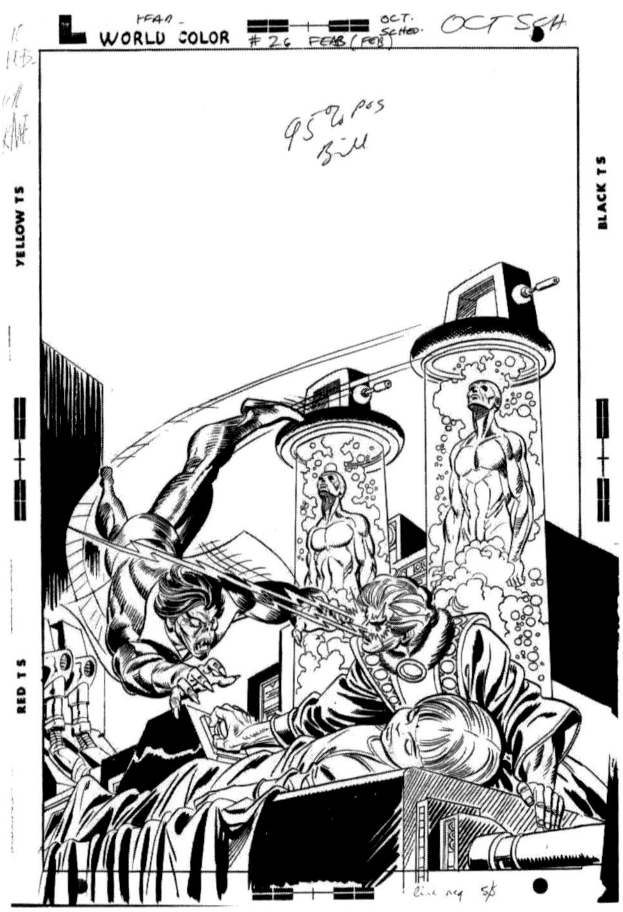

Original artwork for the cover for *Fear* #26, February, 1975, Gil Kane, pencils.

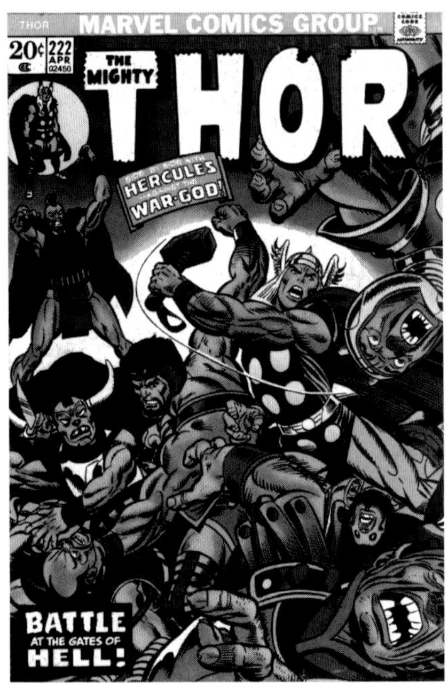

Cover for Thor #222, April, 1974, Gil Kane, pencils.

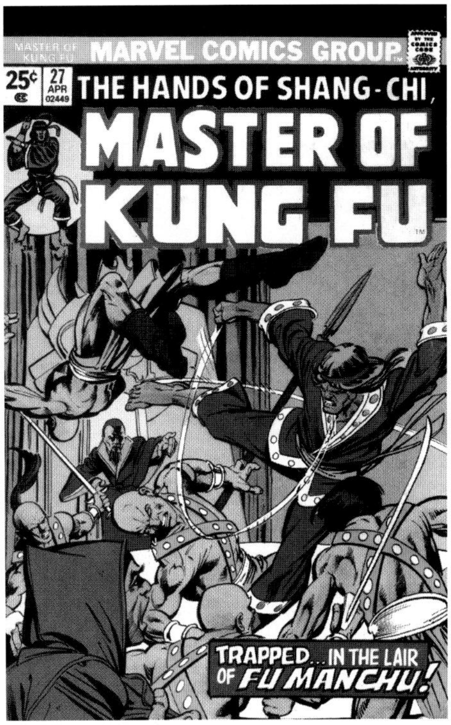
MARVEL COMICS GROUP
25¢ 27 APR 02449
THE HANDS OF SHANG-CHI,
MASTER OF KUNG FU
TRAPPED... IN THE LAIR OF FU MANCHU!

Cover for *Master of Kung Fu* #27, April, 1975, Gil Kane, pencils.

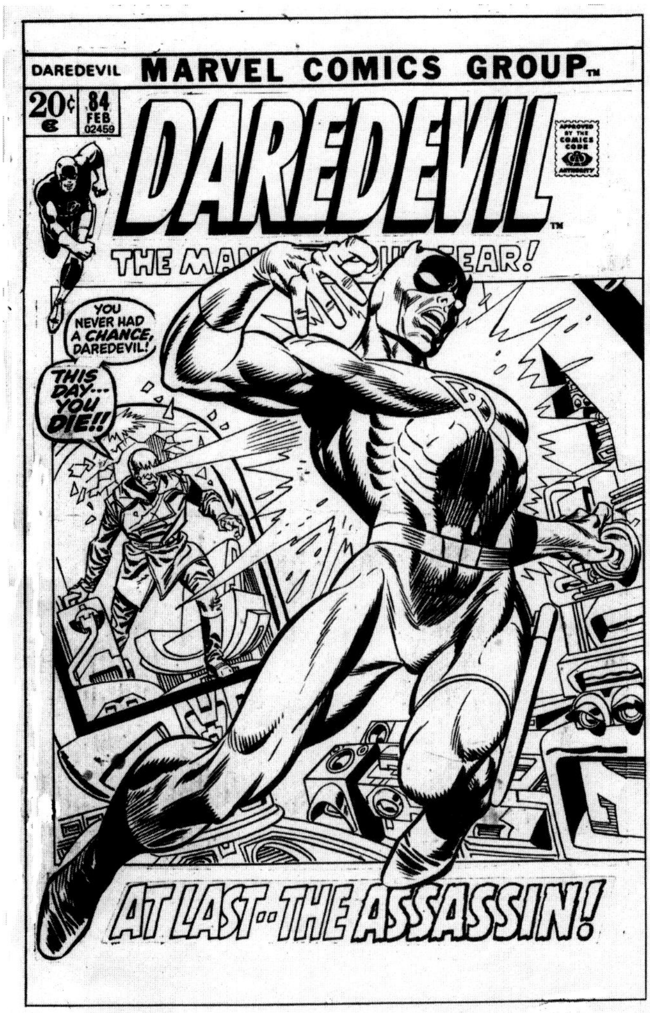
DAREDEVIL MARVEL COMICS GROUP
20¢ 84 FEB 02459
DAREDEVIL
YOU NEVER HAD A CHANCE, DAREDEVIL!
THIS DAY... YOU DIE!!
AT LAST--THE ASSASSIN!

Cover (a photostat of the original artwork with title and text paste ups on board, to be used for production purposes) for *Daredevil* #84, February, 1972, Gil Kane, pencils.

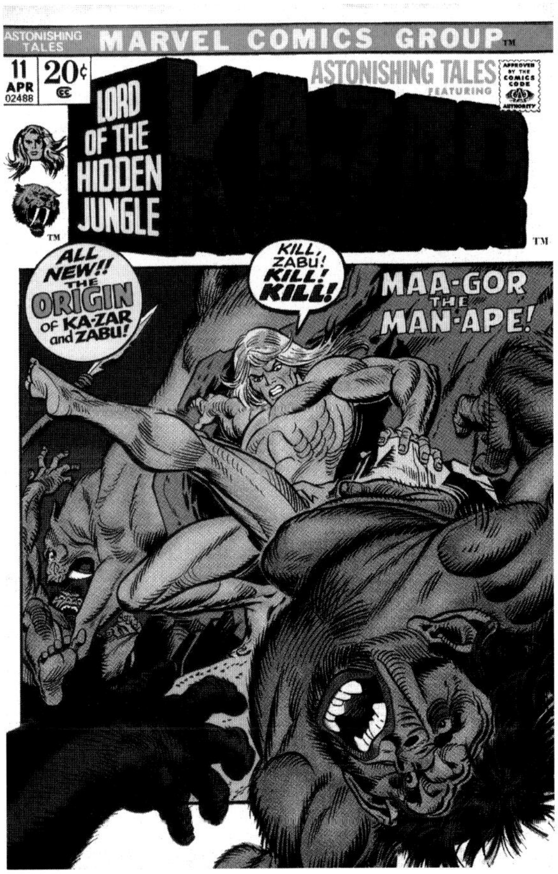
ASTONISHING TALES MARVEL COMICS GROUP
11 APR 02488 20¢
ASTONISHING TALES FEATURING
LORD OF THE HIDDEN JUNGLE
ALL NEW!! THE ORIGIN OF KA-ZAR and ZABU!
KILL, ZABU! KILL! KILL!
MAA-GOR THE MAN-APE!

Cover for *Astonishing Tales* #11, April, 1972, Gil Kane, pencils, Frank Giacoia, inks. Right: cover for *Supernatural Thrillers* #15, October, 1975, Gil Kane, pencils, Tom Palmer, inks.

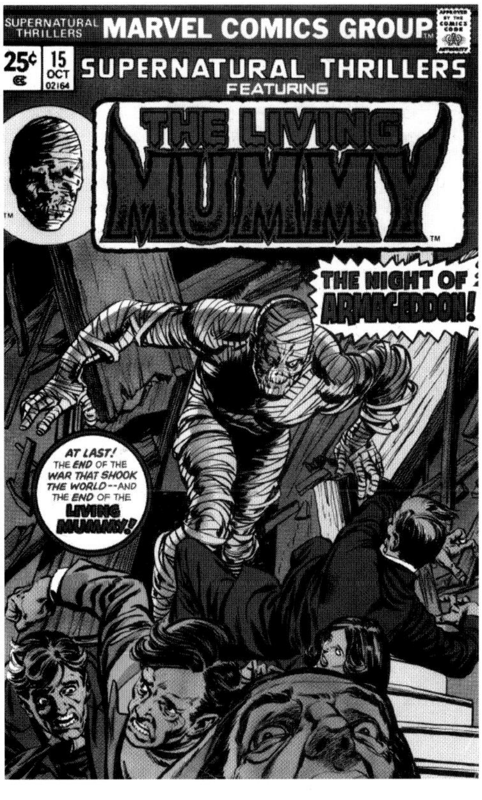
SUPERNATURAL THRILLERS MARVEL COMICS GROUP
25¢ 15 OCT 02164
SUPERNATURAL THRILLERS FEATURING
THE LIVING MUMMY
THE NIGHT OF ARMAGEDDON!
AT LAST! THE END OF THE WAR THAT SHOOK THE WORLD--AND THE END OF THE LIVING MUMMY!

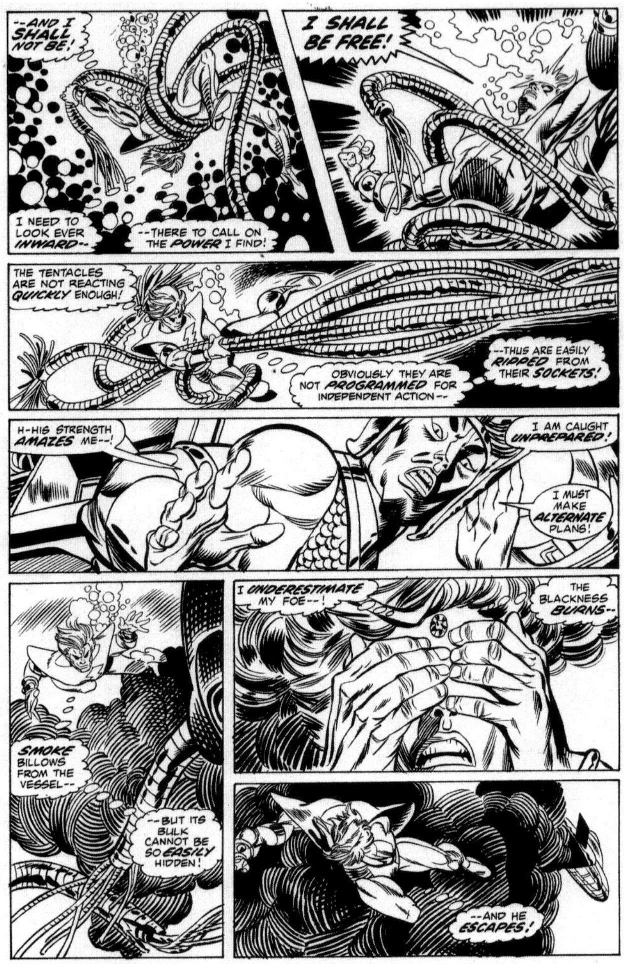
--AND I SHALL NOT BE!
I SHALL BE FREE!
I NEED TO LOOK EVER INWARD--
--THERE TO CALL ON THE POWER I FIND!
THE TENTACLES ARE NOT REACTING QUICKLY ENOUGH!
OBVIOUSLY THEY ARE NOT PROGRAMMED FOR INDEPENDENT ACTION--
--THUS ARE EASILY RIPPED FROM THEIR SOCKETS!
H-HIS STRENGTH AMAZES ME--!
I AM CAUGHT UNPREPARED!
I MUST MAKE ALTERNATE PLANS!
SMOKE BILLOWS FROM THE VESSEL--
--BUT ITS BULK CANNOT BE SO EASILY HIDDEN!
I UNDERESTIMATE MY FOE--!
THE BLACKNESS BURNS--
--AND HE ESCAPES!

Original artwork for an interior page from *Warlock*, Gil Kane, pencils, Tom Sutton, inks, ©2001 Marvel Characters, Inc.

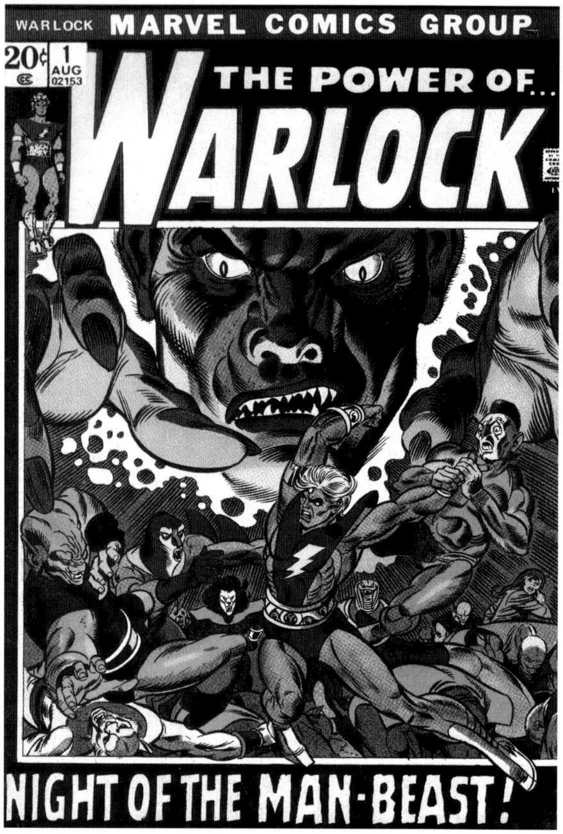
WARLOCK
MARVEL COMICS GROUP
20¢
1
AUG
02153
THE POWER OF...
WARLOCK
NIGHT OF THE MAN-BEAST!

Cover for *Warlock* #1, August, 1972, Gil Kane, pencils, Tom Sutton and John Romita, inks, ©2001 Marvel Characters, Inc.

Conan character, Howard's work, and the genre. Kane made memorable contributions to the many forms of Conan comics released by Marvel.[3]

In 1969, Kane and Thomas revamped the character Captain Marvel. This Captain Marvel, as opposed to the original 1940s Fawcett character of the same name, was a superhero alien. In Kane's incarnation of the character, Mar-Vell was imprisoned in another dimension called the Negative Zone. He came to earth by trading places with Rick Jones, a young man known to Marvel fans as a sidekick of both the Marvel superhero team, the Avengers, and to the

Incredible Hulk. Kane's artwork during his short run on this character, was thoughtful and handsome. Dan Adkins' inking of Kane's pencils kept with the spirit of his work rather than obscuring it.

Kane worked on many titles for Marvel during the 1970s. He worked on *The Amazing Spider-Man, Daredevil, Iron Man, Ka-Zar,* and *Conan the Barbarian*, among others.[4] Much of the time, however, Kane's interpretation of the characters on his covers was at odds with the interior stories, which were pencilled by different artists. In an effort to create a more consistent product, Kane's covers were frequently inked by inkers not sensitive to Kane's dynamics. Although these covers remain unmistakably Kane's work, the often heavy-handed manner in which they are

Kane's "rough"cover, side-by-side with the finished cover for *Giant-Size X-Men* #1, May, 1975, Gil Kane, pencils, Dave Cockrum, inks, ©2001 Marvel Characters, Inc.

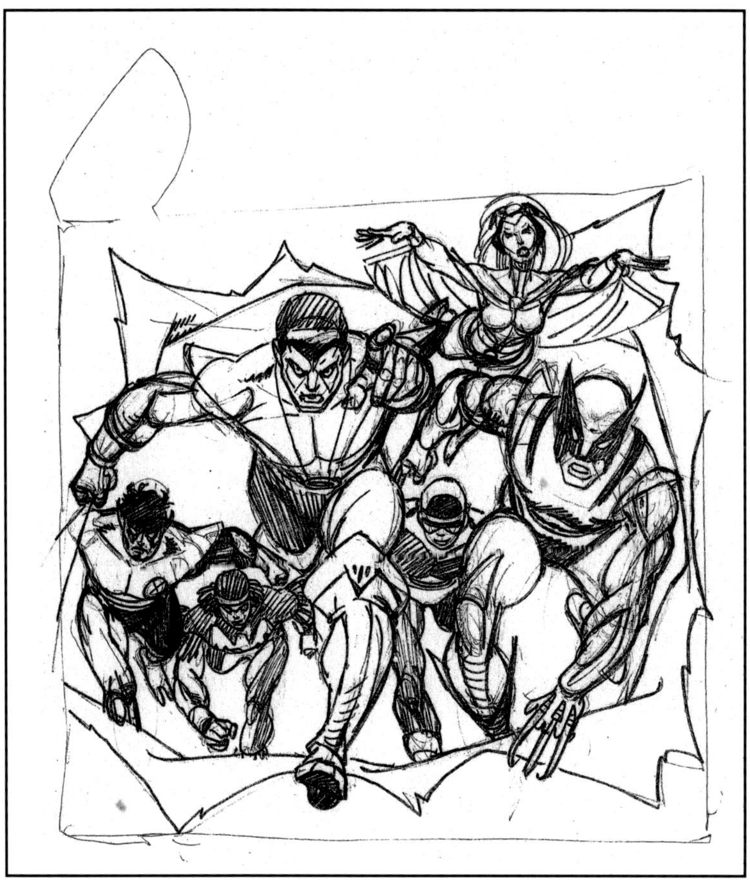

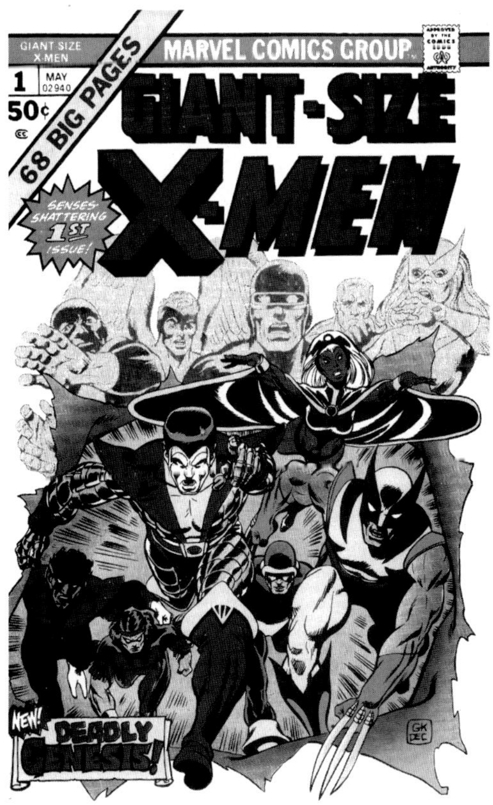

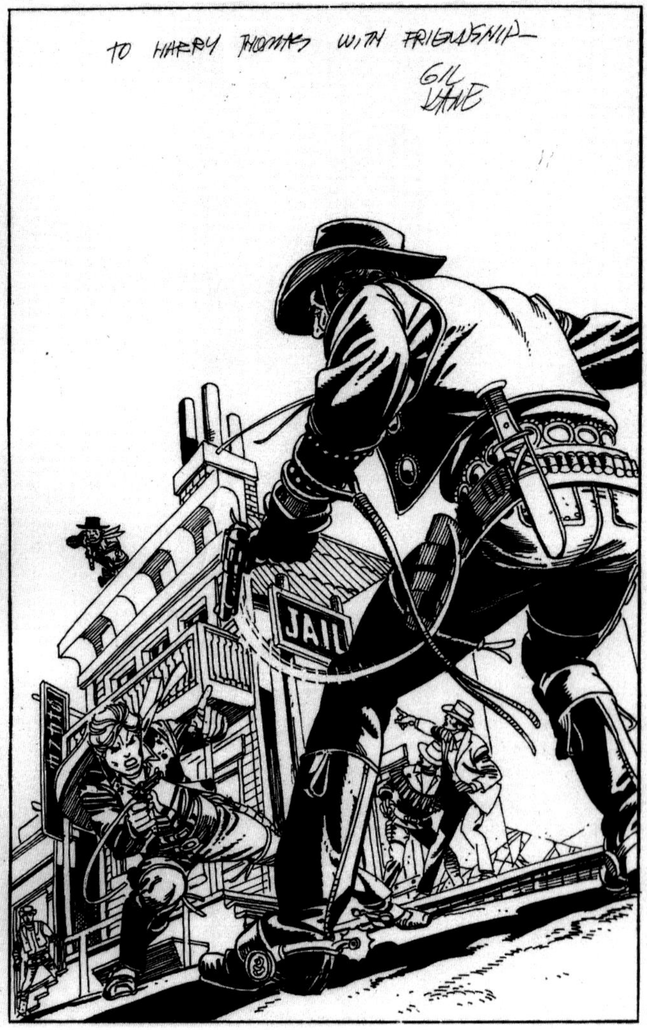

Original artwork for the cover for *Western Gunfighters* #30, July, 1975, Gil Kane, pencils and inks, ©2001 Marvel Characters, Inc. This cover has had all logos and text removed.

inked obscures the line and flow of Kane's drawing. Kane was not content to just create covers, however. Kane and Thomas created the character of Warlock, which was featured in *Marvel Premier* # 1, released in April, 1972. Kane, however, never committed to doing any one character for an extended period of time. He referred to himself as sort of "a hired gun" who came in, did his job and quickly went on to the next. The failure on Kane's part, to firmly identify himself with any one character for an extended period of time, was extremely short sighted, as artists gain popularity with fans through their long-term associations with the characters they work on.[5] While Kane contributed superlative work on many different titles, his fame rests on the extended work he did on the *Green Lantern* and *Atom* series, rather than on the work he did at Marvel.

Interestingly, while Kane is primarily associated with superheroes at Marvel, he experienced significant satisfaction working

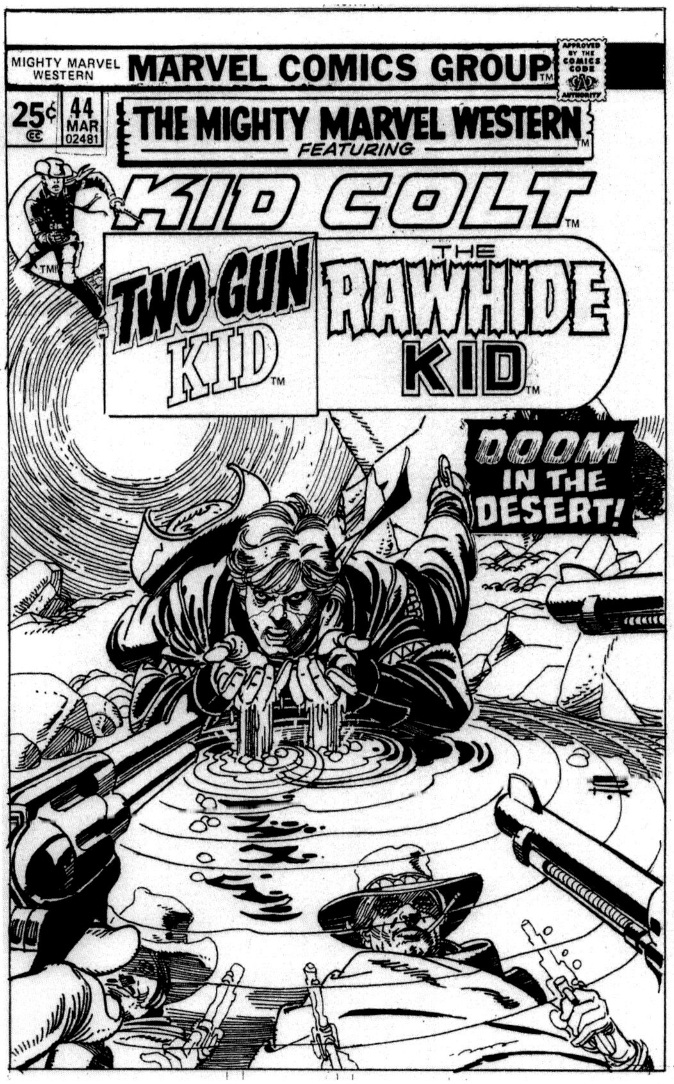

Original artwork for the cover for ***The Mighty Marvel Western* #44, March, 1976, Gil Kane, pencils and inks, ©2001 Marvel Characters, Inc. One of Kane's best western covers, this cover is beautifully composed and staged. Kane's inking perfectly suits the drawing. Of all the western covers Kane drew during his career, this was his favorite.**

on the cover art for western comic books. Since his days with *All-American Western, All-Star Western,* and *Hopalong Cassidy*, Kane had loved working on westerns. Indeed, some of Kane's favorite work, during his tenure at Marvel, was in drawing westerns rather than with the heroic, powerful, and omnipresent superheroes.

Kane's tenure with Marvel broke no new ground. During this period he did not venture back to attempt any extended graphic narratives. He did continue attempting to sell ideas for graphic novel projects with no success. The industry was not interested. Nevertheless, the industry was now following Kane's lead

Right: another Kane western cover, for *Western Gunfighters* #17, September, 1973, Gil Kane, pencils and inks, ©2001 Marvel Characters, Inc. This dynamic cover shows Kane's mastery of composition.

and publishing comic books in larger, black and white formats. For Kane it would be almost another twenty years before he would return to the extended narrative form. Kane had to be content with mainstream fare and to hope and dream for other opportunities.

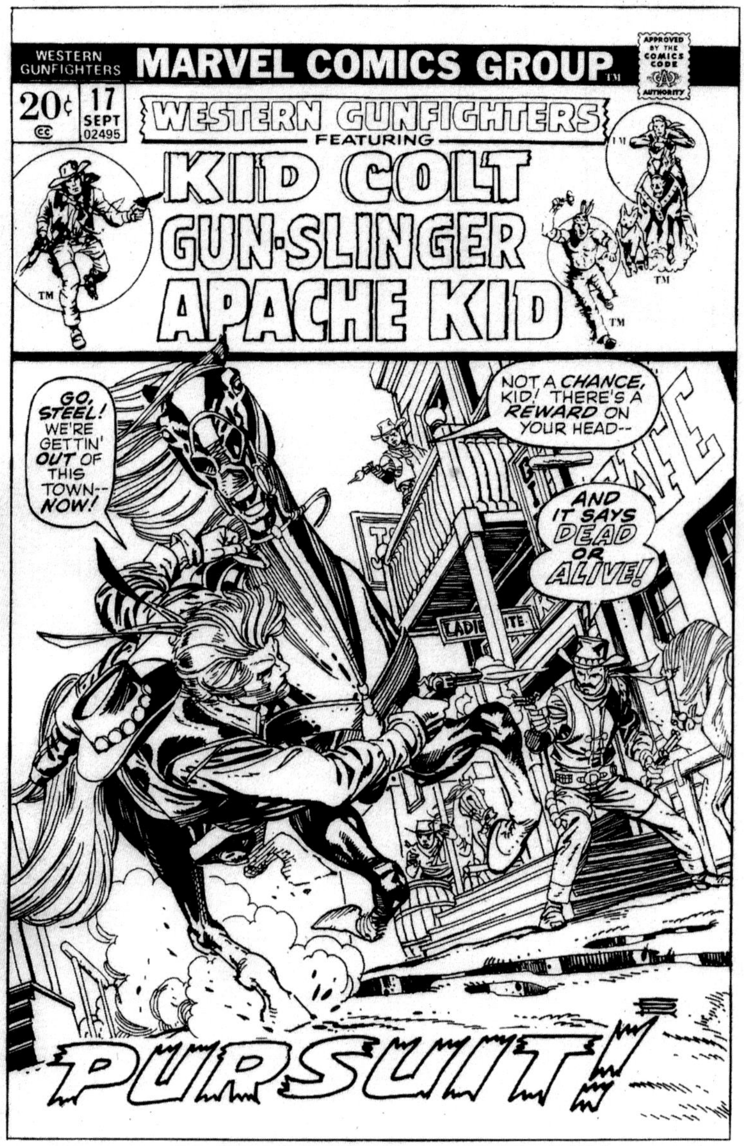
WESTERN GUNFIGHTERS
MARVEL COMICS GROUP
APPROVED BY THE COMICS CODE AUTHORITY
20¢ 17 SEPT 02495
WESTERN GUNFIGHTERS
FEATURING
KID COLT
GUN-SLINGER
APACHE KID
GO, STEEL! WE'RE GETTIN' OUT OF THIS TOWN-- NOW!
NOT A CHANCE, KID! THERE'S A REWARD ON YOUR HEAD--
AND IT SAYS DEAD OR ALIVE!
PURSUIT!

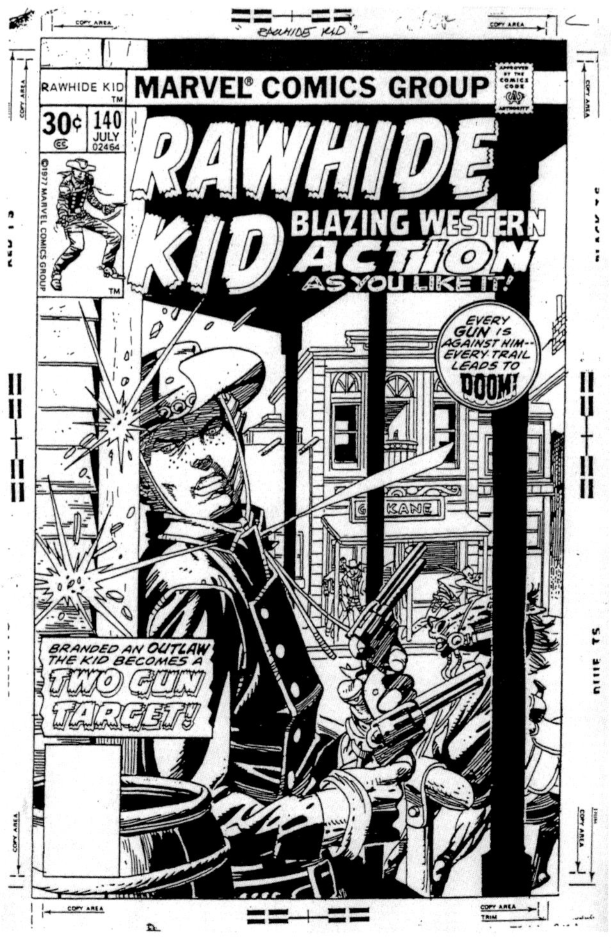
RAWHIDE KID
MARVEL COMICS GROUP
30¢ 140 JULY 02464
©1977 MARVEL COMICS GROUP
RAWHIDE KID
BLAZING WESTERN ACTION
AS YOU LIKE IT!
EVERY GUN IS AGAINST HIM-- EVERY TRAIL LEADS TO DOOM!
KANE
BRANDED AN OUTLAW THE KID BECOMES A TWO GUN TARGET!

Left: original artwork for the cover for *Rawhide Kid* #140, July, 1977, Gil Kane, pencils and inks, ©2001 Marvel Characters, Inc.

9 NEW ADVENTURES AND OPPORTUNITIES WITH STAR HAWKS

Kane was always looking for new opportunities.[1] He had always wanted work on a newspaper strip and in 1976, writer Ron Goulart, who was preparing a space/science fiction strip contacted him to see if he wanted to be the artist for the feature. Ultimately the strip was called *Star Hawks*. Initially, Goulart had been approached by John "Flash" Fairfield, the features editor of the Newspaper Enterprise Association (NEA) branch of United Media, who wanted to publish a science fiction strip with satirical elements.

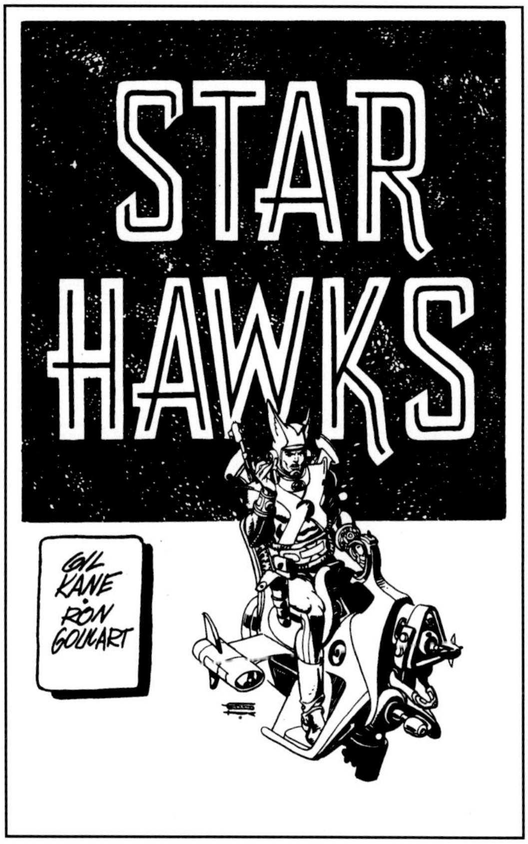

Goulart had worked out roughly two weeks of the continuity and was looking for an artist to collaborate with on the strip.[2] Goulart knew Kane previously as they had met at a party in Connecticut where they both lived. They had spoken at length about science fiction, newspaper

Above: the logo used for *Star Hawks* Sundays, all artwork in this chapter, Gil Kane, pencils and inks, ©2001 United Features Syndicate, Inc. Kane inked his *Star Hawks* strip with a fine line marker pen. This type of pen has a narrow point, which gave Kane's artwork a uniform line. For the rest of his career he inked with similiar marker pens.

strips, and comic books. Later, Kane introduced Goulart to Roy Thomas and, as a result, Goulart wrote several stories for Marvel. Kane and Goulart collaborated on some of this work, and worked comfortably together. Goulart told Fairfield that Kane would be perfect for the strip and he was right.

By Kane's account, when he was approached by Goulart the concept of the feature differed in many respects from the final version of the strip. Kane convinced Goulart that the strip should be a classic adventure with both romantic and satirical elements.

Star Hawks, unlike any daily strip before it, was planned in two tiers and, therefore, took up the space of two strips. Fairfield had planned for the strip to be presented in two equal sized horizontal tiers. Kane insisted that the

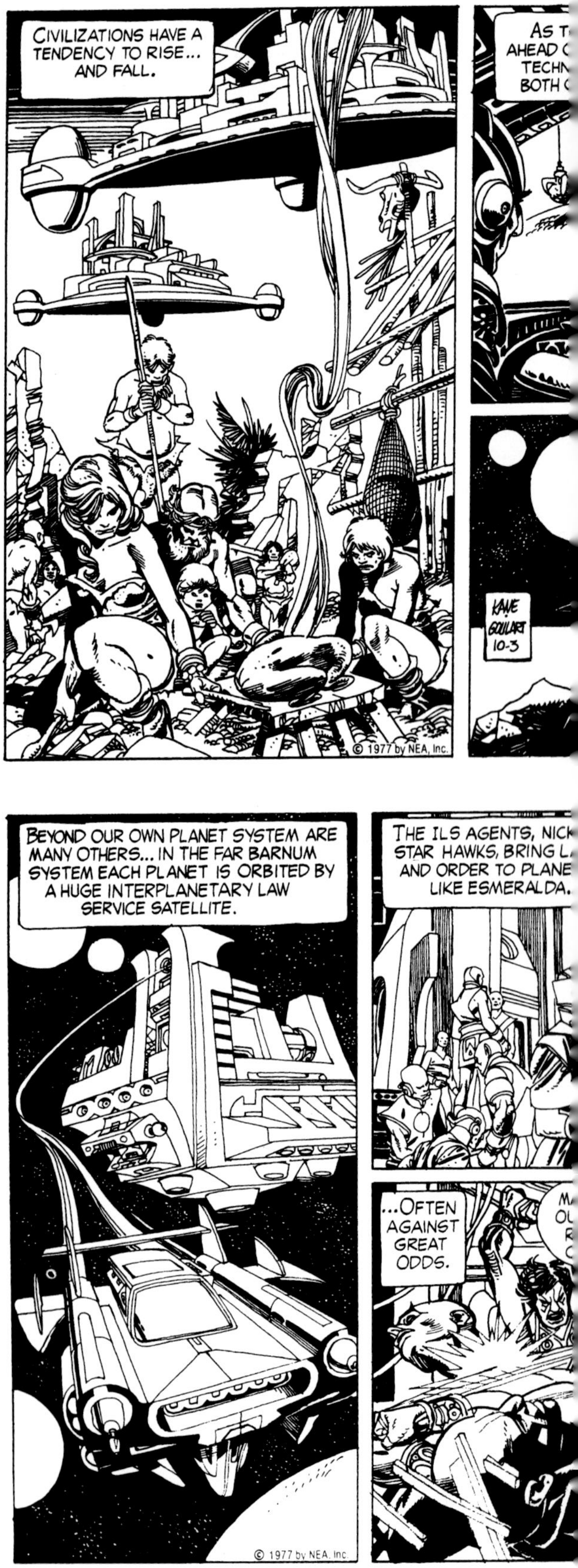
CIVILIZATIONS HAVE A TENDENCY TO RISE... AND FALL.
KANE GOULART 10-3
© 1977 by NEA, Inc.
BEYOND OUR OWN PLANET SYSTEM ARE MANY OTHERS... IN THE FAR BARNUM SYSTEM EACH PLANET IS ORBITED BY A HUGE INTERPLANETARY LAW SERVICE SATELLITE.
...OFTEN AGAINST GREAT ODDS.
© 1977 by NEA, Inc.

Center: the first two *Star Hawks* dailies, rarely reproduced in reprint versions of the strip. These dailies brought the art of comic books to the pages of daily newspapers, October 3-4, 1977.

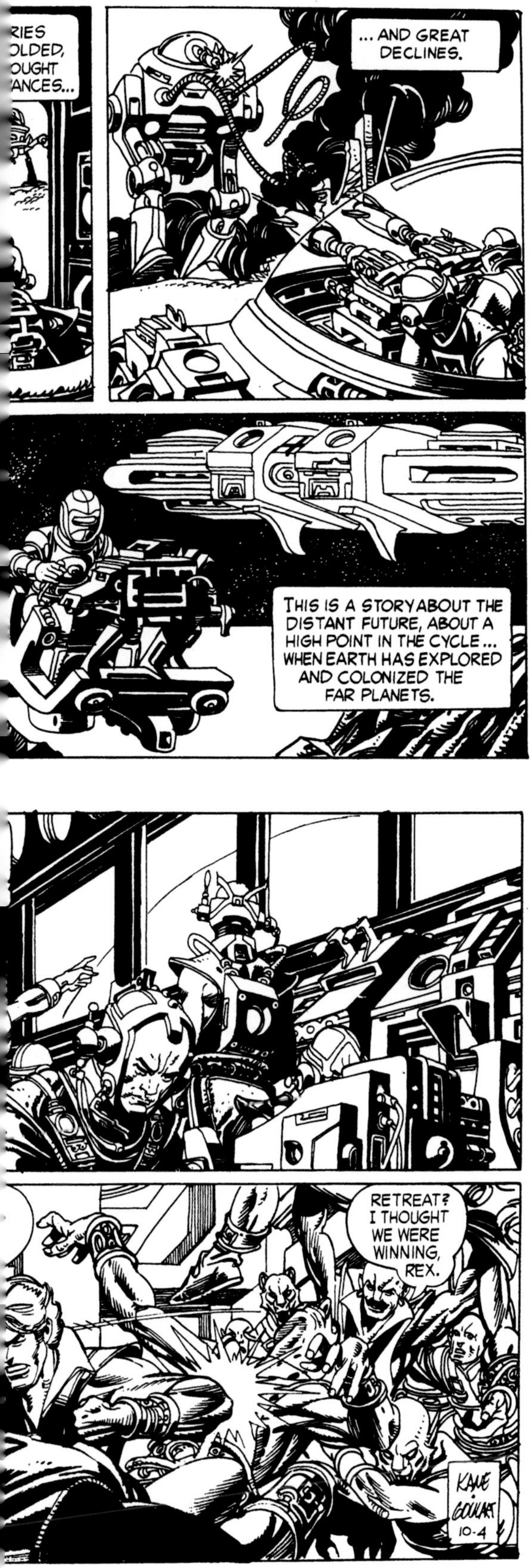
... AND GREAT DECLINES.
THIS IS A STORYABOUT THE DISTANT FUTURE, ABOUT A HIGH POINT IN THE CYCLE ... WHEN EARTH HAS EXPLORED AND COLONIZED THE FAR PLANETS.
RETREAT? I THOUGHT WE WERE WINNING, REX.
KANE GOULART 10-4

strip be laid out like a comic book page, using both the vertical and horizontal space available. Kane argued that if NEA published the strip as planned, it would have no visual impact. He insisted that to have a dramatic effect, the strip **had** to take advantage of the storytelling devices developed by comic books. Kane prevailed.

The format of the strip, as developed by Kane, allowed him to expand the potential of the story and to provide more visual impact than had ever been possible in a **daily** newspaper cartoon. Kane's sense of how to stage an adventure, together with his well-developed skill presenting figures and action, combined with Goulart's satirical sense and humor, made for many memorable adventures.

Although *Star Hawks* began by taking a swipe at *Star Wars*, it had nothing to do with the film and was conceived well before the release of the motion picture. *Star Hawks* was

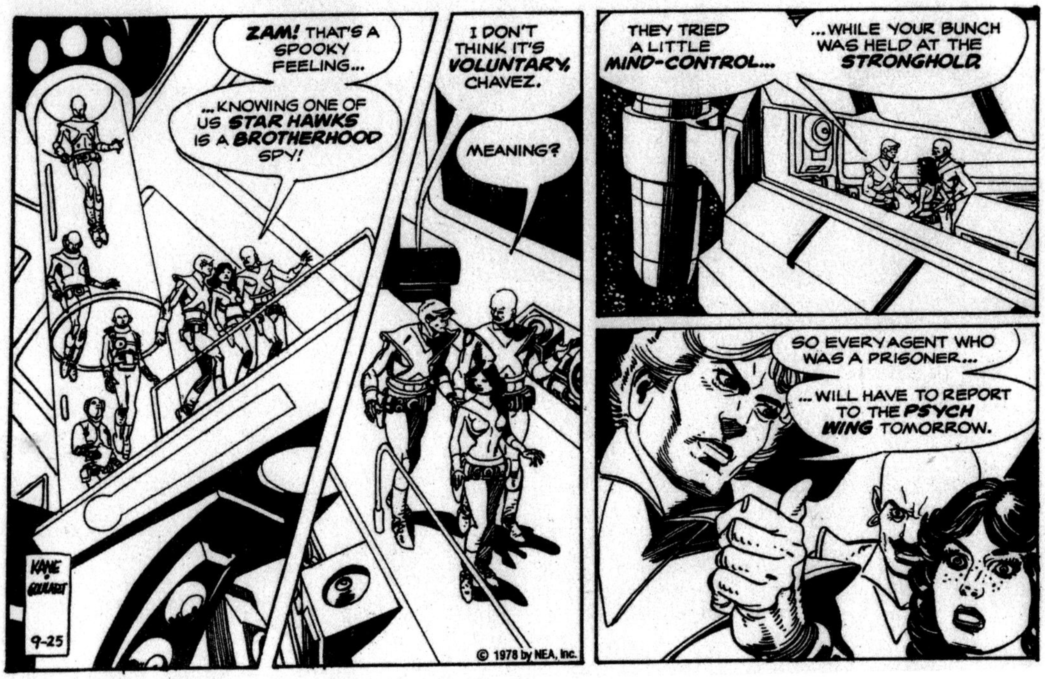
ZAM! THAT'S A SPOOKY FEELING...
...KNOWING ONE OF US STAR HAWKS IS A BROTHERHOOD SPY!
I DON'T THINK IT'S VOLUNTARY, CHAVEZ.
MEANING?
THEY TRIED A LITTLE MIND-CONTROL...
...WHILE YOUR BUNCH WAS HELD AT THE STRONGHOLD.
SO EVERY AGENT WHO WAS A PRISONER...
...WILL HAVE TO REPORT TO THE PSYCH WING TOMORROW.
KANE GOULART
9-25
© 1978 by NEA, Inc.

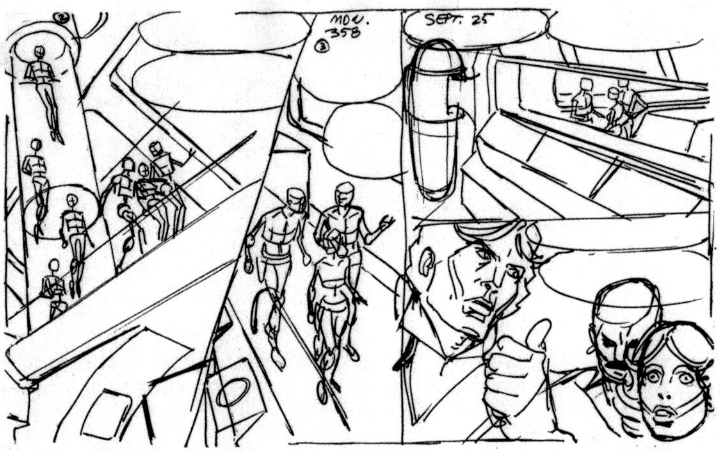
SEPT. 25

Above and left: ***Star Hawks*** **daily for September 25, 1977, with the corresponding layout drawing. The next two pages show two more strips in the continuity with their accompanying layout drawings. After the layout drawing was finished, Kane would enlarge it on a copying machine, place the copy on a lightbox, and use it as a guide for the finished strip.**

criticized for being nothing more than a *Star Wars* imitation, and nothing could have been further from the truth. First, there was very little that was original about *Star Wars*, as many of the characters, plot elements, and concept designs came directly from comic books (despite director George Lucas' attributing his influences to other, high minded, sources). Second, Kane had been working with science fiction material, as an artist, for over thirty-five years at the time of the creation of *Star Hawks*. He and Goulart were both extremely familiar with the conventions of pulp science fiction. In fact, rereading *Star Hawks,* more than twenty years after it was written, shows it to be classic pulp/ science fiction/adventure, with a sense of humor, augmented by Kane's lean, fluid drawing and choreography. The two-tier format, moreover, allowed Kane to develop the action and the story more cinematically **every day**. Prior to *Star Hawks,* only Sunday comic strips could boast the ability to develop an action story effectively in the space of one installment. The limited space afforded daily strips required that the

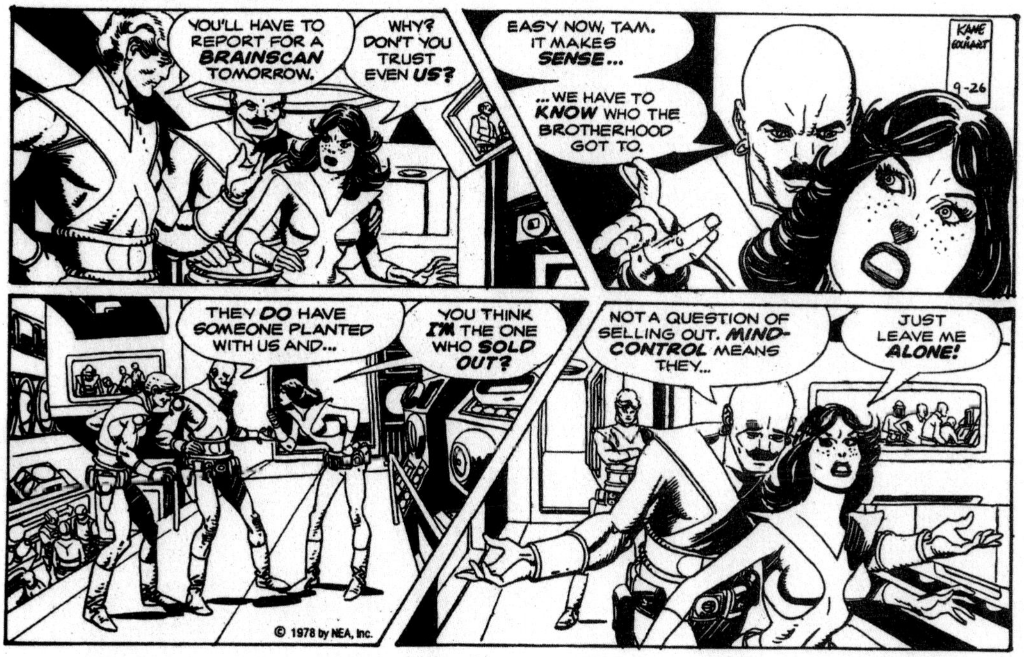
YOU'LL HAVE TO REPORT FOR A BRAINSCAN TOMORROW.
WHY? DON'T YOU TRUST EVEN US?
EASY NOW, TAM. IT MAKES SENSE...
...WE HAVE TO KNOW WHO THE BROTHERHOOD GOT TO.
KANE GOLDHART
9-26
THEY DO HAVE SOMEONE PLANTED WITH US AND...
YOU THINK I'M THE ONE WHO SOLD OUT?
NOT A QUESTION OF SELLING OUT. MIND-CONTROL MEANS THEY...
JUST LEAVE ME ALONE!
© 1978 by NEA, Inc.

***Star Hawks* daily for September 26, 1978, with its accompanying layout drawing.**

action and story be broken down and serialized. *Star Hawks* was a pioneering effort because it

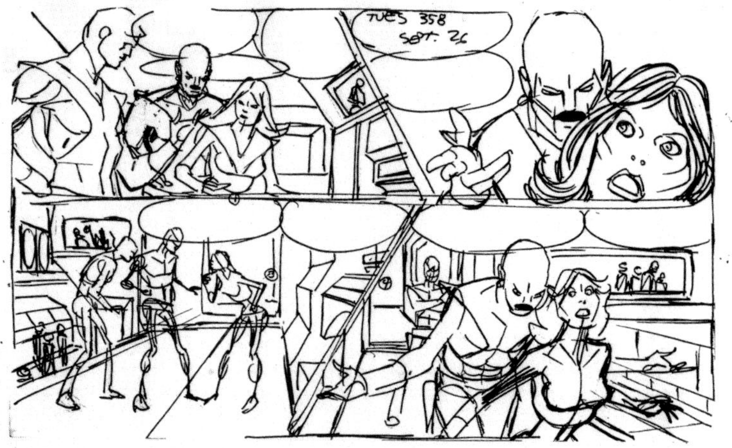
TUES 358
SEPT. 26

successfully told its story using an extended format.[3] *Star Hawks* is also interesting in the respect that it brought a comic book style to daily newspaper strips. Kane had come full circle, not only was he working as a newspaper strip artist, he was now bringing the art of comic books to the hallowed pages of newspaper strips. Although Kane was hardly the first comic book artist to work on a strip, he brought the unique perspective of comic books to newspaper strips, something his predecessors, who had

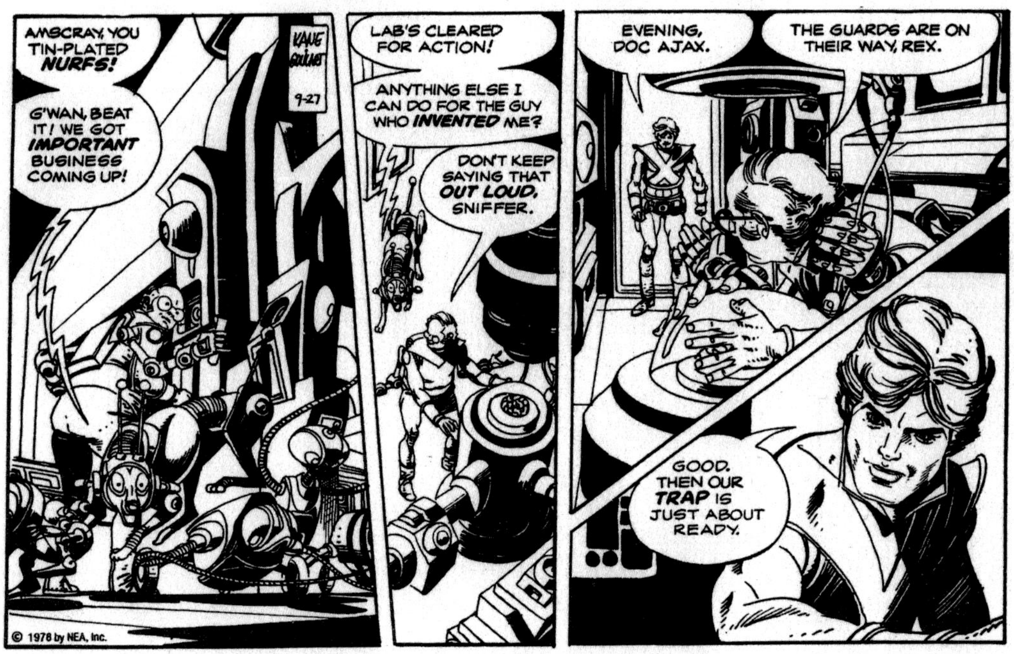
AMSCRAY, YOU TIN-PLATED NURFS!
G'WAN, BEAT IT! WE GOT IMPORTANT BUSINESS COMING UP!
KANE GOLDEN
9-27
LAB'S CLEARED FOR ACTION!
ANYTHING ELSE I CAN DO FOR THE GUY WHO INVENTED ME?
DON'T KEEP SAYING THAT OUT LOUD, SNIFFER.
EVENING, DOC AJAX.
THE GUARDS ARE ON THEIR WAY, REX.
GOOD. THEN OUR TRAP IS JUST ABOUT READY.
© 1978 by NEA, Inc.

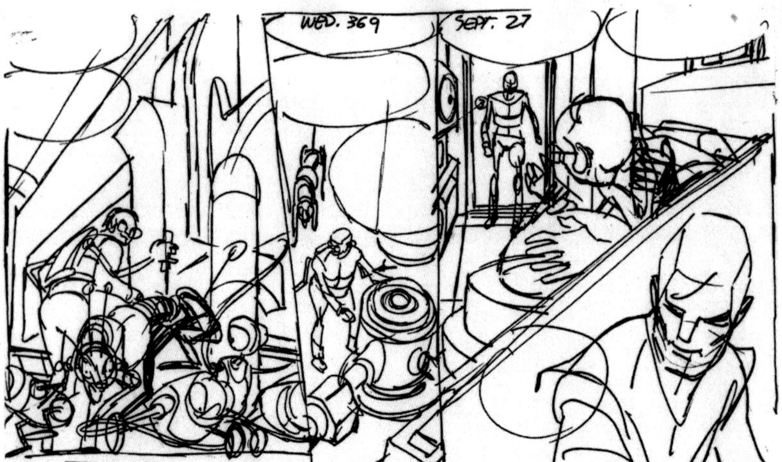
WED. 369
SEPT. 27

The final strip, in the three strip continuity, for the *Star Hawks* daily for September 27, 1978, with its accompanying layout drawing.

graduated from the comic books to strips, had failed to do. Kane never lost sight of his roots in comic books, and this served the *Star Hawks* strip well.

During Kane's run on the *Star Hawks* strip, he also drew the continuity for the *Tarzan* Sunday strip. Since Kane's youth, he had admired the work that Hal Foster and Burne Hogarth had contributed for the *Tarzan* Sundays, and finally, Kane too, had an opportunity to interpret the Tarzan myth.

Star Hawks ran for three and a half years before being cancelled.[4] In 1979, Kane became ill with gall bladder problems, and for the first time in his life was unable to work. He briefly turned to his one time assistant, Howard Chaykin, and to Ernie Colon to ghost the feature.[5] Kane made a quick recovery and returned to work, but this would not be the last time illness would intervene in his life.

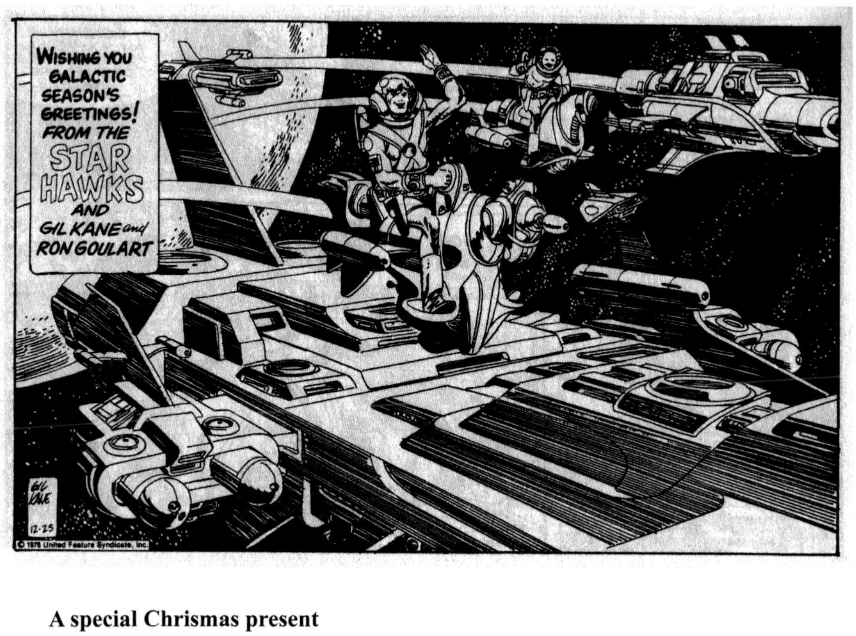
WISHING YOU GALACTIC SEASON'S GREETINGS! FROM THE
STAR HAWKS
AND
GIL KANE and RON GOULART
12-25

A special Chrismas present to readers from Kane and writer Ron Goulart from December 25, 1978.

10 BACK IN THE MAINSTREAM AND ON TO HOLLYWOOD

By the end of Kane's run with *Star Hawks* he was approaching sixty, an age when most artists of comics are either burned out, have gone on to other professions, or are contemplating retirement. Kane, however, continued to produce high quality work, which he considered the best of his career. His work was now mature and more completely realized than ever before. Kane was able to tell stories and depict the human figure in action, effortlessly.

During the 1980s, Kane continued to appear at comic book conventions and frequently spoke at length regarding his views on the art of the comics and comics in general.[1] He also gave many interviews in which he made his opinions on the art of the comics, and everything else regarding the comics, well known. Notable among these

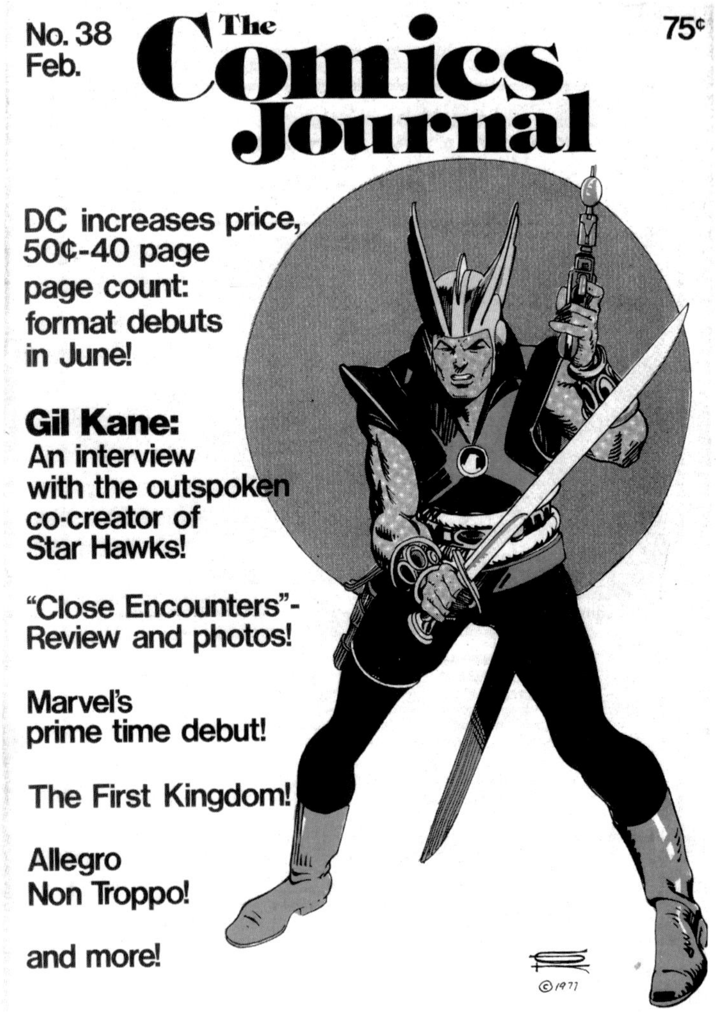
No. 38
Feb.
The Comics Journal
75¢
DC increases price, 50¢-40 page page count: format debuts in June!
Gil Kane:
An interview with the outspoken co-creator of Star Hawks!
"Close Encounters"- Review and photos!
Marvel's prime time debut!
The First Kingdom!
Allegro Non Troppo!
and more!
©1977

Cover for *The Comics Journal* #38, February, 1977, ©2001 Fantagraphics Books, Inc. Kane was interviewed many times by the editor of *The Comics Journal*, Gary Groth.

interviews were those given to *The Comics Journal*. Gary Groth, who published *The Comics Journal*, interviewed Kane in many of these edited dialogues and his familiarity with Kane was helpful in

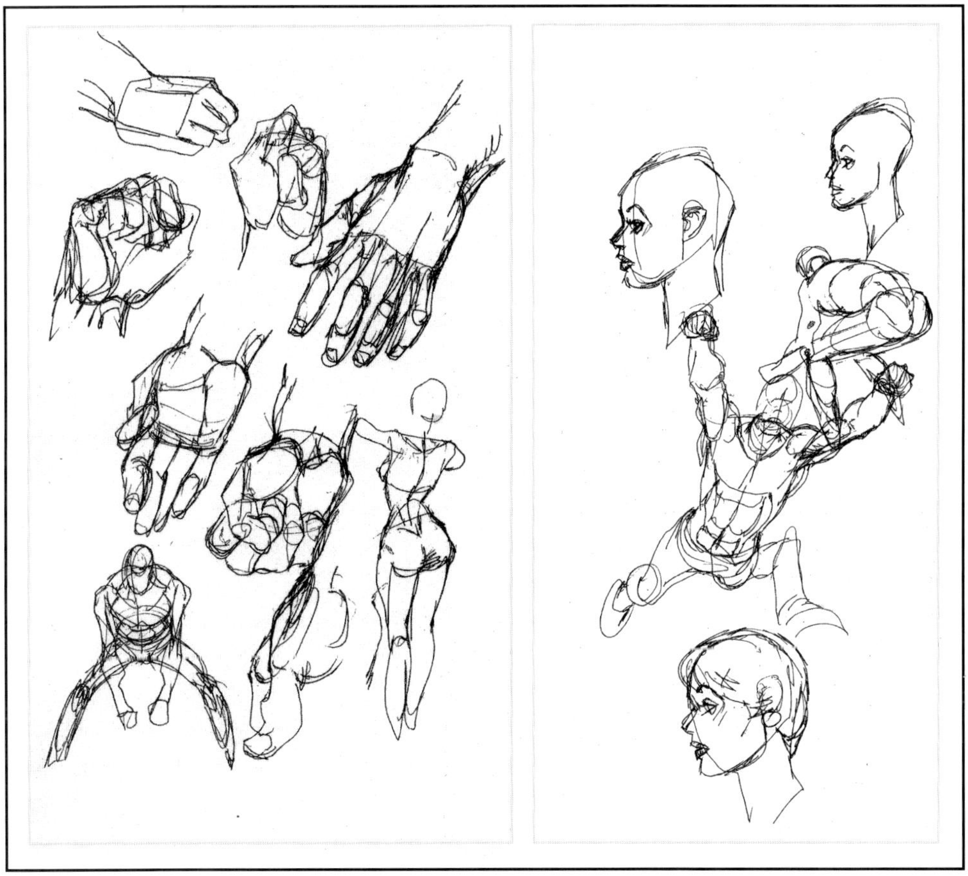

developing a better understanding of Kane and his work. Kane, through these interviews and through his candid comments at many conventions, became one of the most significant oral chroniclers of the history of comic strips and comic books. Kane's strong personality and

Kane did warm-up or practice sketches every day. He focused great energy and care in drawing and redrawing the human form. Above: two examples of his warm-up sketches.

acerbic style dominated many informal discussions with panels of other artists and writers at such conventions. Kane was keenly aware of the history of cartooning and how comic books, as a medium, fit within the greater context of twentieth century culture. He made it clear to all those who asked, and to those who would listen, that for the most part,

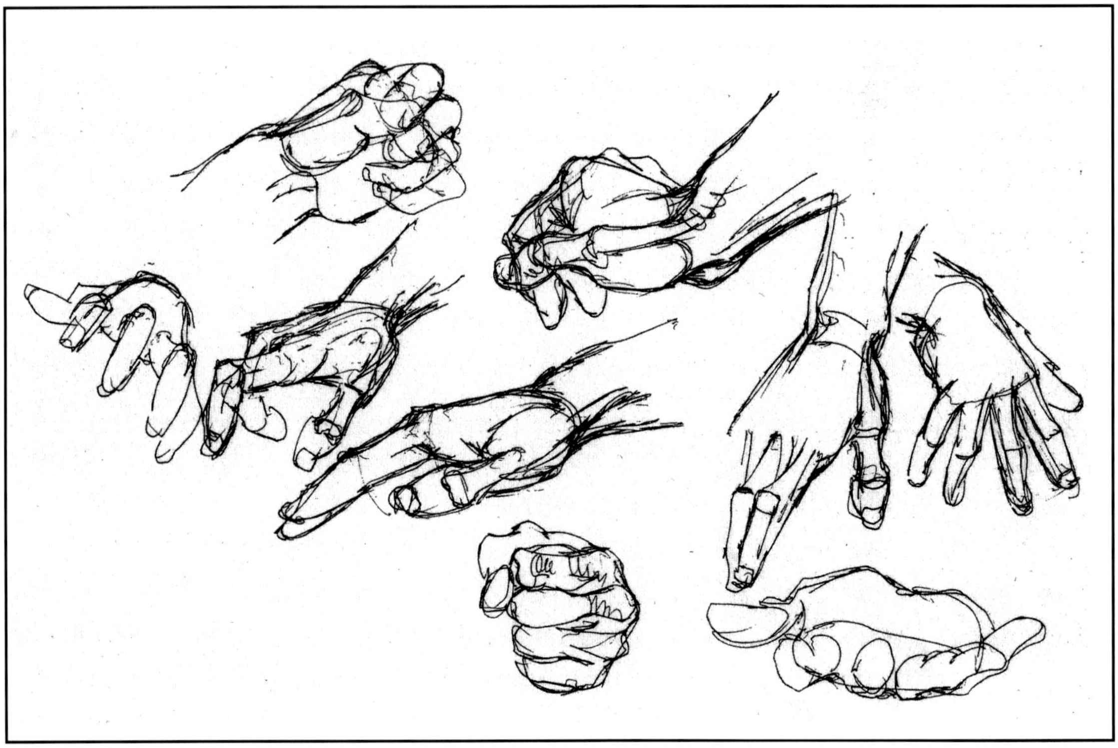

comic books never succeeded in being more than a craft which churned out a product with such speed that the artists and writers involved could produce very little of significance and artistic import. Frequently, during extended monologues on his own work, he expressed

Kane took great pains to practice drawing every facet of human anatomy.

disappointment with his inability to more fully develop his work.

Indeed, publicly and privately with his friends, Kane often professed a

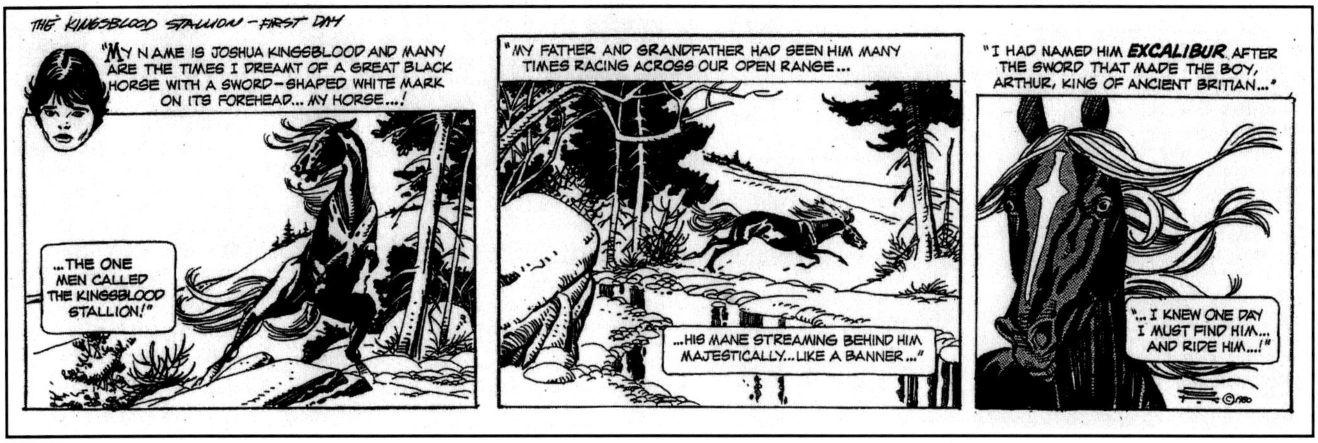
THE KINGSBLOOD STALLION - FIRST DAY
"MY NAME IS JOSHUA KINGSBLOOD AND MANY ARE THE TIMES I DREAMT OF A GREAT BLACK HORSE WITH A SWORD-SHAPED WHITE MARK ON ITS FOREHEAD... MY HORSE...!
...THE ONE MEN CALLED THE KINGSBLOOD STALLION!"
"MY FATHER AND GRANDFATHER HAD SEEN HIM MANY TIMES RACING ACROSS OUR OPEN RANGE...
...HIS MANE STREAMING BEHIND HIM MAJESTICALLY...LIKE A BANNER..."
"I HAD NAMED HIM EXCALIBUR AFTER THE SWORD THAT MADE THE BOY, ARTHUR, KING OF ANCIENT BRITIAN..."
"... I KNEW ONE DAY I MUST FIND HIM... AND RIDE HIM...!"

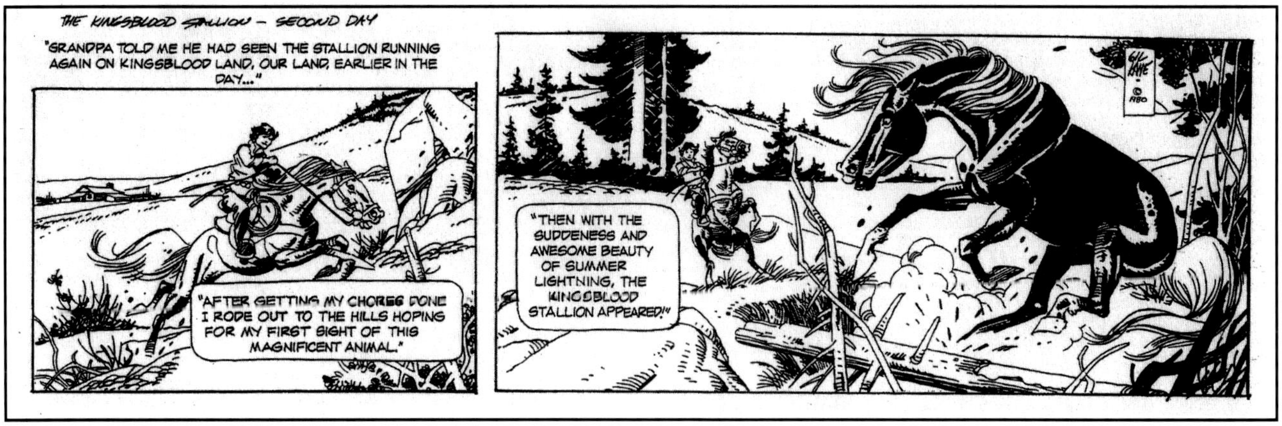
THE KINGSBLOOD STALLION - SECOND DAY
"GRANDPA TOLD ME HE HAD SEEN THE STALLION RUNNING AGAIN ON KINGSBLOOD LAND, OUR LAND, EARLIER IN THE DAY..."
"AFTER GETTING MY CHORES DONE I RODE OUT TO THE HILLS HOPING FOR MY FIRST SIGHT OF THIS MAGNIFICENT ANIMAL."
"THEN WITH THE SUDDENESS AND AWESOME BEAUTY OF SUMMER LIGHTNING, THE KINGSBLOOD STALLION APPEARED!"

dissatisfaction with the quality of his work. He openly acknowledged that he could produce hundreds of finished pages over a several month period, and that he sacrificed artistic integrity in the name of being paid to deliver large amounts of

In 1980 Kane prepared a continuity of six daily strips for a proposed series entitled *The Kingsblood Stallion*. The strip, a western, shows Kane's affection for the genre and is beautifully composed and drawn. Unfortunately, the strip never sold. Above: the first two dailies for the proposed strip. All dailies from this continuity, Gil Kane, pencils and inks, ©2001 The Estate of Gil Kane.

finished work. Kane's self doubt, however, was not entirely justified. Despite his production of large quantities of work, in retrospect, the quality of the design and execution, is extremely high in quality. Although much of the work Kane produced during the last twenty years of his life was not inspired, there are numerous examples which extend beyond mere craft, and exhibit what Kane was truly capable of. As with many disciplines within the greater context of twentieth century art, comic art, at its best, transcends its commercial origins and achieves the status of art. Despite his own reservations, during the last two decades of his career, Kane produced extremely rigorous and well-developed graphic stories. It is important to note the emphasis here is

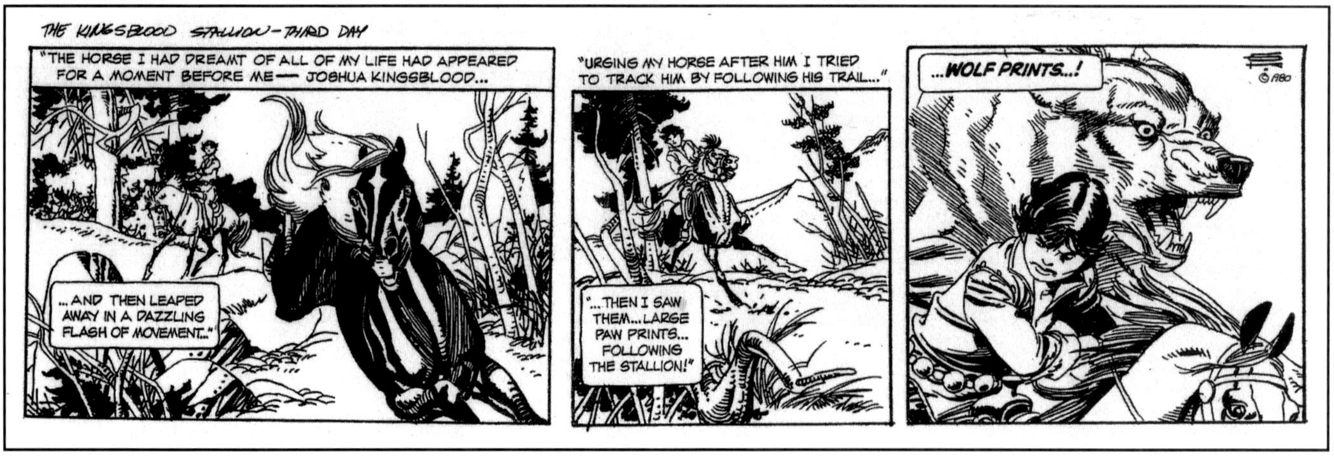
THE KINGSBLOOD STALLION—THIRD DAY
"THE HORSE I HAD DREAMT OF ALL OF MY LIFE HAD APPEARED FOR A MOMENT BEFORE ME— JOSHUA KINGSBLOOD...
"...AND THEN LEAPED AWAY IN A DAZZLING FLASH OF MOVEMENT..."
"URGING MY HORSE AFTER HIM I TRIED TO TRACK HIM BY FOLLOWING HIS TRAIL..."
"...THEN I SAW THEM...LARGE PAW PRINTS... FOLLOWING THE STALLION!"
...WOLF PRINTS...!

The third consecutive strip in the continuity, from Kane's unpublished western strip, *The Kingsblood Stallion.*

on the importance of **storytelling** because, ultimately, to transcend its roots as mere commerce, comic art must be completely and seamlessly integrated with its story. Due to Kane's understanding of his medium, he was able to accomplish this fusion.

Kane continued trying to pitch stories and ideas to publishers. In 1983, with the help of writer Jan Strnad, Kane took *The Atom* and gave the strip a well-developed contemporary treatment. Kane had decided to take the Atom away from his superhero orientation and to recast the character in a primitive setting where the Atom would wield a sword and rely upon his wits. Kane submitted an outline to DC Comics, which was approved. He plotted the material and Strnad made contributions to the plot and wrote the dialogue and text. The result of this four-issue mini-series and two subsequent specials was impressive. Although the story-line did have soap operatic qualities, it gave the main characters depth and set into motion an interesting turn of events, taking the normally rather staid Atom character to the Amazon, where he is unable to return to

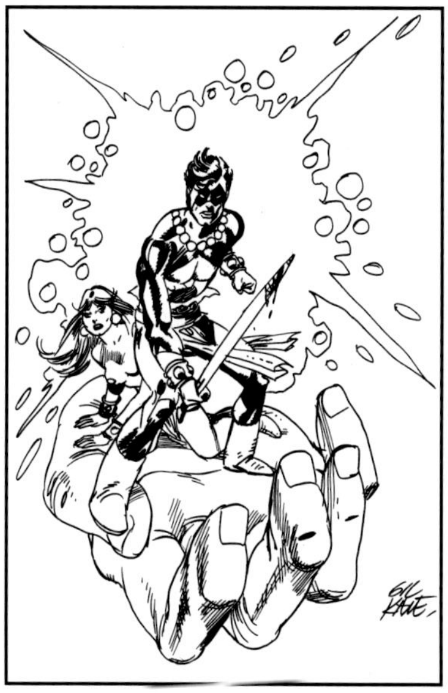

Kane's 1980s rendition of the Atom, *Sword of the Atom*, unpublished original artwork, Gil Kane, pencils and inks, ©2001 DC Comics.

normal size once he is reduced to six inches. There he finds a Lilliputian race in conflict, and lends his talents to overthrow an unwise king. The action is precipitated when the Atom's alter ego, Ray Palmer, discovers that his wife, Jean Loring, is having an affair. Inevitably, Loring travels to South American to find Palmer/the Atom. Kane proved with the *Sword of the Atom* series that he was still at the top of his game as a comic artist. Not only is the *Sword of the Atom* series intelligently assembled and scripted, it is admirably shaped and crafted by Kane. The ease with which Kane handles the staging and development of the story was clear evidence that he had developed his personal language of form beyond a mere craft and to an **art**. The *Sword of the Atom* series was a prime example that Kane, who at the

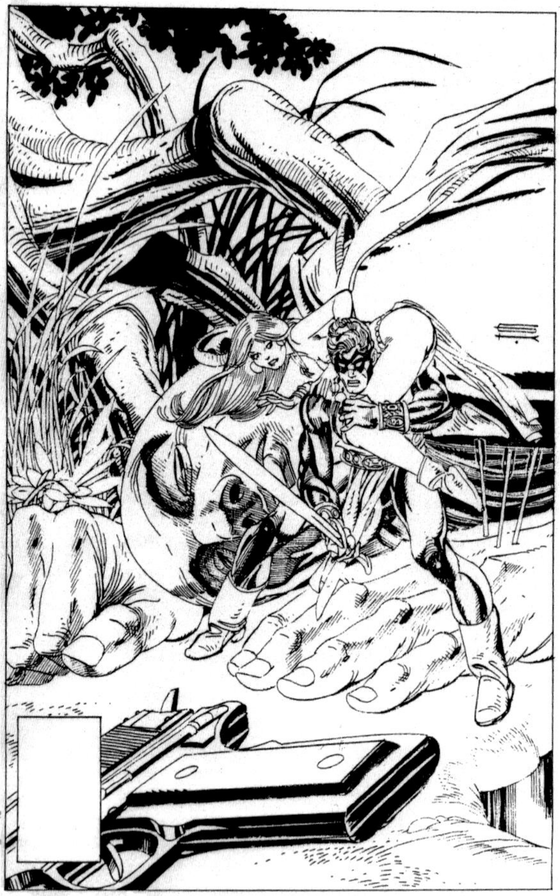

Original artwork for the cover for *Sword of the Atom Special* #1, 1984, Gil Kane, pencils and inks, ©2001 DC Comics.

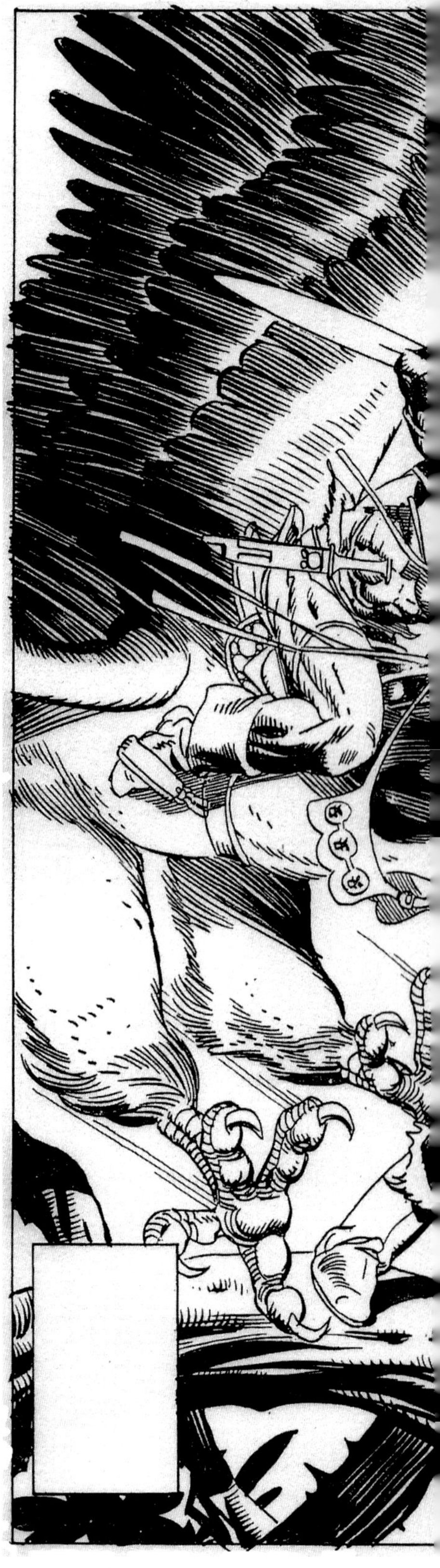

Original artwork for the cover for *Sword of the Atom Special* #2, 1985, Gil Kane, pencils and inks, ©2001 DC Comics.

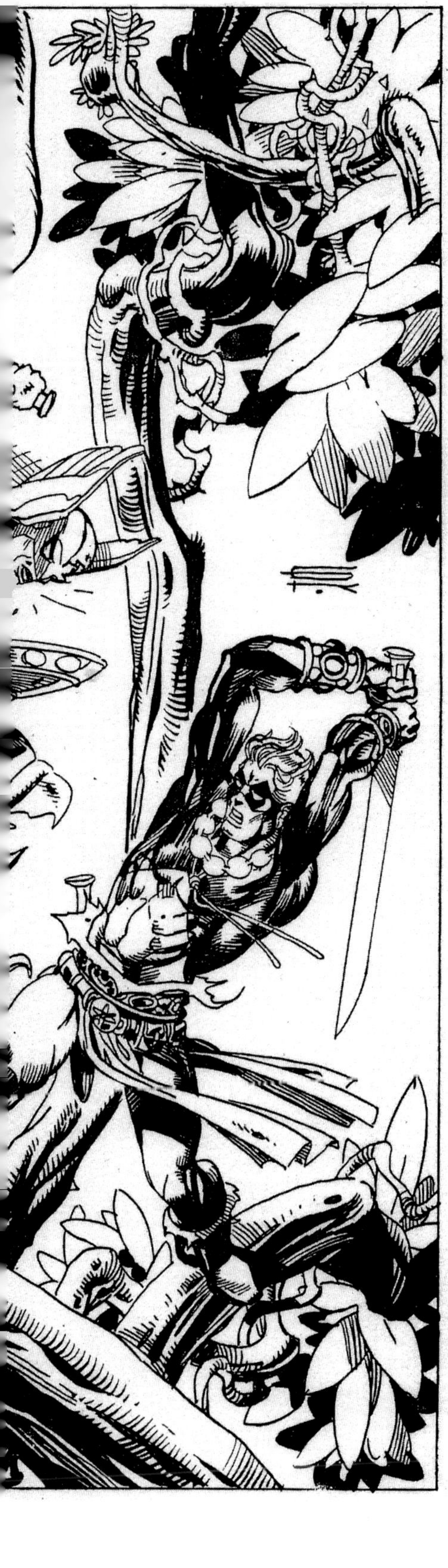

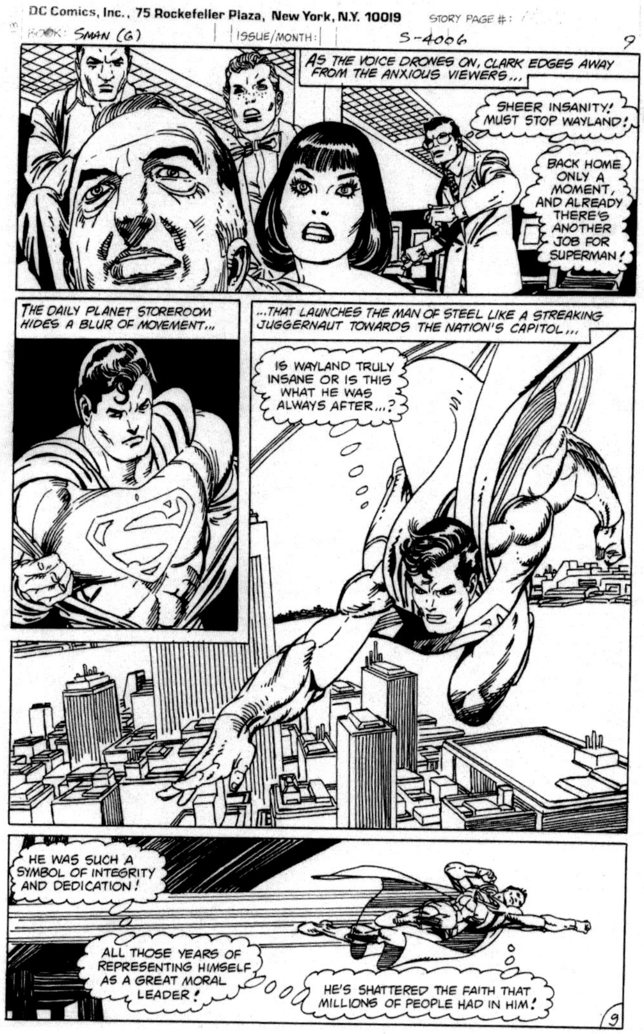
DC Comics, Inc., 75 Rockefeller Plaza, New York, N.Y. 10019
AS THE VOICE DRONES ON, CLARK EDGES AWAY FROM THE ANXIOUS VIEWERS...
SHEER INSANITY! MUST STOP WAYLAND!
BACK HOME ONLY A MOMENT, AND ALREADY THERE'S ANOTHER JOB FOR SUPERMAN!
THE DAILY PLANET STOREROOM HIDES A BLUR OF MOVEMENT...
...THAT LAUNCHES THE MAN OF STEEL LIKE A STREAKING JUGGERNAUT TOWARDS THE NATION'S CAPITOL...
IS WAYLAND TRULY INSANE OR IS THIS WHAT HE WAS ALWAYS AFTER...?
HE WAS SUCH A SYMBOL OF INTEGRITY AND DEDICATION!
ALL THOSE YEARS OF REPRESENTING HIMSELF AS A GREAT MORAL LEADER!
HE'S SHATTERED THE FAITH THAT MILLIONS OF PEOPLE HAD IN HIM!

time was 57 years old, was still capable of producing work which rivaled not only his remaining second generation peers, but also the up and coming stars of the comic book world. The *Sword of the Atom* was also the first time Kane received royalties for his work at DC Comics. Things were indeed changing in the industry, unfortunately, much too late to benefit Kane in a meaningful way.

Kane also turned in attractive work on *Superman* and the *Green Lantern*, along with other

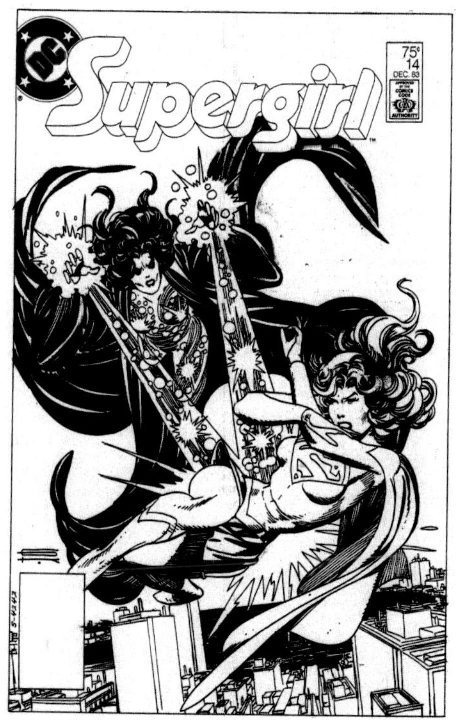
DC
Supergirl
75¢
14
DEC. 83

Above: original artwork for an interior page for *Superman Special* #1, 1983, Gil Kane, pencils and inks, ©2001 DC Comics. Right: original artwork for the cover for *Supergirl* #14, December, 1983, Gil Kane, pencils and inks, ©2001 DC Comics.

Left: original artwork for the cover for *Green Lantern* #166, July, 1983, Gil Kane, pencils and inks, DC Comics. Right: artwork for the inside front cover for *Micronauts* #45, September, 1982, Marvel Characters, Inc.

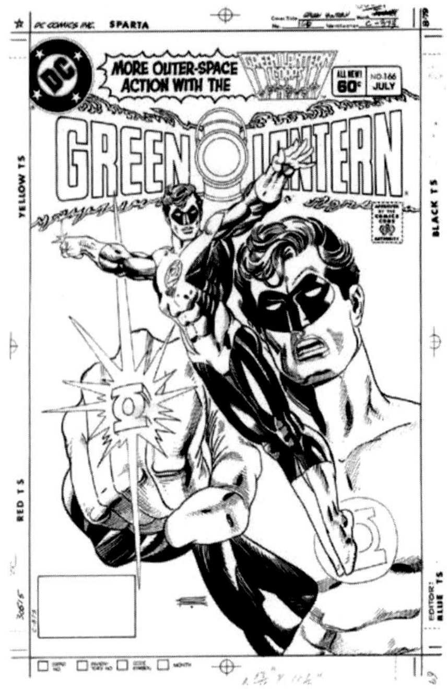
MORE OUTER-SPACE ACTION WITH THE
60¢
GREEN LANTERN

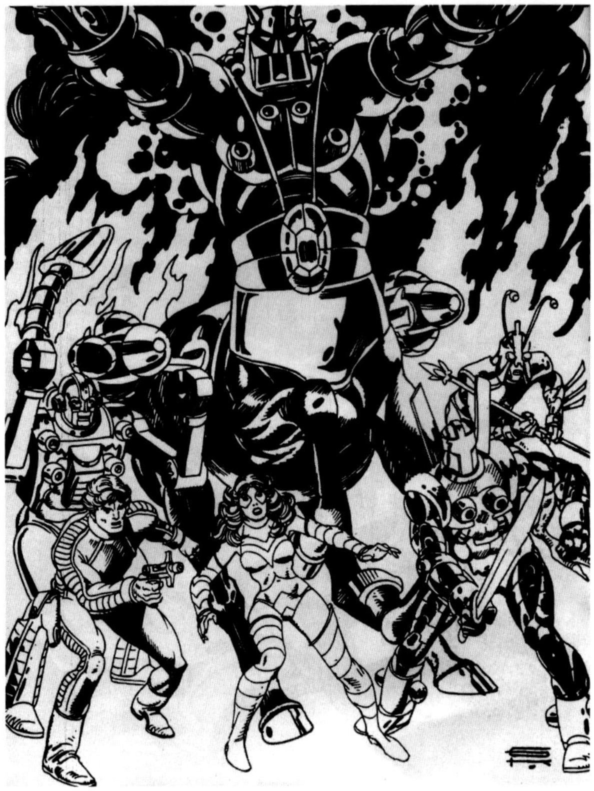

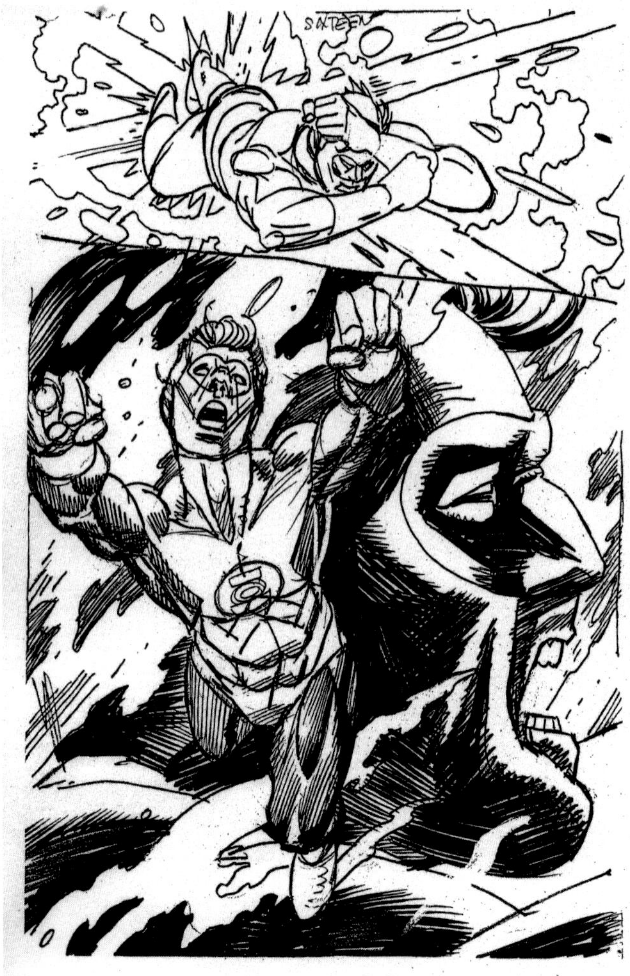

Above: original pencil layout for an interior page for *The Green Lantern Corps* #224, May, 1988, Gil Kane, pencils, ©2001 DC Comics.

work he was doing for DC Comics.

Kane also continued to make contributions to Marvel comics. He worked on Conan stories; did concept designs, stories, and covers for *Micronauts;* and a charming serialization of Rudyard Kipling's *Jungle Book* in *Marvel Fanfare*. Kane's work on the *Jungle Book* stories was very effective and demonstrates the range of Kane's interests. The art, text, and dialogue perfectly narrate Kipling's

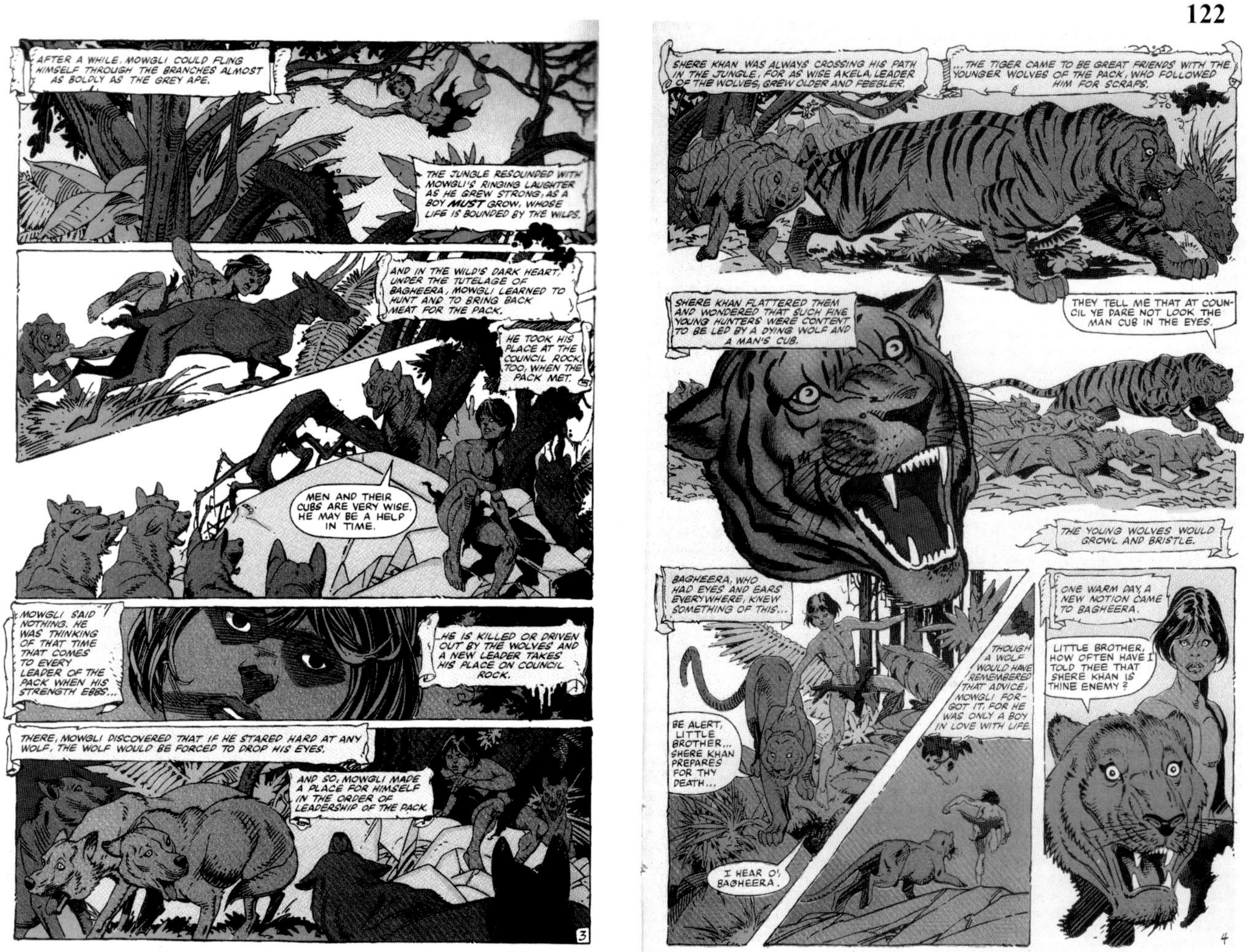
AFTER A WHILE, MOWGLI COULD FLING HIMSELF THROUGH THE BRANCHES ALMOST AS BOLDLY AS THE GREY APE.
THE JUNGLE RESOUNDED WITH MOWGLI'S RINGING LAUGHTER AS HE GREW STRONG; AS A BOY MUST GROW, WHOSE LIFE IS BOUNDED BY THE WILDS.
AND IN THE WILD'S DARK HEART, UNDER THE TUTELAGE OF BAGHEERA, MOWGLI LEARNED TO HUNT AND TO BRING BACK MEAT FOR THE PACK.
HE TOOK HIS PLACE AT THE COUNCIL ROCK, TOO, WHEN THE PACK MET.
MEN AND THEIR CUBS ARE VERY WISE. HE MAY BE A HELP IN TIME.
MOWGLI SAID NOTHING. HE WAS THINKING OF THAT TIME THAT COMES TO EVERY LEADER OF THE PACK WHEN HIS STRENGTH EBBS...
HE IS KILLED OR DRIVEN OUT BY THE WOLVES AND A NEW LEADER TAKES HIS PLACE ON COUNCIL ROCK.
THERE, MOWGLI DISCOVERED THAT IF HE STARED HARD AT ANY WOLF, THE WOLF WOULD BE FORCED TO DROP HIS EYES.
AND SO, MOWGLI MADE A PLACE FOR HIMSELF IN THE ORDER OF LEADERSHIP OF THE PACK.
3
SHERE KHAN WAS ALWAYS CROSSING HIS PATH IN THE JUNGLE, FOR AS WISE AKELA, LEADER OF THE WOLVES, GREW OLDER AND FEEBLER,
...THE TIGER CAME TO BE GREAT FRIENDS WITH THE YOUNGER WOLVES OF THE PACK, WHO FOLLOWED HIM FOR SCRAPS.
SHERE KHAN FLATTERED THEM AND WONDERED THAT SUCH FINE YOUNG HUNTERS WERE CONTENT TO BE LED BY A DYING WOLF AND A MAN'S CUB.
THEY TELL ME THAT AT COUNCIL YE DARE NOT LOOK THE MAN CUB IN THE EYES.
THE YOUNG WOLVES WOULD GROWL AND BRISTLE.
BAGHEERA, WHO HAD EYES AND EARS EVERYWHERE, KNEW SOMETHING OF THIS...
BE ALERT, LITTLE BROTHER... SHERE KHAN PREPARES FOR THY DEATH...
THOUGH A WOLF WOULD HAVE REMEMBERED THAT ADVICE, MOWGLI FORGOT IT, FOR HE WAS ONLY A BOY IN LOVE WITH LIFE.
I HEAR O' BAGHEERA.
ONE WARM DAY, A NEW NOTION CAME TO BAGHEERA.
LITTLE BROTHER, HOW OFTEN HAVE I TOLD THEE THAT SHERE KHAN IS THINE ENEMY?
4

Two sequential pages showcasing Kane's retelling of Rudyard Kipling's *Jungle Book* from *Marvel Fanfare* #9, June, 1983, Gil Kane, pencils, P. Craig Russell, inks, ©2001 Marvel Characters, Inc.

work and present the story as a romantic myth rather than as a silly comedy.

Kane, who had for many years labored under financial problems, was finally in a position where he could free himself from these debts, and with his next move, he would for the first time in his life, gain some degree of financial security. He had been offered work in California, working for Marvel, which was now attempting to produce cartoon television shows.

Kane's children were grown and gone. He and his wife were

finally in a position where they were free to relocate anywhere. He had frequently considered a move to California and there was nothing now to stand in his way. Marvel was putting together a unit in California to prepare concepts for television cartoons. Kane was offered a position with Marvel preparing concept drawings and storyboards. He and his wife, Elaine, packed up and moved to Los Angeles. When Kane arrived at Marvel, his old colleagues from DC Comics, Russ Heath and Mike Sekowsky, were already at work. Stan Lee was also involved with the development of projects, but he had only peripheral contact with Kane. The offer made

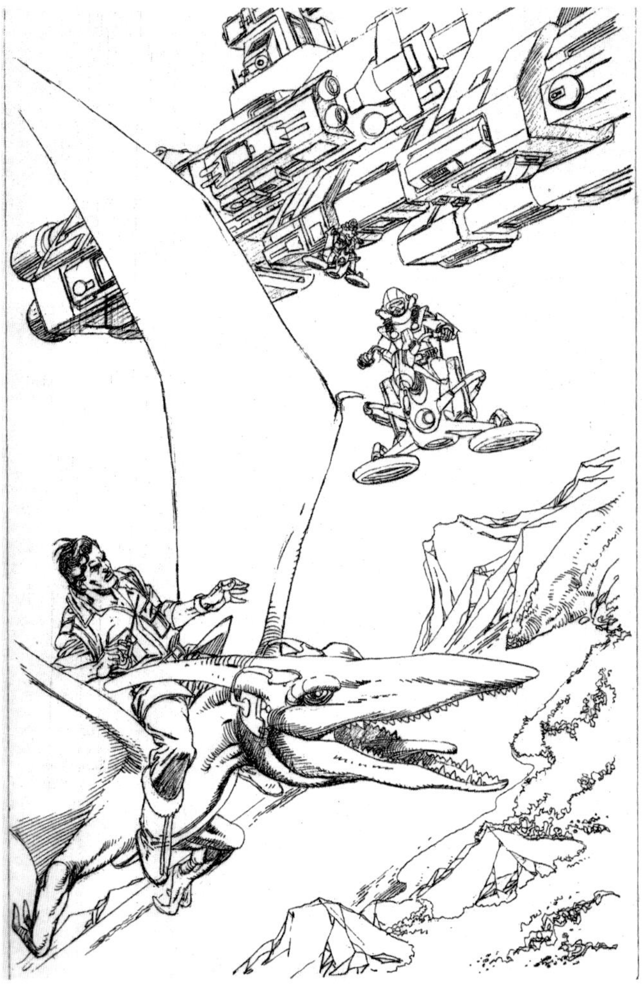

Presentation drawing prepared by Kane for Ruby-Spears Productions, Gil Kane, pencils, ©2001 Ruby-Spears Productions.

by Marvel, which had attracted Kane to Los Angeles, was not entirely as described. Fortunately, Kane was immediately approached by Ruby-

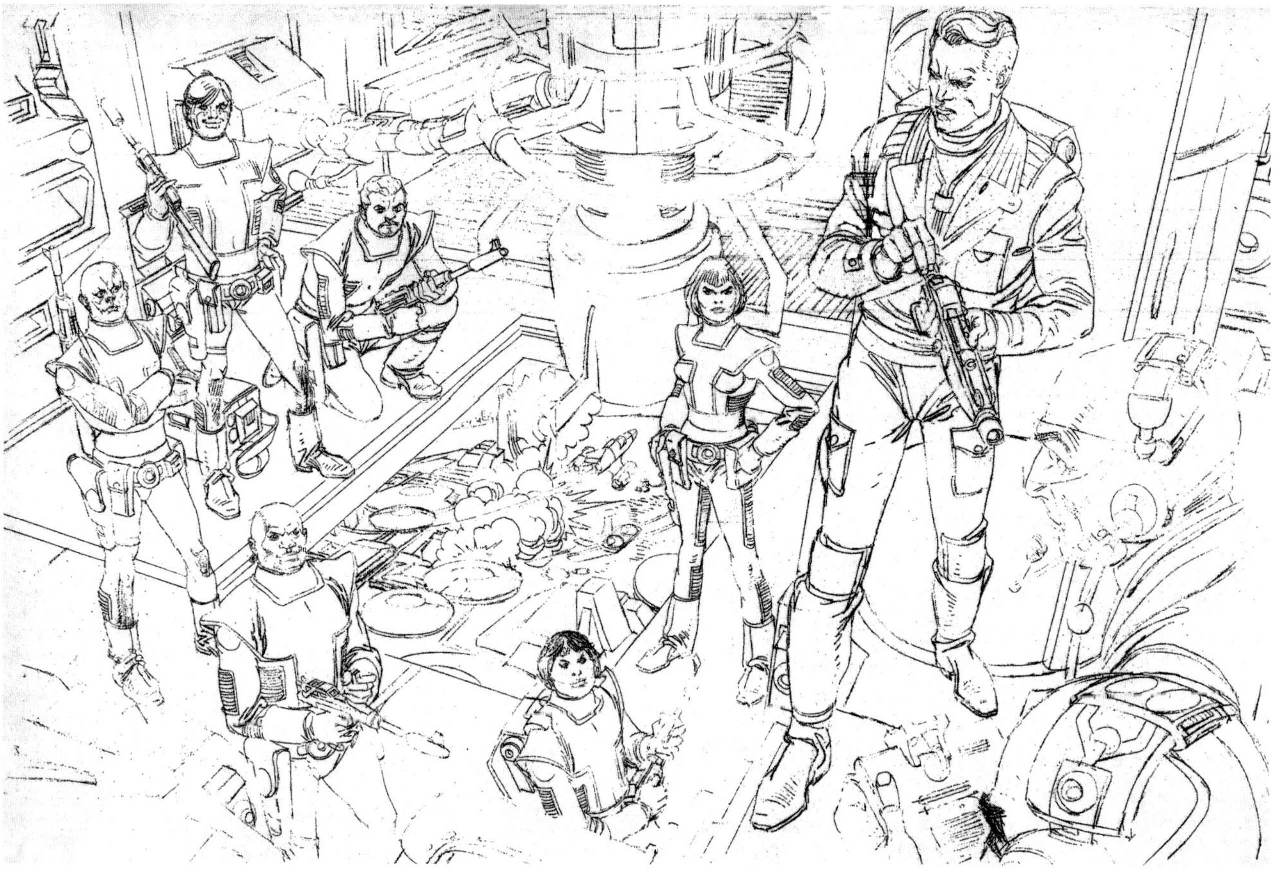

Spears Productions, which was also involved in numerous television cartoon projects.[2] Kane was interviewed by John Dorman and was immediately hired at a significantly higher salary than Marvel had been paying him. Ruby-Spears already had Alex Toth, Jack Kirby, and Doug

Presentation drawing prepared by Kane for Ruby-Spears Productions, Gil Kane, pencils, ©2001 Ruby-Spears Productions.

Wildey working on presentation pieces and story boards, and with the addition of Kane, Ruby-Spears could boast having in its employ some of the most influential comic book artists of both the first and second generations. However, although Jack Kirby turned out impressive work, by this time, at age 67, he had slowed considerably. Unfortunately, Kirby was physically unable to supply work on a regular basis with consistent quality. Kane was called upon to fill this void and to supply Ruby-Spears with a significant portion of its presentation artwork.[3] For the first time in Kane's life, he was not under the pressure of having to produce large

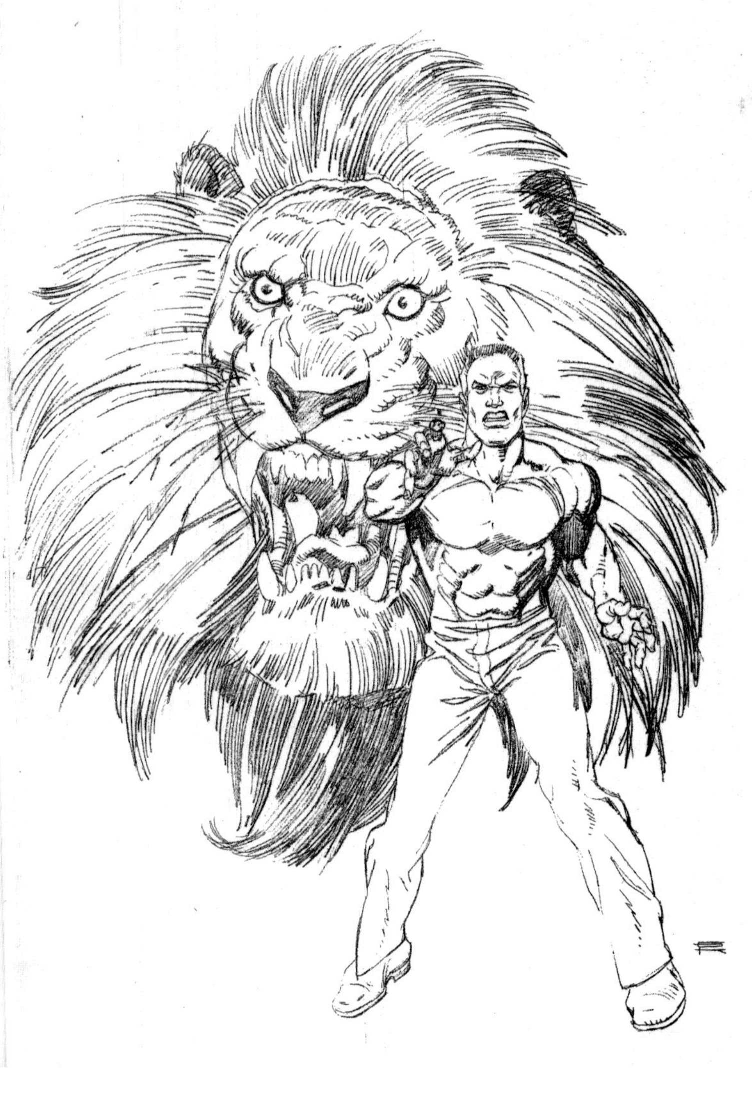

Presentation drawing prepared by Kane for Ruby-Spears Productions, Gil Kane, pencils, ©2001 Ruby-Spears Productions.

quantities of artwork to generate income. He received a generous salary and was able to concentrate on creating giant presentation pieces (routinely the pieces were twenty by thirty inches) which resembled huge splash pages. He also created concepts for projects depicting characters and their futuristic accoutrements. He also enjoyed the camaraderie and upbeat atmosphere at Ruby-Spears. Roy Thomas worked on concepts at Ruby-Spears, and Thomas and Kane were able to renew their old friendship. While Kane's work at Ruby-Spears did nothing to move the art of the comics forward, it did provide a welcome respite from the pressure of the comic book business. Kane occasionally would produce stories for DC Comics, but his energies

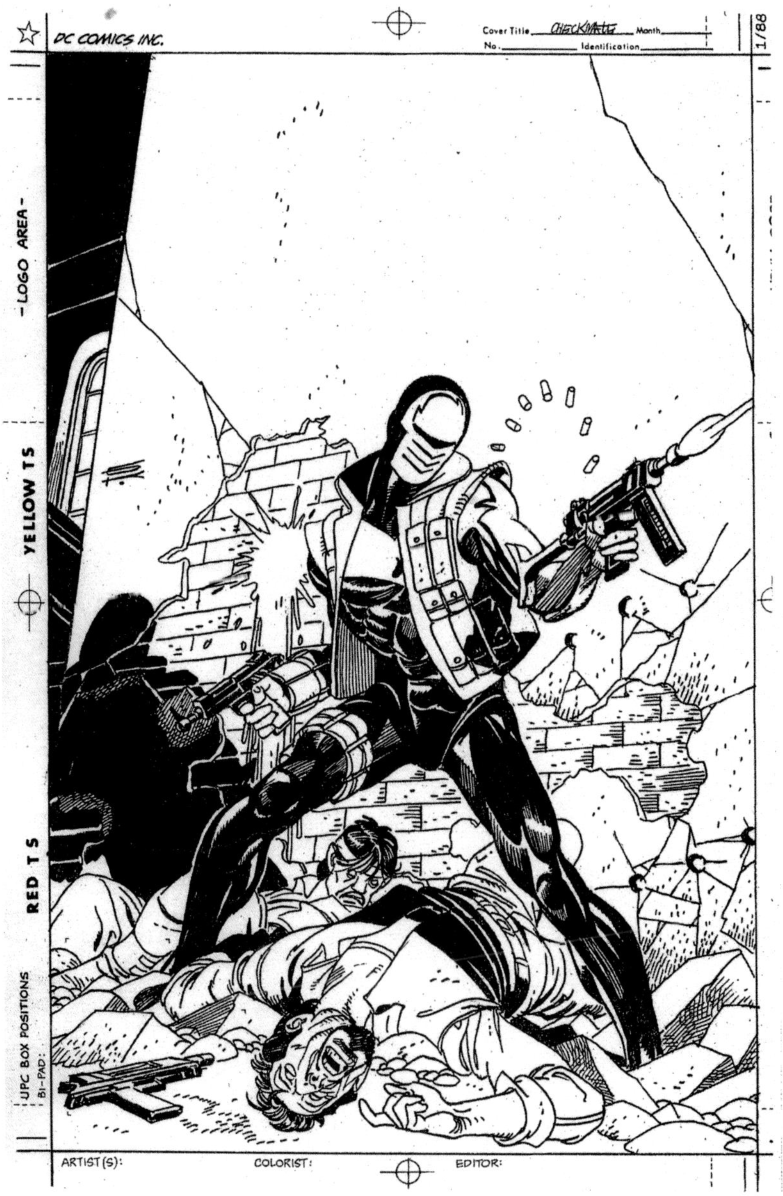

Original artwork for the cover for *Checkmate!* #11, 1988, Gil Kane, pencils and inks, ©2001 DC Comics.

were primarily focused on drawing. One difficulty in assessing Kane's work at Ruby-Spears is that his concepts were transformed into cartoons which represented the triumph of shoddy and thoughtless commercialism, at its lowest common denominator, over any semblance of art. By 1988 Ruby-Spears was having difficulties securing any work, and after the loss of their bid to produce the *Captain Planet* cartoon, the company was forced to lay off most of its employees, including Kane.

The comic book business had gone through significant changes in the almost five years Kane had been away. A new

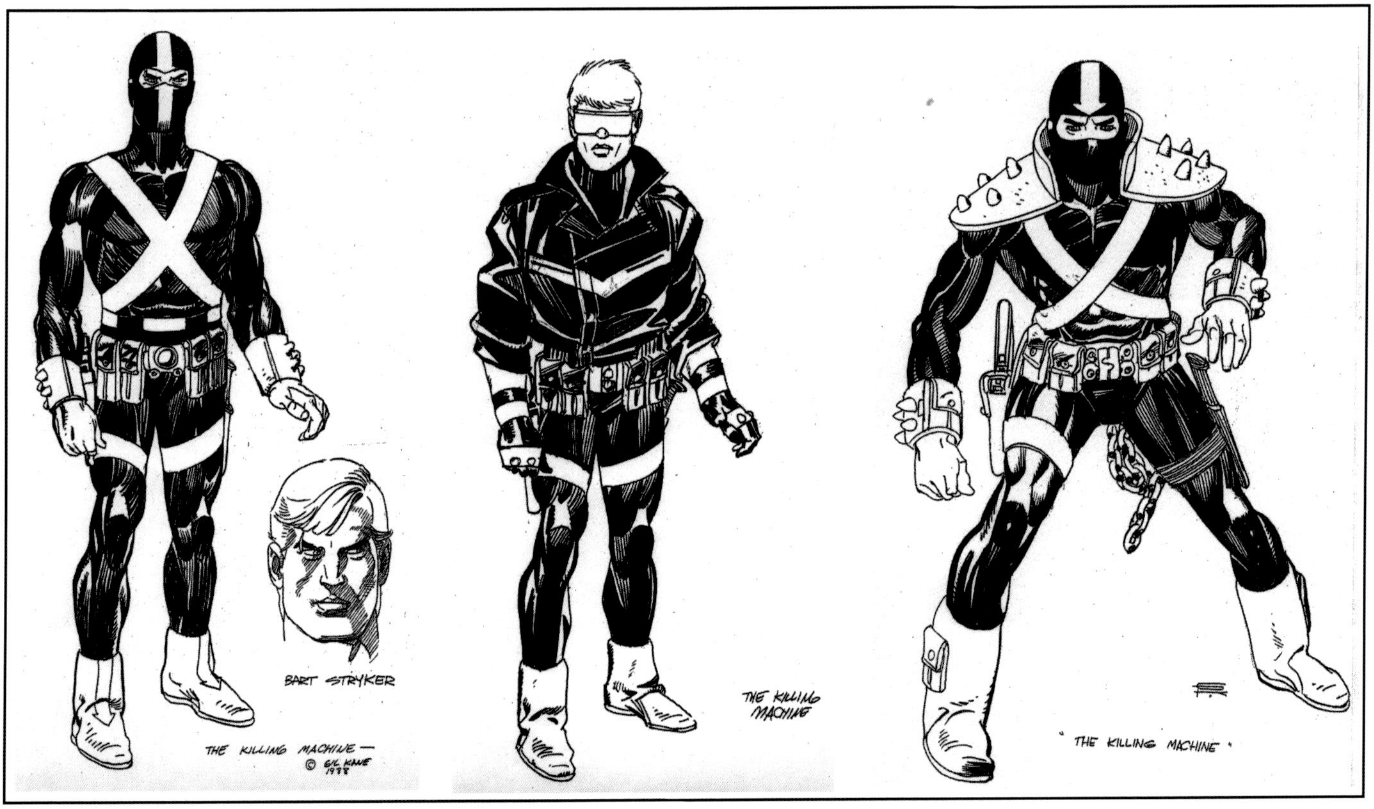

Three model sheets, prepared for Kane's never published *Killing Machine* stories, 1988, Gil Kane, pencils and inks, ©2001 The Estate of Gil Kane.

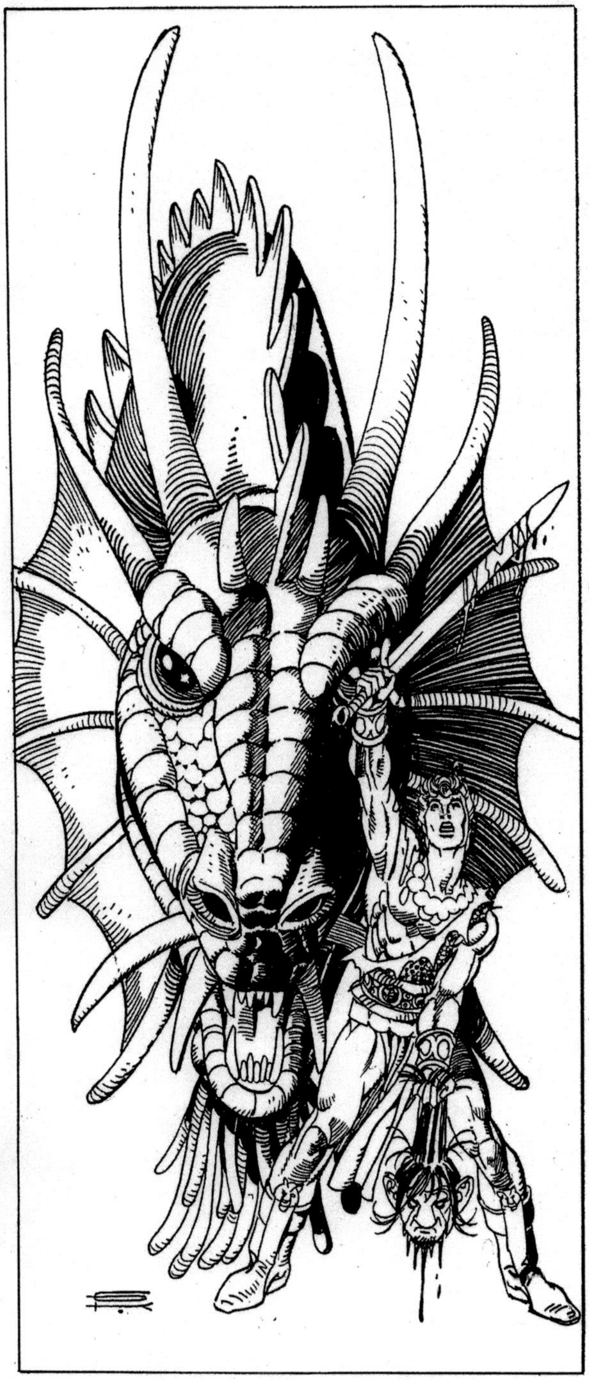

generation of comic book artists had burst onto the scene, many of whom were taking inspiration from Kane's work. The new crop of young artists, instead of finding inspiration from newspaper comic strips, pulp science fiction, literature, illustration, and the cinema, used only comic books as a point of reference. Moreover, many of these artists were impressed by anime (Japanese animation) and manga (Japanese comic books) and their style of

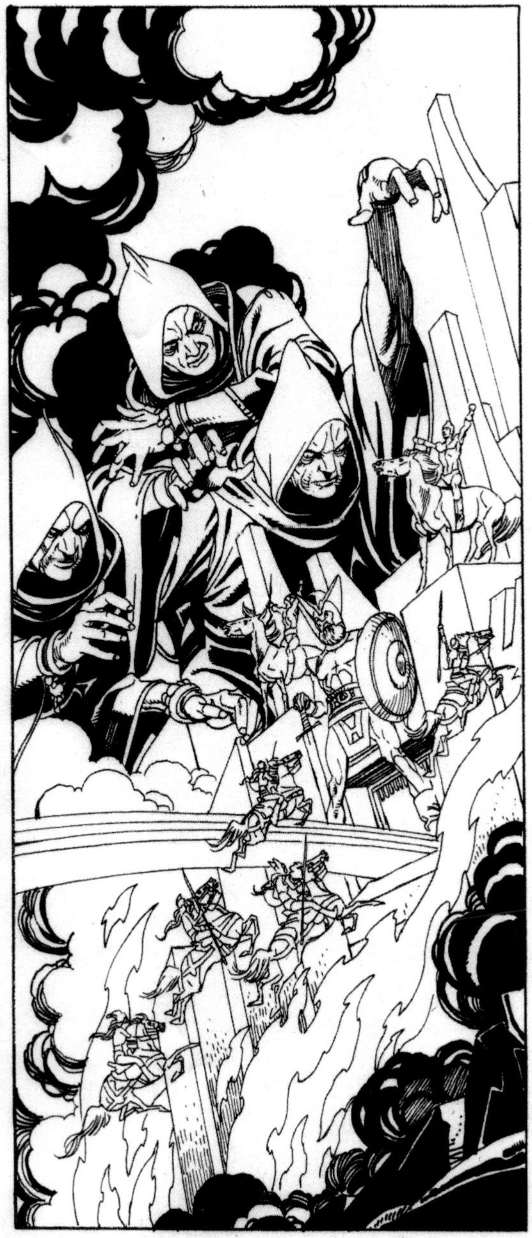

Two back cover designs for *The Ring of the Nibelung*. Above: back cover for *The Ring of the Nibelung* #3, 1990. Right: back cover for *The Ring of the Nibelung* #4, 1990. All, Gil Kane, pencils and inks, all ©2001 DC Comics.

This page and the next: four consecutive pages from *The Ring of the Nibelung* #1, Gil Kane, pencils and inks, © 2001 DC Comics. Kane was back again, in his favorite genre with *The Ring*. Although Kane felt he had rushed work on *The Ring*, his handling of the story successfully illustrates the myth.

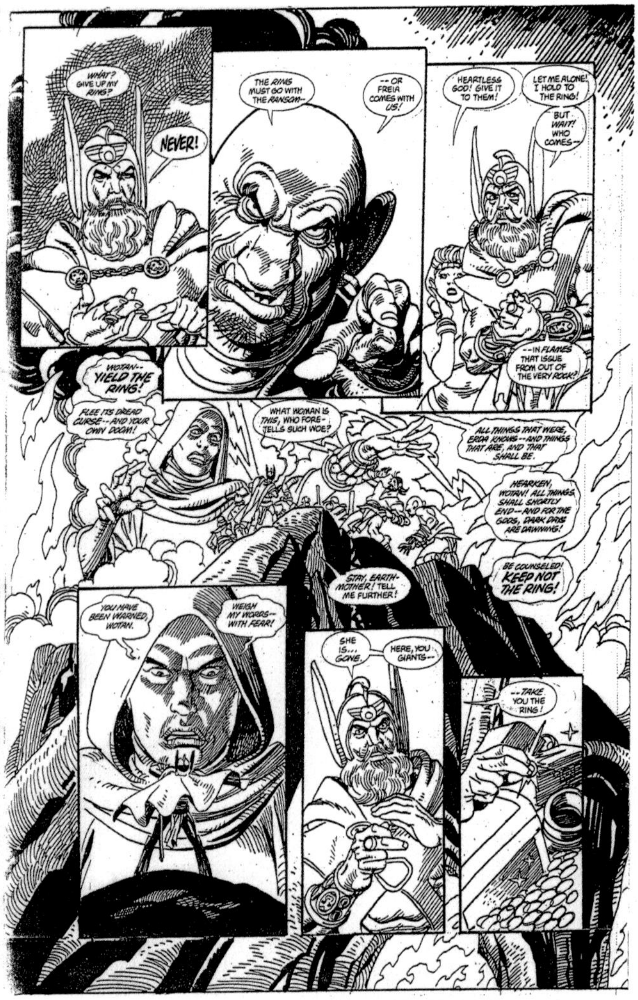

WHAT? GIVE UP MY RING?
NEVER!
THE RING MUST GO WITH THE RANSOM--
--OR FREIA COMES WITH US!
HEARTLESS GOD! GIVE IT TO THEM!
LET ME ALONE! I HOLD TO THE RING!
BUT WAIT! WHO COMES--
--IN FLAMES THAT ISSUE FROM OUT OF THE VERY ROCK!
WOTAN-- YIELD THE RING!
FLEE ITS DREAD CURSE--AND YOUR OWN DOOM!
WHAT WOMAN IS THIS, WHO FORETELLS SUCH WOE?
ALL THINGS THAT WERE, ERDA KNOWS--AND THINGS THAT ARE, AND THAT SHALL BE.
HEARKEN, WOTAN! ALL THINGS SHALL SHORTLY END--AND FOR THE GODS, DARK DAYS ARE DAWNING!
BE COUNSELED! KEEP NOT THE RING!
STAY, EARTH-MOTHER! TELL ME FURTHER!
YOU HAVE BEEN WARNED, WOTAN.
WEIGH MY WORDS-- WITH FEAR!
SHE IS... GONE.
HERE, YOU GIANTS--
--TAKE YOU THE RING!

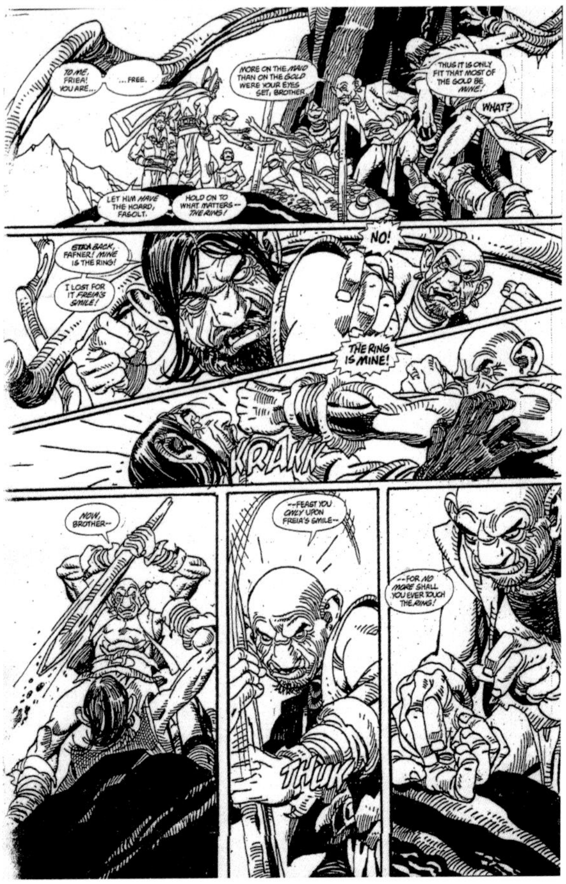

TO ME! FREIA! YOU ARE...
...FREE.
MORE ON THE MAID THAN ON THE GOLD WERE YOUR EYES SET, BROTHER.
THUS IT IS ONLY FIT THAT MOST OF THE GOLD BE MINE!
WHAT?
LET HIM HAVE THE HOARD, FASOLT.
HOLD ON TO WHAT MATTERS-- THE RING!
STAND BACK, FAFNER! MINE IS THE RING!
NO!
I LOST FOR IT FREIA'S SMILE!
THE RING IS MINE!
KRAKK
NOW, BROTHER--
--FEAST YOU ONLY UPON FREIA'S SMILE--
--FOR NO MORE SHALL YOU EVER TOUCH THE RING!
THUK

drawing and inking emphasized elongated and exaggerated anatomy. They inked with a fine, razor thin, line. For many in the industry, Kane was a dinosaur. Kane, however, aggressively moved forward designing a character called the "Killing Machine," which was very much in step with the trends in comic books. Indeed, unlike many of his second-generation contemporaries, Kane's style set the tone for the hot new artists in comic books. Kane had collected books about anime and manga, and had assimilated this information into his approach to his art years before. *The Killing Machine* was sold to DC Comics as three completely pencilled books, where they have sat, unused since 1988. Kane was

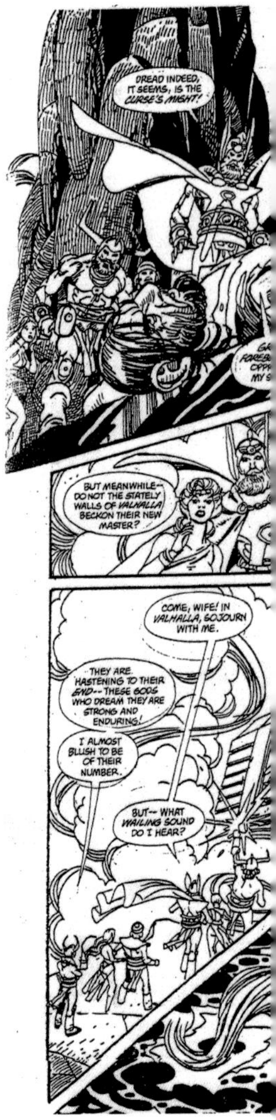

DREAD INDEED, IT SEEMS, IS THE CURSE'S MIGHT!
BUT MEANWHILE-- DO NOT THE STATELY WALLS OF VALHALLA BECKON THEIR NEW MASTER?
COME, WIFE! IN VALHALLA, SOJOURN WITH ME.
THEY ARE HASTENING TO THEIR END-- THESE GODS WHO DREAM THEY ARE STRONG AND ENDURING!
I ALMOST BLUSH TO BE OF THEIR NUMBER.
BUT-- WHAT WAILING SOUND DO I HEAR?

again at a crossroad in his life and he elected, despite the possible obstacles, to return to the world of comic books. Kane's luck was about to change.

Fortunately for Kane, Roy Thomas had not forgotten him. Thomas was moving forward with an idea to serialize *The Ring of the*

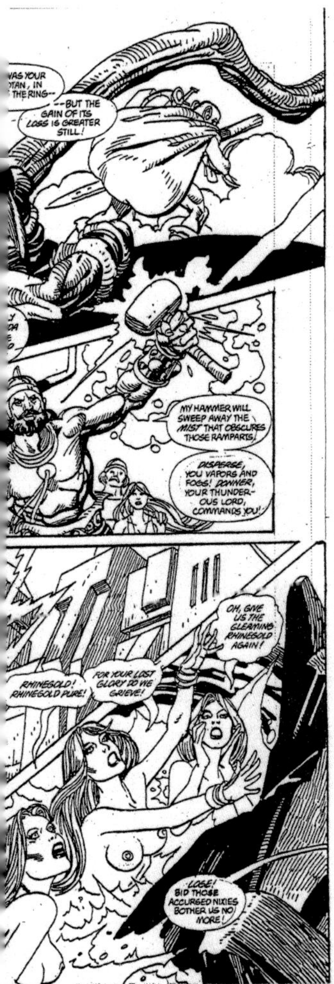
--BUT THE GAIN OF ITS LOSS IS GREATER STILL!
MY HAMMER WILL SWEEP AWAY THE MIST THAT OBSCURES THOSE RAMPARTS!
DISPERSE, YOU VAPORS AND FOGS! DONNER, YOUR THUNDEROUS LORD, COMMANDS YOU!
OH, GIVE US THE GLEAMING RHINEGOLD AGAIN!
FOR YOUR LOST GLORY DO WE GRIEVE!
RHINEGOLD! RHINEGOLD PURE!
LOGE! BID THOSE ACCURSED NIXIES BOTHER US NO MORE!

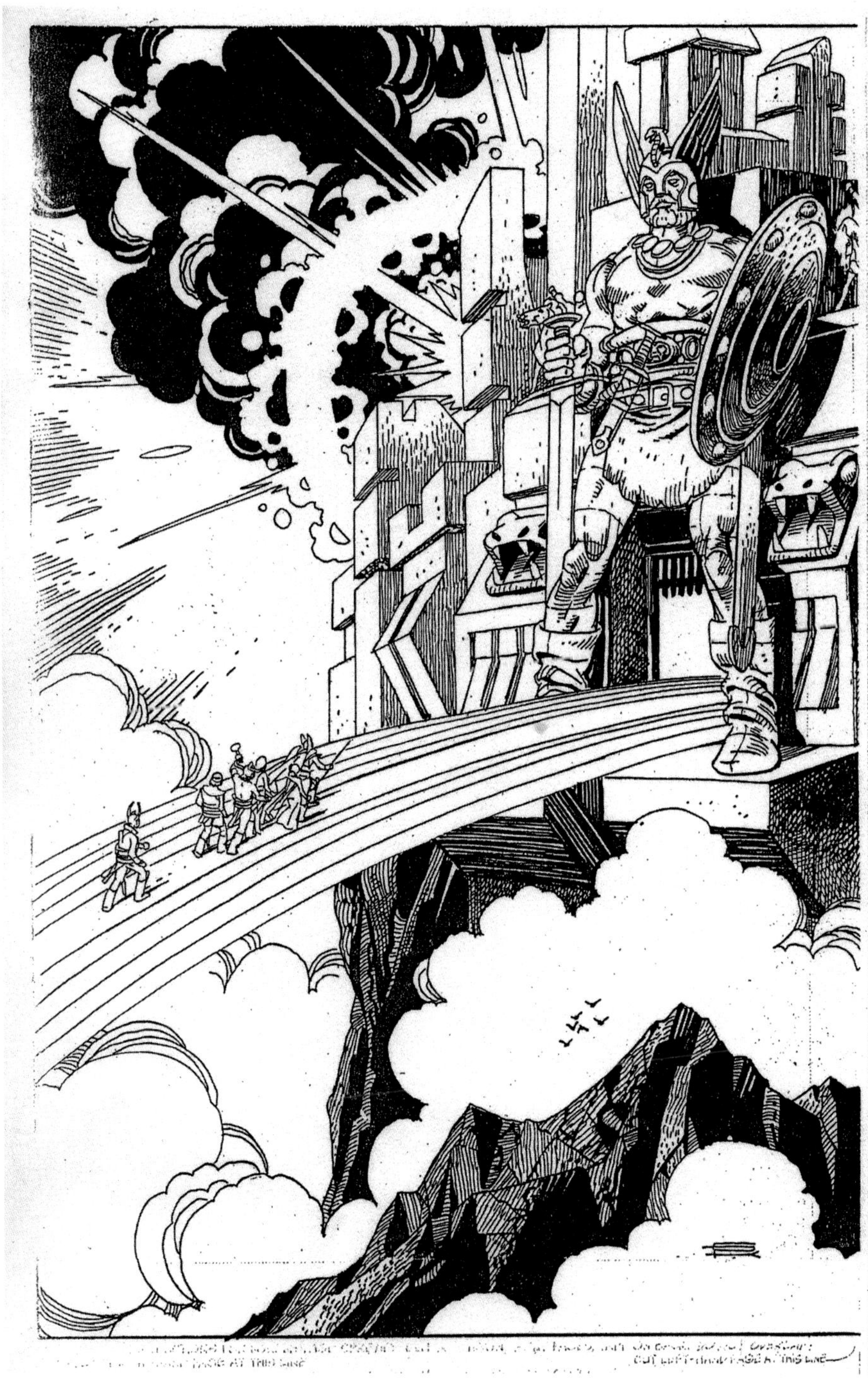

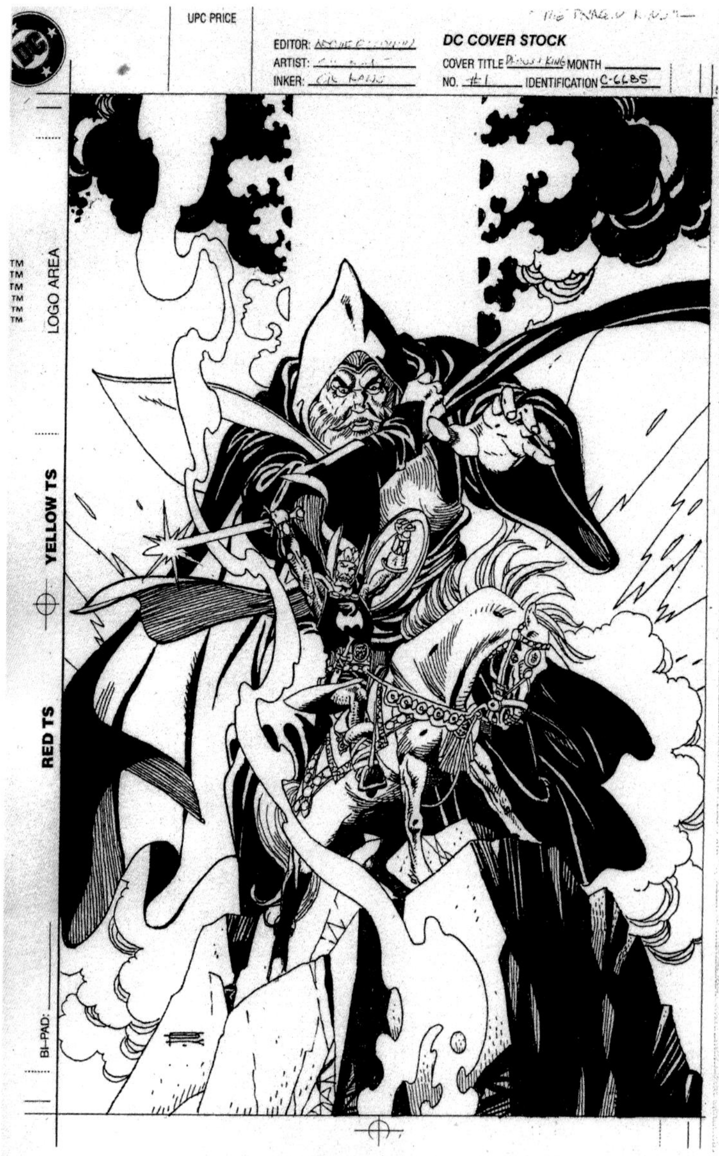

Right: the original artwork for the unpublished cover for Kane's retelling of the Aurthurian legend, *The Dragon King*, Gil Kane, pencils and inks. Coming after the successful reception of *The Ring*, Kane tackled one of his favorite myths, the story of King Arthur. Over the years Kane had read and reread the many versions of this archetypal myth. The uninked layout pages to the story are beautiful, and only hint at what the finished artwork would have looked like. Unfortunately, DC Comics lost interest in this project and it never was completed. Below: the layout for the splash page for *The Dragon King*. All artwork ©2001 The Estate of Gil Kane.

Nibelung using Richard Wagner's librettos. Thomas was familiar with the mythology surrounding the Norse legends but was determined to use Wagner's operas as the basis for a serialized comic version.[4] Kane, true to form, was more interested in using the myths as a basis for the story. Thomas insisted that they stick to the operas and in the end Thomas won out. The final product, four comic books issued in 1989 and 1990, effectively retold the story of *The Ring*. Kane and Thomas composed these books as a quartet and they were subsequently assembled in graphic novel form. *The Ring* received strong reviews not

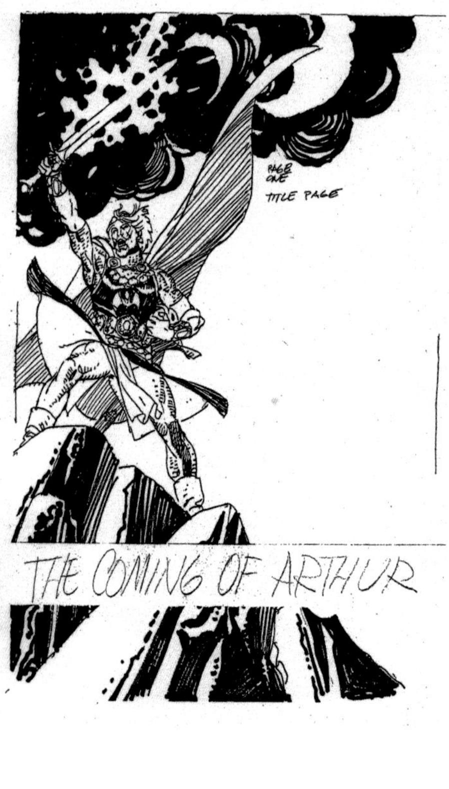

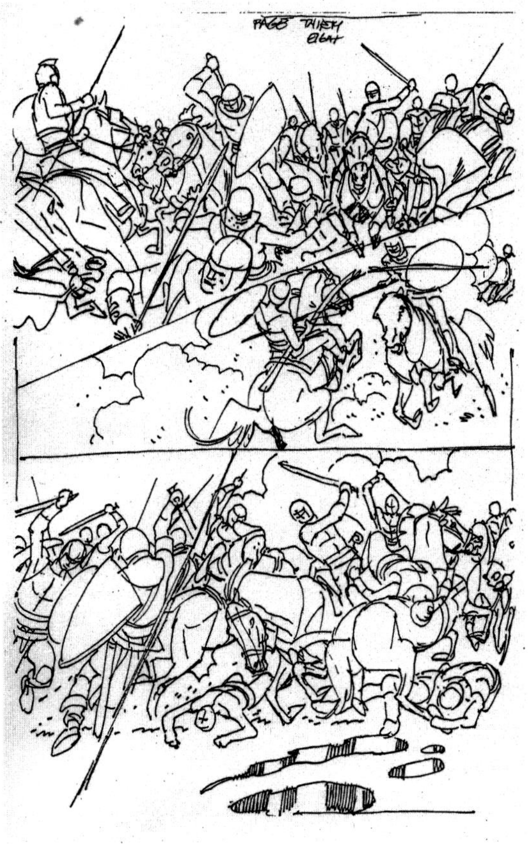

only from the comic book press but also from John Rockwell in the New York Times. As a result of his work on *The Ring,* Kane once again had credibility with comic book publishers and he set out on a number of assignments.

With the success of *The Ring,* Kane proceeded to pitch to DC Comics the idea of doing a comic book treatment of the Arthurian legend. Kane had studied the many versions of the myth of King Arthur for most of his mature life, and he saw the interest generated by *The Ring* as an opportunity to finally proceed with such a project. Kane had seriously been considering a graphic novelization of these legends since his involvement with John Jakes and the paperback novel, *Excalibur*. The book was to be called *The Dragon King*. The cover was completed, and an entire story was pencilled, but DC Comics never gave the go ahead to proceed with the story. This, unfortunately, would not be Kane's last disappointment.

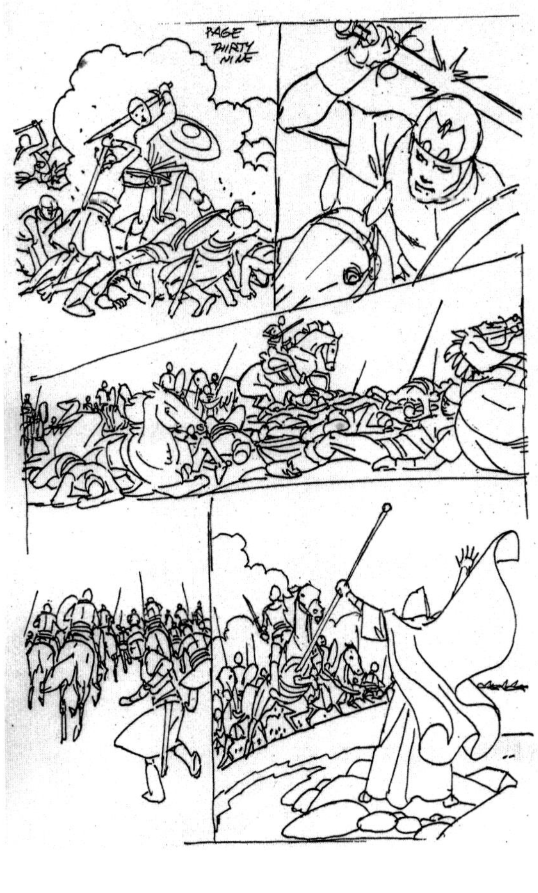

Two layout pages from Kane's unpublished *The Dragon King*, ©2001 The Estate of Gil Kane.

11 CHALLENGES

In 1989, Kane was diagnosed with non-Hodgkin's lymphoma and he began a trial of radiation and chemotherapy. The treatments made him extremely weak. Kane found not being able to work irritating, but the treatments he had received were debilitating. In 1990, John Dorman approached Kane to create presentation pieces and concepts for a planned cartoon series called *The Pirates of Dark Water*.

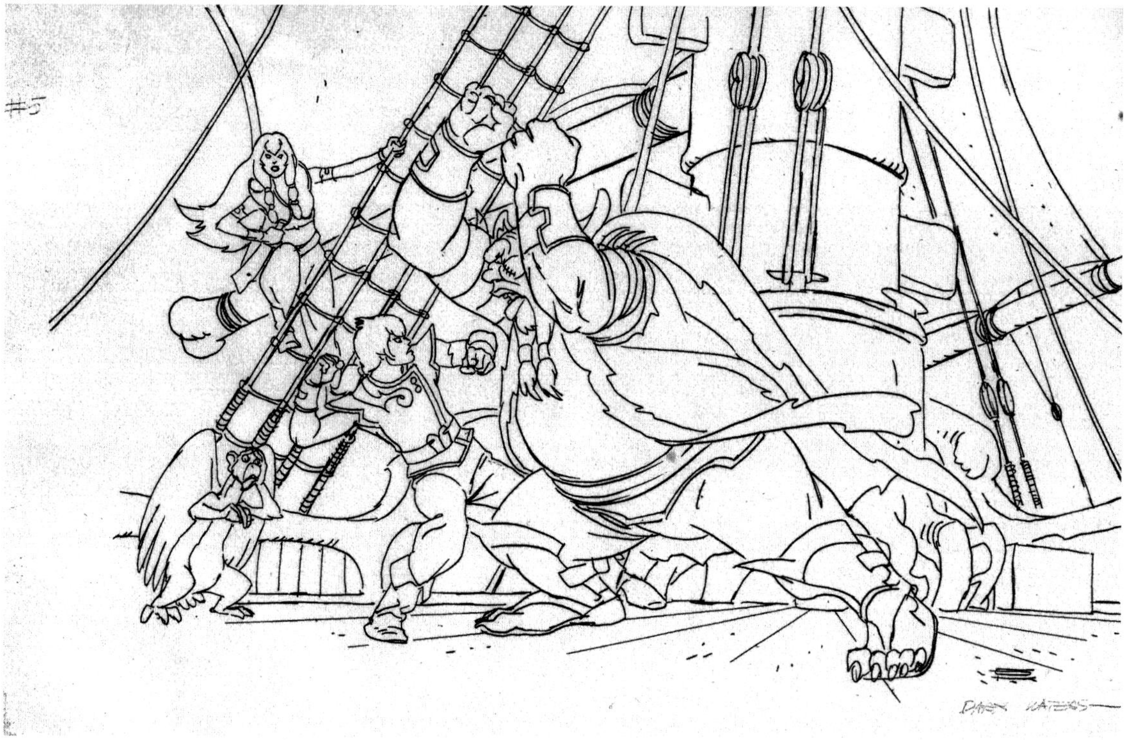

Kane demurred, but Dorman persisted, ultimately Kane did detailed presentation work for the project. After Kane's treatments were finished he was pronounced cancer free but the extensive radiation

Presentation piece for *Dark Waters*, later known as *The Pirates of Dark Water*, released as a television cartoon for Hanna-Barbera, Gil Kane, pencils and inks, ©2001 Hanna-Barbera.

therapy had severely damaged his heart which required radical surgery.

As soon as he was able, Kane wanted to get back to work. He tried to resuscitate *The Dragon King* and the *Killing Machine*, to no avail.

The 1990s were not a productive period for Kane, even though he worked on a number of projects. He did a series of comic books for the baseball card manufacturer, Topps, which were based on the plot for the motion picture, *Jurassic Park*. Kane was required to work on the book without the benefit of seeing the film, which was in postproduction. He was given a script outline and photographs of some of the actors. Kane was required to imagine portions of the movie and did a convincing job. The uninked pencils for *Jurassic Park* were beautifully rendered by Kane, but the books

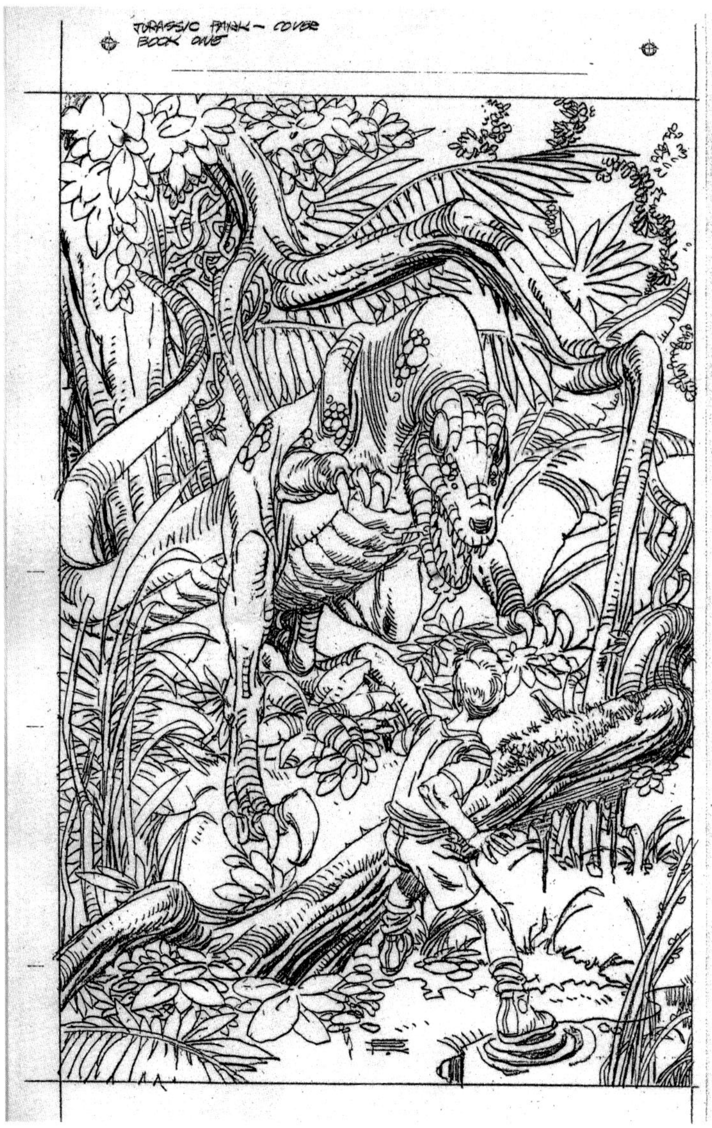
JURASSIC PARK – COVER
BOOK ONE

Original artwork, uninked pencils, for the cover for *Jurassic Park* #1, June, 1993, Gil Kane, pencils, ©2001 Topps Comics, Inc., Universal City Studios, Inc. and Amblin Entertainment, Inc.

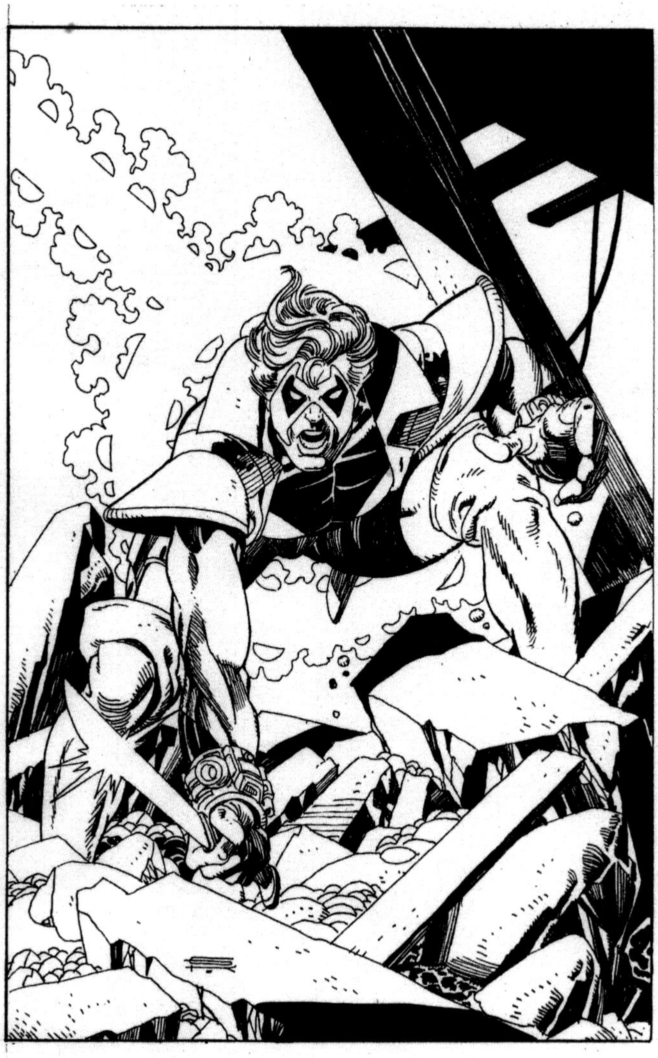

were ruined by clumsy and insensitive inking by George Perez. Perez managed to ruin the flow, plasticity, and line of the drawing. Perez made much of the artwork inarticulate and unattractive.

Kane fared better on the *Edge* series, which he created with writer Steven Grant for Malibu Comics. Kane inked his own work and again demonstrated his skill as a graphic storyteller. Much to Kane's disappointment, the publication of the four book series was interrupted by a change in climate in the

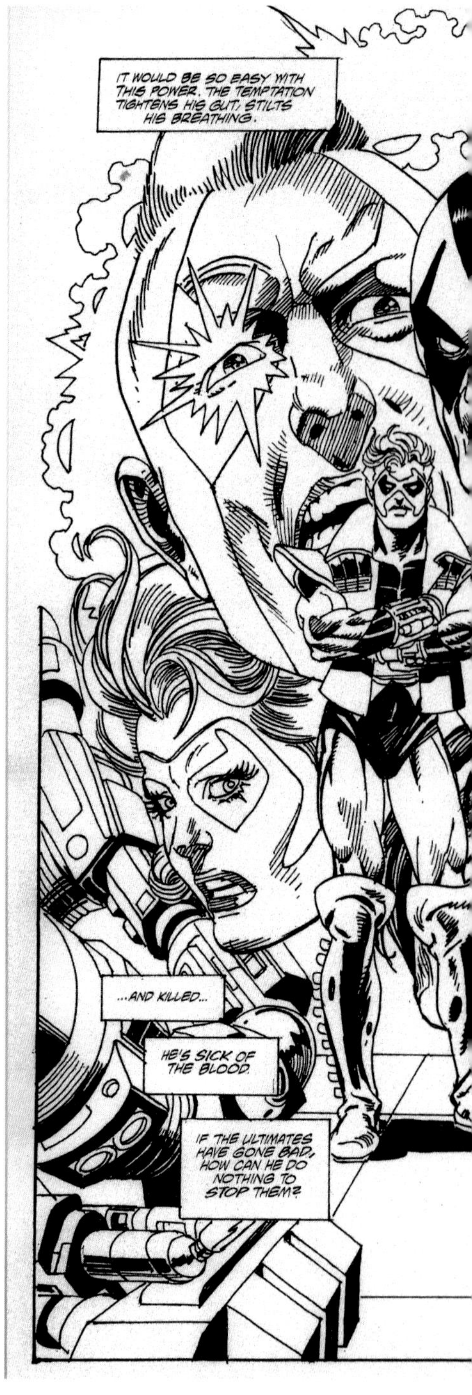
IT WOULD BE SO EASY WITH THIS POWER. THE TEMPTATION TIGHTENS HIS GUT, STILTS HIS BREATHING.
...AND KILLED...
HE'S SICK OF THE BLOOD.
IF THE ULTIMATES HAVE GONE BAD, HOW CAN HE DO NOTHING TO STOP THEM?

Above and right: original artwork for the cover and the splash page for *Edge* #2, August, 1994, Gil Kane, pencils and inks, ©2001 The Estate of Gil Kane and Steven Grant.

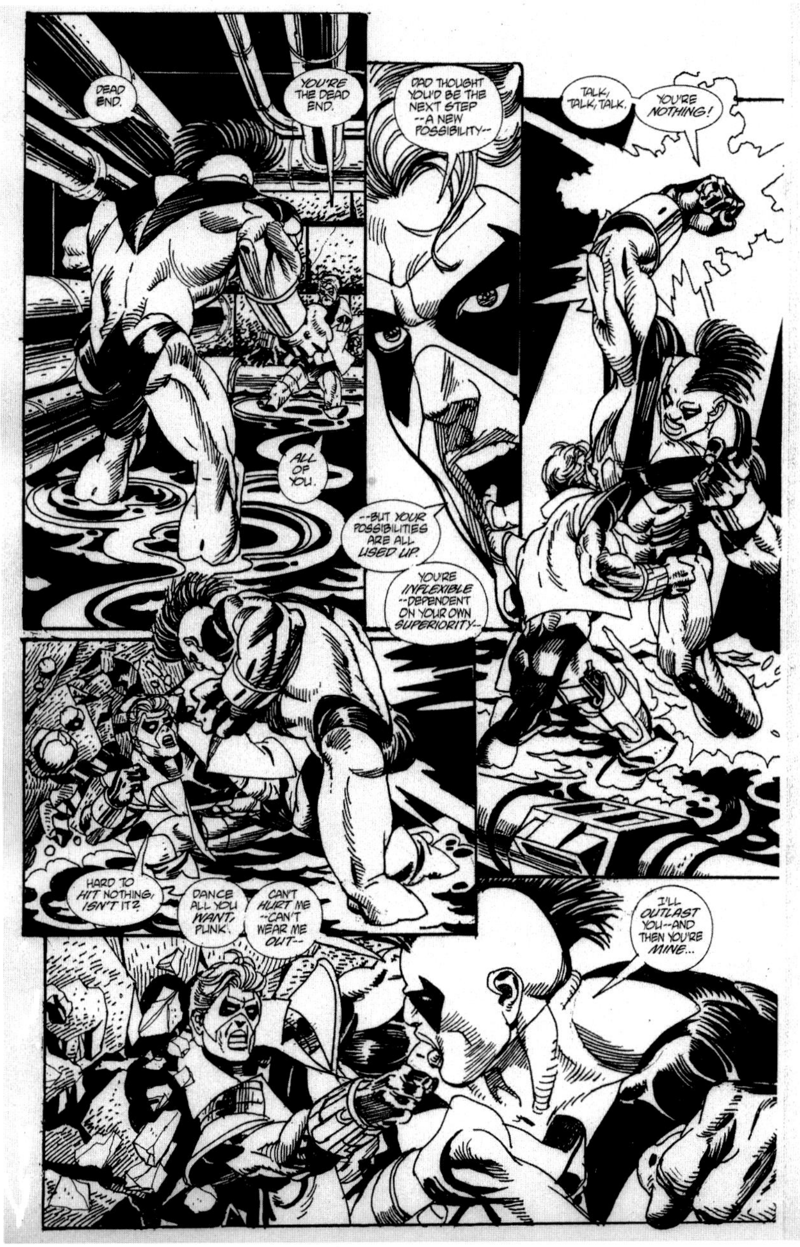
DEAD END.
YOU'RE THE DEAD END.
DAD THOUGHT YOU'D BE THE NEXT STEP --A NEW POSSIBILITY--
TALK, TALK, TALK.
YOU'RE NOTHING!
ALL OF YOU.
--BUT YOUR POSSIBILITIES ARE ALL USED UP.
YOU'RE INFLEXIBLE --DEPENDENT ON YOUR OWN SUPERIORITY--
HARD TO HIT NOTHING, ISN'T IT?
DANCE ALL YOU WANT, PUNK.
CAN'T HURT ME --CAN'T WEAR ME OUT--
I'LL OUTLAST YOU--AND THEN YOU'RE MINE...

Original artwork for an interior page for *Edge* #2, August, 1994, ©2001 The Estate of Gil Kane and Steven Grant. As these examples from the *Edge* series show, Kane had fully recovered from his illness and was in top form.

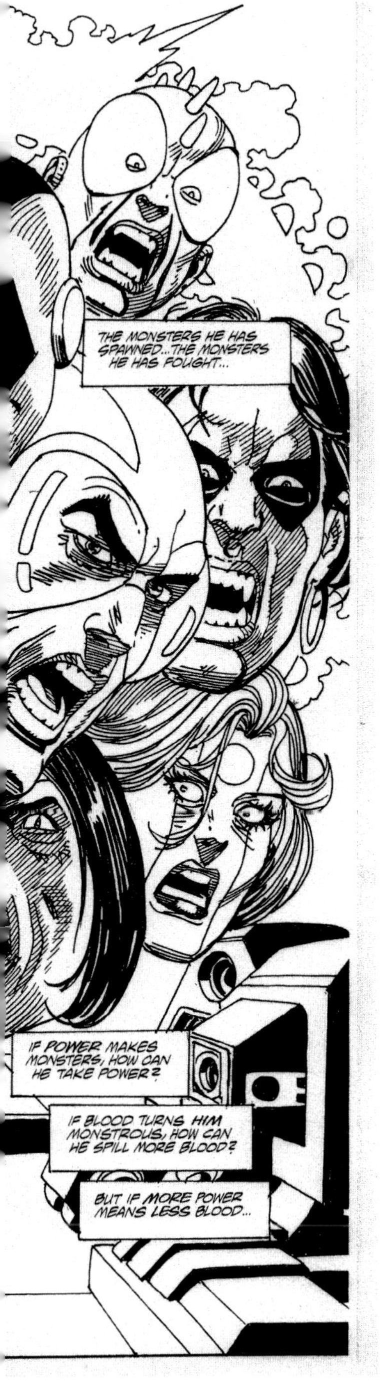
THE MONSTERS HE HAS SPAWNED...THE MONSTERS HE HAS FOUGHT...
IF POWER MAKES MONSTERS, HOW CAN HE TAKE POWER?
IF BLOOD TURNS HIM MONSTROUS, HOW CAN HE SPILL MORE BLOOD?
BUT IF MORE POWER MEANS LESS BLOOD...

comic book business and the series was cancelled, with the fourth volume remaining unpublished. Kane also directed his energies to various projects for DC Comics including work on extended stories on Batman, Superman, and duties on the Green Lantern and Atom.

In 1997, Kane again was diagnosed with lymphoma. He spent the next two-and-a-half years valiantly fighting this disease. His last published works were Green Lantern and Atom stories. Gil Kane died on January 31, 2000, leaving countless unfinished projects. The little boy who at sixteen had wanted to draw comics, had changed the craft of comic story-telling, and in the process had helped elevate the comic book story to an art form.

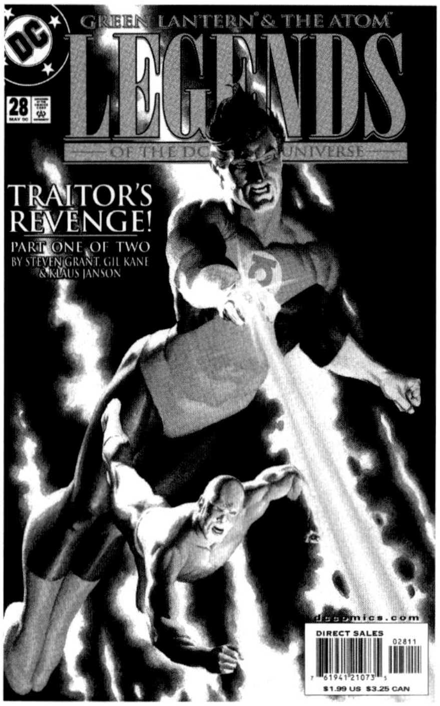
GREEN LANTERN & THE ATOM
LEGENDS
OF THE DC UNIVERSE
28
TRAITOR'S REVENGE!
PART ONE OF TWO
BY STEVEN GRANT, GIL KANE & KLAUS JANSON
dccomics.com
DIRECT SALES
$1.99 US $3.25 CAN

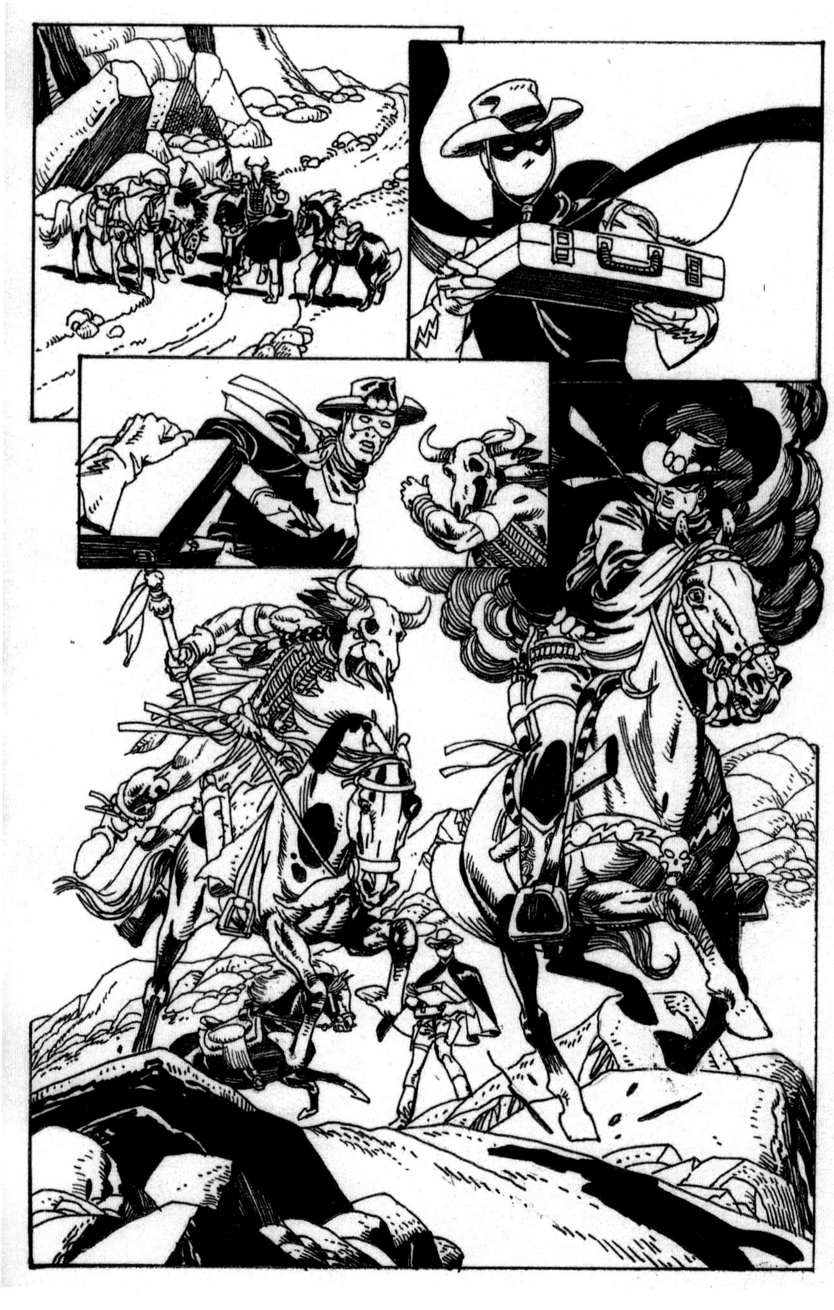

Right: Kane's work for *Judgment Day*, although only amounting to a four page sequence in the story, was impressive. This page showcases his skill in choreographing a classic western scene, with the hero galloping away on his horse. Original Artwork for *Judgment Day*, June, 1997, Gil Kane, pencils and inks, ©2001 Awesome Entertainment, LLC. Above: cover for *Legends of the DC Universe* #28, May, 2000, Gil Kane, pencils, Alex Ross, paints, ©2001 DC Comics. This is one of the last covers Kane pencilled. Kane also pencilled the interior pages to the comic book which were inked by Klaus Janson. The book was published posthumously.

12 EPILOGUE

The twentieth century witnessed a radical redefinition of the concept of what constitutes art. The artists at the core of the modernist movement expanded and redefined art by enlarging the meaning of art to include "high" craft and "high" design. Comic books and comic book art fit within this context. The creation of the comic book was intended only with the purpose of selling a product and making money. The same motive can generally be attributed to early twentieth century cinema, advertising, and commercial design, all of which in the hands of talented practitioners transcend their origins. As a storytelling medium, the comic book was transformed by a small group of artists and writers. Gil Kane was one of these men. Through Kane's efforts at DC Comics, he developed commercial comic book storytelling and gave it an individual voice and vision. Limited by politics, personalities, and the bottom line mentality that is pervasive in business, Kane ventured outside of the

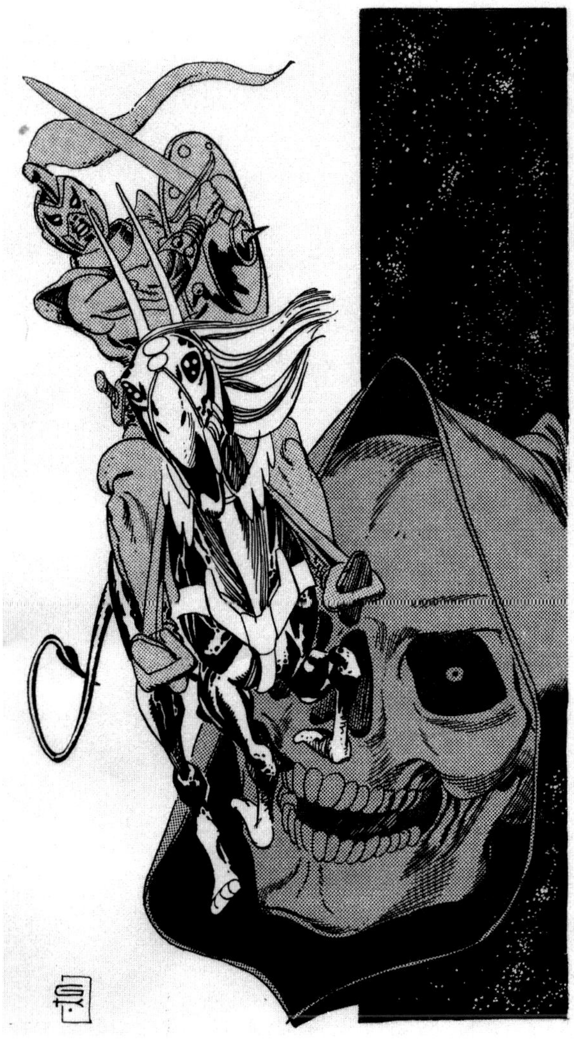

Interior page from the original artwork for Chapter II of *Blackmark*, 1971, Gil Kane, pencils and inks, ©2001 The Estate of Gil Kane.

Kane in the 1970s.

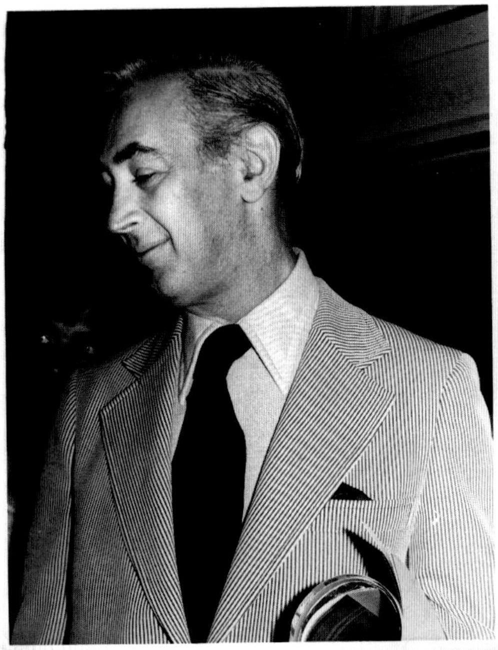

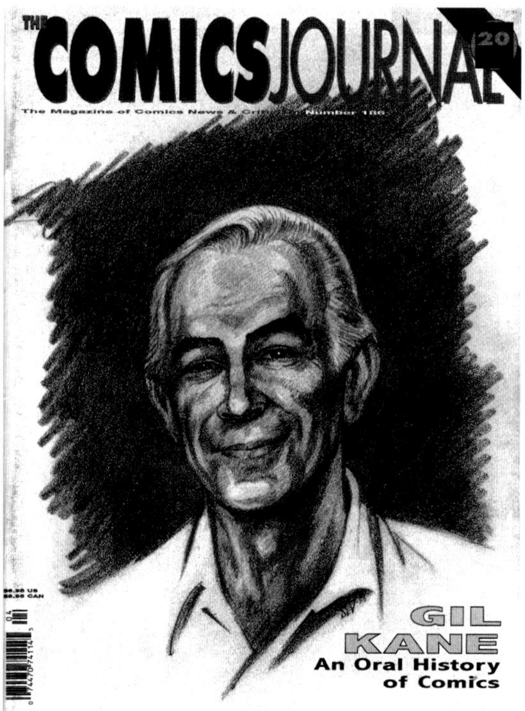
THE COMICS JOURNAL
GIL KANE
An Oral History of Comics

Cover for *The Comics Journal* # 186, April, 1996, cover artwork by Marie Severin, ©2001 Fantagraphics Books, Inc. This issue of the *Journal* contained the first of two extended interviews between Kane and Gary Groth.

mainstream with *Savage* and *Blackmark.* In retrospect, both *Savage* and *Blackmark* were far more influential upon other artists and writers in the comic book field than anyone ever imagined. Both *Savage,* and *Blackmark*, in its original version, were successful in demonstrating that graphic storytelling had its own legitimate niche within the greater scope of twentieth century art. Unfortunately, market forces and the politics of the comic book industry forced Kane back into the mainstream. For almost thirty years after Kane's two experiments in graphic storytelling he toiled with standard comic book fare, only infrequently venturing back to uncharted waters. Kane continued to grow as an artist and during the 1970s he helped shape and influence the house style at Marvel. His successful work at Marvel was followed with his co-creation of *Star Hawks,* which brought the art of the comics to daily newspaper strips.

Kane pushed his art and the art of the

comics to develop an aesthetic which emphasized the plasticity of form, simplicity of line, and fluidity of motion. Kane's language of story-telling evolved into a highly influential and effective voice among other comic book artists and for millions of readers. Kane's language of form and composition, which eschewed background and lighting effects for the energy of movement, further transformed comic book art from its dependence on illustration, to an art form on its own terms. He combined these elements with a compositional style that exaggerated and forced perspective to further heighten the drama and action of the stories he told.

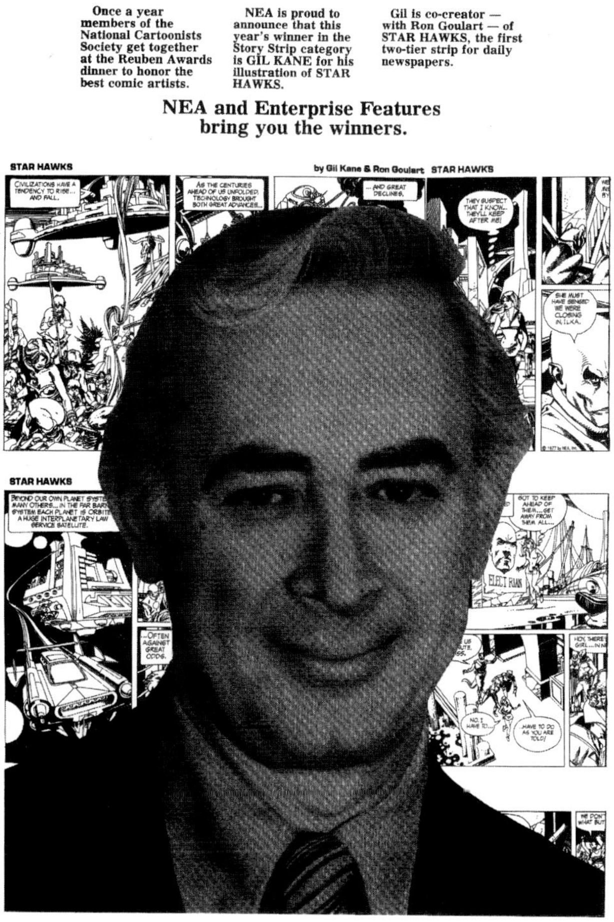
Once a year members of the National Cartoonists Society get together at the Reuben Awards dinner to honor the best comic artists.
NEA is proud to announce that this year's winner in the Story Strip category is GIL KANE for his illustration of STAR HAWKS.
Gil is co-creator — with Ron Goulart — of STAR HAWKS, the first two-tier strip for daily newspapers.
NEA and Enterprise Features bring you the winners.
STAR HAWKS
by Gil Kane & Ron Goulart STAR HAWKS
CIVILIZATIONS HAVE A TENDENCY TO RISE... AND FALL.
AS THE CENTURIES AHEAD OF US UNFOLDED, TECHNOLOGY BROUGHT BOTH GREAT ADVANCES...
... AND GREAT DECLINES.
THEY SUSPECT THAT I KNOW... THEY'LL KEEP AFTER ME!
STAR HAWKS

An announcement distributed by NEA to celebrate Kane's receiving a Rueben award for his work on *Star Hawks.*

In developing his personal language of form and composition,

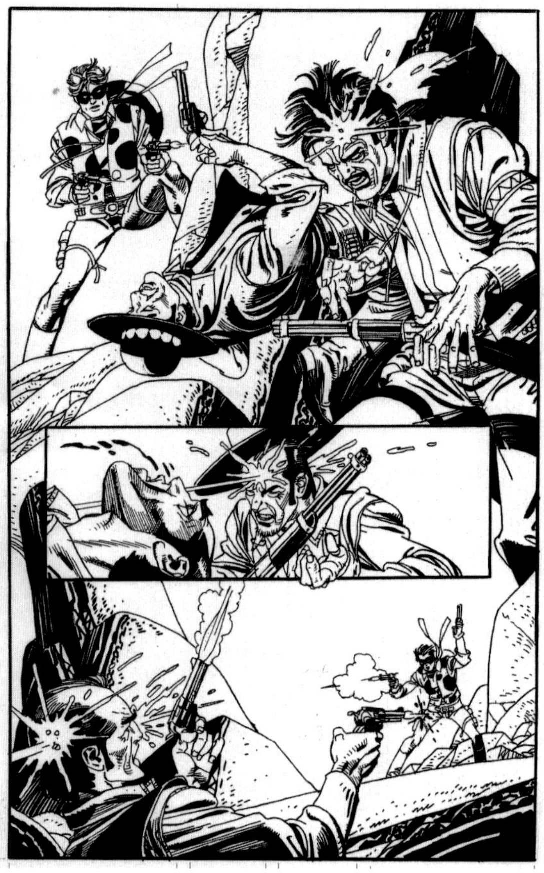

Kane was always keenly aware of his predecessors and their influences, not only on him, but on the art of the comics. Kane freely shared this intimate knowledge with thousands of fans, and also with thousands of students as a teacher. He taught a class on the art of the comics at New York University in the 1970s. He taught numerous classes on the subjects of drawing and composition, with a hearty dose of history thrown in.

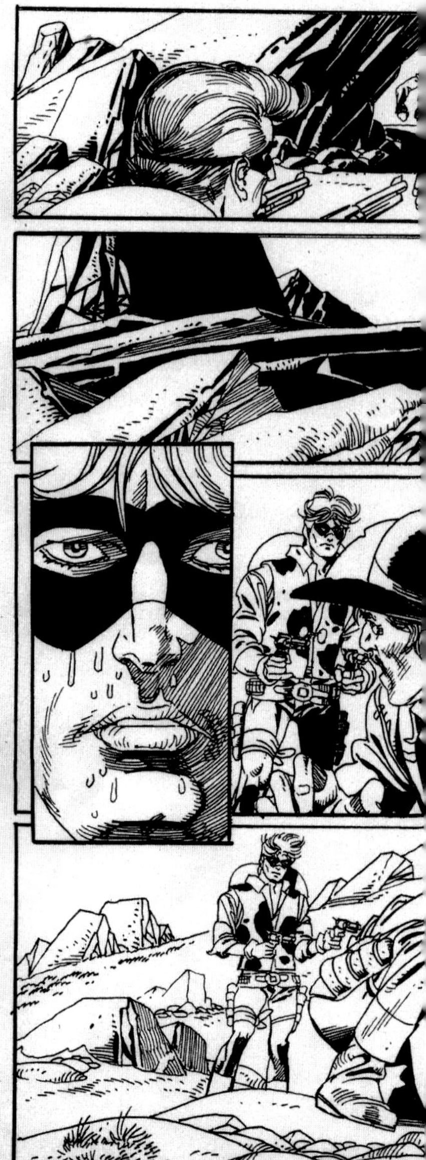

Three interior pages of Kane's original artwork, in the western genre, which demonstrate his impeccable panel composition, Gil Kane, pencils and inks, ©2001 the respective copyright holder.

Kane lived not only to see those he worked under and with pass into the history of comics, but, also to become a figure of historical significance, himself. Kane's importance as a teller of graphic stories should not be limited to the comics world, however. Kane's legacy demands wider appreciation among those not familiar with comic books, as his language of form is much more broad based in its appeal and significance within the broad scope of twentieth century art. Kane was quick to point out that his comic book stories were not high art and had no aspiration to be. Nevertheless, his art occupies a place of singular significance in the uniquely American art form of the comic book. Indeed, while Kane would hotly debate it, he ultimately became a better and more influential graphic storyteller than many of those who influenced him.

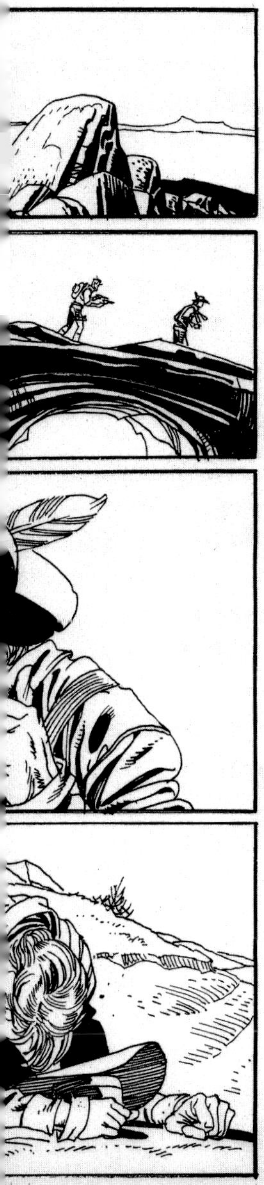

As has been demonstrated in this book, Kane drew literally thousands of stories in the 1970s, 1980s, and 1990s, not to mention thousands of covers. While Kane, ever critical of his own work, admitted that among this large body of work were some "stinkers,"

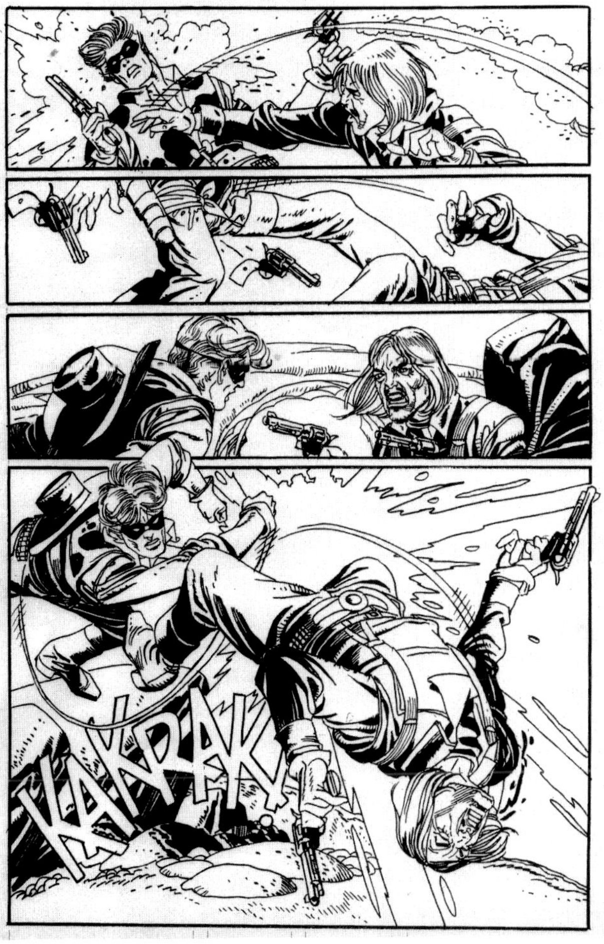

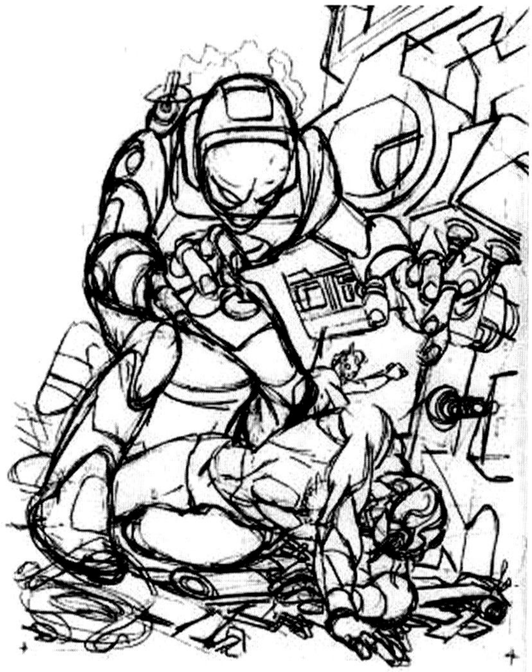

on the whole, Kane's work was well designed and crafted.

Kane's life story is the archetypal American myth. He came with his immigrant parents to the new world in search of a better life. He grew up in the Jewish immigrant neighborhood in Brooklyn, New York, and was educated in the streets, museums, and libraries of New York City. He was a child of the depression and he carried with him a romantic optimism which pervaded his work. He was a kid from the "city" who loved horses and the old west, and who dreamed of distant planets, space ships, and maidens in distress. All of these things are reflected in his oeuvre. As with other immigrant artists, Kane chose a new name for himself. He learned over time to dress in an elegant manner and carried himself with an air of assurance and confidence, but he never forgot his roots. He spoke often, well, and passionately, to fans of his work, always

Layout drawing for the cover for *Captain Marvel* #18, November, 1969, ©2001 Marvel Characters, Inc.

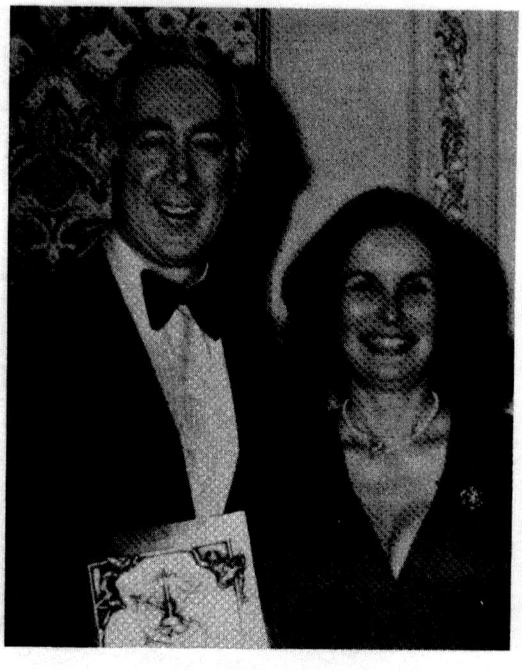

Gil and Elaine Kane in the 1970s.

punctuating his answers with the phrase "m'boy."

Kane changed the face of the art of the comics. Kane's style is indelibly stamped on contemporary comics, whether the current crop of artists is aware of it or not. Late in his life Kane felt that the comic book as a medium had seen its day because current comic books are, to a great extent, self-referential, depending solely on past comic books for inspiration. When Kane started in the industry, artists and writers had to make things up as they went along, which forced them to look to numerous sources, and to create a mélange of influences. Kane was right in this conclusion, as today's comics lack the flavor and infectious enthusiasm injected by the first and second generation of comic book artists.

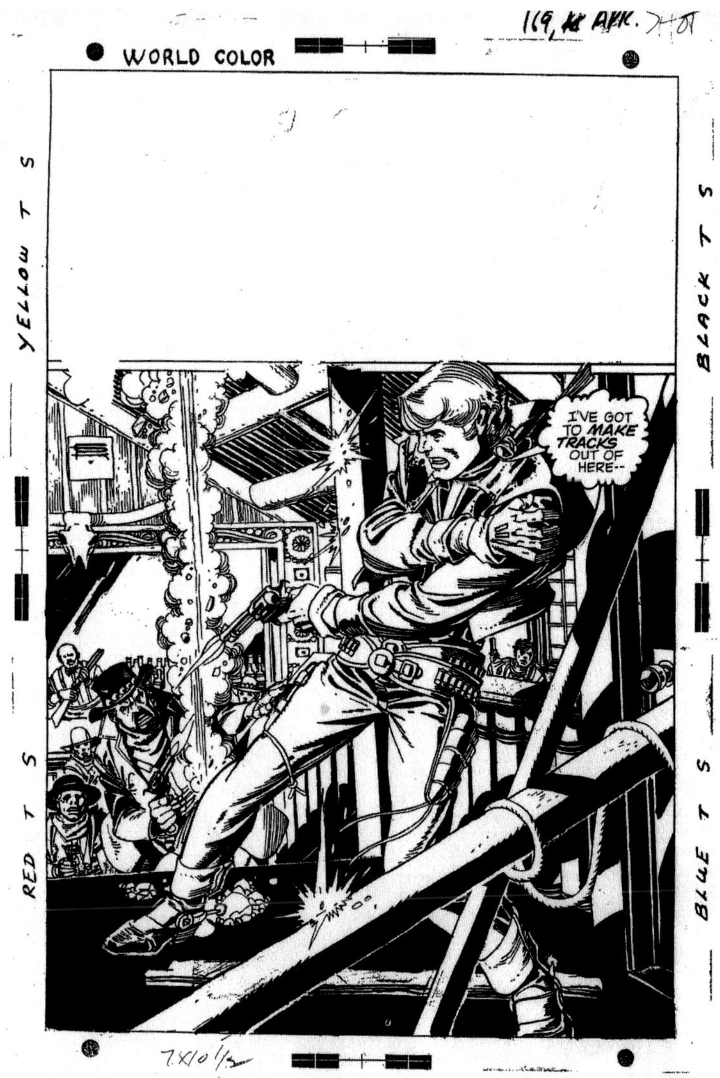
WORLD COLOR
I'VE GOT TO MAKE TRACKS OUT OF HERE--

Although Kane never reaped the financial reward of his efforts, he indelibly

Original artwork for the cover for *Kid Colt* #169, April, 1973, Gil Kane, pencils and inks, ©2001 Marvel Characters, Inc.

influenced the art of the comic book as one of its most eloquent advocates.

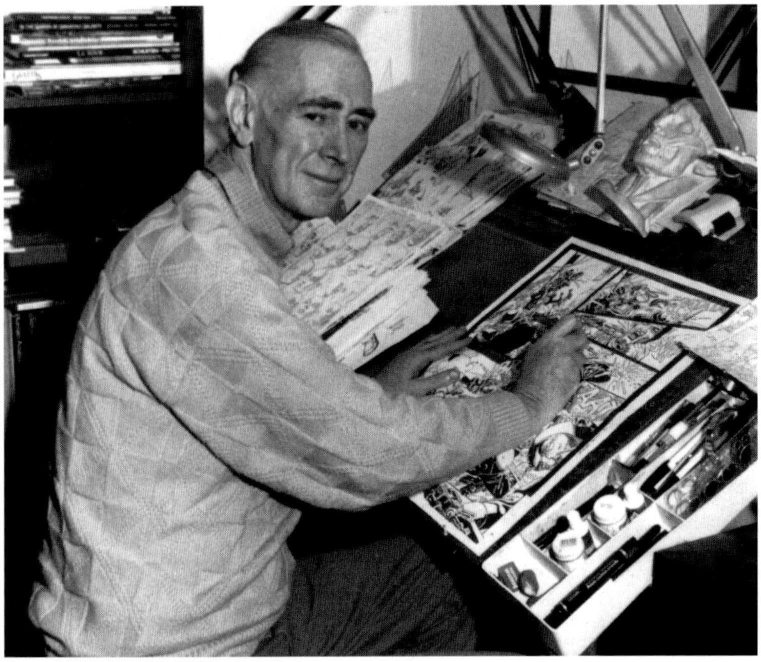

Kane in 1997, photograph by Alex Chun, ©2001 Alex Chun, used by permission.

Despite Kane's many comments to the contrary, he was an incurable idealist. This does not mean that every story he told, should or does have a happy ending. Kane, however, was happiest struggling to tell stories of adventures or quests where the motive of the main character was a just and noble one. To Kane, the struggle to tell the story was part of the adventure of being a comic book storyteller. In Kane's own quest as a storyteller, while he did not always prevail in the market place, he always came through on the page and for the reader.

Gil Kane once commented that the best cartoonists were possessed. In Kane's case he was possessed with a romantic's love of the mythical. Kane was able to imbue his images with an enthusiasm that has rarely been rivaled. Above all else, Kane was a master storyteller who created an imagery that stands as a high water mark in the art of the comics.

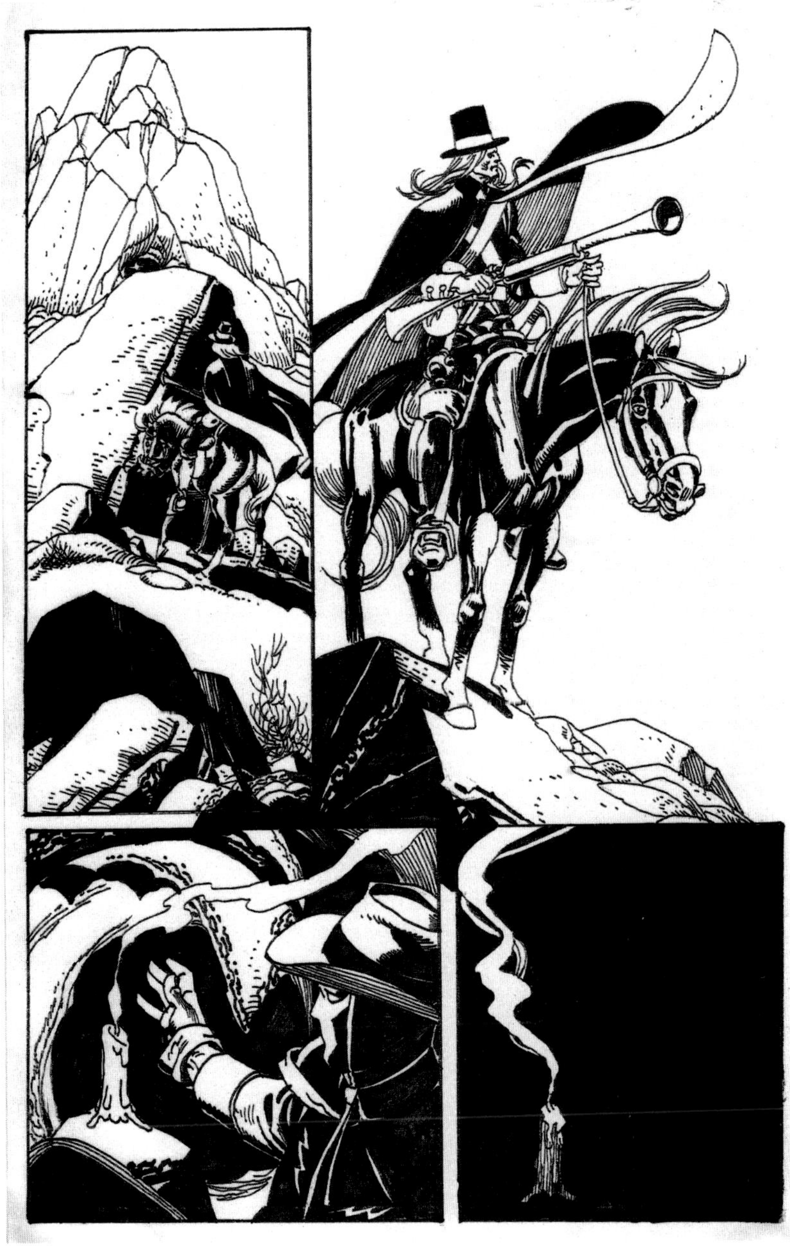

Right: final page of a four page continuity from *Judgment Day*, June, 1997, Gil Kane, pencils and inks, ©2001 Awesome Entertainment, LLC. One of the last western stories on which Kane ever worked, this page's concluding panel is strangely poetic.

FOOTNOTES

INTRODUCTION

1. During the five decades that spanned his career, Kane worked in a number of industries which used comic illustration. He primarily worked drawing comic book stories. He also drew story boards for television (story boards, like comic book stories, lay out the action and plot development of a story in the form of drawings, which are used in the production and direction of television and film), introduced the modern "graphic novel" (a graphic novel is an extended, developed story, told in comic book fashion, which substantially addresses its plot and characters), worked drawing newspaper comic strips, and worked in the production of story boards, presentation pieces, and character designs for cartoons. Kane, also, briefly worked designing advertising.

CHAPTER 1

1. Newspaper comic strips or "strips" run in daily newspaper sections in a horizontal row, usually broken down into several panels or frames and are more elaborate in their Sunday incarnations. The word, "strip," generally refers to a comic book story title, or newspaper comic title. A "continuity" of a comic book or comic strip is the continuation of the story, story line, or feature, through successive issues, daily strips, or installments.

CHAPTER 2

1. An artist who pencilled a strip could provide very precise or "tight" pencils which merely had to be traced over in ink, or could provide a rough layout which required much more on the part of the inker. Inkers could, depending on the completeness of the pencil drawing supplied, do little more than fill in areas with ink, or they could add background detail, and significant substance to the composition of pages and stories.

CHAPTER 3

1. DC Comics is the current incarnation of what was originally known as Detective Comics. Detective Comics was the publisher of such comic books as its namesake, *Detective Comics*, which featured the first Batman story, and *Action Comics*, which featured Superman, and a host of other comic books featuring mysteries, superheroes, and humor. In 1961, Detective Comics changed its name to National Periodical Publications. In 1971, its name was finally changed to DC Comics, Inc.

CHAPTER 4

1. The influence of Crane, Sickles, and Caniff was clearly pervasive among the second generation in their handling of figures, lighting, and inking. The storytelling techniques of Foster, Raymond, and Hogarth, together with their interpolation of illustration and cinematic storytelling methods, were also the basis for many of the best of the second generation's work in comic books (all of these artists were also influential upon the first generation of comic book artists). These strip artists were but one of the resources considered by the second generation of comic book artists. The second generation also took inspiration from those in the vanguard of the first generation. Kane frequently acknowledged these debts publicly. Kane had also informally interviewed many of the most prominent first generation artists and influential strip artists.
2. Indeed, the witch hunts and paranoia of post World War II America were not limited to Senator Joseph McCarthy and his Senate Permanent Investigations Subcommitte, and the House UnAmerican Activities Committee. Before McCarthy, as early as 1948, comic books became the target of a small group, who blamed juvenile delinquency, among other things, on them. The grand inquisitor of the comic book witch hunt was Dr. Fredric Wertham, a psychiatrist for the New York Department of Hospitals. Wertham, much like McCarthy, made sweeping accusations, which were unsupported by empirical study. Wertham maintained that in every single case of juvenile delinquency he had studied, comic books were a factor. The magazines *Colliers* and *The Saturday Review* focused on these assertions and lent them legitimacy, although *Colliers* subsequently reconsidered its previous conclusions. By 1954, Wertham had published his book, *Seduction of the Innocent*, which further bashed comic books, and went as far as to suggest that the relationship between Batman and Robin "may stimulate children to homosexual fantasies." It was in this environment that censorship came to comics.

CHAPTER 5

1. The repackaged *Green Lantern* was very much in step with the pulse of the late 1950s. The origin story tells of an interstellar policeman, Abin-Sur, who accidentally crashes his space ship on Earth. Instead of a gun to enforce the laws of the cosmos, he wears a ring which gives him superpowers. The ring must be charged every twenty-four hours, with a green lantern, hence the name of the strip. Dying from his injuries, Abin-Sur instructs his ring to seek out someone worthy to wield its power. The ring searches the world and finds test pilot Hal Jordan, who is brought, through the power of the ring - - while he is in a stationary aircraft simulator - - to the alien policeman's side, where

he receives the ring, and his assignment, and becomes the Green Lantern.

2. The New York Times obituary of Kane prominently featured a picture of the cover of *Showcase* #22, the first comic book appearance and origin of the Green Lantern. Kane pencilled and inked this cover.
3. Despite this established practice, Kane had asked to ink his own pencils for *Green Lantern,* but Editor Julius Schwartz demurred. He wanted Kane to pencil as many pages as possible. Kane's inking his own work would have substantially reduced his production. It should be noted that Kane was permitted to ink his own work on secondary features, such as stories in *Strange Adventures*. Finally, toward the end of Kane's tenure on *Green Lantern*, he pencilled and inked both the covers and stories. Kane's ability to control his work more completely can clearly be attributed to the change in atmosphere in the comics industry, due to social and societal changes, and the accompanying demands by artists for more control over their work in the late 1960s. Substantive rights for artists would not be realized for almost another twenty years.
4. There are differing accounts of who first had the idea to reintroduce the Atom. Julius Schwartz maintained that it was his idea, whereas comics fan, and later comics historian, Jerry Bails, has maintained that he suggested bringing back the Atom in a letter to writer and *Atom* scripter Gardner Fox, which was in turn shown to Julius Schwartz. Kane, however, strongly believed that the *Atom* received a second chance as a comic book character, based on his pitch. Kane also specifically remembered preparing the original presentation artwork, which depicted the new, improved, Atom in several poses, including, sitting on the head of a German Shepherd similar to Rex the Wonder Dog. Irrespective of who originated the idea to reintroduce the character, it was Kane's work in redesigning the character, and drawing the strip for all but the last few issues of the run of the comic book, that defined the title, and made the stories work.

CHAPTER 6

1. *Savage* was published in a magazine size format, and printed in black and white, which emphasized the graphic nature of the artwork.

CHAPTER 7

1. Kane was divorced and subsequently remarried. Due to this situation he was required to support two families. This put significant pressure on him to produce large quantities of work to satisfy his financial obligations.
2. Brand worked as an assistant for Kane from 1967 to 1969. He also

become a talented comic artist in underground and mainstream comics until his death, due to alcoholism, in 1985.

3. Kane's wife, Elaine, helped inking black areas of art, called "spotting blacks," and typing the dialogue, and text. Kane also received an assist from Harvey Kurtzman, who did several "breakdowns" or rough layout drawings, which indicate the positioning of characters, camera angles, and framing of shots. Kane, additionally, received help from comic artist Neal Adams, who inked several of the pages for *Blackmark*.

CHAPTER 8

1. When Infantino became Editorial Director, he went as far as to tell Kane his rate for drawing pages was too high and would be reduced. Schwartz was powerless to help him, and Kane decided it was time to go.
2. Thomas' recollection of events differs significantly from Kane's. Thomas maintains that the decision to use the Conan character was based on fan mail suggesting the use of such a character coupled with his interest in using Conan. Thomas' recollection is quite clear that the idea was his, and that the decision was discussed and approved by Stan Lee (it would be an understatement to say that Lee had a hand in everything that happened at Marvel in the late 1960s/early 1970s). Thomas does indicate that once he made the decision to proceed with the use of Conan in a comic book title, Kane was a highly visible, and vocal supporter of this move.
3. Kane also did an effective adaptation of Howard's *Valley of the Worm* in *Supernatural Thrillers*, #3, April, 1972. Kane admired this story, and, in fact, had purchased the rights from the Howard estate. The script, by Thomas and Jerry Conway, together with Kane's effective storytelling, dramatically tell this archetypal story.
4. Kane pencilled covers for Marvel for just about every title the company put out, including Kung Fu titles, horror titles, mysteries, occult stories, and suspense titles.
5. Kane's focus on covers was primarily motivated by the rate he received to pencil a cover, versus the rate he received to pencil a page. Kane openly acknowledged that it took him less time to pencil a cover and he received a higher rate, hence his motivation to do as many covers as he could.

CHAPTER 9

1. During the 1970s Kane negotiated with Isaac Asimov to script a graphic novel version of *Buck Rogers*, but Asimov's publisher, Doubleday, vetoed the idea. Kane also attempted, in vain, to secure the rights to produce Asimov's *Foundation* series as a graphic novel.

Kane was additionally involved in a short-lived partnership with Burne Hogarth. Hogarth, who became a close friend of Kane's, was peripherally involved in an attempt to publish a novel about the Arthurian legend. Kane developed the idea with author John Jakes and presented Jakes with an outline of the first portion of the proposed story. Jakes authored 132 pages of text before dropping out of the project. Kane considered publishing the work in its original form, but was concerned about its commercial viability. He accordingly wrote an outline further developing the story and hired a ghostwriter to add the additional pages. Kane also considered using the 132 pages of text written by Jakes as the basis for a graphic novel, which never materialized. Ultimately, the book was published by Dell under the title *"Excalibur,"* giving Kane first name credit, with Jakes as coauthor.

2. Toward the end of the run of the strip, Archie Goodwin replaced Goulart as the scripter of *Star Hawks.*
3. Kane's work on *Star Hawks* was recognized by his contemporaries and he received the National Cartoonists Society's Reuben Award for his efforts in 1978.
4. *Star Hawks* ran from October 3, 1977 to April 25, 1981.
5. Chaykin would later go on to make a significant impact in comics in the 1980s with his comic book *American Flagg*. Subsequently Chaykin worked in television as a story editor and writing scripts while continuing his involvement with comic books. Chaykin has acknowledged Kane's importance to the art of the comics and has described Kane as the most important influence on him in his career.

CHAPTER 10

1. Fans of comics come together in the thousands to meet artists and writers of comic books, buy comic books and comic art, to see the wares of publishers, and to listen to panel discussions between artists, writers, and comic book historians. These conventions became a subculture of comic book collecting. Foremost among these conventions is the San Diego Comic-Con, which was established in 1969. In 2000, the San Diego Comic-Con drew over fifty thousand visitors, over the span of the four day convention.
2. Ruby-Spears Productions was, at the time, one of the largest companies producing Saturday morning television cartoons. The company, named for its two principals, Joe Ruby and Ken Spears, was owned by Taft Entertainment, which also owned Hanna-Barbera.
3. Kane took particular pride in the work he did on proposed projects for Superman and Tarzan cartoons.
4. The story, as told in the comic books, begins earlier in the legend than Wagner did.

GIL KANE

ART IN COLOR

AN ESSAY IN PICTURES

Gil Kane spent his entire career working in black and white. Occasionally, he would prepare work in color, but this was the exception, rather than the rule. Although Kane had color preferences for his work, his opinions were most often not used. Kane felt his work was strongest, seen in its original, black and white form. For the public, however, Kane's work was only in color. This section presents a representative sampling of Kane's work, as it was seen in comic books, in color.

Kane worked on *Johnny Thunder* throughout the 1950s. Before his work on the *Green Lantern*, the *Johnny Thunder* strip was one of the features most associated with Kane's artwork. These panels are representative of many *Johnny Thunder* stories, *All-Star Western* #109, Oct./Nov., 1959, Gil Kane, pencils, Joe Giella, inks, ©2001 DC Comics.

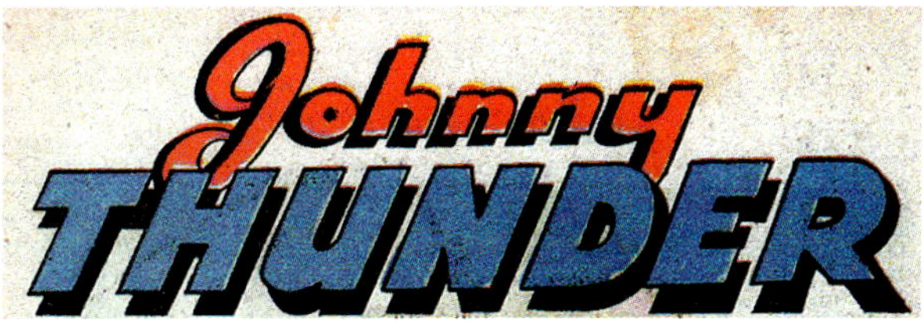
Johnny
THUNDER

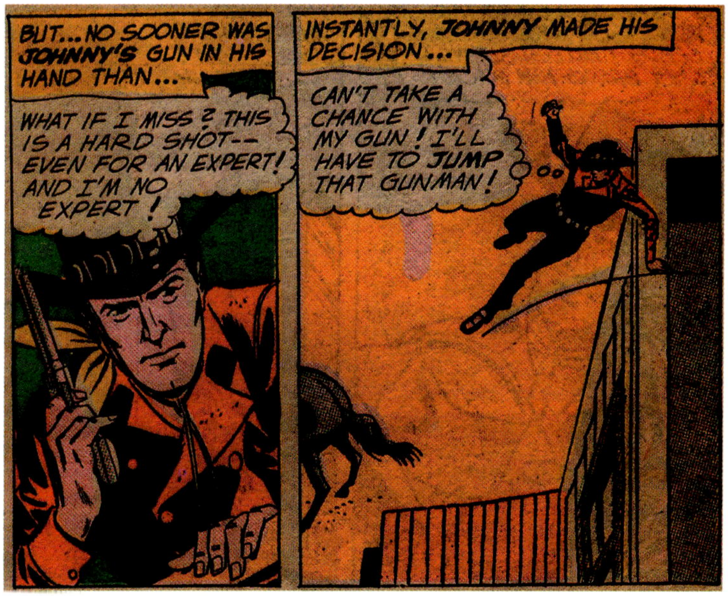
BUT... NO SOONER WAS JOHNNY'S GUN IN HIS HAND THAN...
WHAT IF I MISS ? THIS IS A HARD SHOT-- EVEN FOR AN EXPERT! AND I'M NO EXPERT !
INSTANTLY, JOHNNY MADE HIS DECISION...
CAN'T TAKE A CHANCE WITH MY GUN ! I'LL HAVE TO JUMP THAT GUNMAN !

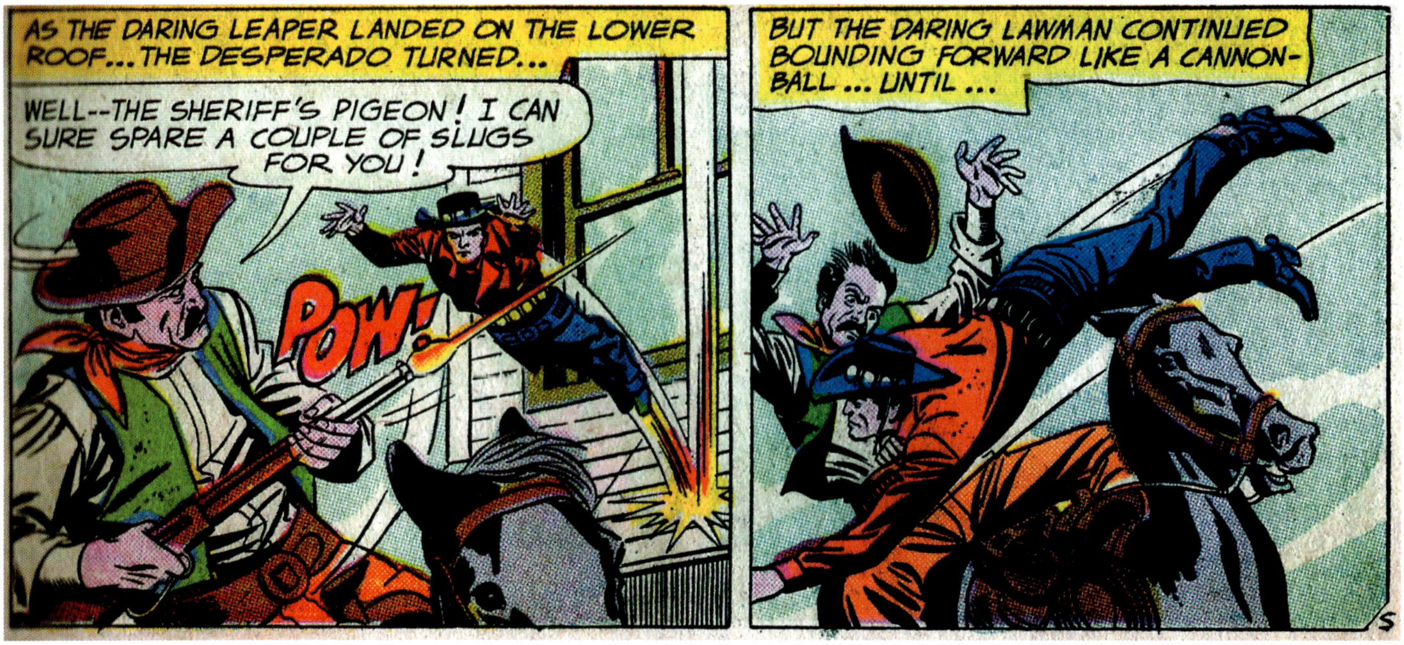
AS THE DARING LEAPER LANDED ON THE LOWER ROOF... THE DESPERADO TURNED...
WELL--THE SHERIFF'S PIGEON ! I CAN SURE SPARE A COUPLE OF SLUGS FOR YOU !
POW!
BUT THE DARING LAWMAN CONTINUED BOUNDING FORWARD LIKE A CANNON-BALL ... UNTIL ...

GREEN LANTERN

As this book demonstrates, Kane made many significant contributions to the art of the comics. Despite that his most noteworthy efforts occurred after the late 1960s, and subsequently thereafter, Kane is most closely associated, by fans of comic books, with the work he did on *Green Lantern* in the 1960s.

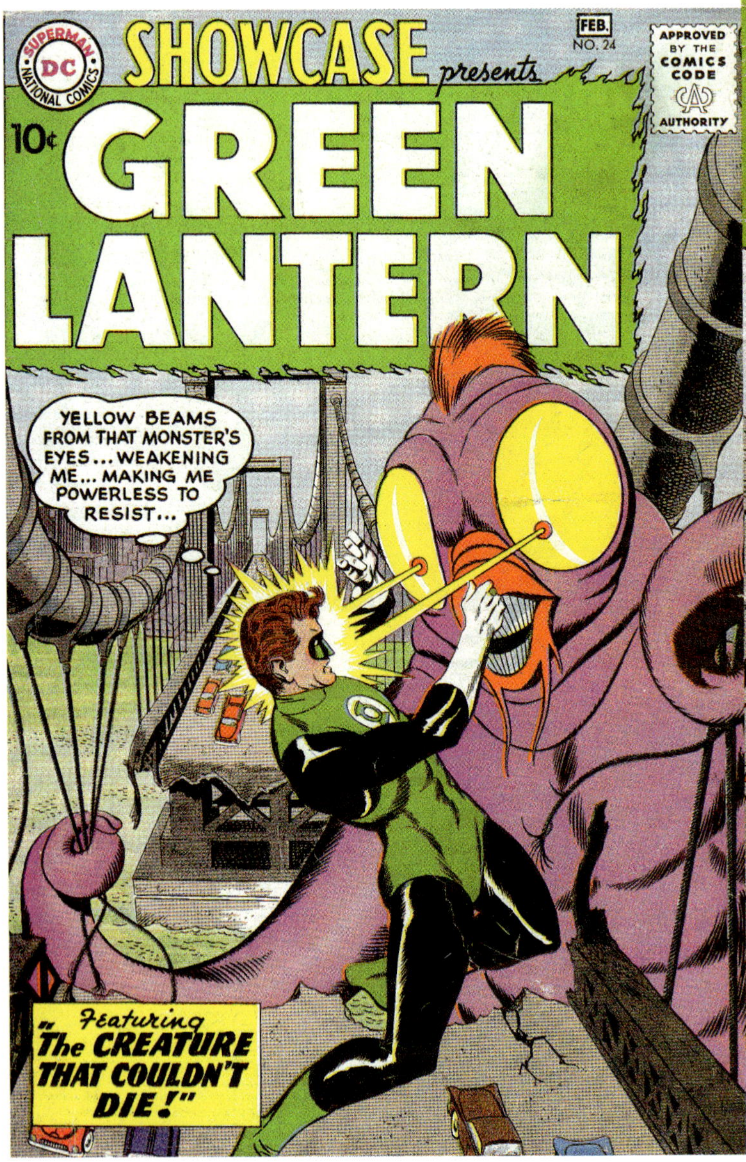
SUPERMAN DC NATIONAL COMICS
SHOWCASE presents
FEB. NO. 24
APPROVED BY THE COMICS CODE AUTHORITY
10¢
GREEN LANTERN
YELLOW BEAMS FROM THAT MONSTER'S EYES... WEAKENING ME... MAKING ME POWERLESS TO RESIST...
Featuring "The CREATURE THAT COULDN'T DIE!"

Cover for *Showcase* #24, January/February, 1960, Gil Kane, pencils, Joe Giella, inks. All artwork in this section ©2001 DC Comics. The third comic book appearance of the Green Lantern offers a classic cover that showcases everything that is most frequently associated with comic books: monsters, superheroes, and a cliff-hanger- - will the Green Lantern save the city?

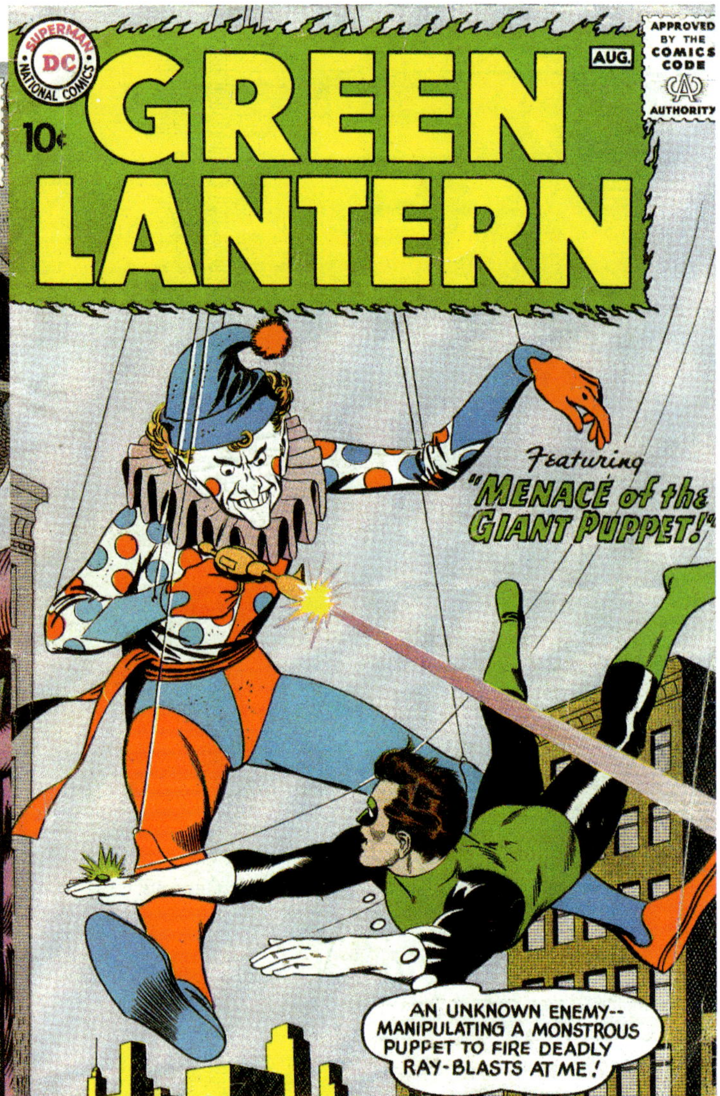
SUPERMAN DC NATIONAL COMICS
AUG.
APPROVED BY THE COMICS CODE AUTHORITY
10¢
GREEN LANTERN
Featuring "MENACE of the GIANT PUPPET!"
AN UNKNOWN ENEMY-- MANIPULATING A MONSTROUS PUPPET TO FIRE DEADLY RAY-BLASTS AT ME!

Cover for *Green Lantern* #1, July/August, 1960, Gil Kane, pencils, Joe Giella, inks. This cover is frequently associated with Kane. The design, while not one of Kane's best, offers an image which is archetypal for comic books.

Below: cover for *Green Lantern* #26, January, 1964, Gil Kane, pencils, Murphy Anderson, inks. Contrast this color version of the cover with the original artwork for the cover in Chapter 5. The original black and white artwork is bold and graphic. The addition of bright, primary yellow, refocuses the composition and lends a hot visual edge to the cover.

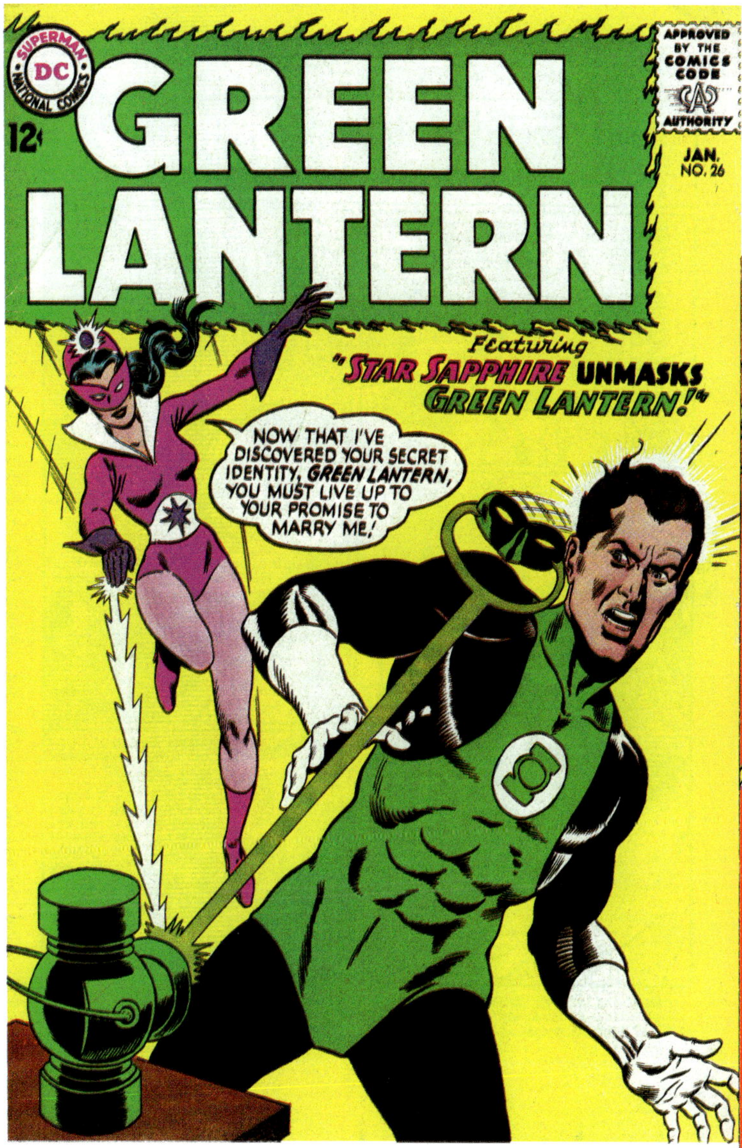
SUPERMAN DC NATIONAL COMICS
12¢
GREEN LANTERN
APPROVED BY THE COMICS CODE AUTHORITY
JAN. NO. 26
Featuring "STAR SAPPHIRE UNMASKS GREEN LANTERN!"
NOW THAT I'VE DISCOVERED YOUR SECRET IDENTITY, GREEN LANTERN, YOU MUST LIVE UP TO YOUR PROMISE TO MARRY ME!

Cover for Green Lantern #60, April, 1968, Gil Kane, pencils, Murphy Anderson, inks. The use of primary red, coupled with Kane's cropped shot of the Green Lantern's face, makes this cover one of the best designs of the series. This cover could easily have been used as a movie poster design. The original artwork for the cover can be found in the Introduction.

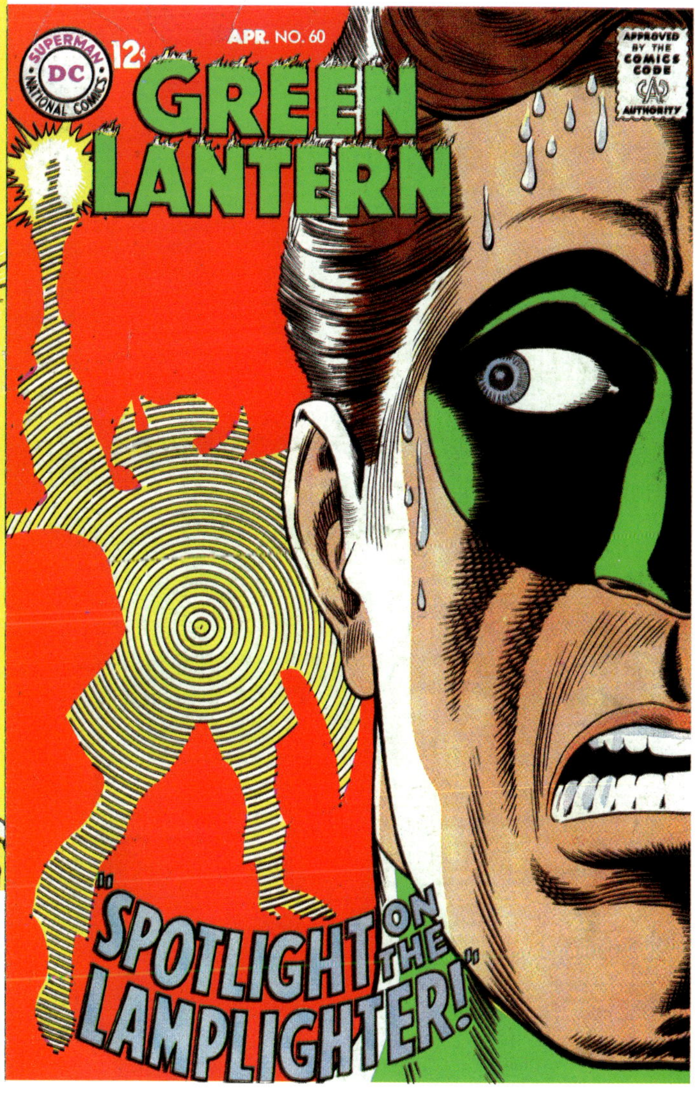
SUPERMAN DC NATIONAL COMICS
12¢
APR. NO. 60
GREEN LANTERN
APPROVED BY THE COMICS CODE AUTHORITY
"SPOTLIGHT ON THE LAMPLIGHTER!"

Comic book covers were designed to immediately attract the attention of their young audience and to inspire quick purchase. Because their function was to quickly get the attention of potential buyers, covers had to have visual impact. Obviously, the dynamics of designing covers, verses the stories contained inside comic books, were dissimilar, as they served different purposes. Interestingly, many comic books are more frequently remembered for their covers than their content. These covers are fondly remembered by fans of the Green Lantern more than the stories that were contained inside.

Examples of Kane's handsome work for *Green Lantern*. Left: interior page from *Green Lantern* #32, October, 196 Gil Kane, pencils, Sid Greene, inks. Right: interior page from *Green Lantern* #48, October, 1966, Gil Kane, pencils Sid Greene, inks. Below left: panel from an interior page from *Green Lantern* #75, March, 1970, Gil Kane, pencils, Joe Giella, inks. All ©2001 DC Comics.

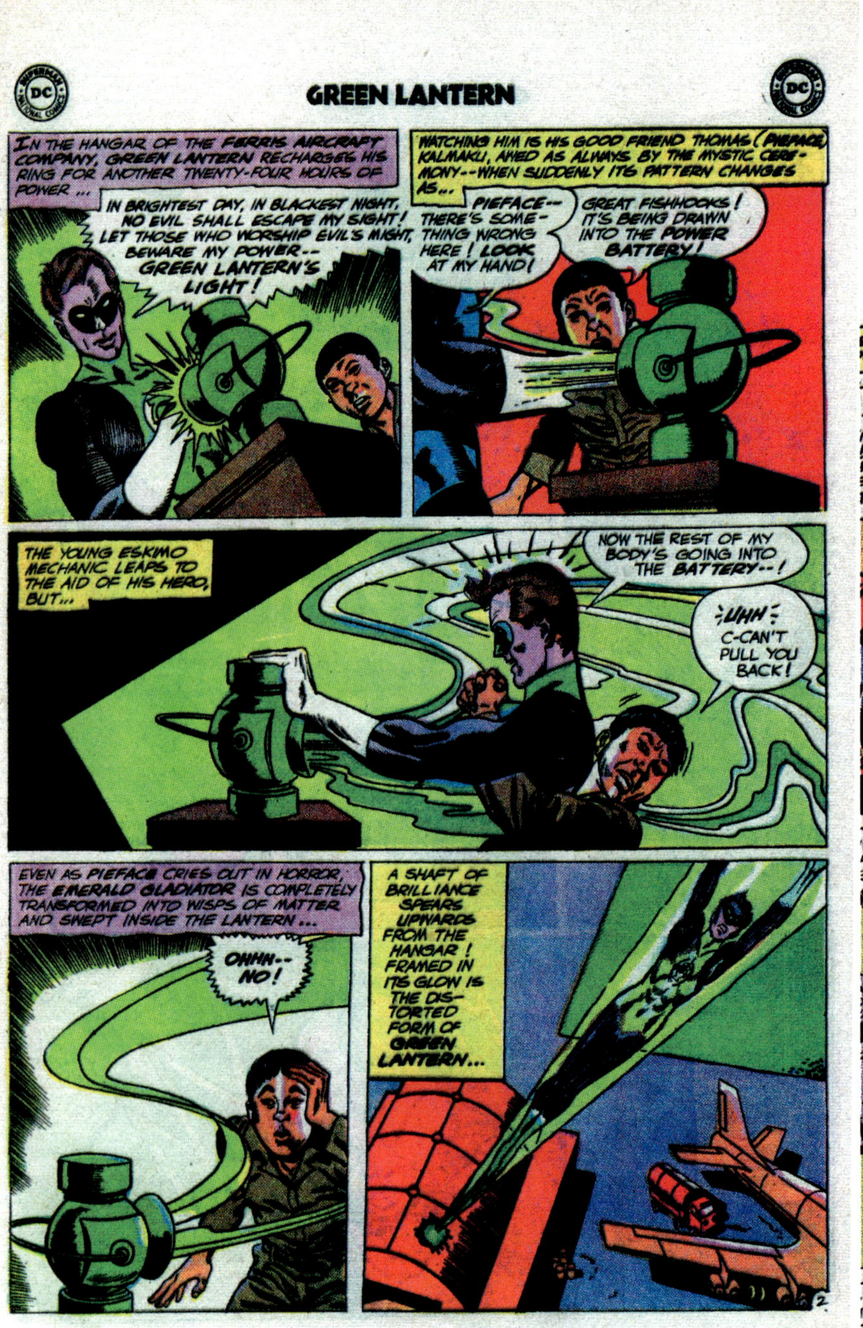

GREEN LANTERN
IN THE HANGAR OF THE FERRIS AIRCRAFT COMPANY, GREEN LANTERN RECHARGES HIS RING FOR ANOTHER TWENTY-FOUR HOURS OF POWER ...
IN BRIGHTEST DAY, IN BLACKEST NIGHT, NO EVIL SHALL ESCAPE MY SIGHT! LET THOSE WHO WORSHIP EVIL'S MIGHT, BEWARE MY POWER-- GREEN LANTERN'S LIGHT!
WATCHING HIM IS HIS GOOD FRIEND THOMAS (PIEFACE) KALMAKU, AWED AS ALWAYS BY THE MYSTIC CEREMONY--WHEN SUDDENLY ITS PATTERN CHANGES AS...
PIEFACE-- THERE'S SOMETHING WRONG HERE! LOOK AT MY HAND!
GREAT FISHHOOKS! IT'S BEING DRAWN INTO THE POWER BATTERY!
THE YOUNG ESKIMO MECHANIC LEAPS TO THE AID OF HIS HERO, BUT...
NOW THE REST OF MY BODY'S GOING INTO THE BATTERY--!
UHH! C-CAN'T PULL YOU BACK!
EVEN AS PIEFACE CRIES OUT IN HORROR, THE EMERALD GLADIATOR IS COMPLETELY TRANSFORMED INTO WISPS OF MATTER AND SWEPT INSIDE THE LANTERN ...
OHHH-- NO!
A SHAFT OF BRILLIANCE SPEARS UPWARDS FROM THE HANGAR! FRAMED IN ITS GLOW IS THE DISTORTED FORM OF GREEN LANTERN...
2

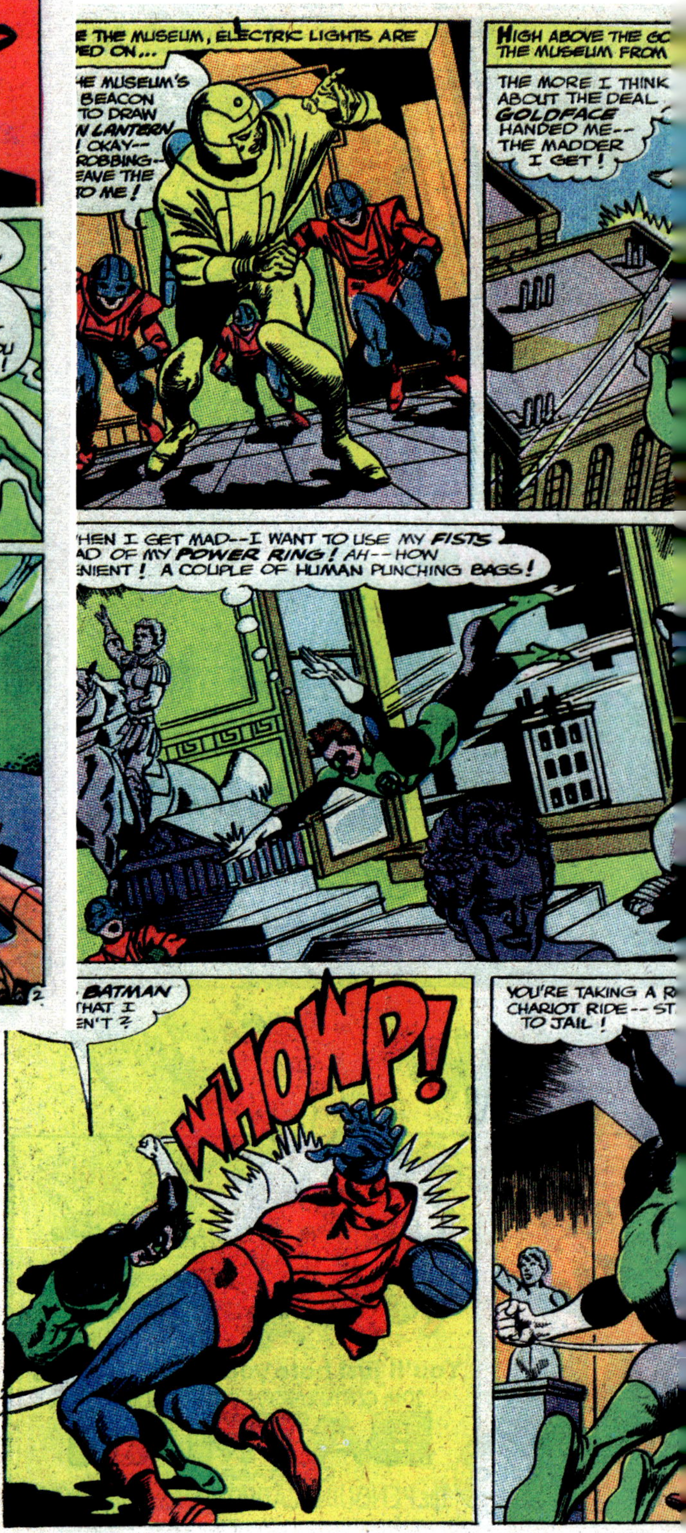

E THE MUSEUM, ELECTRIC LIGHTS ARE
ED ON...
HE MUSEUM'S BEACON TO DRAW N LANTERN ! OKAY-- ROBBING-- EAVE THE TO ME!
HIGH ABOVE THE GO THE MUSEUM FROM
THE MORE I THINK ABOUT THE DEAL GOLDFACE HANDED ME-- THE MADDER I GET!
HEN I GET MAD--I WANT TO USE MY FISTS AD OF MY POWER RING! AH--HOW ENIENT! A COUPLE OF HUMAN PUNCHING BAGS!
BATMAN THAT I EN'T ?
WHOMP!
YOU'RE TAKING A R CHARIOT RIDE--ST TO JAIL!

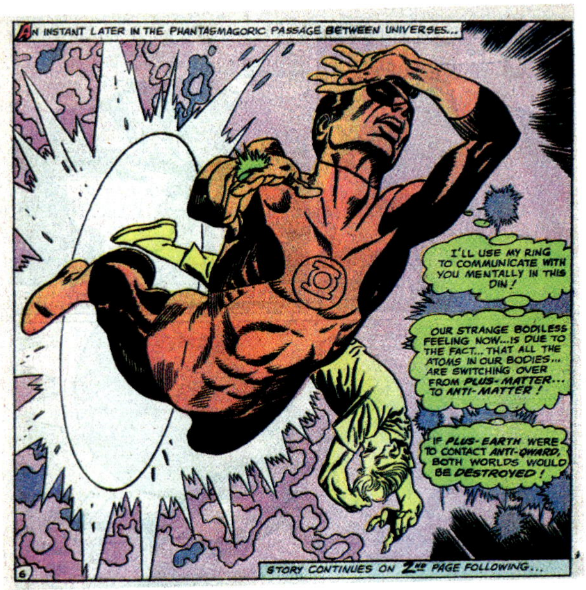

AN INSTANT LATER IN THE PHANTASMAGORIC PASSAGE BETWEEN UNIVERSES...
I'LL USE MY RING TO COMMUNICATE WITH YOU MENTALLY IN THIS DIN!
OUR STRANGE BODILESS FEELING NOW...IS DUE TO THE FACT...THAT ALL THE ATOMS IN OUR BODIES... ARE SWITCHING OVER FROM PLUS-MATTER... TO ANTI-MATTER!
IF PLUS-EARTH WERE TO CONTACT ANTI-OWARD, BOTH WORLDS WOULD BE DESTROYED!
STORY CONTINUES ON 2ND PAGE FOLLOWING...
6

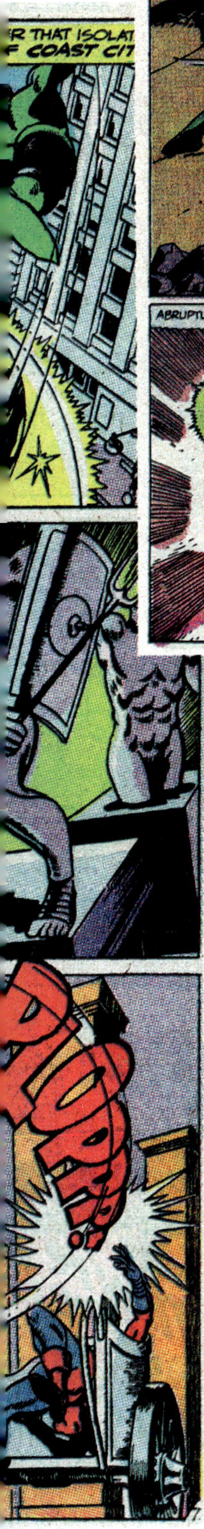

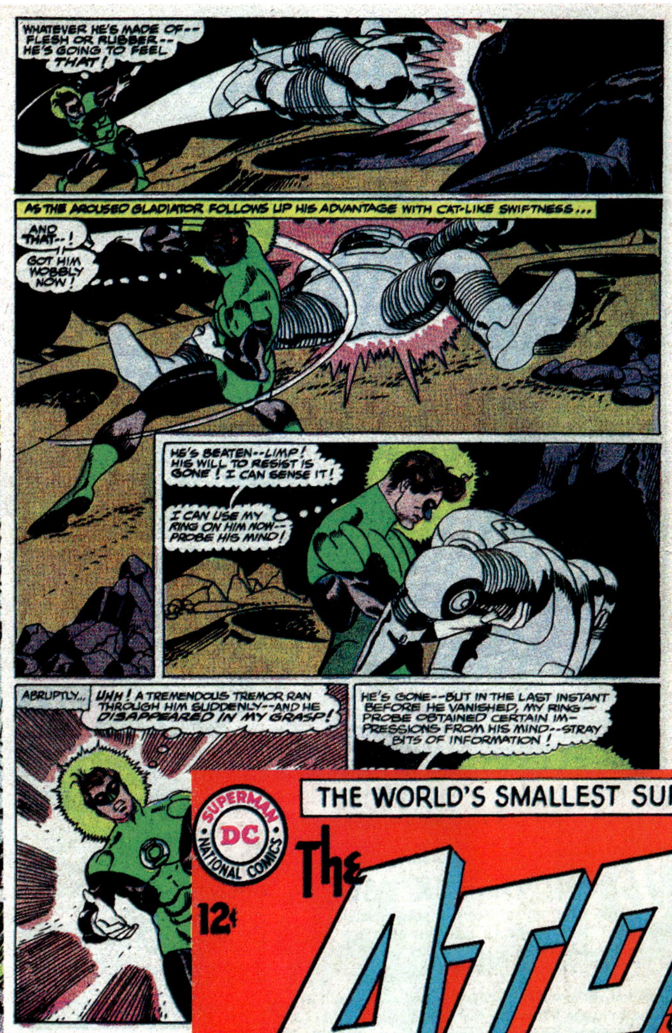
WHATEVER HE'S MADE OF-- FLESH OR RUBBER-- HE'S GOING TO FEEL THAT!
AS THE AROUSED GLADIATOR FOLLOWS UP HIS ADVANTAGE WITH CAT-LIKE SWIFTNESS...
AND THAT--!
GOT HIM WOBBLY NOW!
HE'S BEATEN--LIMP! HIS WILL TO RESIST IS GONE! I CAN SENSE IT!
I CAN USE MY RING ON HIM NOW-- PROBE HIS MIND!
ABRUPTLY...
UHH! A TREMENDOUS TREMOR RAN THROUGH HIM SUDDENLY--AND HE DISAPPEARED IN MY GRASP!
HE'S GONE--BUT IN THE LAST INSTANT BEFORE HE VANISHED, MY RING-PROBE OBTAINED CERTAIN IMPRESSIONS FROM HIS MIND--STRAY BITS OF INFORMATION!

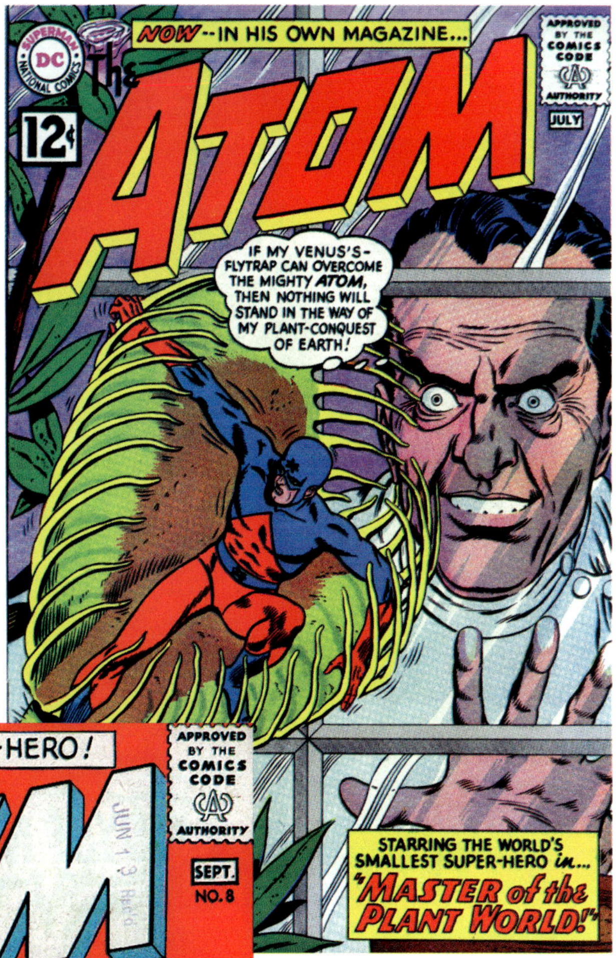
NOW--IN HIS OWN MAGAZINE...
APPROVED BY THE COMICS CODE AUTHORITY
JULY
12¢
The ATOM
IF MY VENUS'S-FLYTRAP CAN OVERCOME THE MIGHTY ATOM, THEN NOTHING WILL STAND IN THE WAY OF MY PLANT-CONQUEST OF EARTH!
STARRING THE WORLD'S SMALLEST SUPER-HERO in...
"MASTER of the PLANT WORLD!"

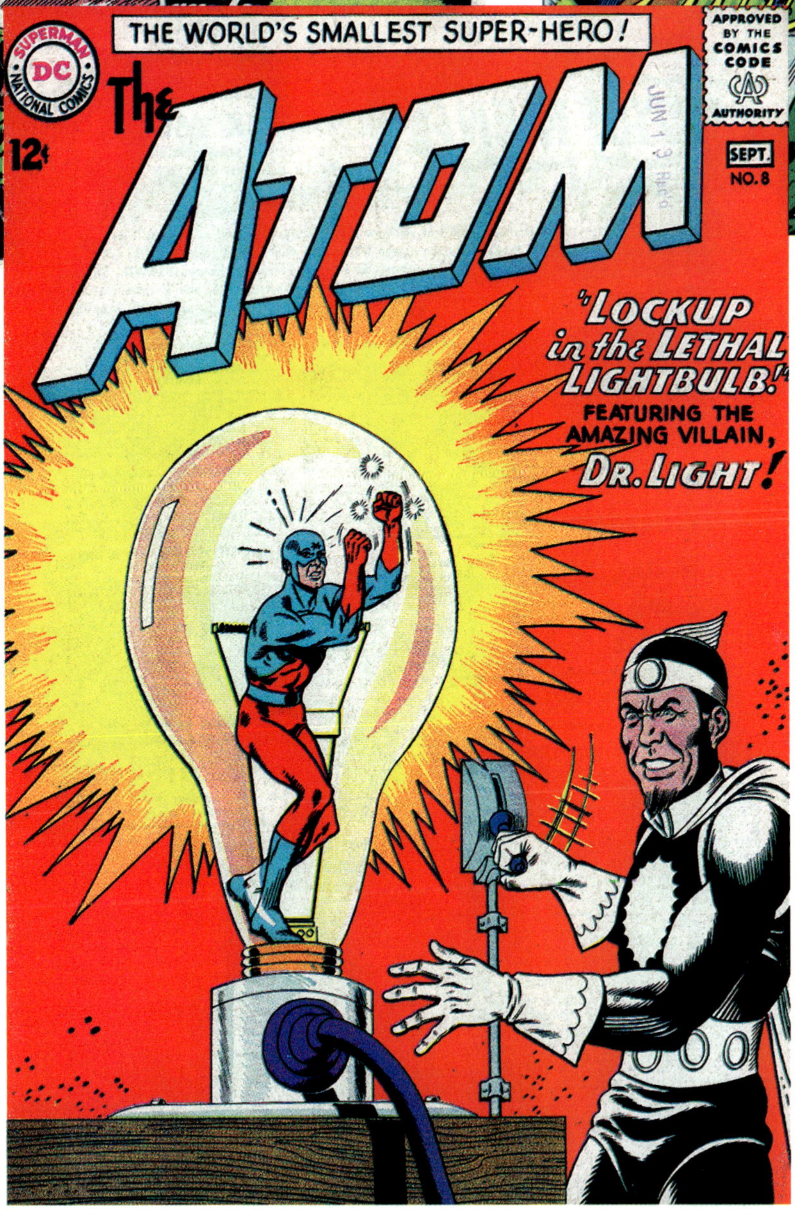
THE WORLD'S SMALLEST SUPER-HERO!
APPROVED BY THE COMICS CODE AUTHORITY
12¢
The ATOM
SEPT.
NO. 8
"LOCKUP in the LETHAL LIGHTBULB!"
FEATURING THE AMAZING VILLAIN, DR. LIGHT!

These images have undeniable eye appeal. The covers and interior pages pictured here, feature arresting artwork, which is fanciful and surreal. Above: cover for *The Atom* #1, June/July, 1962, Gil Kane, pencils, Murphy Anderson, inks. Left: cover for *The Atom* #8, August/September, 1963, Gil Kane, pencils, Murphy Anderson, inks. Above left: interior page from *Green Lantern* #55, September, 1967, Gil Kane, pencils and inks. All ©2001 DC Comics.

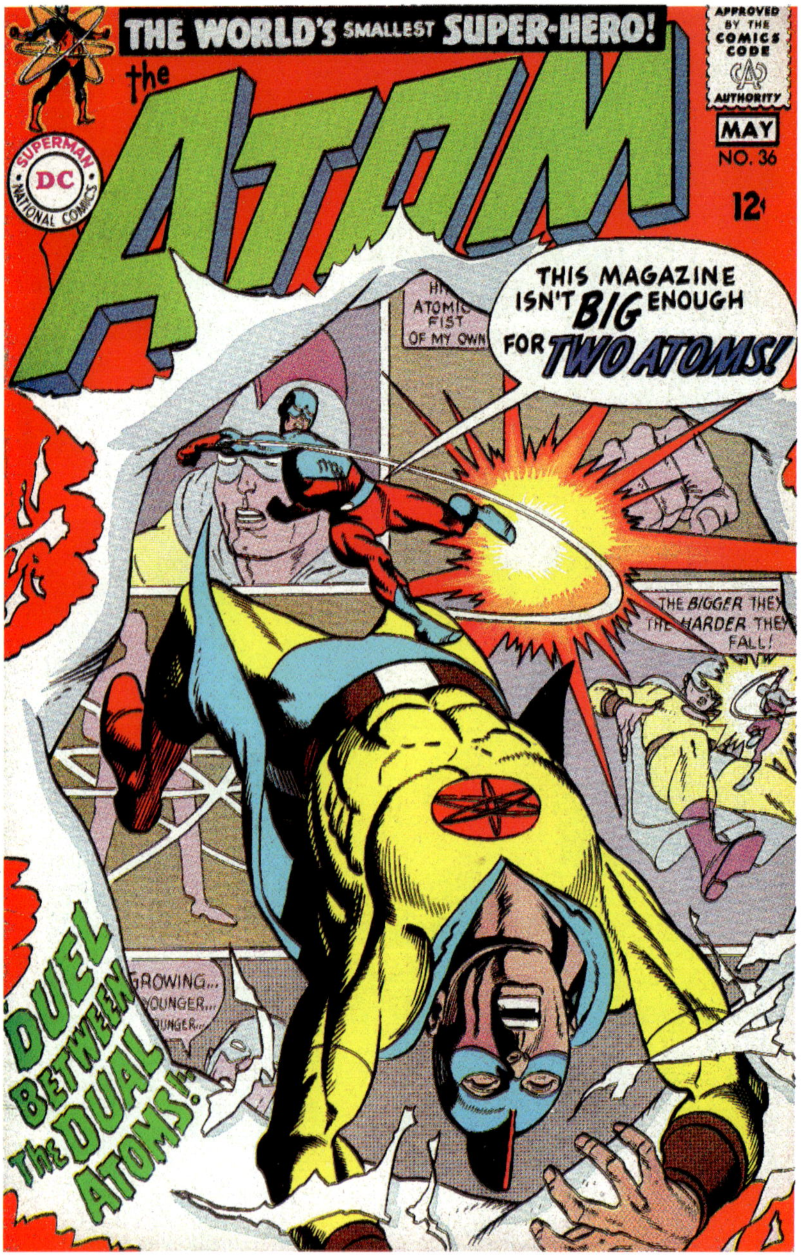
THE WORLD'S SMALLEST SUPER-HERO!
APPROVED BY THE COMICS CODE AUTHORITY
the ATOM
SUPERMAN DC NATIONAL COMICS
MAY
NO. 36
12¢
THIS MAGAZINE ISN'T BIG ENOUGH FOR TWO ATOMS!
THE BIGGER THEY THE HARDER THEY FALL!
GROWING... YOUNGER...
DUEL BETWEEN THE DUAL ATOMS!

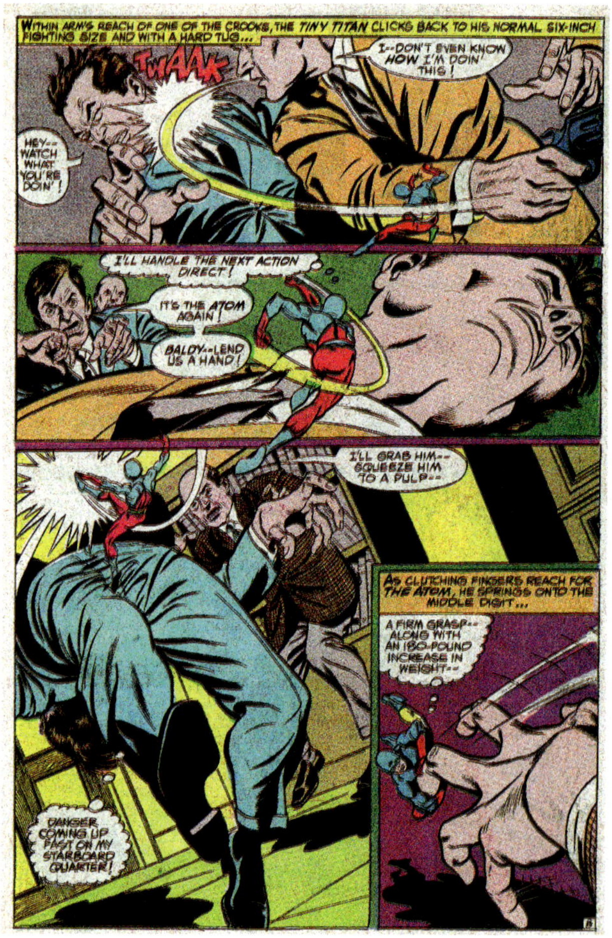
WITHIN ARM'S REACH OF ONE OF THE CROOKS, THE TINY TITAN CLICKS BACK TO HIS NORMAL SIX-INCH FIGHTING SIZE AND WITH A HARD TUG...
TWAAK
I--DON'T EVEN KNOW HOW I'M DOIN' THIS!
HEY-- WATCH WHAT YOU'RE DOIN'!
I'LL HANDLE THE NEXT ACTION DIRECT!
IT'S THE ATOM AGAIN!
BALDY--LEND US A HAND!
I'LL GRAB HIM-- SQUEEZE HIM TO A PULP--
DANGER COMING UP FAST ON MY STARBOARD QUARTER!
AS CLUTCHING FINGERS REACH FOR THE ATOM, HE SPRINGS ONTO THE MIDDLE DIGIT...
A FIRM GRASP-- ALONG WITH AN 180-POUND INCREASE IN WEIGHT--

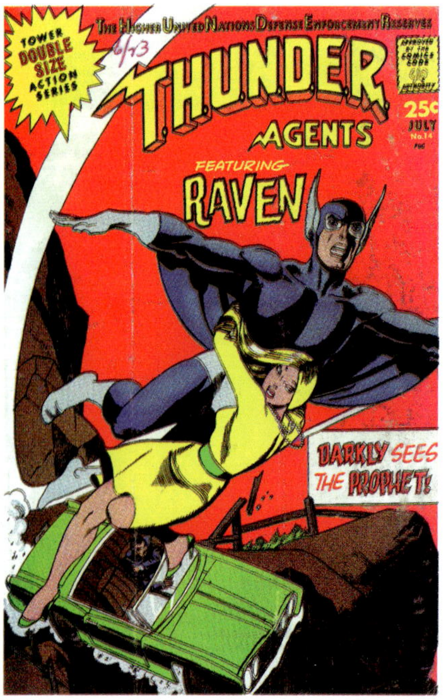
TOWER DOUBLE SIZE ACTION SERIES
THE HIGHER UNITED NATIONS DEFENSE ENFORCEMENT RESERVES
T.H.U.N.D.E.R. AGENTS
25¢
JULY
FEATURING RAVEN
DARKLY SEES THE PROPHET!

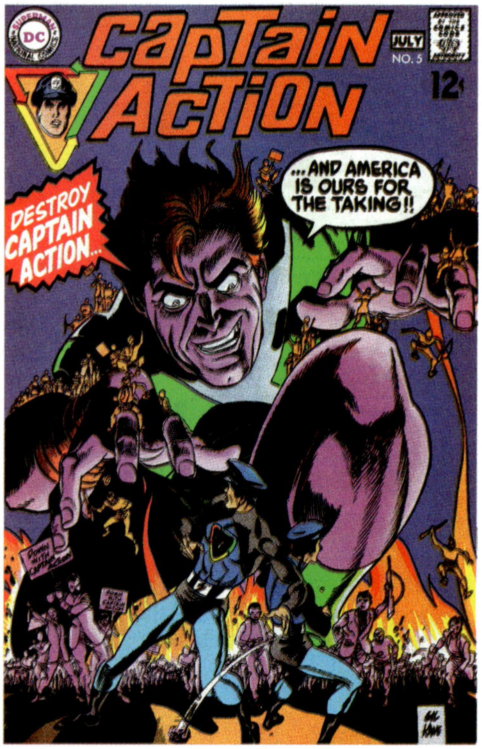
SUPERMAN DC NATIONAL COMICS
Captain Action
JULY
NO. 5
12¢
...AND AMERICA IS OURS FOR THE TAKING!!
DESTROY CAPTAIN ACTION...

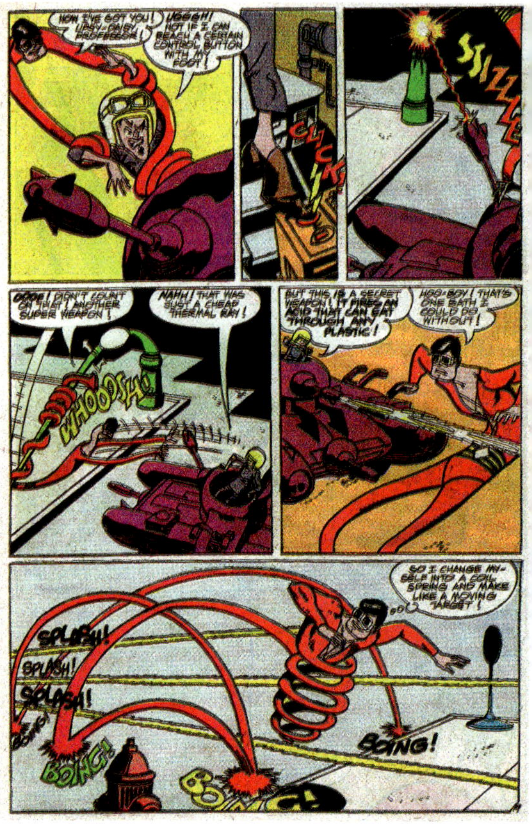
USSSH!! NOT IF I CAN REACH A CERTAIN CONTROL BUTTON WITH MY FOOT!
CLICK!
SSIZZLE
NAHH! THAT WAS JUST A CHEAP THERMAL RAY!
WHOOSH!
HOO-BOY! THAT'S ONE BATH I COULD DO WITHOUT!
SO I CHANGE MY-SELF INTO A COIL SPRING AND MAKE LIKE A MOVING TARGET!
SPLASH!
SPLASH!
BOING!
BOING!

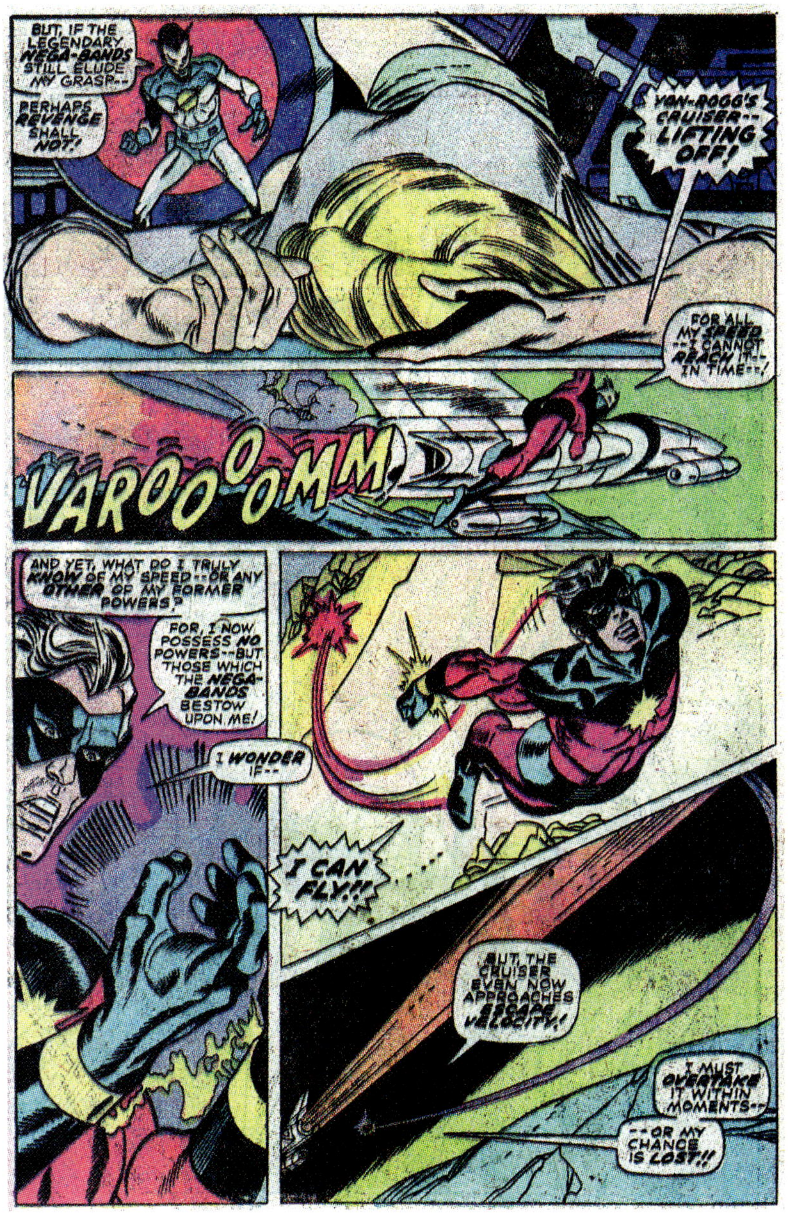
BUT, IF THE LEGENDARY NEGA-BANDS STILL ELUDE MY GRASP--
PERHAPS REVENGE SHALL NOT!
YON-ROGG'S CRUISER--LIFTING OFF!
FOR ALL MY SPEED--I CANNOT REACH IT--IN TIME--!
VAROOOOMM
AND YET, WHAT DO I TRULY KNOW OF MY SPEED--OR ANY OTHER OF MY FORMER POWERS?
FOR, I NOW POSSESS NO POWERS--BUT THOSE WHICH THE NEGA-BANDS BESTOW UPON ME!
I WONDER IF--
I CAN FLY!!
BUT THE CRUISER EVEN NOW APPROACHES ESCAPE VELOCITY!
I MUST OVERTAKE IT WITHIN MOMENTS--
--OR MY CHANCE IS LOST!!

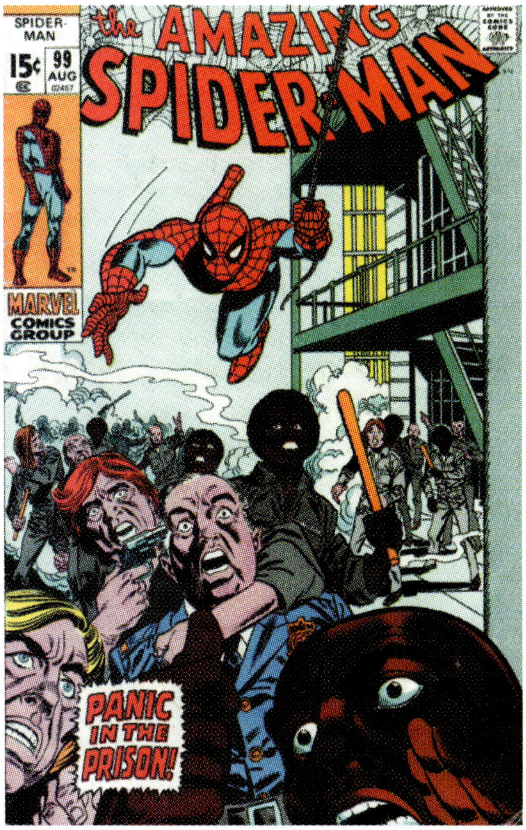
SPIDER-MAN
15¢
99
AUG
the AMAZING SPIDER-MAN
MARVEL COMICS GROUP
PANIC IN THE PRISON!

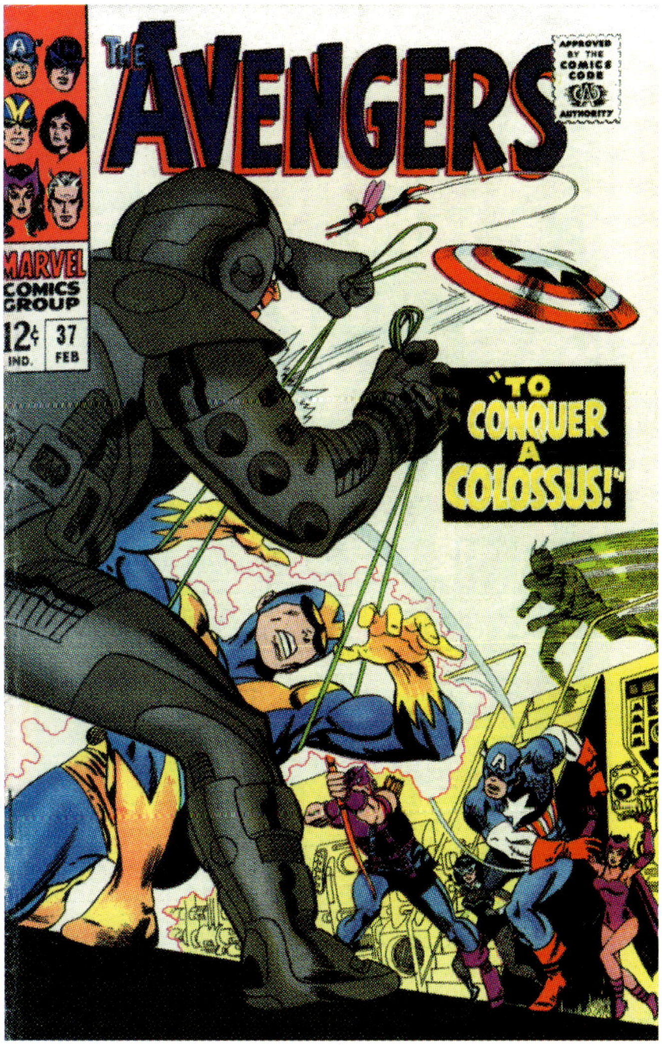
THE AVENGERS
MARVEL COMICS GROUP
12¢
37
FEB
"TO CONQUER A COLOSSUS!"

Toward the end of the 1960s, Kane's handling of the human form became more fluid and assured. These two pages of *Art in Color* attest to Kane's maturity as an artist of comic book stories. Kane's composition was solid and his drawing fully realized the fantastic action demanded by these stories. Opposite page, top left: cover and an interior page from *The Atom* #36, April/ May, 1968, Gil Kane, pencils and inks (cover), Sid Greene, inks (interior page). Opposite page, cover for *THUNDER Agents* #14, July, 1967, Gil Kane, pencils and inks, ©2001 Tower Comics. Center: cover for *Captain Action* #5, June/July, 1969, Gil Kane, pencils and inks. Left: Kane's homage to Jack Cole's Plastic Man, *Plastic Man* #1, November/December 1966, Gil Kane, pencils and inks. All, unless otherwise noted, ©2001 DC Comics. This page, above: interior page from *Captain Marvel* #17, October, 1969, Gil Kane, pencils, Dan Adkins, inks. Kane felt that Adkins was one of the handful of inkers who understood his work and who sensitively and successfully inked his pencils. Above right, cover for *The Amazing Spider-Man* #99, August, 1971, Gil Kane, pencils, Frank Giacoia, inks. Right: cover for *The Avengers* #37, February, 1967, Gil Kane, pencils and inks. All ©2001 Marvel Characters, Inc.

Below: the original logo for *His Name is...Savage*, seen in Chapter 6 on the unused cover for *His Name is...Savage* #1. Pictured below: the cover for the 1982 Fantagraphics reissue of *Savage,* renamed *Gil Kane's Savage*. Kane created a new cover for his second attempt to reach a wide audience with his ground-breaking graphic novel, ©2001 The Estate of Gil Kane.

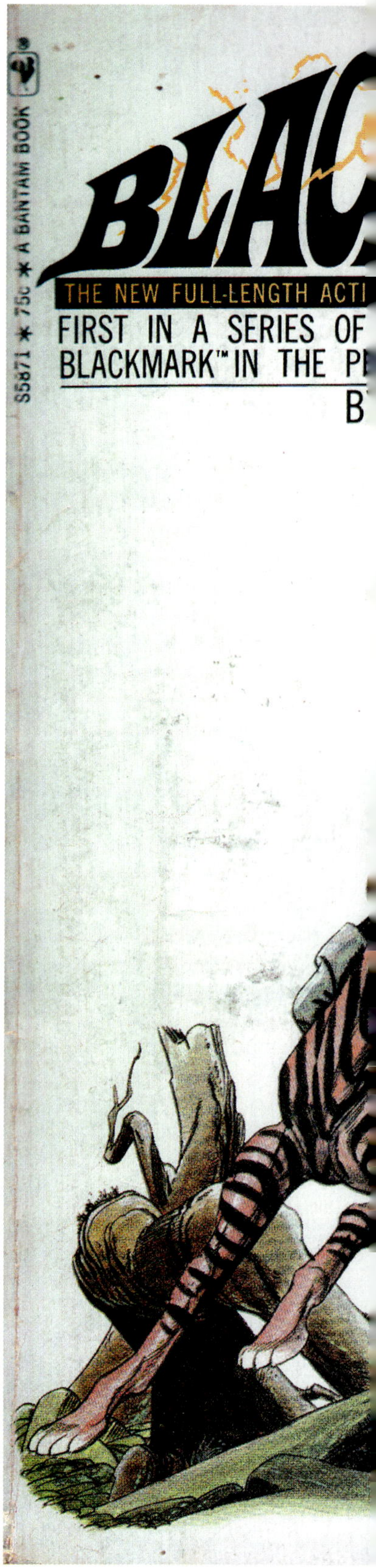

S5871 ★ 75c ★ A BANTAM BOOK
BLAC
THE NEW FULL-LENGTH ACTI
FIRST IN A SERIES OF
BLACKMARK™ IN THE P
B

SAVAGE !

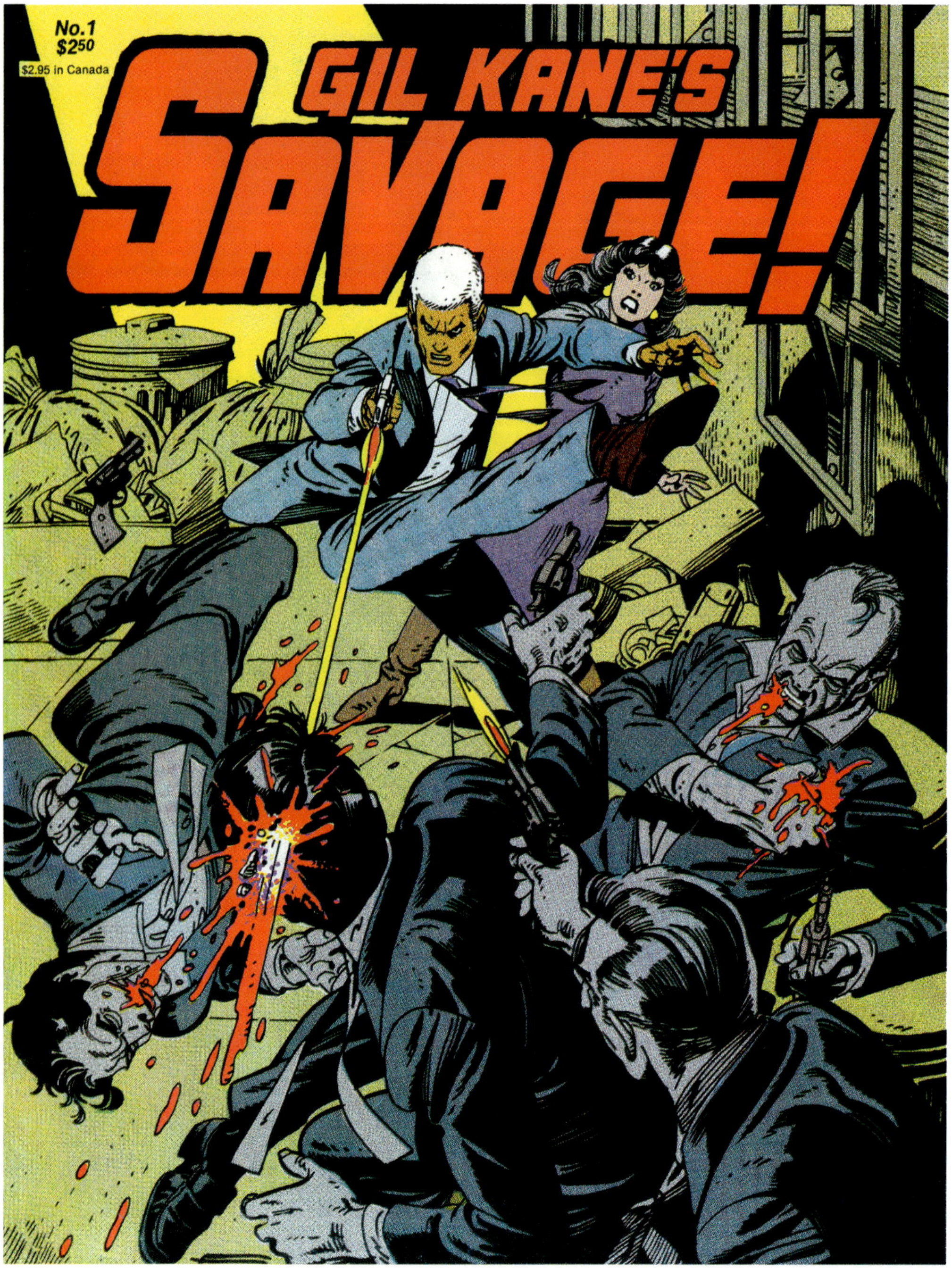

No.1
$2.50
$2.95 in Canada
GIL KANE'S
SAVAGE!

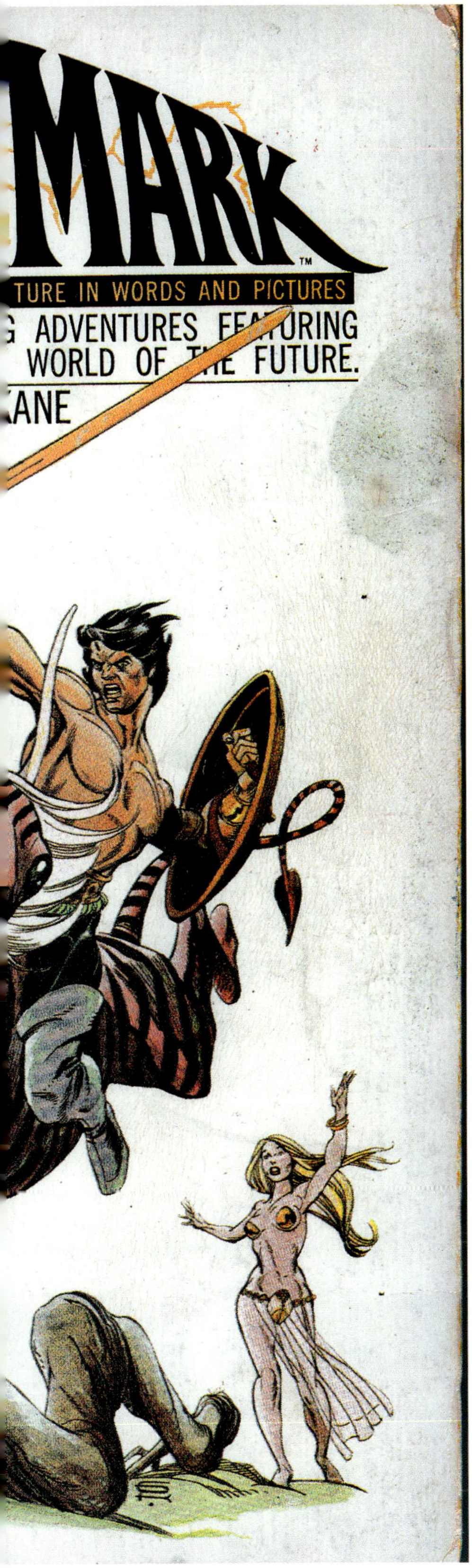

Cover for *Blackmark*, 1971, Gil Kane, pencils and inks, ©2001 The Estate of Gil Kane. The cover for Kane's second graphic novel, issued by Bantam Books as a pocket book.

Below: Kane created this cover for a reprint of his *Star Hawks* newspaper strip. *Star Hawks*, reprint, cover, Gil Kane, pencils, inks, and colors, ©2001 United Features Syndicate, Inc.

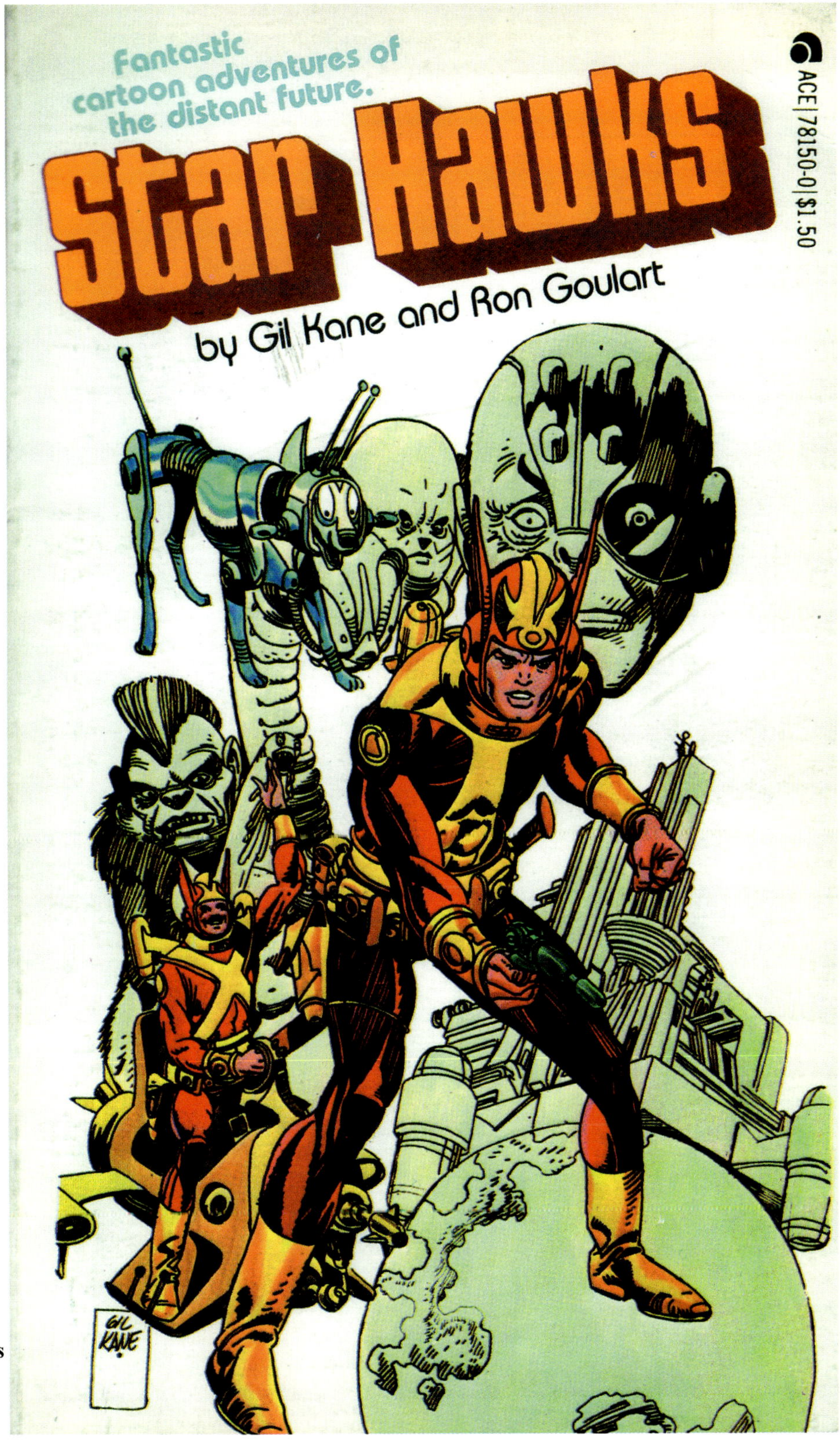

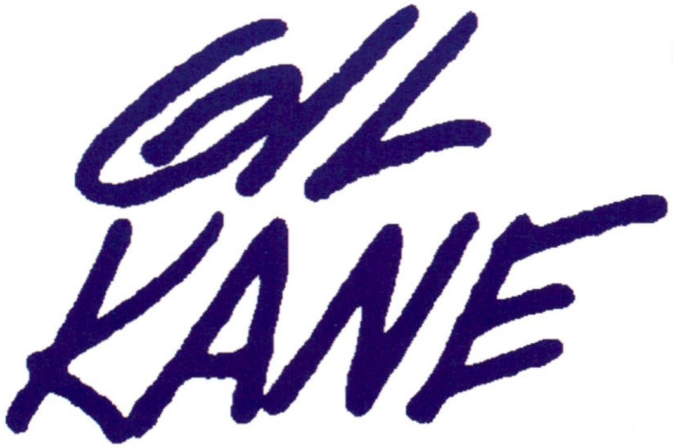

COVERS FOR MARVEL COMICS

During his tenure as chief cover artist for Marvel Comics, Kane pencilled over 800 covers. Of all these covers, Kane enjoyed composing the covers for western genre comics the most. Kane received free rein in his composition of the artwork for these covers. He felt that these covers displayed his best work and referred to them as truly being "his." Kane's favorite western cover, for *The Mighty Marvel Western* #44, is pictured below and the original artwork for this cover can be found in Chapter 8.

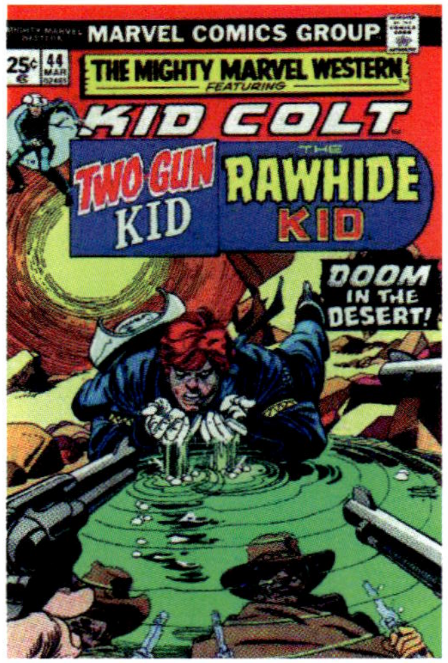

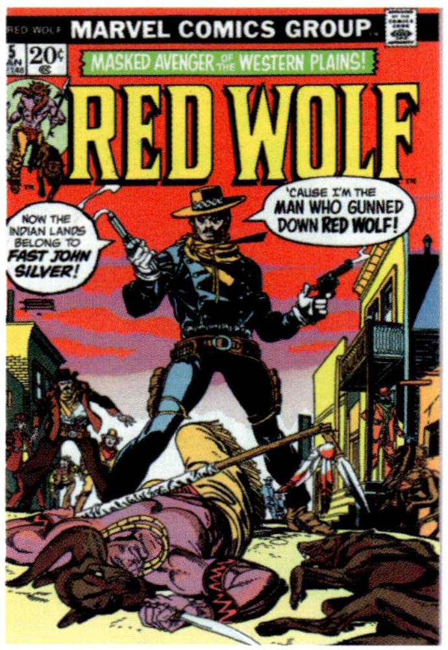

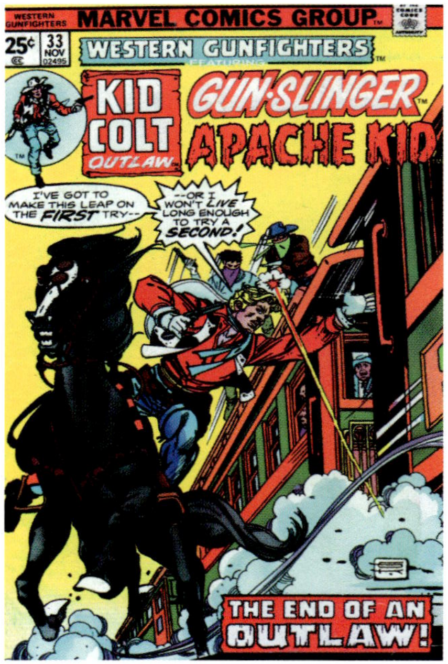

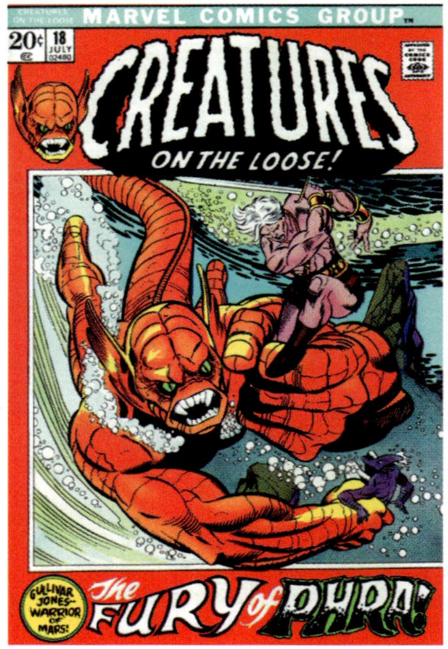

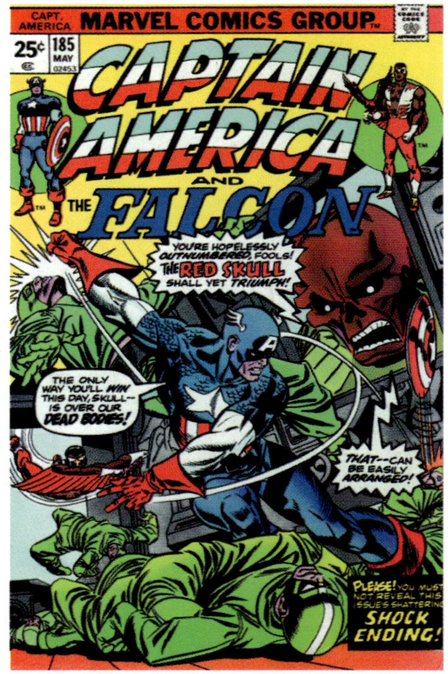

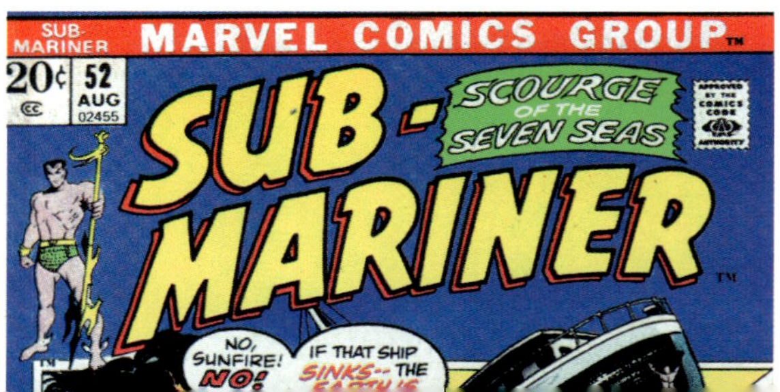

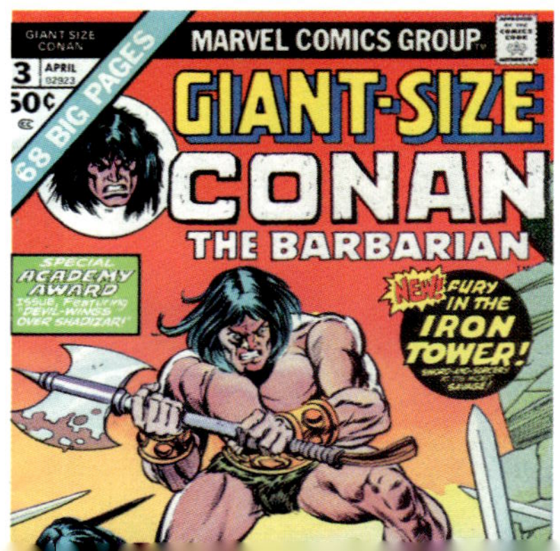

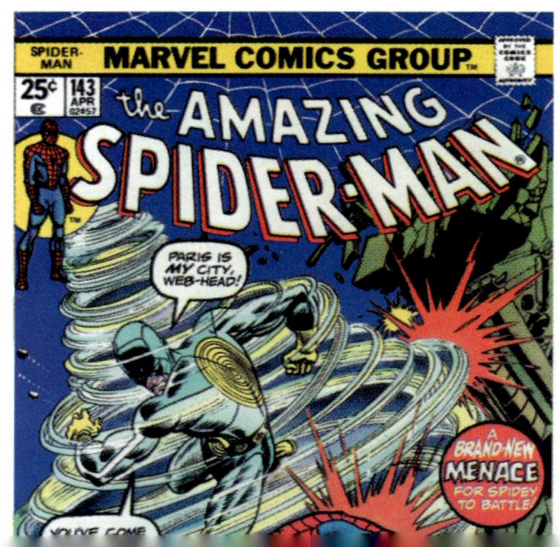

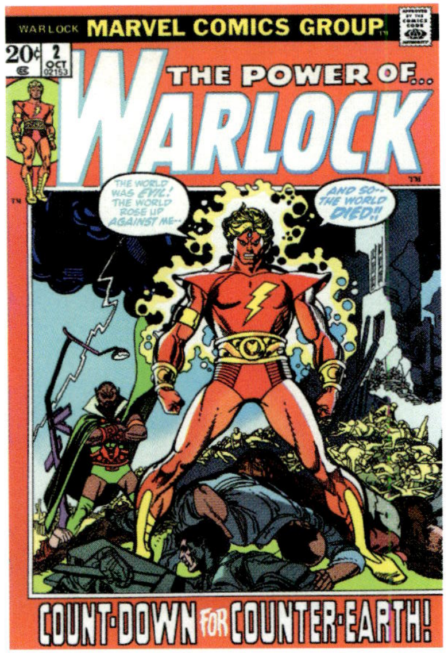

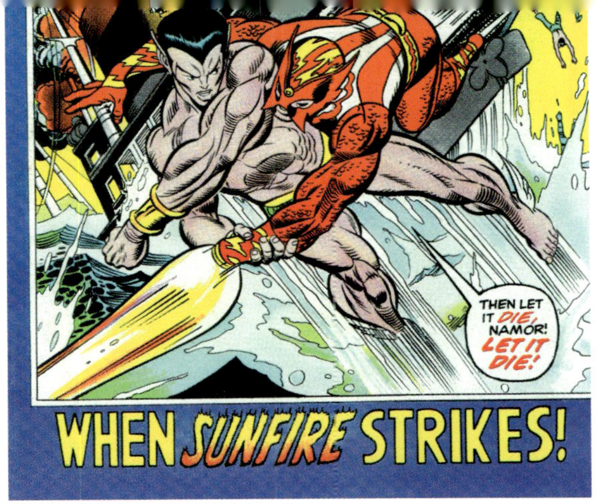

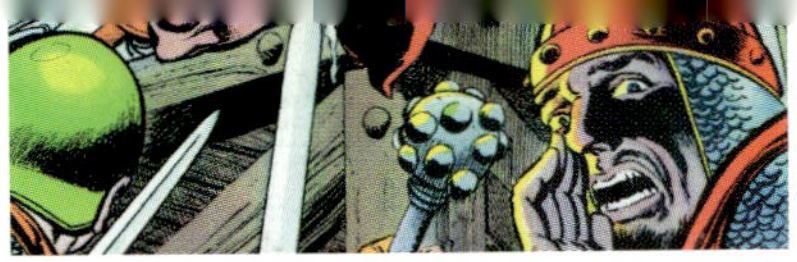

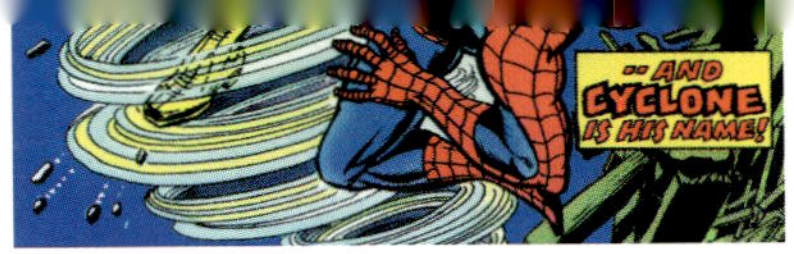

From left to right: *The Mighty Marvel Western* #44, March, 1976, *Western Gunfighters* #33, November, 1975, *Creatures on the Loose* #18, July, 1972, *Captain America* #185, May, 1975, *Red Wolf* #5, January, 1973, *Warlock* #2, October, 1972, *Submariner* #52, August, 1972, *Giant-Size Conan* #53, April, 1975, *The Amazing Spider-Man* #143, April, 1975, *Ghost Rider* #1, September, 1973, *Ka-Zar* #11, October, 1975, and *Daredevil* #127, November, 1975. Gil Kane, pencils, all, various inkers. All covers ©2001 Marvel Characters, Inc. It is clear that the tone and detailing of several of these covers were significantly changed by the inkers. Kane inked the three western covers and the cover for *Warlock* #2.

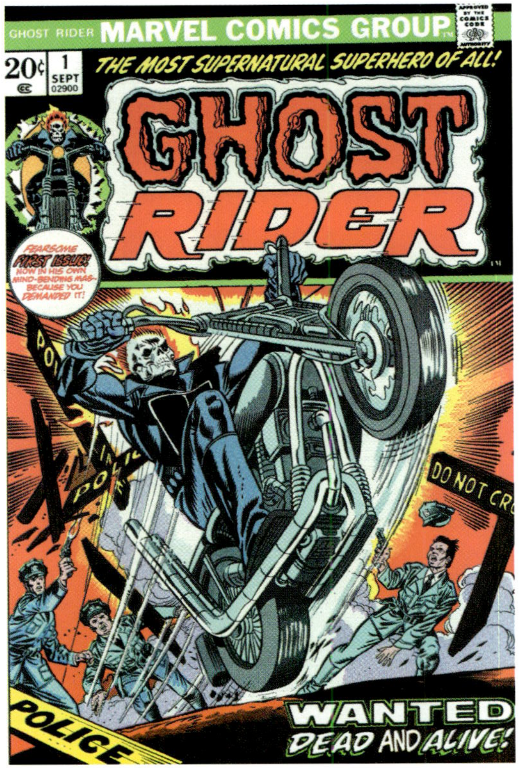

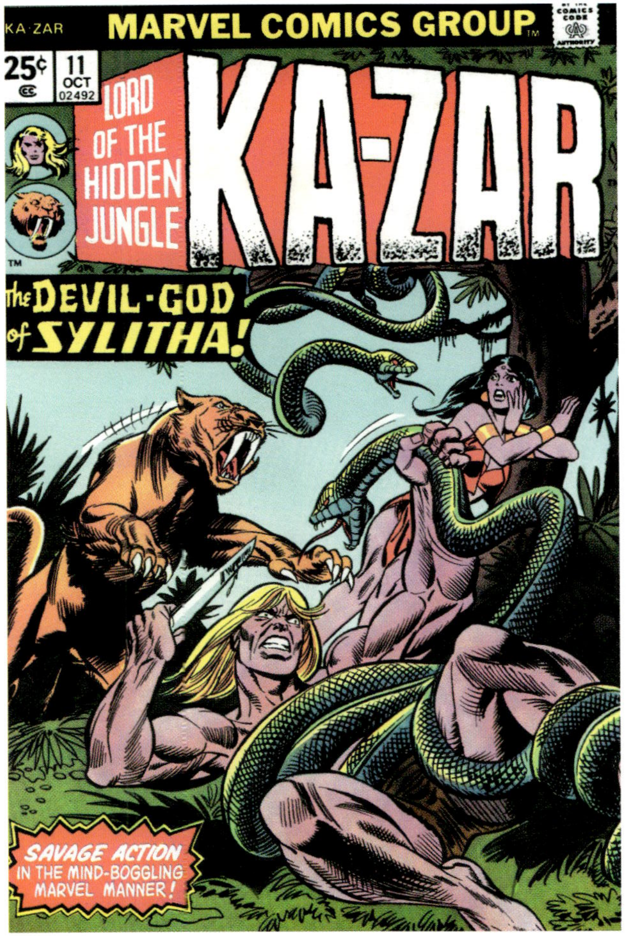

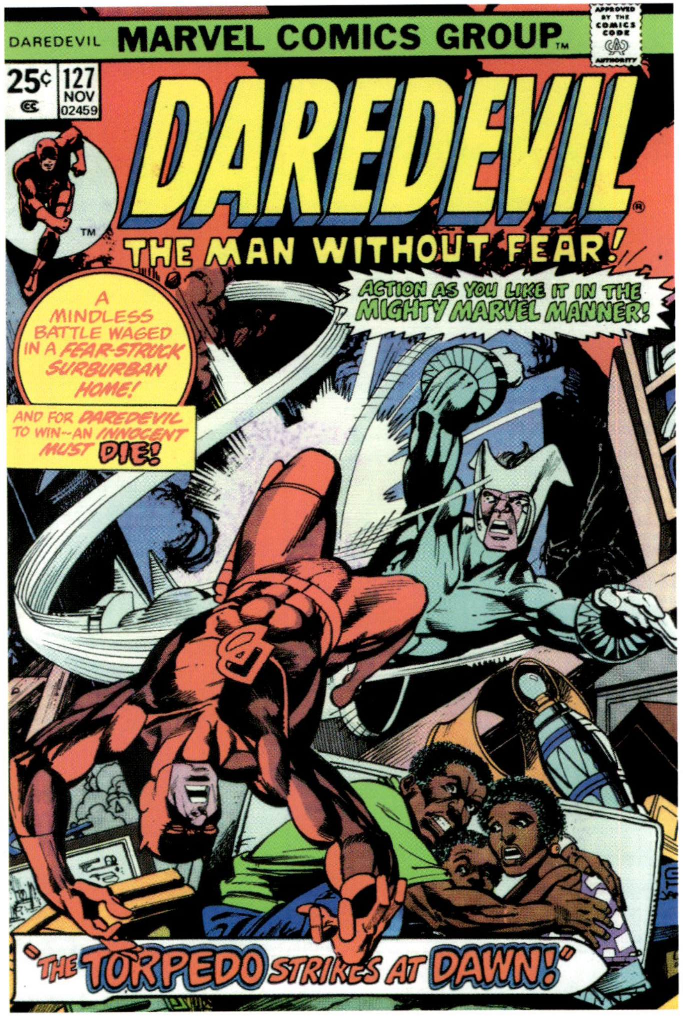

During the 1980s, Kane did beautiful work for both Marvel and DC Comics. He worked in a number of diverse genres and did outstanding work for *The Micronauts* and *Superman*. Kane also did a thoughtful adaptation of Rudyard Kipling's *Jungle Book* for Marvel. Left: cover for *The Micronauts* #44, August, 1982, Gil Kane, pencils and inks, ©2001 Marvel Characters Inc. Right: interior page from *Marvel Fanfare* #10, August, 1983, Gil Kane, pencils, P. Craig Russell, inks (the *Jungle Book* adaptation), ©2001 Marvel Characters, Inc. Bottom left: interior page from *Superman Special* #1, 1983, Gil Kane, pencils and inks, ©2001 DC Comics. Middle: cover for *Superman* #377, November, 1982, Gil Kane, pencils and inks, ©2001 DC Comics. Left: cover for *Wonder Woman* #303, May, 1983, Gil Kane, pencils and inks, ©2001 DC Comics.

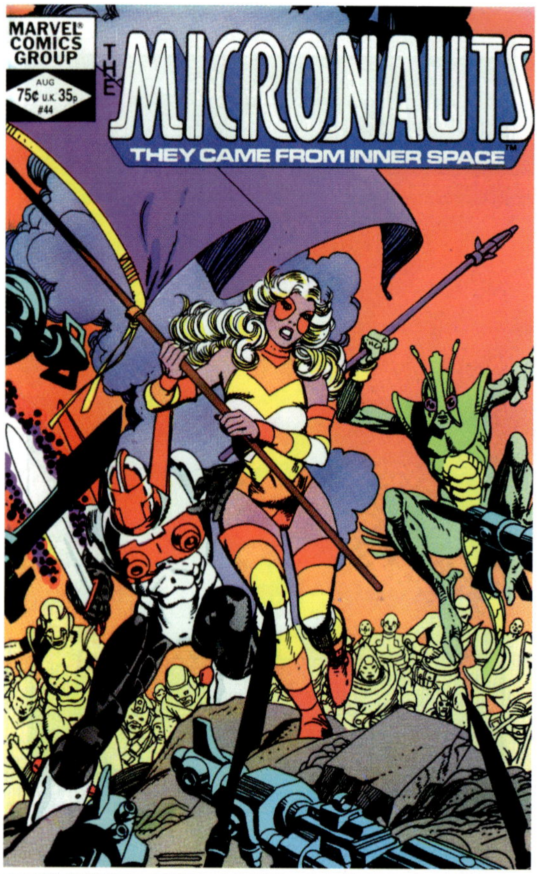
MARVEL COMICS GROUP
AUG 75¢ U.K. 35p #44
THE MICRONAUTS
THEY CAME FROM INNER SPACE

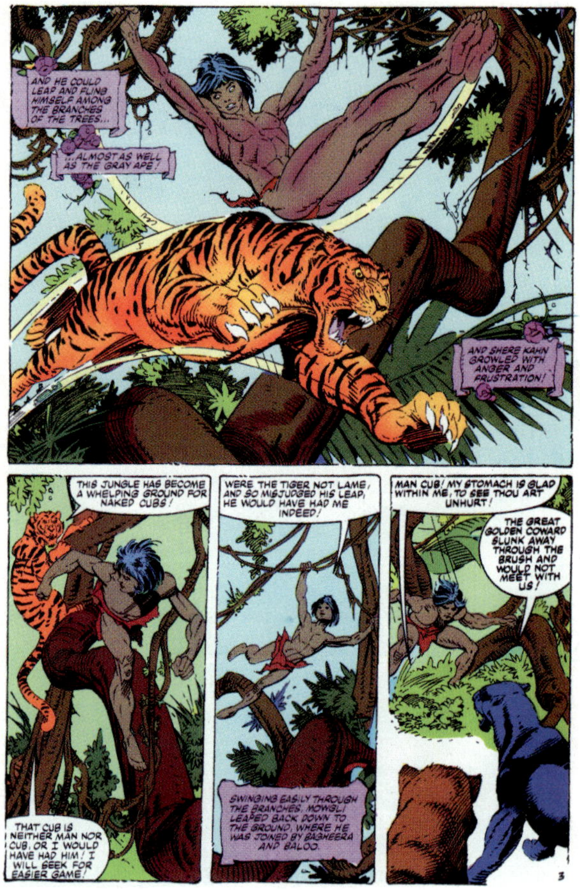
AND HE COULD LEAP AND FLING HIMSELF AMONG THE BRANCHES OF THE TREES...
...ALMOST AS WELL AS THE GRAY APE!
AND SHERE KAHN GROWLED WITH ANGER AND FRUSTRATION!
THIS JUNGLE HAS BECOME A WHELPING GROUND FOR NAKED CUBS!
THAT CUB IS NEITHER MAN NOR CUB, OR I WOULD HAVE HAD HIM! I WILL SEEK FOR EASIER GAME!
WERE THE TIGER NOT LAME, AND SO MISJUDGED HIS LEAP, HE WOULD HAVE HAD ME INDEED!
SWINGING EASILY THROUGH THE BRANCHES, MOWGLI LEAPED BACK DOWN TO THE GROUND, WHERE HE WAS JOINED BY BAGHEERA AND BALOO.
MAN CUB! MY STOMACH IS GLAD WITHIN ME, TO SEE THOU ART UNHURT!
THE GREAT GOLDEN COWARD SLUNK AWAY THROUGH THE BRUSH AND WOULD NOT MEET WITH US!
3

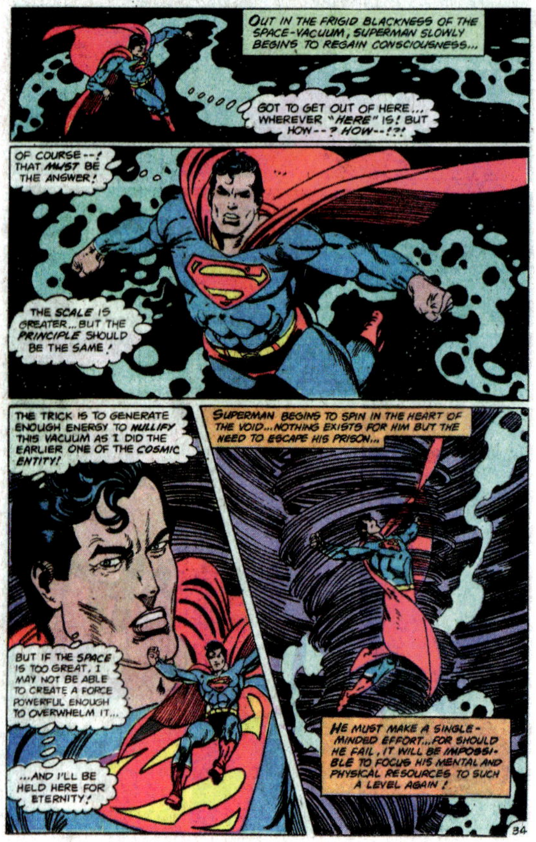
OUT IN THE FRIGID BLACKNESS OF THE SPACE-VACUUM, SUPERMAN SLOWLY BEGINS TO REGAIN CONSCIOUSNESS...
GOT TO GET OUT OF HERE... WHEREVER "HERE" IS! BUT HOW--? HOW--!?!
OF COURSE--! THAT MUST BE THE ANSWER!
THE SCALE IS GREATER... BUT THE PRINCIPLE SHOULD BE THE SAME!
THE TRICK IS TO GENERATE ENOUGH ENERGY TO NULLIFY THIS VACUUM AS I DID THE EARLIER ONE OF THE COSMIC ENTITY!
BUT IF THE SPACE IS TOO GREAT, I MAY NOT BE ABLE TO CREATE A FORCE POWERFUL ENOUGH TO OVERWHELM IT...
...AND I'LL BE HELD HERE FOR ETERNITY!
SUPERMAN BEGINS TO SPIN IN THE HEART OF THE VOID... NOTHING EXISTS FOR HIM BUT THE NEED TO ESCAPE HIS PRISON...
HE MUST MAKE A SINGLE-MINDED EFFORT... FOR SHOULD HE FAIL, IT WILL BE IMPOSSIBLE TO FOCUS HIS MENTAL AND PHYSICAL RESOURCES TO SUCH A LEVEL AGAIN!
34

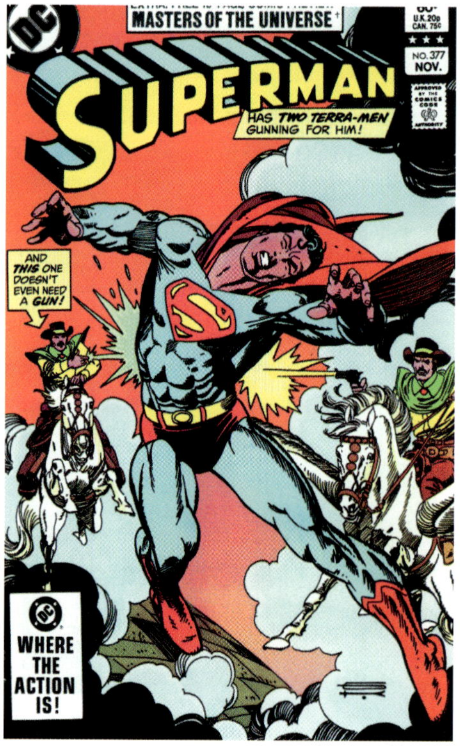
MASTERS OF THE UNIVERSE
U.K. 20p CAN. 75¢
NO. 377 NOV.
SUPERMAN
HAS TWO TERRA-MEN GUNNING FOR HIM!
AND THIS ONE DOESN'T EVEN NEED A GUN!
WHERE THE ACTION IS!

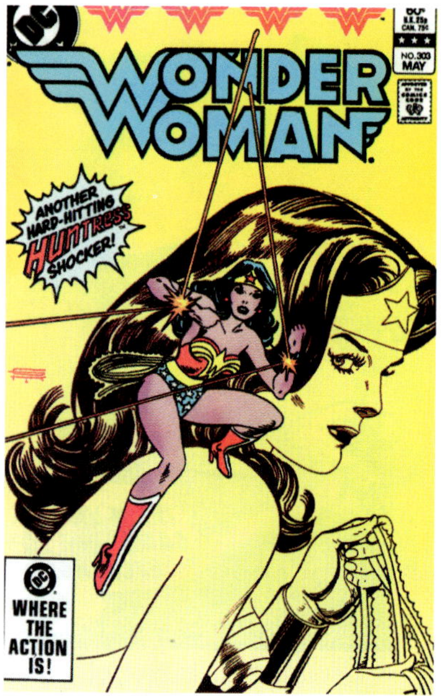
NO. 303 MAY
WONDER WOMAN
ANOTHER HARD-HITTING HUNTRESS SHOCKER!
WHERE THE ACTION IS!

In 1983, Kane revisited the Atom with an overhaul. The new series, *Sword of the Atom*, brought the strip into the 1980s and more fully developed the character. Kane also continued duties with the *Green Lantern* strip. Shortly, Kane would direct most of his energies toward television cartoons, designing presentation art for Ruby-Spears Productions. Left: interior page from *Sword of the Atom* #3, November, 1983, Gil Kane, pencils and inks. Below: interior page from *Sword of the Atom Special* #1, 1984, Gil Kane, pencils and inks. Below left: cover for *Sword of the Atom Special* #2, 1985, Gil Kane, pencils and inks. Below right: cover for *Green Lantern* #171, December, 1983, Gil Kane, pencils and inks. All ©2001 DC Comics.

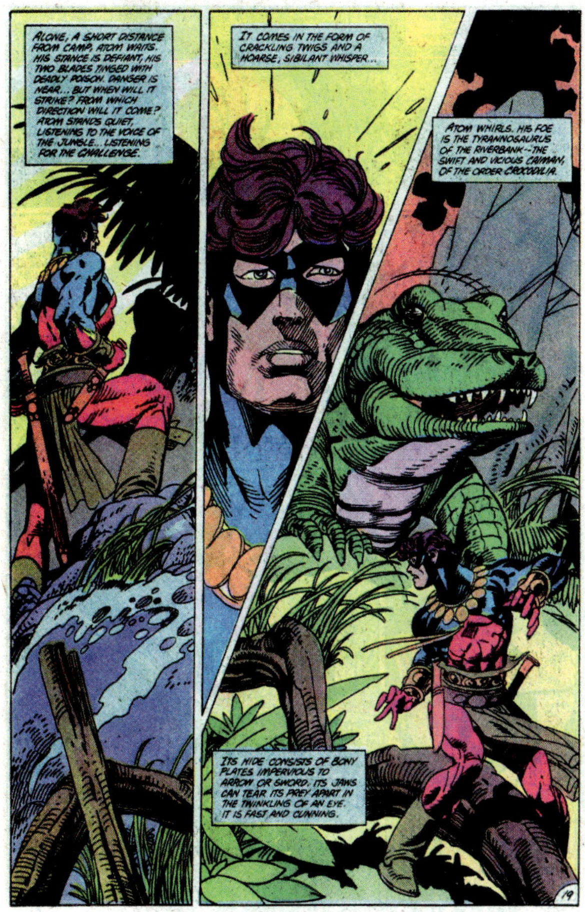
ALONE, A SHORT DISTANCE FROM CAMP, ATOM WAITS. HIS STANCE IS DEFIANT, HIS TWO BLADES TINGED WITH DEADLY POISON. DANGER IS NEAR... BUT WHEN WILL IT STRIKE? FROM WHICH DIRECTION WILL IT COME? ATOM STANDS QUIET, LISTENING TO THE VOICE OF THE JUNGLE... LISTENING FOR THE CHALLENGE.
IT COMES IN THE FORM OF CRACKLING TWIGS AND A HOARSE, SIBILANT WHISPER...
ATOM WHIRLS. HIS FOE IS THE TYRANNOSAURUS OF THE RIVERBANK--THE SWIFT AND VICIOUS CAIMAN, OF THE ORDER CROCODILIA.
ITS HIDE CONSISTS OF BONY PLATES IMPERVIOUS TO ARROW OR SWORD. ITS JAWS CAN TEAR ITS PREY APART IN THE TWINKLING OF AN EYE. IT IS FAST AND CUNNING.
19

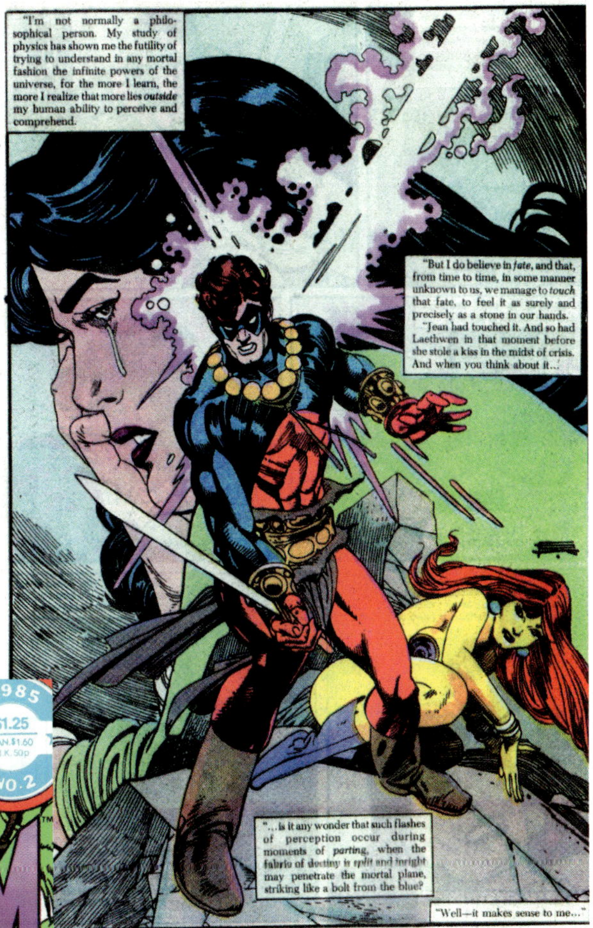
"I'm not normally a philosophical person. My study of physics has shown me the futility of trying to understand in any mortal fashion the infinite powers of the universe, for the more I learn, the more I realize that more lies *outside* my human ability to perceive and comprehend.
"But I do believe in *fate*, and that, from time to time, in some manner unknown to us, we manage to *touch* that fate, to feel it as surely and precisely as a stone in our hands.
"Jean had touched it. And so had Laethwen in that moment before she stole a kiss in the midst of crisis. And when you think about it...'
"...is it any wonder that such flashes of perception occur during moments of *parting*, when the fabric of destiny is *split* and insight may penetrate the mortal plane, striking like a bolt from the blue?
"Well—it makes sense to me..."

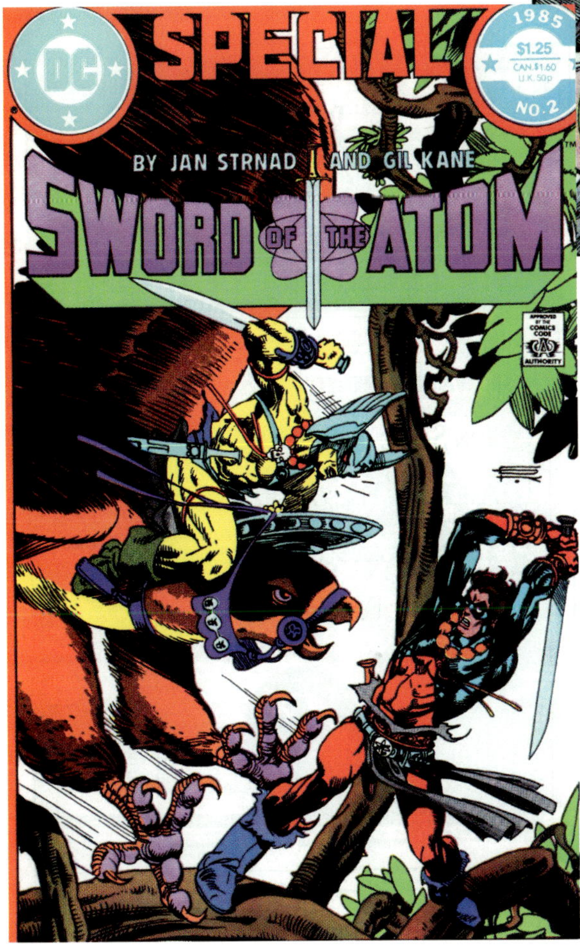
DC
SPECIAL
1985
$1.25
CAN $1.60
U.K. 50p
NO. 2
BY JAN STRNAD AND GIL KANE
SWORD OF THE ATOM

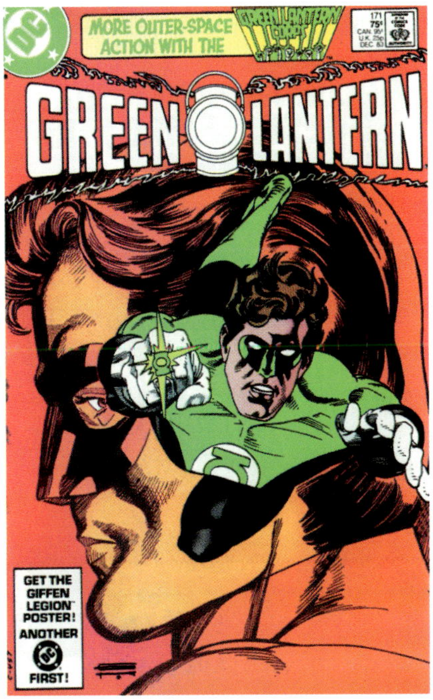
DC
MORE OUTER-SPACE ACTION WITH THE
171
75¢
CAN 95¢
U.K. 25p
DEC 83
GREEN LANTERN
GET THE GIFFEN LEGION POSTER! ANOTHER FIRST!

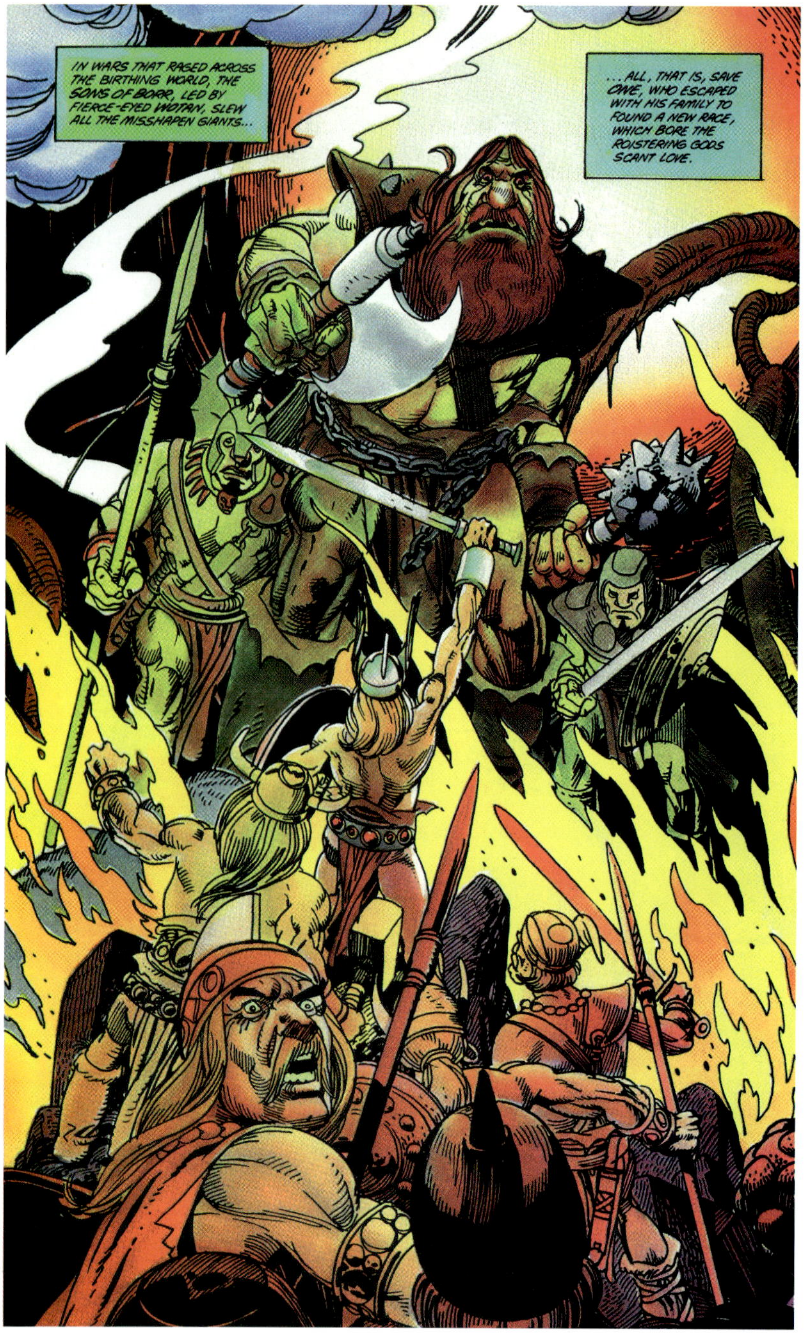
IN WARS THAT RAGED ACROSS THE BIRTHING WORLD, THE SONS OF BORR, LED BY FIERCE-EYED WOTAN, SLEW ALL THE MISSHAPEN GIANTS...
...ALL, THAT IS, SAVE ONE, WHO ESCAPED WITH HIS FAMILY TO FOUND A NEW RACE, WHICH BORE THE ROISTERING GODS SCANT LOVE.

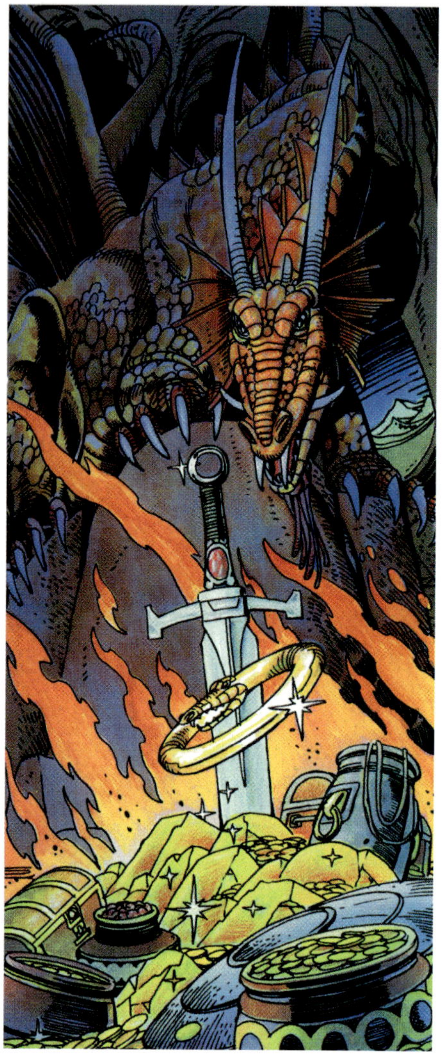

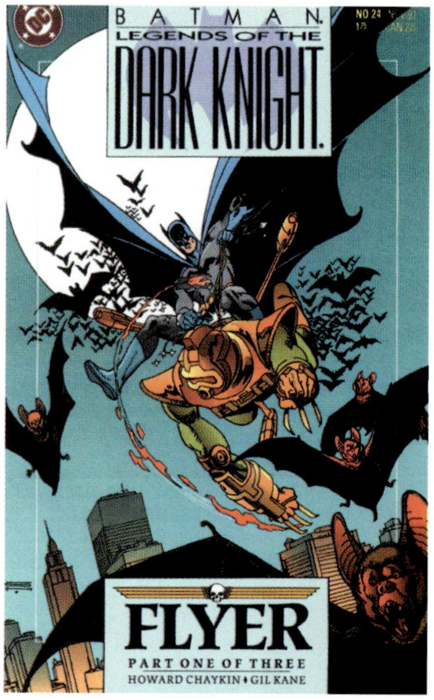
BATMAN
LEGENDS OF THE
DARK KNIGHT
FLYER
PART ONE OF THREE
HOWARD CHAYKIN • GIL KANE

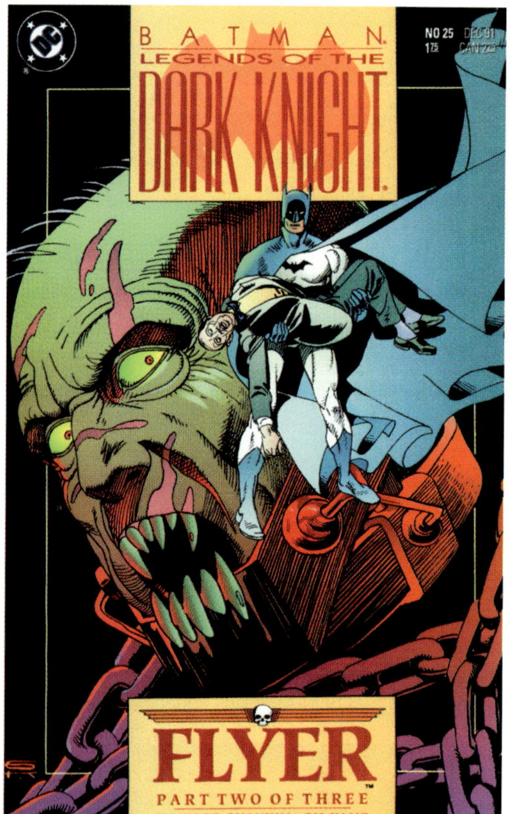
BATMAN
LEGENDS OF THE
DARK KNIGHT
NO 25
FLYER
PART TWO OF THREE
HOWARD CHAYKIN • GIL KANE

During the late 1980s and early 1990s, Kane worked on a number of projects. The art on this page is a small sample of Kane's work during that period which illustrates the diversity of his efforts. Above, interior page and the back cover from the *Ring of the Nibelung* #1, 1989, Gil Kane, pencils and inks, ©2001 DC Comics. Right: covers for *Batman: Legends of the Dark Knight, Flyer, Parts One and Two*, Gil Kane, pencils and inks, November and December, 1991, ©2001 DC Comics.

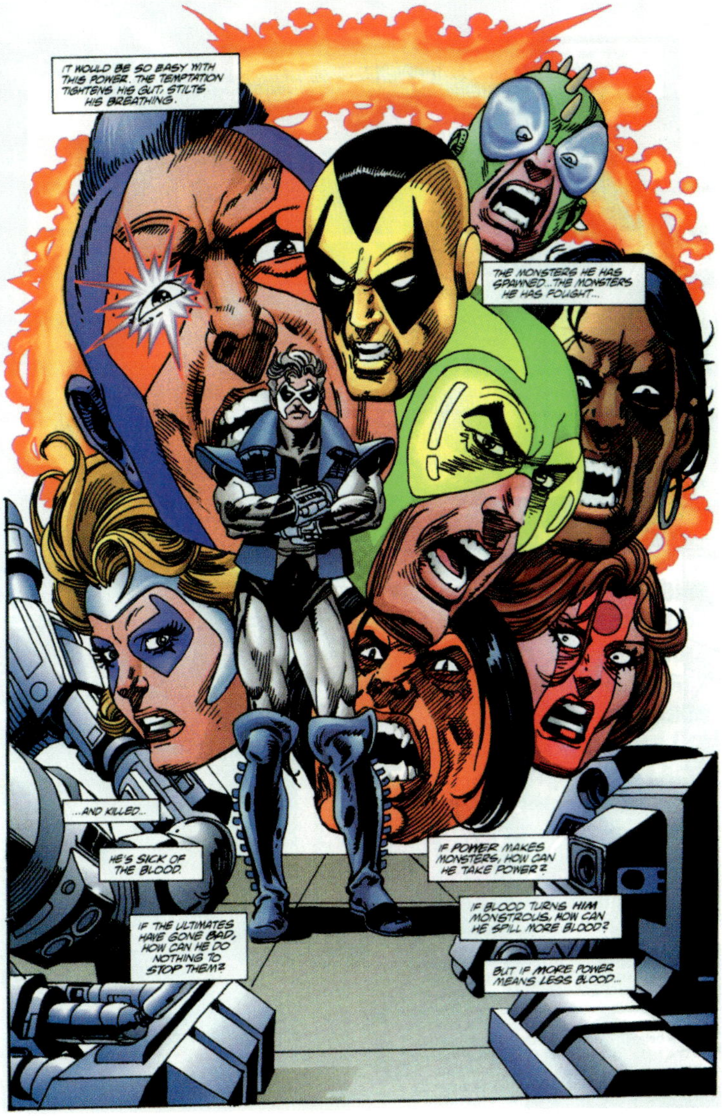
IT WOULD BE SO EASY WITH THIS POWER. THE TEMPTATION TIGHTENS HIS GUT, STILTS HIS BREATHING.
THE MONSTERS HE HAS SPAWNED...THE MONSTERS HE HAS FOUGHT...
...AND KILLED...
HE'S SICK OF THE BLOOD.
IF THE ULTIMATES HAVE GONE BAD, HOW CAN HE DO NOTHING TO STOP THEM?
IF POWER MAKES MONSTERS, HOW CAN HE TAKE POWER?
IF BLOOD TURNS HIM MONSTROUS, HOW CAN HE SPILL MORE BLOOD?
BUT IF MORE POWER MEANS LESS BLOOD...

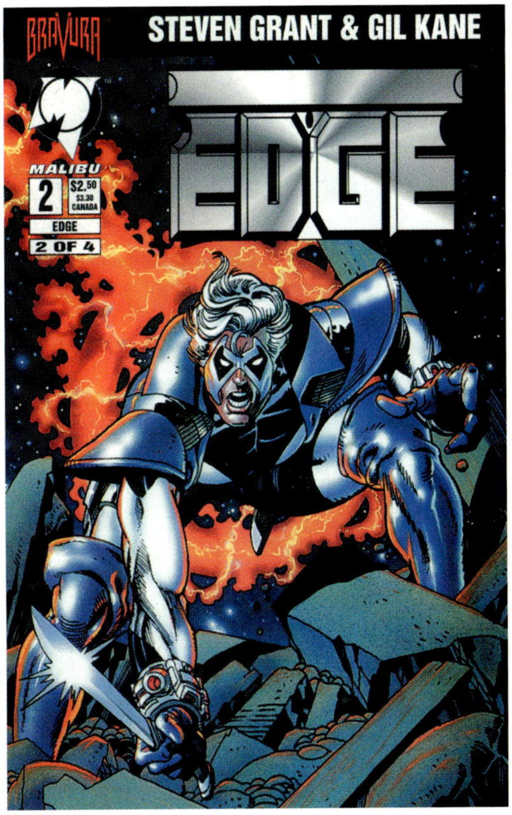
BRAVURA
STEVEN GRANT & GIL KANE
MALIBU
2
$2.50
$3.30 CANADA
EDGE
2 OF 4
EDGE

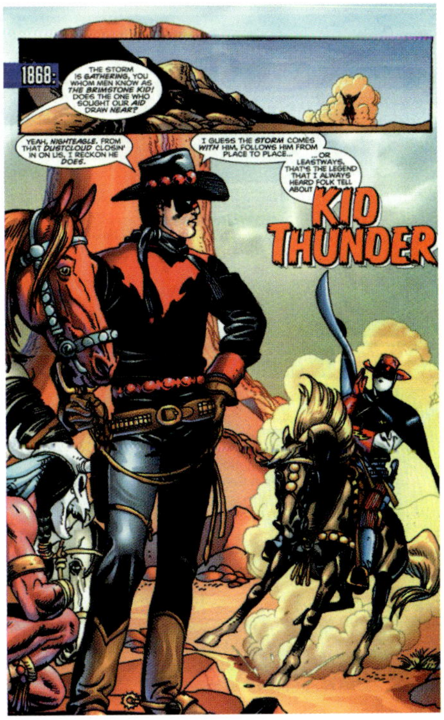
1868:
THE STORM IS GATHERING, YOU WHOM MEN KNOW AS THE BRIMSTONE KID! DOES THE ONE WHO SOUGHT OUR AID DRAW NEAR?
YEAH, NIGHTEAGLE. FROM THAT DUSTCLOUD CLOSIN' IN ON US, I RECKON HE DOES.
I GUESS THE STORM COMES WITH HIM, FOLLOWS HIM FROM PLACE TO PLACE...
...OR LEASTWAYS, THAT'S THE LEGEND THAT I ALWAYS HEARD FOLK TELL ABOUT
KID THUNDER

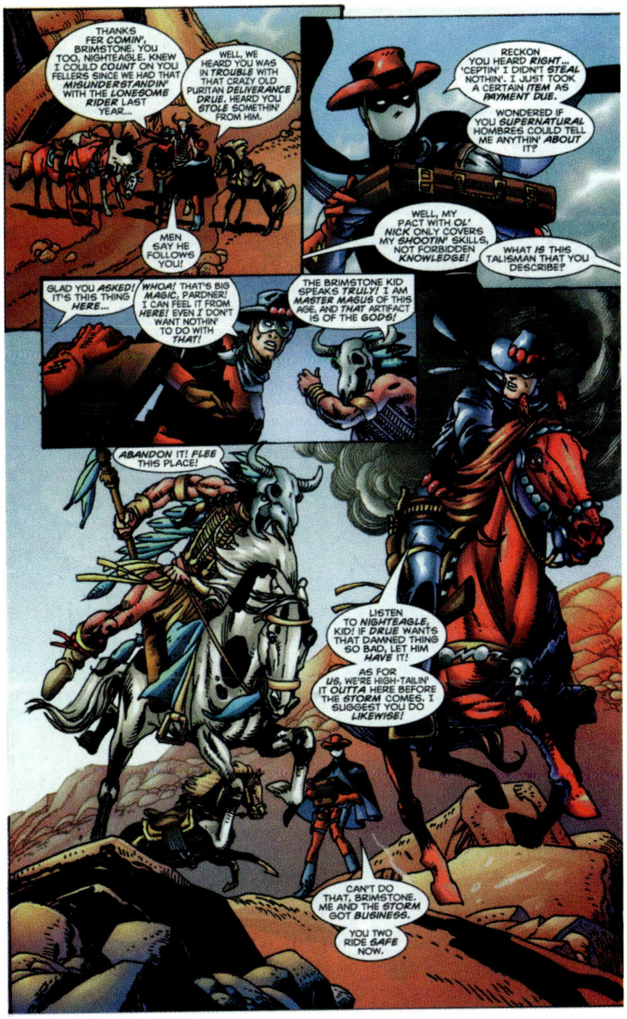
THANKS FER COMIN', BRIMSTONE. YOU TOO, NIGHTEAGLE. KNEW I COULD COUNT ON YOU FELLERS SINCE WE HAD THAT MISUNDERSTANDIN' WITH THE LONESOME RIDER LAST YEAR...
WELL, WE HEARD YOU WAS IN TROUBLE WITH THAT CRAZY OLD PURITAN DELIVERANCE DRUE. HEARD YOU STOLE SOMETHIN' FROM HIM.
MEN SAY HE FOLLOWS YOU!
RECKON YOU HEARD RIGHT... 'CEPTIN' I DIDN'T STEAL NOTHIN'. I JUST TOOK A CERTAIN ITEM AS PAYMENT DUE.
WONDERED IF YOU SUPERNATURAL HOMBRES COULD TELL ME ANYTHIN' ABOUT IT?
WELL, MY PACT WITH OL' NICK ONLY COVERS MY SHOOTIN' SKILLS, NOT FORBIDDEN KNOWLEDGE!
WHAT IS THIS TALISMAN THAT YOU DESCRIBE?
GLAD YOU ASKED! IT'S THIS THING HERE...
WHOA! THAT'S BIG MAGIC, PARDNER! I CAN FEEL IT FROM HERE! EVEN I DON'T WANT NOTHIN' TO DO WITH THAT!
THE BRIMSTONE KID SPEAKS TRULY! I AM MASTER MAGUS OF THIS AGE, AND THAT ARTIFACT IS OF THE GODS!
ABANDON IT! FLEE THIS PLACE!
LISTEN TO NIGHTEAGLE, KID! IF DRUE WANTS THAT DAMNED THING SO BAD, LET HIM HAVE IT!
AS FOR US, WE'RE HIGH-TAILIN' IT OUTTA HERE BEFORE THE STORM COMES. I SUGGEST YOU DO LIKEWISE!
CAN'T DO THAT, BRIMSTONE. ME AND THE STORM GOT BUSINESS.
YOU TWO RIDE SAFE NOW.

Above: an interior page and the cover for *Edge* #2, August, 1994, Gil Kane, pencils and inks, ©2001 The Estate of Gil Kane and Steven Grant. The original artwork for these pieces can be found in Chapter 11. Right: two sequential pages from *Judgment Day* #1, June, 1997, Gil Kane, pencils and inks, ©2001 Awesome Entertainment. The original artwork for the page on the extreme right can be found in Chapter 11.

Even though he was extremely ill at the time, Kane continued to work. The art which appears on this page was completed shortly before Kane's death. The quality of this work clearly attests to the fact that even though seriously ill, Kane was still able to produce beautifully crafted work. Left: cover for *Green Lantern* #1, July, 2000, Gil Kane, pencils, Kevin Nolan, inks. Below: cover for *Legends of the DC Universe* #29, June, 2000, Gil Kane, pencils, painted by Alex Ross. Below right: interior page from *Legends of the DC Universe* #28, May, 2000, Gil Kane, pencils, Klaus Janson, inks.

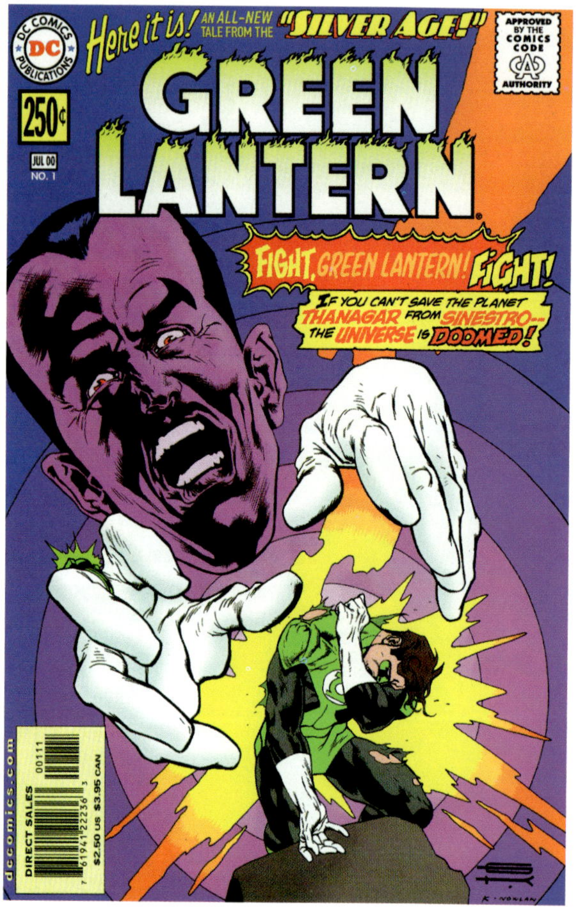
Here it is! AN ALL-NEW TALE FROM THE "SILVER AGE!"
GREEN LANTERN
250¢
JUL 00 NO. 1
FIGHT, GREEN LANTERN! FIGHT!
IF YOU CAN'T SAVE THE PLANET THANAGAR FROM SINESTRO--THE UNIVERSE IS DOOMED!
dccomics.com
DIRECT SALES
$2.50 US $3.95 CAN
K. NOLAN

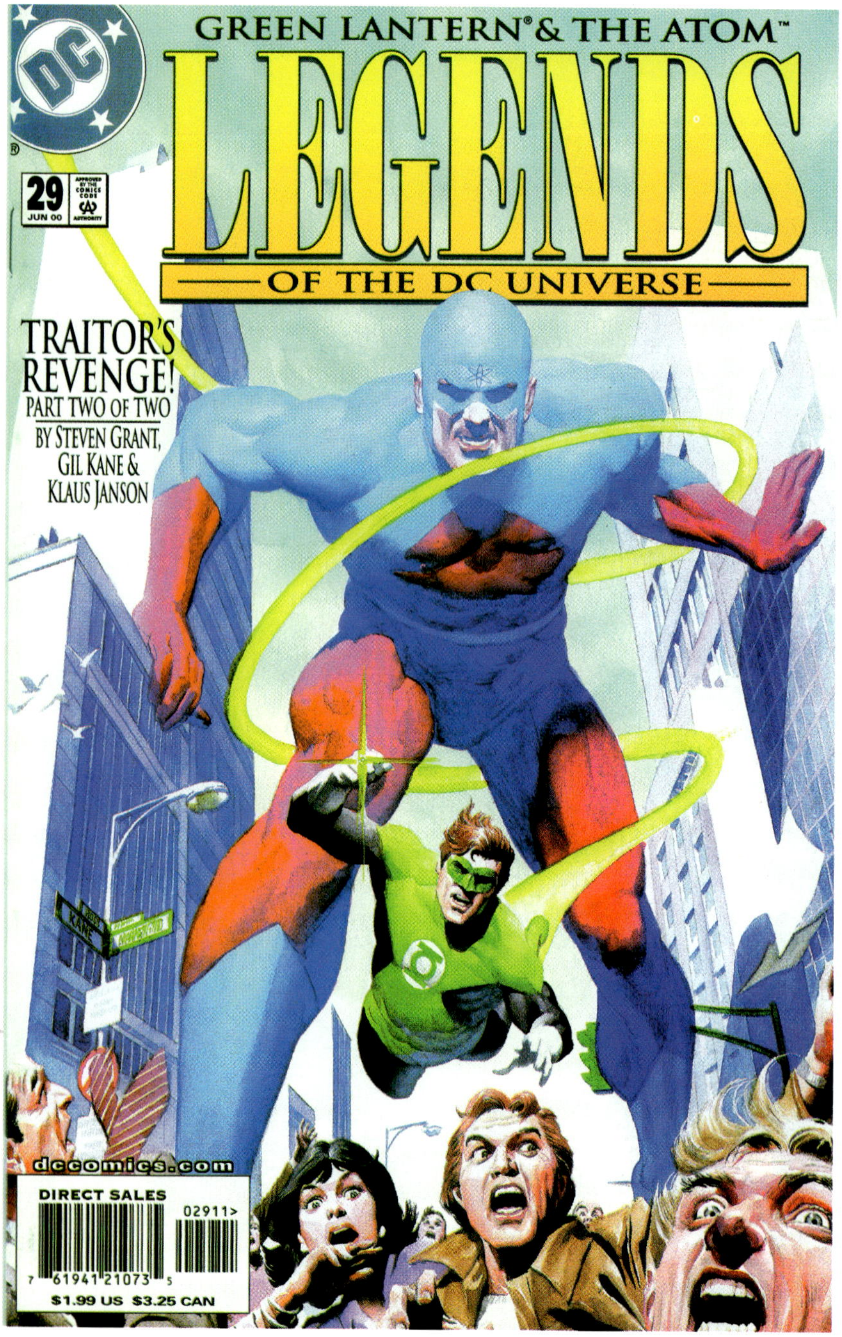
GREEN LANTERN® & THE ATOM™
LEGENDS
OF THE DC UNIVERSE
29
JUN 00
TRAITOR'S REVENGE!
PART TWO OF TWO
BY STEVEN GRANT, GIL KANE & KLAUS JANSON
dccomics.com
DIRECT SALES
$1.99 US $3.25 CAN

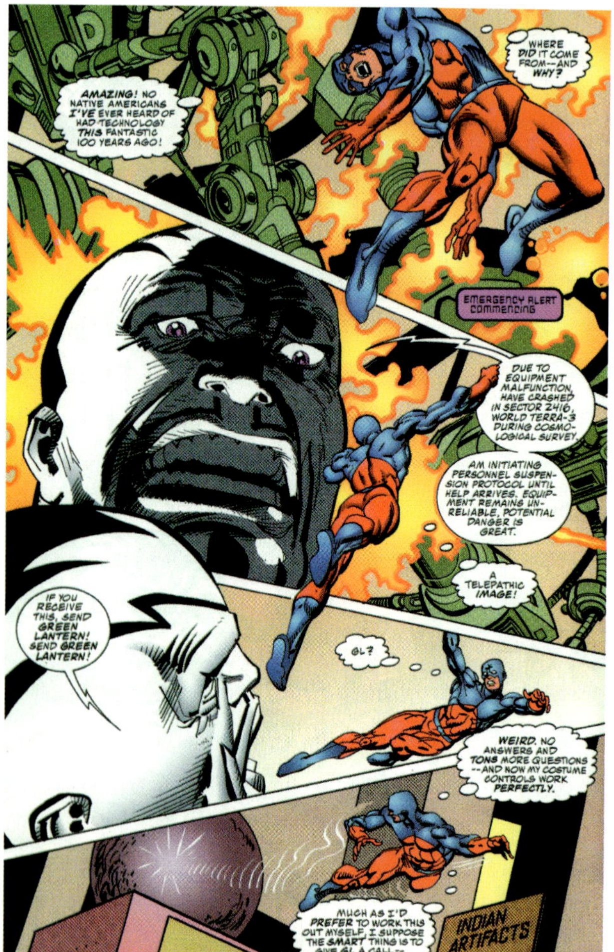
AMAZING! NO NATIVE AMERICANS I'VE EVER HEARD OF HAD TECHNOLOGY THIS FANTASTIC 100 YEARS AGO!
WHERE DID IT COME FROM--AND WHY?
EMERGENCY ALERT COMMENCING
DUE TO EQUIPMENT MALFUNCTION, HAVE CRASHED IN SECTOR 2416, WORLD TERRA-3 DURING COSMO-LOGICAL SURVEY.
AM INITIATING PERSONNEL SUSPEN-SION PROTOCOL UNTIL HELP ARRIVES. EQUIP-MENT REMAINS UN-RELIABLE, POTENTIAL DANGER IS GREAT.
A TELEPATHIC IMAGE!
IF YOU RECEIVE THIS, SEND GREEN LANTERN! SEND GREEN LANTERN!
GL?
WEIRD. NO ANSWERS AND TONS MORE QUESTIONS --AND NOW MY COSTUME CONTROLS WORK PERFECTLY.
MUCH AS I'D PREFER TO WORK THIS OUT MYSELF, I SUPPOSE THE SMART THING IS TO GIVE GL A CALL--
INDIAN ARTIFACTS

GIL KANE: CHECKLIST

This checklist was compiled for use in conjunction with the text of this book. There is inconsistent documentation as to exactly what material Kane worked on at the beginning of his career. For that reason we have chosen to list only those sources which have been confirmed by several sources. Kane's recollection on precisely what he did in 1942, 1943, and 1944, was not exact and only generally aided in this list. This list is not a definitive listing of all Kane's work nor is it a complete listing of all his work. This list primarily focuses on Kane's work in comic books. Information regarding his work in animation is not readily available. This list uses abbreviations as follows: c – cover attributed, and p – pencilling attributed, and i – inking attributed.

1941

Hillman Periodicals
Air Fighters V.2#5pi
MLJ
Zip Comics 14i

1942

Hillman Periodicals
Flying Dutchman 1

1943

MLJ
Black Hood Comics 9i
PEP 38pi, 39pi, 40pi, 41pi

1944

DC Comics
Adventure Comics 92p, 93pi, 94pi,
Star Spangled Comics 31cp, 32cp
Hillman Periodicals
Air Fighters Comics v2 5pi
MLJ Comics
Black Hood Comics 11i
PEP 47pi, 49i, 50pi
The Shield 47
Timely Comics
Young Allies 11i

1945

DC Comics
Adventure Comics 96pi, 97pi, 98pi, 99cpi

1946

DC Comics
Adventure Comics 102i

1947

DC Comics
Sensation Comics 70pi, 71pi, 72pi

1948

DC Comics
Flash 98p
Sensation Comics 73pi, 74p
Western Comics 1, 2, 3, 4, 5, 6
Famous Funnies
Heroic Comics 49
Fawcett Movie Comics
Monte Hale Western 33, 34

1949

Avon Periodicals
Wild Bill Hickcock 1
DC Comics
All-American Western 107p, 108cp
Girls' Love Stories 32
Sensation Comics 87pi, 88pi, 89pi
Western Comics 7, 8, 9, 10, 11

1950

DC Comics
All-American Western 114p, 115cp, 116cp, 117p
All Star Comics 53p
Girls' Romances 25
Jimmy Wakely 6p, 7p, 8p
Mr. District Attorney 15p
Western Comics 12, 13, 14, 15, 16, 17, 18

1951

DC Comics
All-American Western 119cp, 120cp, 121, 122p
All Star Comics 56
All-Star Western 58cp, 59cp, 60p, 61cp
Jimmy Wakley 9p, 10cpi, 11cpi, 12cpi
Mystery in Space 3p, 4p
Sensation Comics 105
Strange Adventures 7p, 8p, 11p, 12cpi, 13cpi, 14cpi, 15cpi

1952

DC Comics
Adventures of Rex, the Wonder Dog 2cp, 3cp, 4cp, 5cp, 6cp
All-American Western 123cpi, 124cpi, 125p, 126p
All-Star Western 62cp, 63cp, 64pi, 65p, 66p, 67cp, 68cp
Big Town 17cp, 18cp
Jimmy Wakely 15cpi, 16cpi, 17cpi, 18cpi, 19
Mystery in Space 7cp, 11cp
Our Army at War 1p, 3cp
Sensation Mystery 108, 109, 110cp, 111, 112cp
Strange Adventures 16cpi, 17cpi, 20cpi, 22, 25cp, 26p, 27p

Marvel Comics
Mystic 8

1953

DC Comics
Adventures of Rex, the Wonder Dog 7cp, 8cp, 9cp, 10cp, 11cp, 12cp
All-Star Western 68cp, 69cp, 70cp, 71cp, 72cp, 73cp
Big Town 19cp, 20cp, 21cp, 22cp, 24cp
Mystery in Space 12p, 13p, 14p
Sensation Mystery 113, 114cp, 115cp
Strange Adventures 28p, 29p, 31cp, 35p, 36p, 37p, 38p, 39p

Dell Comics
Frogmen 11p

Marvel Comics
Mystic Comics 24
War Comics 19

1954

Atlas
Lovers 58

DC Comics
Adventures of Rex, the Wonder Dog 13cp, 14cp, 15cp, 16cp, 17cp, 18cp
All-American Men of War 12p
All-Star Western 74cp, 75cp, 76cp, 77cp, 78cp, 79cp
Big Town 25cp, 26cp, 27cp, 28cp, 29cp, 30cp
Girls' Love Stories 32p
Girls' Romances 25p
Mystery in Space 18p, 19p, 20p, 21p, 22p, 23p
Secret Hearts 22p
Strange Adventures 40p, 41p, 42p, 43p, 44p, 45p, 46p, 47p, 48p, 49p, 50p, 51p
Western Comics 44p, 45p, 46p, 47p, 48p

1955

DC Comics
Adventures of Rex, the Wonder Dog 19cp, 20cp, 21cp, 22cpi, 23cp, 24cpi
All-Star Western 80cp, 81cp, 82cp, 83cp, 84cp, 85cp
Big Town 31cp, 32cp, 33cp, 34cp, 35cp, 36cp
Mystery in Space 24p, 25p, 26cp, 27p, 28p, 29cp
Strange Adventures 52p, 53p, 54p, 55p, 56p, 57cp, 58cp, 59cp, 60cp, 61cp, 62cp, 63cp
Superboy Adventure Book 1p
Western Comics 49p, 50p, 51p, 52p, 53p, 54p

Holoyke/Continental
The Blue Beetle

1956

DC Comics
Adventures of Rex, the Wonder Dog 25cpi, 26cpi, 27cpi, 28cpi, 29cp, 30cpi
All-Star Western 86cp, 87cp, 88cpi, 89cp, 90cp, 91cp
Big Town 37cpi, 38cp, 39cp, 40cp, 41cp, 42cp
Falling In Love 3p, 5p
Mystery in Space 30cpi, 31cpi, 32cp, 33p, 34cpi, 35cpi, 36c
Secret Hearts 35 p
Strange Adventures 64cpi, 65cpi, 66cpi, 67cpi, 68p, 69cp, 70p, 71p, 72p, 73p, 74p, 75cp
Western Comics 55p,56cpi,57cp,58cp,59cp,60cp

1957

DC Comics
Adventures of Rex, the Wonder Dog 31cpi, 32cp, 33cp, 34cp, 35cp, 36cp
All-Star Western 92cpi, 93cp, 94cp, 95cp, 96pi, 97cp, 98cp
Big Town 43cp, 44cp, 45cp, 46cp, 47cp, 48cp
Hopalong Cassidy TV 123cp,124cp,125cp, 126cp
Mystery in Space 37cp, 38cpi, 39cp, 40cp, 41cp
Robin Hood Tales 7cp
Showcase 8p (short)
Star Spangled War Stories 55p
Strange Adventures 76cp, 77cp, 78cp, 79cp, 80cp, 81cp, 82cp, 83cp, 84cp, 85cp, 86cp, 87cp
Western Comics 61cp, 62cp, 63cp, 64,cp, 65cp, 66cp

1958

DC Comics
Adventures of Rex, the Wonder Dog 37cpi, 38cpi, 39cpi, 40cpi, 41cp, 42cp

All-Star Western 99cp, 100p, 101cp, 102cp, 103cp, 104cpi, 105cpi, 106cpi
Big Town 49cp, 50cp
Hopalong Cassidy 127cp, 128cp, 129cp, 130cp, 131cpi, 132cp
Mystery in Space 42cpi, 43cpi, 44cpi, 45cp, 46cp, 47cpi, 48cp
New Adventures of Charlie Chan 1, 2, 3, 4
Showcase 17cpi
Strange Adventures 88cp, 89cp, 90cp, 91cp, 92cp, 93cpi, 94cpi, 95cp, 98cpi, 99cpi
Western Comics 67cp, 68cp, 69cp, 70cp, 71cp, 72cp

Dell Publishing Company

Cadet Gray of West Point, April
Four Color TV Comic Books, Have Gun Will Travel 13pi

1959

DC Comics

Adventures of Rex, the Wonder Dog 43cpi, 44cp, 45cp, 46cp
All-Star Western 107cpi, 108cpi, 109cpi, 110cp
Hopalong Cassidy 133cp, 134cp, 135cp
Mystery in Space 49cpi, 50cp, 51cpi, 52cpi, 53cp, 54cp, 55cp, 56cp
New Adventures of Charlie Chan 5, 6
Showcase 18cp, 19cp, 22cpi, 23cp
Strange Adventures 100cp, 101cp, 102cp, 103cpi, 104cpi, 105cpi, 106cp, 107 cp, 108cpi, 109cpi, 110cp, 111cp
Western Comics 73cp, 74cp, 75cp, 76cp, 77cp, 78cpi

1960

DC Comics

All-Star Western 111cpi, 112cp, 113cpi, 114cp, 115cp, 116cp
Falling in Love 32p
Green Lantern 1cp, 2cp, 3cp
Mystery in Space 57cp, 58cp, 59cp, 60cp, 61p
Showcase 24cp
Strange Adventures 112cp, 113cpi, 114cp, 115cp, 116cpi, 117cp
Western Comics 79cp. 80cp, 81cp, 82cp, 83cp

Dell Comics

Four Color Television, Tales of Wells Fargo 1075p,
The Lost World 1145p

1961

DC Comics

All-Star Western 117cp, 118cpi, 119cp
Green Lantern 4cp, 5cp, 6cp, 7cp, 8cp, 9cp
Mystery in Space 67p
Rip Hunter…Time Master 29
Secret Origins 1cp
Showcase 31cp, 34cp
Strange Adventures 124p, 125p, 130p
Western Comics 85cp

Dell Comics

Have Gun Will Travel 10pi, 13pi

1962

DC Comics

Atom 1cp, 2cp, 3cp, 4cp
Green Lantern 10cp, 11cp, 12cp, 13cp, 14cp, 15cp, 16cp, 17cp
Showcase 35cp, 36cp
Strange Adventures 138p, 146p

Dell Comics

Four Color Movies, Brain Boy 1330pi

1963

DC Comics

Atom 4, 5cp, 6cp, 7cp, 8cp, 9cp, 10cp
Metal Men 30, 31
Green Lantern 18cp, 19cp, 20cp, 21cp, 22cp, 23cp, 24cp, 25cp
Strange Adventures 148p, 151p, 153p, 154cp, 155cp, 157p, 159p

1964

DC Comics

Atom 10cp, 11cp, 12cp, 13cp, 14cp, 15cp, 16cp
Falling In Love 70p
Green Lantern 26cpi, 27cp, 28cp, 29cp, 30cp, 31cp, 32cp, 33cp
Secret Hearts 95 p

1965

DC Comics

Atom 16cp, 17cp, 18cp, 19cp, 20cp, 21cp, 22cp
Brave & Bold 59cpi
Falling in Love 73p
Giant Magazine 8p
Girls' Romances 107pi
Green Lantern 34cp, 35cp, 36cp, 37cp, 38cp, 39cp, 40cp, 41cp
Mystery In Space 101cpi,102pi
Rip Hunter…Time Master 21, 22, 23, 24, 25, 26, 27, 28, 29cpi
Strange Adventures 173pi, 174pi, 176pi, 179pi, 182pi
Tales of the Unexpected 88pi

Dell Comics
Kona 16cpi
Naza 5cpi
Tower Comics
T.H.U.N.D.E.R. Agents 1p, 5, 6c, 14, 15, 16

1966

DC Comics
Atom 22, 23cp, 24cp, 25cp, 26cpi, 27cpi, 28cpi
Batman 178cp, 179cp, 180cp, D2939cp
Brave & Bold 64cpi
Green Lantern 42cp, 43cp, 44cp, 45cpi, 46cpi, 47cpi, 8cpi,49cpi
Plastic Man 1cpi
Strange Adventures 184cpi, 185pi, 186pi
Harvey Comics
Unearthly Spectaculars 2pi
King Comics
Flash Gordon 2cpi
The Phantom 19pi, 20
Marvel Comics
Sgt. Fury & His Howling Commandos 37cpi
Tales to Astonish 76p
Tower Comics
NoMan 1p
T.H.U.N.D.E.R. Agents 19
Undersea Agent 3pi, 4cpi, 5cpi, 6
Green Lantern 58cp, 59cp, 60cp, 61cp

1967

DC Comics
Atom 27, 28, 29cpi, 30cpi, 31cp, 32cp, 33cp, 34cp
Detective Comics 368p, 369cp, 370p, 373, 374
Green Lantern 50cpi, 51cpi, 52cpi, 53pi, 54cp, 55cp, 56cp, 57cp
Phantom 19, 20pi
Strange Adventures 204p
Marvel Comics
Avengers 37cpi, 38cpi
Daredevil Annual 4
Fantasy Masterpieces 7cpi
Marvel Super-Heroes 34, 42-46
Tales of Suspense 88cpi 89pi, 90cp, 91cp
Tales to Astonish 76, 87cpi, 88pi, 89cpi, 90pi, 91cpi
X-Men 33cp
Tower Comics
Dynamo, Man of High Camp nnp
Tales to Astonish 87, 88, 89, 90, 91
T.H.U.N.D.E.R. Agents 14cpi,15cpi,16p
NoMan, the Invisible T.H.U.N.D.E.R. Agents nnp
Undersea Agent 6pi
Warren Publications
Creepy Magazine 15pi, 16pi

1968

Adventure House Press
His Name is … Savage, in magazine format, pi
DC Comics
Atom 33, 34, 35cp, 36cpi, 37cp, 38
Captain Action 2cpi
Detective Comics 371p, 372p, 373p, 374p
Green Lantern 58cp, 59cp, 60cp, 61cp
Hawk and the Dove 3cpi
Metal Men 30p, 31cpi
Tales of the Unexpected 105p
World's Finest Comics 174p
Tower Comics
T.H.U.N.D.E.R. Agents 19cpi

1969

DC Comics
Batman 208p
Beware the Creeper 6cpi
Captain Action 3cp, 4cpi, 5cpi
Captain America 2c, 3c, 4c, 5c
DC Special 3p
Detective Comics 384p, 385p, 388p, 389p, 390p, 391p, 392p, 393p, 394p
Giant Magazine G55p
Green Lantern 67cp, 68cpi, 69cpi, 70cpi, 71cpi, 72cpi, 73cpi
Hawk and the Dove, 1st Series 3c, 4cpi, 5cpi, 6cpi
House of Mystery 180p, 184
Strange Adventures 219p
Teen Titans, 1st Series 19p, 22p, 23p, 24p, 39
Marvel Comics
Captain Marvel 12cp, 17cp, 18cp, 19cp, 20c
Marvel's Greatest Comics 34, 37

1970

DC Comics
All Star Western 3pi, 4, 6
DC Special 6p, 8p
Detective Comics 395p, 396p, 397p, 398p, 399p, 400p, 401p, 402p, 403p, 404p, 405p, 406p
Flash 195p, 197cpi, 198cpi, 199cpi
From Beyond the Unknown 3p, 6p, 7p, 8p
Green Lantern 74cpi, 75cpi
House of Secrets 85p
House of Mystery 180, 184p, 196, 198, 253, 300
Justice League of America 78cpi
Outlaw Kid 10, 12, 15
Strange Adventures 222cp, 227p
Super DC Giant 1970
Marvel Comics
Amazing Spider-Man 89p, 90cp. 91p
Captain Marvel 20cp, 21cp

1971

Bantam Books

Blackmark paperback, cpi

DC Comics

Action Comics 404p
All-Star Western 4pi, 6pi, 8p
DC Special 13p
DC 100-Page Super Spectacular 7p
Detective Comics 407p, 408p
From Beyond the Unknown 9p, 11p, 13p, 14p
Green Lantern 85p, 87p
Ringo Kid 15, 18, 24, 26, 27, 28, 29

Marvel Comics

Amazing Spider-Man 92p, 93, 94, 95, 96cpi, 97p, 98cp, 99cp, 100p, 101cp, 102cp, 103cp
Astonishing Tales 9cp
Conan, the Barbarian 12cp
Daredevil 80c, 81c, 82c
Iron Man 43cp
Marvel Spotlight 14, 15, 17-27, 32
Savage Tales 4
Strange Adventures 228p, 230p, 231p

1972

DC Comics

Action Comics 408p
Adventure Comics 414p, 425pi
From Beyond the Unknown 19p, 20p
Fantastici Quattro 43p, 44p, 45p, 46
Green Lantern 88p
Green Lantern and the Green Arrow 1p, 2p
Mitico Thor 44p
Outlaw Kid 27, 28, 29
Teen Titans 39p
Tomahawk 139p, 140p
Wanted, The World's Most Dangerous Villains p1, 5
Weird Western Tales 15p

Marvel Comics

Amazing Adventures 10cp, 11cp, 12cp, 14cp
Amazing Spider-Man 104cp, 105cp
Astonishing Tales 10cp, 11cp, 14cpi, 15cp
Avengers 97cp
Captain America, Giant Size 1c
Captain America 145p, 147cp, 149cp, 150cp
Captain Marvel 21c, 22cp, 23cp, 24c
Chamber of Chills 1cp
Conan, the Barbarian 17cp, 18cp
Creatures on the Loose 15cp, 16cpi, 17cpi, 18cp, 19cpi, 20cpi
Daredevil 84c, 85c, 88c, 90c, 91c, 92c, 93c, 94c
Defenders 3cp
Fear 6cp, 7cp, 9cp
Iron Man 44cp, 45cp, 46cp, 47cp, 48cp, 49cp, 50cp, 51, 52cp, 53cp
Journey into Mystery 2nd Series 1cp, 2cp
Jungle Action 2cpi
Kid Colt Outlaw 157cp, 161cp, 162cp
Marvel's Greatest Comics 34cp, 37cp
Marvel Feature 3cp
Marvel Premiere 1cp, 2cp
Marvel Tales 34cp, 35cp, 40cp
Marvel Team-Up 1cp ,2cp, 3cp, 4cp, 5cp
Marvel Triple Action 2cp, 3cp, 9, 10
Mighty Marvel Western 18cpi, 19cp
Outlaw Kid, 2nd Series 10cpi, 11cp, 12cp, 15c
Rawhide Kid 96cp, 101pc
Red Wolf 1cp, 2cp
Ringo Kid 15cp
Sgt. Fury 37c, 94cpi, 95cp, 96cp, 100cp, 102, 103cp
Sub-Mariner 45cp, 46cp, 47cp, 48cp, 49cp, 50cp, 51cp, 52cp
Thor 201cp, 205cp
Two-Gun Kid 102cp, 103cp, 104cp, 105cp
Tomb of Dracula 3cp, 5cp, 9
Warlock 1cp, 2cp, 3cp, 5, 7
Western Gunfighters 2nd Series 11cp
Western Kid 2nd Series 5cp
Where Monsters Dwell 13cp, 16cp, 17cp
X-Men 74cp, 75cp, 76cp, 79cp

1973

DC Comics

Adventure Comics 496, 497, 498, 499c, 537
All-Star Western 67
Detective Comics 438p (1937 Series)
Forbidden Tales of Dark Mansion 13
Green Lantern 85, 87, 88 (unpublished)
Johnny Thunder 2p, 3p
Secret Origins 2p
Super Spectacular 14p,15p,18p,20p(as G. Stack)i

Marvel Comics

Amazing Spider-Man 120p, 121p, 122p, 123p, 124p
Astonishing Tales 21cp
Avengers 110cp
Captain America 160cp
Captain Marvel 24cp
Chamber of Chills 2cp
Conan, the Barbarian 23, 25cp, 27cp, 28cp, 29cp, 30cp, 31cp, 32cp
Conan Annual 6
Creatures on the Loose 25cpi
Daredevil 95c, 96c, 97c, 104
Dead of Night 11
Defenders 7
Doc Savage 4cp, 5cp, 6cp
Fantastici Quattro 47p, 48p
Fear 19cp

Ghost Rider 1cp, 2cp
Gunslinger 2cpi
Iron Man 54cpi, 62cp, 63cp, 64
Journey into Mystery 3cp, 5cp, 8cp
Jungle Action 4cp
Kid Colt, 2nd series 166cpi, 169cpi
Marvel Double Feature 9, 14
Marvel Feature 7cp
Marvel Tales 41cp
Marvel Team-Up 6cp, 7cp, 12cp, 13cp, 14cp, 15cp, 16cp
Marvel Two-in-One 1
Marvel Triple Action 9cp, 10cp
Marvel Super-Heroes 34c
Monsters Unleashed 3p
Outlaw Kid 15cp
Red Wolf 5cpi
Ringo Kid, 2nd Series 18cpi
Sgt. Fury and His Howling Commandos 107cpi
Strange Tales 170cp, 171cp, 172
Star Spangled War Stories 169pi
Sub-Mariner 58cp, 66cp
Supernatural Thrillers 3cp, 6cp
Thor 207cp,208cp, 209cp, 210cp, 211, 212, 216
Tomb of Dracula 10cp, 13cp, 14cp
Two Gun Kid 108cpi
Wanted: The World's Most Dangerous Villains 5p
Warlock 4cp, 5cp, 7cp
Werewolf by Night 12cp
Western Gunfighters 17cpi, 18cpi
Weird War Tales 115, 116, 118
Weird Western Tales 20
Weird Wonder Tales 1cpi
Where Monsters Dwell 19cp, 20cp
Worlds Unknown 1p, 2p
Wyatt Earp 32cpi
X-Men 80cp ,81cp

Time Magazine
Illustration

1974

Aurora Plastics Co,
Aurora Comic Scenes Instruction Booklet
Aurora Models 183-140

DC Comics
Action Comics 437p
Batman 257p
Brave & Bold 112cpi, 115p
Detective Comics 439p
The Flash 229p
Superman 272
Superman Family 221, 222

Marvel Comics
Adventures into Fear 21c
Amazing Adventures 25cp
Amazing Spider-Man, Giant Size 1, 2
Amazing Spider-Man 129cp, 131cp, 132cp, 137cp, 138cp, 139cp
Astonishing Tales 23cp
Avengers, Giant Size 1, 2cp
Avengers 122cp, 127cp, 128cp, 130cp
Captain America 170, 172cp, 173cp, 174cp, 177, 180cp
Captain Marvel 35cp
Conan, the Barbarian Giant Size 1cp, 2p
Conan, the Barbarian 34cp, 35cp, 38cp, 39cp, 41cp, 42cp, 43cp, 45
Creatures on the Loose 29cp, 30cp, 31cp
Daredevil 108, 109c, 112c, 114c, 115, 116c
Deadly Hands of Kung Fu 23
Defenders Giant Size 1cp, 2cp, 3c
Defenders 13cp, 16cp, 18cp
Dracula/Bram Stoker's Giant Size 3cp
Fantastic Four Giant Size 2cp, 3
Fantastic Four 143cp, 145cp, 146cp, 150cp, 153cp
Fantastici Quattro 77p, 78p, 80p
Fear 20cp, 21cpi, 23cp, 24cp, 25cp
Frankenstein 10cp, 13cp
Ghost Rider 4cp, 5cp, 8cp, 9cp
Giant-Size Super-Heroes 1p
Human Torch 2cp
Iron Man 66cp, 67cp
Jungle Action 8, 9cp, 10cp, 11cp
Ka-Zar 2nd Series 3cp, 5cp
Kull, the Destroyer 15cp
Man-Thing 4, 10, 12cp, 13, 14, 15, 16, 17, 18, 19, 20
Marvel Premiere 15, 16cp, 17cp, 18cp, 19cp
Marvel Spotlight 14cp, 15cp, 17cp, 18cp, 19cp
Marvel Superheroes 42cpi, 43pi, 44cpi, 45pi, 46cpi
Marvel Team-Up 17cp, 18cp, 19cp, 20cp, 21cp, 23cp, 24cp, 25cp, 26cp, 28cp
Marvel Treasury Edition 1p
Marvel Two-in-One 1cp ,2p ,3cp
Master of Kung Fu 19cp, 20cp
Mighty Marvel Western 31cpi
Power Man 17cp, 18cp, 19cp, 20cp
Savage Sword of Conan 1p, 2p, 3p
Savage Tales 4p
Sargent Fury and His Howling Commandos 120cp
Strange Tales 174cp
Sub-Mariner 70cp, 71cp
Supernatural Thrillers 9cp,10cp
Tarzan 232p,233p
Thor 220cp,222cp,223cp
Tomb of Dracula 17cp, 18cp, 19cp, 20cp, 23cp, 24cp, 25cp, 26cp, 27cp
Vampire Tales 4, 5p
War is Hell 9cp, 10cp\
Weird Mystery Tales 10pi
Weird Wonder Tales 2cp
Werewolf Giant Size 2cp

Werewolf by Night 17cp, 18cp, 19cp, 20cp, 21cp, 22cp, 23cp, 24cp
Western Gunfighters 2nd Series 22cp
Worlds Unknown 5cp, 6cp, 8cp

1975

DC Comics
Action Comics 443p, 449p
Batman 261p
Batman Family 2cp
DC Special Presents 17p, 18cp, 19p
Flash 232p
Flash Gordon n1cp
Super-Team Family 1p

Marvel Comics
Amazing Adventures 28,2 9cp, 30
Amazing Spider-Man Giant Size 3cpi, 4cp, 5cp
Amazing Spider-Man 140cp, 143cp, 144cp, 145cp, 148cp, 149cp, 150cp, 151
Avengers, Giant Size 3cp, 4cp
Avengers 131cp, 133cp, 134cp, 136cp, 138cp, 139cp, 140cp, 141cp, 142cp, 143c, 144c
Captain America, Giant Size 1cp
Captain America 181cp, 183cp, 184cp, 185cp, 186cp, 187cp, 188cp, 189cp, 190cp
Captain Marvel, Giant Size 1p
Captain Marvel 37cp, 44c
Champions 1cp
Conan, the Barbarian Giant Size 3cp, 4cp, 5p
Conan, the Barbarian 47cp, 48cp, 49, 50cp, 51cp, 52, 53, 54cp, 55, 57cp
Creatures on the Loose, Giant Size 1
Creatures on the Loose 33c, 35cp, 36cp, 37cp, 38
Daredevil, Giant Size 1cp
Daredevil 117, 119c, 120c, 121c, 122c, 124c, 126c, 127c, 128c
Dead of Night 11cp, 20, 21, 22, 23, 24, 25, 26
Defenders, Giant Size 3cp, 4cp, 5cp
Defenders 19cp, 20cp, 21cp, 22cp, 23cp, 24cp, 25cp, 26
Doctor Strange Giant Size 1cp
Doctor Strange, 2nd Series 8cp, 9cp, 10cpi
Dracula Giant Size 4cp, 5cp
Fantastic Four 154cp, 155, 160cp
Fantastici Quattro 103p, 105p, 107p, 108p
Fear 26cp, 27cp, 28cp, 31cp
Frankenstein 15cp
Ghost Rider 11cp, 12cp, 13cp
Hulk, Giant Size 1cp
Human Torch 3cp, 5cp, 6cp, 8cp
Incredible Hulk 193cp, 194cp
Inhumans 1cp,4
Invaders 2cp
Iron Fist 1cp,2cp
Iron Man, Giant Size 1cp
Iron Man 72cp, 73cp, 74cp, 75cp, 77cp, 78cp, 79cp, 80cp
Jungle Action 13cp, 14cp, 15cpi, 16cpi, 17cp
Ka-Zar 2nd Series 8cp, 9cp, 10cpi, 11cp, 13cp, 14
Kid Colt 194cpi, 195cpi, 197cpi, 199cpi, 200cpi, 201cpi
Kid Colt, Giant Size 2cpi, 3cpi
Kull & the Barbarians 1p, 2pi
Kull, the Destroyer 21c
Man-Thing 13cp, 15cp, 16cpi, 17cp, 18cp, 19cpi
Man-Thing, Giant Size 2, 3
Marvel Chillers 1cp
Marvel Double Feature 9cp
Marvel Feature 1cp
Marvel Premiere 20cp, 21cp, 22cp, 23cp, 24cp, 25cp, 27cp
Marvel Presents 1cp
Marvel Preview 16,17
Marvel Spotlight 20cp, 21cp, 22cp, 23cp, 24cp, 25cp
Marvel Team-Up 30cp, 31cp, 32cp, 33cp, 34cp, 35cp
Marvel Treasury 13
Marvel Two-in-One 8cp, 9cp, 10cp, 11cp
Master of King-Fu, Giant Size 3cp, 4cp
Master of King-Fu 24cpi, 26cp, 27cpi, 28cp, 29cp, 30cp, 31cp, 32cp, 33cp, 35cp
Masters of Terror 1p, 2p
Mighty Marvel Westerns 37cp, 38cpi, 39cpi, 40cpi, 41cpi, 42cpi, 43cpi
Monsters Unleashed Annual 1
Night Rider 6
Outlaw Kid 27cpi, 28cp, 29cp
Power Man Annual Giant Size 1cp
Power Man 24cp, 25cp, 26cp, 27, 28cp
Ringo Kid 24cpi
Savage Fists of King Fu 1
Savage Sword of Conan 4p, 5p, 8p
Savage Tales Annual 1cp
Skull, the Slayer 1c, 2c
Son of Satan 1cp
Spider-Man, Giant Size 3, 4, 5
Spidey Super Stories 4cp
Strange Tales 182cp
Super-Heroes, Giant Size 1
Super-Villain Team-Up Giant Size 2cp
Supernatural Thrillers 12cp, 13cp, 14cp, 15cp
Thor, Giant Size 1cp
Thor 231cp, 233cp, 234cp, 235cp, 236cp, 237cp, 238cp, 239cp, 240cp, 242cp, 243
Tomb of Dracula 30cp, 31cp, 32cp, 33cp, 34cp, 35cp, 36cp, 37cp, 38cp, 39cp
Two Gun Kid 124cpi
X-Men 94cp, 95cp, 99
X-Men, Giant Size 1cp, 2cp
War Is Hell 11cp, 12cp, 13cp, 14cp
Weird Wonder Tales 10cp
Werewolf Giant Size 3cp, 4cp, 5cp

Werewolf by Night 25cp, 26cp, 27cp, 28cp, 29cp, 30cp, 31cp, 32cp, 33cp, 34cp, 39c, 44c
Western Gunfighters, 2nd Series 27cp, 28cpi, 29cpi, 30cpi,
31cpi, 32cpi, 33cpi
Where Monsters Dwell 33

1976

DC Comics
DC Special Presents 20p, 21p
DC Super-Stars Presents 1pi, 2pi, 10p19
Four Star Spectacular 3p
Marvel Comics
Adventures on the Planet of the Apes 8cp
Amazing Spider-Man Annual 10cp
Amazing Spider-Man 152cp, 153cp, 158cp, 159cp, 160cp, 161cp
Avengers 143cp, 144cp, 145cp, 146c, 159
Black Goliath 5cp
Captain America 84cp, 93cp, 94p, 97p, 188c, 189c, 190c
Captain Britain 36-38
Captain Marvel 44cp
Champions 8cp, 9cp
Conan, the Barbarian 60,61,62cp,63cp,65,66,67 68cp, 69cp
Daredevil 133c, 139
Daredevil Annual 4cp
Deadly Hands of Kung Fu 23p
Defenders 31cp, 32cp, 33cp, 35cp, 36cp, 37cp, 40cp, 41cp
Defenders Giant 1c, 2, 4c
Ghost Rider 19cp, 20cp, 21p
Incredible Hulk 196cp, 198cp
Inhumans 5p, 6p, 7cp, 8cp
Iron Fist 4cp, 5cp, 6cp
Iron Man 82cp, 84cp, 88cp
Jungle Action 19cp, 24cp
Ka-Zar 2nd Series 15cp, 19cp, 20
Kid Colt 205cpi, 206cpi, 207cpi, 208cpi, 210cpi, 211cpi, 213cpi
Kull, the Destroyer 17cp
Marvel Chillers 3cp
Marvel Classics 1, 2c, 3c, 4c, 5c, 6c, 7c, 8c, 9c, 10c, 11c, 12c
Marvel Premiere 28cp
Marvel Presents 5cp
Marvel Spotlight 26cp, 27cp
Marvel Tales 71
Marvel Team-Up 41cp, 43cp, 44cpi, 45cpi, 47cp, 50cp, 51cp
Marvel Treasury Edition 13cp
Marvel Two-in-One 14cp
Master of Kung-Fu 36cp, 38cp, 39cp, 40cp, 41cp, 42cp, 45cp
Mighty Marvel Western 44cpi, 46cpi
Omega the Unknown 3cp
Power Man 29cp, 38cp
Ringo Kid 26cpi, 27cpi, 28cpi, 29cpi
Son of Satan 2cp, 3cp, 6cp, 7cp
Super-Villain Team-Up 9cp
Thor 243
Two Gun Kid 129cpi, 130c, 132cpi

1977

DC Comics
DC Super-Stars 14p
House of Mystery 253
Marvel Comics
Amazing Spider-Man Annual 11cp
Avengers 159cp
Captain America 98cp, 99p, 100cp, 101cp, 102p, 115p, 116, 215cp, 216cp
Captain Britain 37p, 38p
Captain Marvel 53cp
Champions 11cp, 14cp, 15cp, 16cp
Conan, the Barbarian 70cp, 71cp, 72cp, 73cp, 74cp, 76cp, 77cp, 78cp
Daredevil 141cp, 146cp, 147cp, 148cp
Defenders 52cp
Ghost Rider 24cp, 25cp, 26
Invaders 13cp, 17cp, 18cp, 19cp, 20cp, 21cp, 22cp, 23cp
Iron Fist 11cp
Iron Man 96, 98cp
Island of Doctor Moreau 1c
John Carter, Warlord of Mars Annual 1cp
John Carter, Warlord of Mars 1cp, 2cp, 3cp, 4cp, 5cp, 6cp, 7cp
Ka-Zar 20cp
Kid Colt 212c, 216cpi, 218cpi, 220cpi, 221cpi
Kull, the Destroyer 21cp
Marvel Classics 13c, 14c, 15c, 16c, 17c, 21c, 22c, 24c, 32
Marvel Movie Special 1c
Marvel Premiere 36cp, 37cp, 38cp
Marvel Spotlight 32cp
Marvel Tales 79, 80, 81, 82, 83cp
Marvel Team-Up 53, 54cp, 62cp
Marvel Treasury Edition 14cp, 15p, 16
Marvel Two-in-One 28cp, 29
Master of Kung Fu 59cp, 63
Omega, the Unknown 5,8cp, 9cp
Power Man 44cp, 47cp, 48cp
Rawhide Kid 139cpi, 142cpi
Red Sonja 5cp
Son of Satan 8cp
Spectacular Spider-Man 3cp
Star Wars 4cp
Super Spider-Man 240 cp

Super-Villain Team-Up 10cp
Two Gun Kid 135cpi, 136cpi
What If? 2c, 3cp, 4c

Newspaper Strips
Star Hawks 1977-1981 33

1978

DC Comics
DC Comics Presents 28,35,48,56

Marvel Comics
Amazing Spider-Man 181cp
Amazing Spider-Man Annual 12p
Captain America 220cp, 221cp
Captain Marvel 56cp
Daredevil 150, 151cp, 152
Defenders 55cp
Incredible Hulk nn
Invaders 24cp, 25cp, 26cp, 27cp
John Carter, Warlord of Mars 1cp, 2cp, 3cp, 8cp, 9cp, 10cp, 15cp
John Carter, Warlord of Mars Annual 1, 2
Kid Colt Outlaw 222cpi
Marvel Classics 25
Marvel Preview 16p
Marvel Tales 98p, 99, 100, 101, 117
Marvel Treasury Edition 16cp,1 8p
Master of Kung-Fu 59, 63cp
Ms. Marvel 8c,13cp
Rawhide Kid 143cpi, 144
Spectacular Spider-Man 15, 17cp, 18cp, 23cp
Star Wars 7cp, 8cp, 9cp, 11cp, 15cp
What If? 7cp, 8

1979

DC Comics
Flash 229, 232
Green Lantern 123cpi, 125
Time Warp 2p

Heavy Metal
Heavy Metal V2 10

Marvel Comics
John Carter 1cp, 2cp, 4cp
Marvel Preview 17pi
Marvel Tales 100p
Marvel Treasury Edition 22 p
Savage Sword of Conan 47p

Newspaper Strips
Tarzan Sunday Page 1979-1981

Simon and Schuster
The Amazing Spider 1

1980

DC Comics
DC Comics Presents 28pi
DC Special Blue Ribbon Digest 4 p, 5p
Justice League of America 81,200
Legion of Super-Heroes 300
Mysteries in Space: The Best of DC Science Fiction Comics 1p
Time Warp 2

Marvel Comics
What If? 24p
King Conan 8
Marvel Tales 120

1981

DC Comics
Best of DC 10p,18p
DC Comics Presents 35p, Annual 3
DC Special Blue Ribbon Digest 9p, 14p, 15p
Justice League of America 201

Krupp Comic Works
The Spirit 28pi

Marvel Comics
Conan, the Barbarian Annual 6cpi
Conan, the Barbarian 127cpi, 128cpi, 129cpi
Marvel Tales 125cp, 126, 127, 130, 137, 138, 139, 140, 141, 142, 143, 144, 145, 146, 147, 148, 149, 150, 151, 152, 153, 154, 155
Rawhide Kid 139, 141, 142, 143
Savage Sword of Conan 63pi, 64pi, 65pi, 67pi
Star Trek 15pi

1982

DC Comics
Action Comics 535cp
Atari Force 2i, 3p
Best of DC 30p, 31cpi
Daring New Adventures of Supergirl 6, 8, 9, 11, 12
DC Comics Presents 48cp
DC Special Blue Ribbon Digest 22p
Detective Comics 520pi
Flash 312cp
Fury of Firestorm 30
Green Lantern 154cpi, 156cpi
House of Mystery 300p
Justice League of America 200pi
New Adventures of Superboy 32cpi, 33cp, 35cpi
Superman 342, 367pi, 372pi, 374cp, 375cp, 377c
Superman Annual 9
Superman Family 221cp, 222cp
Warlord Annual 6
Weird War Tales 115cpi, 116cpi, 118cpi
Wonder Woman 294cp
World's Finest Comics 281cpi, 282cpi, 283p, 289c

Fantagraphics Publ
Gil Kane's Savage, Reprint
Marvel Comics
Conan, the Barbarian 130cpi, 131cpi, 132cpi, 133cpi, 134cpi
Ka-Zar, 11pi, 12pi, 14
Marvel Tales 135cp, 136cp
Micronauts 38pi, 40cpi, 41cpi, 42cpi, 43cpi, 44cpi, 45cpi, 46
Thor 318cpi

1983

Archie Comics Group
Hall of Fame 1p, 2p, 3p
DC Comics
Action Comics 539cpi, 540cpi, 541cpi, 544cpi, 545cpi, 546cpi, 547cpi, 548cpi, 549cpi
Adventure Comics Digest 496cpi, 497cpi, 498cpi, 499cpi
Atari Force 5cp
Blackhawk 263cpi, 264cpi
Daring New Adventures of Supergirl 6cpi, 8cpi, 9cpi, 11cpi, 12cpi
Daring New Adventures of Supergirl Annual 1, 2c
DC Comics Presents 56cpi, 58cpi, 60cpi, 62cpi, 64cpi, 66
DC Comics Presents Annual 2cpi
Green Lantern 163cpi, 165cpi, 166cpi, 167cpi, 168cpi, 169cpi 170cpi, 171cpi
Legion of Super-Heroes 300cp
New Adventures of Superboy 39cpi,41cpi,42cpi, 43cpi, 44cpi, 45cpi, 46cpi, 47cpi, 48cpi
Supergirl 14
Superman Annual 2, 9cpi
Superman 381cpi, 382cpi, 384cpi, 385cpi, 386cpi, 387cpi, 388cpi, 389cpi, 390cpi, 391c
Superman Special 1, 2
Sword of the Atom 1cpi, 2cpi, 3cpi, 4cpi, Spec 1, 2
Wonder Woman 303cpi, 304cpi, 305cpi, 307cpi
World's Finest Comics 174, 281, 282, 283, 289cpi
Heavy Metal Magazine
Vol 7 #1p
Marvel Comics
Ka-Zar, the Savage 14pi
Kree-Skrull War Starring Avengers 2
Marvel Fanfare 8p, 9p, 10p, 11p
Savage Sword of Conan 85p, 86p

1984

DC Comics
Action Comics 551cpi, 552cpi, 553cpi, 554cpi
Best of DC 44cpi
Blue Devil 7pi
DC Comics Presents 68cpi
DC Presents Annual 3cpi
Fury of Firestorm 29cpi
Green Lantern 177cpi, 184
New Adventures of Superboy 49cpi
Superman 392cpi, 395cpi
Superman Special 2cpi
Sword of the Atom Special 1cpi, 2
Tales of the Green Lantern Corps Annual 1
Vigilante 12pi, 13cpi
Wonder Woman 312cpi, 313, 314cpi

1985

DC Comics
Batman 382cpi
Best of DC 61pi
Deadman 2p,3p
Green Lantern 184cpi
Sword of the Atom Special 2cpi
Tales of the Green Lantern Corps Annual 1
Web of Spider-Man Annual 6
Who's Who: The Definitive Directory of the DC Universe 1pi, 2pi, 3pi, 4pi, 5pi, 6pi, 7pi, 8pi, 9pi, 10pi

1986

DC Comics
Action Comics 580cpi
DC Challenge 4cpi
Secret Origins 2cp, 3, 4, 5, 6, 7, 8, 9, 10, 11, 12, 13, 14, 15, 16 17, 18, 19, 20, 21, 22, 23, 24, 25, 26, 27, 28, 29, 50
Who's Who: The Definitive Directory of the DC Universe 11pi, 13pi, 14pi, 16pi, 19pi, 21pi, 22pi
Fantagraphics Publ
Anything Goes 1cpi

1987

DC Comics
Talos of the Wilderness Sea 1cpi
Warlord Annual 6pi
Who's Who: The Definitive Directory of the DC Universe 23pi, 25pi, Update '87 1pi
Fantagraphics Publ
Doomsday Squad 7cpi

1988

DC Comics
Action Comics 551, 552, 553, 554, 580, 601pi, 602pi, 603pi, 604p, 605p, 627cpi, 642
Blue Beetle 4, 7, 8, 10, 22p
Checkmate! 2cpi, 4cpi, 7cpi, 8cpi, 10cpi, 11cpi
Green Lantern Corps 222, 223cpi, 224cpi

Green Lantern Corps Annual 1
Secret Origins 28pi
Showcase 1pi
Marvel Comics
Conan Saga 10

1989

DC Comics
Action Comics 642pi
Checkmate! 15cpi, 16cpi, 17cpi, 18cpi, 19cpi
Ring of the Nibelung 1cpi
Sandman 11pi
Marvel Comics
Conan Saga 23, 24,2 9
Marvel Comics Presents 116, 122
Marvel Masterworks 11cp
Marvel Tales 224, 225, 226, 227

1990

DC Comics
Greatest Fifties Stories Ever Told nnp
Greatest Team Up Stories Ever Told
Justice League 5cpi, 6cpi
Ring of the Nibelung 2cpi, 3cpi, 4cpi
Who's Who in the DC Universe 2pi, 4pi, 5p
Harvey Comics
Monster in my Pocket
Marvel Comics
Amazing Spider-Man Annual 24
Marvel Tales 234
Web of Spider-Man Annual 6
Spectacular Spider-Man 10pi

1991

DC Comics
Batman: Legends of the Dark Knight 24cpi, 25cpi,
Challengers of the Unknown 6cpi
Forgotten Realms Annual 1cpi
Green Lantern, 3rd Series 19pi
Emerald Dawn II 4
Sandman 26pi, 27pi
Harvey
Monster in My Pocket 2cpi, 3cpi, 4cpi
Marvel Comics
Marvel Tales 249, 251, 252, 253

1992

DC Comics
DC Silver Age Classics 5cpi
DC Silver Age Classics Showcase 22
Essential Showcase 1
Legends of the Dark Knight 26cpi
Tomahawk
Harvey Comics
Back to the Future 3, 4
Impact
Web 5cpi, 9cpi, 10cpi, 12cpi, 13cp, 14cpi
Marvel Comics
Marvel Comics Presents 116pi
Star Magazine
Magazine 19p,21cp

1993

DC Comics
Superman Gallery 1pi
Topps Comics
Jurassic Park 0, 1cp, 2cp, 3cp, 4cp
Malibu Comics
Edge 1cpi,2cpi

1994

Marvel Comics
Marvel Magazine 4p, 6pi
Savage Fists of Kung Fu 1cp
Spider-Man Magazine 4p, 6pi
Tomb of Dracula (Vintage Pack) 25

1995

DC Comics
Action Comics 715
Doomsday Annual 1
Superman 99, 101, 102, 103
Superman: Man of Steel Gallery 1pi
Malibu Comics
Edge 3cp
Marvel comics
Scarlet Spider
Spider-Man 63
Spider-Man Magazine 4p, 5p, 6p
X-Men Classic 1p
Milestone DC Comics
Static 31
Penthouse
Omni Comix 3

1996

DC Comics
Green Lantern 81pi
Power of Shazam! 14p, 19p
Superman: The Wedding Album 1p
Superman: Distant Fires 1p
Tales of the Unexpected 88

179

Marvel Comics

Incredible Hulk Magazine 1pi
Marvel: Heroes & Legends 1 cp
Untold Tales of Spider-Man #nnpi

Tekno

I-Bots 4

1997

DC Comics

Life Story of the Flash, p

Image Comics

Stormwatch 44p

Lightning Comics

Judgment Day 1pi

1998

DC Comics

Doctor Tomorrow 8pi
Green Lantern Annual 1cp
Secret Origins Replica Edition 1cpi
Welcome Back to the House of Mystery 1

Image Comics

WildC.A.T.S./Aliens 1p

Lightning Comics

Judgment Day: Aftermath 1p

2000

DC Comics

Green Lantern 1cp
Legends of the DC Universe 28c, 29c

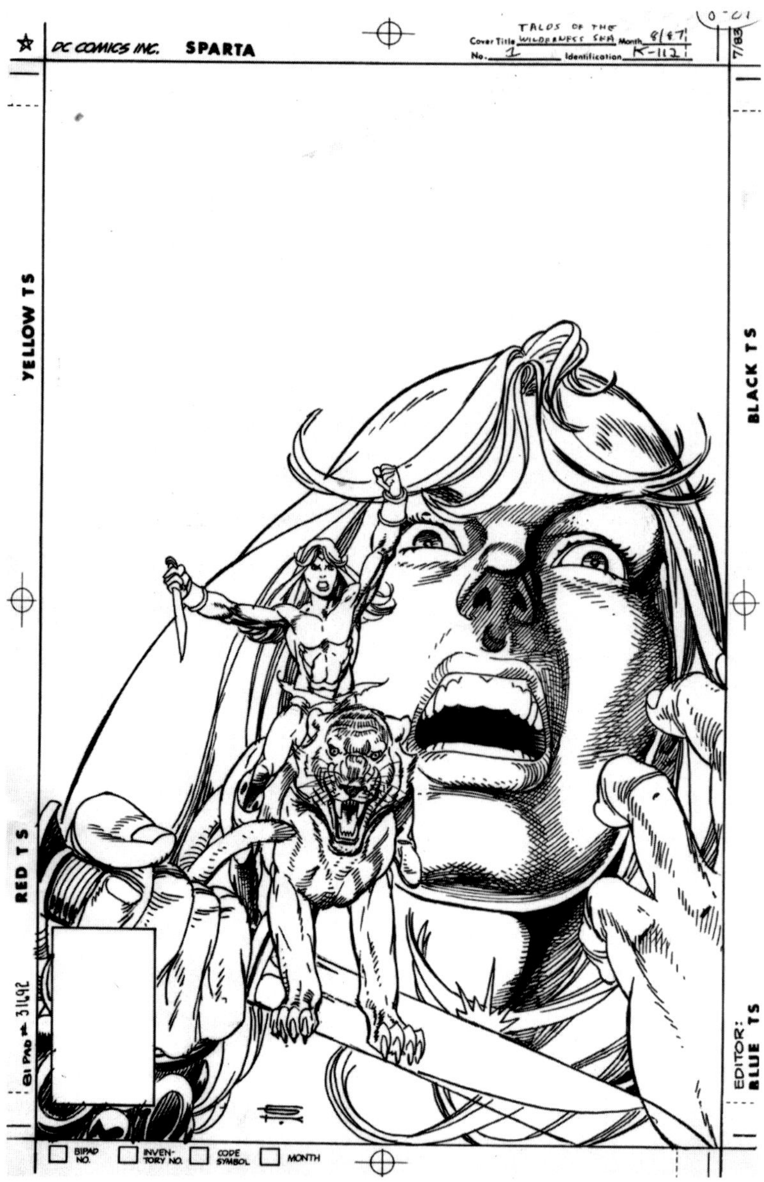

Above: original artwork for the cover for *Talos of the Wilderness Sea* # 1, August, 1987, Gil Kane, pencils and inks, ©2001 DC Comics.

GIL KANE: AN INTERVIEW

In preparation for this book, I conducted a number of interviews with Gil Kane. Many aspects of Kane's opinions and experience with the art of the comics, the history of comics, and the development of comic books as a story telling medium were explored. What follows is a small excerpt from one interview. This interview has been edited for publication.

Q. Gil, consciously or not, artists who draw comic book stories have to deal with a number of design problems. Over your career, you have had to design stories, splash pages and covers. When you go about designing a cover or a splash page, what are you looking to do that is different from the design of the interior pages?

A. First of all, let me tell you that page layout, page design is different from compositional design. I mean the elements of design that are utilized in narrative composition are different. From the 1940s on I was interested in page layout and there were a lot of excellent guys doing first rate page layout. It simply was not terribly popular with editors because they always complained that it was hard to follow the narrative line, panel to panel and most artists weren't that interested in it. Everything that they would design was to advance the narrative. I mean page design is something people have been doing since about the early 1940s. I got interested watching all of these people. I always wanted to do more elaborate page design than I was allowed to do. But editors insisted primarily that you stick with the traditional grid because the traditional grid had been introduced by the newspaper strips and comic books in the beginning were nothing except a cheap imitation of the newspaper strips.

Q. DC, even though it had a very conservative house style in the 1950s and 1960s, was a little more open minded about the format they would allow because they would allow three-quarters splash pages with a boxed panel inside them to develop the story. Was that the artist or was that the DC editors?

A. Essentially, if it didn't get too complicated that was the artist. It was at DC that I had enormous difficulty when I worked with Julie [Schwartz], or practically any of those guys. The editors were very rigid about allowing any variation from traditional grid styles. I tried it every now and then. [Joe] Kubert used to do it on occasion but while he broke from the regular grid, the fact is that his page designs were not really revolutionary in any way. It wasn't until later on when I did *Blackmark* that I really thought about page design. In order to accommodate balloons, text and pictures on a very small area and at the same time allow for some white space I didn't look at other comic books, I went to *House Beautiful* and the best layout design in publishing. I tried to use that stuff for months. I came away with what I needed to know. I started the *Blackmark* books in that style. It turned out to be, for me, the answer to everything. It wasn't for everybody else, though a lot of people objected to it and would have preferred a traditional style.

Q. When you did *Star Hawks*, its design deviated from standard newspaper design. Was that your idea?

A. They suggested to me at first a two-tier strip but in effect there were three panels on each tier just like an ordinary strip. I said, what the hell is the use of that, why do we not give them a comic book page in each strip? I broke it up unevenly. There was a certain amount of resistance to it but ultimately they allowed me leeway. I broke it up as though I was doing a comic book page. Actually I was a little freer than if I was doing a comic book page. Ultimately after a very short while I began to be radical with it. I used all sorts of layouts. I noted that finally every now and then I would see it in a traditional strip. I saw Joe Kubert try to use it in strips he worked on. Panel design or page design is different from composing a picture for a cover or an illustration. An interior illustration, whether it is for a splash or for an interior panel, is exactly the same. The props are the same. The thing you want to do on a splash page is to make it as distinctive as possible. But, you also must follow the needs of the narrative to keep it chugging on.

Q. How much actual input did they give you when you were doing a cover in designing the color of the cover and the layout of the text and logo?

A. First of all, most of that stuff such as the cover logo are designed before you even do the book. Second, the color itself was, in those days, done by the production department. What I did in the beginning is pencil and ink the cover but we would talk over the cover idea. I would design the cover, submit it and if they approved it, then I would finish it. That's the way it got done.

Q. One of the things that I always found attractive about some of the covers is they used really bright primary colors, which is very attractive and which is clearly something that you see in twentieth century design, rather than having all kinds of different shadings and different colorings.

A. That was only because they were limited in the palates. They used a very cheap process.

Q. Did they get good design as a result of economy rather than out of intent?

A. It gave comics a distinctive look so that ultimately comic books, even though they came down from newspaper strips, ultimately developed a look that was different from newspaper strips. The lettering was different and the whole slam, bang quality that was associated with comic books was a step away from newspaper strips.

Q. When you did your graphic novels, *Savage* and *Blackmark*, the story telling is more like a motion picture. It is close to cinema. Did you feel like an artist/director?

A. Well, I certainly tried. Film was only one of the things I had in mind when I was working on *Savage*. Those 40 pages were done in 30 days.

Q. Judging by your output, you seemed to be able to work really fast.

A. Well, I did. As a matter of fact, I was finishing the last page on *Savage* while they were assembling the first part of the book.

Q. You have to be one of the most prolific comic artists along with Jack Kirby.

A. Jack Kirby exceeded me.

Q. In the late 1960s and 1970s you were pumping out tons of covers for Marvel.

A. The 1970s was my time. The 1970s was when I was turning out the most work that I ever turned out. I was turning out the equivalent of a story a week, that is I pencilled a story a week. After a while, when Roy [Thomas] became the editor, I stopped that in favor of doing the covers. Sometimes I would do 25 covers a week. It was a little bit of one and a little of the other. But it was my most prolific period in terms of production if not the quality. My best stuff started in the late 1970s and began to really show up strong in the mid 1970s. I was already working on *Star Hawks* in 1977 so I was beginning to kick up my heels a little before that. I started to kick up where I felt a certain amount of artistic authority. I guess it was in the early 1970's in comics and later in animation, and it was during animation that I thought I had done my best work.

Q. You worked for Marvel and then for Ruby-Spears?

A. Yeah, I worked for Marvel for a very short while. Then I worked for Ruby-Spears for years. Jack Kirby and I and Doug Wildey did the presentation work. Wildey would take three weeks to do a picture and Jack would get an assignment and spend about two days on it, come back a week later with his full assignment, six boards. But Jack was beginning to go into decline. He was having problems with his eye-sight, age, and whatever. He would do six boards. Out of the six, two or sometimes three would be really good and three were almost unusable. Since I had a style that was somewhat reminiscent of Jack, except it was more literal and more representational, they started giving me most of the stuff to do. Finally I became the presentation artist. Wildey quit. Jack didn't quit but he slowed down until he was doing very little.

Q. When you do presentation art do you have to develop an idea and then do character drawings, backgrounds and so forth?

A. I would do these 20" x 30" boards. I would do about six or seven or eight of them a week. They would be ultimately painted and submitted as the presentation for or to the network. Before I did that, I would also design the characters that were going to appear on that board. I would be given a script or my art director, who was John Dorman would tell me what he wanted to see and I would try to come through with the characterizations he asked for. Once it was approved I would then work out some of my presentation boards with him. They would nearly always have a narrative aspect.

Q. Let's address your technique of inking your work for a moment. Do you just use a pen as opposed to using a brush to do the inking?

A. Well, actually I used a marker. They manufactured the perfect marker. I was able to get away for years with the kind of inking that I did because the weight of the marker was just the right weight to offset the fact that I wasn't using a light source. Finally, in the last two years I started to use light source inking but unfortunately most of the time all they wanted was pencils.

Q. Did you ever use technical or rapidograph pens?

A. I could have used a rapidograph pen. The rapidograph pen only emphasizes those qualities I never should have had and creates a dead line. It doesn't give the line any depth and it doesn't give it any value. I prefer to use a marker. The markers I use work like a pencil so I was able to use them comfortably. The reason I used markers was that speed was always of the essence. Everything I used was really a replacement for a pencil, something that worked just like a pencil except that it dispensed ink. I began experimenting with markers and I was one of the first guys in the country to use them. I kept looking. I found one marker that I liked. It worked just like a pencil. The fact is that it gave me the effect of a brush so I got away for years with a much softer line. It wasn't until I started pushing myself to the limit when I was assigned a Conan Story. I had about two-and-a-half weeks in which to get out thirty-seven pages. I remember one day I inked seven pages. I just kept inking roughly about the rate of five to six to seven pages a day. It was a black and white Conan book. When it came out I was surprised that it looked as reasonable as it did. My problem was that without a light source I wasn't giving sufficient weight to my figures. I did do one thing fairly well. I could always pencil. I could always get beautiful whites in there and I knew how to design a panel. The only problem is that when you ink and you don't use a back light source or have a superb sense of spotting like Wally Wood. Wally didn't always use a light source but he had such a great sense of spotting and had such a special hand with a brush that the page always looked finished. I did a whole set of Superman Books for about a year-and-a-half and all of the covers were always done with just a single marker and yet they came out pretty well because the weight was just right so it softened up. My pencilling was always reasonable in ink but it was just the fact that I wasn't getting the most out of it. In other words I wasn't supporting my pencils to the extent that they should have been supported and that's been one of my big failures even though I thought I liked my own pencils best when I inked them myself. I improved the pencils as I worked on it with the ink. If I had been a more practiced inker working with a light source, I would have enhanced it because I would have made it tighter and better as I inked it. I also would have given it substance. I never gave it mood because mood depends on blacks and I was always going too fast for that so I never managed to do that, so I wasn't always a good inker. For instance look at Ruby Nebres. That son-of-a-bitch used to do a finished page that was simply incredible. I couldn't believe how polished it was. What I hated was that he would change the heads and so forth. They totally lacked character, they lacked any sort of grace but the god-damned finished page looked like a Michaelangelo Painting. He would follow all the pencilling on the figure and everything else but his inking style has such vitality that he brought to the work. Even though I still preferred my own inking, the fact is that he brought a professionalism and vitality. Ultimately he became a very limited inker because his light source was very shallow. He became a series of feathering effects, all done with incredible vitality, but that's what it came down to. He stopped being the kind of inker he was when he first came to the United States.

Q. A big problem with comic artists is the separation between the person who draws and the person who inks and in many cases inkers do not follow the intentions of the person who pencils.

A. There can be a different personality. If there is a collaboration it is between a writer and an artist. Even then I prefer to do everything myself. It is only in comic books that they introduce the inker as somebody with a professional status. When these strips were done artists had assistants. They would do all the important stuff and leave the finishing of certain background details, the minor things such as the lettering. Milton Caniff, for instance, would pull an inker on occasion, aside from Noel Sickles, who used to do the strip. Sickles inked a lot of the material. A lot of the material was pencilled by Sickles and inked by Caniff. During the war Caniff continued to employ a whole series of inkers who worked with him who went on to do strips of their own. They were very, very limited. They were good Caniff inkers but they weren't pencillers and each one of them ultimately led a less than distinguished career. Alex Raymond had an excellent inker, who turned into a better artist than Raymond, Austin Briggs. Raymond started Flash Gordon and did all of it up until about the Tournaments of Mongo from about 1935-36. Austin Briggs inked all of that stuff for about the next three or four years. At the end of the 1930s Briggs left to do a daily Flash Gordon Strip, which was lousy. Raymond inked most of his own stuff. He pencilled and inked both of his own stuff which at this point became photographic and then he ultimately went into the service. Briggs came in with a brush style that was superior to Raymond even though he couldn't draw Flash Gordon, he could pencil it well. He was a good draftsman. Briggs simply couldn't make up pictures and compositions. Raymond would do the pencilling. When Austin Briggs would do the inking that stuff had a majesty that I have never known Flash Gordon to have before or after. In fact it's my favorite period. It wasn't Williamson's favorite period. Al Williamson likes that period in the early 1940s when everybody looked like Ruritania. Instead of it being in the early days, it was all breast plates and swords. By 1940 or so, people were wearing boots and it looked like something out of middle Europe in 1890.

Q. Why do you force perspective right down the viewers throat?

A. First, I would put the head forward then tipping it backwards. I would do a lot of nostril shots. The big thing is it makes you learn how to draw. I don't know why I was a late developer. I tell you I am not being modest. I was always smarter than Carmine [Infantino]. We all grew up together. I knew Kubert since we were kids. All of these guys exceeded me, you known, when we were younger. In my 20s they just left me in the dust. I didn't really start developing until my late 30s. It wasn't for lack of trying. I always looked for the stars and only saw the ceiling. Finally there was some beginning, some sort of a breakthrough and I began to see possibilities. Once I saw the first possibility in terms of what was wrong I began to see what I could do and adjust it. Each theme would lead to another theme but it took me a long time. Al Toth, when he was twenty years old, had a spell-binding vitality not too far from where he is now. By the time that he was about twenty-one or twenty-two he was as good as he ever got to be. The thing is that I still don't understand why it took me so much longer to begin any kind of really professional development. It wasn't until my mid-late 30s, when I was thirty-six or thirty-seven, that I really started to plan how to do composition and design. When I was a kid about sixteen, Irv Novick said all you have to do in order to create a design is to have people looking into a panel and from both sides of the picture and not to have anything go out of the frame. I just went on, little by little, doing informal study of composition and design. I am still at it. The point is that it took me years to get to a point where I could use it a little bit. It wasn't until I was about thirty years old that I discovered Roy Crane. With the discovery of Roy Crane, everything began to open up for me in the smallest way but I began to understand a little about design and deep space. I hadn't even thought about deep space as a concept. In my late twenties I began to be satisfied with what I was doing but there weren't any significant differences until my early thirties when I found Crane and once I found Crane I tackled George Bridgman again.

Q. Did you look at Frank Robbins and Noel Sickles?

A. I never got anything out of those guys because they were designers. They didn't register and I couldn't penetrate it. I just didn't know what made it tick. After I had Roy Crane and deep space and his compositional approaches which I only was beginning to understand a little bit, I tackled George Bridgman for about the tenth or twelfth time. I have never been able to conquer George Bridgman.

Q. In designing your work did you want to use Zip-a-tone and Craftint more often?

A. That's part of design, but that is also part of inking. You can't use that stuff without a light source. I really never used that stuff until *Blackmark* and *Savage,* then I started to use it. I finally tackled Bridgman. I approached Bridgman through one of my old-time pals, Reed Crandall. He was one of my absolute favorites. He and Louie Fine and of course, Jack.

Q. Lets shift gears. I prefer to characterize the developments in comic art by focusing on the artists. I characterize the first group of comic book artists from the late 1930s as the first generation and the artists that began their mature work, after the Second World War, as the second generation. Were you in the first or second generation of comic artists?

A. I was three-quarters through the first generation. The first generation started somewhere around 1937. I came in in 1942. They were beginning to go into the service. At fifteen I was working along side all of these guys who were all active professionals at the time. The only one who had left the field by 1942 was Lou Fine and actually he hadn't left the field he went on to do the *Spirit*.

Q. I was thinking that you have created a lot of images for comic book covers, splash pages, interior pages, and stories which are very, very dynamic and very striking. Do you feel uncomfortable when someone, an artist of "serious art" for instance, takes one panel out of context? An example would be, Mel Ramos or Roy Lichtenstein.

A. No, no I don't. As a matter of fact I think the whole point of comics is that it's a medium of where it's visually dynamic and the story serves as a lyric in a song and you're still listening to the melody all the time and the thing is that, I don't feel that we have a moral, to me the thing with comics is that they ultimately present a series of aesthetic problems and the only thing that I recognize is that I spent my whole life trying to resolve them. You know, trying to resolve them upwards to elevate my craft through these aesthetics and the more I do it, I still feel like I haven't even scratched the surface. It's simply a problem that goes beyond, I think, what most people are interested in or even want to hear about when it comes to comics. It's like some intricate effort and years after everyone's lost interest in looking at it you're still stuck with working it through and you find that it keeps evolving and evolving enough to keep your mind and personality occupied to the point where it becomes, besides from your family, my chief preoccupation.

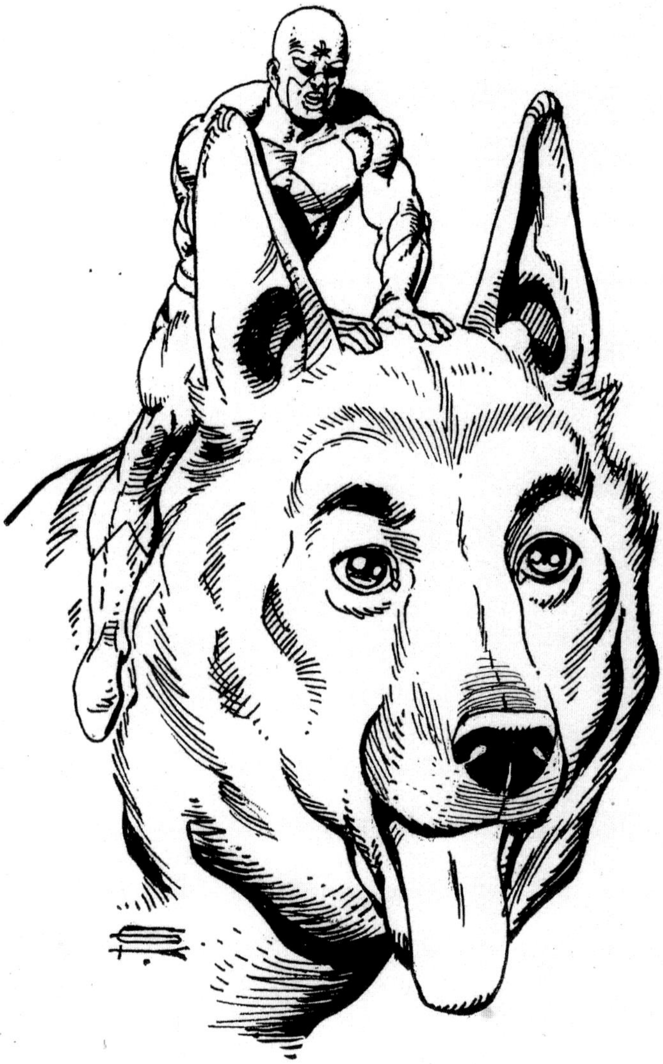

The original artwork for Kane's recreation of one of his concept pieces for the Atom, Gil Kane, pencils and inks, ©2001 DC Comics. Kane prepared the original and now lost artwork to pitch the character to DC Comics executives, which inevitably led to the character's reintroduction in 1961.

INDEX

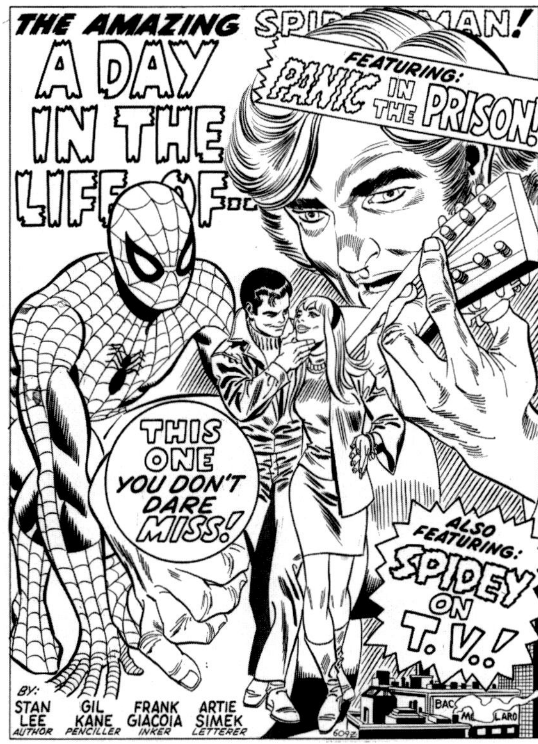

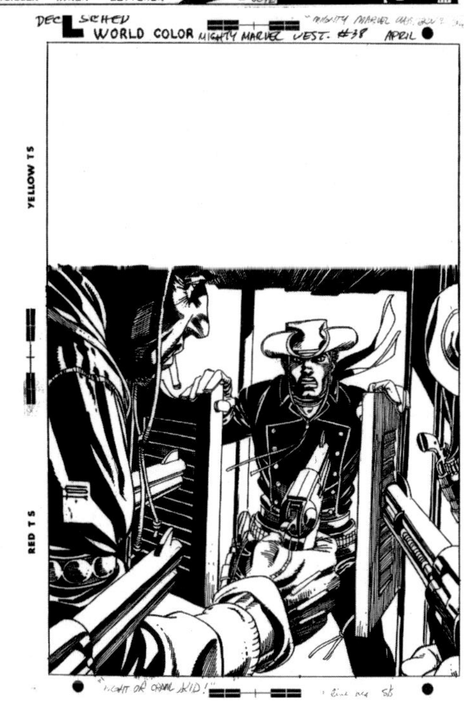

Above: original artwork for the splash page for *The Amazing Spider-Man* #99, August, 1971, Gil Kane, pencils, Frank Giacoia, inks and the original artwork for *The Mighty Marvel Western* #38, April, 1975, Gil Kane, pencils and inks, both ©2001 Marvel Characters, Inc.

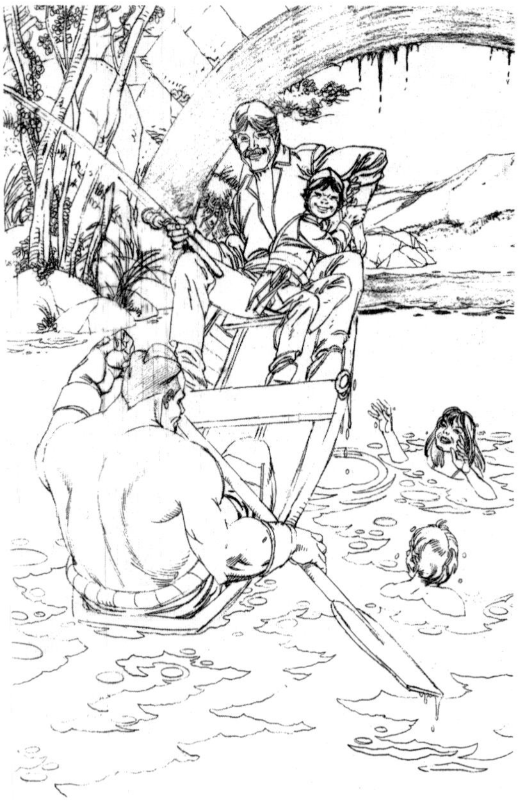

Above: original presentation artwork for Ruby-Spears, Gil Kane, pencils, ©2001 Ruby-Spears Productions.

Below: original pencils for two sequential pages for *Green Lantern Corps* #224, May, 1988, Gil Kane, pencils, ©2001 DC Comics.

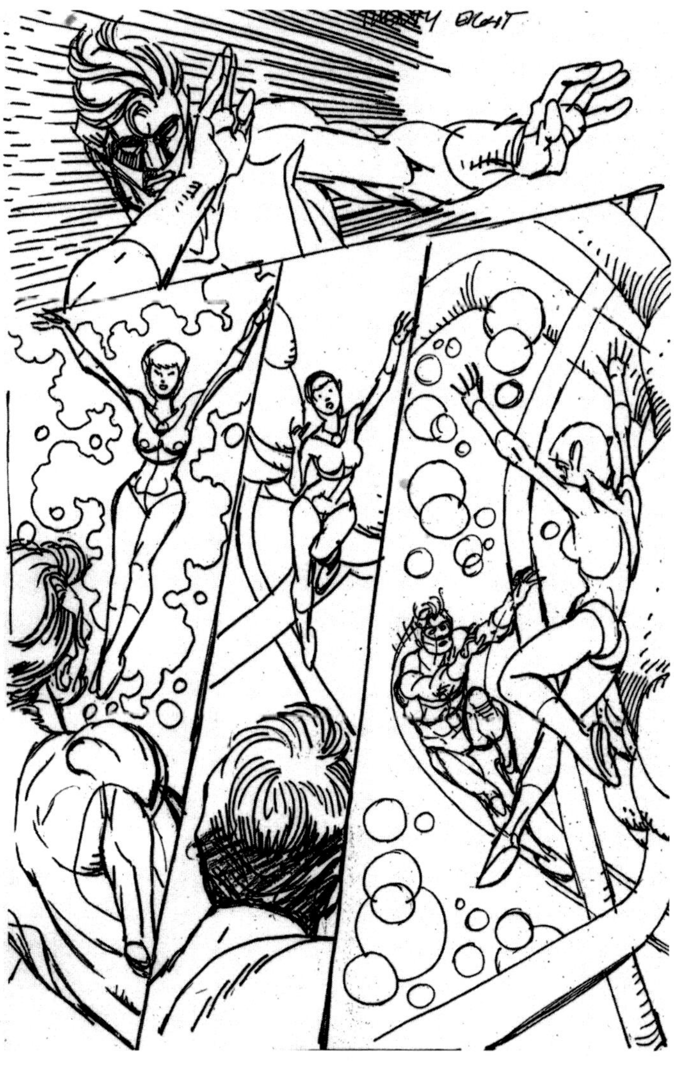

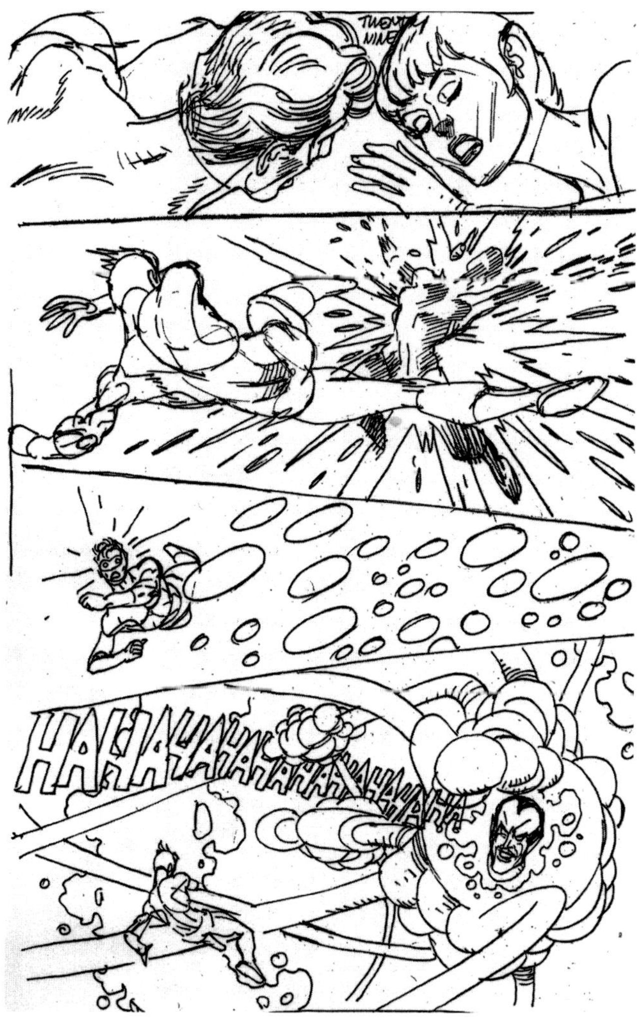

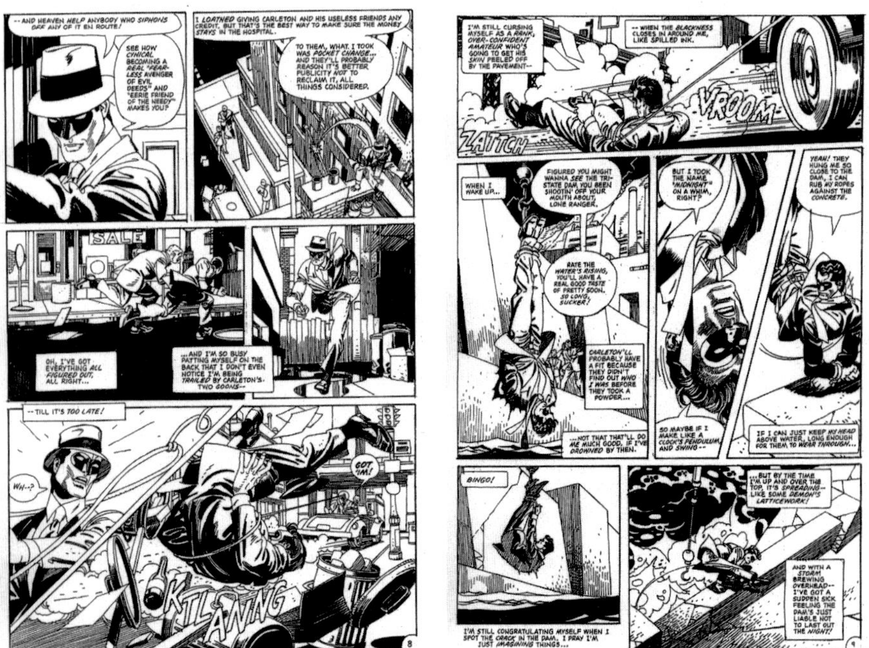
--AND HEAVEN HELP ANYBODY WHO SIPHONS OFF ANY OF IT EN ROUTE!
SEE HOW CYNICAL BECOMING A REAL "FEARLESS AVENGER OF EVIL DEEDS" AND "EERIE FRIEND OF THE NEEDY" MAKES YOU?
I LOATHED GIVING CARLETON AND HIS USELESS FRIENDS ANY CREDIT, BUT THAT'S THE BEST WAY TO MAKE SURE THE MONEY STAYS IN THE HOSPITAL.
TO THEM, WHAT I TOOK WAS POCKET CHANGE... AND THEY'LL PROBABLY REASON IT'S BETTER PUBLICITY NOT TO RECLAIM IT, ALL THINGS CONSIDERED.
SALE
OH, I'VE GOT EVERYTHING ALL FIGURED OUT, ALL RIGHT...
...AND I'M SO BUSY PATTING MYSELF ON THE BACK THAT I DON'T EVEN NOTICE I'M BEING TRAILED BY CARLETON'S TWO GOONS--
--TILL IT'S TOO LATE!
WH--?
GOT 'IM!
KTLANNG
8
I'M STILL CURSING MYSELF AS A RANK, OVER-CONFIDENT AMATEUR WHO'S GOING TO GET HIS SKIN PEELED OFF BY THE PAVEMENT--
-- WHEN THE BLACKNESS CLOSES IN AROUND ME, LIKE SPILLED INK.
VROOM
ZATTCH
WHEN I WAKE UP...
FIGURED YOU MIGHT WANNA SEE THE TRI-STATE DAM YOU BEEN SHOOTIN' OFF YOUR MOUTH ABOUT, LONE RANGER.
RATE THE WATER'S RISING, YOU'LL HAVE A REAL GOOD TASTE OF PRETTY SOON. SO LONG, SUCKER!
CARLETON'LL PROBABLY HAVE A FIT BECAUSE THEY DIDN'T FIND OUT WHO I WAS BEFORE THEY TOOK A POWDER...
...NOT THAT THAT'LL DO ME MUCH GOOD, IF I'VE DROWNED BY THEN.
BUT I TOOK THE NAME "MIDNIGHT" ON A WHIM, RIGHT?
SO MAYBE IF I MAKE LIKE A CLOCK'S PENDULUM, AND SWING--
YEAH! THEY HUNG ME SO CLOSE TO THE DAM, I CAN RUB MY ROPES AGAINST THE CONCRETE.
IF I CAN JUST KEEP MY HEAD ABOVE WATER, LONG ENOUGH FOR THEM TO WEAR THROUGH...
BINGO!
I'M STILL CONGRATULATING MYSELF WHEN I SPOT THE CRACK IN THE DAM. I PRAY I'M JUST IMAGINING THINGS...
...BUT BY THE TIME I'M UP AND OVER THE TOP, IT'S SPREADING-- LIKE SOME DEMON'S LATTICEWORK!
AND WITH A STORM BREWING OVERHEAD-- I'VE GOT A SUDDEN SICK FEELING THE DAM'S JUST LIABLE NOT TO LAST OUT THE NIGHT!
9

Left: two sequential pages from the original artwork for *Secret Origins* #28, 1986, Gil Kane, pencils and inks, ©2001 DC Comics.

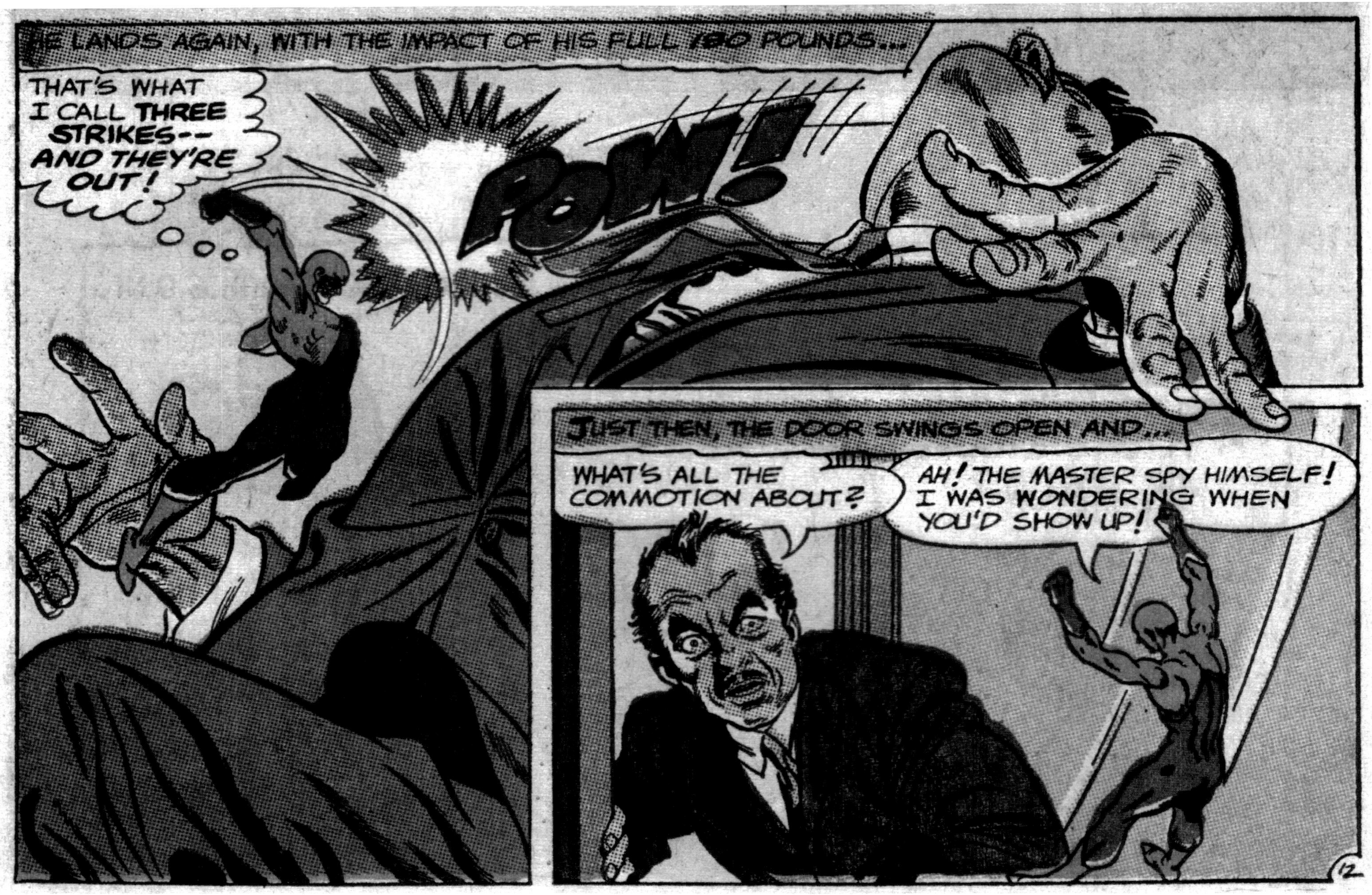
HE LANDS AGAIN, WITH THE IMPACT OF HIS FULL 180 POUNDS...
THAT'S WHAT I CALL THREE STRIKES-- AND THEY'RE OUT!
POW!
JUST THEN, THE DOOR SWINGS OPEN AND...
WHAT'S ALL THE COMMOTION ABOUT?
AH! THE MASTER SPY HIMSELF! I WAS WONDERING WHEN YOU'D SHOW UP!
12

A partial interior page from *The Atom* #21, Oct./Nov., 1965, Gil Kane, pencils, Sid Greene, inks, ©2001 DC Comics. The vitality of Kane's artwork is obvious.

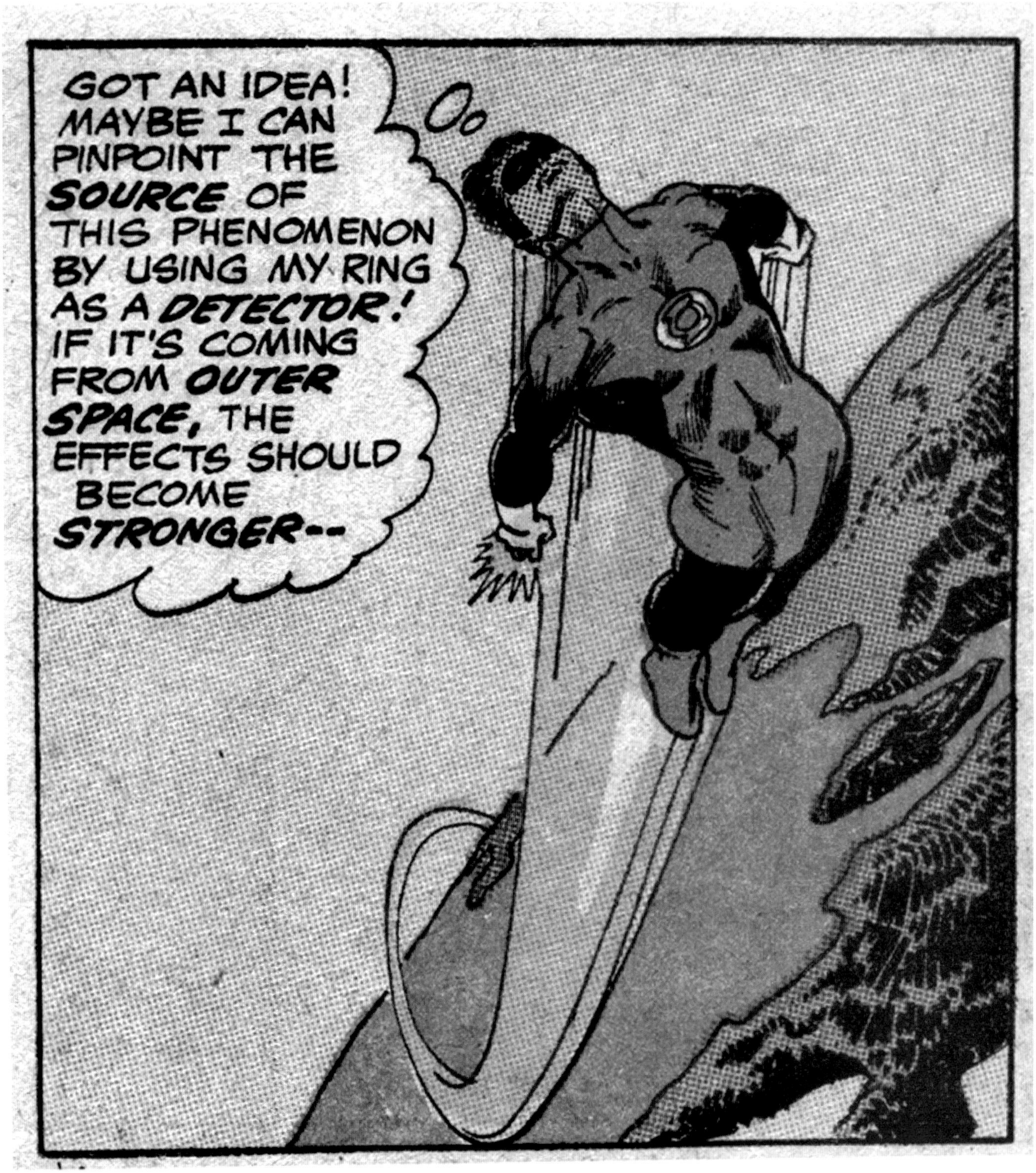
GOT AN IDEA! MAYBE I CAN PINPOINT THE SOURCE OF THIS PHENOMENON BY USING MY RING AS A DETECTOR! IF IT'S COMING FROM OUTER SPACE, THE EFFECTS SHOULD BECOME STRONGER--

Flying never looked so effortless. Kane's artwork from an interior page from Green Lantern #71, September, 1969, graces the next two pages. These images need no explanation. Gil Kane, pencils, Joe Giella, inks, ©2001 DC Comics.

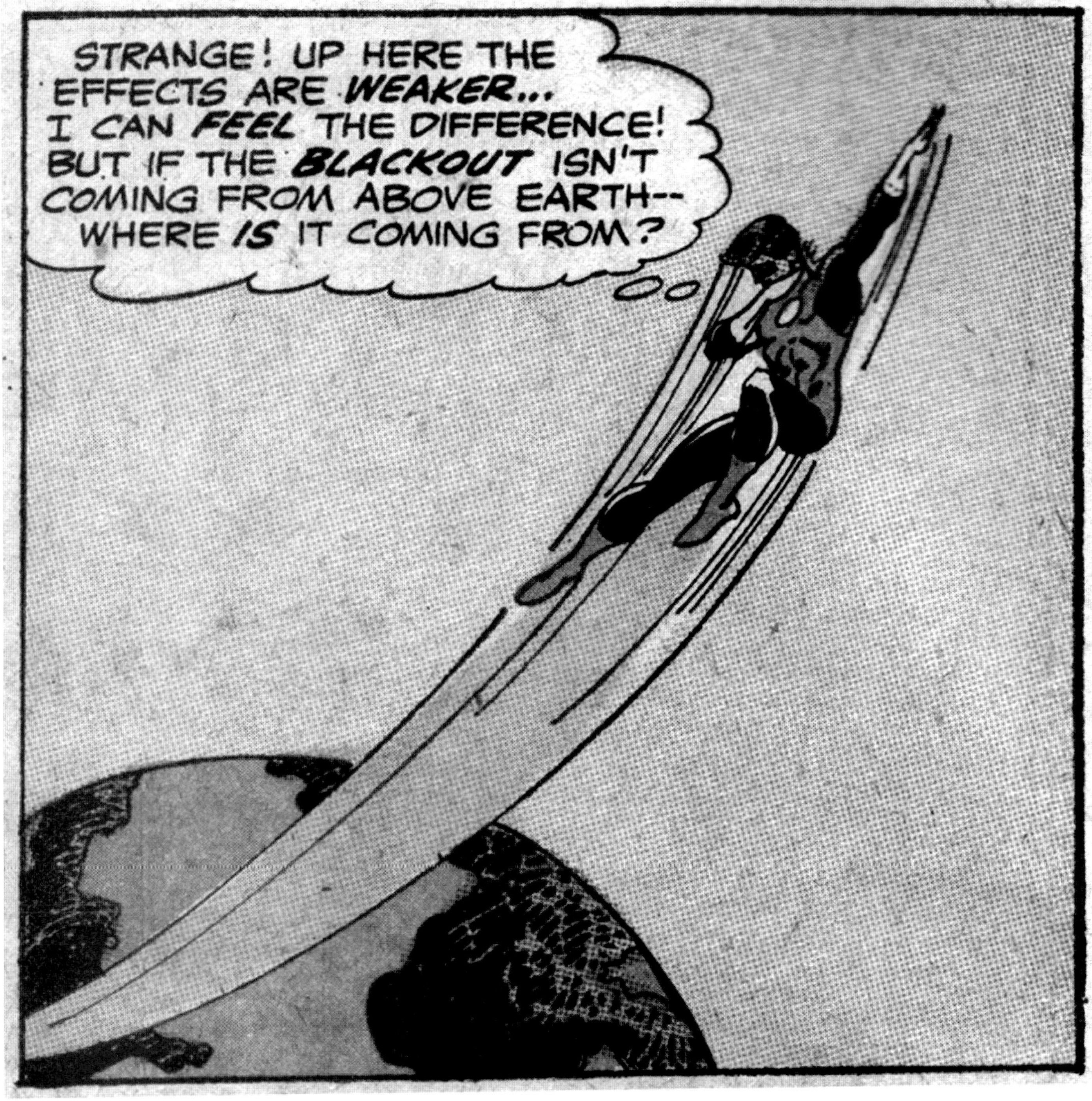
STRANGE! UP HERE THE EFFECTS ARE WEAKER... I CAN FEEL THE DIFFERENCE! BUT IF THE BLACKOUT ISN'T COMING FROM ABOVE EARTH-- WHERE IS IT COMING FROM?

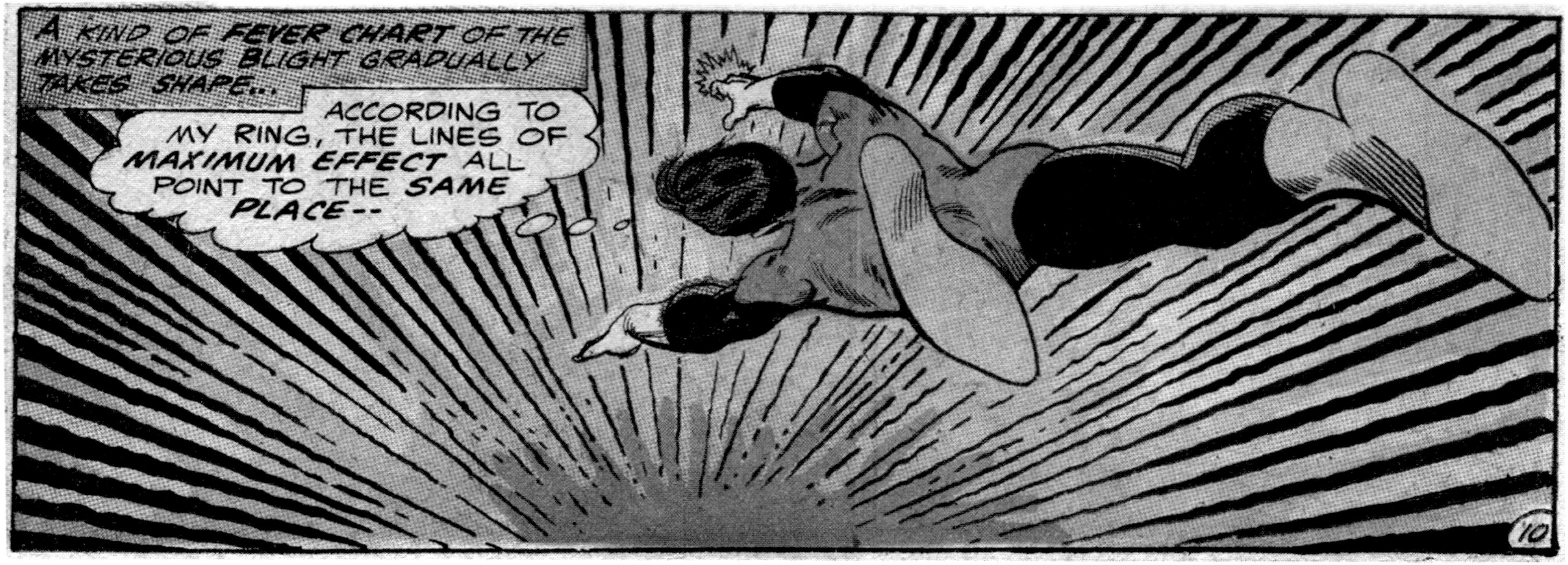
A KIND OF FEVER CHART OF THE MYSTERIOUS BLIGHT GRADUALLY TAKES SHAPE...
ACCORDING TO MY RING, THE LINES OF MAXIMUM EFFECT ALL POINT TO THE SAME PLACE--
10

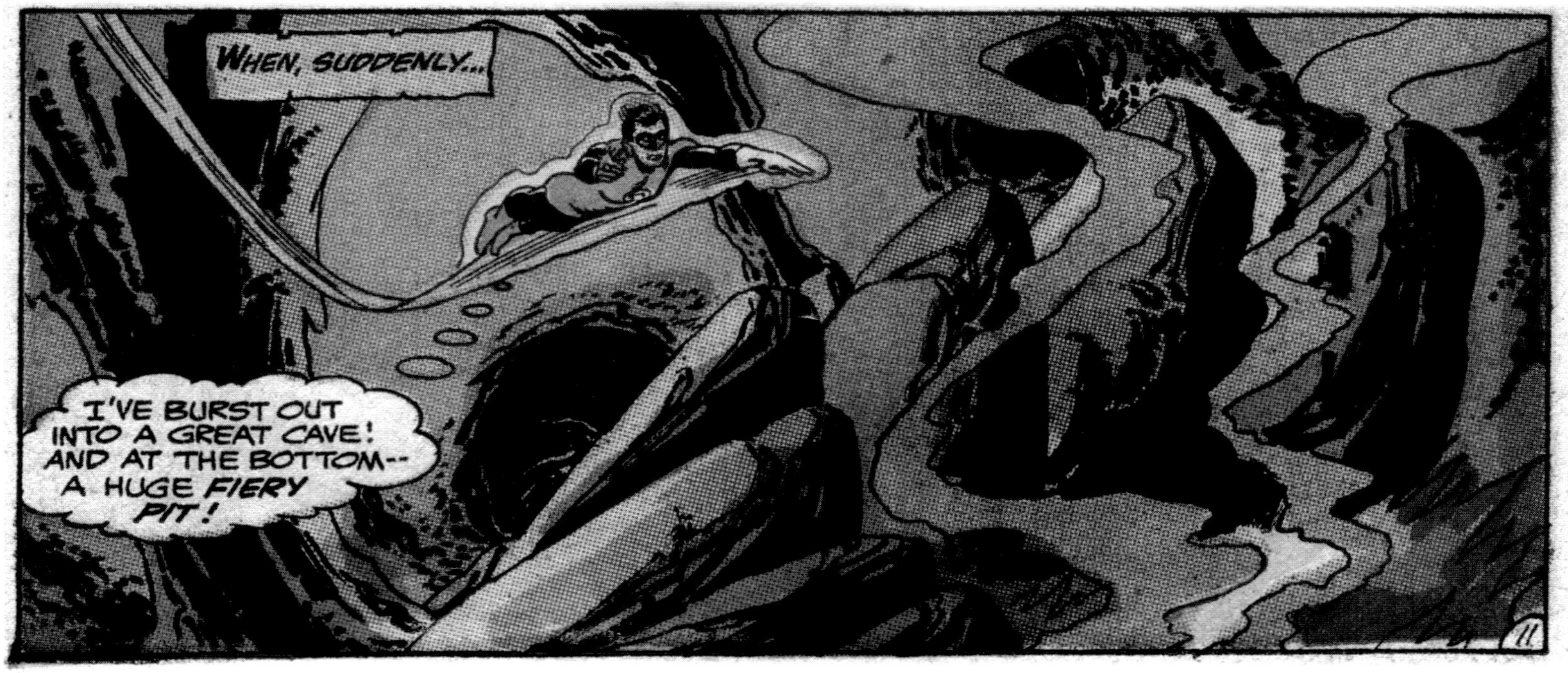
WHEN, SUDDENLY...
I'VE BURST OUT INTO A GREAT CAVE! AND AT THE BOTTOM-- A HUGE FIERY PIT!
11

Additional panels from the interior artwork for *Green Lantern* #71, September, 1969, Gil Kane, pencils, Joe Giella, inks, ©2001 DC Comics.